FIX YOUR OWN PC

4TH EDITION

COREY SANDLER

Henry Holt and Co., New York

MIS:Press
A Subsidiary of Henry Holt and Company, Inc.
115 West 18th Street
New York, New York 10011
http://www.mispress.com

Fourth Edition—1997

```
Sandler, Corey, 1950-
   Fix your own PC / by Corey Sandler. -- 4th ed.
      p.   cm.
   ISBN 1-55828-548-2
   1. Microcomputers--Maintenance and repair. I. Title.
TK7887.S33 1997
621.39'16'0288--dc21                              97-12284
                                                     CIP
```

MIS:Press and M&T Books are available at special discounts for bulk purchases for sales promotions, premiums, and fundraising. Special editions or book excerpts can also be created to specification.

For details contact: Special Sales Director
                     MIS:Press and M&T Books
                     Subsidiaries of Henry Holt and Company, Inc.
                     115 West 18th Street
                     New York, New York 10011

10 9 8 7 6 5 4 3

Associate Publisher: Paul Farrell   **Editor:** Michael Sprague

Managing Editor: Shari Chappell   **Copy Edit Manager:** Karen Tongish

Production Editor: Anthony Washington   **Copy Editor:** Gwynne Jackson

Dedication

To my father, who showed me the way things work. Ask me how to drive to the post office, and I'll explain how a carburetor works.

—Corey Sandler

Acknowledgments

Let's take a look under the covers of this book.

At MIS:Press, thanks to old friend Paul Farrell who championed this book in its new and improved fourth edition, and to Michael Sprague, who edited it with good cheer. Thanks, too, to Jono Hardjowirigo, who helped sketch out the book's logic on a Las Vegas cocktail napkin many years ago. Appreciation also goes to production editor Anthony Washington and copy editor Gwynne Jackson.

Photographer Jack Weinhold explored with me the new world of digital photography. Most of the pictures in this book were created without benefit of film: the image went from a high-resolution camera to disk, from there to a page makeup program at the publisher, and onward to the printing plant. They look great, too. Weinhold can be reached at jack@nantucket.net.

Dalco Electronics was an invaluable source of information, expertise, and parts. We recommend Dalco as one worthy source for repair and upgrade projects. Thanks to Scott Stanforth and Dale Dittmer for working with us.

Dalco Electronics

275 S. Pioneer Blvd.

Springboro, OH 45066

Retail Sales: (800) 445-5342

Dealer Sales: (800) 228-9859

Customer Support: (800) 543-2526

Local: (513) 743-8042

Internet: http://www.dalco.com

We also worked with some of the latest and greatest pieces of add-in hardware. They include:

- ATI 3D Xpression 3D and video accelerator graphics card. ATI Technologies, Inc., 33 Commerce Drive East, Thornhill, Ontario, Canada L3T 7N6. (905) 882-2600. http://www.atitech.ca.

- Cardinal MVPV341, 33.6 internal V.34 fax modem and Cardinal MVP34XF, 33.6 external V.34 fax modem including Windows 95 Plug and Play compatibility. Cardinal Technologies, 1827 Freedom Rd., Lancaster, PA 17601. (800) 775-0899 or (717) 293-3124. http://www.cardtech.com.

- Diamond Edge 3D 3240XL and other Diamond 3D and video accelerator graphics cards. Diamond Multimedia Systems, Inc., 2880 Junction Ave., San Jose, CA 95134-1922. (800) 468-5846. http://www.diamondmm.com.

- 9FX Reality 332 3D and video accelerator graphics card. Number Nine Visual Technology, 18 Hartwell Ave., Lexington, MA 02173. (800) 438-6463. http://www.nine.com

- Sound Blaster Discovery CD 12X kit, with Sound Blaster 32 PnP wave-table sound card, 12X CD-ROM, and 10 watt speakers. Creative Labs, Inc., P.O. Box 1452, Stillwater, OK 74076. (800) 998-5227 or (405) 742-6600. http://www.soundblaster.com.

Here are some of the most valuable pieces of software in our toolkit for the fourth edition of Fix Your Own PC:

- DisplayMate for Windows. SONERA Technologies, P.O. Box 565, Rumson, NJ 07760. (800) 932-6323 or (908) 747-6886. E-mail: sonera@displaymate.com. http://www.displaymate.com.

- Norton Utilities. Symantec Corp., 175 W. Broadway, Eugene, OR 97401. (800) 441-7234 or (541) 334-6054. http://www.symantec.com.

- PhoneDisc. An invaluable collection on CD-ROMs of telephone numbers and Web sites for companies and individuals. Phone Disc, 6931 Arlington Rd. #405, Bethesda, MD 20814. (800) 284-8353. http://www.PhoneDisc.com.

- QAPlus/Win-Win. DiagSoft Inc., 6200 Courtney Campbell Cswy, Suite 320, Tampa FL 33607. (800) 342-4763 or (408) 438-8247. http://www.diagsoft.com

- WinCheckIt. TouchStone Software Corp., 2124 Main Street, Suite 250, Huntington Beach, CA 92648. (800) 531-0450, (714) 969-7746. http://www.checkit.com.

- WINProbe 4. Quarterdeck Software Corp., 13160 Mindanao Way, Marina Del Rey, CA 90292. (800) 683-6696 or (310) 309-3700. http://www.checkit.com.

Contents

CHAPTER 1

Under the Cover of a Personal Computer

What? You want me to take the covers off of my PC and poke around inside?

Yes, actually. That's the reason you bought this book, right?

Don't worry, I'll be *very* gentle.

I will be the first to admit that I once trembled at the thought of applying a screwdriver to a brand-spanking-new PC.

I can also tell you that after you've changed your first CMOS battery, plugged in your first video card, or installed your first hard disk, you'll find yourself prowling the corridors of your office or the streets of your town in search of more challenging electronic territory to explore.

This is the fourth edition of *Fix Your Own PC*, and over the years we've helped tens of thousands of readers understand how their PCs work and how to solve the knotty modern-day problems that sooner or later afflict our electronic desktop companions.

This newest edition has been completely updated and expanded, and it includes details on new technologies including Enhanced IDE controllers, OverDrive chips, MMX extensions to the Pentium processor, the Universal Serial Bus, and much more.

Repairing a PC is much less physically challenging than fixing a toaster or a bicycle or an automobile, but it does require quite a bit more logical energy. In other words, this is a job that exercises the muscle between your ears.

This chapter introduces you to your computer's anatomy and to its individual components. We'll come back to discuss the components in much greater detail later in the book.

Dinosaurs and Modern Machines

Throughout this book, I am going to make a very important distinction between what I will call "dinosaur" and "modern-machine" systems:

- *Dinosaurs* are based on the obsolete 8088, 8086, and 80286 microprocessors—including IBM PCs, PC-XTs, and PC-ATs, and dozens of clone machines that use the same chips. With this, the fourth edition of *Fix Your Own PC*, we welcome the venerable 80386 processor to the realm of the dinosaur.
- *Modern machines* are those that can work with current operating systems (Windows 3.1, if you must, or Windows 95) and can use current hardware peripherals. Included in this group are machines based on the Intel 486 (in SX, SL, DX, DX-2, and DX-4 versions), Pentium, Pentium Pro, and Pentium with MMX chips, as well as non-Intel designs from Cyrix, AMD, and IBM.

    Some of these machines use an *AT bus*, an extension of the motherboard used in the original PC-AT and sometimes called the *ISA bus*; others use more advanced bus designs including EISA, VL, and PCI.

Don't let your eyes glaze over with this sudden introduction to the alphabet soup of the PC world. We'll translate most technical terms as we introduce them, and there's a glossary in the back of this book.

We'll also help you figure out exactly what type of machine lies beneath the cover.

Don't feel that all is lost if you happen to be the proud owner of a dinosaur. It is still possible to do a reasonable amount of work with an older machine, and it is also possible—in some cases—to upgrade a dinosaur to near-modern capabilities in a cost-effective manner. We'll discuss your options in this book.

Preparing for Open-Case Surgery

Before you go any further, be sure to turn off the computer *and* unplug it before you remove its cover. Why do both? It's a great habit to get into to protect yourself from mental lapses—sort of a belt-and-suspenders kind of thing.

There is no electricity in the computer when it's off and unplugged. Actually, there is very little shock hazard when the computer is on, as long as you never disassemble the sealed power supply or the monitor. The computer bus runs on the 5- or 12-volt DC current that comes out of a properly functioning power supply.

There is, however, the potential danger of short-circuiting components of the system if you touch a screwdriver to the traces of the motherboard or drop a bracket into the works. For that reason, you should generally not perform any repairs or adjustments to a powered-on PC.(Almost always but not always.)

One more thing about electricity: you can very easily damage the microprocessor, memory chips, and other components if you stroll across the carpeted floor of your office or den and deliver a static electricity shock of a few thousand volts from your fingertips.

We recommend that you find a way to ground yourself before you lay hands on the innards of a PC. One easy way to do that is to touch the center screw that holds the plastic cover over the nearest electrical outlet—don't stick your finger in the outlet, just touch the screw. If you're going to be doing repair work regularly, a more elegant and safer means of grounding yourself while working under the covers of a PC is to wear an antistatic wrist strap; a wire from the bracelet connects to a known ground (Figure 1.1). It's worth the investment of a few dollars.

Place the computer on a sturdy table under a good light. You'll probably need to remove most or all of the cables that attach to the computer to comfortably remove the cover (Figure 1.2).

I recommend having a small box at hand to hold screws and other parts, a notepad, a roll of masking tape, and a marker pen. Keep notes on any unusual steps in disassembling the case and use the tape and pen to mark cables with their intended destination.

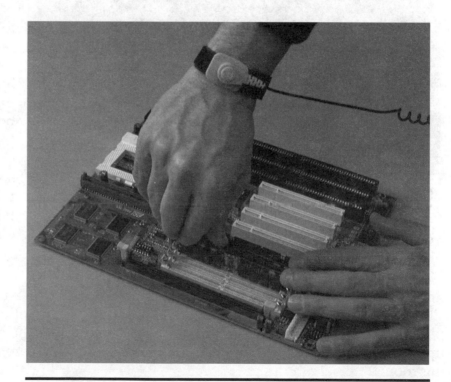

Figure 1.1 A good way to protect the electronics of your PC from static electricity is to wear a grounded antistatic wrist strap, an inexpensive solution to a potentially dangerous problem.

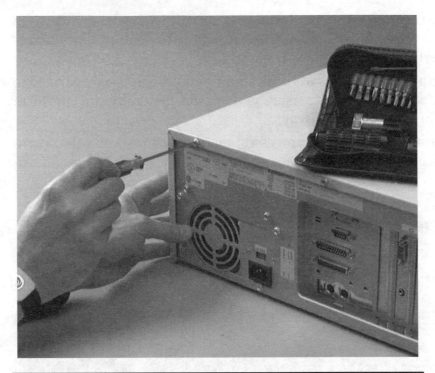

Figure 1.2 To take off the cover on most cases, remove the screws on the back panel. On some ultra-compact desktop cases, the screws may be on the sides. Be careful not to remove the four screws that surround the power supply.

A Case of PCs

There are dozens of types of PC cases, but nearly all follow the same basic design: a heavy metal shell that slides tightly into place over a metal frame holding the computer's motherboard and all the internal devices attached to it. Portable and laptop computers use a metallized plastic shell and are generally not intended to be serviced by users.

Why all this heavy metal? Blame it on the government, the Federal Communications Commission (FCC) to be exact. All electronic devices, including microprocessors, generate electrical signals that can create interference. As personal computers become faster, the likelihood that they may become tiny local radio transmitters increases. To avoid interference with your neighbor's garage door opener, your kids' television set, or the PC in the next cubicle, the FCC requires all computers to be tested for radio frequency (RF) leakage. The solution to passing the test generally involves heavy metal cases, internal shielding, and less-obvious solutions such as little copper "fingers" that help extend an electronic girdle around your interfering PC.

Cases are available in either desktop (full or "baby" sizes) and tower (full- and mini-sized). A *baby case* is a tightly packed, slimmed-down box with limited options for expansion. My strong preference is for tower designs that sit under the desk and offer plenty of space for drives and other devices, usually include larger capacity power supplies, and generally have more room to work with under the cover. A compromise is a mini-tower, which may take up a bit less space—make sure it is not merely a desktop case turned on its side without the benefits of more working room.

On most cases, you will find the cover secured in place by four to eight large screws on the back of the computer. A standard Phillips screwdriver will remove them; you may also be able to use a socket wrench or nut driver. On many systems you'll see a few smaller screws around the air exhaust for the power supply. You don't need to remove them to take the cover off. Consult the instruction manual for your PC if you have any doubts about the location of the screws.

You'll also learn how to slide the cover off. On some systems you'll have to remove a plastic false front to gain access to some of the disk drives. Other designs attach drives to a card cage that bolts into place within the case. This design allows you to remove a group of drives with a few turns of a screwdriver. Some computer manufacturers have introduced screwless cases that substitute simple latches or thumbscrews.

Whatever the design, remove the case slowly and evenly (Figure 1.3). You want to avoid pinching or cutting any misbehaving wires that may have crept up near the top of the case, and you want to avoid tumbling the whole assemblage onto the floor with a misguided yank.

Take a Good Look

Now comes your chance to look around inside the computer. In a typical machine, you will see the main motherboard, several plug-in circuit boards, gray ribbon cables, a metal box holding the power supply, a hard drive, and one or more floppy drives.

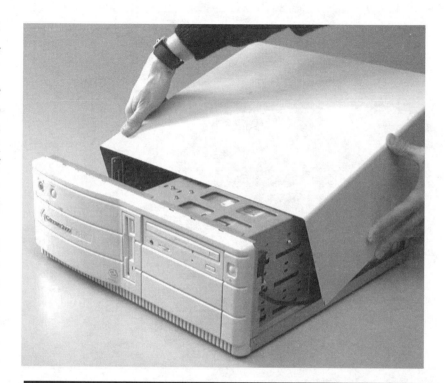

Figure 1.3 Slide the cover back away from the flange at the front of the case and then lift the cover up and away. On some machines, you'll find copper fingers that are part of system's defense against release of RF radiation; take care to avoid dropping them into the case. If any of the fingers do end up in the case, be sure to remove them before the power is turned back on. Leaving them to rattle around within could cause a short.

There are hundreds of thousands of possible combinations of add-in cards, drives, memory modules, and other devices. Even a room full of IBMs or Dells or Compaqs is likely to have very different combinations of parts under the hood—users may have had different requirements when the machines were purchased, technologies may have changed over the course of a series of orders, or the manufacturer may have had a mix-and-match assembly line where Brand X disk drives were installed on Mondays and Wednesdays, Brand Y on Tuesdays and Thursdays, and whatever was on sale was stuck in boxes put together on Fridays.

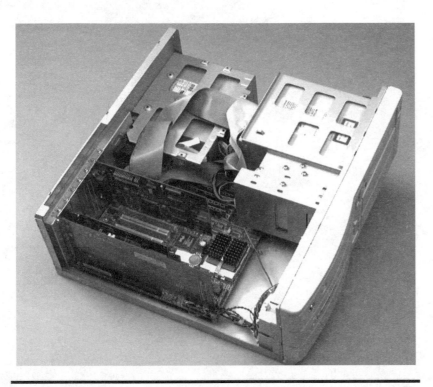

Figure 1.4 A basic modern machine with PCI and ISA bus slots, a Pentium 100 MHz CPU with heat sink, power supply, hard drive, and CD-ROM.

That said, most computers—from the very first IBM PC to the latest state-of-the-art 200 MHz Pentium with MMX—are more alike than they are different (Figure 1.4).

The Modular Design of a PC

One of the most important features of the PC is its modular design. Nearly every PC uses this modular design: motherboard, expansion cards, power supply, drives connected by cables to internal controllers, and (mostly) external keyboard and monitor. Nearly every personal computer is made up of interchangeable parts that can be attached or removed with relative ease. This allows users to make many types of repairs and to upgrade their systems (that is, of course, the reason for this book).

The biggest circuit board in your computer is the *motherboard*, sometimes called the *mainboard*. The motherboard is the home of the *CPU* (central processing unit), also called the *microprocessor*. The CPU is the brain of the computer, where the bulk of the actual manipulation of data and instructions takes place.

Expansion cards, or *adapters*, are smaller, special-purpose circuit boards that plug into sockets on the motherboard. These sockets are called *bus slots* or *expansion slots*. The computer *bus* is functionally an extension of the address lines of the microprocessor. The particular kind of bus slot on your motherboard tells us a lot about the motherboard and your computer's capabilities.

Your computer also has a *power supply*, a transformer that converts 110-volt AC current into low-voltage DC current to run the computer. The power supply is easy to identify, since the computer's AC power cord plugs into the back of it. It's usually a large shiny or black metal box sprouting many wires and connectors to power the guts of your computer.

Floppy drives and hard drives are electromechanical boxes connected to the rest of the computer with gray, flat-ribbon cables and four-wire power connectors from the power supply box. The diskette-insertion slot on the front of the PC should be a familiar landmark to users.

You'll also notice some thin wires that lead to the drive indicator light, the speaker, and the power-on indicator.

If your PC is a dinosaur, the memory chips—marked with identifying numbers—are probably arranged in rows of nine and are in a segregated section of the motherboard by themselves.

If your computer is a modern machine, it most likely uses SIMM (single in-line memory module) strips instead of individual memory chips. SIMMs are strips of circuit board with a row of eight or nine chips that plug into special connectors on the motherboard or—occasionally—into a plug-in board that attaches to the motherboard. A near-cousin is a SIP (single in-line processor), an earlier version that uses tiny pins as a connector to the motherboard; SIPs were used only for a short period of time and have been supplanted by SIMMs. As we write this book, SIMMs typically hold from 1 to 32 MB of RAM.

We'll discuss memory types and configuration in much greater detail in Chapter 7 of this book.

It's okay to press down on the chips and strips to make sure they're seated firmly, but don't poke around inside the computer with a screwdriver.

Notice the expansion cards, lined up in neat rows and plugged into a set of black plastic and metal slots on the motherboard. The cards are held in place by the clamping action of the metal fingers within the slot and locked down with a single screw that screws through a bracket and into the support frame of the computer case. To remove a card, you'll need to disconnect any external cables attached to the card and then unscrew the bracket screw; the last step is to carefully work the card out of the slot in the motherboard. Installing a card is just as simple—just make sure that the card is fully inserted into the slot.

Some baby and other mini case designs use a *riser card* that installs into a single slot on the small motherboard. Add-on cards plug into slots on the riser.

Finally, take a look at the motherboard itself. In most designs, the board floats above the bottom or side of the case on plastic standoffs. You'll see a handful of screws holding it in place. At the back of the machine are ports for serial and parallel cables to external devices, a video port to connect to the monitor, and connectors for a keyboard and mouse. On some systems you may see other connectors including ports for SCSI devices, joysticks, and more (Figure 1.5).

PCs by the Numbers

Just how modular is a PC? Here are the basic parts for most systems; we've indicated where you will find more details about this particular part in this book:

- **Keyboard** (attaches by cable to port on the motherboard). Chapter 5.
- **Monitor** (attaches by cable to port on video card). Chapter 13.
- **Case.** Chapter 1.
- **Power supply.** Chapter 5.
- **Motherboard.** Chapter 5.
- **CPU.** Chapter 2.
- **BIOS.** Chapter 3.
- **RAM (Random Access Memory).** Chapter 7.
- **Video adapter** (on some systems, part of the motherboard). Chapter 12.
- **Floppy- and hard-drive controllers** (on some systems, part of the motherboard). Chapters 8 and 9.

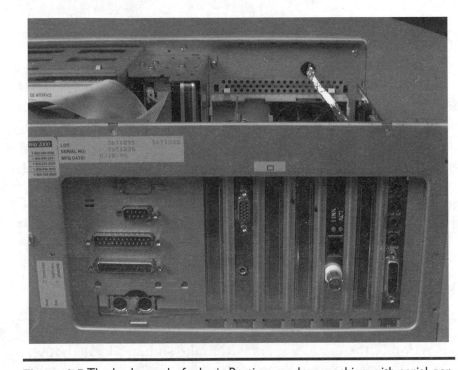

Figure 1.5 The back panel of a basic Pentium modern machine with serial, parallel, video, mouse, keyboard, and Ethernet connections.

- One or more **floppy disk drives.** Chapter 8.
- One or more **hard disk drives.** Chapter 9.
- One or more **serial ports** (On most modern machines, these are part of the motherboard; on most dinosaurs, they are usually on an I/O card or part of a multifunction adapter). Chapter 14.
- One or more **parallel ports.** Chapter 16.
- An internal or external **modem.** Chapter 15.
- **Printer**. Chapter 17.

On multimedia-capable systems, you'll also find a few more modular parts:

- **Sound card**. Chapter 11.
- **CD-ROM controller** and internal or external **CD-ROM drive** (on some systems, the CD-ROM controller is part of the sound card, and on others the controller may be a SCSI adapter shared by other devices including scanners and hard drives). Chapter 11.
- **Game controller.** Chapter 11.
- One or more **high-capacity removable** drives. Chapter 10.

Even more adventuresome users trick out their systems with devices such as scanners, video capture cards, and video editing cards.

Many computers in offices and even those in some small home offices add a *network card*. Almost anything else can be and has been tucked into the obliging slots of a PC. Here are some other exotic devices: *A/D* (analog-to-digital) or *D/A* (digital-to-analog) boards to monitor scientific experiments or control machinery; *IEEE* (Institute of Electrical and Electronics Engineers) devices to monitor lab equipment; *EPROM* burners to create new ROMs; *IC* (integrated circuit) testers, and *3270* or other terminal emulation cards for connecting to mainframe computers.

What Kind of PC Do You Have?

The first step in analyzing a PC is to understand what type of system it is: is it a dinosaur or a modern machine? Does it have an ISA, EISA, VL, or PCI bus? Is it possessed of a poky 8 MHz or a zippy 200 MHz processor? Is the hard disk an old ST506, an obsolete ESDI, a modern IDE, or a high-performance SCSI or EIDE model?

Again, don't worry about the jargon. We'll define the terms later when we discuss repairs and upgrades. If you need an immediate explanation, consult the glossary at the back of this book.

The first place to look on many systems is on the front *bezel*—the plastic faceplate where the computer manufacturer may proudly hang an advertising sign. In many cases, the model name for the computer gives you a great deal of information about what lies within.

For example, here are a few sample names for machines we have worked with

Intel Processors

- **P6-200.** The "P6" is an unofficial industry label for Intel's current server champion, the Pentium Pro, in this case running at a blazing 200 MHz clock speed. Virtually all modern P6-based computers use a combination of PCI and ISA buses to interconnect various elements.

- **P5-100-PCI.** A *P* or more commonly *P5* in a product name usually means that the computer uses a Pentium processor, in this case running at 100 MHz. The letters after the number tell us that the motherboard uses a PCI bus.

- **P5-200 with MMX.** A hot Intel 200 MHz Pentium processor with MMX technology, plus 512 K of Pipeline Burst SRAM cache, 32 MB of SDRAM DIMM memory, and a PCI local-bus 3D graphics accelerator with 2MB SGRAM video memory.

- **4DX2-66V.** Are you getting the clues here? The processor is a 486DX2 running at 66 MHz. The *V* at the end means that this particular motherboard uses a *VL*, or local, bus, a popular design of several years ago now mostly pushed aside by PCI bus models.

- **Pentium 100ES.** The Pentium part is easy, and the 100 stands for the use of a 100 MHz chip. The ES, though less obvious, is an important distinction: this model, intended for use as a high-performance file server, uses an EISA bus, a design that has been mostly supplanted by PCI over the past few years. If you've got one of these, your upgrade and repair path is sharply limited.

- **486DX4-100.** A top-end 486 system, this one uses an Intel DX4 chip, which despite its enumeration is actual-clock *tripled* rather than quadrupled. It runs at 100 MHz internally.

- **4SX-33.** This is a 486SX model running at 33 MHz. You'll have to poke around under the covers or in the instruction manual to determine the type of bus it uses; this somewhat underpowered chip came out near the end of the VL bus era and the dawn of the PCI age—some motherboards included slots to serve both designs.

- **216.** One of the dinosaurs, this is an 80286 running at an anemic 16 MHz. The motherboard almost certainly uses a very basic AT (also called *ISA*) 16-bit bus. We keep this one around as a museum piece; it is like a wheel-less sled among racing cars.

- **IBM Personal Computer.** Even deeper in the closet is the original IBM PC, with an 8088 processor running at 4.77 MHz, a pair of gigantic 5.25-inch 360 K floppy drives, 64 K of memory chips on the motherboard, and a crude CGA video adapter. We haven't fired it up in years, but we can't quite bring ourselves to deliver it to the dump: it cost almost $5,000 when we bought it.

Machines Using Non-Intel CPUs

- **Cyrix 6x86-P166+, IBM 6x86-P200+,** and **SGS 6x86-P200+.** The Cyrix series of processors are the same as but different from Intel equivalents. The company employs some special tricks to eke more speed out of their designs while maintaining near-perfect compatibility with Intel equivalents. They do make things a bit difficult with their naming scheme, though. The Cyrix 6x86-P166+ actually runs at 133 MHz, but is claimed to outperform an Intel Pentium 166 MHz chip—isn't marketing fun? One more issue: IBM has manufactured chips for Cyrix for some time, and some machines may have chips with the IBM name instead of Cyrix. So an IBM 6x86-P200+ runs at 166 MHz, acts like a 200 MHz Intel CPU, and is the same as a Cyrix 6x86-P200+. Similarly, SGS-Thomson also makes chips for Cyrix and some systems may have an SGS logo.

- **AMD K5 100 MHz.** AMD is another relatively major competitor to Intel, offering comparable and compatible performance, usually at a price discount. Its chip numbering scheme is relatively simple: a K5 is equivalent to a Pentium P5.

- **Nx586 P100.** This system uses the NexGen Nx586 processor, a now-discontinued competitor to Intel's Pentium chip. The Nx586 was not pin-compatible with the Pentium and because of that it required special motherboards and chip sets and it lacked an on-chip floating-point unit (FPU). The chip model here is the P100, which actually runs at 93 MHz but is claimed to rival a Pentium at 100 MHz. NexGen was bought out by AMD and that company may be able to support the chip, but serious problems with a NexGen-based machine may require a change of motherboard and CPU.

The next place to look is in the documentation—what mere mortals call the *instruction manual*—that comes with the system.

If you don't have the manual or if it is one of those annoying books that attempts to explain many different types of systems within one set of covers, there's a quick and easy way to check on most of the elements of a PC if you have a copy of MSD (Microsoft Diagnostics). This is a capable utility supplied as part of MS-DOS 6.X and Windows 3.1. Boot up the system and go to the DOS prompt. Microsoft warns that not all of the readings of MSD are accurate if you run it from within Windows or from a DOS window opened under Windows, so exit Windows if it is running and execute MSD from the DOS prompt.

You can also use one of several diagnostic programs that will give you a full report. In Chapter 20 we show you how to use MSD and reproduce a full report.

The final way to determine the nature of your machine is to look for yourself. Locate the CPU chip on the motherboard. The processor's manufacturer and number are printed on the chip. Although some computers tuck the CPU chip and part of the motherboard under the drives to save space, the CPU itself is still pretty easy to find. It is usually the largest chip on the motherboard and is surrounded by a network of copper circuit traces.

The 8088 CPUs of a dinosaur are rectangular, about two inches long and half-an-inch wide. 80286 chips are roughly an inch square. On modern machines, 80386, 486, and Pentium CPUs are big square chips that are hard to miss. Some 486 and Pentium chips are mounted in large chip carriers that make them easy to remove for upgrades; you'll also see aluminum heat sinks atop some of the advanced chips.

The CPU might be labeled 8088, 80286, 80386, 80486, Pentium, or Pentium Pro; some dinosaur XT-style clones used an NEC V20 or V30 chip, while some modern machines use chips from manufacturers including AMD, NexGen, and Cyrix. TI (Texas Instruments) and IBM also have variants of the Intel CPU with their names on them.

See Chapter 2 for a fuller discussion of the CPU march of time from the dawn of the dinosaurs to the arrival of the modern machine.

Reinstall the Cover

Now that you've looked around inside the machine, put the cover back on the computer, tucking in the cables. The computer should boot up when you turn it on, but if it doesn't, don't panic. If the machine worked before you took the cover off, the problem almost certainly is an accidentally dislodged, misconnected, or pinched cable.

CHAPTER 2
The CPU March of Time

Intel has owned the heart of the PC market from its very birth, when IBM chose the company's 8088 processor as the brains for the first PC. Today Intel is still inside most PCs, although a small but significant slice of the market is now claimed by AMD, Cyrix, and IBM.

Intel's 8088 was not the fastest processor available at the time of the birth of the IBM PC, but IBM felt the chip offered the best combination of speed, price, and availability of peripherals; perhaps most importantly, the 8088 did not seem to present much of a threat to "real" computers. That choice by IBM ended up hobbling the expansion capabilities of PCs for many years, and is still a factor in today's backwards-compatible hardware and operating systems.

The Intel family of processors has gone through six major generations. The first four generations used "8" as a family name, beginning with the 8088/8086/80186 family and running through the 80286, 80386, and 80486 series.

Within the 80386 and 80486 family line, some chips were subdivided into SX and DX, DX2, and DX4 groups; another set of categories involves the clock speed of the chips. Intel also dropped the "80" prefix from the names of the chips for marketing purposes; today you'll see references to 386 and 486 processors.

With the introduction of the Pentium, Intel changed its naming convention; some technical types maintain a link to the family by calling the Pentium the P5, a reference to its once-intended 80586 name. In 1996, Intel began widespread shipments of the Pentium Pro (the P6 to some). And in 1997, the MMX multimedia extensions were added to the Pentium family.

Dinosaurs: The 8088 Family and Relatives

Intel 8086 (Introduced 1978)

Bypassed for the original PC, it was used in a few relatively unimportant later versions. A true 16-bit chip, the 8086 processed information internally 16 bits at a time and communicated externally with the PC's bus across a 16-wire data connection.

Intel 8088 (1979)

The chip that launched the PC revolution was a hybrid device that processed information internally in 16-bit chunks, but communicated externally to the bus in 8-bit words. Used as the brain of the original IBM PC and clones as well as the PC XT and the PCjr, the chip ran at a poky 4.77 MHz clock speed and could only address up to 1 MB of memory—an upper limit of 640K of random access memory (RAM), with the top 384K set aside for memory addresses for the video card, the hard disk, and the read-only memory basic input/output system (ROM BIOS). Some early XT clones managed to boost the clock speed a bit, but machines based on the original PC CPU are still glacially slow compared to modern machines.

NEC V20, NEC V30 (1981)

Functional equivalents of the 8088 and the 8086 respectively, machines using these chips made by Japanese maker NEC could boost processing speed by as much as 30 percent over original PC designs.

NOTE

MS-DOS, the operating system designed for the 8088 microprocessor, is limited to the capabilities of the least common denominator—the original 8088 microprocessor. Consequently, programs operating under MS-DOS cannot use memory over 1 MB without a special program to open up that RAM. To get around the memory limit of DOS, many programs are able to use what is called *expanded memory*. Expanded memory cards can be added to dinosaur XTs and ATs, although there is little cost justification for doing so today. The issue of memory management for DOS pretty much ended with the arrival of Windows 95 for modern machines, some of which use as much as 64 MB of RAM for a desktop system engaged in complex graphics or database work.

Intel 80286 (1982)

The 80286 was a true 16-bit chip able to address as much as 16 MB of memory and able to work with *virtual memory*, a scheme which uses disk-based storage to simulate up to 1 GB of memory.

The 286 also took the first baby steps toward multitasking and introduced the concept of *real mode* (an emulation of the 8086) and *protected mode* (the ability to multitask with multiple programs running in their own separate world; DOS was unable to take advantage of that ability, but future operating system enhancements, including Windows, would.) IBM built its Advanced Technology PC AT around the chip. When introduced, the 286 ran at 6 MHz, but was soon raised to 8 MHz by IBM; clone makers found ways to boost it to as much as 20 MHz.

Some versions of the 80286 chip were manufactured under license by other companies, including Harris (Figure 2.1).

Figure 2.1 A Harris version of an 80286 chip on a dinosaur motherboard.

Intel 386 (1985), Intel 386SX (1988)

The 386 family brought the first 32-bit processor for personal computers, able to crunch twice as much data with each clock cycle internally and able to communicate with 32-bit peripherals. It could also address as much as 4 GB (gigabytes) of real memory and 64 TB (terabytes) of virtual memory. The 386 could also work with a separate math coprocessor chip called the 80387; it was of value in certain types of applications, including graphics and very large spreadsheets.

The standard AT/386 hardware design limited physical memory to 16 Mb. The last 15 Mb of this memory is extended memory, which can be used either as extended or as expanded memory in 386 or 486 computers if you run a memory manager (such as the EMM386 program that is a part of the later versions of DOS, or QEMM386, a third-party utility).

Virtual memory gets its name because computer programs think this memory exists, even though it isn't really there. For the ordinary DOS user, the most important difference between 386 and earlier chips was the virtual 8088 mode, which made the 386 computer look like several 8088 computers running simultaneously on the same machine. During much of the useful life of the 386, though, there were few peripherals and chips able to operate on a full 32-bit-wide highway—and not that many users truly needed that much speed then.

Intel's reduced version of the CPU, the 386SX, processed 32 bits internally but communicated to the rest of the system over 16-bit data lines. The SX chip allowed manufacturers to produce lower-cost computers, albeit with lesser capabilities. 386 clock speeds ran from 12.5 MHz to 33 MHz. The chip also introduced the first small processor cache (a mere 16 bytes), which permitted the storage of some program instructions before they were needed.

Intel 386SL (1990), IBM 386SLC (1991)

Intel developed a special low-power variant of the 386DX with an eye on the developing portable computer market. In addition to low demands on battery power, the chips included special circuitry that could manage the shutdown of other elements of the system. SL CPUs could also work with flash memory.

IBM took the SL concept one step further with its SLC design, which added an 8 KB cache and other enhancements that in certain situations could nearly double the performance of a plain 386.

The Dawn of the Modern Machine

Intel 486 (1989), Intel 486SX (1991)

The next generation brought together in one chip the brains of the 386, the formerly external math coprocessor and cache controller, and other enhancements that permitted increased processing speed. The 486 was pushed as fast as 120 MHz clock speed in doubled and quadrupled versions.

The 486 was different from the 286/386 line in some important ways. In fact it was only pretending to be an 80x86 chip. Inside, it was talking RISC. *Reduced instruction set chips* (RISC) do only a few things, but they do them very fast. Workstations like the SUN, Hewlett-Packard, and others are RISC machines.

The 486 was available in DX and SX versions, but the distinction was different from the 386 models. Both 486 DX and SX chips operate at 32 bits internally and externally, but the SX lacks the internal math coprocessor. (Actually, it's still there, but disabled.)

The 486SX operates at about twice the effective speed of a 386DX chip, and is therefore a very worthy upgrade in most systems.

> Most 486 and Pentium processors include a built-in cache—a small amount of high-speed memory intended to hold the most recently requested instruction and the computer's guess at the next most likely instruction—called a *Level 1 cache*. The CPUs also support a secondary external cache, known as a *Level 2 cache*. If the CPU cannot find the data or instructions it wants in the internal cache, it looks in the Level 2 cache. If it still cannot find what it is looking for, the cache controller will find the data or instruction in system memory and copy it into one of the caches.

NOTE

Intel 486SL (1992), IBM 486SLC2 (1993), Cyrix 486SLC (1993), Cyrix 486DLC (1994)

The SL versions of the 486 CPU, designed for use with portable systems, were able to work at 3.3 volts instead of 5 volts, and offered shutdown monitoring capabilities. Lower voltage means better suitability for battery-operated portable PCs, and less heat production inside the case of a desktop machine.

IBM's SLC2 design, produced under license from Intel, included the energy-saving features of the SL, plus a 16-KB cache and clock-doubling circuitry, which we will discuss below.

In later chips, Intel incorporated the low-power draw design to standard 486DX chips as a matter of course; in desktop systems, going to low-voltage versions has the benefit of reducing the damaging effects of heat generated by high-speed CPUs.

Cyrix chips are clones of the Intel original with their own microcode. The Cyrix 486SLC was actually more like a 386SX than a 486, and in fact plugged directly into a 386SX socket without any modification. It offered 32-bit internal registers and 16-bit communication with a standard bus. It included a small 1 KB cache but lacked the math coprocessor circuit.

The Cyrix 486DLC added 32-bit communication with the data bus, but still lacked the coprocessor. In some systems designers paired the DLC chip with an external coprocessor, but the result was still below that of an Intel original, although the net price was usually lower.

Intel 486DX2 (1992), Intel 486DX4 (1994), AMD Am486DX4-100 (1995)

The DX2 and DX4 designs are very powerful speedups to the 486 chip family, able to run internally at twice (DX2) or three times (DX4) the external bus speed. The most popular versions of the chips are the 486DX2-66, which runs at 66 MHz, and the 486DX4-100, which reaches to just short of 100 MHz. Systems based around the DX4-100 rival the processing power of the low-to mid-range Pentium processors at a lower price.

Why did Intel name the fastest 486 chip as DX4 instead of a more accurate DX3? The answer lies in an arcane argument between engineering and marketing about whether the name relates to tripling the speed of a 33 MHz bus or quadrupling the speed of a less-common 25 MHz bus; either way, a DX4 tops out at about 99 MHz.

The Intel DX4 processor is functionally identical to and 100 percent binary compatible with the original Intel 486 DX microprocessor, including the same RISC technology CPU, a floating-point unit, and memory management unit.

The 16-KB Intel DX4 processor cache has twice the capacity of the cache in the DX2 microprocessor. Based on advanced 0.6 micron fabrication for its 1.5 million transistors, the DX4 runs at 3.3 volts. The Intel DX4 processor includes all the SL technology features, including static design, Stop Clock, Auto Halt Power Down, Auto Idle Power Down, I/O restart, and Intel's System Management Mode. Static design enables the processor to operate at 0 MHz while maintaining its state and consuming minimal power. The Auto Idle feature allows the Intel DX4 processor to hibernate when it is idle during a memory cycle, waiting for I/O or memory to respond. According to Intel, Auto Idle Power Down feature saves at least 10 percent on processor power consumption with no impact on performance.

AMD's Am486DX4-100 is a clock-tripled 486 clone from American Micro Devices, a major U.S. fabricator of integrated circuits.

iCOMP Index of Intel Processors

The iCOMP (Intel Comparative Microprocessor Performance) index shows relative performance of various current Intel chips. A creation of Intel, it is a weighted combination of four industry-standard benchmarks that test integer, floating-point, graphics, and video performance: PCBench 7.0 (68 percent), SPECint92 (25 percent), SPECfp92 (5 percent), and Whetstone (2 percent). The higher the iCOMP rating, the higher the relative performance of the microprocessor.

In 1996, Intel updated and recalculated the iCOMP index to better reflect modern 32-bit software and multimedia applications. The iCOMP Index 2.0 is a weighted average based on five industry standard benchmarks: CPUmark32, Norton SI-32, SPECint95, SPECfp95, and the Intel Media Benchmark.

The new base processor for the iCOMP 2.0 is a Pentium 120 MHz processor, rated at 100 on the new scale. Although the new index does not exactly track backwards into older Intel processors, it is fair to say that an Intel Pentium 120 MHz is about 30 times faster than an i386 SX-20 CPU, and about three times as fast as the 486DX-22 66 MHz workhorse. Going the other direction, this same Pentium 120 MHz processor is less than half the speed of a Pentium Pro 200 MHz.

In the table that follows, you'll find scores for nearly every microprocessor produced by Intel from the dawn of the dinosaur to the latest and greatest of today's modern machines. The test results span four different scales employed by Intel over the years, but there is enough of an overlap to show the steady onward march of speed and capability.

Table 2.1 iCOMP Index of Intel Processors

INDEX	INTEL iCOMP	INTEL iCOMP 2.0	MIPS	SPEC Rating
8088 4.77 MHz			0.33	
8088-8			0.75	
80286-8			1.20	
80286-10			1.50	
80286-12			2.66	
i386 DX-16			5.00-6.00	
i386 DX-20			6.00-7.00	
i386 SX-16			2.50	
i386 SX-20	32		4.20	
i386 SL-20	u/c		4.21	
i386 SL-25	41		5.30	
i386 SX-25	39		u/c	
i386 DX-25	49		8.50	
i386 SX-33	56		u/c	
i386 DX-33	68		11.40	

Table 2.1 iCOMP Index of Intel Processors (continued)

INDEX	INTEL iCOMP	INTEL iCOMP 2.0	MIPS	SPEC Rating
i486 SX-16	u/c		13.00	
i486 SX-20	78		16.50	
i486 SX-25	100		25.00	12.00 SPECint92
i486 SL-25	122		u/c	
i486 DX-25	122		20.00	
i486 SX-33	136		27.00	15.86 SPECint92
i486 DX-33	166		27.00	22.40 SPECint92
i486 SL-33	166			
i486 DX2-40	182			
i486 DX2-50	231		41.00	29.90 SPECint92
i486 DX-50	249		41.00	33.40 SPECint92
i486 DX2-66	297		54.00	39.60 SPECint92
i486 DX4-75	319		53.00	41.30 SPECint92
i486 DX4-100	435		70.70	54.59 SPECint92
Pentium 60 MHz	510		100.00	70.40 SPECint92
Pentium 66 MHz	567		112.00	77.90 SPECint92
Pentium 75 MHz	610		126.50	2.31 SPECint95
Pentium 90 MHz	735		149.80	2.74 SPECint95
Pentium 100 MHz	870	90	166.30	3.30 SPECint95
Pentium 120 MHz	1000	100	203.00	3.72 SPECint95
Pentium 133 MHz	1110	111	218.90	4.14 SPECint95
Pentium 150 MHz		114		4.27 SPECint95
Pentium 166 MHz		127		4.76 SPECint95
Pentium 166 MHz with MMX		160		5.59 SPECint95
Pentium 200 MHz		142		5.47 SPECint95
Pentium 200 MHz with MMX		182		6.41 SPECint95
Pentium Pro 150 MHz		168		6.08 SPECint95
Pentium Pro 166 MHz		u/c		7.11 SPECint95
Pentium Pro 180 MHz		197		7.29 SPECint95
Pentium Pro 200 MHz		220		8.09 SPECint95

Intel Pentium (1993)

Intel brought the PC into the world of 64-bit processing with the Pentium, a microprocessor with power greater than that of many room-sized minicomputers of only a decade ago. The 3 million switches of the Pentium can perform an incredible 100 million instructions per second (MIPS) in its slowest 60 MHz version, and about 300 MIPS in its 200 MHz version.

The Pentium chips at the low end of the spectrum—60 and 75 MHz clock speed—were certainly speedy, but they were not necessarily markedly faster than a well-designed machine based on a 486DX4/100 chip. The main improvement offered by the Pentium lies in its speed in processing floating point math calculations. Before you try to tell us that the only math going on in your house occurs on a pocket calculator next to your checkbook, consider the fact that graphics programs are very math intensive. And graphics programs include your basic Intergalactic Monster Ping Pong game as well as Windows itself, which is a graphical user interface.

Subsequent speed boosts to as much as 200 MHz have removed any question about the value of the Pentium. A 233 MHz CPU is expected to top out the Pentium class by the end of 1997.

The chip communicates with the bus across an interface that is 64 bits wide (its socket includes 273 or 238 pins for connection); internally, the Pentium is actually a pair of 32-bit chips that can be chained together to perform a task split between them. The Pentium's standard 16K internal cache can handle program instructions and can also buffer some of the data coming in and out of the chip.

The processor is fully compatible with earlier Intel PC chips. True speed comes with the use of Pentium-optimized software; the split-processor design is not as efficient at running DOS applications as it is with Windows and OS/2 programs.

Figure 2.2 A Pentium 100 MHz CPU with a heat sink in place. This passive cooling device is very dependent on a proper flow of air through the PC as drawn by the fan on the power supply, and often by a supplementary cooling fan at the front or back of the case.

One concern with Pentium chips was their propensity for building up heat. Nearly all early Pentium systems included vaned heat sinks intended to draw away heat (Figure 2.2); many later designs include tiny fans atop the chips, and there have even been a few models that included tiny electronic cooling systems. Intel has reduced much of the heat problem with its later versions of the chip, which were made with super-efficient technology that permits them to run at 3.3 volts, instead of the original 5 volt draw.

Inside the Pentium Processor

The Pentium, like other Intel CPUs, builds upon the base of previous X86 chips, but includes more significant enhancements and new features than any processor before it. New architectural features include superscalar architecture, a totally redesigned floating point unit, branch prediction, and separate code and data caches.

Figure 2.3 A 133 MHz Pentium chip slips into a waiting socket on a motherboard.

Other enhancements to the architecture include speedy hardwired instructions for common operations, enhanced microcode, increased page size, pipelining, and a 64-bit data bus.

A good deal of the raw speed gain for the Pentium comes from the shrinking size and tighter integration of the chip (Figure 2.3). Individual elements of the latest chips are created at less than a *micron* (one-millionth of a meter) in size, with 3.1 million transistors on a single chip. The integration of elements such as math coprocessors and caches onto the CPU chip dramatically decreases the time required to access them.

The Pentium processor is a superscalar device, built around two instruction pipelines that are each capable of performing independently.

The pipelines permit the Pentium to execute two integer instructions in a single clock cycle, nearly double the performance of a 486 chip operating at the same frequency.

In certain circumstances, the Pentium processor can issue two instructions at once—one to each of the pipelines—in a process known as *instruction pairing*. Each pipeline is like a mini-computer itself, with its own arithmetic logic unit (ALU), address generation circuitry, and interface to the data cache.

While the 486 processor offered a dual-purpose 8-Kbyte cache, the original Pentium processor featured two 8K caches, one for instructions and one for data. The caches serve as temporary storage places for instructions and data obtained from slower main memory; the theory is that data and instructions are often used multiple times, and it is much faster to retrieve information from an on-chip cache than from main memory.

The chip manages the use of the caches through the use of an *LRU* algorithm that discards least recently used copies of data. *Dynamic branch prediction* is a technology that allows the processor to preload into the cache an instruction it expects to execute soon. Together, these two features speed operations considerably. According to Intel, a single iteration of the Sieve of Eratosthenes benchmark requires only 2 clock cycles on a Pentium processor, compared to 6 clock cycles on a 486 chip.

Completely redesigned in the Pentium is the floating point processor (FPU). (Alas, in the process, the Pentium's famous math flaw was introduced in some early models of the chip; more about that later.) The FPU includes an 8-stage pipeline, capable of executing one floating point operation every clock cycle. In certain circumstances, it can perform two operations per cycle.

The Pentium processor uses a 32-bit bus for its internal processing, the same as the 486DX and 386DX chips. However, Pentiums communicate to the external data bus across a 64-bit-wide highway. This doubles the amount of data that can be transferred in a single bus cycle. In addition, a Pentium processor burst mode can load 256-bit chunks of data into the data cache in a single bus cycle.

The 64-bit data bus allows a Pentium processor to transfer data to and from memory at rates up to 528 MB/sec. This is more than triple the peak transfer rate of a 50 MHz 486 chip.

In the CPU itself, Intel designers have taken several of the most commonly used instructions—including MOV and ALU—and hard wired them into the processor instead of the microcode library of instructions.

The Pentium processor includes a number of built-in features for testing the reliability of the chip. These include a Built-In Self Test that tests 70 percent of the Pentium processor's components upon resetting the chip.

In addition to speed boosts, Intel has made a basic change to the packaging of the chip itself, moving away from the ceramic container it has used more or less since the birth of the microprocessor. Newer high-speed Pentiums use a plastic pin grid array (PPGA) that includes a copper-nickel alloy heat sink directly above the chip to help draw away heat. In addition, the traces of the chip itself use copper instead of tungsten to improve conductivity and reduce heat.

Floating Point Flaw in the Pentium Processor

The year 1995 brought the highest-tech flub ever to come to the attention of the general public. Well beyond snipes at PC user clubs and flames on the Internet, it also became the source of a hundred late-night talk show jokes.

The offender was the floating point processor unit of Intel's proud new Pentium processor. In Intel's defense, the error was something that was likely to come up extremely rarely among technical and scientific users and almost never for home and office users. But Intel made some very serious public relations errors in dealing with the problem: it took several weeks for the company to decide it would replace the chip from any user who wanted to remove a suspect processor.

The problem affects the accuracy of the floating point divide instruction for certain combinations of numbers. According to Intel, the mistake will occur once in about 9 billion possible independent divides. According to Intel, the largest group of PC users have the least chance of running into the problem.

How can you tell if your processor has the floating point problem? If you took delivery of your system prior to Jan. 1, 1995, it is very likely that your processor has the floating point flaw. After that date, it is still possible that the machine you purchased was sitting in the retail channel long enough to have been built before the problem was identified. The affected chips were slower models, running at 60, 66, 75, 90, or 100 MHz.

It is not easy to tell if your Pentium chip has the flawed section by looking at it, especially if the top of the chip is covered with a heat sink or fan. You can call the manufacturer of your PC system and ask about your particular model; be sure to have your system's serial number and date of purchase available.

A more precise way to determine whether your Pentium is an "old" version is to run one of several identification programs. Intel has developed a utility called **CPUIDF.EXE** which tests your chip and reports on its lineage. The program is available on many BBS systems as well as on Intel's own Web page. For a Frequently Asked Questions (FAQ) paper on the problem, check Intel's page at: **http://support.intel.com/oem_developer/gen_q_and_r/other/8804.HTM**

Should you replace your Pentium? Intel says you don't need to—and they are probably correct—unless you are using your PC to redesign the Space Shuttle or to control your personal artificial heart. For most of the rest of us, the chances of seeing the flaw are very remote, and the effect of the error if it occurred would probably be very evident.

But a lot of PC users can't stand the thought of their machine being less than perfect. After all, that's why we have a computer on the desk: so it won't make the sort of dumb mistakes we constantly commit. And perhaps more rationally, there is also the consideration that it's next to impossible to predict what sort of software we will use in coming years. So, we recommend you take advantage of the chip swap; you can do it yourself or let Intel arrange for the changeover.

Upon request, Intel will replace a flawed Pentium processor with an updated chip any time during the life of the user's computer. This means you do not have to ask for the chip now.

Some computer makers (including ALR, AST, AT&T, Compaq, Digital Equipment Corp., Dell, and IBM) will service their customers directly. Contact the maker for assistance. Owners of systems from other manufacturers can obtain a new CPU from Intel and replace it themselves, or obtain information from Intel on the location of a walk-in service center where the work will be done.

For information on the process of replacing a chip, contact Intel in the United States at (800) 628-8686. You'll need to tell Intel your computer manufacturer and model as well as CPU speed. Intel will request a credit card number as a security deposit; no charge will be applied if the flawed chip is returned within 30 days of the shipment of the replacement CPU.

According to Intel, it asks for return of the old CPU to avoid illegal resale of the parts and to minimize market confusion. This is not a minor issue: fees range from $495 to $995 (depending on clock speed) for failure to return the old chip. The old chips will be ground up so that some of the precious metals used in their manufacture can be recovered.

Pentium Pro Processor (1995)

The latest and greatest Intel processor, the Pentium Pro, arrived near the end of 1995 in high-end servers and special-purpose machines; in 1996, the new CPU became the chip of choice in most high-demand applications. Increasing numbers of business and home users adopted the chip for use in workstation applications. The Pentium Pro chip began at the middle of the Pentium speed range, with a 166 MHz model, and as this book goes to press tops out at 200 MHz with a 233 MHz version moving toward the door.

A Pentium Pro-based system should work with any software intended for a Pentium machine, but it will be at its best when it is paired with a 32-bit operating system, such as Windows NT or OS/2 Warp. Even if you are not using those systems now, though, a Pentium Pro system puts you in a good position for OSes to come, including later versions of Windows 95.

The Pentium Pro is superpipelined (its pipelines are deep and multistaged), and it uses what Intel calls *dynamic execution* (a speculative, out-of-order design) to enhance performance over the Pentium chip. (Translation: It's fast.)

The Pentium Pro contains 8K of instruction and 8K of data Level 1 (L1) cache, the same as within the Pentium. However, it moved beyond that to add the Level 2 (L2) cache in the same chip-carrying package. There are models of the Pentium Pro with either 256K or 512K of four-way, set-associative L2 cache. Since the cache is essentially on the

CPU chip itself, it runs at the CPU speed, and performance is therefore much faster than in a system using an L2 cache on the motherboard.

The Pentium Pro integrates about 5.5 million transistors on the chip, compared to approximately 3.1 million transistors on the Pentium processor. The Pentium Pro operates at a low 3.3 volts.

Prices of Pentium Pro chips, as with other CPUs, go up with speed. As this book goes to press, a special version of the chip with a clock speed of 200 MHz and an L2 cache of 512K was the most expensive. To most observers, the best price/performance ratio is the 200 MHz chip with the smaller 256K cache. Note that the 180 MHz Pentium Pro chip—not the most popular version—runs at a slower 60 MHz bus speed; in some tests this version of the Pentium Pro did not run appreciably faster than a Pentium.

Pentium Pro

Clock Speed (MHz)	166	180	200	200
Bus Speed (MHz)	66	60	66	66
L2 Cache	512K	256K	256K	512K

According to Intel, the high performance of the Pentium Pro makes it well-suited for upcoming desktop applications such as speech recognition and multimedia authoring, as well as for more demanding server and workstation applications.

The Pentium Pro delivers superior performance through use of new technology called *dynamic execution*, a combination of three processing techniques the Pentium Pro uses to speed up software:

- **Multiple Branch Prediction**. The processor looks multiple steps ahead in the software and predicts which branches, or groups of instructions, are likely to be processed next.
- **Dataflow Analysis**. Next, the Pentium Pro analyzes which instructions are dependent on each other's results and then creates an optimized schedule of instructions.
- **Speculative Execution**. The processor then carries out instructions on a speculative basis. In theory, it will guess right more often than wrong, and keep the chip's superscalar processing power busy while boosting overall software performance.

Cache and Carry

Optimizing a Pentium Pro processor is a bit more complex than it was for earlier, simpler CPUs.

You should think about the intended use for the machine and then consider the particular Pentium Pro chip you use, and the associated chipset on the motherboard. In some instances, for example, a 166MHz Pentium Pro CPU with a 512K cache can offer better performance than a 200MHz Pentium Pro chip with more raw speed potential but with a 256K cache.

The Pentium Pro is actually two chips—the CPU and a memory chip for caching—mounted within what Intel calls a *Multi-Chip Module.*

Intel engineers say most workstation users will be well served by a 256K cache, while machines used as application servers or World Wide Web sites would most likely benefit from the larger 512K cache.

The next decision involves the chip set (also made by Intel in most instances) on the motherboard; these chips interface between the CPU and the BIOS and bus.

As this book goes to press, the high-end chip set is the 450GX, which supports four CPUs and 4GB of RAM; it also permits bridging multiple PCI buses to expand the number of PCI slots available to the system.

A notch below are the 440FX and 450KX chip sets, both of which support two CPUs and 1GB of RAM. The 440FX also supports the Universal Serial Bus, bus-mastering, and EDO (extended data out) RAM.

Obviously, a super server with more than two CPUs demands the 450GX; for the rest of us, the 440FX with its support for the developing Universal Serial Bus is a better deal than the 450KX.

The 430VX and 430HX, and the popular 430FX (also known as the Triton chipset) are members of an older series. The VX chip set supports high-performance synchronous DRAM (SDRAM) while the HX does not.

The time to look at the PCI chipset is when you buy a motherboard or a system. In most cases the motherboard is optimized for a particular chipset, and the support chips may even be soldered into place and not changeable.

Pentium MMX Extensions (1997)

Pentium with MMX (Multimedia Extensions) arrived at the start of 1997 in 166 and 200 MHz versions; as usual, the hardware was ahead of the ability of the software to make use of it. MMX-enabled software was expected to arrive later in the year.

According to Intel, MMX technology enables higher quality, high-performance technologies for graphics, video and audio. Specifically, Intel is looking toward video conferencing, full-motion video, and more advanced technologies.

Early tests showed speed boosts of 10 to 20 percent over Pentiums of the same clock speed. Software makers were expected to unleash a flood of MMX-enabled products later in 1997. Observers expected that among the first gee-whiz

applications of MMX would be playback of MPEG-2 video without the need for costly hardware accelerators, a feature that will mesh nicely with the arrival of MPEG-2 capable DVD-ROM drives in 1997.

Among changes in the new version, Intel includes a larger L1 cache, with 16K instruction and 16K data—double the size of the cache used on earlier Pentiums.

The Pentium processor with MMX technology is a dual voltage chip, operating at 3.3 volt I/O and 2.8 volt at the core. The lower voltage requirement should help move the chip into notebooks and lower the load and heat production in desktop machines. A special version of the chip with a 2.5 volt demand is intended for notebook applications.

Because of the change in voltage level, the first group of MMX CPUs cannot be plugged into most existing Pentium motherboards. (New motherboards for MMX CPUs need to add a voltage regulator to accommodate the new voltage levels and in most cases previous versions of the system BIOS will not work with the new chip.)

As this book goes to press, the only Intel chipset that supports the dual voltage is Intel's 430HX. Another issue involves the use of Socket 7 CPU carriers which do not support MMX processors. The motherboard needs wiring and a socket to support both Socket 5 and Socket 7 pin-outs.

Intel's "Tucson" motherboard is built around that chipset and socket, although other boardmakers may use the chips and socket as elements of their own designs.

Finally, you may need to update your version of Windows 95 to make an MMX chip work properly with an EIDE CD-ROM. Intel offers a utility on its Web site to make the fix: **ftp://ftp.intel.com/pub/patch/ideinfup.exe**

In any case, Intel promises that a Pentium OverDrive processor with MMX technology will be available by the end of 1997 to allow upgrade of Pentium processor-based systems.

In addition to tweaks to the hardware, Intel added 57 powerful new instructions to its architecture—the first significant change to the x86 instruction set since the introduction of 80386—to speed up certain compute-intensive loops in multimedia and communications applications. While the loops typically occupy 10 percent or less of the overall application code, they can account for up to 90 percent of the execution time.

The 57 new instructions are specifically aimed at media and signal processing tasks including video playback, graphics, and advanced audio functions; MMX-enabled programs are able to call for a single operation of the CPU instead of requesting a series of complex operations.

Intel chose to make the MMX instructions an extension of the existing Pentium chip, and as such had to make some compromises to fit them in; principal among them is the fact that MMX CPUs cannot execute MMX and floating point instructions at the same time. For most users, though, this will not be a significant problem since current applications do not make much use of the floating point unit. In the relatively uncommon situations where a program is written to use both floating point and MMX operations, there could be a slowdown in performance; it seems unlikely that software designers will go out of their way to create situations where this penalty is applied.

MMX instructions process multiple data elements in parallel using a technique called *Single Instruction Multiple Data* (SIMD). In simulations and preliminary tests on development systems, Intel claims performance benefits have ranged from 50 to 400 percent, depending on the application.

Microsoft plans to support MMX technology in its Direct3D* API, a set of API services for real-time, interactive 3-D graphics; ActiveMovie, its next-generation video technology; and its Visual C++ compiler.

The first Pentium Pro with MMX was due to join the family midway through the year. By the end of 1997, Intel plans to include the MMX extensions in all of its Pentium chips. The chips were expected to demand a relatively small premium of about $100 to $200 over the previous Pentium versions when first introduced, and then follow Intel's regular downward price spiral in coming years.

MMX Clones

AMD and Cyrix have both indicated they will add MMX compatibility to their own chips. AMD signed a cross-licensing deal with Intel for the rights to the MMX technology and its instruction set, and was expected to add MMX to its next-generation K6 chip. Cyrix was expected to add MMX to its new M2 series chip.

Pentium Clones

Three major chipmakers have introduced their versions of the Pentium chip. As was the case with the first 486 clones, the competitive chips seem to require tradeoffs of one sort or another. Early chips were less expensive than the Intel versions, but ran slightly slower.

AMD5K86 (1995), Nx586 P100 (1995)

AMD's introduction of its K5 was delayed because of performance problems. When it finally arrived as the AMD5K86, it received good marks for compatibility and speed; its main advantage is a price break compared to the comparable Intel Pentium chip. It includes some advanced features, including out-of-order speculative execution, a 16K instruction cache (twice that of the standard Pentium), and an 8K data cache.

The Next Generation Nx586 P100 model actually ran at 93 MHz, but was claimed to rival a Pentium at 100 MHz. It had the disadvantage of not being pin-compatible with a Pentium chip, and therefore required a special motherboard

and support chips. In 1996, Next Generation was purchased by AMD and its research and development labs were incorporated into AMD.

Cyrix 6x86 (1996)

The Cyrix 6x86 processor is pin-compatible with the Pentium. In magazine lab tests, the 6x86 generally outperformed equivalent Intel processors, but fell short of the results turned in by Pentium Pro processors.

One other issue noted in 1996 were reports of overheating and heat-related failures on some 6x86 systems; Cyrix says its chips should not overheat if system vendors follow their recommendations for heat sinks and high-volume fans as well as sufficient airflow ducts in cases. If you have a 6x86-based system, you should make certain the cooling system is appropriate and take care to avoid blocking air vents.

The next chip in the pipeline for Cyrix is the M2, which if the company follows its current naming scheme will likely be called 7x86. The chip is expected to include the MMX extensions and run at higher clock rates.

AMD K6 (1997)

Among the expected results of AMD's purchase of NexGen was incorporation of NexGen's 686 design in AMD's plans for the K6 chip, which is expected to be a competitor to IBM's Pentium Pro chips. Release of the K6, which will also include the MMX extensions, was expected sometime in 1997.

About Clone Names

As we discussed in Chapter 1, both AMD and Cyrix have contributed to the complexity of chip-naming schemes. The problem arose out of the success both companies had in optimizing the speed of their clones: a Cyrix 6x86 runs at 133 MHz, but benchmarks show it performing at a level equivalent to a 166 MHz Pentium. In 1996, chip designers Cyrix and AMD, together with contract chipmakers IBM and SGS-Thomson, came up with something they called the P-Rating Specification. This is intended to relate the performance of their CPUs to an Intel equivalent. Therefore, a P166+ is supposed to indicate that the chip performs at a speed comparable to an Intel Pentium at 166 MHz.

According to the specification, if a clone chip's score is within 1.5 percent of a particular Pentium on Ziff-Davis' Winstone 96 benchmark, it can carry a rating equivalent to the Pentium.

Table 2.2 Intel Processors

	8086	8088	80286
Address Bus	16 bit	16 bit	24 bit
Data Bus	16 bit	8 bit	16 bit
FPU?	No	No	No
Memory Management?	No	No	No
Internal Cache?	No	No	No
Clock Speed (MHz)	5, 8, 10	5, 8, 10	6, 8, 10, 12
Avg. Cycles/Instruction	12	12	4.9
Frequency of FPU	=CPU	=CPU	2/3 CPU
Upgradeable?	No	No	No
Address Range	1 MB	1 MB	16 MB
Freq. Scalability?	No	No	No
Voltage	5v	5v	5v
Number of Transistors	29,000	29,000	134,000
Date of Introduction	June, 1978	June, 1979	Feb., 1982

	i386 SX	i386 DX	i386 SL
Address Bus	24 bit	32 bit	24 bit
Data Bus	16 bit	32 bit	16 bit
FPU?	n/a	n/a	n/a
Memory Management?	Yes	Yes	Yes
Internal Cache?	No	No	Control
Clock Speed (MHz)	16, 20, 25, 33	16, 20, 25, 33	16, 20, 25
Avg. Cycles/Instruction	4.9	4.9	<4.9
Frequency of FPU	=CPU	=CPU	=CPU
Upgradeable?	No	No	No
Address Range	16 MB	4 GB	16 MB
Voltage	5v	5v	3v or 5v
Number of Transistors	275,000	275,000	855,000
Date of Introduction	June, 1988	Oct., 1985	Oct., 1990

Table 2.2 Intel Processors (continued)

	i486 SX	i486 DX	i486 SL	i486 DX2	i486DX4
Internal bus	32 bits	32 bits	32 bits	32 bits	32 bits
External bus	32 bits	32 bits	32 bits	32 bits	32 bits
Virtual Address Space	64 Terabytes	64 TB	64 TB	64 TB	64 TB
Physical Address Space	4 Gigabytes	4 GB	4 GB	4 GB	4 GB
Clock Speed (MHz)	16, 20, 25, 33	25, 33, 50	25, 33	50, 66	75, 100
Math Coprocessor	Available	Built-in	Built-in	Built-in	Built-in
Cache Control?	Built-in	Built-in	Built-in	Built-in	Built-in
1st-Level Cache?	Built-in	Built-in	Built-in	Built-in	Built-in
OverDrive Support?	Yes	Yes	No	Yes	Yes
Number of Transistors	1.2 Million	1.2 Million	1.4 Million	1.2 Million	1.6 Million
Date of Introduction	April, 1991	April, 1989	Nov., 1992	March, 1992	March, 1994

	Pentium		Pentium Pro	Pentium with MMX
Internal bus	32 bits		32 bits	32 bits
External bus	64 bits		64 bits	64 bits to front, 64 bits to L2 cache
Virtual Address Space	64 TB		64 TB	64 TB
Physical Address Space	4 GB		4 GB	64 GB
Clock Speed (MHz)	60, 66, 75, 90, 100, 120, 133, 150, 166, 200		166, 200	166, 180, 200
Math Coprocessor	Built-in		Built-in	Built-in
Cache Control?	Built-in		Built-in	Built-in
1st-Level Cache?	Built-in		Built-in	Built-in
OverDrive Support?	Yes		To come	To come
Number of Transistors	3.1-3.3 Million		4.5 Million	3.1-3.3 Million
Date of Introduction	March, 1993		January, 1997	November, 1995

OverDrive Processors

Kicking an Intel CPU into OverDrive is like attaching a turbocharger to an old flivver, delivering a "mid-life" kick. OverDrive chips are a generally cost-effective bridge between an underpowered older machine and new technology. Intel has delivered OverDrive processors for 486SX and DX-based machines, and for Pentium processors from 60

MHz to 100 MHz in speed. As this book goes to press in 1997, Intel was about to release hot OverDrives that take Pentium processors into the realm of Pentium with MMX at 166 and even 200 MHz.

Intel recommends its Pentium OverDrive processor for upgradable Intel SX2 and Intel DX2 CPU-based PCs, and upgradable Intel 486 SX- and DX-based PCs with 237- or 238-pin sockets. Two versions of the Pentium OverDrive processors were available at the start of 1997: 63-MHz Pentium OverDrive processors for 25 or 50-MHz systems and 83-MHz Pentium OverDrive processors for 33 or 66-MHz systems.

The Overdrive CPU still interconnects with the external bus at its original clock rate, enabling it to work with the rest of the original system and any of its installed peripherals.

If possible, I recommend you upgrade all the way from a 486 to Pentium power; there is no good reason to save just a few dollars and go part of the way. Unfortunately, not all 486 systems are capable of accepting an Intel Pentium OverDrive.

Until 1996, Intel also offered upgrade processors for 486SX and 486DX microprocessors that brought them to DX/2 or DX/4 equivalencies, applying the same speed-doubling technology used in the development of the 486DX2 CPU; they allowed the chips to operate internally at twice the clock speed of the CPU they replaced. Two versions of the Intel DX4 OverDrive processor were offered for Intel 486 SX and DX processor-based systems: the 75-MHz Intel DX4 OverDrive processors for 20/25-MHz systems, and the 100-MHz Intel DX4 OverDrive processors for 33-MHz systems. Intel discontinued production of the chips in 1996, claiming low demand after the first round of 486 owners made their upgrades. The good news: if you can't find an Intel 486 OverDrive, you should be able to find other upgrade options from other companies employing AMD or Cyrix CPUs (we'll discuss their devices later).

Intel planned to continue to offer Pentium OverDrive processor upgrades for Intel 486 processor-based systems which have the larger 237/238-pin socket ("Socket 2" or "Socket 3").

If you do find an Intel DX4 OverDrive still available, pay attention to the part number. There were two types of chips offered. BOXDX4ODPR parts have 168 pins and are designed to upgrade Intel 486 DX CPU-based systems, using the same jumper settings as the original part. BOXDX4ODP parts have 169 pins and are designed to upgrade Intel 486 SX CPU-based systems, most of which use a "keyed" upgrade socket with one extra pinhole to ensure correct orientation of the OverDrive processor. These parts use jumper settings specific to the OverDrive processors and the old Intel 487 SX math coprocessors. Consult your system maker or Intel for further details before using this DX4 upgrade. See Figure 2.4.

Figure 2.4 On some motherboards an Intel OverDrive replaces the original 486 or Pentium chip in the processor socket, while some older designs had a separate OverDrive socket on the motherboard.

Fixing a Rare Pentium Problem

Some early Pentium systems were designed with instructions that incorrectly support the WriteBack mode of the Pentium OverDrive processor. In order to upgrade these systems to Pentium processors, you'll need to use a special "interposer" chip carrier that sits between the OverDrive and the CPU socket on the motherboard; the interposer disables the WriteBack mode. If your system manufacturer advises you that the interposer is required, they may be able to supply the part or you may need to deal directly with Intel, which supplies the part for free or at very low cost.

Table 2.3 Intel iCOMP INDEX for Microprocessors with OverDrive Processors

CPU	iCOMP Index	With OverDrive	Equivalent after upgrade
i486 SX-20	78	182	i486 DX2-40
i486 SX-25	100	231	i486 DX2-50
i486 DX-25	122	231	i486 DX2-50
i486 SX-33	136	297	i486 DX2-66
i486 DX-33	166	297	i486 DX2-66

Table 2.3 Intel iCOMP INDEX for Microprocessors with OverDrive Processors (continued)

CPU	iCOMP 2.0 Index	With OverDrive	Equivalent after upgrade
Pentium 60	51	75	Pentium 83
Pentium 66	57	84	Pentium 90
Pentium 75	67	92	Pentium 105
Pentium 90	81	114	Pentium 150
Pentium 100	90	127	Pentium 166

486 Socket Types

Intel's plans for OverDrive chips developed during the early days of 486 motherboards. As a result, there are three types of 486 systems on the market:

- Motherboards that come equipped with a special OverDrive socket that supplements your CPU
- Motherboards where the user must remove the CPU and replace it with a new OverDrive CPU in a special 168-pin version of the DX2 OverDrive processor
- Motherboards that will not work with an OverDrive chip.

If you have any doubts about the design of your system's motherboard, consult the instruction manual or contact the PC's manufacturer.

Intel publishes the *OverDrive Compatibility Guide*, which contains a list of systems that have been tested and confirmed as compatible with the OverDrive chip. Intel recommends against using the OverDrive in any system not on the list, and will not honor warranty claims for chips damaged as a result of improper usage.

Note also that Intel's certification applies to systems rather than motherboards because of variables, including the types of peripheral components in a system and whether the system has sufficient airflow to properly cool the OverDrive processor. Because of this position by Intel, many no-name 486 machines are not certified as compatible.

Some single- or two-socket systems may have a larger socket. These models are upgradeable with a 486 or Pentium OverDrive.

Getting a Handle on 486 Sockets

Two common types of sockets for OverDrive processors are those with a handle (also called *Zero Insertion Force* or *ZIF sockets*) and those without a handle (sometimes called *Low Insertion Force sockets*).

You have, of course, turned off your computer and removed the power plug before attempting any work inside the box. Ground yourself by touching the chassis of the PC or by touching a grounding strap.

To open a socket with a handle, push down and away on the handle to unhook it from the small catch that holds it in place. Lift the handle to a 90° upright position, then remove the processor or insert a new one. Place the old processor on a soft, non-conductive surface like the piece of foam usually provided with the replacement chip. To close the socket, lower the socket handle and hook it under the catch.

If your system's processor socket does not have a handle, you should obtain a chip removal tool (basically a small, non-conductive, spatula-like device that slips under the chip and gives you a fulcrum point to push up on the chip from its underside). Work carefully and slowly here and be careful not to bend or break the pins on the chip you are removing. When the chip is removed, carefully align the replacement processor over the proper holes and push it into place evenly, again taking care to avoid bending or breaking pins.

There are several socket designs on 486 processor systems of different sizes. If your system has a socket with 17 pin-holes per side (168- or 169-pinhole socket), you cannot upgrade with Intel's Pentium OverDrive processor (although you may find a processor upgrade available from other makers, usually employing an AMD or Cyrix CPU.)

In order to use an Intel OverDrive in a 486 system, the socket must have 19 pinholes per side (237- or 238-pinhole socket). An easy way to tell if you have such a socket is to examine the original 486 processor in place; look for an extra row of pinholes around the processor.

Some 486 systems offer a second, special socket intended for the OverDrive processor upgrade. In this design, all you have to do is install the OverDrive processor in the empty socket; the system will automatically disable the 486 processor.

Installing an OverDrive in a Single Socket 486 Motherboard

1. Turn off the PC and unplug the power cord. Remove the PC's covers. Before handling the internals of the computer, ground yourself by touching the metal backplate of the PC or by touching the center screw of an electrical outlet cover.

2. Locate the 486 CPU on the motherboard or on a removable CPU card. On some systems, it may be necessary to take apart much of the system to gain access to the chip, including the removal of cards and hard drives.

3. Using an extraction tool, carefully remove the 486 CPU. Remove the chip with a firm, even pull that does not bend the pins or damage the motherboard.

4. Install the OverDrive processor into the socket. Align Pin 1 of the chip with the marked hole in the socket and press down firmly and evenly. Take care not to bend any of the pins of the chip under its body or outside of the socket.

5. If necessary, set jumpers or switches on the motherboard so that it will recognize the presence of the OverDrive. Consult your instruction manual or call the system manufacturer for further details. Some systems may require new BIOS chips or software updates to configuration programs.

6. Reinstall any boards or cables removed to make room for the installation of the OverDrive. Plug the system into electrical current and turn it on to test the processor.

Installing an OverDrive in a 486 Motherboard with an Upgrade Socket

1. Turn off the PC and unplug the power cord. Remove the PC's covers. Before handling the internals of the computer, ground yourself by touching the metal backplate of the PC or by touching the center screw of an electrical outlet cover.

2. Locate the empty OverDrive socket. Some systems have standard sockets, while others have Low Insertion Force (LIF) sockets or a Zero Insertion Force (ZIF) socket.

3. Orient the OverDrive processor correctly before installing it. There are several designs for sockets:

   - A "keyed" socket has four rows of pin holes and a key pin hole; match the key pin on the chip with the key pin hole on the socket.
   - If the socket has fewer than three rows of pin holes, or does not have a key pin hole, your computer may still be upgradeable with the OverDrive processor. Consult your computer system's manufacturer for more information.

4. Insert the OverDrive processor in the empty socket. If the socket is a Zero Insertion Force design, be sure to unlock or release the socket before inserting the chip and close the lock/unlock lever or turn the lock/unlock screw to the closed position after the chip is in place.

    If the system has a standard socket, you may have to press firmly to seat the pins in the socket; be sure to press evenly and watch that none of the pins bend underneath the chip or outside the socket. And do not press hard enough to bend the motherboard.

5. If necessary, set jumpers or switches on the motherboard so that it will recognize the presence of the OverDrive. Consult your instruction manual or call the system manufacturer for further details.

Installing an OverDrive in a Pentium Motherboard

1. Turn off the PC and unplug the power cord. Remove the PC's covers. Before handling the internals of the computer, ground yourself by touching the metal backplate of the PC or by touching the center screw of an electrical outlet cover.

2. Locate the original Pentium processor. If the original Pentium processor has a fan cooling system, unplug the cable; it will not be needed for the Pentium OverDrive processor. Unfasten any clips holding the processor and heatsink to the socket.

3. 75, 90, or 100 MHz systems: open the socket handle and remove the original Pentium processor. Orient the Pentium OverDrive processor so that the side with the processor speed mark is next to the number in the socket label.

    60 or 66 MHz systems: open the socket handle and remove the original Pentium processor. Orient the Pentium OverDrive Processor so that the speed mark on the processor is next to the "S" in the socket label.

4. Close the socket handle, put the cover back on your computer, plug it in, and test the system using your standard applications, a utility benchmark program, or the special diagnostic software that comes with the Pentium OverDrive processor.

Troubleshooting an Intel OverDrive

Problem: You have installed an Intel OverDrive, but the computer does not power up when the switch is turned on, or the operating system prompt does not appear on the screen.

Solution:

- Check that the power cord is attached to the system and is plugged into the wall socket. If that does not solve the problem, unplug the wire and check that cables and connectors inside the computer are attached correctly, and that any boards you may have removed are reinstalled correctly.

- Check that the OverDrive processor is oriented correctly in the socket, especially if it is installed in an overlarge 238-pin socket. All chips should be fully inserted into the socket with only about a dime's width between the bottom of the chip and the top of the socket.

- Be sure that you have installed the OverDrive in the upgrade socket and have not put it into the Weitek 4170 math coprocessor socket that is present on some motherboards.

- IBM PS/2 computers require the running of the Reference Diskette to update the system information. Other systems may require setting jumpers and sockets.

- Does your computer require a BIOS upgrade? Contact Intel Technical Support at (800) 321-4044 for information.

Problem: The OverDrive processor fails the Intel Diagnostics program.

Solution:

- Is the OverDrive Processor fully inserted in its socket? If you are using a ZIF socket, is the socket lever fully locked or the screw fully closed?

- Does your computer require an update to its BIOS? Consult with the manufacturer of your computer or with Intel.

- Check jumpers and switches to be sure they are set correctly.

- You can remove the OverDrive processor and install it in another identical or similar PC to see if it performs properly. Be sure that you have the correct model of OverDrive for the second computer. If the chip works, there is a problem with the first computer; if the chip fails, it is probably defective.

- If the OverDrive Processor still fails the diagnostic tests, remove it and return it to your dealer or Intel.

Problem: The PC does not run any faster with the OverDrive processor installed.

Solution:

- Are jumpers or switches on the motherboard set correctly, as described in your computer's manual? (Some systems require no changes to settings.)
- Have you run any necessary setup programs, such as the Reference Diskette for IBM PS/2 systems?
- Use the Intel Diagnostics to be sure the OverDrive is installed properly. Use a general system diagnostic program to check on the entire computer as well.
- Does the system have a second level cache? Check the CMOS setup screen to assure that it is turned on.
- Check the integrity of your cache. With the OverDrive installed, go to the CMOS setup and switch off the cache. Using an application such as a spreadsheet, database, or word processor run a specific number of commands on a lengthy file and time how long they took to execute. Then perform the identical test with the cache switched on. If there is no performance difference, you may have a problem with your second level cache. Contact your computer manufacturer for more assistance.

Problem: The OverDrive feels hot to the touch.

Solution:

- The OverDrive processor (and many other high-speed chips) generate heat when operating. According to Intel, the heat sink that is part of the chips will draw away heat so that a chip fan is not necessary.
- Be sure that your PC's fan is operating properly, that input air ports are not blocked with dust, and that exhaust ports are not blocked by being too close to a wall or other obstruction.

Problem: The computer boots up and runs normally for a while and then hangs or shuts down.

Solution:

- Check that the OverDrive is fully inserted into the socket, and properly oriented—is the key pin aligned with the socket's key pin?
- If you are using a ZIF socket, is the lever fully locked or the screw fully closed?
- Are jumpers or system switches set correctly, if changes are necessary? Consult your computer manual or the manufacturer of the system.

- Do you need to update your system's BIOS? Owners of IBM PS/2 Models 90 or 95 must run the latest Reference diskette. Consult your computer manual or Intel's customer support.

- Do you have to wait for the computer to cool off before it boots? Your computer may not be producing enough airflow to cool the OverDrive. Check with Intel's customer support for information about using an alternate OverDrive processor.

Problem: After about a month's use of the OverDrive Processor, the computer quits booting.

Solution:

- Assuming no other changes have been made to the system, the problem may be that the OverDrive Processor needs to be reinstalled. Take the motherboard out of the computer and place it on a firm surface, being careful not to damage the solder joints on the under side. Reinstall the OverDrive Processor, being sure to firmly push down on the part. This will solve your problem.

CPU Upgrades from Other Makers

Intel is not the only game in town when it comes to upgrading older CPUs to more modern capabilities and performance. A number of companies offer replacement chips that bring a 386 to near-486 power, 486s to Pentium-like performance, and older Pentiums to faster models.

The chips, which generally will work in either an OverDrive socket or the primary socket, use an AMD or Cyrix processor. Here's a sampling of some of the upgrade offerings:

Table 2.4 Original CPUs and their replacement equivalents

Evergreen Technologies (Uses AMD CPUs)

ORIGINAL CPU	REPLACEMENT EQUIVALENT
386SX 16, 20, 25 MHz	486 32, 40, 50 MHz
386SX 16, 20, 25 MHz	486 48, 60, 75 MHz
386DX 16, 20, 25 MHz	486 48, 60, 75 MHz
486SX or DX/25, 33, 40, 50 MHz	486 75, 80, 100 MHz
486 20, 25, DX2/50	586 80 or 100 MHz
486 33, 40, DX2/66	586 120 or 133 MHz

Table 2.4 Original CPUs and their replacement equivalents (continued)

Evergreen Technologies (Uses AMD CPUs)

Gainbery (Uses Intel CPUs and other chips)

60 MHz Pentium	90 MHz Pentium
66 or 75 MHz Pentium	100 MHz Pentium
66 MHz Pentium	586 133 MHz
60 MHz Pentium	586 150 MHz

Trinity Works (Uses AMD CPUs)

486 SX, SX/2, DX, DX/2	586 75 MHz
Pentium 60 or 66 MHz	586 120, 133, 150 MHz
Pentium 75 or 90 MHz	586 150 MHz

Kingston Technology TurboChips for 486 Systems

Kingston Technology's TurboChip processor upgrades are chip-for-chip upgrades for most 486DX or SX systems. They are based on Advanced Micro Devices 486-compatible chips.

TurboChips come in several versions. The TC486/75 provides 486 clock-tripling performance for 16, 20, and 25 MHz 486 systems. The TC486/100 upgrades 486-based 33 MHz systems to 100 MHz. Both versions come equipped with an 8-KB internal cache and a cooling fan. Another version is the TurboChip 133, which includes a 16-KB internal cache.

Note that the TurboChips will not provide much of an improvement in performance on 50 MHz or 66 MHz systems.

Installation is straightforward, without the need for alterations to the system board, switch settings, or device drivers on most systems. The only consideration for some users is the fact that the TurboChip, with its cooling fan, sits 7/8″ higher than the chip it replaces. A small number of PCs may have disk drives or other parts that sit close to the microprocessor socket and could cause a problem here.

The TurboChip replaces your existing processor, or plugs into an Intel OverDrive socket if the original processor cannot be removed. If you use the OverDrive socket, you will probably have to set jumpers or switches to disable the existing CPU.

Many 486 computers use Zero Insertion Force (ZIF) sockets with a lever or retaining screw to permit easy removal of the CPU. Kingston also provides a PGA socket extender to use with certain types of ZIF socket installations using an overhead locking bar that would not ordinarily close with the higher TurboChip in place.

The most important step in installing a Kingston upgrade involves the same precautions as would be involved in working with any chips on your system: be sure to switch off and unplug the system before working under the covers; ground yourself before touching a chip; use even pressure to remove the existing CPU if necessary; take special care to align Pin 1 of the TurboChip with Pin 1 of the socket, and install the new chip with even pressure. Watch carefully to be certain you do not bend or misalign any pins as you install the new chip.

A Real World Test

We installed a TurboChip 100 and then a TurboChip 133 into a Gateway 2000 486SX-33 computer, a capable—but relatively slow—home computer.

Before installing the chip, I ran the Landmark Speed 2.0 benchmark program on the Gateway machine. It reported that the 33 MHz SX chip was the functional equivalent of a 112.5 MHz PC-AT; another way to state this comparison is to say that the unimproved Gateway machine was running about 14 times faster than an 8 MHz PC-AT. After the TurboChip 100 was put in place, the Landmark Speed 2.0 benchmark indicated the presence of a 100 MHz 486DX chip at the functional equivalent of a 334 MHz PC-AT; the Gateway's speed had been tripled.

For the fourth edition of this book, we worked with the newer TurboChip 133. This time the Landmark Speed 2.0 benchmark reported the functional equivalent of a 431 MHz PC-AT, more the quadrupling the raw speed of the CPU.

Of course, the raw clock speed rating of the CPU is not a true measure of the power of the computer. More realistically, you can expect a near doubling of speed.

The installation took a total of 15 minutes, with 5 minutes of the time devoted to a careful check, double-check, and triple-check of the orientation of the chip in the ZIF socket of the Gateway machine. The only trick consists of carefully noting the notched corner of the Intel original chip and orienting the replacement Kingston chip's notch in the same place on the socket.

I checked the installation one more time before powering up the system. After the covers had been replaced, the final step consisted of pasting a Kingston TurboChip sticker over the outdated 486-33SX label.

Lightning Upgrades for 386DX Systems

Kingston also offers the Lightning 486 Processor Upgrade, a small board and CPU that provides 486 clock-doubled performance for 386DX-based 25-and 33 MHz systems, and 486 clock-tripled performance for 386DX-based 16-and 20 MHz systems.

An unusual offering from Kingston is a version of its Lightning 486 product aimed at IBM PS/2 models 70 and 80 that boosts those devices to 66-MHz performance and includes a specialized cache buffer which optimizes the capabilities of the Micro Channel architecture.

The Lightning upgrades will not work with systems based on 386SX processors.

Intel's Future Development

Intel's announced plans call for microprocessors capable of delivering up to 2,000 MIPS at a 250 MHz clock rate by the year 2000. Such chips could contain as many as 100 million transistors and include multiple CPUs, special units for high-speed math, and an "intelligent" interface to handle such functions as full-motion video, image processing, and speech and handwriting recognition.

The top end of the Pentium class of chips is expected to be a 233 MHz CPU with MMX extensions, expected by mid-1997. The zippy chip was added to Intel's product list after AMD's K6 CPU proved to be a tough competitor in Pentium systems.

According to the computer press, Intel has at least more five CPUs in development for release between now and 1998. Internal code names for the processors have a decidedly green flavor: all are named after American rivers and parks.

Intel was expected to release 200 MHz, 233 MHz, and 266 MHz versions of the code-named Klamath processor, a Pentium Pro with the MMX extensions in the second half of 1997. Klamath was to sport a larger L1 cache than the Pentium Pro, but not to include an internal L2 cache; removing the L2 cache will reduce the cost of the chip and give system vendors more flexibility in designing their offerings.

Near the end of the year, Intel was expected to release Deschutes, a smaller version of the Pentium Pro suitable for notebook use, initially released at 300 MHz. Katmai, an even smaller Pentium Pro chip, is expected to process more instructions per clock cycle than the original CPU.

By the middle of 1998, Intel is expected to release Willamette, with further speed and efficiency improvements.

Out on the horizon is a very fast promise: the P7 (code name Merced) chip in joint development by Intel and Hewlett-Packard Co.

The 64-bit chip is expected to eventually reach a clock speed of 1,400 MHz, with somewhat slower earlier versions expected late in 1998 and the top speed arriving a few years later. According to analysts, Merced should be able to bite off chunks of x86 or Unix code at five to seven instructions per clock cycle, resulting in at least a doubling of the efficiency of the Pentium Pro.

The ultra speed of the chip may force Intel to abandon the traditional silicon base for the chip; alternatives may be expensive gallium arsenide, or silicon germanium, which was used to make the very first transistors in the 1950s but was abandoned because of cost.

Dinosaur Arithmetic: Math Coprocessors

A math coprocessor is a specialized form of microprocessor that is capable of performing certain types of floating point math calculations much faster than a general-purpose CPU. It works in cooperation with the CPU, taking charge of some jobs ordinarily performed by the microprocessor. It adds speed to your system by doing the calculations faster than the main chip *and* by reducing some of the CPU's workload.

Math coprocessors are an add-on to dinosaur 386 and 286 CPUs; a floating point unit is included within 486DX and all current Pentium chips.

What is a floating point calculation? First of all, floating-point is a way of expressing a number, not a particular type of number like an integer or a rational or irrational number. A floating-point number is a value in which the decimal point can move one way or the other as the result of mathematical manipulations. It's easier to define by saying what is *not* a floating-point number: whole numbers (integers) and predetermined values like dollars and cents where there are always two numbers to the right of the decimal point.

A floating-point number has three parts: the *sign*, which indicates whether its value is greater than or less than zero; a *significant* (also called a *mantissa*) which includes all of the mathematically meaningful digits; and an *exponent*, which expresses the order of magnitude of the significant, which would be the location to which the decimal point floats.

Just because you are running a spreadsheet model of the economy of France from 1870 to 1999, don't automatically assume that your application makes much use of floating point calculations.

PC Magazine conducted some interesting tests a few years back that illustrate this: the magazine found that a coprocessor delivered little or no benefit in most spreadsheet applications based on database sorts. It also found that most financial calculations involve mostly addition and subtraction, which yield no benefit. And even with most commercial applications that perform heavy-duty calculations, only a relatively small amount of their work is actually related to the math, with the rest devoted to overhead including display and sorting.

The real boost came in custom software for very complex calculations, including manipulation of arrays of irrational numbers and trigonometric functions. (An *irrational number* is an infinite value such as pi or 2/3 which must be rounded off by the computer.)

And one more interesting finding by the magazine: no matter what combination of 386 chip and coprocessor it tried, a 486 chip with its built-in math coprocessor was always faster. This would apply in spades for Pentium chips.

Therefore, unless you are running some very strange and demanding software, it would seem that the most cost-efficient upgrade for owners of a 386 modern machine would be to install an OverDrive or similar replacement technology that would move your PC to the 486 or Pentium class. Not only will you pick up the floating-point math unit but you'll also improve the overall abilities of the CPU. This option is not available to owners of most dinosaurs, though.

How Do You Choose the Proper Math Coprocessor?

The best-known maker of math coprocessors is Intel, the designer and prime manufacturer of nearly all microprocessors used in PCs. Other makers of coprocessors over the years have included Advanced Micro Devices, Cyrix Corporation, Integrated Information Technology, ULSI, and Weitek.

Start by checking the instruction manual from your computer's maker; you may need to call the manufacturer's technical support line. Intel's FaxBACK Service also contains compatibility listings for Intel math coprocessors for many widely used computers.

Some general guidelines:

- **Pentium**, **486DX**, **486DX/2**, **486DX/4**, **486SL**. These CPUs include a built-in math coprocessor, and do not need an external chip.

- **486SX**. The 486 SX can be brought near to the capability of a 486DX CPU through the addition of an i487 math coprocessor chip. In 486SX-based computers, the microprocessor and math coprocessor run at the same speed.

  A better solution, though, is to use an OverDrive Processor instead of the 487; the OverDrive unit includes the math coprocessor and will also boost overall system performance by up to 70%.

- **386DX, 386SX, 386SL.** None of the members of the 386 class of CPUs have an integral math coprocessor; the SX and SL versions of the chips differ in their compatibility with 16-bit data buses rather than the 32-bit bus lines of the DX version.

   You will need to select the appropriate 387DX or 387SX math coprocessors. Note that the 387 DX is not certified to operate with non-Intel microprocessors that operate faster than 33MHz, and the 387SX is not certified to operate with non-Intel microprocessors that operate faster than the speed rating of the math coprocessor.

   Users with 386DX systems and CAD or scientific applications can also consider Intel's RapidCAD Engineering coprocessor which can boost math operations by up to 70% over the performance of a 386DX and 387DX combination.

   Systems based on the 386SX 16-, 20- or 25-MHz microprocessor or the 386SL 16, 20 or 25 MHz microprocessor can use the 387SL math coprocessor.

- **80286-based Computers.** Most computers based on the 286 processor drive the math coprocessor at two-thirds the microprocessor speed. The 287 math coprocessor is capable of running at speeds of up to 12.5 MHz.

   Some laptops, including the Compaq 286/LTE and the Tandy 2800, employ a nonstandard design and can use a special small-form coprocessor, the 287XLT.

   We're in the realm of the dinosaurs here, of course; the effort may not be worthwhile. In any case, consult your instruction guide and speak to the manufacturer before you attempt to upgrade such a system.

- **8088- and 8086-based Computers.** In the original design for 8088 and 8086 computers, the microprocessor and math coprocessor usually run at the same speed. This class of computer started out with a clock speed of 4.77 MHz, and subsequent models operated at 8 or 20 MHz. The math coprocessor must match the computer's fastest operating speed.

Intel's Math Coprocessor Identification System

Intel has used two different marking schemes for its math coprocessors. The original notation, used in many old machines and some that were more current, used a different system.

Table 2.5 is a listing of Intel chips, with the old and new names.

Table 2.5 Intel Math Coprocessors

PRODUCT NAME	RATED SPEED	NEW INTEL PART	OLD INTEL PART
OverDrive SX	33 MHz	BOXDX2ODPR66	BOXODP486SX-33
OverDrive SX	25 MHz	BOXDX2ODP50	BOXODP486SX-25)
OverDrive SX	16, 20 MHz	BOXDX2ODP50	BOXODP486SX-20
OverDrive DX	25,33 MHz	BOXDX2ODP66	BOXODP486DX-33
OverDrive DX	25 MHz	BOXDX2ODPR50	BOXODPR486DX-25
OverDrive DX	33 MHz	BOXDX2ODPR66	BOXODPR486DX-33
OverDrive SX	25 MHz	BOXSX2ODP50	n/a
i487 SX	16,20,25 MHz	BOX487SX	
RapidCAD	16,20,25,33 MHz	BOXRAPIDCAD	
i387 DX	16,20,25,33 MHz	BOX387DX	
i387 DX-33	33 MHz	Not current	
i387 DX-25	25 MHz	Not current	
i387 DX-20	20 MHz	Not current	
i387 DX-16	16 MHz	Not current	
i387 SL	16,20,25 MHz	BOX387SL	
i387 SX33	33 MHz	BOX387SX33	
i387 SX	16,20,25 MHz	BOX387SX	
i387 SX-25	25 MHz	Not current	
i387 SX-20	20 MHz	Not current	
i387 SX-16	16 MHz	Not current	
287XL	Up to 12.5 MHz	BOX287XL	
287XLT	Up to 12.5 MHz	BOX287XLT	
8087-10 (-1)	10 MHz	BOX8087-1	
8087-8 (-2)	8 MHz	BOX8087-2	
8087 (-3)	4.77 MHz	BOX8087	

How to Install a Math Coprocessor

Before you begin, be sure that you have the proper math coprocessor, rated at a speed equal to or greater than that of the microprocessor. Check your system's instruction manual and acquaint yourself with the location and orientation of the socket for the coprocessor. Finally, inspect the chip itself, looking for damage including bent pins. You may not want to try to repair bent pins; return the chip to the vendor for a new one.

1. Ground yourself. Touch the metal back or side panel on your computer, or the center screw on an electrical outlet, to ground yourself and prevent static electricity from damaging your system or the math coprocessor.

2. Switch off the power and unplug the computer. When the system is disconnected from power, remove the covers.

3. Locate the socket. The empty socket for the coprocessor is almost always next to the CPU itself. It may be marked with name or number; consult your instruction manual or call your computer's technical support line if you have any doubts about its location.

4. Orient the math coprocessor correctly. Chips are marked with a dot for pin 1 (387 and 487 coprocessors) or the chip is marked with a dot and beveled edge (8087s and 80287s). The socket is marked with a similar dot or bevel and both should match location when installed.

5. Insert the math coprocessor. Align the chip with pin 1 above socket 1 and lightly press the chip into place. Watch to be sure that none of the pins become bent under the chip so that they will not make contact. Be sure that each pin is above its corresponding socket before you press down firmly. Depending on the design of the particular chip and the socket you may have to press down fairly hard to seat the chip. Take care not to make the motherboard bend as you insert the chip, or you could end up damaging the delicate circuitry beneath its surface.

6. Set switches or jumpers on motherboard. On some systems you will need to set switches or jumpers or both on the motherboard to let the computer know you have added a math coprocessor. Consult the PC's instruction manual, or contact the system's manufacturer for more information. Information for some motherboards is available on Intel's FAXBack system.

   In most cases, if you have correctly inserted the math coprocessor, an incorrect jumper or switch setting will not damage the chip; it will simply not work properly.

   Some systems are capable of recognizing the presence of the coprocessor, while others will adjust based on a configuration program.

7. Restart the computer. Put the cover back on the computer, reconnect all the cables and cords, plug the power cord into the wall outlet, and turn on the computer.

8. Run reference or system configuration program. Some computers have a System Installation, Reference, or System Configuration program that must be run to enable the system to work with a math coprocessor. The program may be in ROM or on a disk. See your system manual for more information.

9. Test the math coprocessor. Use the diagnostics software program on the utilities diskette that came with your math coprocessor to test the chip. If the program shows that the math coprocessor isn't operating correctly, verify that switches or jumpers have been set properly and that the chip is properly installed; if you are unable to proceed, contact the supplier of the chip.

Installing an Intel 387 Math Coprocessor in a Weitek Socket

Some 386 motherboards were designed to work with coprocessors by Weitek, a design competitive to Intel's chip. Many of these systems have a square socket that will accommodate either a Weitek or Intel coprocessor.

This socket has three rows of holes on all four sides. In many such computers—including the Compaq 386—the inner two rows of pins are compatible with the Intel 387. To install, place the pins of the Intel 387 over the inner two rows of holes and align pin 1 with the key pin hole before pressing down.

Some computers, including the Tandy 4000, have the Weitek socket but do not support the Intel 387DX. Consult your computer manual or contact the manufacturer for further information on using the Weitek socket.

Math Coprocessor Troubleshooting Advice from the Experts

Intel's technical support staff offers these answers to common problems with math coprocessors.

Problem: The system won't boot with the new math coprocessor installed. The diagnostics program hangs when the math coprocessor is tested, or the coprocessor is not recognized by the system or diagnostics.

Solution: There are several possible sources of the problem.

- Check your instruction manual to see if there are any jumpers or switches that need to be set on the motherboard to enable the math coprocessor.
- Check your system manual to see if you need to run a setup program to enable the math coprocessor.
- Turn off the power, unplug the system and remove the covers. Examine the math coprocessor to be certain that the chip is completely and evenly seated in its socket. None of the corners of the chip should be higher than any other.
- Make certain the chip is installed in the correct direction in the socket, with the chip's notch or marker matching its equivalent in the socket. Consult the instruction manual for details.

- It may be necessary to remove the math chip and look for any bent or broken pins. Carefully restore any bent pin to be parallel to those around it; don't move the pin back and forth too much or it will snap off. While the chip is out of the socket, check that the receptacle on the motherboard is clean and free from dust.

- You can try installing the chip in another system with the same bus and CPU. If the chip works, your problem lies in the installation in the original system or in that system's motherboard; if the chip does not work, the chip itself may be defective.

- If the computer boots partially but you have new problems with drives or other accessories, check that any internal cables and cards you may have dislodged while installing the chip are properly seated.

Problem: You receive an error message after installation of a math coprocessor.

Solution:

- **Configuration Error.** If you remove an Intel Math Coprocessor from an IBM PC/AT computer and fail to make changes in the computer's SETUP program to show that a change has been made, the computer will search for a chip that is not there.

- **Weitek Coprocessor Not Installed.** You may have set a software switch in the EMM386 utility that leads the BIOS to believe you are using a Weitek math coprocessor rather than an Intel device. Consult your DOS manual or Microsoft technical support for assistance.

- **OS2 1107 Error.** This message will appear if you try to run the Intel Math Coprocessor diagnostics on a system running OS/2 versions 2.0 or 2.1. The Intel tests will not work with OS/2. TO run the test, boot your computer with a DOS system diskette and type the following command:

      mcpdiags   <Hit the **Enter** Key>

- **162 Error in IBM PS/2 Model 50, 60, and 70**. On these systems, you must run the computer's reference diskette after the math coprocessor is installed. Boot from the IBM reference diskette and run the setup program. Select **Automatic** if you haven't changed the configuration of any add-in cards, and the computer will configure itself to run correctly with the math coprocessor.

CHAPTER 3
BIOS

A computer *BIOS* (Basic Input Output System) is the lowest-level set of instructions for your computer, defining your PC's personality and handling essential tasks—including bringing the machine to life when the power is first turned on, running startup diagnostics, managing the interpretation of signals from the keyboard, and the interchange of information through ports. The operating system (MS-DOS or Windows 95 on most modern machines) sits atop the BIOS, overseeing its actions *after* initial bootup.

For many users, it is not necessary to upgrade your PC's BIOS chips during the typical usable life of a PC (three to five years); most modern machines are capable of working with most current hardware or can be updated with device drivers. Similarly, most existing BIOS chips can work with enhanced versions of operating systems.

But there are situations where major alterations—usually improvements—are beyond the predictions made by BIOS designers. In the early days of personal computers, the original PCs were quickly locked out of using higher-capacity floppy and hard disk drives, and were unable to keep pace with advances in video standards. In more modern machines, some earlier BIOS chips had difficulties working with SCSI controllers, CD-ROMs, and even some advanced versions of operating systems (including Windows 3.1 and Windows 95).

One other important BIOS improvement arrived in 1994 when new codes permitted the use of hard disk drives larger than 500 MB. Without a current BIOS, your system may only be able to work with the first 500 MB of a drive, even if it has a listed capacity much larger than that. For many users, an update to a new BIOS is worthwhile for that feature alone.

A number of hard drive manufacturers, though, have come up with workarounds that allow you to create a "logical" hard drive on a physical device. For example, a 2 GB hard drive could be logically divided into four 500 MB drives as far as the BIOS is concerned.

BIOS Failure

The BIOS chip or chips themselves are fairly reliable. Nevertheless, because of the importance of the boot-up information included within them, the very first thing the BIOS chip does when it is turned on is to check its own validity, examining every single bit. Under some designs, this can amount to a million bits. A *checksum* is calculated—a mathematical summation of the value of the bits—and it is compared with the official checksum stored in the BIOS ROM. If the numbers do not agree, the BIOS will stop the boot and a **BIOS Checksum Error** message will be displayed. If you receive that message, try turning off the machine and then starting over again. If the error does not recur, you can (nervously) hope that the problem was a once-in-a-very blue moon occurrence.

If you get past the BIOS self-check, the chances are very strong that any problems you encounter do not lie within the BIOS.

The only cure to a problematic BIOS chip or chips is replacement. On some modern machines, the BIOS chips can be upgraded in place through the use of "flash" RAM. A new version is loaded into the BIOS from a floppy disk or even directly over a telecommunications line. Unfortunately, if your system is unable to boot because of a damaged BIOS chip, this option is not available to you.

Sources for BIOS Chips

To replace a BIOS chip, begin by contacting a distributor who works with the existing code within your system. Although it is theoretically possible to upgrade a Phoenix BIOS with a set of new AMI or Award chips, you may run into compatibility problems with custom VLSI or ASIC chips on the motherboard.

There are a number of sources for replacement and upgrade chips; you may have to go no farther than the original supplier of your PC or the motherboard within, or you may need to go to a specialized supplier. A set of chips typically sells for about $50 to $100 plus shipping.

Micro Firmware sells chips including those from Phoenix and Quadtel; you can call them at (800) 767-5465 or visit their site on the World Wide Web at **http://www.firmware.com**. AMI, Phoenix, Award, and other chips are offered by

Unicore; they can be reached at (800) 800-BIOS, or at **http://www.unicore.com**. A range of BIOS chips is also available from TTITech, through their Web page at **http:/www.ttitech.com**.

Determining Your BIOS Needs

The first step is to determine the type of BIOS in your system, the number of chips, and their sizes. Dinosaurs may use one or more 128K chips, while modern machines typically use 256K, 512K or 1 MB chips. In dinosaurs, the 128K BIOS may have been made up of eight 16K chips.

Your computer's instruction manual may not be all that helpful in disclosing the exact model of BIOS in your system; the reason for this is that manufacturers sometimes change the BIOS to updated versions over the life of a machine. The best way to be certain of the identity of your BIOS is to take off the covers and do some exploration. Follow the standard precautions, please: turn off and unplug the system before removing the covers and ground yourself before touching the motherboard.

The chips may be clearly labeled on top, or you may need to carefully peel away a covering label. Look for a number marked on the chip, usually on the end opposite the notch. Find a number that begins with 27 or 28. Chips numbered *27* or *27c* are standard EPROMs, while those labeled with a *28* are flash chips that can be upgraded in place.

To install the chips, turn off your machine and remove the power cord. Ground yourself before touching the innards of the PC. You may need to remove hard drives and adapter cards that block access to the BIOS chips. Use a chip-removal tool (often supplied by the BIOS distributors) to gently and evenly pry the chips from their sockets. Install the new chips in their place. Follow any special instructions from the makers for setup routines.

Installing New BIOS Chips

It's relatively easy to upgrade the BIOS chips on your motherboard if necessary. In fact, some of the most modern of the modern machines use a special type of ROM chip called Flash Memory that can be upgraded by running a software program from disk; the contents of the new BIOS are recorded electrically into the nonvolatile memory of the chips. The other way to upgrade BIOS chips involves a bit of careful work with a screwdriver and chip extraction tool.

Before you remove any BIOS chips, make a copy of all of the entries on your system's CMOS Setup screen. You will need to fill out a new Setup configuration for the new BIOS chips.

Most BIOS sets are made up of a pair of chips, referred to as the "odd and even" chips. Both must be replaced at the same time, and installed in the proper socket.

Turn off the power and remove the power cord. Locate the BIOS chips, using the instruction manual or a diagram provided by the replacement BIOS vendor. It may be necessary to remove some adapter cards or even disk drives to gain access to the BIOS chips.

Ground yourself before touching any internal part of the computer, and then use a chip extractor—the BIOS vendor may supply a simple U-shaped tweezer or you can purchase fancier and better models from a tool catalog or store—and carefully remove the chips one at a time. Be sure to work the chips out of their sockets evenly; try to avoid bending the pins to permit you to reinstall the chips if necessary.

As with most other electronic circuit and memory devices, the chips are marked at one end with a dot or a notch to indicate the end that is to match a corresponding dot or notch on the socket. Spend a few moments to be certain that you have the chips oriented properly and that they are intended for the specific socket.

On some new chips, the pins are set a bit wider than the corresponding holes on the socket; before installation, gently rock the chips on a firm surface to push the pins inward a tiny amount. Be sure that you do not twist any of the pins.

Gently insert the chips into the sockets; be sure to apply pressure evenly so that pins are not bent or misaligned. When the chip is about halfway into the socket, stop your work and examine the socket from all four sides; look for any pin that may be bent under or outside of its intended hole. If you find any wrongly positioned pins, use your extractor and remove the chip and carefully straighten the pin or pins. Be careful not to bend a pin back and forth too much or it will break off. If a pin breaks, the chip is ruined.

After the new BIOS chips are in place, reinstall any components you removed and power up the system. You will have to run a new Setup program and inform the system of memory, drives, and other elements of your PC.

Flash Updates for BIOS Chips

An increasing number of modern machines use a form of BIOS chip that can be upgraded in place by reading a new set of instructions from a floppy disk, or from your hard drive after a download over the Internet or directly from the manufacturer.

Contact the maker of your system or a distributor of BIOS upgrades; be sure to correctly identify the brand and model number of the BIOS in your present system. Follow the instructions provided for the flash upgrade carefully; in most instances, the upgrade is done from the DOS prompt or from a special boot disk that takes control of the system independent of the BIOS.

CHAPTER 4
Driving the Computer Bus

The bus that interconnects the peripherals and memory of your computer with the microprocessor is a mass transit highway. Following the analogy, any commuter knows that even a superhighway can have slowdowns, dangerous curves, and bottlenecks.

There are currently six routes to choose (that is there are six standard bus designs in use with PCs): PC, ISA (AT), EISA, MCA, VL, and PCI Motherboards. And you can add to that a pair of outrigger buses: SCSI and PC Card systems.

You cannot change the design of your bus while it is in place, unless you engage in a massive engineering makeover: a new motherboard. However, many modern machine motherboards are combinations of more than one type of bus, allowing a mix and match of expansion cards. The only fly in the ointment is this: if your system has, for example, slots for four ISA and three PCI expansion adapters and your have four PCI cards to install, you've got a problem.

In this chapter, we're going to look at the various buses in the order of most common use on your desktop. We'll begin with the ISA (AT) bus and its closely paired PCI extension, which is the combination you'll find in nearly every current modern machine. Then we'll move on to the VESA VL Bus that was popular in the early generation of modern machines, and then the PC Card system which is used in most laptops and as an outrigger bus on some desktop machines.

From there we'll move on to a pair of nearly abandoned special purpose buses: MCA and EISA. And finally, we'll re-enter the world of the dinosaur with a backwards glance at the original 8-bit PC bus.

The Modern Machine Bus

Industry Standard Architecture (ISA) or AT-Bus

The PC bus doubled the width of its internal highway with the introduction of the PC-AT in 1984. The arrival of the new machine came at the moment of explosion of the clone industry, and the bus was widely imitated. Clonemakers dubbed the bus the *Industry Standard Architecture*.

The original AT was a 16-bit machine, with many internal data transfers made 16 bits at a time. The major difference between an AT-type computer and the original IBM PC and PC-XT-type computer is the size of the expansion slot. ISA buses have longer 16-bit expansion slots, sometimes mixed with shorter 8-bit slots, while an XT has only the short 8-bit slots (Figure 4.1).

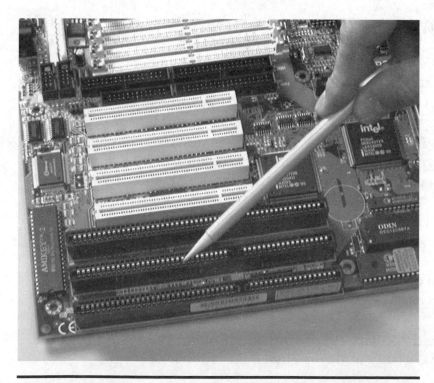

Figure 4.1 Three ISA slots are available on the Micro-Star motherboard for compatibility with older adapter cards and those that do not need the high speed of the PCI bus.

Peripheral Component Interconnect (PCI)

The PCI bus was developed by Intel Corporation. In technical terms, it is actually not a bus at all but an extension of the microprocessor capable of running closer to the speed of the microprocessor itself than earlier designs. It includes arbitrated bus mastering, parity checking for all devices in the system, and the ability to set system configuration without jumpers or switches.

The Peripheral Interconnect Bus, or PCI, is the current speed demon of most desktop PCs. The initial implementation of the PCI standard set it up as a parallel superhighway that ran alongside an ISA, EISA, or VL bus. The CPU and memory attach directly to the PCI, while a PCI bridge connects the bus to the second bus in the system. The PCI, in its early versions, was capable of working with as many as three peripheral devices plugged directly into it; the best uses of those slots were for devices that would benefit most from the speed, including video display adapters, disk controllers, and network adapters.

Some early modern machines, then, will have a PCI bus that coexists with other local bus standards, and is relatively limited in its scope and capabilities.

With the introduction PCI Release 2.0, the standard took full flight and became the bus of choice for nearly every Pentium machine aimed at consumer and small business users. PCI 2.0 can work with the existing bus of a system or stand by itself; it is best used to boost the performance of devices including network adapters, hard disk drives, full-motion video, and high-performance graphics adapters.

CHAPTER 4

Running at a clock speed of 33 MHz, the PCI local bus employs a 32-bit data bus that supports multiple peripheral components and add-in cards at a peak bandwidth of 132 MB/second—a substantial improvement over the 5 MB/second peak transfer rate of the standard ISA bus. This increased bandwidth allows the PCI local bus to provide more than four times the graphics performance of the ISA bus.

The PCI local bus, however, offers much more than high bandwidth. It allows peripherals to take full advantage of available processing power without being dependent on processor speed or architecture. It also supports auto-configuration of Plug and Play-enabled add-in cards, and offers system designers a standardized design path. Finally, PCI provides built-in upgradability to accommodate future technical advances.

PCI was designed to permit future enhancement to 64-bit data transfer. A 64-bit extension to basic PCI adds another 60 pins to the 120 available for standard 32-bit cards, doubling potential data transfer speed to 264 MB per second.

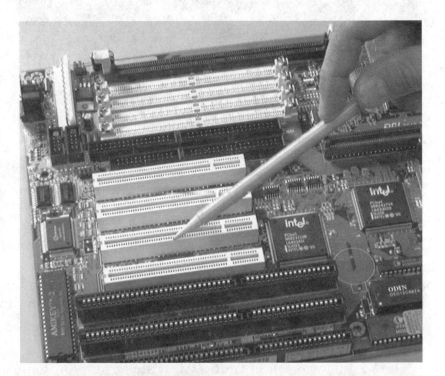

Figure 4.2 The Micro-Star motherboard from Dalco Electronics has four high-density PCI slots. Many modern video cards and some network adapters make use of the high capacity and speed of the PCI bus.

Figure 4.3 This dinosaur 286 AT used a low-profile case. The motherboard had only one ISA bus slot, which was occupied by a riser card with slots branching off to the left and right. This design of case was sometimes prone to overheating, could not work with some full-size adapter cards, and had very limited expandability.

Among the special features of the PCI is automatic configuration of cards, so-called "Plug and Play" installation where each add-in card includes information on board that can be read by the processor and used in setup. PCI devices can be either targets (devices which accept commands) or masters (devices which can perform some processing independent of the CPU and the bus).

VESA VL Bus

The VL bus was created to develop a way to connect the video adapter directly to the processor and avoid traveling the relatively slow bus.

Established by the Video Electronics Standards Association, a group of manufacturers of video adapters, the VL bus is actually a secondary—faster—bus that is used together with the principal data bus of a computer.

The most common implementation of VL buses are as enhancements to ISA bus systems. Some VL bus systems have the video circuitry mounted directly on the motherboard, which saves some of the expense of a separate adapter but may limit the ability to enhance or repair the adapter. Subsequent designs added as many as two additional VL bus slots (the specification recommends a limit of three VL slots) that could be used for other devices. But nearly every VL design also extended the expansion capability of the system with a set of standard ISA slots.

Because the VL bus design is tied to the processor's speed, not every VL bus card is compatible with every VL bus-based system.

The VL bus was widely adopted in the design for many advanced 486 systems. But in 1995, it was mostly pushed aside by the widespread adoption of PCI bus designs for Pentium systems.

PC Cards (PCMCIA)

The PCMCIA standard defines a removable credit-card-size device that can be used in a wide range of portable computers and desktops. The circuit card, a bit larger than 2 by 3 inches, can be used for memory, tiny hard drives, modems, network adapters, sound cards, SCSI adapters and more. Future versions of PC Card specifications are expected to permit video and even processor upgrades.

When it was first introduced, we poor users were forced to memorize its tongue-twisting acronym of a name: PCMCIA. Luckily, more sensible heads prevailed and the working title for cards that use the PCMCIA standard was dubbed *PC Card* in 1995.

The standard was set by the Personal Computer Memory Card International Association, a group of more than 300 manufacturers. Among the advantages of the card are its tiny size and easy plug-in insertion; many of the cards permit *hot swapping*—removing and inserting cards without turning off the computer. And using a technique called *Execute in Place*, software installed on a PCMCIA-compatible ROM card can be executed directly from the card itself instead of being loaded into RAM first, permitting an expansion of the ROM capabilities of the computer without using up precious RAM.

The 68-pin interface connects the card to the motherboard or the system's expansion bus.

Although the first uses of the PC Cards were as add-ins to portable computers, some users have added PCMCIA sockets to desktop machines to permit quick changes to the capabilities of the devices.

There are three types of PC Card slots, measured by the thickness of card they will accept. Be sure to check on the capability of your PC Card reader before making a purchase. A properly designed Type III socket will work with Types I and II as well; a Type II socket should accept Type I cards as well.

- **Type I**. 3.3 mm thick, commonly used for RAM, flash memory, electronically erasable programmable read-only memory, and other such devices. Type I slots are most often seen in personal digital assistants and handheld devices.
- **Type II**. 5 mm thick, and fully I/O capable. They are used for memory enhancements, or for I/O devices such as modems and network connections.
- **Type III**. 10.5 mm thick, and designed primarily for removable hard drive devices.
- A fourth design, **Type IV,** is expected to be approved at a later date, with common use for large-capacity but still-tiny hard drives. The thickness may be 18 mm.

CHAPTER 4

Hot Swap

One of the advanced features of a PC Card is something called *hot swap*. In theory, this permits you to insert and remove cards while the PC power is still on, without damaging the card or system or losing data. However, not all applications or versions of operating systems can recognize when cards have been inserted or removed; it is always worthwhile to save data before trying this feature.

Using a PC Card with a Desktop PC

The first uses of the PCMCIA slot were almost entirely as expansions to laptop computers. But as with most impressive new developments in personal computing, the best and the smallest technologies quickly spread. Over the next few years, expect to see credit-card technologies in increasing use among desktop users.

Why use a PC Card with a desktop?

- **Security**. Essential corporate or personal information can be stored on a memory card and removed to a safe at the end of the day.
- **Transportability**. Carry a few megabytes of information across the room or across the country in your pocket.
- **Ease of Upgrade**. PC Card network adapters, sound cards, and hard disk drives are nearly perfect "plug and play" upgrades that do not require installation of adapters or switch settings. See Figure 4.4.

Figure 4.4 The SCM PC card/floppy combination drive occupies a single drive bay but demands one of your ISA slots for the PC card controller.

A Neat Desktop PC Card Solution

A number of companies offer internal and external PC Card readers that work with desktop computers. They connect to your PC's bus through the use of an adapter card, or through a connection to the PC's parallel port.

One especially elegant line of devices is offered by SCM Microsystems with their SwapBox products. We installed a SwapBox Classic Combo, a combination PC Card slot (Type I, II or III) and a 3.5-inch high-density disk drive, squeezed together into a box that fits in a single standard floppy disk drive bay.

Other SwapBox devices include the Premium, which offers two PC Card slots—one on the front of the PC and the second on the back—opening into the adapter in the bus.

Outdated Modern Buses

Micro Channel Architecture (MCA)

Micro Channel was IBM's proprietary 32-bit bus with bus mastering. Unlike EISA, MCA is not compatible with ISA devices. Special features include the ability of the bus to reach out and identify any adapter plugged into it, permitting automatic configuration. And the bus is smart enough to be able to shut off a misbehaving adapter. Finally, MCA adapters generate less electrical interference, which reduces the chance for errors on high-speed buses.

Many of IBM's PS/2 machines used the MCA bus and there were a handful of clones built with the same design, but the MCA bus did not become a predominant design and has been mostly supplanted by VESA and PCI designs.

The Micro Channel design departs in several significant and interesting ways from the Industry Standard Architecture used by most other modern machines. However, the basics of processor, power supply, video adapter, memory, and data storage are very similar. We'll concentrate in this section on the differences you'll need to understand in order to troubleshoot problems that may arise with a Micro Channel machine.

Connectors on an MCA Motherboard

A Micro Channel computer can have a combination of 16- and 32-bit connectors on the motherboard. You can install an 8-bit or 16-bit adapter in a 16-bit slot; a 32-bit slot can accommodate 8-, 16-, and 32-bit adapters.

Some of the connectors of a Micro Channel machine have an extension, which is an additional set of connectors for special purposes. The three types of Micro Channel extensions are:

- **Base Video**. Used in computers that do not have video adapter circuitry built into the motherboard, base video is the minimal video function that displays messages on your screen during boot-up diagnostics.

- **Auxiliary Video**. Permits a machine to have more than one display attached to the computer; this extension works in conjunction with the base video function.
- **Matched Memory**. A special fix used in some systems to match the speed of some 32-bit memory adapters to the speed of the microprocessor.

The Micro Channel Bus

IBM's bus has 32 signal paths for data, which allows 32 bits of data to be sent through the channel at the same time, but (as with most other designs) only one device at a time can use the bus to send or receive data. The three functions of the bus are:

- **Expansion Bus**. The channel can be used to provide paths for transferring data and control information to and from adapters.
- **Address Bus**. Every memory location and I/O device attached to the Micro Channel bus is assigned a unique number, known as an address. A device wishing to transfer data begins by sending out the address of the device that is its target.
- **Data Bus**. The Micro Channel's data bus is capable of supporting data bus widths of 8, 16, or 32 bits, depending on the capabilities of the sending and receiving devices. (A 32-bit device sending data to an 8-bit device effectively works as an 8-bit unit, sending four consecutive 8-bit transfers instead of a single 32-bit burst.)

There are, of course, only benefits to be had from using 32-bit devices within a Micro Channel system. A 32-bit bus is capable of addressing as much as 4 GB of memory.

Arbitration

When more than one device wants to use the Micro Channel bus at the same time, the computer uses a system called *arbitration*. Every device is assigned an arbitration level that is unique to it; the listing of priorities for each device is held in a software file called an *adapter description file*.

The Micro Channel includes a fairness feature intended to make sure than every device gets a turn to control the bus, even if it has a much lower arbitration level than another active device. The Micro Channel configuration process allows the user to turn off the fairness feature for one or more devices. You should do so only with caution, however, since a busy—or ill-behaved—device could end up locking out all other adapters.

Masters and Slaves

The Micro Channel bus categorizes the two ends of a data-transfer process as either *master* or *slave*. When a master has control of the bus, it can send or receive data from a slave without demanding the direct involvement of the CPU.

There are three types of masters:

- **System Master**. A device that assigns system resources and issues the commands of the primary operating system.

- **Bus Master**. A device that takes control of the bus to transfer directly to and from I/O devices and memory without using the CPU or the DMA controller. A bus master can have its own microprocessor, instruction cache, and memory. A Micro Channel computer can have as many as 15 bus masters, permitting some level of multiprocessing.

- **DMA Controller**. Circuitry that manages data transfer between DMA slaves and memory slaves.

A *slave* is a device that is selected by a master as the source or target of a transfer. There are three types of slaves in a Micro Channel system:

- **Memory Slave**. A device that provides a block of system memory. A memory slave responds by putting requested data on the bus, or by writing data from the bus to RAM. A memory slave can be selected by the system master, bus master, or DMA controller.

- **I/O Slave**. A device that communicates with or controls a peripheral, including printer and modem. An I/O slave can be selected by the system master or a bus master.

- **DMA Slave**. A device that requires the DMA controller to manage data transfers. This is the only type of slave that can initiate arbitration. A DMA slave can be selected by the DMA controller or by a bus master.

Dual Bus

Some advanced PS/2 machines have a *dual bus* that provides both a data bus from the microprocessor to the memory controller and another data bus from the Micro Channel devices to the memory controller. A dual bus design permits the microprocessor to read and write to system memory at the same time a bus master is controlling the Micro Channel bus.

The Dinosaur Bus

Certified Dinosaur: The Original PC Bus

The original design for the IBM PC offered a handful of slots capable of accepting cards that dealt with 8 bits of information at a time. The bus itself extended 62 wires from the processor; 20 of the lines were available as "address lines" that helped direct information to and from locations in memory, and eight lines were dedicated to the transmission of data. The remainder of the lines were given over to electrical needs, interrupts, and control circuits.

The PC Bus was used for the very first machines from IBM and the early PC clones; the IBM PC-XT, which brought the first internal hard drive to the family used a slightly modified version.

No modern machines use the PC Bus. However, you may be able to use an old 8-bit adapter card in a 16-bit ISA slot, which are actually made up of an 8-bit connector and a second, extended bus line connector. However, an 8-bit card will only fit in a 16-bit slot if it has a high "skirt". Before you get too excited about that concept, here's what it means: the original design for an 8-bit card had the gold-plated electrical contact fingers stick down from the body of the card, leaving about a half an inch of vertical clearance (the skirt) on either side of the contacts. Some card designers, though, tried to cram electronics onto every available square inch of space and integrated the fingers into a solid expanse of card from front to back. This sort of card would fit properly in an 8-bit slot, but would end up butting into the slot for the extended bus lines on a 16-bit slot.

NOTE

If you have a PC-XT, there is one special consideration on the use of the slots: IBM, which once considered PCs as slaves to its huge mainframes, reserved slot eight (the one nearest to the power supply) for special-purpose adapters, including mainframe emulation cards. This slot is electrically isolated from the rest of the bus; many ordinary cards will not work in that slot. Check the instruction manuals (if you still have them) or the maker of your old cards (if they are still in business), if you have any questions.

IRQs: Irksome Essentials

The various pieces of hardware that are attached to the CPU through the system bus need the attention of the microprocessor to perform services or to supervise the movement of information from place to place. Happily, not all of the

devices need the CPU's attention all the time—if they did, the computer would not be able to deal with more than one thing at a time.

Some devices, such as keyboards, are in heavy use while other pieces of hardware, such as sound cards or floppy disk drives, may only be operated for a few seconds at a time over the course of a day's work. The computer solution is to use something called *interrupts* which do exactly what their name suggests: they are electronic flag-wavers that grab the CPU's attention when necessary.

The interrupts are signals that run along the wires of the bus. They are carried out in order of their importance to the system, according to a pecking order set by interrupt numbers; in computer terminology, these are called *IRQs* (Interrupt Requests.)

The original PCs had a single Intel 8259A PIC (programmable interrupt controller), which was capable of arbitrating among eight requests for attention. They were numbered IRQ 0 through 7; the essential system timer was assigned IRQ 0 with the highest priority, and the keyboard used IRQ 1.

As PCs became more capable and complex, it became obvious that there was a need for additional interrupts to service new devices including network adapters, sound cards, and more. The PC-AT and all modern machines therefore have a second interrupt controller with eight more lines, numbered IRQ 8 through 15. In order to maintain compatibility with older hardware and operating systems, the eight new interrupts are cascaded to the first controller over the IRQ 2 line. This results in a total of 15 IRQs.

Because the eight additional IRQs enter into the system between IRQ 1 and 3, interrupts 8 through 15 have a higher priority than do IRQs 3 through 7. On a modern machine, the system claims permanent ownership of IRQs 0, 1, 8, and 13. The remaining 11 are open to assignment.

It is important to understand that on a standard PC no two devices can use the same IRQ at the same time without causing serious problems, including a lock-up of the system. In theory, two devices can have the same assignment if they are never in use together; this is a dangerous practice, though.

MCA and EISA systems are capable of allowing multiple hardware devices to share a single IRQ.

Most devices come preset to use a particular IRQ; their instruction manuals should inform you which other interrupts they can be set to and how to make the reassignment. Older devices used connector blocks or DIP switches to change interrupts; some modern devices can change their settings with a software command.

In theory, IRQ 7 is assigned to the first parallel port (LPT 1), and IRQ 5 to the second possible parallel port (LPT 2.) But for most users and in most situations, the parallel port does not make use of any interrupts. It is common for other devices to lay claim to these two interrupts.

Here are some typical assignments for IRQs on a modern machine:

IRQ0	System Timer
IRQ1	Keyboard
IRQ2	Cascade from second 8259A PIC
IRQ3	Serial Port COM2
IRQ4	Serial Port COM1
IRQ5	Sound Card
IRQ6	Floppy Disk Controller
IRQ7	Parallel Port LPT1
IRQ8	CMOS Real-Time Clock
IRQ9	Software Redirected to IRQ2
IRQ10	Available for use
IRQ11	Available for use
IRQ12	Available for use
IRQ13	Math Coprocessor
IRQ14	Hard Disk Controller
IRQ15	Available for use

For the record, here are the typical assignments for IRQs on a dinosaur:

IRQ0	System Timer
IRQ1	Keyboard
IRQ2	Available for use
IRQ3	Serial Port COM2
IRQ4	Serial Port COM1
IRQ5	Hard Disk Controller
IRQ6	Floppy Disk Controller
IRQ7	Parallel Port LPT1

IRQs: What Goes Where?

As we've discussed already, two devices are not supposed to share the same IRQ. And as you'll find out very quickly as you expand a modern machine with multimedia capabilities, you can soon end up with only a few options to avoid conflicts.

First of all, realize that some IRQs are permanently assigned; the interrupts for System Timer, Keyboard, COM ports, and disk controllers are immutable.

Make a Little List. We recommend that you establish and keep current a listing—write it down inside the cover of your machine's instruction manual. As you install any adapter, make note of IRQ, DMA, and Memory Addresses to which it lays claim.

While you are at it, keep a record of any settings you make to DIP switches or jumpers on adapter cards; it's a lot easier to open a manual and read the listings than to have to open the covers of a PC and remove the cards. Not all DIP switches are consistent in their labeling, either. In computer terms, 0 means off and 1 means on; Open means off and Closed means on. Here's a chart of equivalence:

N O T E

ON	OFF
1	0
CLOSED	OPEN

After the fact, you can use a diagnostic program to check on IRQ settings, although the reports are not 100 percent accurate because not all devices may be active when the test is run. One of the simplest testers is Microsoft's MSD utility which is provided as part of Windows 3.1 and DOS 6.X. (If you upgrade to Windows 95, MSD is not ordinarily included, but you can keep your copy from the previous operating system.)

To load MSD, exit Windows if it is running, and go to the DOS prompt. Type **MSD** and press the **Enter** key. Once Microsoft Diagnostics is on screen, press **Q** to select the IRQ Settings screen. Consult the IRQs list in search of a **RESERVED** listing; these IRQs are likely to be available for use.

DMA: Mind Transfers Made Easy

The other half of the communication process for many hardware devices including some disk controllers, sound cards, and other I/O cards, is something called *Direct Memory Access* (DMA). DMA is a facility that allows transfer of data directly, without intervention by the microprocessor. This allows for greater speed in data transfer and avoids bogging down the CPU with unnecessary tasks.

The dinosaur PC had a single Intel 8237A four-channel DMA controller, capable of 8-bit data transfers. DMA line 0 was reserved by the system for dynamic RAM refresh, with DMA 2 assigned to floppy disk transfers, and DMA 3 was to be used for hard disk transfers.

With the arrival of the PC-AT and other modern machines capable of 16-bit operations, a second DMA controller was added. The output of the first controller is routed to the first input of the second chip.

CHAPTER 4

Therefore, a modern machine has seven DMA lines, numbered 0 through 3 and 5 through 7. The lower lines still are used only for transfers between 8-bit devices and 8- or 16-bit memory; DMA lines 5 through 7 are available for full 16-bit transfers in either direction.

Because of the improved speed of CPUs beginning with the 80286, DMA is no longer needed for RAM refresh operations, and DMA 0 is therefore available for reassignment on modern machines. So, too, DMA 3 is not used for hard disk transfers on 16-bit machines.

Here are some typical assignments for DMA Channels:

0	(8-bit)	Available for data transfer
1	(8-bit)	Sound card
2	(8-bit)	Floppy controller
3	(8-bit)	Available for data transfer
4		Cascade channels 0-3
5	(16-bit)	Available for data transfer
6	(16-bit)	Available for data transfer
7	(16-bit)	Available for data transfer

CHAPTER 5

Basic Hardware Skills

In this chapter, we'll explore the basic components of the computer in more detail, including:

- System unit case and cover
- Motherboard
- Expansion cards
- Setting the system configuration
- Power supply
- Keyboard

Tools of the Trade

Before you do any repair work on your PC—in fact, before you even think about taking off the cover of your computer—we recommend that you assemble a computer tool kit. We're not talking about hundreds of dollars here; you can obtain all you need for less than $50 from a computer dealer or mail order house, or a from a well-equipped hardware store.

Your computer tool kit should include a good quality set of needle-nose pliers, and small-blade straight-edge and Phillips head screwdrivers. The next step up is a set of nut drivers, one or more tweezers, and a set of chip insertion and extraction tools. Also of value are Torx blades, which work with special screws used by some manufacturers in hopes that you won't try to open their magic boxes by yourself. To clean the connectors of adapter cards, have a small supply of rubbing alcohol and a set of cotton swabs.

You can assemble the pieces yourself or pick up a package like those offered by companies such as Dalco Electronics or Jensen Tools. Dalco has a range of kits from as low as $10 to electronic kitchen sinks topping out at more than $300. We worked with a small Dalco kit that included a set of appropriate flat head and Phillips screwdrivers, a set of torque bits and nut drivers, an IC inserter and extractor, tweezers, and parts holders.

A low-tech nicety is a small compartmentalized plastic or wooden box, such as a sewing kit. Mark the compartments with letters or numbers, and keep a notepad and pen in the box; as you remove screws and parts, put them into individual sections and make a note of where they go.

You should have a way to ground yourself before touching the static-sensitive chips under the covers of the PC. The official way to do this is with something called a grounding strap, which attaches to your wrist or ankle and connects to an electrical ground; you can purchase a grounding strap for less than $10 from Dalco Electronics or other electronics supply houses. Another useful and even less expensive device is a static touch pad or touchstrip that can be anchored on the desktop and connected to a ground (Figure 5.1).

You can also make your own antistatic device by running a wire from the center screw of an electrical outlet plate—be careful not to insert the wire into the blades of the outlet itself—and taping the other end to your desktop. Touch the bare end of the wire to discharge any static in your body before touching any electronic parts.

In any case, it is also useful to check all the outlets in your office or home to assure that they are properly grounded; simple plug-in ground fault detectors are available at Radio Shack or other suppliers. If they indicate a problem, contact a professional electrician.

Another useful tool for advanced troubleshooters is a simple multimeter that can check DC and AC voltage and DC current. Older designs use a meter with a needle, while more modern (and more sturdy) devices have digital readouts. Use the meter to check for proper output from a power supply and to check voltage levels on connectors; some devices also permit you to check the continuity of

Figure 5.1 A good practice is to install an antistatic device on your desktop, like this touchpad, or a keyboard mat or touchstrip.

cables. Meters sell for about $20 to $100 for consumer grade devices, and are available from sources such as Dalco Electronics or Radio Shack. Be sure to study and understand the instruction manual before you use a multimeter. Be especially careful not to short across connectors or traces on the motherboard.

More sophisticated testers are used for serial and network cables. An RS232 Breakout Box from Dalco Electronics, for example, includes a set of jumper wires to reconfigure cables, DIP switches to cross over connections, and LEDs to monitor signals on a live cable, and sells for about $30. A similar breakout box is available for the eight lines of an RJ45 cable used in Ethernet 10Base-T cable.

If you are going to make your own cables, you should invest in a fine-point soldering iron, a set of wire strippers, and some needle-nose pliers. You'll also need raw cable and a set of connectors for the cables you want to make. All are available from the same sources we've already mentioned. All that said, we haven't built a cable from scratch in years—cables are more standardized than they used to be, and most cables are available at reasonable prices from mail order houses or computer retailers.

System Unit Case and Cover

The computer case provides physical strength to support internal and external devices, and electromagnetic insulation to keep radio radiation within. In order to pass Federal Communications Commission (FCC) regulations, when the PC is sold the case must present an essentially unbroken wall, with all openings filled to keep electromagnetic waves generated by the computer inside the chassis.

Once the computer is in your hands, there is nothing to prevent you from leaving slot covers off, or even running the PC without its cover. Neither is a good idea, though. In addition to permitting broadcast of stray radio signals, operating the computer without covers is a way to introduce dirt into the disk drives and onto the electrical contacts, allow metal objects to fall in and short the wires, and interfere with the cooling flow of the PC's fan.

And though stray electromagnetic radiation will not harm the computer or cause it to malfunction, it may cause interference with televisions, FM radios, portable and cellular telephones, and other devices whenever the computer is on. (It is also said that electromagnetic radiation is not a threat to human beings, at least at the levels present in a PC. In any case, it is good practice to stay at arm's length distance from your computer and the monitor . . . and to keep slot covers and cases on.)

The problems of radio frequency (RF) interference become worse as PCs operate faster and faster. As this book was written, the top end of microcomputing was a Pentium chip running at 200 MHz, with 233 MHz processors on the

Figure 5.2 Vertical or tower cases offer maximum expandability. This sturdy case from Dalco Electronics has a pair of drive cages that can hold three 5.25-inch devices and four 3.5-inch drives. The case comes with a 250-watt power supply to support the devices. Even fully stuffed, there is ample room for working within the case.

Figure 5.3 An empty case waiting the arrival of its innards.

horizon. Leaving aside the tremendous capabilities of the Pentium, consider for a moment that the clock speed of the original IBM PC was an anemic 4.77 MHz.

Lightweight laptop or portable computers have electromagnetic shielding too, even those with plastic cases. Some portables, for example, have aluminum plates embedded in the plastic. Other clone makers use aluminum paint over the plastic parts.

How to Test the System Unit Case and Cover

In general, if the case looks all right, it works all right. But not always. Believe it or not, even the case occasionally causes system troubles. A really poorly designed case with mis-shapen pieces of metal in the wrong places can cause intermittent shorts.

We have come across defective cases where part of the case sat very close to rough, soldered component leads on the bottom of the motherboard. Sometimes the motherboard actually touched the case, with only the black paint film on the case providing insulation. Over time, the hard disk caused the motherboard to vibrate enough to rub away the paint on the case, causing intermittent shorts and other vexing symptoms.

In another instance, the high-tech and expensive case on a modern machine included a row of small copper "fingers" that were part of the protection against RF leakage. Unfortunately, a few of the fingers worked loose in the process of removing and reinstalling the cover, with the result that a few of these pieces of metal were rattling around on the motherboard, just waiting to short out the machine.

Figure 5.4 A vertical case's cover lifts up and away to expose both sides of the internal frame within.

As we said, either a case works or it doesn't. However, you can usually detect RF leakage by bringing a television set or FM radio near the PC. If you see a pattern that changes as the PC performs various assignments, or if the reception on the FM radio is affected by a whine or pulsing beat that changes as the PC responds to keyboard commands, you have an RF radiation problem.

Should it be fixed? RF radiation is in most cases just an annoyance. In the most severe instances, though—where it interferes with television reception in the home, changes the channel on the office Muzak system, or opens and closes your neighbor's garage door—you're going to want to seal up all of the openings in the PC case properly. (Be sure not to block air intakes and vents, of course.)

How to Remove and Install the System Cover

Start by turning off the computer and unplugging the 110-volt power cord from the back of the computer. (Remember our "belt and suspenders" advice?)

Next, remove any cables attached to the back of the PC. Move the computer to a sturdy desk beneath a good light.

Desktop Models

Consult your instruction manual to see if your computer's case uses any unusual fasteners or means of closing. The screws holding the cover in place are usually hidden on the back. Most computers have five machine screws: four at the extreme corners and one in the center top of the back surface. A few desktop models use four screws, two on each side of the case. You'll need a standard blade or Phillips screwdriver to remove the machine screws.

You might also find a system that employs one of several quick release systems such as Curtis Computer Speed Screws, large plastic thumbscrews for internal boards and computer cases. Some other cases use latches instead of screws. Finally, a handful of mini-desktop units have screw attachments along the side of the cover rather than at the back.

If you are disassembling a computer with a plastic case, take care not to overtighten screws that enter into plastic threads in plastic posts. If you go too far you will strip the threads or break off the plastic posts.

Once you've removed the screws or fasteners, slide the cover off the chassis. Some cases pull back toward the rear of the PC, while others lift straight up; consult your instruction manual. The cover might be a bit sticky until it breaks loose, but once it starts sliding it should move smoothly.

It's easy to catch the power supply wires or the floppy drive ribbon cable on the sharp edges of the case cover. Be gentle and use good sense when removing or reinstalling the cover; ripping these wires loose will increase the diagnostic challenge.

Tower Models

Under the cover, tower computers are sometimes identical to the manufacturer's desktop models, but the disk drives are usually rotated to mount horizontally in the tower and the motherboard is rotated to stand on its end.

Towers usually offer considerably more room for additional internal hard drives, CD-ROMs, Syquest drives, and the like. And they usually include larger power supplies to support those extra devices; in general, a larger power supply is a good thing, allowing a healthy margin for those times when the CD-ROM drive is loading to the hard drive while the network card is pumping data across the Ethernet.

Another advantage of a tower unit is that it is designed to sit on the floor and therefore does not take up precious desk space. However, any computer can be mounted on its side; just take care to support it properly so that it does not tip over. (The only problem might arise with using certain CD-ROM drives on their side, especially those that use a tray-loading mechanism; older CD-ROM drives that used a caddy to carry the disc can usually be operated on their side.)

Consult your instruction manual to see if your computer's case uses any unusual fasteners or means of closing.

A tower case usually has five to ten cover screws, rather than four or five. Remove the cover screws, then pull the cover forward and up, or backward and up, depending on the design.

The tower case usually has a full-length plastic face plate with lights and cutouts for the floppy drives. Some models won't let you remove the floppy or hard disk drives until you snap this plastic cover off. Other tower models mount this face plate semipermanently with screws and let you slip the drives out from the back. Examine your computer's manual and use your own judgment.

Cover Reinstallation

Before you reinstall the cover, look down inside it and check to see if there are any pegs or other protrusions on the inside front surface. If there aren't any pegs, simply tip the cover up extra high in front as you slide it onto the chassis, then slide it straight back into place. Tighten the machine screws gently; force is neither necessary nor helpful. If there is a peg or two on the inside of the cover, installing the cover is a bit trickier; you must wiggle the cover up and down a bit to make it slide that last half-inch into position. Once in place, install the screws and test-boot the computer.

The Mother of All Boards

The *motherboard* is also known as the *system board* or the *mainboard*. Figure 5.5 shows a motherboard from a modern machine.

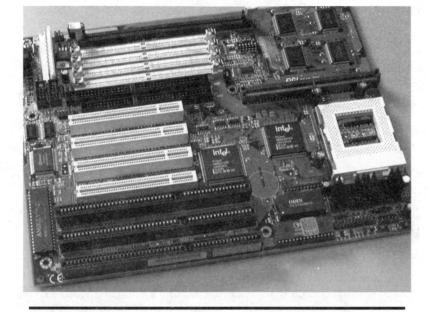

Figure 5.5 A bare Micro-Star Pentium motherboard, a board offered by Dalco Electronics and other suppliers for replacement and upgrade projects.

Modern machines may also have the following:

- OverDrive socket
- Integrated IDE or SCSI I/O circuitry
- Integrated video circuitry

Dinosaurs may have the following:
- Math coprocessor socket or chip

All PC motherboards include the following in one form or another:

- CPU (Central Processing Unit or Microprocessor)
- System ROM BIOS (Read-only Memory Basic Input/Output System)
- RAM (Random Access Memory)
- DMA (Direct Memory Access) channels
- System Bus
- Setup system: CMOS, DIP switches, or jumpers
- Clock crystal

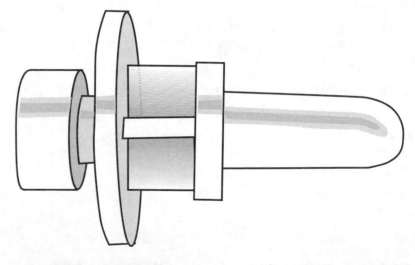

Figure 5.6 The motherboard needs to be supported from beneath, especially under the slots where cards are inserted; sturdy plastic spacer supports like these pop into holes in the board and then slip into channels on the case. One or two screws lock the board into place. Upgraders can obtain replacement supports in several designs from parts suppliers like Dalco Electronics.

CPU (Microprocessor)

The microprocessor is the engine of the computer, the place where data is actually processed. We've already discussed the lineage of CPU chips in Chapter 2; a review appears in Table 5.1.

Table 5.1 CPU Chip Lineage

CPU Chip	Used in Systems of This Type
Dinosaurs	
Intel 8088	IBM PC, PC-XT, PCjr
NEC V20, NEC V30	PC clones
Intel 80286	PC-AT and clones
Modern Machines	
Intel 386, 386SX	ISA machines, EISA, PS/2s
Intel 386SL, IBM 386SLC	Portables
Intel 486DX, Intel 486SX	ISA, EISA, PS/2, VL, PCI
Cyrix 486SLC, Cyrix 486DLC, AMD Am486DX4-100	ISA, VL, PCI
Intel 486DX2, Intel 486DX4	ISA, VL, PCI
Intel Pentium	ISA, EISA, VL, PCI
Cyrix 6x86, AMD5K86	ISA, PCI
Intel Pentium Pro, Intel Pentium with MMX	ISA, PCI

The CPU is almost always been located on the motherboard, although a few designs moved the microprocessor to a back-plane card that attached to a system board; this design was intended to allow for easy upgrades of the processor. In the most modern of modern machines, though, this scheme has been replaced by CPUs mounted in zero insertion-force (ZIF) sockets, or additional OverDrive sockets that accept upgrade chips.

BIOS ROM (System ROM)

The computer power-on self-test (POST) and the boot instructions are stored in the *BIOS* (Basic Input/Output System) *ROM*, a read-only memory chip. The ROM also provides the most basic level of hardware control while the computer is running.

Originally, BIOS chips were rarely replaced. Then came a period when computer users were regularly offered upgrades to the BIOS chips which required that they be pried out of their sockets and replaced. The pace of change has slowed a bit lately, mostly because the Pentium microprocessor is deep into maturity, but some buyers of late-model 486 and early-model Pentium machines are a step behind. In 1995, many owners of modern machines found that they were shut out from the use of new high-speed, low-cost hard disk drives over 508 MB in size because their AT-class BIOS chips were designed with a limit on the number of cylinders they could work with.

Some manufacturers have made the BIOS upgrade process easier through the use of "flash" chips that can have their contents changed by reading a new program into them from disk; this special class of memory device can retain a set of instructions without power being applied.

BIOS replacement is discussed in detail in Chapter 3.

RAM (Random Access Memory)

RAM, also called *system memory*, provides a temporary storage area for DOS, programs, and data. Under DOS, 640K of system memory can be used, and that has become an absolute requirement for current software. Modern machines and 386-based dinosaurs are able to work with expanded or extended memory that lies above system memory. Such memory is essential for use with Windows and many DOS multimedia programs.

The IBM PC, the original dinosaur of dinosaurs, came equipped with as little as 16K or 64K of memory. If you have an antique with just that little, or just 256K of memory, you will not be able to run modern software and it is probably not economically feasible to upgrade such an outdated system; it would be cheaper to buy a new motherboard capable of accepting high-capacity memory chips.

On all machines, the first 64K of memory is filled with housekeeping information (data the computer needs to operate itself). Consider the example of the interrupt vector table, an element of the operating system that tells the microprocessor what to do if a particular piece of hardware requires its attention. The table must be correct and in the proper place in order for the computer to do any work. (It is because of this that most memory test diagnostic programs cannot read from or write to the first 64K of memory without crashing the computer.)

The original dinosaur PC had its memory installed directly on the motherboard. The next step in the evolution of PCs moved the memory to an add-on card that plugged into the bus, and later into a special memory slot. The current design of modern machines has brought high-capacity memory SIMMs back to special slots on the motherboard.

We'll discuss memory in more detail in Chapter 7.

DMA (Direct Memory Access)

DMA channels allow direct information transfer from peripherals to system memory without the involvement of the microprocessor; this change both speeds up the transfer and removes some of the workload from the CPU.

Some dinosaur clones did without DMA, but virtually every member of the PC family has utilized them for modern machines.

DMA is routinely used for most of the peripherals of the PC, with the exception of floppy disk drives; some backup programs, though, are capable of rerouting floppy disk transfer to the DMA channels to pick up speed in making massive archival backups.

DMA chips are almost always soldered into place on the motherboard, making it nearly impossible to replace them if they fail. Such failures are relatively rare in modern machines. If these chips do fail, you are probably due for a replacement of the motherboard.

Bus

The *bus* is the main information path inside the computer. It connects the microprocessor, memory, ROM, and all expansion cards. As we have seen, PC buses have gone through an ever-improving progression from 8-bit PC to 16-bit AT to ISA, EISA, MCA, VL, and PCI designs. They are all essentially the same: a series of thin wires, called *traces*, that run from connectors on the motherboard to control chips and the CPU itself. High-performance buses are wider (capable of handling more parallel pathways) and faster; advanced systems also include intelligence that can arbitrate among multiple demands for access to the bus at the same moment.

The design essentials of computer buses is discussed in Chapter 4.

Bus Connectors for Expansion Cards

PC/XT clones use an 8-bit bus with a single 62-pin connector for each expansion card.

AT-style computers have a 16-bit bus, with two connector sockets for each expansion card. This 16-bit AT bus is also called the *Industry Standard Architecture* (ISA) bus. The 62-pin socket on the ISA bus is identical to the PC/XT 62-pin socket; cards designed to use this single socket (8-bit cards) will usually work in a 286, 386, 486, or Pentium ISA bus computer too. You'll often see one or two bus connector positions on ISA motherboards with only the single 62-bus socket. The single sockets sometimes make it easier to install one of the bulky old 8-bit cards.

EISA computers use a versatile bus connector socket that can accept ordinary 8-bit cards, ordinary 16-bit ISA-style cards, or (if you've got the bucks to buy them) EISA cards.

MCA buses include 16-bit and 32-bit designs. Cards for 16-bit devices have 58 fingers, with signals available on each side of the card for a total of 116 connections. Cards for 32-bit devices have 93 fingers, again with connections on both sides of the card for a total of 186 wires. MCA cards generate less electrical interference than other adapters, which enhances system reliability and the integrity of data.

VL or VESA local bus systems are extensions to an ISA or EISA motherboard that connect directly to the CPU. Some early designs for local buses used proprietary cards and connectors, but standardization was eventually achieved. VL motherboards place an MCA connector in line with a standard ISA connector; VL cards include pins that plug into both.

The *Peripheral Component Interconnect* bus, or PCI, usually exists as a parallel bus alongside an ISA, EISA, or VL bus. Standard 32-bit cards have 120 active connections, with four pin locations used for card keying for a total of 124 pin locations. A 64-bit extension to the standard card can add another 60 pins for a total of 184.

System Setup: Dip Switches, Jumpers, or CMOS Memory

Until the most modern of the modern machines—EISA and Plug and Play PCI/ISA combos—users have had to find a way to instruct the system on what type of parts are installed. As machines have progressed the process of doing so has become simpler; put another way, the machines have become smarter.

PC/XT

Dinosaurs used *DIP switches* to tell the BIOS ROM what hardware is installed on the machine. Technicians or users set the switches to reflect the amount of memory and number of floppy drives installed, the video type, and the presence or absence of a numeric coprocessor.

Jumpers are small pins with plastic and metal devices that can be moved into place to open or close the electrical connection between the pins. In this way they work just like switches, although they are more trouble for users. Be sure to save any of the connectors if you are asked to remove them. Each motherboard manufacturer uses jumpers and switches slightly differently. You must have the motherboard manual to know which function a particular jumper controls.

Modern Machines

Nearly all current machines use a Setup or configuration program to write system hardware information to a *CMOS* memory chip. Here the system records the amount of memory, the type of floppy and hard drives installed, the video adapter type, and whether a math coprocessor is installed. CMOS also keeps track of the date and time. CMOS memory chips hold onto their information with the assistance of a small, rechargeable battery so that configuration information is not lost while the power is shut down overnight.

EISA computers also use an extended setup routine called the *EISA configuration utility* (ECU). The ECU stores information about any expansion cards installed in the computer.

Plug and Play

Nearly all machines introduced just before and since the introduction of Windows 95 include a feature called *Plug and Play* that allows the system to notice the presence a new card or other device and to install new drivers and adjust other settings if possible, or to request of the human operator that the requisite adjustments be made. Plug and Play adapters including video cards, disk controllers, and special purpose devices are available; some hard drives, monitors, and even uninterruptible power supplies can also announce their presence to the system in this way. Plug and Play systems can also notice if a card or other device has been removed from the system and make necessary adjustments.

You'll find more details about Plug and Play later in this chapter.

Clock Crystal

The CPUs of all PCs beat to an internal clock, calibrated with a quartz crystal that vibrates at a known frequency when electricity is applied. With each beat of the clock, the CPU moves a block of information through its set of microscopic switches. The tempo of the internal clock is measured in MHz; a megahertz represents one million cycles per second.

Although a 486 CPU is by itself faster than a 386 chip, and a Pentium faster than a 486, the speed of the clock crystal has a major effect on processing throughput. The original IBM PC had a clock crystal that beat at a somnolent 4.77 MHz. As this book is written, the current speed champion is a 200 MHz Pentium, with even faster devices on the horizons.

Faster is better, although high speed also brings with it heat buildup and RF radiation. For these reasons, a properly designed case and ventilation system is essential; do not modify a PC case or block its air holes.

Clock crystals are almost always soldered onto the motherboard. Some early dinosaurs had crystals in sockets, and there were some early upgrade kits that gave a CPU a quick boost by speeding up the crystal. On modern machines the crystal beats at a high speed and can then be downwardly adjusted by dividing the number of pulses accepted by the processor. Crystals rarely fail; if you do have a problem with the clock the motherboard will likely have to be replaced or professionally repaired.

Real Time Clock/CMOS Battery

Modern machines have a battery-powered clock that keeps track of the date and time and communicates it to the operating system for such important tasks as recording that information with files as they are saved. The clock is located within a chip on the motherboard; the battery can be located in a socket on the motherboard or in a holder attached to the chassis.

The most modern of modern machines employ something called a *Real Time Clock*. This is a special low-power clock and low-demand backup for CMOS with a special battery that can have a useful life of ten years or more. On some motherboards the real time clock and battery is installed in a DIP-type socket and can be replaced. On other boards, the clock and battery are soldered in place on the motherboard; the maker is gambling (with your money, no less) that the life of the battery will be longer than the useful life of the motherboard.

Some older machines employed a short-sighted solution: the battery was soldered into place on the motherboard. Not only did this make replacement of the battery very difficult, it also opened the system to the possibility of serious and sometimes fatal damage from a leaking battery. If you have such a system you should keep a close eye on the health of the battery and consider bringing the system to a technician in hopes that the battery can be surgically removed and a socketed replacement installed.

Modern machines with removable batteries typically use one of several designs:

- A small holder that accepts a round coin-shaped battery, like those used in some clocks and cameras
- A larger battery pack that can hold either a set of rechargeable cells or in some designs a group of AA or AAA alkaline batteries
- A connector cap that attaches to the top of a special rechargeable cell shaped somewhat like a standard 9v battery.

The battery pack or connector cap design sometimes places the battery on a clip that attaches to the drive cage of your PC case, while the small coin-shaped batteries are often directly on the motherboard. If you have any doubt as to the location of the battery, consult the instruction manual for your system or call its manufacturer.

When you purchase a PC or a replacement battery, there should be specifications from the battery maker telling you the typical life of the cells; good practice is to replace the battery a few months ahead of the recommended life. One tipoff that the batteries are at or near the end of their useful life is a message at bootup that warns of "Invalid System Settings." If you have not made changes to the CMOS yourself or made changes to the hardware in the system, your next logical assumption would be that the battery is failing to hold its charge while the machine is turned off.

In most cases, when you remove the old battery to replace it with a new one, the contents of your CMOS setup will be lost. That's why we strongly urged earlier in this book that you maintain a current copy of your settings—write them down in a notebook or use the facility of some Setup screens to produce a hard copy of your settings on a printer.

Dinosaur PCs and PC-XTs did not have a clock on the motherboard. Instead, some of the first multifunction cards developed for those systems added a clock along with communication ports.

CHAPTER 5

Dinosaur Days: Math Coprocessor Socket

This socket can accommodate an optional mathematics chip for heavy number-crunching work. Math coprocessors are of benefit in heavy graphics and spreadsheet work; only a relatively small proportion of PC owners, though, actually install the chip. Beginning with the 486DX chip and including all Pentium CPUs, a math coprocessor is built into the microprocessor. The 486SX chip has the math coprocessor section disabled or removed.

Nearly all PC motherboards have an available socket for a coprocessor. Some 486DX motherboards have a socket that can accommodate a Weitek coprocessor, which operates even faster than the math coprocessor built into the 486 chip.

OverDrive Sockets

Modern machines, beginning with late-model 486 motherboards and continuing into Pentium-based PCs, usually include a specialized socket near the CPU intended to accommodate an Intel OverDrive chip. These chips are capable of upgrading the processor to faster and more efficient chips as they are developed. Other versions of OverDrive chips are intended to physically replace older CPUs.

In addition, some third-party makers offer their own CPU upgrade chips that may work in the OverDrive socket or in the original CPU socket. Such manufacturers include Kingston and Evergreen.

OverDrive and CPU upgrade chips are discussed in Chapter 2.

Integrated I/O and Video Circuitry on the Motherboard

Serial and parallel ports were originally adaptations to the PC, installed as single-purpose adapter cards, or as elements of "multifunction" cards such as a video adapter and printer port, or a combination game port, clock, and serial port. Modern machines now typically have most or all of these functions as part of the motherboard.

So, too, hard and floppy drive controllers began life as separate adapter cards that plugged into the bus. Although many modern machines still put high-performance drive controllers on add-in cards, other current machines make use of IDE and EIDE adapters that are integrated onto the motherboard.

Video adapters began as separate cards that plugged into the bus, although some integrated designs of modern machines placed the video circuitry on the motherboard itself. Current machines generally pick up some speed with video adapter cards that plug into special local bus slots or into VL or PCI local bus slots.

One advantage of integrating many functions onto the motherboard is the ability of the manufacturer to fine-tune and test all the components together and guarantee the complete product—no more worries about subtle incompatibilities between your floppy drive controller and your motherboard.

Integration can also reduce the overall price of a system since there is no need for redundant electronics on the adapter cards, plus the cost of the cards themselves. And another advantage lies in the fact that integrated functions do not demand use of any of the limited slots on the motherboard.

The principal disadvantages of integration are the limitations they place on buyers. If you want to use a SCSI controller instead of an IDE system, for example, you may have to disable the IDE circuitry on the motherboard (and pay for it, whether you use the integrated controller or not). See Figures 5.7, 5.8, and 5.9.

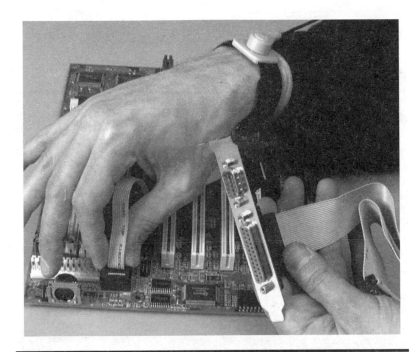

Figure 5.7 The serial connector on a motherboard with integrated I/O functions. In this system a cable connects to the motherboard and leads to a bracket with ports that poke through the rear panel of the case.

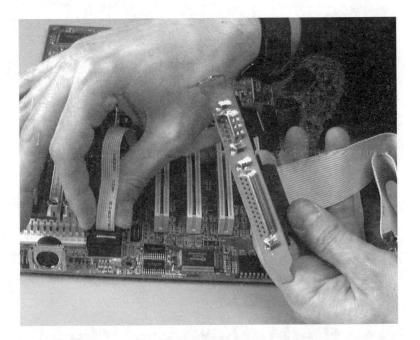

Figure 5.8 The parallel connector on a motherboard with integrated I/O functions.

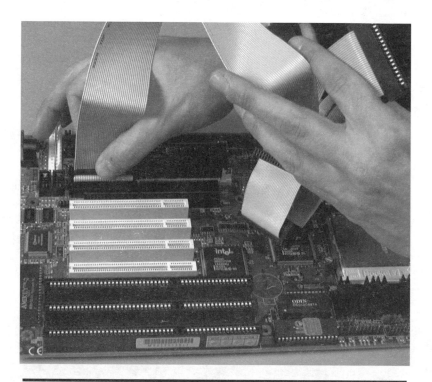

Figure 5.9 A FDD (floppy drive) connector and one of two HDD (EIDE circuitry for hard drives or CD-ROM drives) on an integrated motherboard.

The riser card makes for a compact box, but a sometimes difficult repair and upgrade assignment.

Tower systems place the motherboard on its end along one side of the box with add-in cards mounted horizontally.

How the Motherboard Works

The mother of all boards in your PC is the home of the CPU and its supporting chips, including the BIOS ROM.

Where to Find the Motherboard

In a desktop machine, the motherboard lies beneath the add-in cards and internal peripherals of the PC. In most systems, several add-in cards stand upright in slots on the motherboard.

In another type of design, a "riser card" stands up a slot on the motherboard like a Christmas tree with slots branching off on either side for add-ins. Riser card systems are often used in low-profile desktop machines.

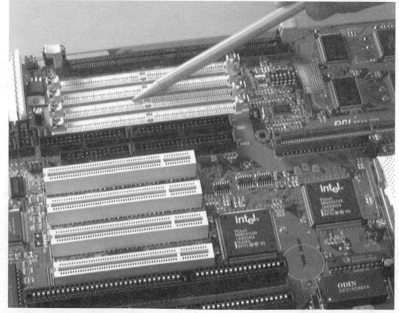

Figure 5.10 This Micro-Star motherboard includes two banks of memory slots for 72-pin SIMMs; each bank (made up of two matched slots) can hold 4, 8, 16, or 32 MB of memory. This particular board also offers a third bank of memory using a 168-pin DIMM module of 8, 16, or 32 MB.

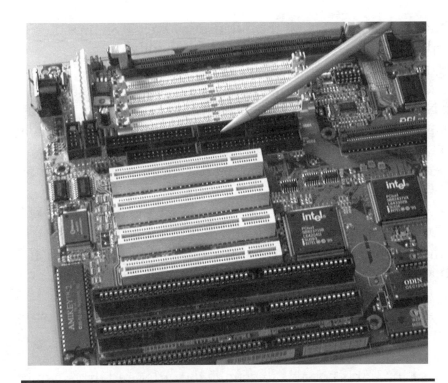

Figure 5.11 Modern motherboards with integrated I/O circuitry offer connectors for two serial and one parallel port, one floppy disk cable (capable of controlling two devices), and two EIDE ports. The EIDE controller can work with as many as four devices, including hard drives and CD-ROM drives.

As we've already discussed, system memory may lie on the motherboard or on an add-in card; other elements that may be integrated onto the motherboard include serial and parallel ports, the video adapter, and floppy and hard drive adapter. The motherboard is also connected to a power supply that provides low voltage DC power and a fan that helps keep the closed box cool.

To understand how the motherboard components interact, consider what happens when we turn on the power. What follows is a generic description of a modern machine coming to life.

The computer's first steps are hard-wired into the circuitry. When you flick on the power switch, the power supply takes a few fractions of a second to get ready to transform the voltage and spin its fan; when it is ready, it sends a "power good" signal to the clock reset chip on the motherboard. The clock reset chip in turn sends a reset message to the microprocessor. The CPU resets and initializes itself with its ordinary start-up instructions; the early steps include the running of a self-test.

The final, hard-wired step as the computer comes to life is an instruction to look in a specific very high address for further instructions. There, the microprocessor will find a pointer that will send it to the place in memory where the BIOS ROM is waiting.

At this point, the computer marches according to the instructions programmed into the ROM. It is important to remember that ROMs are replaceable; they can be upgraded or changed to provide different instructions to the microcomputer. Some major computer manufacturers are large enough to produce their own BIOS ROMS (IBM among them), while others are important enough to request customization of the BIOS routines. Today the largest manufacturers of BIOS chips are IBM, Phoenix, Award, and American Megatrends (AMI). There are also more than a few Asian sources.

The various BIOS chips all use some form of Power-On Self Test (POST), but the details may vary from machine to machine. The error messages or informational messages displayed on screen may also differ slightly.

The ROM BIOS usually begins by writing its name, date, and copyright information on the screen; then it checks the keyboard (on many systems you can see the CapsLock and NumLock lights flash on and off). The test usually extends to the controller chip inside the keyboard itself. Next it reads the DIP switches on a dinosaur PC or consults the CMOS settings on a modern machine to learn what equipment it should expect. On EISA and MCA machines, the BIOS may be able to interrogate devices plugged into the bus to find out what their capabilities are.

On many BIOS ROMs the next step is to conduct an inventory and test of system memory; you may see a countdown on screen as it checks the chips or SIMMs.

The ROM also checks many of the other parts of the system during the POST, including the CPU itself, the DMA chips, and other critical elements of the system.

The BIOS ROM checks the floppy drives (the floppy drive light flashes, and the drive spins as its doing this). If a printer is attached to the parallel port and turned on at bootup, the POST will initializes the printer, clearing its memory, and preparing it to accept output.

In addition, the ROM checks for ROM BIOS extensions—those extra ROMs installed on a hard disk controller or an EGA or VGA video card—and follows the initialization instructions in each of these ROM extensions in turn.

The ROM next tries to boot a disk in drive A, looking at track 0, sector 1 (the DOS boot sector). If no disk is present, it tries drive C, the hard disk, again checking only track 0, sector 1. It is possible to change the order and drive names for bootup on many systems, either through the use of switches or changes to the CMOS setup.

When the selected drive spins to life, the drive heads look to the boot sector to load two hidden DOS files, **IO.SYS** and **MSDOS.SYS**. These files are dedicated to low-level hardware control. **IO.SYS** contains resident device drivers (the software instructions for operating standard hardware devices, such as the keyboard, the disk drives, the printer, and the serial ports).

NOTE Under Windows 95, there are new boot sector files but the basic process remains the same.

The boot sector then looks for a **CONFIG.SYS** file. This file contains directions to the operating system about specific keyboards, device drivers, and other important settings for the system. Typical device drivers cover mice, sound cards, CD-ROMs, scanners, and certain unusual data storage devices.

As a final step, the computer loads a command-line processor or a shell (the interface between the keyboard/mouse and the DOS commands). Most people use **COMMAND.COM** from the DOS disk, but shells from sources other than Microsoft can be used.

Windows 3.1 is loaded on top of DOS, but it doesn't use most DOS functions. In fact, Windows is really an alternative operating system that accesses the CPU chip independently. That's why DOS will run on any of the 8088 family of CPU chips, but Windows 3.1 won't. Windows was written to take advantage of the improvements engineered into 386 and higher chips.

Windows 95 is even more of an operating system by itself; the installation of Windows 95 writes new boot tracks on your hard drive. DOS is still there, somewhere, but it basically comes into play only when you launch a DOS window or instruct the system to restart as a DOS machine instead of a Windows 95 machine.

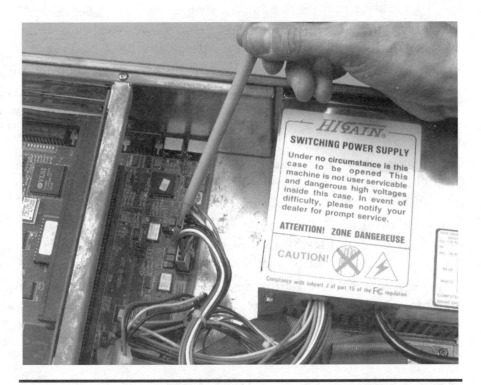

Figure 5.12 On most motherboards, a pair of power supply connectors marked P8 and P9 provide all of the power for the CPU, logic chips, and devices plugged into the bus.

How to Test the Motherboard

Very few of the motherboard components are individually serviceable. Here's a list of what you can do:

- RAM chips can be replaced if they are not soldered into place; RAM SIMMs or SIPPs are held in place in sockets and can be easily changed
- ROM BIOS chips are usually held in sockets and can be replaced because of failure or for upgrading. Some BIOS chips hold instructions in "flash memory" that can be changed in place by reading in new code from a floppy disk or other source

- The clock/CMOS battery is a simple slip-out/slip-in replacement on most motherboards, but some poorly designed dinosaurs had the battery soldered into place

- Most dinosaur CPU chips are installed in sockets and can be removed for replacement or upgrade, although some machines including a family of relatively inexpensive 386SX machines produced in the early 1990s had the CPU soldered into place. Modern machines almost always have their CPU in sockets, and the most current machines often have ZIF (zero insertion force) sockets that permit easy interchange.

On most motherboards, the clock generator and timer chips, the clock crystal and clock reset chip, dip switches, the CMOS chip, the bus controller chip, the DMA controller chip (for direct disk drive to RAM memory information transfer), and all the chip sockets are soldered on.

The board itself is a maze of printed circuits, none of which is readily repairable. Therefore, whenever the problem is stickier than bad RAM, bad ROM, a dead CMOS battery, or incorrect dip switch/jumper settings, it's often necessary to replace the entire motherboard.

Ironically, a soldered-chip design makes the troubleshooting process a bit easier, but makes the problem more expensive to solve. If the chips cannot be replaced, you don't have to bother to identify the specific cause of the problem; instead, the process consists of eliminating any causes that are off the motherboard.

Anatomy of an NMI Error

An NMI error is often the signal that something has gone seriously wrong your PC's motherboard. NMI stands for Nonmaskable Interrupt. An *interrupt* is a signal from a particular device that it wants the attention of the microprocessor.

A *nonmaskable* interrupt is one that the hardware is not permitted to mask, or ignore while processing another task. When an NMI occurs, the NMI error message goes up on the screen and everything is deadlocked until you address the NMI error, no matter what else is going on.

One common source of an NMI interrupt is a memory parity error. See the discussion of NMIs in Chapter 7's section on memory.

How to Remove a Motherboard

To get to the motherboard, start by turning off the computer and unplugging it from the wall. Remove the system cover. Ground yourself before reaching into the case.

In most systems you will have to remove add-in cards and some or all of the hard drives, floppy drives, CD-ROMs, and other internal devices. On tower cases and some desktops, you may want to unbolt one or more drive cages that hold add-in drives; many of these cages overhang parts of the motherboard.

We suggest you keep a notepad close at hand and make a sketch of the innards of the case to help you put things back where they were. Use sticky-tab papers to mark pieces, or make notes on masking tape to identify the parts. Assign numbers to any cables you remove and place matching numbers on the connectors to which they attach. Put screws into envelopes or containers marked with their purpose. Trust us on this one: a few minutes spent organizing the parts you take out can save hours when it comes to putting it all back together again.

Once everything is out of the way, unplug the motherboard from the electrical cable that connects it to the power supply.

Here's a step-by-step walkthrough of a typical project; your case may be slightly different:

1. Remove the cover. Turn off the power and unplug the PC from the wall. Remove the screws that hold the cover in place and store them in a safe place. Slide the cover off.

2. Ground yourself. Touch a grounding strip or the center screw of an electrical outlet plate to release static electricity in your body. Even better, wear a properly grounded antistatic wrist strap.

3. Remove cards. Remove all the expansion cards, marking any cables or wires you must disconnect in the process.

4. Mark and remove wires. Attach labels to all wires connected to pins on the motherboard. Such wires typically include a pair of wires to the tiny internal speaker on PCs, a wire that powers the small "in use" light on disk drives, and similar wires to other indicators on the face of the PC. Mark them well so that you can properly reinstall them. Finally, remove the wires that run from the power supply to the main electrical connections on the motherboard.

5. Remove power supply if necessary. A desktop computer case is pretty crowded. It may be necessary—or you may find it easier—to remove the power supply screws and slide the power supply out of the case so you'll have some working room.

6. *Dinosaurs*: Remove mounting screws and slide motherboard out. Most PC/XT motherboards have nine stand-offs (little metal or plastic legs) that attach the board to the bottom of the case. Look for screws on the bottom of the computer which correspond to the nine screws or nuts on the top of the motherboard. You can remove either the top nuts or the bottom screws. Other XT clones use two screws and a handful of insulated plastic pegs.

After you remove the nuts or screws, slide the motherboard out of the chassis. On some older systems you'll find paper or plastic insulating washers on both the top and bottom of the motherboard at each of the nine

Figure 5.13 Non-conducting plastic standoffs are installed from the underside of a motherboard to support the board and keep it from touching the metal case. A replacement motherboard should come with an appropriate set of new standoffs; for unusual cases you can order specialized supports from companies like Dalco Electronics.

Look for an insulating washer under the screw heads. Remove the screws, then slide the motherboard 1/2-inch sideways, moving it away from the power supply; it might make sense to remove the power supply and possibly the drive cage on a larger case to make room to remove the board. Lift it up and wiggle it out of the chassis. Sometimes it's easier to squeeze the tops of the stand-offs and lift the motherboard out.

stand-offs and/or screws. You may need to reuse these insulating washers, the stand-offs, and the screws to mount a new motherboard.

Modern Machines: Remove mounting screws and slide the motherboard out. Many modern motherboards are mounted with as few as one or as many as half a dozen small screws, with the motherboard reinforced and electrically insulated at the screw holes. At other places, especially beneath the bus slots, you'll find plastic stand-off supports that pop through the board and slip into slots on the case beneath.

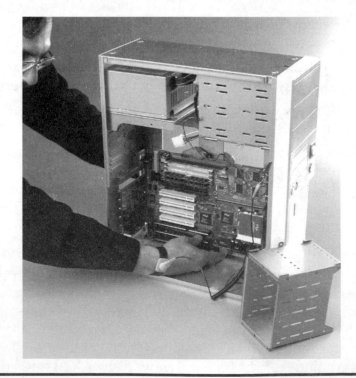

Figure 5.14 You may find it worthwhile to remove drive cages on some cases to make it easier to remove or install a motherboard. Within some compact cases it is necessary to remove the power supply which overhangs the motherboard.

Save the washers and stand-offs to mount the new motherboard. You can also purchase new hardware from sources like Dalco Electronics.

Installing a New Motherboard

In theory, installing a new motherboard is simply the reverse process from removing the old one. Unfortunately, there are only the loosest of standards on motherboard sizes, location of mounting holes, and electrical connection points. And board makers are (thankfully) constantly striving to improve their products, make them smaller and more tightly integrated. We have never seen a replacement go perfectly smoothly, but we have never failed to complete the job sooner or later. This is an indoor job, no heavy lifting.

For this book, we worked with a new Micro-Star Pentium motherboard from the Dalco Electronics catalog. The motherboard was well-labeled at most of its attachment points, and the instruction manual was almost clear enough to understand at first reading. The board was installed in a sturdy vertical tower case with plenty of room to maneuver; the only problem we had was the lack of an instruction manual for the case. Some of the electrical connectors, especially those to front panel indicators, were unlabeled; we made a telephone to Dalco's support desk and a technician there walked us through identifying the cables and changing a few jumpers to adjust the front-panel display lights on our case. The lesson: buy from a reputable company willing to support you after they have your cash in hand.

1. Prepare the case and motherboard. Gently place the new motherboard into the case so that the keyboard connector is lined up exactly with the keyboard hole at the back of the case. Lift up the motherboard slightly to determine where you must install plastic standoffs onto the new motherboard so that it is secured and cannot touch the metal case at any point. The more standoffs you install, the more stable the motherboard installation will be.

   On most cases you will find slotted grooves that accept the underside of the standoffs and lock them into place. In some places you may have standoffs that merely sit atop the bare metal bottom of the case. Don't pass up a chance to add support to the motherboard anywhere you can.

   Find the location on the chassis itself of the one or two brass hexagonal studs that actually hold the motherboard in place. You may have to reposition this metal connector to match a different hole location on the new motherboard.

2. Set switches or jumpers. It may be necessary to make changes to the default settings of switches or jumpers on the motherboard to indicate the type or speed of CPU. Consult the instruction manual.

3. Install the motherboard. Once you have determined the proper location for all of the standoffs, you can lay the motherboard into the case by sliding the plastic standoffs into the grooves of the case. Be careful not to warp the motherboard as you slide it into place; a warped motherboard can short out or break the electrical traces.

    Attach the board with a screw into the brass stud, with a non-conductive paper or plastic washer between the screw and the motherboard.

4. Connect electrical cables to the motherboard. Locate the two white rectangular power leads that come from your power supply; they are usually (but not always) marked P8 and P9.

    Stop, look, and think: a mistake here could fry your motherboard. The good news is that it is pretty difficult to make a mistake with these connectors; they are keyed so that they should only fit in the proper direction, and color coded for position. The most important color code is this: the two connectors line up alongside each other with black wires adjacent to each other. On most cables, the color order goes like this: orange, red, yellow, blue, black, black, black, black, white, red, red, and red. On most motherboards, these leads plug into a connector near the keyboard port at the back end of the board.

    Next, connect the power indicator, turbo, reset, and hard drive light connectors to pins on the motherboard indicated in the manual that accompanies it. The pins are usually marked with numbers or labels printed directly on the motherboard. Pay special attention to the polarity of the plugs you install; the instruction manual usually indicates the color of wire for each pin or whether a particular pin is + or - voltage. In general, power supply wires are as follows: red or yellow are +, blue or white are -, and black is ground.

5. Install CPU and RAM. If the microprocessor and memory are not already installed, you'll need to do so now. We prefer to wait until this stage in the installation if there is room to work inside the case; if your case is very crowded, you might want to put the CPU and memory into place before the motherboard itself is installed. Either way, take care not to damage the somewhat delicate pins on the CPU and be sure to take appropriate antistatic precautions.

    Read the instruction manual for your motherboard carefully to determine memory options; some boards require banks to be filled in matched pairs, while others may not work with certain types of memory such as EDO. If you want to reuse memory SIMMs from the original motherboard be sure they are appropriate for the board. We discuss ways to adapt older style memory carriers to new boards in Chapter 7.

    On some high-speed machines you'll need to connect a CPU fan to the power supply to help remove the heat produced by the microprocessor.

6. Install add-in cards. Reinstall expansion cards into appropriate slots on the motherboard. If you are upgrading to a motherboard with a different slot design, make sure your old cards will fit into the new board. Some full-

size dinosaur-era PC cards are too large to fit in 8/16 bit slots on an AT motherboard. Some cards are wider than others and you'll need to give some thought about which cards can safely sit next to each other.

And just to make things interesting, most ISA 16-bit cards have their components on the opposite side of those on PCI cards. The place where ISA and PCI come together on the motherboard can be a very crowded neighborhood.

7. Reinstall drive cages if they have been removed. Reattach power connections to hard drives and floppy drives if they were disconnected.

8. Attach data cables. If your system's hard drive, floppy drive, and CD-ROM drive connect to an EIDE port on the motherboard, you'll need to attach those cables so that they can communicate with the bus. If the drives instead connect to an adapter card, the cables were probably not removed during the installation of the motherboard.

9. Double-check everything. Take a few moments to check the inside of the case once more. Look for any unattached cables. (There are likely to be a few extra power leads from the power supply, but indicator lights, speaker, and other such elements of the motherboard should all be attached.

10. Attach external components. Plug in the keyboard, mouse, and a video display.

11. Turn on the system. Plug in the computer, and turn it on. If everything has been done correctly, you will go to the new motherboard's CMOS Setup screen to inform it of the elements of your computer. Consult the instruction manual for your motherboard to understand the specifics of your ROM BIOS.

What If the New Motherboard Doesn't Run?

Stop, look, and listen: you don't want to see smoke or sparks and you want to hear a power supply fan and you want to hear the correct audio tones from the speaker. If anything looks or sounds wrong, turn off the computer.

There's not much else to do except to reverse all of the installation steps and check and double-check everything you've done. Here are some common reasons why a new motherboard may not work:

- Power supply not properly connected to the board
- Memory SIMMs not properly seated in slots
- CPU not oriented properly in socket
- Traces on bottom of motherboard shorting out to case
- Improper settings on switches or jumpers

Of course, it is also possible that you have received a bad motherboard, although dead-on-arrival boards are much less likely with modern devices. Once again, though, this is a time when you will be very thankful if you are dealing with a reputable vendor who will offer technical assistance and/or replacement if necessary.

Working with Expansion Cards

The time has come to lay hands on your computer. Before you begin, we'll review how to remove and install an expansion card, and how to inform the computer about what you have just installed. We'll discuss setting switches or jumpers and running the setup or configuration program on a modern machine.

We've already discussed how to remove the system cover in Chapter 1; review that section if you need to. Be sure to turn off the power and remove the power cord before going under the cover. And we recommend use of a grounding strap or grounding pad.

How to Remove an Expansion Card

An expansion card becomes part of the computer through the bottom connector that plugs into the system bus expansion slots on the motherboard. The connector picks up electrical power as well as tying into data and communication lines through the slot.

The card is held firm in its slot by a bracket that attaches to the back wall of the system unit chassis with a single screw. That same bracket may also hold serial, parallel, video, mouse, SCSI, telephone, or other ports to the outside world. In dinosaurs and some modern machines, the other end of the card slips into a plastic groove that holds it in place laterally; new high-density integration has permitted modern expansion cards to become smaller and smaller, and today few cards extend all the way across the length or width of a motherboard.

To remove an expansion card, begin by disconnecting any external cables connected to the port at the back of the computer. Next, take out the screw that attaches the card to the system unit chassis; set it aside in a safe place. Some people like to work with magnetized screwdrivers to help hold onto the screw; this is a good idea in theory, so long as you take care not to lay the screwdriver down on a floppy or hard disk drive. The magnetic power of the screwdriver is relatively low, but magnetism is the enemy of data stored on a disk.

Removing these cards doesn't take much force, but watch your fingers—the card bristles with prickly solder blobs and little metal legs. Put your fingers in comfortable places before lifting. It's also helpful to rock the card back and forth slightly from end to end—*not side-to-side*—to dislodge it from the slot.

Installing a New Card to Replace a Bad Card

Most of the time the replacement card will look a lot like the card you take out of the system. Unless you are upgrading the machine with an adapter of greater functionality, you will want to replace an 8-bit hard disk controller with another 8-bit hard disk controller, an 8-bit video card with another 8-bit video card, and so forth. Compare the bus connectors on the two cards. If they are the same, just slide the new card into the old card's expansion slot.

Carefully line up the card edge connector with the slot on the motherboard, then press down firmly, applying even pressure at front and back. If the card has external connectors for ports on the back, you may have to angle the card slightly to come under the lip of the PC chassis before you position it above the slots.

When the card is in place, the screw hole on the card lines up with the screw hole in the back of the chassis. Reinstall the screw and test the machine.

If the bus connectors are not the same, consult the instruction manual or speak with the manufacturer to be certain the device is compatible with your system. SCSI host adapter cards, for example, are available in versions with 8-bit, 16-bit, EISA, and PCI edge connectors. So are network cards and many video cards.

Some computers have slots that can accommodate more than one kind of bus connector. ISA machines, for example, can usually handle 8 bit as well as 16-bit cards. Modern PCI machines often can work with VL, 16-bit, and 8-bit cards. Consult your instruction manual or call the manufacturer if you have any doubts about the capabilities of specific slots.

Installing an Additional Card

Did you ever carry an air conditioner into the house, set it up carefully in the window, then find out that the plug won't fit the electric outlet? Perhaps the air conditioner is looking for 220 volts while the outlet is an ordinary 110-volt line.

PC expansion cards, like electric appliances, plug right in when the card edge connector matches the motherboard bus connector. When the connectors don't match, there's no action.

Don't be concerned about the specifics of the size or shape of these cards; card manufacturers often seek to save money by making modern cards as small as possible. Concentrate your attention on the card edge connector—the place where the card plugs into the motherboard.

To choose the slot where you will install the new card:

- If you are installing an 8-bit card with the short, single bus connector, any bus expansion slot in any of the clones will do. These 8-bit cards fit in XT clones, in 286/386/486/Pentium ISA computers, and in EISA computers. Don't worry about long versus short slots; if the board will physically fit into the slot, it will work.
- If you have an ISA 16-bit expansion card, it will fit in either an AT-style ISA computer or an EISA computer.
- EISA cards fit only in EISA motherboards, though ordinary 8-bit and 16-bit cards will fit in EISA motherboard connectors.
- MCA cards fit in high-end PS/2 computers with the MCA bus. Use only MCA cards in MCA computers; nothing else will fit.
- VL and PCI bus designs are generally paired with a separate ISA bus. This allows you to use any ISA cards you want, reserving special high-speed adapters for the VL and PCI slots with their extra connectors.

To install your new card, remove the screw at the back of the chassis that holds the slot cover to the case. The slot covers are slender metal strips (usually 3/4 of an inch wide) at the back of the chassis. The slot covers are part of your PC's defense against the leakage of RF radiation that can interfere with radio, television, and other signals in your home or office.

You'll see one slot cover for each unused expansion slot; the cover will be replaced by the bracket of the new card. Remove the cover for the slot you want to use and save the screw. Put that cover away in your computer tool kit; you'll want to put it back into place if you ever remove a card from the bus and don't replace it.

Line up the card with a motherboard expansion slot and the empty slot cover. Press the card down firmly. When it bottoms out and the screw hole on the card lines up with the screw hole on the chassis, reinstall the screw.

Note that some slim-line PC designs call for adapter cards to be installed sideways into a riser card that comes up from the motherboard. The same principles apply to the use of a riser card, except that you will be pushing in toward the center of the riser card instead of down to the motherboard itself.

Similarly, PCs using tower cases generally have the motherboard turned on its side. With a tower case, it may be easier to turn the PC on its side for removal and installation of adapter cards.

The final step after installation is to attach any necessary external cables to the port on the back of the card.

A Computer's BIOSed View of the World

Your computer needs to know what pieces of hardware are installed in it. The oldest systems may need to be instructed about every last piece of equipment, from keyboard to floppy disks and hard drives to video cards, parallel ports and serial ports. On an XT and some early AT machines, you'll have to set switches or make other mechanical notification to the system. Modern systems may be able to detect the presence of some devices, or you may have to inform the system of devices through use of the Setup or Configuration program.

As we discussed, computers in the PC family are equipped with a basic input/output system, read-only memory (BIOS ROM) chip. The BIOS chip contains the nitty-gritty directions your computer needs to connect to a floppy drive, video card, or another device.

The BIOS ROM in the original IBM PC computer was a true dinosaur. IBM didn't bother to put directions to allow it to work with a hard disk, because nobody thought users would ever want or could ever afford hard disks. In fact, the original IBM PC came with a cassette port so that users could save data on an ordinary audio cassette recorder, a painfully slow process. If anyone ever actually made regular use of that port, that fact has been lost in the mists of history; however, to maintain compatibility, support for the cassette port continued to be part of the BIOS ROM for many years to follow.

IBM XTs and their clones were a bit smarter. These computers were instructed to search for additional ROMs located on cards plugged into the bus—for example, ROMs on a hard disk controller card or on a video card.

The BIOS chips in ATs and AT clones were even smarter. They knew about hard disks, and actually had directions built in for the most popular hard disks then available. The AT computers (ISAs) kept the search for other-ROMs feature, too.

EISA computers are smarter yet. They include the full instructions of ISA computers and add to them accommodations for special EISA adapter cards, which transfer data at extraordinarily high speeds. But you, the installer, must tell the EISA computer which EISA cards are installed.

MCA computers, like EISA computers, demand that you run a Micro Channel setup program from the reference disk shipped with your computer whenever you install a new card.

PCI and VL Bus systems have standard ISA or adapted ISA setup screens that are part of their ROM BIOS code.

Plug and Play

By now, every man, woman, child, and Shetland sheepdog has heard of Windows 95, Microsoft's operating system introduced late in 1995 (and due for some important incremental updates in late 1997.)

One of the most intriguing features of Windows 95 is the Plug and Play specification. In theory, this allows Windows 95 to reach out and interrogate every piece of hardware within and without the system to determine its presence and its need of interrupts, DMA channels, port addresses, and other elements of the PC.

Plug and Play works through the use of BIOS chips on hardware and a huge list of devices maintained by Windows. In theory, when you turn on your PC, Windows 95 will know everything it needs to know about your system and will be able to manage devices so that they do not conflict with each other.

By the way, this is one feature that Apple's Macintosh has had for years; before you allow an Apple fan to rant and rave about the supposed superiority of that system, remember that Apple was able to enforce its will because it was a closed architecture. Manufacturers were forced to comply with Apple's directives, which resulted in higher prices and limits on availability of devices. The open PC architecture, like most democracies, presented a wild, disorganized, and lively marketplace.

Sometime between now and forever, all of the elements of your PC just may conform to the Plug and Play (PnP) specification and all will be well with the world. In the meantime, you can expect to have a mix of PnP and old-style devices in your machine and on the market for years to come. Users will still have to configure non-PnP devices manually, and may even run into some conflicts with automatically set devices.

Telling the Computer about the Card You Have Just Installed

Each branch of the PC family uses slightly different techniques to tell the computer and the BIOS ROM what parts are installed.

XTs and XT Clones

XT-style computers are the least flexible. XTs look at the settings on switches on the motherboard for an inventory of hardware devices for such elements as floppy drives, memory, and what kind of video is installed. There is also a switch on the motherboard to set if you have installed an 8087 math coprocessor chip.

Set the switches according to the instructions shipped with the motherboard; if the maker of your machine is still in business, you may be able to obtain information from technical support.

Table 5.2 is a generic listing of switch settings based on the original IBM PC-XT. Remember, though, not all clone makers designed these same generic switch settings into their XT motherboard. The wrong settings won't blow up the computer, but it won't work right either.

Table 5.2 Typical XT Switch Settings

Switch	Typical Setting
Switch 1	Normally off
Switch 2	OFF = 8087 math coprocessor installed
	ON = No math coprocessor installed
Switches 3 and 4	Instructs the motherboard on the amount of memory installed. This is an area where one motherboard can differ greatly from another. Consult the motherboard maker; you may be able to obtain help from a memory chip vendor, although few companies still sell the antique 64K RAM chips that were used on early machines.
Switches 5 and 6	Indicates the video display.
	5 ON, 6 OFF = CGA color, with 80 characters per line
	5 OFF, 6 ON = CGA color, with 40 characters per line
	5 OFF, 6 OFF = Monochrome adapter
Switches 7 and 8	Indicates number of floppy drives installed. Note that XTs worked only with double-density 5.25-inch floppy drives.
	7 ON, 8 ON = 1 floppy
	7 OFF, 8 ON = 2 floppies
	7 ON, 8 OFF = 3 floppies (!)
	7 OFF, 8 OFF = 4 floppies (!)

Look for a bank of eight switches in a row on the motherboard. They will be either rocker switches or slide switches. The switches may be marked ON and OFF, or CLOSED and OPEN, or sometimes 1 and 0. (On, Closed, and 1 all mean that the switch is closed, which in electrical terms means it is on. Off, Open, and 0 mean that the switch is open, and therefore disabled.)

You will need a ball-point pen, a toothpick, or a tiny screwdriver to change the switches. Set rocker switches by pressing the rocker down on the side of the switch you want; for example, press down on the Off side of switch 1 to turn the switch off.

Slide switches are moved laterally toward the setting you want to use.

AT-Class (ISA) Computers

IBM AT computers and their offspring, modern machines with an ISA bus, are more flexible. ISA computers use a Setup routine to tell the computer what devices are installed.

As a general rule, software is more flexible than hardware, but hardware is faster. When IBM designed the AT they wanted to get the advantages of both, so they stored the configuration information in a battery-protected CMOS (complementary metal oxide semiconductor) chip and they stored the actual how-to-operate-a-hardware-device information in the BIOS ROM.

It's easy to change the settings in the CMOS chip with software (no poking around on the motherboard looking for switches). In addition, if your BIOS ROM becomes hopelessly outdated you can pry it out of its socket on the motherboard and replace it with a new BIOS ROM. (On the most modern of modern machines, the ROM BIOS can be updated by running a software program that can "flash" new information that will be recorded within the chip.)

Early ATs and AT clones used a separate system setup disk. Running the system configuration software program (often called SETUP) allowed the user to edit the list of drives, memory type, video type, and so on in the CMOS chip. Since the CMOS chip is backed up with batteries, it remembers what hardware is installed in the computer, even when the power is off.

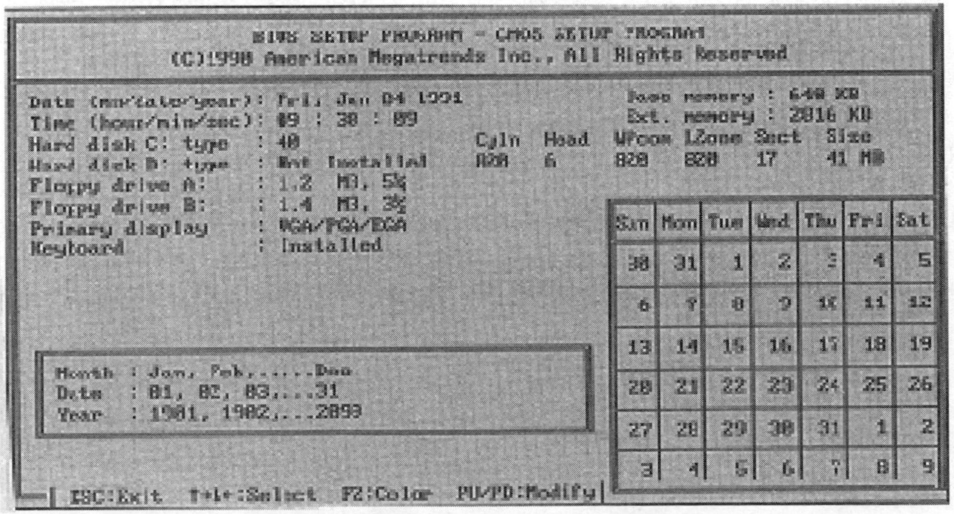

There were several problems with putting the setup program on the floppy disk. First of all, the disk could become lost or damaged. Secondly, the disk would be of no use if somehow the setting that enabled the computer to recognize the presence of a floppy disk drive was damaged. The next step in the development of PC systems, then, was to put the setup program right into the BIOS ROM.

On most such machines with Setup in the BIOS you will see a message like this during bootup: "Press **Del** if you want to run SETUP or DIAGS" or "Press **<Ctrl> <Esc>** for setup" or something similar. Press the keys they tell you to, then follow the directions on the screen (see Figure 5.15).

Figure 5.15 A typical BIOS setup screen.

Consult the instruction manual for your PC if you are unable to display the setup screen with one of these common key sequences.

Before you make any changes to the Setup screen, make a copy of the settings and place it in the instruction manual for your computer. Some Setup programs allow you to print the settings to a file that can be edited within a word processor, or to print settings directly to an attached printer. If you can't obtain such an automatic copy, use a pen and piece of paper for the task.

Take care with the entries you make in the Setup file; you shouldn't be able to damage your computer with a software setting, but some instructions could make things difficult. Pay special attention to the hard drive setting; enter the wrong hard disk type and your hard disk and all of its data will seem to disappear. It's still there somewhere, so don't panic. You'll have to make the correct setting before the system can find the drive and its contents.

When in doubt, check your computer's instruction manual or call the manufacturer for more details on Setup settings.

CHAPTER 5

Running an EISA Configuration Utility

Because EISA computers are compatible with ISA computers, you must run the standard ISA Setup routine described above for most EISA PCs whenever you add hardware devices to your EISA computer. Once that is done, you must also run an EISA configuration utility.

EISA configuration utility (ECU) instructions come with all EISA computers. After installing a card, run the ECU, copy the EISA card configuration file for your new card into your computer, then use the ECU to configure your computer. EISA computers use these card configuration files to manage the expansion cards in your computer.

ISA cards (the 8-bit and 16-bit AT-style cards) use jumpers and switches. An ISA computer doesn't manage the card for you; you have to do it yourself.

What do we mean by *manage the cards*? Expansion cards use resources, much as automobiles in a parking lot use up floor space. If the owners will be self-parking the cars, each owner must cruise until a free space is found. In a lot with valet parking the owners can rely on attendants to arrange the cars efficiently. Think of EISA as valet parking. Once the EISA computer knows what resources (floor space) your expansion card requires, it shuffles the assigned spaces for the cards, parking them here or there, until it finds a free space for all of them. To do this, though, EISA must know each card's vital statistics. That's where the EISA configuration file comes in.

All new EISA cards come with an EISA configuration file disk. In addition, most EISA computer vendors provide a generic configuration file for ISA cards. On some EISA computers you don't have to inform the system about the presence of ISA cards, and therefore won't have to use this generic ISA file. Other EISA computers make it mandato-

ry. In either case, ISA cards are not as convenient as EISA cards because you may have to remove the computer cover and reset the jumpers on the ISA card if you want to change the resources it uses.

On the other hand, ISA cards are much cheaper than EISA cards. Network servers often need high-speed EISA network cards and hard disk adapters cards, but ordinary workstations often run just fine with the ISA versions.

Using the Boot Reference Disk on a PS/2 Computer with MCA

The MicroChannel Architecture (MCA) is off by itself, completely incompatible with ISA and EISA architecture. The MCA was developed by IBM and it was used in many, but not all, IBM PS/2 computers.

PS/2 computers with the Micro Channel bus use a boot reference diskette to load and edit the configuration information for your computer. The reference diskette is self-booting. Simply put it in the A drive and reboot the computer with **Ctrl-Alt-Del** (that means hold down **Ctrl** and **Alt** keys, then hit the **Del** key once and release everything). You should ask the boot diskette to automatically reconfigure the computer whenever you add a new piece of hardware to an MCA computer. Some new expansion boards require a special Configuration file, which is shipped on a diskette with the new board. Just follow the instructions that come with the board.

In PS/2s, the configuration is backed up with a lithium battery. Since the chips forget this configuration information slowly, you can replace the lithium battery without losing the configuration information if you do it quickly. In an emergency, you may be able to cause the system to lose its configuration information (for example, you have installed a password and can't remember it) you can try to leave the lithium battery disconnected for at least 20 minutes, then reconfigure the computer with the reference diskette.

Power Supplies

The *power supply* is a transformer that changes 115 volts of AC (alternating current) from the power line into 5 and 12 volts of DC (direct current) for the components of the computer.

The power supply is inside the computer case; it's easy enough to find—just look for a big shiny or black box with a fan and a power plug coming out the back. To remove a power supply start by unplugging it from the wall, and then disconnect each of the power connectors from the supply to the motherboard and internal devices. You might want to label each connector as you remove it to help you in installing a new power supply. In most computer designs, the power supply is attached to the case by four screws that come through from the rear panel. On some PCs, especially compact desktop units, it may be necessary to remove some adapter cards or device cages to gain access to the power supply.

A modern machine's power supply typically has two large power connectors marked P8 and P9 that send voltage to the motherboard itself; on most systems the two connectors attach to a single attachment point with the black wires on each connector next to each other. Next, there are five or six connectors that are intended for internal devices such as floppy, hard, and CD-ROM drives. The larger power connectors (see Figure 5.16) are generally used by hard drives and CD-ROMs, and the mini-plugs are employed by 3.5-inch floppy drives. No matter what the size of the connector, the voltage level and type are the same.

In Table 5.3 you'll find the assignments for the wires from a standard PC power supply.

Table 5.3 Wire Assignments

Device connector

Pin	Wire color	Function
1	Yellow	+12V DC
2	Black	Ground
3	Black	Ground
4	Red	+5V DC

P8 connector to motherboard

Pin	Wire color	Function
1	Orange	Power good signal
2	Red	+5V DC
3	Yellow	+12V DC
4	Blue	-12V DC
5	Black	Ground
6	Black	Ground

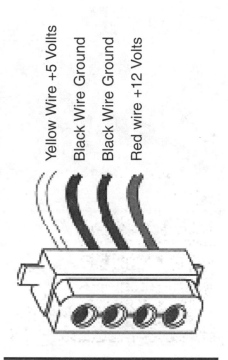

Figure 5.16 A four-wire power supply connector.

CHAPTER 5

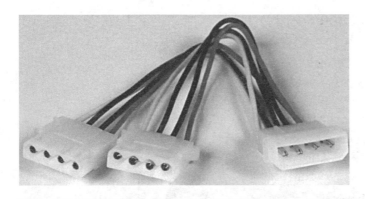

Figure 5.17 A variety of Y cable designs, like this disk drive Y cable, can be used to split off power to multiple devices.

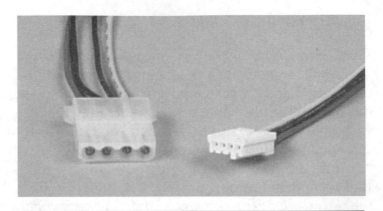

Figure 5.18 Some dinosaurs and other machines may need an adapter to convert a power lead intended for a 5.25-inch drive to work with a 3.5 floppy drive and other modern devices (Dalco catalog).

P9 connector to motherboard

Pin	Wire color	Function
1	Black	Ground
2	Black	Ground
3	White	-5V DC
4	Red	+5V DC
5	Red	+5V DC
6	Red	+5V DC

How the Power Supply Works

The power supply has a very simple job: to provide clean smooth power at +12 volts DC, -12 volts DC, +5 volts DC, and -5 volts DC. It monitors its own power output on startup and sends a "power good" signal to the motherboard when the voltages have stabilized at their required levels. The microprocessor resets and bootup starts when the motherboard receives this signal.

The electronics inside the power supply are not repairable by amateurs and are usually not worth the expense of a professional repair. Do not open the power supply itself!

WARNING

Power supplies are rated by the wattage they will support: the higher the wattage, the more peripherals the unit will work with. Modern machines typically have a power supply rated at least 200 watts; some companies, including major makers like IBM and Compaq, have produced underpowered PCs in recent years that are not capable of supporting internal CD-ROMs and multiple hard drives.

CHAPTER 5

Modern machines can work with an astonishing variety of devices, and you may find that you have run out of power connectors running off the power supply. Assuming you have enough available power—add up the wattage demands of peripherals and be sure to leave an unclaimed overhead of about 30 watts to handle startup power for hard drives and CD-ROMs—you can use a power cable splitter that connects into a power lead at one end and branches into two available connectors.

Dinosaur PCs had power supplies as small as 65 watts, Modern machines have as much as 200 watts in a typical configuration.

Here is an estimate of the power demands of elements of your system:

Motherboard	20 to 35 watts
CD-ROM drive	20 to 25 watts
3.5-inch floppy drive	5 watts
5.25-inch floppy drive	5 to 15 watts
3.5-inch hard drive	5 to 15 watts
Full-size hard drive	10 to 30 watts
Memory	5 watts per MB
Adapter card	5 to 15 watts

A typical early PC with two old-style floppy drives, a full-size hard drive, a few adapter cards, and 1 MB of RAM, then, would demand about 100 watts.

A modern machine with new low-power floppy and hard drives plus a CD-ROM and 16 MB of RAM would ask for about 150 watts.

If you're going to replace a power supply, it's always a good idea to go up a level or two in wattage. Another consideration for some users is the noise level for the cooling fan; some power supply makers offer near-silent fans at a slight premium.

How to Test the Power Supply

Loss of CMOS setup in modern machines is often caused by a bad power supply. The CMOS chip requires at least 4.5 volts to reliably hold the configuration setup information (date, time, installed hardware). It is powered by batteries whenever the computer is turned off. When the 5-volt line climbs above 5 volts or the "power good" line to the motherboard is on, the CMOS battery backup disengages. If a defective power supply has sent the "power good" signal before the 5-volt line is high enough, the setup information is lost. Be sure to check the batteries first. They tend to wear out after a year of service. If you replace the batteries and run the CMOS Setup routine, but the problem still remains, then you probably have a faulty power supply.

Power supplies are not serviceable in the field. Besides, replacements are cheap. If your power supply is not performing correctly, do not attempt to repair it—just throw it away. New power supplies range in price from about $30 to $125. Nearly all power supplies come from obscure Asian manufacturers; we'd pay more attention to the warranty claims of the store or mail order house than to any brand name for the power supply.

You can easily test the voltages produced by your power supply with a hand-held voltmeter. To do this, you must hook the power supply up to 115 volts and to a load of some kind—a disk drive or the motherboard will do. All the four-wire connectors are identical, so you can use any one of them to test your power supply while it is hooked into the computer. This is probably the best way to test the power supply since it should perform properly when fully loaded with all add-on boards, drives, and other such devices. You're looking for +5, -5, +12, and -12 volts.

If the DC voltages are low, consider the external circumstances before condemning the power supply. It's smart to test the AC line current. 104 volts AC is the minimum acceptable standard; if your power is marginal, we recommend you purchase an uninterruptible power supply or a power line conditioner.

Unfortunately, power supplies will occasionally fail for only a microsecond, perhaps on bootup or during drive access. In addition, a defective unit may send the "power good" signal prematurely, causing the microprocessor to reset while voltages are unstable. Premature reset can cause a problem in almost any part of the computer, since random errors may be introduced any place in memory. If you turn the computer power switch off and on again, the same problem may recur, or a different one, or no problem at all. The ordinary voltmeter does not respond rapidly enough to catch a momentary dip or surge in power. In this case substitute a known good power supply and retest the machine to confirm the bad power supply diagnosis.

Occasionally, one of the four-wire power connectors will fail while the others remain functional. If you suspect a problem with one of the four-wire connectors—because disk drive B doesn't function at all, for instance—you can try switching the suspect power connector with the known good one from drive A. If you establish that as the problem, you can try rewiring a new connector; don't go under the covers of the power supply, though.

How to Remove and Replace the Power Supply

Before you remove the power supply, unplug the 110-volt power cord and disconnect the four-wire power supply connectors from disk drives, tape drives, and other devices.

The motherboard receives power from a single long connector or from two multiwire connectors. Examine these connectors closely before removing them, and place labels on them to help with reinstallation. They must be reinstalled properly. If you jam the connectors on backward and turn on the computer, you will damage the motherboard.

Remove the four screws that hold the power supply to the back panel of the chassis. On some designs you'll need to slide the power supply forward an inch or two to clear the lugs on the bottom of the case and lift it up out of the case.

To install a power supply, perform the steps in reverse order. Make sure you reinstall the power connectors on the motherboard correctly.

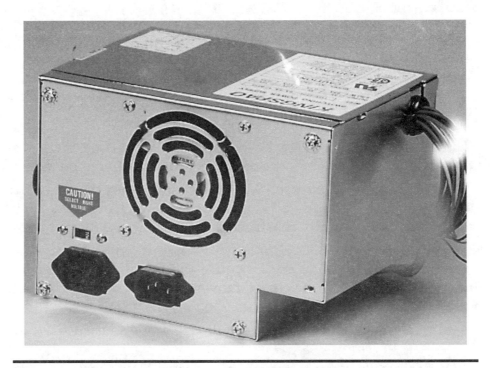

Figure 5.19 Make sure to take the measure of your power supply before ordering a replacement; we found 17 different models in the Dalco Electronics catalog. Common sizes include PC/XT, AT Compact, AT Standard, AT Square, and AT Full Size like the one pictured here. Also pay attention to wattage ratings and the location of power switch, which can differ within various sizes.

CHAPTER 5

Keyboard

It's easy to overlook the keyboard, but don't do that. The device that sits beneath your fingers is critical to the operation of your computer and it is also essential that it fit your style of work like a glove.

There are two basic types of "feel" to a keyboard—soft and click. The original IBM PC came with Big Blue's computer equivalent of its famed Selectric typewriter keyboard; each press of the keys was a smooth passage to a firm bottom, accompanied by a solid click. Soon thereafter, though, many PC clone makers began adopting a soft-touch keyboard where the key presses did not reach a bottom and the click was gone.

Both types of keyboards work, and some users barely notice the difference between the two types of feel. But some of us are strong partisans of one style or another.

The primary maker of click keyboards these days is Lexmark, a spin-off of IBM; IBM also sells its famed keyboard under the IBM Options brand. Soft keyboards are offered by many companies.

There is absolutely no reason why you cannot select the keyboard of your choice to work with your old or new PC; with only a few exceptions, all keyboards are interchangeable. Whichever design you prefer, we suggest you spend a little extra to buy a solidly constructed model. The cheapest of the keyboards are just that: very cheap and ultimately short-lived.

The next issue involves the layout of the board. There are full-sized keyboards with 102 to 105 keys including numeric keypads, separate cursor movement keys, and 12 function keys; there are also 80 to 84-key small footprint models that give you just the basics.

Again, they'll all work; we prefer full-size models because we spend hours at the keyboard.

New Keyboard Features

There are three interesting new variants on the basic keyboard design.

One design uses a tiny round button set into the middle of the keys and used as the controller for the mouse cursor; slight pressure on the button in any direction will move the cursor just as sliding a mouse on a desktop will. The built-in controller began as a space-saving solution for laptop computers, but is beginning to show up in some desktop models. It's an acquired taste, but for some users it is faster and less fatiguing than moving a hand to operate the mouse.

Another interesting trend involves ergonomic keyboards. These designs reject the rectangular, straight-line layout of the keyboard in favor of one that is said to be more like the shape of the human hands. One design, the Microsoft Natural Keyboard, splits the left and right sides of the keyboard along a curved shape. Adesso's TruForm Extended Keyboard is more angular, but also splits the left and right sides. Both keyboards include an extended wrist support in front, intended to help avoid strains in the hands.

Whatever works for you is fine with us; in our experience, though, long-time users of traditional keyboard will have a long and sometimes difficult adjustment period for ergonomic keyboards. In my case, I never became comfortable with the split design.

Finally, we come to keyboards that offer Windows 95-specific keys. One such model is the Qtronix Scorpius 104 Plus, available from Dalco Electronics and other sources. The board includes a button that summons a pop-up Start list and another that duplicates the context-sensitive effect of pressing the right mouse button.

How the Keyboard Works

All keyboards are essentially boxes full of switches. When you press or release a keyboard key, the keyboard sends a signal to the computer over a cable (or through a wireless infrared link in a few models) to a keyboard port on the motherboard.

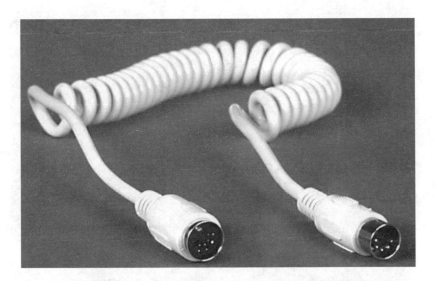

Figure 5.20 Use a keyboard extension, like this PC/XT/AT cable, to allow placement of the computer on the floor or at a distance from the keyboard.

Beneath the keys on the keyboard is a grid of circuits. When you press a key, two wires on the grid are connected. These wires send a signal to the keyboard microprocessor, which converts the grid signals to standard scan codes (signals identifying which key was pressed or released). The scan codes are sent through the keyboard cable to the motherboard.

Inside dinosaur PCs, the ROM converts the keyboard scan code into an ASCII character code representing letters, numbers, and function keys. On modern machines, there is a dedicated keyboard controller on the motherboard to make this translation.

Because XT and AT machines use the five pins of the keyboard cable for different signals, many keyboards are manufactured with an XT/AT switch on the back. A keyboard set to work with an XT and plugged into a modern machine will send only gibberish. If the monitor displays a keyboard error message on bootup, this XT/AT switch is the first place to check.

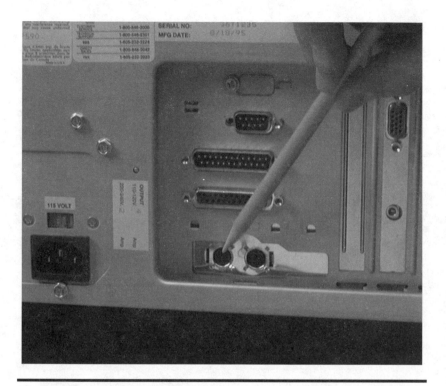

Figure 5.21 A small PS/2-style keyboard connector on the back panel of a PC. Older machines use a larger AT-style connector; adapter plugs are available to convert cables to work with either type of connector.

The original PC keyboard used a large round plug to connect to the keyboard port; newer models use a smaller DIN plug. You will need to match the cable and port to your setup. There are conversion devices that plug into the end of the keyboard cable to make it fit in an unfriendly port (Figure 5.21).

Preventive Maintenance for Keyboards

Every few months, run the keyboard test that is part of most diagnostic programs to test the electronic logic of the keyboard and the motherboard's keyboard controller; the test will also force you to run through all of the keys on the board, including a few you may not ordinarily use.

Essential to keyboard health is keeping it clean and dry. You shouldn't have a cup of coffee or a can of soda or anything else liquid or sticky anywhere near your keyboard (or your PC, for that matter). Although it may be possible to clean up a keyboard that has been doused with a soda, this is a problem you don't need. If your keyboard is bound to be in a wet or sloppy environment—in a kitchen or a restaurant, for example—you should look into purchasing a keyboard "skin" that covers all of the keys with an impervious plastic but permits you to peck away through it.

To clean a keyboard, turn off the power to the PC and unplug the device, then turn it over to dump dust and dirt. For an even better cleaning, use a can of compressed air to blow between individual keys.

You can use a cloth dampened with a weak plastic cleaner to polish up the keys; the most fastidious among us may want to use a cotton-tipped stick to clean between them. If it is absolutely necessary, you can also remove individual keys using a special tool that is supplied with many keyboards. Do so very carefully to avoid breaking the plastic keycaps or the somewhat delicate switches beneath.

Finally, we recommend that you have a replacement keyboard in the closet; like hard drives and other mechanical elements of the PC, keyboards are bound to fail sooner or later.

To remove the keyboard, turn off the PC and simply unplug it from the system unit. Check the XT/AT switch on the new keyboard. Rotate the new keyboard's plug until the pins fit into the connector on the motherboard, then push it in firmly. The system may have to be rebooted to recognize a new keyboard.

It is not a good practice to attach or remove a keyboard while the PC is powered on; it is possible to generate a short or static surge which could damage the PC or the keyboard in this way.

How to Test the Keyboard

Before you try to correct a keyboard problem, analyze the situation. Does the problem involve just one or two keys? If so, try cleaning the bad keys with compressed air or with a good quality, noncorrosive electronic circuit cleaner to clean out the contamination.

If you have any working keys and a whole row or column of nonworking keys, the grid has failed because of a broken wire or short. This is not worth repairing; you'll have to replace the whole keyboard.

Sometimes no portion of the keyboard works properly. It's possible that there's a bad microprocessor chip in the keyboard, but before you discard the keyboard, check that the XT/AT switch is properly set and the keyboard tightly plugged in at the system motherboard. Also don't forget to check for a stuck key. If you can't fix the problem at the plug or through the keys, it's time for a new keyboard.

Dinosaur Time: Clock Card

Early PCs often have a clock card that provides the date and time of day to the system for use in the file management system. Single-purpose clock cards existed for only a short period of time; a bit later in the early days of the PC, clock functions were commonly part of multifunction cards that also included serial and parallel ports and game controllers.

Modern machines include a clock function as part of the motherboard; consult your instruction manual for any information about batteries that may have to be changed every few years.

Locate the clock card or multifunction card. The clock will usually have a silver, disk-shaped battery about the size of a quarter. A few clock cards use a cylindrical battery about 3/4-inch long and 1/2-inch in diameter.

The battery on the clock card powers the clock/calendar chip whenever the computer's power is below 5 volts. This enables the clock chip to continue calculating the date and time, whether the computer is running or not.

You need special software to read the date and time inside the clock card. Because there are a number of possible clock card addresses and date/time formats, you must use the correct software with each clock card. Mismatched software looks for the clock at the wrong address and returns a "no clock found" message, even if a fully functional clock is present.

The batteries on the clock card need to be replaced every few years; consult the instruction manual for details.

It is highly unlikely that you will be able to obtain a replacement clock card or multifunction card for an early PC anywhere but at a swap meet. The good news is that if the clock gives up the ghost, you can continue to use your elderly machine. You'll just have to manually set the time and date each time you boot up.

CHAPTER 6

Shopping for PC Parts

We have some good news and some bad news.

First the good news: Today's modern machines are a hundred or more times faster than the original dinosaurs and cost, on average, less than half as much.

CPUs seem to double in speed every one to two years. Hard disk drives have grown like Topsy, with speedy drives of several gigabytes selling for less than the price of 40 MB storage devices of just a few years ago. Memory has dropped so fast that it no longer is much of a significant issue in calculating the cost of repairs and upgrades.

Now the bad news: With prices on almost every part of a modern machine plummeting so fast and so often, it is sometimes foolish to even bother to repair a dinosaur, and often not worthwhile to perform major surgery on last year's model of modern machine.

In this chapter, we'll try to help you calculate cost-benefit bottom lines for repair jobs.

The Windows 3.1 Minimum Configuration

Windows 3.1 is the lowest acceptable Windows configuration for a modern machine. We much prefer Windows 95 because of its flexibility in hardware configuration and other features.

If you are determined to run Windows 3.1, here are the minimum hardware elements it requires:

- 386SX-25 processor at a minimum, although a 486DX-33 is a more reasonable starting point

- 4 MB of RAM, although systems with less than 8 MB will suffer serious slowdowns
- A VGA video card with at least 512 KB of RAM, although an SVGA video card with 1 MB or 2 MB will reduce display delays
- High-resolution VGA color monitor, although SVGA is necessary for some software applications
- A large, fast hard drive with 50 to 100 MB of available space
- A mouse or other pointing device, officially optional but virtually a necessity.

The Windows 95 Minimum Configuration

Windows 95 is more demanding than Windows 3.1. Here are its minimum requirements:

- A 486DX2-66 CPU is a reasonable starting point, although we have successfully run the operating system on 486SX-33 machines
- Officially, 4 MB of RAM, although we wouldn't bother to install Windows 95 on a machine with less than 8 MB and recommend you go up one more notch to 16 MB
- High-resolution VGA color monitor, although SVGA is necessary for some software applications
- A VGA video card with at least 512 KB of RAM, although an SVGA video card with 1 MB or 2 MB will reduce display delays
- A large, fast hard drive with 50 to 100 MB of available space (you should note that Windows 95 itself can eat up 50 to 100 MB of disk space on its own, not including any installed applications)
- A mouse or other pointing device, officially optional but virtually a necessity

The State of the Art

This is a very dangerous area for predictions, but here we go: here's a guess at the state of the art for a consumer-level PC at mid-1997. (By mid-1998, this will seem like hopeless old . . .)

A 233 MHz Pentium Pro or Pentium with MMX technology, plus 256K or more of cache

32 MB of high-speed EDO RAM

17-inch SVGA monitor

3-D SVGA graphics accelerator with 2 MB of video RAM

A high-speed hard drive with 3 GB of available space

A three-button or two button plus wheel mouse or other pointing device

The Obsolescence Factor

It's said that by the time you pick up a PC part at the back of the store and carry it to the checkout counter, it is already outdated and devalued. To a great extent, that is true: new products are constantly spilling out of the laboratories and factories and the very last place they appear is on the shelves or in the mail order catalogs.

However, it is also true that if you keep waiting for the latest and greatest you will always be waiting. Sooner or later you've got to jump in an make a purchase.

There are three possible buying decisions you can make:

- Buy the hottest new technology as soon as it is offered to the public. You'll pay top dollar, and likely have to put up with some troublesome bugs and incompatibilities until software catches up with hardware, but for a period of time you'll be as current as the magazine covers.

- You can buy the cheapest closeout products. There are some incredible savings to be had if you're willing to help a retailer or mail order operator clear out back inventory. But the truth is that saving money in this way can become expensive in terms of time and money down the road. Settling for an older 486 CPU in the age of the Pentium Pro can mean that you won't be able to run the latest and greatest software; buying an inexpensive smaller hard drive can be pennywise and pound-foolish if you end up having to pull it out in six months because it is much too small for your applications. And you may end with hardware that is no longer backed up by technical support desks at manufacturers.

- In many instances, the best deals come when you buy one step behind the state of the art. You may end up with a slightly slower or smaller device, but you'll benefit from the inevitable price reduction when an item moves off the magazine covers and into the back of the book. For example, as this book goes to press, the hottest Pentium CPUs are 200 MHz speedsters; the best price/performance ratios are for systems based on 166 or 133 MHz chips. The older chips run about 10 to 20 percent slower, but are priced several hundred dollars

CHAPTER 6

below the top of the line. One warning: don't buy older technology if it has been pushed aside because of a flaw. That kind of headache is not worth any price.

The Rules of the Shopping Game

Here, then, are Sandler's Basic Rules for Shopping:

1. Do your own research in this book, in computer magazines, and on-line before making a buying decision.
2. Ask lots of questions before you place your order.
3. Make the rapid pace of improvement work to your advantage: buy the latest and greatest for the longest active life, or buy one step behind the curve for the best price-performance.
4. Always pay with a credit card.

A Bang-for-the-Buck Price Matrix

	Top of the Line	Most Bang for the Buck	Rock-Bottom Minimum for a Modern Machine
Computer Case	Full Tower 300W power supply 8 expansion slots 6 externally accessible 5.25-inch bays. About $136.	Mid-Tower 250W power supply 8 expansion slots 3 externally accessible 5.25 inch bays, two externally accessible 3.5-inch bays. About $80.	Desktop 200W power supply 8 expansion slots 3 externally accessible 5.25 -inch bays, two externally accessible 3.5-inch bays. About $60.
Motherboard	Pentium PCI/ISA with Pentium Pro with MMX socket, EDO RAM, 256K Pipeline burst cache included, four enhanced IDE devices, two 16550 high-speed serial ports, one EPP printer port. About $200.	Pentium PCI/ISA. Supports Intel, Cyrix and AMD processors from 75-200 MHz, EDO RAM, 256K Pipeline burst cache included, four enhanced IDE devices, two 16550 high-speed serial ports, one EPP printer port. About $150.	486 PCI/ISA. Supports most 486 Intel, AMD, and Cyrix processors as well as OverDrive chips. About $150.

	Top of the Line	Most Bang for the Buck	Rock-Bottom Minimum for a Modern Machine
CPU	Pentium MMX 233 MHz. About $600.	Pentium 133 MHz. About $200. IBM or Cyrix 6x86 P166+. About $175.	Intel DX4-100, Cyrix DX4-100 or AMD DX4-120. About $100.
Memory	32 MB EDO. About $190.	16 MB EDO. About $95.	16 MB. About $90.
Video Card	64-bit 3D graphics PCI bus card with 4 MB VRAM. About $280.	64-bit 3D PCI bus graphics card with 2 MB EDO DRAM. About $190.	64-bit VL-bus 2D graphics card with 2 MB DRAM. About $100.
Hard Drive	3.1 to 3.5 GB Enhanced IDE. About $325 to $350	2.1 to 2.5 GB Enhanced IDE. About $250 to $275.	1.2 GB Enhanced IDE. About $175 to $200
Floppy Drive	3.5 inch 1.44 MB. About $40 to $50.	3.5 inch 1.44 MB. About $40 to $50.	3.5 inch 1.44 MB. About $40 to $50. 3.5 inch/5.25-inch combo drive. About $90.
Keyboard	Alps Glidepoint with cursor-controlling touchpad. About $100. Scorpius 95 with Trackball. About $53.	Qtronix Scorpius '95 with Windows 95 keys. About $20.	Qtronix Scorpius i95 with Windows 95 keys. About $20.
CD-ROM	12X EIDE, 1,800 KBps transfer rate. About $125.	8X EIDE, 1,200 KBps transfer rate. About $100.	4X EIDE, 600 KBps transfer rate. About $50
Sound Card	Sound Blaster AWE32 PnP 32-bit wave-table card. About $250.	Sound Blaster 16-bit card with IDE connector. About $95. House brand 32-bit wave-table card. About $140.	16-bit sound card with Sound Blaster compatibility and IDE connector. About $40 to $50.
Monitor	Sony 17-inch Multiscan Trinitron. About $700 to $800. NEC M Series 17-inch. About $800.	ViewSonic, Magnavox, other major brand 15-inch models. About $300 to $400.	House brand 15-inch monitors. About $250 to $300.
Modem	56 Kbps External fax/data modem. About $250.	33.6 External fax/data modem About $130.	33.6 Internal fax/data modem. About $100.

Figure 6.1 Somewhere out there, you'll find every replacement part you need for your PC, including screw-in rubber feet for the bottom. (Dalco catalog.)

Where to Put Your Money Down

We've already discussed the components of a PC. The next step in understanding the financial side of repairs and upgrades is to consult a full-line mail order catalog or a good retail outlet.

Every PC owner has his or her own level of comfort to satisfy. Speaking for myself, I am perfectly comfortable ordering items over the telephone, from a set of screwdrivers to a complete PC system costing several thousand dollars (see Figure 6.1). Others, though, like to squeeze the cellophane and make their purchases at a retail store.

Which is best for you?

Mail Order	Retail Store
+ Generally lower prices	- May be more expensive, although computer superstores approach mail order prices
+ May have larger selection	- Sometimes more limited in selection
+/- The best mail order houses have first-rate technical support desks; some, though, are only order-takers	+/- The best retailers offer on-site technical experts or toll-free help desks
+/- The best outfits have liberal return and replacement policies	+/- The best outfits have liberal return and replacement policies
+ May not charge sales tax	- Will charge sales tax if applicable
- Adds shipping charges	+ Put your packages in your backseat
+/- Convenience factor: Overnight courier delivery to your home or office	+/- Convenience factor: Immediate pickup if you drive to the store

What about mail order fraud? First of all, most mail order operations are honest and can be counted on to deliver. However, there is one very important thing you can do to increase your leverage: always pay with a credit card, and always monitor your credit card statements carefully. The bank that issues your credit card is required by law can be counted on to deliver. However, there is one very important thing you can do to increase your leverage: always pay with a credit card, and always monitor your credit contact the issuer of your credit card immediately and follow their procedures to protest the charge.

What about support? It has been my experience that you can obtain excellentres to pr—technical support from a mail order outfit or at a retail store. I make it a point to ask lots of questions before I make a purchase. If Iím not satisfied with the answers, I take my business elsewhere. If a company is not very helpful to you before you make a purchase, what makes you think they'll be of assistance after they have your money?

In preparing this book, we made good use of the services of Dalco Electronics, a supplier of a wide range of parts from high-end motherboards and CPUs to the little rubber feet that screw onto the bottom of a case. We are also partial to the services of mail order suppliers including PC Connection.

The Upgrade Upset

Letís start out with two basic understandings about personal computers:

First of all, there are only a handful of true computer companies that build their own circuit boards, memory, and hard drives. Instead nearly every computer company could more accurately be called a computer ìassembler.î Companies like Gateway 2000, for example, buy cases and power supplies from one source, motherboards from other, memory and CPUs from a chipmaker, hard drives from other manufacturers, and so on.

For an individual, though, the sum of the parts is more expensive than the whole. In most cases, assembling a complete computer from its component parts is more expensive than buying a complete package from a computer maker.

Why? Because when you buy your component parts you are paying retail prices for each element, with a profit margin built into every piece by the dealer. When Gateway builds its machines, it puts its profit margin on top of the total wholesale price. I would estimate that a typical home-assembled machine will cost you 10 to 20 percent more than the price of a factory-built equivalent, and you will be pretty much on your own as far as technical support for the components.

And so, I cannot recommend that you build your own PC if your sole aim is to save some money. The only reason to do so would be the psychic value of knowing that you have selected every component of the machine, making choices based on cost or quality or speed or a particular custom need.

If you do choose to build your own, buy from a reputable parts dealer that has a technical support department willing to spend some time with you to decipher illiterate instruction sheets and unlabeled cables and circuit boards. A company like Dalco Electronics, for example, sells nearly all of the components necessary to make your own PC, and their technical staff is capable of helping you integrate the pieces together.

Fixing What's Broken

A more logical task is the replacement of parts of a machine that have failed or have become hopelessly outdated. Here a careful shopper can save hundreds or even thousands of dollars by reusing pieces of an older computer that are still working, substituting only what needs to be replaced.

A careful shopper can replace a bad motherboard for a few hundred dollars and reinstall memory, hard drives, and adapter cards from the previous system. And while youíre at it, you can often upgrade to near state of the art for just a few dollars more.

Worthwhile Upgrades

When does an upgrade make sense? The bottom line is different for every user, and every userís pocketbook, but I would say that it is worth upgrading a PC when there are several major components worth recycling. For example, if you have a current motherboard (a PCI or a VL-bus) it probably makes sense to consider changing CPUs. Figure out the replacement cost for the components of your machine and subtract them from the price of a new system.

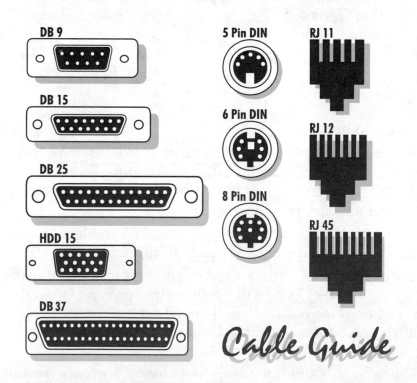

Cable Guide

FIGURE 6.2 Some common cable connectors are illustrated here; note that connectors are drawn to scale but are not actual size (Dalco catalog).

- For 486 machines, the most bang for the buck generally comes from a combination of boosting RAM to 16MB and upgrading the CPU with a Pentium OverDrive or similar chip from a non-Intel source. In a magazine test, a 486-DX2 66 MHz machine was boosted by nearly 50 percent at a cost between $200 and $500 depending on whether older memory SIMMs could be reused. (The 8 MB of additional RAM is probably worth about 25 percent just by itself.)

- For slower Pentiums (those with speeds below 100 MHz) with 8MB of RAM, the most cost-efficient upgrade is generally the addition of an extra 8MB. The memory transplant can be counted on to improve performance by at least 25 percent, at a cost of less than $100.

- For faster Pentiums with 16MB of RAM, the magazine found that the possible benefits of additional RAM or a speedier Pentium OverDrive were hard to justify on a cost basis.

It might seem that if 16 MB was good, then going to 32 MB must be great . . . but experts say otherwise. The extra memory (selling for about $200 to $250 at current prices) was worth only a few percent of speed improvement. Of course, if your particular software application or combination of programs demands extra RAM, you have no choice.

The Motherboard Trap

If youíve read this far in this book, you are a good candidate for the most major of repair and upgrade tasks: changing the motherboard. The job is not all that difficult, but it does require a great deal of attention to detail. If youíre the sort of person who can read a roadmap in a strange place; keep track of half a dozen different sets of screws, clips, and wires; and doesn't mind blazing a sometimes uncharted path from time to time, replacing the motherboard can be an entertaining electronic puzzle.

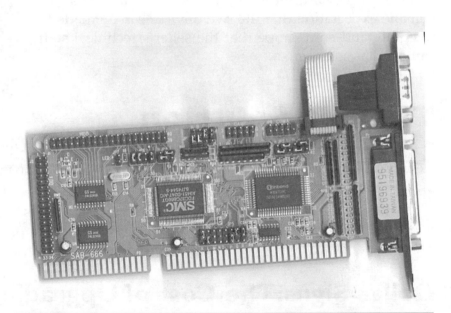

FIGURE 6.3 One way to bring a dinosaur or older modern machine up to I/O speed is to use an adapter like the Super Multi I/O Card which adds support for two IDE drives, two floppy drives, a pair of 16550 serial ports, a high-speed bi-directional parallel port, and a game port. (Dalco catalog).

Before you buy and install a new motherboard, though, consider the hidden costs of the change. A new board may use a different busc puzzle.

job is not all that difficult, but it does require a great deal of attention to detail. If youíre the sort of perso, the memory configuration of your old motherboard may be different from the new card.

And then there are the other costs of an upgrade: will you want to upgrade to a graphics accelerator card, a larger hard drive, a faster CD-ROM?

In any case, we suggest you buy your motherboard and case from same supplier; this way you'll have a reasonable expectation that the two devices can be made to integrate and some hope that the seller's technical staff can be of assistance.

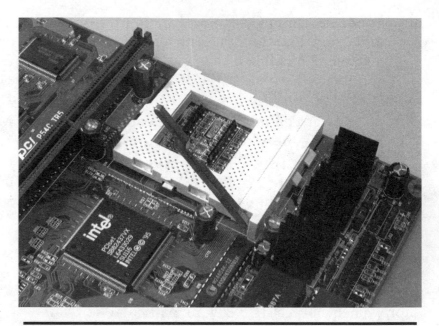

FIGURE 6.4 An empty processor socket, its ZIF handle in the up position, awaits the arrival of a Pentium CPU.

The Kit Solution

One interesting way to upgrade your system is to buy a "kit" that includes a motherboard and CPU pre-installed in a case with power supply. This saves you from some of the more demanding details of the upgrade process, including connecting the motherboard to the half dozen power leads from the power supply.

Check out these kits from sources like Tiger Electronics, Dalco Electronics, or other suppliers. If you can transfer your existing hard drive, RAM, and video card, for example, the kit may make economic sense. However, if you'll need to buy new memory or drives, there may not be any real savings here.

Dollar Signs: The Cost of Upgrading

The cost to upgrade an older PC completely is not trivial, although in certain situations, the cost is less than buying a new system. Let's assume you have an outdated modern machine with some parts that are to be kept and others that need to be upgraded.

A sampling of some prices for individual parts available from national mail order houses and some discount retailers in early 1997 follows:

16 MB RAM	$100
2 GB Hard drive	$200
SVGA Adapter	$100–200
15î SVGA Monitor	$300–$400
Pentium motherboard with 133 MHz CPU	$400

Just for the record, in the second edition of this book, we figured the upgrade cost for a move to a 386 CPU to be about $1,400. Three years later for the third edition the whole package—with a 486 instead of a 386 CPU and a hard drive twice the size—was priced at about $1,000. And now, for the fourth edition, you could do the same shopping trip86 CPU and a hard drive twice the size—st for and some discount retailers in be kept and others that need to be upgraded.

or ex, for about $1,000 to $1,200.

All that said, you may find that the cost of a complete upgrade as outlined above comes very close to the price of a new machine with a new warranty and new software and some additional parts such as a CD-ROM and a keyboard. Of course, you may not need all of the parts listed.

You'll need the proper CPU, of course; a 286 or 386SX is simply not going to cut it for Windows 95, and there is absolutely no reason to save a few dollars by buying a 486-based motherboard rather than a Pentium unless you have some hardware that will not work with a more modern motherboard.

If you have that as a starting point, you may want to do the upgrade in stages, starting by increasing the RAM; going to 8 MB of RAM is the most cost-effective way to boost the ability of your machine to work with Windows.

FIGURE 6.5 A Pentium 133 MHz slips into place in a processor socket on a Micro-Star PCI/ISA motherboard (Dalco).

Improving Your Life Under Windows

Windows is a graphical user interface; it presents a bitmapped screen with components that can be picked up and moved on screen, and graphic and text elements that can be moved among multiple applications available at the same time.

If we analyze the above description, we can understand why Windows is especially demanding of memory, processor capability and speed, video adapter, and hard disk space.

Here's a basic rule of Windows configuration: Whatever you've got will sooner or later not be enough.

Some suggestions about improving Windows life follow.

FIGURE 6.6 High-speed Pentium CPUs need assistance in removing the heat they generate. Some systems use passive heat sinks to conduct the heat away from the chip; Dalco Electronics supplies a clip-on cooling fan for use with this Pentium 133 MHz CPU (Dalco).

Slow Display

Windows applications make heavy demands on the computer, especially the video card. Waiting for the screen to catch up can drive you nuts, especially in graphics-intensive programs such as drawing or image-editing software.

Graphics and publishing packages can use as fast a video card as you can afford. Look for SVGA graphics accelerator cards with at least 1 MB of RAM; 2 MB will allow greater resolution or more colors. For even faster video, you can pay $50 to $100 more for 1 or 2 megabytes of VRAM (Video RAM).

Be sure to take advantage of any special-purpose bus extensions your PC may offer, including VL Local Bus and PCI bus slots. Graphics cards can pick up significant speed boosts by direct connection to the CPU through these slots.

Nearly all modern graphics cards lay claim to an "accelerated" graphics label. Computer magazine reviews of the latest crop of cards will show their rankings on standardized benchmark tests.

In our opinion, we recommend that you stay away from "no-name" video cards at the bottom of the price lists; these cards are also offered by some storefront PC makers who concentrate entirely on price. The price difference between Brand X and an established name is usually less than $100, and for that money you can expect more current and advanced technology, better technical support and warranty, and availability of software driver and hardware upgrades. Among recognized brands are ATI, Diamond, Genoa, Hercules, Matrox, MGA, Number Nine, and STB.

As soon as you install a new graphics card, contact the manufacturer of the card to determine if you have received and installed the latest device driver; new drivers are often produced after boxes of hardware are in the sales channel, and they are also often updated to improve speed and fix bugs.

Memory

We recommend you have at least 8 MB of RAM in your system in order to run Windows of any flavor. Power users will want 16 MB; the extra memory will allow you to efficiently have multiple applications open at the same time.

Consult the instruction manual for your motherboard or contact the maker of your PC to determine the type of RAM (chips, SIMMs, SIPs), its speed, and the upgrade path. Some motherboards require you to upgrade in blocks of a particular amount. Other PCs cheat their owners by inefficient use of the motherboard; these designs may require you to throw away perfectly good SIMMs of small capacity and replace them with larger blocks of memory. (Did we say "throw away" SIMMs? Perhaps that won't be necessary. Check the ads in the back pages of computer magazines for memory specialists who may buy used memory, or accept it in trade for new, larger blocks of memory.)

Memory prices are sometimes very volatile; the best price for RAM can shift from one source to another, based on supply. In general, you will find good prices at mail order companies specializing in memory during times when RAM is plentiful; these companies usually buy on the "spot market" and can take advantage of downturns quickly. When RAM is scarce, you may find better prices through major manufacturers who have long-term contracts with memory makers that may predate current price increases.

Bigger Hard Drive

In Chapter 9, we show how to replace a hard drive and controller. Don't bother to upgrade from a 20-MB drive to a 40-MB device; the prices of hard drives have dropped so steeply in recent years and the storage demands of modern applications have grown so sharply that it makes no sense to skimp here. We consider the minimum size for a Windows-based installation to be 400 MB, and the cost of a few hundred more megabytes is only a little more.

One nonhardware solution is a compression program such as Microsoft's DoubleSpace or DriveSpace, or third-party products including Stacker. These products can compress the size of many programs and data files by as much as half, effectively doubling the capacity of a drive (including floppy disks and some backup storage devices.)

The products perform their magic by using codes to represent blocks of repeated data, and interposing a device driver between the output of the disk controller and memory that expands information back to its real size. They also create a "compressed drive" that occupies a partition on your physical drive; it is not directly readable without the use of the disk compression program.

Some users swear by disk-doubling software, while others swear at these products. In the early days of these products there were some problems with corrupted data; current versions of the products seem stable.

In our opinion, the sharp drop in cost of hard disk drives makes disk-doubling software less important. We are willing to use these products on nonessential data and applications, but not on irreplaceable data. And in any case, we always maintain current backups of important data.

In this day of sharply reduced hard drive prices, we're a lot more comfortable with buying a 2.7 GB hard drive for $300 than using a disk-doubling program.

Faster Hard Drives

If you find yourself going for coffee while your computer cranks through a database sort, you may really want a faster hard drive, not a faster machine. Modern hard drives have disk access rates of 10 ms or less, twice as fast as devices of a few years ago and as much as ten times faster than early disks.

To pick up even more speed, upgrade to a new hard disk controller that includes a disk cache or that works with a cache on the drive electronics itself.

The pace of development in hard drives has picked up dramatically in recent years. You may need to change the hard drive controller, too, in order to use a modern machine drive. And some systems just a few years old may need a change to their ROM BIOS chips in order to work with drives larger than about 508 MB; consult your computer's manufacturer for details.

Math Coprocessors for Dinosaurs

If you are using a 286 or 386-based machine, you may be beneath the threshold of power for the most advanced software. However, you may still be able to pick up a surge of number-crunching speed by adding a math coprocessor chip.

Floating point calculations (that just means numbers after the decimal point) choke up an otherwise speedy microprocessor. Add an Intel 80287 or 80387 chip or a similar Weitek or Cyrix or other third-party coprocessor, at prices from about $50 to $100, for better performance. An 80287 chip makes an AT computer about ten times as fast on certain calculations as a 386 clone.

Locate the empty coprocessor socket on the motherboard when you're inspecting the computer's interior. It's clearly labeled, usually right next to the CPU. If you add an 80387 coprocessor chip, be careful. There are many little pins on the chip that bend and break easily. You might want your local computer repair shop to do the installation if you have a tendency to mash delicate parts.

CHAPTER 6

CHAPTER 7
Thanks for the Memory

Memory is the workspace for your computer. The most powerful processor and the speediest hard disk won't let you do much without the workroom to keep the program and data close at hand.

First, let's go over a critical distinction:

- Data or instructions stored in chips is called *Random Access Memory* (RAM). Random access means that the processor can jump directly to a particular bit of data.

- Data or instructions located on a floppy, hard, or CD-ROM disk can be called *storage* or more sensibly, *disk storage.* Storage is not quite so instantly accessible because the read/write head must wait for the sector on the spinning disk to move into position. (And data stored on a tape system is the least accessible of all memory, since the piece of information you need may be at the very end of a reel of tape.)

Some users like to think of RAM as the desktop, where the work of the moment is gathered temporarily and worked on; storage is the file cabinet crammed with all the transactions of your work as well as the instruction manuals for all the devices in your home or office. One more thing to complete this analogy: at the end of the day your desktop is swept clear and dumped into the trash, while the file cabinets are closed and locked away until they are needed next. RAM is a temporary workspace that goes away when power is turned off, while the hard disk drives are more or less permanent storage.

In this chapter we'll give you a few hints on dealing with common memory problems and some clues on tracking down offending chips.

Dinosaur PCs have rows of individual memory chips on the motherboard or on memory cards. Modern machines generally use Single Inline Memory Modules (SIMMs) instead, although a few machines manufactured during the evolution to modernity required the use of expensive proprietary memory cards.

Memory is another high-tech commodity that has plummeted in price as it has expanded in capacity and speed. When I first began writing about personal computers in 1982, an add-in card with 256K of memory sold for $995. As this book goes to press in 1997, memory was available for as little as $10 per megabyte; the memory on that quarter of a megabyte expansion card of 1982 would sell at retail today for about $2.50.

Even in the space of just the past two years, memory capacities and speeds have gone up while prices have gone down sharply. RAM prices today are about 20 percent of their level in 1995. There is no reason to skimp on memory for a modern machine.

But how much memory is enough? In general, more is better—the new "basic" level for a Windows 95 machine is 16 MB of RAM, with servers and other high-end machines starting out at 32 MB and going up from there. You need more memory because operating systems like Windows 95 and Windows NT need more working space, in order to have multiple applications open and running under them.

CHAPTER 7

How Much Memory Do You Have?

You can watch the digit counter fly as your machine boots up, but detailed information about how much memory is present in your system and how it is allocated is a bit harder to come by. The easiest way to take a reading of your system's memory capacity is to go to the DOS prompt and execute the **MEM** command. (It is best not to execute MEM as a command from the DOS window of Windows 95, since Windows 95 does its own memory allocation while it is in charge.)

Type **MEM** and press the **Return** key. Here is a sample report from two of the systems in our lab.

First is our hard-working 486 DX/2 66 MHz machine. Second is a report from our new homegrown PC, a Pentium 133 MHz machine assembled from parts as described in Chapter 6. Note that the style of the two reports varies slightly because of minor changes made in the versions of DOS that underlie Windows 95.

Table 7.1 Results of the MEM Command on Two Different PCs

486DX2/66

Memory Type	Total	Used	Free
Conventional	640K	59K	581K
Upper	0K	0K	0K
Reserved	384K	384K	0K
Extended (XMS)	15,360K	68K	15,292K
Total memory	16,384K	511K	15,873K
Total under 1 MB	640K	59K	581K
Largest executable program size	581K (594,784 bytes)		
Largest free upper memory block	0K	(0 bytes)	

MS-DOS is resident in the high memory area.

Pentium 133 MHz

Type of Memory	Total	Used	Free
Conventional	655,360	90,896	564,464
Upper	0	0	0
Reserved	393,216	393,216	0
Extended (XMS)	15,728,640	69,632	15,659,008
Total memory	16,777,216	553,744	16,223,472
Total under 1 MB	655,360	90,896	564,464
Largest executable program size	564,448	(551K)	
Largest free upper memory block	0	(0K)	

MS-DOS is resident in the high memory area.

CHAPTER 7

Inside Memory: Binary Math and Word Length

If computers are so darned smart, how come they only understand two things: 0 and 1? The answer is that machines are not smart at all, but they are very fast.

Computers do all of their work using an alphabet made up of just two symbols: 0 and 1. And even the meaning of those symbols are different for the machine: 0 means that there is no value assigned, and 1 means that there is a value assigned. You can also think of 0 as "No" or "Off", and 1 as "Yes" or "On" (this explains, by the way, the sometimes cryptic marking on computer power and setup switches: 0 and 1.)

The machine uses the 0s and 1s to construct numbers using the binary mathematical system. It's not anywhere as complex as it seems. Each place in a binary number is a doubling of the value in the smallest (rightmost) position. Each position is either "on" or "off". Here's a quick and painless lesson.

In binary notation, the number 154 would be represented as:

```
1 0 0 1 1 0 1 0
```

The way to translate that number in decimal terms is to read it, from right to left, as:

```
No 1s, one 2, no 4s, one 8, one 16, no 32s, no 64s, and one 128
```

or

```
0x1 + 1x2 + 0x4 + 1x8 + 1x16 + 0x32 + 0x64 + 1x128
```

As you can see, deciphering this value as 154 is a lot more work in binary math, but it is a lot simpler for the machine to manipulate values when they can only be on or off; a computer makes up for the relative awkwardness of its counting method with its blazing speed.

In the binary system used in a computer, numbers are divided into groups of eight binary digits called a *word*. Each of the positions in the word is called a *bit*, a termed that derives from the term *bi*nary dig*it*. A group of eight bits is called a byte, or word.

(When a computer is called upon to display a character from the alphabet on screen, it receives an instruction in the form of a byte of information. The value of that byte corresponds to a particular character. In this way, the entire contents of this book—or any other data file—is made up entirely of 0s and 1s gathered into words.)

As microcomputers have advanced from dinosaur to modern machine, the size of the word length has increased. A computer *word* is a collection of data bits that are processed as a unit. The original microcomputer CPUs only had the horsepower and bandwidth to deal with 8-bit words. Subsequent improvements have pushed into 16-bit and 32-bit words.

The longer the word length, the bigger the chunk of information processed by the CPU. At the same time, the memory in your PC must be fast enough to keep up with the demands of the CPU.

The dinosaurs processed data in 8-bit chunks. Today's fast Pentiums are 64-bit CPUs, meaning they can accept 64 bits (8 bytes) at a time.

A 30-pin SIMM can move 8 bits at a time with each transaction between the CPU and its memory (each transaction is called a *bus cycle*). This is just fine for a dinosaur. If you are using a modern machine CPU such as a 486 processor, you would need four 30-pin SIMMs per bank to deliver 32 data bits to the processor.

If your more current machine uses 72-pin SIMMs (see Figure 7.2), a 486 processor can draw all 32 bits from a single bank at one time. A 64-bit Pentium can draw a full word from two banks of memory.

You will need to buy upgrades in the correct configuration. The manual that came with your computer should be quite clear about what you need; you may also need to contact the manufacturer. Most dealers that sell RAM chips and SIMMs can tell you what type of device your machine requires.

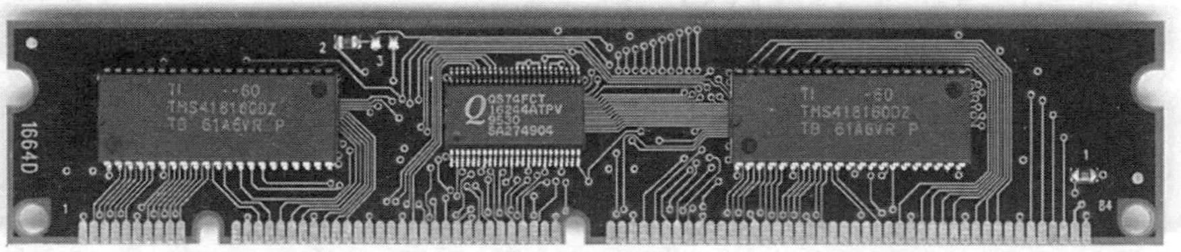

Figure 7.1 168-pin DIMM; as this book goes to press, these strips typically hold 8, 16, or 32 MB of RAM. (Dalco Electronics.)

Where Do You Put Your Memory?

Way back in the days of the dinosaurs, memory chips were mounted directly on the motherboard. Some early designs had them soldered into place, which made it very difficult to replace them in the event of failure. These were quickly supplanted by rows of small sockets to hold the memory.

Figure 7.2 72-pin non-parity SIMM; typical capacities are 4, 8, 16, or 32 MB of RAM. (Dalco Electronics.)

The capacities of the early memory chips were small, and they were expensive. The motherboard of the original PC was only designed to hold 64K of RAM, which was considered more than any user had need for.

As the operating system and applications began to become more demanding and the hardware more accommodating, memory expansions began to move to add-in cards that plugged into the PC's expansion bus.

When machines became faster and faster, memory moved back to the motherboard, which allowed a speedier direct connection to the CPU. By the time modern machines were on the market, nearly every PC accepted memory that plugged into the motherboard using high-capacity chip carriers. One carrier for a block of memory is a SIMM (Single In-line Memory Module). This small printed circuit board was originally available with a 30-pin connector; Modern machines are likely to have 72-pin slots for SIMMs, which must match that number of pins.

Recycling Memory

What do you do if you have a bunch of older 30-pin SIMMS with perfectly good memory chips, and a new motherboard with 72-pin slots? Until fairly recently, your choices were to buy new SIMMs and throw away the old SIMMs or sell them at a greatly reduced price to a used memory dealer.

In 1996, though, came an interesting fixer-upper part that allows you to plug two, four, or even eight 30-pin SIMMS into a small circuit card that in turn plugs into the 72-pin slot on the motherboard. In the Dalco catalog we found half a dozen variations on the them with product names including Simmstack (Figure 7.5) and Simm 4 Recycler. We also found the Simm Doubler, which accepts two 72-pin SIMMS for use in a single 72-pin slot—a good solution for boosting the capacity.

Figure 7.3 Check the instruction manual for your motherboard to learn about specific needs for memory upgrades. On many boards, SIMMs need to be installed in pairs; on this Micro-Star board, the manufacturer warns that the system will not operate with only a single SIMM in place. In this picture, a SIMM is being put in place in slot one of bank one; be sure to align pin 72 on the SIMM with pin 72 on the slot and push the assembly firmly into place. You may need to hold back the locking clip to allow the SIMM to slide into place properly.

Error Detection and Correction

When personal computers first came on the market, a great deal of attention was paid to detecting errors in memory chips. There were two main reasons for this: the early memory chips were somewhat prone to electronic hiccups, and the original designs for computers were done by engineers who were taught that it was better to stop a machine dead in its tracks than to allow it to make an error, no matter how minor the problem.

There are two common methods used to examine the integrity of data: *Parity Checking* and *Error Correcting Code*.

Nearly every dinosaur and most early modern machines used a parity scheme, adding an extra bit of memory as an error-checking device. Although they used 8 bits to make up a computer word, a ninth bit was present in each memory chip to record whether the sum of the other eight bits in the computer word was odd or even. All of the circuitry had to accommodate this ninth bit of information, adding expense to the manufacture of the chip and the motherboard, and demanding a bit of

Figure 7.4 The second SIMM goes into place on the first bank of memory on the motherboard. Note the antistatic strap.

precious time for processing the information.

Parity schemes were either "even" or "odd", meaning that a good report can be a 1 (odd) or a 0 (even), depending on the design of the system.

And in any case, parity was a rather primitive means to see if somehow the contents of any of the hundreds of thousands or millions of bytes of information had somehow failed. (Think about this: If an even number of bits in a particular byte fail, the errors will cancel each other out and the parity check gives a false positive report.

Today, we look at things a bit differently. First of all, memory chips are much more reliable than they were 15 years ago. The likelihood of a single bit going bad is not that great; more likely is the failure of an entire chip, which would be brought to the attention of the user by the system. Secondly, there came a realization that for most users, a minor error in one bit was not likely to cause a major problem—it might make one character in a long document come out wrong (and the computer's spelling checker would likely find it), or it might cause a very tiny problem with an on-

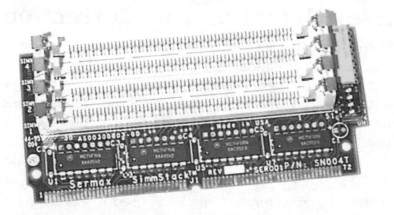

Figure 7.5 One way to recycle older memory is a device like the Simmstack. The unit pictured here converts four 30-pin SIMM modules into a single 72-pin module. (Dalco Electronics.)

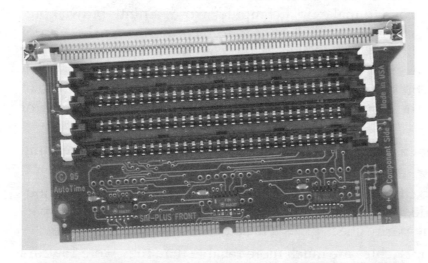

Figure 7.6 This high-capacity converter, called the Simm 72 Plus 4, accepts four 30-pin SIMM modules plus an additional 4 MB or 16 MB 72-pin SIMM, occupying only a single 72-pin slot on the motherboard. (Dalco Electronics.)

screen graphic. In today's way of thinking, only a relatively small number of users need to spend the extra money and effort to try to track down and correct every possible rare error. If you are controlling the launch of the Space Shuttle or monitoring a heart-lung machine you may want a redundant error-correcting computer; otherwise, we're willing to let our software programs perform their own internal error-checking processes and take them out of the hardware.

Today, nearly all consumer and business modern machines (and a small group of dinosaurs) use nonparity memory. They are less expensive—something that takes on even greater importance with machines with 32 MB or even more inside—and there is somewhat less overhead for the CPU to process.

(At one point during the transition from dinosaur to modern machine, some manufacturers used a "fake parity" scheme. In this design, a fake parity chip would generate the proper positive report (even or odd, depending on the system) without bothering to examine the contents of the memory chip. Such a design contributes nothing to the user; it is slightly less expensive than a parity-checking design, but the user does not know if an error is present.)

Error correction code is now used in high-end machines including banking and other real-time applications where the computer is directly controlling something (our example of the Space Shuttle or a heart-lung machine would apply here).

The difference between ECC and parity is that ECC can detect a 1-bit error and then fix it. Depending on the type of memory controller in the PC, ECC can also detect less-common 2-, 3-, or 4-bit memory errors, although in most such systems it cannot correct a multi-bit error.

ECC works by computing a value for data bits and comparing that value to decoded data retrieved from memory chips; a similar scheme is used in error detection and correction systems used in telecommunications.

The easiest way to find out if a dinosaur machine has parity chips is to count the number of chips in the system; if they are divisible by nine, then parity checking is in use. Similarly, ECC memory on a modern machine may use a distinctive design of two x36 SIMMs in a bank; the resulting 72 bits are employed as 64 bits of data and 8 bits for ECC code. You may also see a motherboard with 72-pin SIMMs with an x39 or x40 width specification. Call a memory vendor and read off the markings on the memory chips, or check with the instruction manual or the manufacturer of a modern machine if you have any doubts about the type of memory employed.

New Memory Technologies

EDO RAM

Extended-data-out memory (EDO RAM) and Burst-EDO memory are updates to the previous speed champion, fast page-mode (FPM) memory.

FPM memory was more than adequate for 486 processors, but not quite up to the demands of the faster memory bus speeds of Pentium-based systems.

The difference comes down to a matter of persistence of memory: FPM loses data after it has been read, while EDO holds the last data request in a buffer while reading the next request. EDO's extended memory permits the bus speed to match the Pentium, which runs at 60 MHz (or more commonly at 66 MHz), twice the realistic speed limit for FPM and 486-based systems.

You will need a motherboard and controller chipset that recognizes EDO memory; Intel introduced such facilities with its Triton chipset. In a real-world environment, EDO should offer a 10 to 15 percent speed advantage over comparable FPM chips.

EDO memory will work with most current PC controllers, and can be mixed with FPM memory as long as the two types of memory reside in different banks. In our office, we upgraded one older machine with 8 MB of new EDO RAM added to 8 MB of older FPM memory; putting the EDO RAM in the first bank will speed the loading of Windows 95 a bit.

Synchronous DRAM

Another new technology for memory chips is Synchronous DRAM. This scheme uses a clock coordinated with the CPU so that memory cycles are synchronized; the result is improved efficiency.

Cache Memory

Modern machines, beginning with some models of the 486 processor, have a special type of memory dedicated to the use of the CPU called *cache memory*. The purpose of cache memory is to store instructions and data right alongside the CPU in a small block of especially fast memory; we're dealing with nanoseconds (billionths of a second) here, but a few billionths here and a few billionths there quickly add up to some real time on a high-speed system.

Primary cache, also called *Level 1* or *L1 cache*, is usually part of the microprocessor itself and is sometimes called *internal cache*.

Secondary cache, also called *Level 2* or *L2 cache*, is another level of cache memory available to the CPU. In some systems without an L1 cache, the L2 cache functions as primary cache.

Cache memory is managed by a cache memory controller. When this specialized chip retrieves an instruction from main memory, it also grabs hold of the next few instructions and places them in memory on the logical assumption that adjacent instructions will also be called upon. The better the algorithm used to manage the cache controller, the more efficient the use of the cache and the better the speed for the CPU.

In our previous discussion of memory we described RAM as the computer's desktop; think of cache as a notepad for jotting reminders.

Memory Problems

Memory problems can largely be traced to faulty memory chips and SIMMs. There are several different schemes used to code the size and speed of memory chips, depending on the manufacturer and type. Sometimes the code is easily decipherable, but other times there is no obvious reason for the scheme. It's best to call a supplier of memory and read off the chips you find in your memory bank.

Let's look at what happens when your PC develops a memory problem. We're not going to burden you with unnecessary explanations about how DOS handles memory or other memory matters that concern programmers; there are numerous books that cover the technical side of memory. Instead, we'll focus only on fixing the suddenly forgetful machine.

The most common symptom of memory problems is the BIOS message:

```
NMI error at [address]
```

or

```
Memory parity interrupt at [address]
```

If you have a Phoenix BIOS, the message may continue:

```
Type (S)hut off NMI, (R)eboot, (I)gnore
```

An NMI, or *nonmaskable interrupt,* is one that the hardware is not permitted to *mask* (ignore) while processing another task. When an NMI occurs, the NMI error message goes up on the screen and everything is deadlocked until you address the NMI error, no matter what else is going on.

The most important nonmaskable interrupt on dinosaurs and some modern machines is a parity error—a report by the computer that it found something wrong with the contents of at least one byte in memory.

In any case, a memory parity test is performed strictly with hardware. No software or microprocessor is involved. So there is no point thinking about the possibilities of a bad CPU or defective software code when you're considering the causes of an NMI error.

What causes a parity error? There are four possibilities:

- A bad RAM chip
- A drop in voltage (before 4.5 volts on most PCs) that causes the chips to forget the stored data
- Malfunctioning address logic to the memory chips that causes one RAM chip to be mistaken for another
- A bad parity logic chip that reports a parity problem when there is none.

The first two problems (a bad chip or low power) , are the most likely to occur and the easiest to deal with. The last two are somewhat rarer symptoms of bad (and nonreplaceable) chips or circuits on the motherboard.

Let's troubleshoot this NMI error a little further. What can you determine from the address on the screen that's part of the NMI message? Unfortunately, the information does not explain where the problem is located, but instead points to the place in memory where the program was working when it got that error, even though the error could have come from any place in memory.

To correct the problem, try the following possibilities.

First, you will want to run a software memory test. If it finds bad chips, consider yourself lucky and replace them. Note that memory test programs are generally unable to test the lowest 64K of RAM, where the basic elements of the operating system reside. The makers of *QAPlus* say it can test the lowest 64K of RAM by tricking the CPU into momentary stupidity. If you don't receive the answer you feel you need, you'll still end up having to pull SIMMs or chips and running them through a memory tester.

If you are lucky, the offending chip or SIMM may only be loose in its socket. Turn off the PC and unplug it, open up the case, and press firmly on all the memory chips or on the SIMM strips.

Frequently, when an individual chip goes bad, corroded wires are the cause. There are tiny wires inside the memory chip, connecting the actual chip of silicon to the legs on the outside of the memory chip. Run a capable memory utility such as *QAPlus*. If the diagnostic says that a given chip or SIMM is bad, pop it out and replace it.

If the software test doesn't find anything, take all the RAM chips out of the motherboard and run them through a chip-testing machine at a computer repair shop. Have the chips tested at least 20 nanoseconds faster than the manufacturer of the motherboard recommends to cover inaccuracies in speed ratings and the testing machine itself.

If you're nervous about removing the chips or SIMMs, you can bring the PC or the motherboard to the repair shop for testing. Before you do either, get an estimate from the shop personnel on their charges for testing and replacing memory.

SIMMs, because the chips are soldered into place and tested as a unit before they leave the factory, are less likely to fail than chips. As this book goes to press, a SIMM with eight megabytes of RAM sells for less than $50. It may be cheaper for you to purchase one or two SIMMS and experiment with installing the new SIMMs until the error goes away.

If all the chips test as good, it's time to consider low power; the memory is supplied by what is called the "+5 volt line." Do you have good incoming power? Most computers expect power from the wall outlet to be in the range of 104 to 120 volts. What time of the year is it? A summer heat wave could bring a brown-out in many parts of the country; you can call your power company to see if they are experiencing any problems. In some homes and offices, the power lines will dip significantly when a major electrical motor is turned on—are you sharing the line with a refrigerator, or an elevator? If you have any doubts, test the household current at the wall with a voltmeter (basic units sell for less than $20 at Radio Shack; be sure to follow the manufacturer's instruction on working with live voltage).

Once in a while, chips pass the test but still cause NMI errors. In this case, you can experiment to see if temperature variations have an effect on the memory problem. Spray a commercial cooling spray on the chips to chill them before retesting; to go the other way, try heating the chips just a bit with a hair dryer.

If you still have NMI errors, replace the power supply with a known-good unit. (Power supplies sell for about $50 to $100; it is a good idea to have a spare unit available, or at least to know of a retail outlet or mail order service that can deliver a unit within a day.) There is no way to test a power supply for those short-term voltage drops that produce intermittent NMI errors. If the problem doesn't go away after you replace the power supply, there are two other possible solutions, both expensive: replace the motherboard or replace all the RAM chips. Neither solution is more likely than the other to be the correct choice, and you might end up doing both.

If this approach doesn't sound very scientific, you won't get an argument from us. But there is really no other choice. Enormously expensive machines capable of analyzing the current flow on every wire in the motherboard could be built; they would have to be redesigned every time a new motherboard was introduced. There is no way to justify that sort of an expense.

How Much Should You Replace?

If you have a true dinosaur PC or PC/XT clone with memory chips soldered in place on the motherboard and a persistent memory error message, it's time to replace the whole machine, or at the very least the motherboard and its memory. There is no cost-benefit analysis that makes it worthwhile to try to bring a completely extinct creature back from the dead.

When you have a dinosaur XT with socketed memory chips on the motherboard, it may be worthwhile to have the chips pulled and tested. This will involve perhaps a 15-minute investment of your time and a $25 to $50 charge at a computer shop for testing—it's still less than the cost of installing a new board. But you'll still have an XT when you're through. And the memory you may be bringing to the new system may be old, slow, and too small.

It may make sense to replace a dead PC-AT motherboard with a new 386SX or 386DX motherboard, if the rest of the components are fairly new. A few caveats: You *can* put a 386 motherboard in an XT case, but the power supply will probably need to be upgraded to a higher wattage, and in most cases the 8-bit hard disk controller will be too slow to work with the faster CPU. Do the math and see if you wouldn't be better off buying a new machine.

Memory Everywhere

There are other parts of your computer besides the motherboard that use memory chips. These components include the video card and some hard disk controllers that use a cache to store data temporarily. The memory chips in these devices are usually soldered in, so if the memory goes bad, the board needs to be replaced. A few hard drive controllers and video adapters use SIMMs that can be replaced. Consult your instruction manuals.

Ancient Operating Systems

Although this book is concentrating on hardware, we do have to make a few points here and there about the operating system. Here's the most important point: dinosaur-age DOS is almost irrelevant in the modern age.

All things being equal, you should be running the most current version of MS-DOS on any PC; as this book goes to press, the latest and probably the last standalone DOS is labeled version 6.22. Windows 95 brings its own version of DOS that lies beneath; that version of DOS is considered DOS 7.0.

PC-DOS and MS-DOS in versions below 5.0 can only address 640K of RAM. DOS 5.0, 6.0, and later can trick the machine into using a large amount of memory. (The all but forgotten DR-DOS 6.0 has the same capability.)

Programs running under DOS 3.3 and earlier make use of expanded memory through a technique called *bank-switching*. Blocks of 16K are switched in and out of a 64K window in RAM. Up to 8 MB of extra RAM can be added in this manner. Expanded (bank-switched) memory cards still work, but modern machines make use of simpler facilities that are possible under current versions of DOS.

Some dinosaur systems had odd memory configurations in which the system board memory stopped at 512K and picked up again at 768K. Several vendors tried this, but we have never liked it. Clones also exist that can never be expanded beyond 512K of RAM because of the motherboard design. These designs are generally not worth upgrading or fixing.

Table 7.2 Typical System Memory Map

0000 to 9FFF	DOS 640K memory
A000 to BFFF	Video Memory
C000 to C7FF	Video Shadowing
C800 to CFFF	SCSI, ESDI, or RLL controller
D000 to DFFF	Usually free
E000 to EFFF	Copy of main BIOS initially, may be reclaimed after boot
F000 to FFFF	Main BIOS Shadowing

Table 7.3 Types of Random Access Memory

Interleaved Memory	This scheme increases processing speed by dividing the memory into two or four portions that process information alternately. The CPU sends information to one section for processing while another section goes through a refresh cycle.
Page-Mode Memory	A technology that allows back-to-back memory accesses within blocks of memory called *Pages*, thereby avoiding wait states.
Row/Column Memory	The traditional method of accessing data at a memory address. RAM is mapped as a matrix (an indexed array of locations) and each address is given a row and a column number.
Static-Column Memory	Under this scheme, once data has been located at a specific column address, subsequent pieces of related data are allocated to the same column. Because the column is *static*, data retrieval is faster.

Table 7.4 How Modern Machines Divide Memory

Conventional Memory	Also called *Base Memory*, this is the first 640K of memory, the original limit for dinosaurs and dino-DOS.
Lower Memory	The first several hundred bytes within conventional memory, used by the operating system and installable device drivers.
Upper Memory	The area between the top of conventional memory and 1 MB. A total of 384K is available. (For the record, the exact amount is 393,216 bytes. Here's the math: a kilobyte is actually 1,024 bytes in size, making 640K equal to 655,360 bytes. 1 MB is equal to 1024x1024, or 1,048,576 bytes. Therefore, 1 MB minus 640K equals 393,216 bytes.)
	Some sections of upper memory are usually taken over by parts of modern machine hardware, such as for video BIOS. You can (and should) use memory management software to stake your claim to unused sections of upper memory.
Extended Memory	This is one way in which memory located above the 1 MB former limit can be used, but only by modern machines. Some programs can access this memory directly, while others must go through an extended memory manager or device driver. Memory is swapped in and out of use through the use of pages.
Expanded Memory	Memory above the 1 MB ceiling that can be bank-switched under the control of an Expanded Memory Manager on a 386, 486, or Pentium modern machine. (Modern DOS includes EMM386 for this purpose; third-party products such as QEMM386 may offer advantages to some uses. Windows 95 handles memory in a similar manner.)
	Expanded memory was first developed as a specification by a consortium that included Lotus, Intel, and Microsoft, and for that reason was called *LIM memory* for a short period of PC history. The original concept required the use of a special memory expansion card, which may be present in some older modern machines. Expanded memory today is under the control of memory managers that emulate the cards.

Expanded memory divides memory into 16K pages; blocks of four pages, called a *page frame*, are switched in and out of a 64K area in Upper Memory.

Floppy Drives

Floppy Disk Drives

The floppy disk drive has been part of the PC from its very beginnings, although its role has changed dramatically over the years.

The very first dinosaur PCs used slow and relatively low-capacity floppy disk drives as the primary means of data storage. The original IBM PC shipped with one very large 3-inch-tall single-sided standard density floppy disk drive, capable of holding a grand total of 160 Kbytes of information on a fragile 5.25-inch floppy disk. The drives themselves were very prone to mechanical failure, too.

Today, tiny 3.5-inch floppy drives stand less than an inch tall, can hold nearly 10 times more data on a 3.5-inch disk encased in a hard plastic protector, and are extremely reliable.

On some of the most primitive of the dinosaurs, a single 5.25-inch floppy disk drive was intended to hold the operating system, a simple application such as a word processor or spreadsheet, and a small amount of data files. Soon, PC users moved on to a basic setup that consisted of a pair of double-density drives—one for the operating system and the application program, and a second for data storage.

With the arrival of the PC-XT came the first widespread use of hard disk drives for PCs. At that point, most of the previous assignments for the floppy disk drive were taken over by the hard drive, which stored the operating system, applications, and data. The floppy disk drive—by this time expanded in capacity but reduced in size—was relegated to a means to load new information and applications onto the hard drive and to easily transfer data from one machine to another (the "sneaker net" method), and as an emergency boot device in the case of failure to the hard drive or damage to its contents.

A handful of applications attempted to prevent unauthorized copying by requiring that the floppy disk drive hold an "official" copy of the program even if you were operating from the hard drive.

By the time of the full acceptance of modern machines, floppy disk drives were still the source of new programs and data. High-density designs took on a new role: that of a low-cost backup method. And most recently, CD-ROM drives have begun taking over the role as the means of loading huge new multimedia-capable programs and operating system upgrades.

Removable versus Fixed Media

The original IBM PC was capable of controlling one or two single-sided disk drives and a cassette tape drive. Both disk drives and cassette used removable media—you could replace the disk in your disk drive with another or insert a different cassette in the tape recorder. The cassette drive was a joke from the moment of its release: it was painfully slow, of questionable reliability, and very rarely used. As we have noted, floppy disks became the basic vehicle for distributing PC software and were the first reliable means of data storage.

The very first of the dinosaurs used a floppy disk capable of storing 160K of information under DOS 1.0. That was quickly upgraded to 180K with a revision of the operating system. The floppy disks themselves—5.25-inch-square, thin, black plastic envelopes over a fragile circle of plastic coated with metallic particles—were easily damaged and held too little data to satisfy either programmers or users.

About a year into the life of the PC came the first double-sided floppy disk drives, with read/write heads that were capable of looking at both sides of the spinning disk. This brought a doubling of capacity to 360K. It is almost impossible to conceive of a still-functioning PC that might continue to use a 180K floppy disk drive, since today's operating systems and applications typically require many times more capacity than that just to load.

In 1983, IBM introduced the XT, the first member of the PC family with a hard disk (or "fixed disk" as IBM preferred to call it, to distinguish the new sealed medium from the removable floppy drive diskettes).

A few years later came the first 3.5-inch floppy disk drives, an improvement that had its genesis in the Apple Macintosh. These disks are barely floppy because of the hard plastic case, and the circle of thin plastic within is nicely protected by a sliding cover. The initial 3.5-inch disks doubled the capacity of removable floppies to 720K. Subsequently, both 5.25-inch and 3.5-inch disks have doubled again in capacity through the use of high-density magnetic material and new electronics.

In the early 1990s, IBM attempted to introduce super-high-capacity floppies capable of storage of 2.88 MB, but they were not embraced by the market; owners of machines with these drives may have to deal with IBM alone for replacement of the devices.

The fixed/removable distinction still makes sense from a troubleshooting perspective. Fixed media are sealed. If anything goes wrong with either the media or the media-access machinery you'll have to replace the entire hard disk. If something is wrong with a floppy disk, but the drive itself is okay, simply throw away the bad disk.

Not yet a standard, but widely embraced by many users are the high-capacity Zip drives developed by Iomega, and sold under its own name and by manufacturers including Epson. Zip disks, slightly larger than a 3.5-inch floppy, can store as much as 100 MB of data. Zip drives sell for about $150 and the disks are available for as little as $17 each in quantity.

Table 8.1 A PC Floppy Disk Chronology

Floppy Drive Type	Capacity	PC Usage
Single-sided 5.25 inch	160 KB	Original IBM PC.
Single-sided 5.25-inch	180 KB	Original IBM PC, upgraded DOS
Double-sided 5.25-inch	360 KB	PC, PC-XT
Standard density 3.5-inch	720 KB	PC-AT
High-density 5.25-inch	1.2 MB	PC-AT, modern machines
High-density 3.5-inch	1.44 MB	Modern machines
Quad-density 3.5-inch	2.88 MB	Some modern machines

Magnetic versus Optical Media

As PCs have evolved, the bulk of all data storage has used a technology based on magnetism. An electronically controlled read/write head is instructed to record an indication of 1 or 0 across a length of a floppy or hard disk track, down the length of a tape, or on a removable platter of a hard drive cartridge.

Magnetic recording works as follows:

- An intelligent controller instructs the storage device to vary an electrical current fed into an electromagnetic recording device
- The head produces a stream of plus or minus electrical signals that represent the 1s or 0s of digital information
- The information is written onto a medium that is coated with metallic particles able to hold onto a magnetic setting
- The medium moves under the head, either spinning (disks) or streaming past on rollers (tapes)

- The controller reserves a special portion of the disk to itself to keep track of which files were recorded in particular places.

Later, the user can ask the drive to run the same section of the disk or tape under the head. As the changing magnetic field passes beneath the head it induces a variable current flow, recreating the original current flow used to write the data to the disk or tape.

Magnetic recording technology predates the dawn of the PC by many years. Audio tape recorders read and write the same way, and the ubiquitous VCR machines of our time use the same concept, differing principally in the pattern used by the recording heads to store information.

In recent years, though, the PC world has begun to make use of advanced optical media which use nonmagnetic means to write and read data. The leading optical device for PCs is the CD-ROM (Compact Disc Read-Only Memory), a computer adaptation of the CDs produced for audio systems. These disks are increasingly used as a distribution method for operating systems and applications; the standard CD-ROM can hold about 660 MB of information on a platter that costs less than a dollar to manufacture. A variant of the CD-ROM is the DVD-ROM (Digital Video Disc) that can pack as much as 17 GB on a disk of the same size. (See Chapter 11 for more details about CD-ROM and DVD-ROM technology.)

Floptical brand disk drives are a hybrid combination of optical and magnetic technologies, introduced in the mid-1990s. The drives use ordinary magnetic read/write techniques, but they cram over 700 tracks into the space where high-density 3.5-inch diskettes distribute 80 tracks. Flopticals use optical technology to position the magnetic read/write head accurately over the correct track.

And yet one more hybrid technology is the Magneto-Optical (MO) disk. These devices use a highly focused beam of laser light to illuminate and momentarily heat a tiny portion of a special magnetically coated disk. The burst of heat permits recording of a great deal of magnetic information in a small space, with a greater than normal retention rate; in other words, an MO disk is much less likely to lose its information by natural decay of magnetism or by accidental erasure.

Random Access versus Sequential Media

Records and music CDs are both random access media. This means that you can lift the needle on the record or move the laser on a CD directly to a particular song, then play it. Audio and video cassette tapes, by comparison, are sequential. If you want to get from the first song to the tenth one, or from the start of a movie to the end, you have to fast-forward through the length of the tape.

Floppy diskettes, hard drives, removable disk cartridges, CD-ROMs, DVD-ROMs, and Floptical disks are all random access media. Data is easy to find. It's easy to write new data to an empty portion of the disk. And the drive read/write mechanism can quickly move from one location on the disk to another. (It's not quite instantaneous, though; all storage devices are measured in terms of their average seek and access speeds. The *seek speed* is the average amount of time it takes, in milliseconds, for the read head to move to the location of the data; the *access time* includes the time it takes on average to transfer the located data.)

Computer data tapes are sequential, similar to audio and video tapes. (Most tapes use a storage design referred to as *serpentine*. They record several tracks on the tape, moving from one end to the other, and then making a U-turn and continuing on the next track in the opposite direction. They are relatively inexpensive and capable of storing huge amounts of data—as much as 2 GB of information in some forms—but they are slow and difficult to use if you need to retrieve a particular piece of information.

Floppy Disks

Floppy disks—the material within the outside protective casing—are made of plastic (usually Mylar) coated with a ferric oxide capable of holding a magnetic charge. The plastic is flexible, hence the name *floppy*. Because of that, the plastic and coating are very easily damaged. Although it is enclosed in a square protective jacket, the disk can still be damaged. You don't want to:

- Bend a disk in half to fit in an envelope
- Staple a disk to a file folder
- Roll over it with your chair
- Use a disk as a coaster
- Spill a Coke over a stack of disks

Trust us, every one of those acts—and many more even stranger—has been performed by users. The most infamous of all disk-destroying acts is attaching a floppy disk to the side of a file cabinet with a magnet; you probably won't lose the disk, but you'll almost certainly lose some or all of its contents. Also, be aware of less-than-obvious sources of magnetism including some scissors and screwdrivers, and electric motors such as those within pencil sharpeners.

Because they're enclosed in a stiff cover that prevents casual contamination, 3.5-inch floppy disks are sturdier. Under their high-tech cover, standard 3.5-inch disks use the same read/write technology as 5.25-inch floppies.

Extra-high-density (2.88 MB size) 3.5-inch floppy disks use a different coating (barium ferrite), plus a special perpendicular recording technology and twice as many sectors per track as high-density (1.44 MB) floppy disks. The 2.88 MB drive can read 1.44 MB and 720K floppies as well, since it has a separate recording head to maintain compatibility with the older 3.5-inch disk. You'll probably need a device driver in order to use the 2.88 MB drives with standard ROM BIOS chips.

Welcome to the Super Bowl

Imagine a circular stadium, with 40 or 80 concentric rows of seats; these are the tracks of a floppy disk. The stadium has 9, 12, or 18 aisles radiating out from the center, which split the stadium seats into sections (the disk's sectors). The stadium owners sell tickets only to groups, and only in multiple-sector, single-row blocks (clusters). If the group doesn't have enough spectators (bytes of data) to fill a complete block, that's tough; the rest of the seats in the cluster will just have to go to waste and stay empty.

To help visitors or late arrivals find their group, the stadium owners keep a master chart at the ticket office showing where each group has been seated. This chart also tells the stadium owners which clusters are still available, and which clusters are unusable because some seats in the cluster are broken.

Now let's do the technical description.

How a Floppy Disk Drive and Controller Work

When you insert a floppy disk into the drive and close the door, the disk centers on the drive spindle so that it will spin true. At the same time, two read/write heads—one for the top surface of the floppy (side 0) and one for the bottom surface (side 1)—move into position, pressing very lightly on the disk. The heads are now prepared to read the magnetic marks on the disk or to write new ones.

The drive moves these read/write heads according to commands from the controller card. In turn, floppy disk drive controllers get their read or write instructions from DOS. These instructions are quite explicit. For example, DOS might tell the floppy disk drive controller to instruct the floppy drive to move the read/write head to track 15, sector 5, and read the contents of that sector.

The floppy disk drive controller is not a particularly sophisticated device. It doesn't have to keep track of the contents of a disk; DOS does that. It doesn't have to know what parts of the disk are empty and available to store new data; DOS does that, too. Nor does it have to decide which read/write head on the drive it is going to activate. The floppy disk drive controller *does* have to change the DOS instruction "move to track 15" into on/off signals that control the stepper motor that moves the heads from track to track. It also has to know what sector of the floppy disk is under the read/write head at any moment.

For 5.25-inch drives, the floppy disk drive controller locates sectors with the aid of an index hole punched in the floppy disk jacket and in the disk within. When the floppy disk spins, the two index holes line up once every revolution and an electric eye in the disk drive sends a signal to the floppy disk drive controller each time they do. With the knowledge of where the index mark is, the controller then counts the sector markers until the desired sector is under the read/write head. The controller reads the data in the sector, separating housekeeping bits from the actual data, returning a clean stream of data to the microprocessor across the bus.

A 3.5-inch drive works in a similar fashion, except that the mechanism is able to know where it is on the spinning track because of a notch in the center metal spindle of the inner plastic disk; the rotor on the drive motor engages directly into the notch.

Tracks and Sectors

The surface of the floppy is divided into circular tracks and then into sectors so that data can be stored in a particular location and found again easily. Imagine the floppy rotating in the floppy drive, like a record on a turntable. Hold an imaginary felt tip marker 1/2-inch from the outer edge of the record and lower it gently onto the surface. The circle drawn on the surface of the record is track 0. If you could accurately move the marker just 1/50-inch toward the center of the record, that new circle would be track 1 (see Figure 8.1).

You might imagine that information is written uniformly across the entire surface of a floppy disk, but that is not the case. The 360K floppy disk, for example, has all 40 tracks packed tightly together in a band less than an inch wide near the outer edge of the disk. This makes sense because the longest (most spacious) tracks are near the outer edge of the disk. At 48 tracks per inch (TPI), these 360K disks are called *double-density*. By comparison, 1.2 MB floppy disks jam 80 tracks in the same band less than an inch wide. These *high-density* 1.2 MB floppies have 96 TPI. Both the 720K and the 1.44 MB versions of 3.5-inch disks have 80 tracks and are 96 TPI.

A track is a very large space. On a 360K floppy, for instance, a single track holds more than 4,600 bytes of data. The track is divided into 9 sectors. Each sector on a 360K disk holds 512 bytes of data, a more manage-

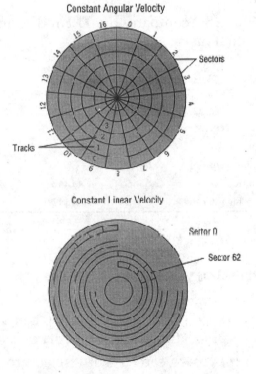

Constant Angular Velocity

Constant Linear Velocity

CHAPTER 8

Figure 8.1 Top: the spiraling Constant Linear Velocity (CLV) method used by CD-ROM drives. **Bottom**: a standard hard or floppy disk with sectors and tracks records data with the Constant Angular Velocity (CAV) method.

able size for the computer to deal with. A 1.2 MB disk has 15 sectors, each with 512K of data. A 720K disk has 9 sectors, each with 512 bytes of data per sector. A 1.44 MB floppy records twice as much data per track, cramming 18 sectors onto each track.

Here's the calculation for the total amount of data storage available on a disk:

```
Tracks x Sectors x Bytes per Sector x Number of Sides = MB data
```

For example, for a 1.2 MB floppy: 80 tracks x 15 sectors x 512 bytes per sector x two sides of the floppy = 1.2 MB of data.

Table 8.2 compares the TPI and sectors per track in double-density versus high-density disks for both 5.25-inch and 3.5-inch disks.

Table 8.2 Physical Disk Configuration for Standard Floppy Disk Types

Type	Size	Capacity	Tracks per side	Sectors per track	Compatible DOS
Double density	5.25 inch	360 K	40	9	2.0 or newer
High density	5.25 inch	1.2 MB	80	15	3.0 or newer
Double density	3.5 inch	720 K	80	9	3.2 or newer
High density	3.5 inch	1.44 MB	80	18	3.3 or newer
Extra high density	3.5 inch	2.88 MB	80	36	5.0 or newer

Directory and FAT

When you format a disk, DOS creates a file allocation table (FAT) and a directory on track 0 so that stored data can be located on a disk. The directory contains the file name, size, date, and time of last modification, file attributes, and physical location of the first part of the file. The FAT contains information about each cluster.

A *cluster* is a conveniently sized group of sectors used to store information. There are typically two sectors per cluster for a floppy drive and four sectors per cluster for a hard drive. All reading and writing on disks is done in whole-cluster increments. If only half a cluster is filled with data from File A, the rest of the cluster will be left blank.

As noted, the FAT stores information about the contents of each cluster. The FAT is a numeric list of all the clusters, with space for a coded entry for each cluster. A zero in an empty cluster's FAT indicates that the cluster is available for use. Physically defective areas on the disk are marked bad by locking out the appropriate clusters in the FAT. Clusters with a nonzero FAT entry contain data.

A file appears to DOS as a chain of clusters. The first cluster is entered in the directory, along with the filename and other directory information. The FAT entry for that first cluster shows the number of the next cluster in the chain. The last cluster containing data for File A is marked as the end.

The Brains of the Outfit: The Floppy Disk Controller

The floppy drive contains the motor and mechanism necessary to spin the disk and move the head to any desired track on the disk. It also has drive-door-closed (for 5.25-inch drives) or disk-present (for 3.5-inch drives) and write-protect sensors.

The brains of the disk reading and writing process are in the floppy drive controller, which is an *interface* (a connection-point) between the computer bus and the floppy disk drives. The controller gets read/write instructions from the microprocessor and data from the bus and then sends both down a ribbon cable to the drives; working the other way, it instructs the floppy drive to locate a particular block of data and then picks it up and sends it across the PC's bus.

Dinosaur PCs used separate floppy and hard drive controllers. Modern machines generally use combination cards that feature both floppy and hard drive controllers; in some cases the controllers also handle CD-ROM drives. Either way, because the electronics for each subsystem are independent, one system might fail while the other continues to work properly.

R.I.P. 5.25-inch Drives

In this section, we will discuss both 5.25-inch and 3.5-inch floppy disk drives. However, the 5.25-inch disk format is all but dead; nearly all new machines have abandoned that older form in favor of advanced 3.5-inch drives.

The only reason to install a new 5.25-inch drive or replace an older one is if you have a large stack of 5.25-inch disks with important information recorded on them. If you have only a few such disks, perhaps you can find a friend or coworker who has a machine with both 5.25-inch and 3.5-inch drives installed and transfer the information to the smaller disks.

There are also combo drives with both 5.25-inch and 3.5-inch drives in a single slim body that occupy just a single bay in your PC.

Advanced Floppy Disk Drives and Dinosaur PCs

Not all DOS versions support 3.5-inch floppy drives—only DOS 3.2 or above. DOS 3.2 supports 720K drives, but not high-density 1.44 MB drives. DOS 3.3 and above can handle either 720K or 1.44 MB drives. DOS 5.0 and later can handle 2.88 MB floppy drives, plus all others.

The message should be clear: run the latest version of DOS (MS-DOS 6.22 or Windows 95 as this book goes to press) if at all possible.

The BIOS chip in modern machines has the ability to operate either high- or low-density 3.5-inch floppy drives. Of course, you'll need to store correct drive configuration data in the CMOS chip with the setup program.

Dinosaur computers, on the other hand, were designed before the 3.5-inch drive became popular. These types of computers need a software device driver to tell DOS that the smaller, higher-capacity drives are in use. These drivers should be available from the maker of the 3.5-inch drive, although there is less and less call for such assistance as the dinosaurs go to their graveyard.

If you need to use a device driver, copy it into your boot directory. You will also need to change your **CONFIG.SYS** file to include the line: DEVICE = xxxx.DRV (substituting the filename of your driver). Consult the specific instructions offered by the manufacturer of the drive.

With such a drive, you should be able to work with low-density (720K) 3.5-inch drives. To use a high-density (1.44 MB) drive, you'll have to use a modern controller; a change in BIOS chips may also be necessary.

Dinosaur Compatibility

Many 5.25-inch high-density (1.2 MB) drives have trouble working with disks formatted at double density because of the design of the read/write heads. Some quick calculation would show you that a 1.2 MB 5.25-inch disk can hold four times as much as a 360K disk. A high-capacity disk drive squeezes all of that information onto a disk by using a write head that has a magnetic gap only one-fourth the size of the equivalent on a 360K drive.

A 1.2 MB disk drive should have no difficulty reading a 360K disk. But if you use a 1.2 MB disk drive to store information on a 360K disk, it writes a thin little track down the middle of a relatively wide space. Take that hybrid disk and try to read it on a dinosaur 360K drive, and the wider head will try to read the entire area, picking up all of the background information garbage as well as the data. For this reason, only a 360K drive should be used to format or write a 360K floppy.

Microfloppies—another name for 3.5-inch disks—are a bit more compatible. The heads for older 720K and 1.44 MB disk drives are the same size, so there is no problem with writing or formatting disks across the two designs.

If 1.44 MB and 720K disks have the same size heads, how does the 1.44 MB disk manage to hold twice as much data? The difference is found in the magnetic capabilities of the disk itself; a high-density disk is capable of storing more bits per inch than is a standard-density device.

In addition, just to make things fun, the write-protect scheme of a 3.5-inch drive is the opposite of the 5.25-inch write-protect notch. On 3.5-inch floppies, the disk is write protected if the notch is open. When the notch is covered, recording is enabled.

How to Judge Which Component Needs to be Replaced

There are four basic components to the floppy drive subsystem:

- Disk drive controller
- Disk drive
- Cable
- Disk

CHAPTER 8

Each component should be tested in turn to determine if it is the cause of the problem with the drive. We're going to turn the order of the above list on its head to make the troubleshooting process a bit easier.

Disks

Try formatting a disk and then copying a file to it. If you get the DOS message **General failure reading**, **Data error**, or **Track 0 failure**, try another disk, preferably a new one. Disks die over time; if two or more disks don't work, then there is a problem.

Make sure you're using the proper type of disk. If you try formatting a high-density disk in a low-density drive, you'll sometimes get a **Track 0 bad** message, even though the disk is okay. It's just the wrong type of disk for the drive heads to cope with.

If you try to format and the drive grinds away with the indicator light on, but does not complete the format, it is possible that the **FORMAT.COM** file of DOS may be damaged. Reinstall that file from your original copy of DOS, or use your emergency DOS boot disk as the source of the new copy for FORMAT.

Be careful not to attempt to mix versions of DOS on the same computer. **FORMAT.COM** from DOS 5 will not work with DOS 6.2, for example, and unraveling such a combination can be a complex mess.

Cables

If the machine has recently been worked on, check to make sure the floppy drive cable is properly installed. If it is correctly in place, check to make sure that the A drive, and only the A drive, has a terminator. If both the cable and the terminator are okay, then break out your diagnostic disk, such as QAPlus, and see if the drive works.

If the diagnostic disk program now says the drive is bad, replace the cable before junking the drive. Run the floppy drive test again. If it still says the drive is bad, replace the drive.

Disk Drive Controller and Power Supply

If a new drive flunks the test and the cables have been checked, you may have a failed controller. The next step down the chain calls for replacement of the controller and retesting. If the drives are still bad, you should try installing a known good power supply. And the end of the line calls for replacement of the motherboard.

Unfortunately, it is very difficult to determine if either the power supply or the motherboard is bad. Often the only symptom is poor floppy drive performance, the exact symptom that brought you here in the first place. So, if you know the disks, the drive, the cable, and the controller are all good, yet you still have floppy drive problems, try installing a known good new power supply.

How to Test a Floppy Disk

As with any other mechanical element of your computer, it is only a matter of time before a floppy disk or a floppy disk drive fails. Not if, but when.

It should be obvious that you should never keep only a single copy of any critical data in one place. Back up any data held on a floppy disk to another floppy disk, or to a hard drive, or to any other backup medium.

In Chapter 19 we cover floppy disk and hard disk data recovery options, particularly the many diagnostic programs to recover data from suspect floppies. These programs look at a floppy disk sector-by-sector, persistently reading and rereading the sector. They check the *Cyclic Redundancy Code* (CRC), a mathematical algorithm that should show up any data corruption in the sector. A CRC number can be calculated from the data read, then compared with the CRC recorded in the sector when the data was originally written to disk. If the CRCs don't match, the data recovery program looks at the *Error Correction Code* (ECC). The ECC algorithm points to the specific bad bit or bits in a corrupted sector. Norton Utilities and PC Tools also contain data recovery utilities to help the frustrated user recover accidentally deleted files or whole directories.

If you're not sure whether or not you have a damaged floppy, continue reading.

Check the suspect disk in a second floppy drive. Find a known good disk drive of the same type as the suspect drive. If you're having problems reading the disk in a 1.2 MB drive, for example, try another 1.2 MB drive. If the disk works fine in one drive but acts poorly in another, then the problems are probably caused by malfunctions in the system unit hardware—the floppy drive or the disk controller, for example—rather than a bad disk. See the troubleshooting charts in Section 3 of this book for diagnostic assistance.

A Known Good Floppy

QA Plus, CheckIt, PC Tools DISKFIX, and Norton Utilities all have excellent floppy disk diagnostic routines. Each diagnostic uses slightly different algorithms to test the disk, so occasionally a floppy will slip past one test only to be flagged bad by the next diagnostic program. In most cases, however, it's unnecessary to run two tests.

If the suspect floppy passes these diagnostics, we can consider it a known good floppy disk.

Where to Find Your Floppy Drive and Controller Card

Floppy drives are easy to locate: just find the drive where it sticks through the chassis of the PC and look inside.

Both 5.25-inch and 3.5-inch floppy drives have a four-wire power cord from the power supply unit and a ribbon cable carrying data to and from the floppy drive controller.

In early dinosaurs, the first 5.25-inch disk drives were gigantic, a full 3 inches tall; as the drive mechanisms and electronics began to get smaller, this size was referred to as "full-height." The next step in the evolution of disk drives was a "half-height" model, which stood just 1.5 inch tall, allowing two drives to fit in the same space as the original occupied. Modern machines use drives that are just an inch tall, and laptop computers now come with tiny floppies that are as little as half an inch in height.

If you are trying to replace a dinosaur full-size drive, you may be out of luck in searching for a direct replacement. You can, however, find adapter hardware that allows you to install a tiny drive in a large space.

The ribbon cable coming off the back of the floppy drive runs to the floppy disk drive controller or to the floppy drive section of a combination hard/floppy controller. Follow the floppy drive ribbon cable carefully. It runs to other floppy drives installed in the system, then terminates at the floppy disk drive controller. (Other ribbon cables in the machine may go to a hard drive or other device, but only the floppy drive cable plugs into the back of the floppy drive).

How to Test a Floppy Drive and Its Controller Card

The proof of a floppy drive is in the reading. Start by placing a known good disk of the proper disk size and density in the suspect drive and see if you can read a directory of the disk. Go to DOS and type:

```
A:DIR        <Enter>
```

substituting the drive letter for the drive under test.

If the drive can't read a known good floppy, go to the troubleshooting charts in the Appendix of this book. Begin at the START chart and work your way through until you locate the problem.

If one of two drives in your system is working, the problem almost certainly does not lie in the disk controller but is due either to a cabling problem or to a dead drive.

If your system has two floppy disk drives—regardless of whether they are both 5.25-inch drives, both 3.5-inch drives, or one of each—one important test is to swap their data cabling. Start by turning off the power and removing the plug, and then taking off the cover of the PC. Locate the floppy drives, their associated floppy disk controller, and the cables that interconnect them. Remove the data cable to Drive A and mark it with a piece of tape or a soft marking pen; do the same with the data cable for Drive B. Now reverse the assignments of the two drives, making the former Drive B your first drive.

Power up the system and see if either of the floppy drives now work. If the formerly inoperative drive is still unresponsive and the other drive continues to work properly, you have a dead drive that must be replaced. If both drives now work, the problem may have been caused by improperly seated cables. Or, if you had just installed new drives before the failure, the problem may have been caused by improper termination settings on the drives.

If the drive still reads and writes unreliably, the problem may be caused by a loose connection on cables or an intermittent failure of the drive electronics. Utilities such as CheckIt, QA Plus, PC Tools COMPRESS, and Norton Utilities read and write to a test disk, repeatedly checking data accuracy at every point on the data storage surface.

How to Determine Whether a Drive is Out of Alignment

If you are having more and more data errors with a drive—especially with disks written on another machine or with older files that you recorded some time before—your floppy drive may be going out of alignment.

Alignment means that the heads of the drive are physically aligned with the tracks on the floppy disk, and the heads write information at the proper level (an electronics term roughly equivalent to "volume" on your stereo).

It is possible to have a brand new disk drive that is out of alignment when you first start using it. You may not realize the problem until you swap disks with someone else or run a diagnostic program.

One way to test this is to purchase a diagnostic program that comes with a preformatted test disk used as a reference point for tests. But before you do so, consider that realigning a floppy disk drive is not a job you can do without some expensive tools and testing devices. And the cost of replacing an old floppy disk drive—less than $50—is sure to be lower than the charge made by a PC repair shop to perform a realignment for you.

Testing the Disk Controller

Test the floppy disk drive controller the same way you test a floppy drive. First make sure that the drive formats disks properly, and then use a diagnostic program to see if the drive reads and writes properly for hours at a time. If the drive functions properly, then the drive controller must be working okay.

The controller is not likely to be at fault when one floppy drive works and the second one doesn't. Conversely, if both drives are bad, it usually means a bad controller, not simultaneous drive failure. The same circuits are used to control both floppy drives, but the hard disk controller has separate circuitry. Therefore, a working hard disk tells us nothing about the state of the controller card, even if the same card controls both floppy and hard drives.

As we have noted, dinosaur PCs used separate floppy disk controllers, while modern machines typically provide combined hard- and floppy-disk controller cards.

The current crop of modern machines almost all have the floppy controller integrated onto the motherboard; the floppy drive cable attaches directly to a connector on the motherboard. If those electronics fail, you should be able to disable the on-board controller with a jumper or by plugging a new controller into the bus.

Low-end disk controllers are a commodity now. No-name replacement controllers that combine IDE hard drive, floppy drive, and serial ports sold for as little as $14 from direct mail sources as this book went to press. Prices for 3.5-inch disk drives ranged from $30 to $50, and 5.25-inch drives sold for about $45. A combination 5.25-inch and 3.5-inch drive, shrunken to fit in a single one-inch bay, sold for about $90.

If you have a dinosaur machine you may not be able to use high-density floppy disk drives; check with the manufacturer of your machine to see if the machine will accommodate more modern drives. A change in the ROM BIOS may be necessary.

How to Install a Floppy Drive Controller

Remove the Old Controller Card

Turn off the computer and unplug the power cord. Remove the system cover. The wide, flat gray cable running from the floppy disk controller to each floppy drive is called a *ribbon cable*. You should examine the ribbon cable connections and routing before you remove any parts. Carefully examine the floppy drive ribbon cable; it's installed so the red (or blue) stripe is toward pin #1 on the controller card's cable-connection pins.

Many controllers, especially those in modern machines, have a "1" silk-screened on the controller next to the connector pins. Mark the cable you are removing with a piece of tape or a soft marker. Plan now, before you take the cable off, to reinstall the cable so the red or blue stripe faces the end with the number 1.

Other controllers, especially those in dinosaur PCs, have a notch cut in the connector on the controller card. The end with this slot is pin #1, and again you will reinstall the cable with the colored edge toward pin #1. Notice that one section of the ribbon cable is split off at the connector and twisted. When you reinstall the cable, the section with the twist must be on the A drive. The B drive is hooked to the straight-through connector in the middle of the cable.

Remove the cables. Then unscrew and save the screw that fastens the controller card to the system unit chassis. Finally, pull the card straight up out of the bus connector.

Put the Replacement Controller Card in the Slot

Press the card down into the motherboard bus connector. Some controller cards are extra long and will only fit in a particular slot on your machine; other than such physical considerations, a disk controller card will work in any slot.

After you install the card, connect the ribbon cable and reattach the screw that holds the card to the system unit chassis. (In some installations, it may be easier to attach the ribbon cable before you place the controller in the slot.)

Test the machine. If it's working, replace the cover and you're through. If not, recheck the cable; the next section tells you how.

Fixing a Problem with a Controller on the Motherboard

If you suspect a problem with the onboard floppy disk drive controller, you should begin by checking the BIOS setup screen for your system. Many modern machines use advanced BIOS code that permits turning on or off the FDD (floppy disk drive) controller from the keyboard. In some instances, power supply or battery backup problems can cause errors to be introduced to the CMOS memory of the machine.

If the FDD has been turned off, reset the option in CMOS and reboot the system to see if this fixes the problem. Try a known good floppy disk drive with the controller, or move your floppy disk drive to a machine with a known good controller to isolate the problem.

If you decide that the FDD controller on the motherboard is bad, disable it from the BIOS setup screen; on some systems you may have to disable it by moving a jumper on a switch block on the motherboard. (And on a few other systems, the act of plugging a replacement FDD controller into one of the slots on the bus will automatically disable the onboard controller.)

Replacement disk controllers, usually combined with IDE hard drive circuitry (which can be disabled to avoid conflicts if necessary) are available from parts suppliers. We found a simple controller for a modern machine for less than $20 in the Dalco Electronics catalog, as well as multiple I/O cards that also include such functions as high-speed serial ports, SCSI ports, and game ports.

How to Install a Floppy Disk Drive

Remove the Old Drive

It is often easier to remove the cables (a ribbon cable and a four-wire power cable) after the drive is loose. Examine the cables carefully before you disconnect them so that you will be able to reinstall them properly. We suggest marking them with a piece of tape or a soft marker to help identify them for reinstallation later.

You will also have to remove the four-wire power connector that comes from the power supply. Hold the connector (not the wires) and firmly pull it out of its attachment point on the drive.

On most dinosaurs, the floppy drives are mounted directly to the chassis. To remove the drive, you must remove the machine screws on the sides of the drive. Occasionally, the screws are installed from below. If that is the case, turn the computer on its side and look for holes in the bottom of the chassis to access these screws.

On most 286 and 386 computers, the floppy drives are installed with rails that slide into slots in the drive bays. Designs vary. Some use a small metal clip that is screwed onto the front surface of the chassis next to the drive.

Remove this clip to slide the drive out of the chassis, like a drawer sliding out of a cabinet. On other systems, the drives are held in place with screws on the side or bottom; once these are removed, the drive will slide out on rails.

Within some PCs, especially those with "slimline" or other low-profile designs, it may be necessary to remove other parts of the system—the power supply, adapter cards, riser cards—in order to gain access to the cage holding the floppy disk drives.

Set Switches/Jumpers on the New Drive

Floppy drives have jumpers or DIP switches to set the floppy's drive selector and terminating resistor options. DOS machines require that the drive selector (DS) on both drive A and drive B be set to the second drive

CHAPTER 8

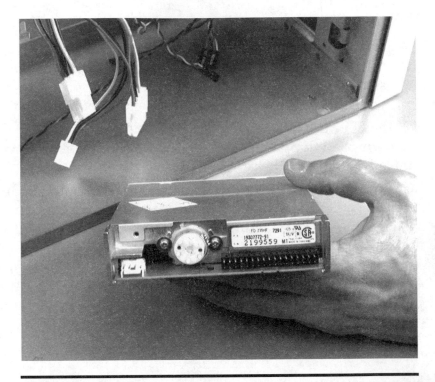

Figure 8.3 Floppy disk drives require juice from the power supply and a data cable. The device that is intended as Drive A takes the connector at the end of the data cable; Drive B attaches to the connector in the middle of the cable. Modern disk drives generally use a 34-pin male connector that mates to a 34-pin female plug on the cable; older drives used a 34-pin edge connector. To deal with this sometime incompatibility, floppy disk drive cables are available with redundant female and edge connectors.

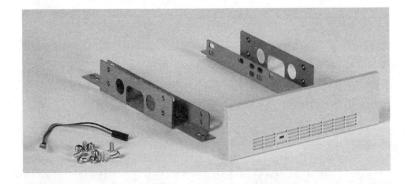

Figure 8.2 To mount a 3.5-inch hard or floppy disk drive in a 5.25-inch drive bay you'll need to install mounting rails; some drive makers include them in installation kits. Standard and specialized rails are available from suppliers like Dalco Electronics.

option. This may not seem to make sense, but the machine won't confuse the two drives when they're set to the same DS; the twist in the ribbon cable straightens everything out (see Figure 8.5).

Figure 8.4 In this roomy vertical case, the 3.5-inch floppy slides into place in a snug lower drive cage. On some machines you may need to install mounting rails to convert a space meant for a 5.25-inch drive and a face plate to fill the space around the front bezel of the case.

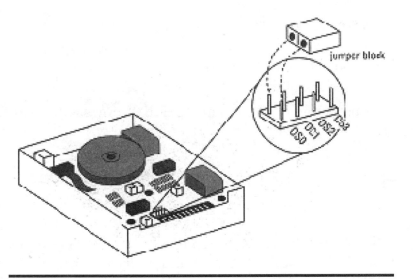

Figure 8.5 Sometimes the drive selector jumpers are numbered DS0, DS1, DS2, DS3 on the circuit board of the floppy drive. Other manufacturers number them DS1, DS2, DS3, DS4. In either case, put the jumper on the second lowest set of DS pins.

Consult the instruction manual that comes with your new floppy drive for the particular settings for that drive and the location of the jumpers or switches.

The floppy drive data cable has three connectors: one for drive B (which is straight-through), one for drive A (which has part of the ribbon cable twisted at the end), and one for the floppy drive controller card. The cable, not the DS jumper, determines which drive is seen by the machine as drive A and which as drive B.

Check Terminating Resistors

Older PCs and floppy drives require the use of a terminating resistor on the drive attached to the end of the data cable; the resistor helps set the proper electrical levels for the signal. Most (but not all) drives come with the resistor in place; if you are installing a floppy drive as the first drive on the cable it may be necessary to remove the resistor.

Consult the instruction manual that comes with your new floppy drive or call the manufacturer to determine if your drive has the resistor in place and whether it is necessary to remove it.

Slide in the Drive and Connect Cables

Once you configure the drive, you can install it. You should be able to reuse the rails and machine screws from the drive you are replacing, but not all floppy drives have the same physical dimensions or screw hole locations.

Screw the new drive down firmly, but not too tightly or you may strip the threads on the hole. After you secure the drive in the chassis, connect the ribbon cable. Most 5.25-inch drives use flat edge connectors to mate with a data cable; most 3.5-inch drives use pin connectors. Reconnect the four-wire power connector. Any of the four-wire power supply cables will do; they are all alike. Note that these connectors are not rectangular; two corners have been cut off on a diagonal. Examine the socket on the floppy drive before installing the connector. It is difficult but not impossible to force the connector in improperly; the result will most likely be a destroyed disk drive and possibly a damaged power supply.

After you install the new drive, turn on the machine and test the drive rigorously. If it passes all the tests, you're through. If it doesn't pass all the tests, recheck everything carefully, looking especially for incorrect switch settings and incorrect or loose cables.

CHAPTER 9

The Hard Life of a Hard Drive

Hard disks were once an expensive, fragile luxury. The first PCs did without them, although owners cast a jealous eye at television-sized Winchester disk drives that delivered what seemed to be a huge 10 MB of storage for only a few thousand dollars!

Over the life of the PC, this (along with processor speed) has been one of the most amazing areas of change. Hard drives have become larger in capacity, smaller in size, faster in speed, and lower in price.

Bigger, Faster, Cheaper

When the PC-XT was introduced in 1982, it came equipped with a 10 MB hard drive with an access time of 80ms; the drive was considered huge and fast. Two years later, the capacity of the new PC-AT was doubled and the access time cut in half. When the third edition of this book went to press in early 1996, a basic hard drive size for a Pentium machine was 540 MB with an 8ms access speed.

And in 1997, any serious Pentium user would expect a hard drive of 1.5 to 2.5 GB, three to five times larger; prices in the meantime continued their sharp drop.

Let's look at the march of disk drive capacity and speed in a graph:

Capacity (MB)		Access speed (ms)
IBM PC-XT (1982)	10	80
IBM PC-AT (1984)	20	40
IBM PS/2 (1987)	115	28
486 Clone (1990)	320	15
Pentium (1995)	540	13
Pentium (1997)	2,500 (2.5 G)	12

Here's a random selection of prices for hard drives from the October, 1982 issue of *PC Magazine*, about a year into the life of the Dinosaur PC:

- 5 MB Winchester in a box about the size of the PC it sat alongside, $1899.
- 19.2 MB Winchester (actually a pair of huge 9.6 MB drives) in a double-sized box, $2799.

When I wrote the third edition of this book, a 1 GB IDE hard drive seemed like a fantastic bargain at about $375, and a huge 9 GB SCSI drive seemed reasonable at $3,215. Well, at the start of 1997, newer and improved versions of those same capacity drives were priced at about $170 and $1,650 respectively—drops of about 50 percent in just over a year. Is that cool, or what?

One last exercise: we'll omit access speeds since it's simply too difficult to compare early PC buses, controller cards, and processors to modern-day systems. We can, though, compare the approximate cost per megabyte (unformatted), as seen in the accompanying table:

Year	Capacity	Price	Cost per MB
1982	5 MB	$1,899	$379.80
	19.2 MB	$2,799	$145.78
1995	428 MB	$183	$ 0.43
	722 MB	$253	$ 0.35
	1 GB	$375	$ 0.37
	9 GB SCSI	$3,215	$ 0.35
1997	540 MB	$139	$ 0.26
	1 GB	$170	$ 0.17
	2.7 GB	$300	$ 0.09
	9 GB SCSI	$1,650	$ 0.18

Back in the early days of the PC, it hardly seemed necessary to have a hard disk, anyhow. After all, word processors fit on a single floppy disk and PacMan was considered the state of the art in multimedia. Today, it is not uncommon for word processors to occupy more than 10 MB of disk space all by themselves, and multimedia games can demand double that room. Microsoft's Windows 95 demands as much as 65 MB all by itself for a full installation. And major application suites like Office 97 can eat up nearly 100 MB before you even put any data files on your disk.

As we go to press, then, the best value would seem to be hard drives in the range of 2 GB to 3 GB. And there is little reason to drop below 1 GB because savings for smaller drives are not significant. Going the other direction, massive hard drives like our 9 GB SCSI example are very cheap and headed down in price, but most users won't need something that large unless they are doing some very sophisticated graphics or video work. (And, we'll admit, we're a bit nervous about putting so many eggs in one basket—if we really had to store that much data, we'd rather have a group of smaller drives in an array so that if one fails it won't take down our entire business at once.)

Meanwhile, those new drives, some as small as a thick credit card, are many times faster and much more reliable than the old behemoths. In this chapter, we will look at standards for modern hard disk drives, including IDE and EIDE drives and adapter cards, and SCSI drives and host adapter cards. And we'll cast a backwards glance at older standards, including ST506 MFM and RLL drives and controller cards as well as ESDI drives and controller cards.

Hard Disk Life Span

Let's start with a universal statement: Hard disks do not last forever. They are a mechanical-electronic device with a motor to spin a disk, another system to move the read/write head to varying positions on the disk, bearings to support the spinning platter, and electronics to communicate with the rest of the computer.

As hard disk drives have gotten smaller, faster, more capacious, and considerably less expensive, they have also become more and more reliable. Some users make the mistake at looking at the older drives with their large cases and heavy motors and assuming that bigger means more sturdy; actually, the miniaturization of drives has brought simpler, less power-hungry circuitry and motors. This extreme improvement in data density has been accompanied by harder platter surfaces and tiny lightweight read/write assemblies that are much less likely to suffer a catastrophic crash.

A typical user who takes ordinary care of his or her system and provides the hard disk drive with a reliable source of electricity can expect several years or more of life from a hard disk. But looking at from the other side, it is also true that you may suffer a catastrophic failure after a few weeks.

Either way, our recommendation is that you always act as if your hard disk drive can fail at any moment, taking with it all of your work.

Hard disks are sealed boxes with high-tech filters designed to prevent particles of dust from clogging the heads or damaging the disks. They are not intended to be opened for service outside of a clean room. And, just as for floppy disk drives, the cost of repairing a hard disk drive is almost always equal or greater than buying a new unit.

In any case, the value of your data is almost always much greater than the value of your computer. For example, this manuscript represents months of work and you can bet that there are multiple copies of the files stored away from the computer on which it is being written. As a matter of fact, we're going to stop writing for a moment right now and update the backup copies we maintain on the hard drive on another machine on the office network and also on a removable Syquest drive . . .

While we're on the subject, permit us to present *Sandler's Top Three Tips for Safe Computing*:

1. Back up your data regularly.

2. Perform Step 1 at least once a week, more often when you are in the middle of a critical assignment.

3. See Steps 1 and 2.

In addition to making backup copies of your data, we also recommend that you run disk drive diagnostic and repair utilities regularly. These programs analyze your drive and ensure that the surface is reliable and any questionable areas are locked out.

What Could Possibly Go Wrong?

If you're lucky, your hard drive will have a full, healthy, and productive life. And then it will die.

We recommend that you read this chapter *before* you need rescue. Then read Chapter 19 if you're hoping to salvage useful data stored on an ailing hard disk. And then when death is in the house, re-read this chapter with the security of knowing you have put away safe backups of everything you should save beforehand.

Hard disks are similar to floppy disks, but the technology is upgraded in every way. Hard disks spin faster, pack in more data per inch, move from track to track more quickly, and accommodate multiple platters in each drive unit.

As with other electronic items, from calculators to digital watches, each generation of hard disks is smaller, faster, and more powerful. Half-height models, which replaced the full-height hard disks of the 1980s, have already given way to inch-high minimonsters. And laptop computers are being delivered with half-inch-tall hard drives with capacities of several hundred megabytes; they are even specially cushioned to protect them from the unusual insults a portable PC may have to endure.

The internal mechanical elements of the drives—always the Achilles heel of data storage devices—are improving too. More precise and reliable voice coil servo mechanisms are replacing cheap stepper motors in high-density, high-capacity hard drives.

A stepper mechanism moves the read/write head in fixed increments, or steps, across the disk surface. The mechanical nature of the drive assures precise positioning when the drive is new, but wear and tear can end up throwing the drives out of alignment. A voice coil mechanism uses servo track information to determine where to move the head in precise increments without the use of preset steps.

How a Hard Disk Works

Despite the changes and the broad spread of designs, all hard disks share the same basic construction. Polished aluminum disks, called *platters*, are spun at a precise speed by a small motor. The platters are coated with an oxide of magnesium, chromium, iron, or other metal particle capable of holding a magnetic charge. Above and below each side of each platter, a read/write head glides on a cushion of air very close to the platter, but not quite touching it. The read/write heads record data as magnetized sections on the platters.

If a modern drive has two platters, it will usually have four read/write heads and four data surfaces. The information of where data is stored is recorded along with the data; in technical terms this is called an *embedded servo*. (An older scheme gave over one entire platter to the storage of servo information; this was called a "dedicated servo." You can tell that sort of system when the specs indicate it has one less data surface than the number of platters multiplied by two. If your machine has such a system, it will almost certainly be necessary to replace your entire disk subsystem—controller and disk, and possibly the ROM BIOS—if your hard drive ever fails or becomes unreliable.)

Some very high-performance and high-capacity drives have several heads on a head assembly, with each one covering a smaller "zone" on the disk. They might therefore have four platters, eight data surfaces, and 16 or more heads.

Because the hard drive platters are not removable like floppy disks, hard drives are also called *fixed disks*.

Treat your hard disk gently. It is a delicate, precision-tooled mechanical device and is easily damaged. Dropping a hard disk might crash a read/write head into the platters. Even if the head is not damaged, the data underneath the head could get scrambled.

As we have noted, hard drives in good quality notebook and laptop computers are designed to take more shocks and wear and tear than ordinary hard drives. Feel free to slap your notebook computer down on the airplane tray table, but don't drop it out of the overhead luggage bin onto the floor. Surprisingly, hard disks and floppies survive X-rays well, but the radio waves generated by a poorly shielded or malfunctioning airport metal detector can destroy the data; we suggest you request hand-inspection for any laptop computer or box of floppy disks you may choose to carry with you on an airplane trip.

There are hundreds of hard disk and controller models, each with idiosyncratic switch settings and jumpers. It is absolutely essential to obtain a complete instruction manual from your disk drive manufacturer; there are also some massive books of settings and specifications for sale, but they do become quickly outdated. If you are transferring a known good disk drive from one machine to another and are missing the documentation, you may be able to obtain information from the drive maker; many manufacturers also have BBS systems and fax-on-demand services that include instructions.

Under the Covers of a Disk Drive

A modern hard disk drive usually has more than one disk within the mechanism. They're called *platters* and are stacked one above another like dishes in the cupboard. There's just enough room between the platters for a read/write head to float above (or below) the disks (see Figure 9.1).

The main element of a standard read/write head is a tiny magnet. One design is made of one or more turns of copper wire on a ring of ferrite; the ferrite core has a hairline gap facing the disk. When current is passed through the coil, the disk surface under the gap is magnetized, and a bit is written to the disk.

The direction of the magnetization from north to south or from south to north depends on the polarity of the current. The disk controller is in charge of rapidly changing the polarity in order to write either 0s or 1s.

To read information from the disk, the device's electronics sense the current caused by the passage of the magnetized sections of the disk as it spins beneath the gap. The electronics sense the change the polarity to decode the difference between a 1 and a 0.

The signal pulses are amplified and converted from the analog waves detected by the read/write head, and then converted to precise digital pulses of 0 or 1. (This is a potential point of failure on a disk drive: if the platter is unable to hold a strong, identifiable marking or if the write head is unable to put one in place, the decoding circuits may mistakenly identify a 0 as a 1.)

Figure 9.1 A hard disk with two platters has four recording surfaces, so the hard disk needs four read/write heads. The heads move together, in and out across the platter surface.

The next step is to separate the data pulses from the clock pulses. A clock signal is a string of precisely spaced pulses that serve as timing references for other signals, including drive control and positioning.

The sector address is examined by the disk controller, and if it matches the address the computer is looking for, the processing continues. If not, the data is ignored.

If the sector is correct, most interfaces then perform some level of error detection. The system computes an error-checking value which is compared to the value that was recorded along with the original value; if an error is found, the controller will try again.

If the data is found to be okay, the stream of data bits must be converted from serial form—one bit behind the other—to the parallel form in which it will move across the computer's bus. On IDE and SCSI drives, this conversion is performed by the drive's integrated electronics in a circuit called a data separator; on most other designs, the data moves from the drive to the controller as serial information and is converted by the controller.

Equally important, though, is an understanding of the logical structure of a hard disk. Hard disks are made up of cylinders and sectors.

Data on a hard disk is stored in concentric circles called *tracks*. Across each track the data is subdivided into small units of storage called *sectors*; common sector counts can be as little as 512 or 1,024 bytes.

A cylinder is defined as the same track on each platter. (If you were to cut the hard disk with a circular cookie cutter, you would end up with a set of cylinders spread across more than one platter.) Large files are recorded across cylinders instead of across tracks to minimize the amount of movement the read/write heads have to make to retrieve data (see Figure 9.2).

There are two popular ways to package information: modified frequency modulation (MFM) and run length limited (RLL) encoding. The first technique, MFM encoding, uses 17 sectors per track. RLL encoding uses 26 sectors per track and packs much more information into the same area, so that a high-quality surface is required. Suitable hard disks are RLL-certified by the manufacturer. In each case, the data coding scheme is built into the controller hardware, not the hard disk. An MFM controller with an RLL-certified hard drive produces MFM data encoding on an overqualified recording surface.

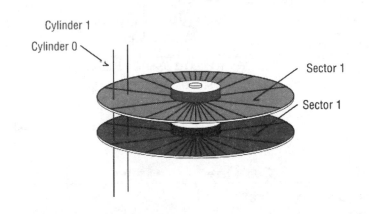

Figure 9.2 Each bit of data is located in a particular sector (pie slice), on a particular track (concentric data storage ring), on the top or bottom of a particular platter. The outermost track on every platter is Cylinder 0. The next track is Cylinder 1, and so on.

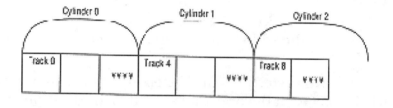

Figure 9.3 DOS sees the data as a continuous stream, like the music on a cassette tape. Tracks 0 and 1 are the outermost tracks on a platter: Track 0 is on the top surface and Track 1 is on the bottom surface. Tracks 2 and 3 are also the outermost tracks, but lie on the second platter. This makes sense, because the read/write heads move together; moving head 0 into position to read Track 0 also moves the other heads into position to read the outermost tracks on the other platters.

To the operating system, the data recorded across sectors, platters, and cylinders appears as a continuous stream of information.

In other words, what you see as two platters is seen by DOS as a long length of tape (see Figure 9.3).

In DOS, the disk is a large string of clusters or, if this is an MFM drive, packets of four sectors. Some drives' clusters are packets of as many as 15 sectors (it depends on the drive type). DOS reads and writes to the disk in increments of sectors and allocates space by the cluster, not by the individual sector.

This is not a minor matter. The larger the capacity of a physical or logical drive, the larger the cluster size it uses. On one of today's massive 1 GB or larger drives, the clusters are usually 32 KB in size. That's fine if you are storing files that are 32 KB, or 64 KB, or some other exact multiple of the cluster size. But if you store a batch file that is 10 bytes in length, it will still be placed into a box that is 32 KB in size; similarly, a file that is 32 KB plus one byte will occupy two clusters, or 64 KB.

It is quite possible to run out of storage space on a 1 GB drive with just 700 or 800 MB of data.

Therefore, if your drive is filled with a great number of short files, your usable space is going to be less than the full capacity. The only way to reduce the cluster size is to reduce the partition size—in other words, to subdivide the drive into smaller logical drives. For example, using **FDISK** to partition a 1 GB hard drive into two logical drives of 512 MB each reduces the cluster size to 8 KB.

Under current versions of DOS, the allowable cluster sizes for various sizes of hard drives are as follows:

Disk Size	Cluster Size
0–128 MB	2 KB
129–256 MB	4 KB
257–512 MB	8 KB
513–1 GB	16 KB
> 1 GB	32 KB

There are two other important concepts to file away in the back of your mind: a hard drive advertised as a 1 GB device may actually be a 1.1 GB drive, or may be capable of holding a mere 900 MB of data. That's because there is no hard-and-fast rule on how data capacity is stated. Any hard drive has to be formatted in order to be used in a computer— the act of formatting adds control information and magnetic markings for the data structure. And, in the process of formatting, some sectors of the drive may be found to be unable to store data reliably and will be locked out of use by the drive electronics. Figure on an overhead of about 10 percent from the raw capacity of a drive.

Some drivemakers will list "formatted capacity" in their specifications, and this should allow a reasonably accurate means of comparing one drive to another.

The second problem involves the sometime loose way in which computer; people use the kilo, mega, and giga prefixes; they are commonly substituted for one thousand, one million, and one billion respectively, but the math is incorrect if you do so. The reason is that computers use binary math, based on powers of two. A computer byte (made up of eight bits) has a maximum value of 1,024. Therefore a kilobyte is 1,024 bytes, a megabyte is 1000*1024 or 1,024,000 bytes, and a gigabyte is one million bytes or 1,000,000*1024 or 1,024,000,000 bytes. The problem arises when one maker calls a drive with 1,000,000,000 bytes a 1 GB drive (overstating its capacity by 24,000,000 bytes) and the other uses the 1 GB label accurately for a drive with 1,024,000,000 bytes. The only way to know whether a particular disk drive maker users true binary accounting for the size of its drive is to ask the manufacturer or study its specs carefully.

The Data Structure of the Hard Disk

The operating system divides a hard disk into two logical sections: the *system* area and the data area.

The system area carries essential programs and directories that help the computer operate and keep records of how information is stored on the disk.

The boot sector holds a short program that gives the computer the very basic instructions it needs in order to bring itself to life (the term "boot" comes from the phrase "lifting yourself up by your own bootstraps," which is a colorful way to look at what DOS is performing when it first starts. Information in the boot sector includes how much, if any, of the disk belongs to DOS (DOS understands that it may have to share the disk with another operating system) and where the DOS boot files are located (see Figure 9.4).

Every disk has a boot sector on it, whether or not it is a *system disk* that is intended to fully start the operating system; system disks add a few other critical files necessary to initiate DOS.

The boot sector is recorded on Track 0, a fixed location on the disk. If that sector is in some way damaged or the files corrupted, you will have to find some other way to boot the system.

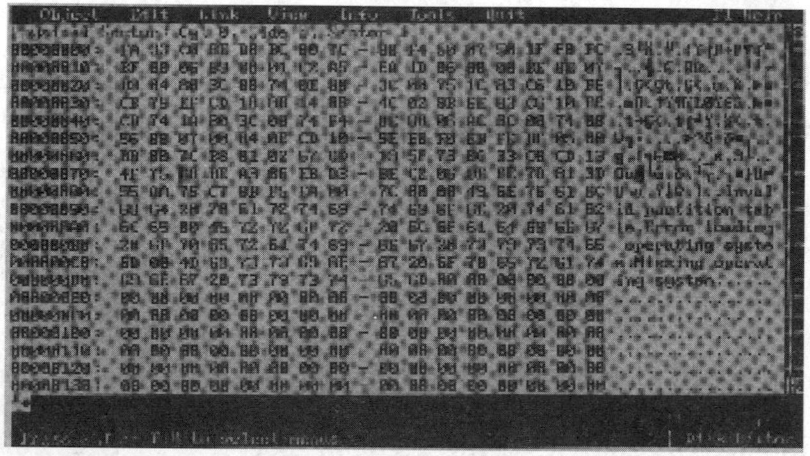

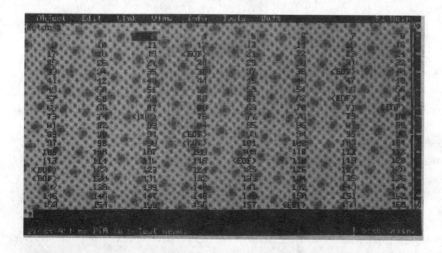

Figure 9.4 The hard disk boot sector (sector 00). Programs like the Norton Utilities (shown here) will allow you to examine the boot area, the FAT clusters and the root directory on a hard drive.

Figure 9.5 Sector 01, the beginning of the File Allocation Table (FAT).

The next section of the disk holds the file allocation tables (FATs), the critical description of the organization of the disk. FAT1 and FAT2 are simple arrays of numbers that indicate, for example, that Cluster X is linked to Cluster Y, Cluster Z is unusable, and Cluster W is free. The system offers some measure of protection by maintaining a pair of identical FATs.

The hard disk boot sector is shown in Figure 11.4. Sector 01, the beginning of the FAT, is shown in Figure 9.5.

If the boot cluster is damaged, DOS will not be able to recognize the disk and will give you a message such as Non-System Disk, if it can give any message at all. Usually the machine just locks up. If the FAT is slightly damaged, the DOS command CHKDSK or the improved SCANDISK program of DOS or a data-recovery program may be able to reconstruct the pointers (the directions to the next cluster in the chain). If the FAT is unreadable, the pointer information and whatever is on the disk are lost. Even though the information is actually still on the disk, there is no way to access it in any meaningful form.

Some utility programs seek to protect you from the irretrievable loss of the FAT by making copies of the file elsewhere on the hard disk or on an emergency recovery disk.

The last part of the system area is the *root directory*, which begins at Cluster 2. It contains the names of the files and subdirectories and indicates the pointer in the FAT that is the marker for the first cluster of each file. If the root directory is badly damaged, data on the disk cannot be retrieved.

Subdirectories are just lists of file names, file sizes, dates created, file attributes, and first cluster numbers. In other words, a subdirectory is structured just like the root directory, but is itself a file.

And here's a secret of DOS: When a file is erased, the first letter of the file name is changed to hex value E5 (E5H, in computerspeak) and the FAT pointer is zeroed out, but the data is not actually erased from the disk. That is how "Undelete" programs perform their magic: so long as no new file has written over the same space, the program can change E5 back to an alphabetic character and the file will once again appear in the disk directory and be available for use.

Speeding Through Life

Faster is better, and drives are becoming faster and faster even as they become larger in capacity, smaller in size, and significantly less expensive. But just what is meant by "speed" on a hard drive? It all comes down to this: when you enter a command from the keyboard or when a program issues an instruction by itself, how long does it take for the disk drive subsystem to deliver the information to the microprocessor or the video adapter?

One of the components of speed is the rotational speed of the drive. A hard disk typically spins about 10 times faster than a floppy disk drive, usually in the range from 2,400 to 3,600 RPM. That's about 40 to 60 times per second.

Perhaps even more important, though, are four other factors: physical seek time, latency, data buffer size, and transfer rate.

One measure of the first three factors is *access time*, which is often expressed as "average access time." The term "average" is an important component of that specification.

If the drive maker wants to fudge the number, it can calculate how fast the drive can get to a bit of information that is already directly under the read/write head; such a number is all but useless as an indicator of true access time.

Access time is supposed to mean the amount of time required for the read/write head mechanism to find the track or cylinder that holds the desired data (this is called *average seek time*), plus the time required for the head mechanism to become stable over the location of the data (called *settling time*), plus the average time required for the proper data to spin under the read/write head (called *rotational latency*). Latency is directly related to the speed of rotation of the disk drive.

Expressed as a formula, then, it would be expressed as:

Average Access = Average Seek + Settling Time + Latency

Some manufacturers have dropped out latency from their access time claims and some ignore settling time. Be sure you are comparing fast apples to fast apples when you look at supposed drive speed.

The final—and very important—component of drive speed is data transfer. This is the rate at which a drive or controller dumps the information it has retrieved to the bus of the computer. This is an area where there are often great mismatches—a slow data transfer system can cause quickly accessed data to back up on the hard drive side of the controller; a very fast data transfer system can stand idle most of the time waiting for a slow disk drive to find and pick up the requested data.

Now that we've (sort of) cleared up the issue of speed on a drive, there is one more issue to bear in mind: the stream of data that comes off a hard drive includes more than just the information you are looking for. The data includes formatting data and on some drives padding bits that mean nothing but are used to deal with speed variations at the narrow or wide parts of the disk. On an IDE or SCSI drive, this information is taken out of the data stream by the drive's integrated electronics; on older designs, the extra stuff is removed by the drive controller card. Either way, a full ten-pound bucket of data may contain only eight pounds of usable stuff.

Interleave Factor

A hard disk's interleave has a great deal to do with the speed of information retrieval from a hard disk drive. The interleave, in turn, is directly related to the speed of the mechanical and logical elements of the drive. The interleave factor tells you how many physical sectors must pass beneath the read/write head before the next logically numbered sector is reached. The factor is equal to the number of physical sectors between two logical sectors, plus 1.

Here's an example of the problem the interleave factor is supposed to fix: a hard disk (unlike many floppy disk designs) is constantly spinning at a predetermined speed. If the drive has a 2:1 interleave factor, after Physical Sector 1 is read, the disk read head is positioned over Physical Sector 2. If the hard disk controller is not fast enough to request data in the few milliseconds between the time the disk moves from the first sector to the second, the controller is forced to wait for a full revolution of the disk before the head is again over Physical Sector 2.

The logical order of sectors on a hard drive, however, can be set by software, and does not have to follow the physical scheme of one after another around the disk. An *interleave*, then, moves the logical sectors around on the disk to give the controller sufficient time to react.

A 1:1 interleave simply places sectors in numerical order; for the very fastest of drives and controllers (or, conversely, the very slowest of electronics), that is sufficient. The accompanying table shows an example of 2:1 and 3:1 interleaves on a drive with 17 sectors:

Interleave	Sector Order
2:1	1,10,2,11,3,12,4,13,5,14,6,15,7,16,8,17,9
3:1	1,7,13,2,8,14,3,9,15,4,10,16,5,11,17,6,12

Some disk-tuning software, including Gibson Research's SpinRite 4.0, is able to examine your controller and drive and choose the optimal interleave factor for your system. We recommend you consult the maker of your hard drive before going down this sometimes technically challenging path.

Form Factor: What Fits Where?

Most desktop PCs have space for 5.25-inch or 3.5-inch devices, in internal case bays.

Dinosaurs were at their height when 5.25-inch-wide devices were considered tiny; modern machines usually offer a few of the wider bays for larger devices including 5.25-inch floppy drives—a vanishing breed—and internal CD-ROM drives.

It is easy to install a 3.5-inch drive into a 5.25-inch bay with the aid of adapter rails and carriers; some drives include the extra hardware while in other cases you'll have to pay a few dollars extra for a few pieces of sheet metal and screws (see Figure 9.6).

Notebook computers usually employ tiny 2.5-inch drives, with increasing capacities and low power requirements; they are priced at a premium over large-size drives. At present, there is little reason to install one of these drives in a typical desktop system.

CHAPTER 9

FIGURE 9.6 This 3.5-inch hard drive fits into a drive cage of the same width; some systems may demand the use of mounting rails to adapt the smaller device to a wider bay. Some technicians try to test the drive before it is screwed into place in the drive cage.

Hard Drive Interfaces

Alphabet Soup: IDE, ATA, EIDE, SCSI, AT, ESDI, and ST506

Computers communicate with hard disks through an *interface* (a set of rules describing the adapter card, the cable, the electronics on the hard disk itself, and the electrical signals running between the hard disk and controller). IDE (also known as ATA in some implementations), the enhanced EIDE standard, SCSI, ESDI, and ST506 have been the most significant interfaces in personal computers. On today's modern machines, we're mostly looking at EIDE and SCSI interfaces.

Think of each interface as an independent contractor. Each of these hard drive interfaces provides the following:

- A standard controller/adapter card which plugs into the computer's motherboard bus, or in the most modern of modern machines, right into a connector on the motherboard with a local bus pathway to the microprocessor;
- The ability to stand as an interpreter between DOS and the computer's ROM BIOS for the purposes of controlling the flow of data, and
- The facility to send data to be stored on the hard disk and instruct the drive to retrieve it when necessary.

Each hard drive interface handles the actual data storage in its own way.

SCSI, for example, uses a separate bus (its own data and control signal path) to carry the data signals and control signals from adapter card to hard disk and back again. The SCSI bus is so separate, in fact, that most SCSI installations tell you to set up your computer as if there were no hard drives installed; SCSI doesn't want the computer messing around with its bus, its data, or its hard disk.

By comparison, the older ST506 specification used on many dinosaurs expects the computer's ROM BIOS to know how many heads and cylinders are on the hard disk, which read/write head should read what data, and what track on the hard disk this head should read. ST506 may be an independent contractor, but it requires a great deal of supervision.

IDE drives allow ordinary computer bus signals on the cable running from the IDE adapter card to the IDE hard drive, which has its own intelligence. But the IDE interface lies to the computer about the hard drive actually installed, cleverly convincing the host computer that a nonstandard hard disk is obeying its commands as an ST506 drive would.

These hard drive interfaces all do the same basic job (store and retrieve data, and connect to the computer mother-board), but in such different ways that none of the parts are interchangeable. An ESDI hard disk controller card won't work with SCSI, ST506, or IDE drives; SCSI cables or adapter cards won't work with anything but SCSI drives.

In addition, the troubleshooting and installation techniques vary from interface to interface. Therefore, we have divided this chapter into SCSI, IDE, ESDI, and ST506 (MFM and RLL) units.

How does your computer talk to its hard disk? Before you proceed any further, we'd suggest you find out what kind of interface and drive you have. The information should be available in your computer's instruction manual; the specification should also be listed in the report of any capable diagnostic or system information program.

Comparing the ST506, ESDI, IDE, EIDE and SCSI Interfaces

Dinosaur: ST506

Almost all early PCs used Seagate's ST506/ST412 interface, named for Seagate's popular ST506 hard disk. ST506-compatible drives are also called MFM (Modified Frequency Modulation) and RLL (Run Length Limited) drives, because of the means by which data is encoded on the disk.

The MFM data encoding technique was used on the first IBM XT hard drives and many systems that followed; to increase speed and data storage capacity, drive manufacturers started using RLL encoding with the ST506 interface. Because RLL encoding stores roughly 1.5 times as much information in the same space, it requires high-quality RLL-certified hard disks and a special RLL hard disk controller.

ST506 was more than adequate for the poky PC-XTs and just about good enough for the first PC-AT machines, but ran out of a reason for being about 1984. ST506 in any form has all but disappeared now except for a few warehouses that hold boxes of old drives waiting to be used to repair early systems.

Dinosaur: ESDI

As the early PCs began to become faster and more capable, a group of hard disk manufacturers created their own improved adaptation of the ST506 design. The Enhanced Standard Device Interface transfers data two, three, or four times as fast as ST506 drives—as much as 20 million bits per second.

ESDI uses the same wiring system as ST-506 drives, but the two types of drives cannot be interchanged under the same controller because of changes to the control signals. And ESDI drives are particularly sensitive to a perfect match to a particular brand or type of ESDI controller.

CHAPTER 9

In addition to significant speed pickups, ESDI improvements include reserved areas on the disk itself for the storage of setup parameters and bad track data.

Modern Machine: SCSI and Wide-SCSI

The SCSI interface (pronounced "skuzzy") was under development about the same time as ESDI, and represents (along with IDE) a new approach to the design of disk drives and controllers. The new concept was intended to move much of the intelligence from the computer to the drive electronics; in doing so, the speed of the drives was improved and compatibility across systems was enhanced.

Because it is a higher-level interface than a mere card in the bus, SCSI can also be used to connect a wide range of other devices to the PC, including scanners and CD-ROMs. SCSI controllers add about $100 to $250 to the cost of a machine, and SCSI drives sell at a premium of about $50 to $100 over EIDE equivalents.

The SCSI specification allows up to seven devices on one controller, and more than one controller in a system. SCSI is well suited for external drives, CD-ROMs, scanners, tape backups and other devices that can be daisy-chained on the desk and beneath the desk.

The original specification for SCSI had a top end of 5 MB per second with an 8-bit data path. That was soon surpassed by SCSI-2 (also called Fast SCSI), which could move as much as 10 MB per second in an 8-bit bus. Beyond that is Wide SCSI, which uses a 16-bit data path and moves twice as much—20 MB per second.

And just arriving on consumer-level machines is SCSI-3, which includes a new mode called Ultra SCSI or Fast 20. This permits another doubling of speed, to 20 MB/second on an 8-bit bus and 40 MB/second on a 16-bit bus.

Modern Machine: IDE

The most common and versatile interface in the day of the modern machine is IDE (Integrated Drive Electronics), and the newer, extended, Enhanced IDE (EIDE). Nearly all current home and small business machines use EIDE; older modern machines commonly use IDE.

And nearly every new motherboard offers the IDE connection without the need to use a controller card in the bus; in fact, the most modern motherboards offer two IDE connectors, one for the primary and one for the secondary IDE circuit. You can plug as many as two devices into each of the cables that attach to the connectors.

IDE is a relatively fast interface, capable of a maximum transfer of 3.33 MB per second, and doesn't require the use of a sophisticated controller card. Most current machines include the interface on the motherboard, while simple adapter cards for other systems are inexpensive.

The original IDE drive specification suffered from a few handicaps, though. As designed, IDE circuitry could not work with hard drives larger than 528 MB, which seemed huge at the time but is not so anymore. Another problem was a limitation to no more than two devices per IDE connector. Finally, IDE was never intended for anything other than hard drives, meaning it could not work with CD-ROM drives and tape backup devices.

Modern Machine: EIDE

Western Digital lead the effort to enhance the IDE specification, coming up with an improved variant that was named, logically, Enhanced Integrated Drive Electronics, or EIDE.

EIDE can support as many as four drives per controller. The drives can be all EIDE, all IDE, or a mix. (However, an IDE drive plugged into an EIDE controller will be limited in capacity to IDE's old maximum of 528 MB.) The maximum size of hard drives supported was boosted all the way to 8.4 GB (although few drives of that size have been produced for EIDE; massive drives today are mostly attached to SCSI controllers).

The speed of the controller was boosted to a potential minimum of 11.1 MB/second, although all drives are limited by other factors including the speed of the drive head in moving from location to location and other factors. If you are looking for the maximum possible potential transfer rate, check the specifications of EIDE hard drives to see if they support PIO Mode 0 (the old IDE definition), PIO Mode 1 (11.1 MB/second), PIO Mode 2 (16.6 MB/second), or one of the newer and improved PIO Mode 3 or 4 specifications. In some systems, the entire EIDE channel will be limited to the maximum speed of the slowest device attached.

EIDE includes the ATA Packet Interface (ATAPI) specification that extends control to other types of devices. ATAPI drivers are available for CD-ROM drives, tape drives, and removable storage devices such as Iomega Zip drives and larger cartridge devices including Iomega Jaz and SyQuest SyJet.

One way to quickly determine if your system uses IDE or EIDE is to go to the BIOS setup screen. If you find you are permitted to define only two drives, you have an IDE system; if there are options for four devices, there is an EIDE controller present.

Examining Your Hard Drive and Interface

If necessary, you can open your computer to examine the drive, its controller/adapter, and their associated cables. Remove the cover and find the hard drive—a solid, rectangular, metal device that is usually mounted in a bay at the front of the chassis, although some designs suspend it elsewhere inside the case.

There will be a 4-wire power cable and one or two ribbon cables attached to the back of the hard disk. Your floppy disk drive or drives will also have a 4-wire power cable and a ribbon cable, but it is easy to tell floppy disk drives from hard drives: each floppy drive has a door in front to insert the floppy disks—a hard drive doesn't.

CHAPTER 9

Once you have found the hard disk, look at the ribbon cable or cables attached to it. Compare them to the descriptions below and to Figures 9.7 and 9.8.

SCSI and IDE/EIDE each use a single ribbon cable running from the hard drive adapter card to the back of the hard disk. SCSI ribbon cables have 50 wires. IDE ribbon cables have 40 separate wires. Both of these cables are straight-through in design, with pin 1 at one end equal to pin 1 at the other.

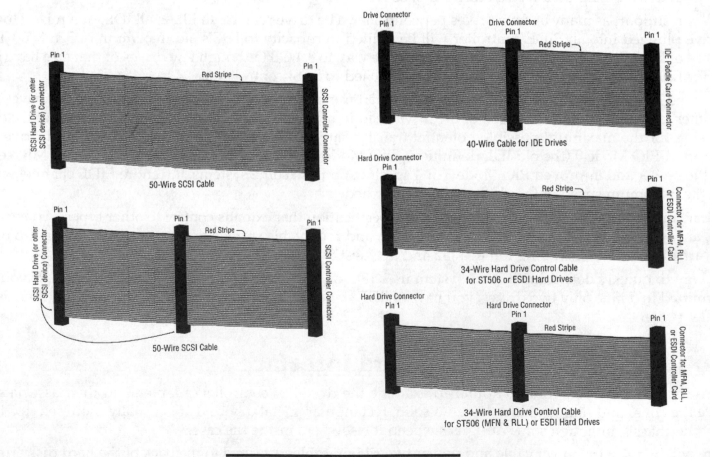

Figure 9.7 Straight-through ribbon cables.

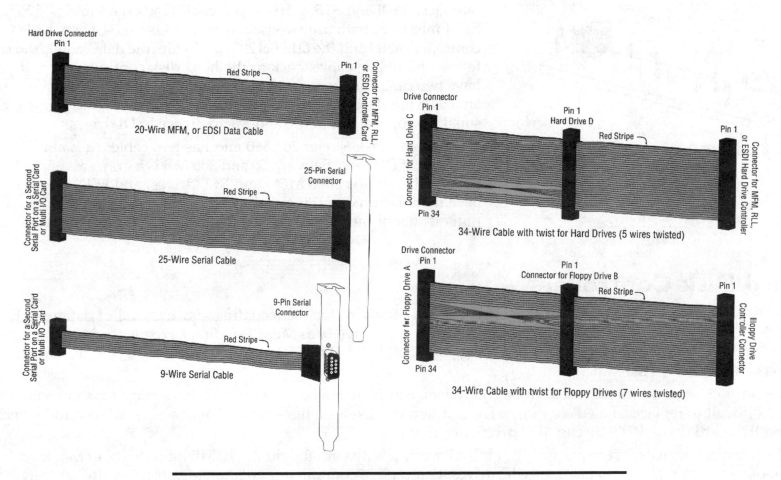

Figure 9.8 (Left) Straight through ribbon cables, (Right) ribbon cables with a twist.

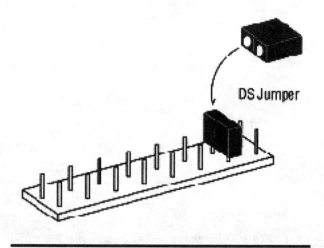

DS Jumper

Figure 9.9 You may need to set a jumper to indicate a master or slave hard disk.

By comparison, a floppy drive cable has a "twist" with seven wires split off from the rest of the ribbon, flipped over, and clipped into the next connector (see Figure 9.9).

Since ESDI is simply a faster (but incompatible) version of the ST506 interface, ESDI and ST506 drives and cables look the same. ST506 and ESDI interfaces both use two ribbon cables. One is 34 wires wide (the controller cable) and the other is 20 wires wide (the data cable). You can follow the ribbon cables back to the hard disk controller card. If you have two cables and your hard disk is under 50 MB, you probably have an ST506 interface. (There are a handful of exceptions, including a few small Micropolis, Rodime's, and Microscience ESDI drives.)

If the hard disk is over 200 MB and has two cables, it is almost certainly an ESDI drive. Between 50 and 200 MB is a gray area, since both ST506 drives (also called MFM and RLL drives) and ESDI drives have been manufactured in this size range. It makes sense to call your computer dealer or the hard drive manufacturer if you have any doubts.

Hard Disk Controllers

There is a dizzying alphabet soup of standards and specifications for the recording and retrieval of data on a hard disk. For our purposes here, it doesn't matter whether your drive uses MFM (Modified Frequency Modulation) or RLL (Run Length Limited) schemes for recording, or ST506, ESDI, IDE, EIDE or SCSI disk controllers: the hard drive platters and heads are the same.

The early PC systems mostly used ST506 controllers, which are now obsolete. If you have such a system, you may find it difficult to replace a failed controller. The solution will likely be the substitution of a new IDE controller and a paired IDE hard drive. We'll discuss IDE drives in a moment.

ST506 controllers used in the original IBM PC-XT worked only with the clunky 10 MB hard drives of that machine, while others were matched to other specific drives. Later ST506 controllers were more flexible, but still severely limited in the size of drive they would work with.

A later standard was the Enhanced Small Device Interface (ESDI), which was a much quicker system but still limited in size. In addition, the ESDI controller had to be matched carefully to the drive so that both had the same trans-

fer rate. ESDI controllers may also be difficult to obtain or justify on a cost-benefit basis; you may need to substitute an IDE controller and new disk to fix a broken ESDI system.

Modern machines now commonly use Integrated Drive Electronics (IDE) or Enhanced IDE controllers, which are inexpensive, quick, and very flexible. The key to understanding these controllers lies in the name: the drive electronics are integrated onto the drive itself. IDE controllers are little more than ports into and out of the computer bus, with the brains on the drive. This placement allows for customization and upgrades by the drive manufacturer.

Many current PCs come with the IDE controller built directly onto the motherboard. (If you don't want to use the IDE controller or if it fails, the system BIOS should permit you to turn off the onboard IDE controllers. If that is not part of the BIOS, the motherboard should include a jumper block or switch that offers a means to disable the controller and recognize a new one plugged into the bus.)

You can also purchase a separate IDE controller on an add-on card. (Some makers call IDE controller cards, "paddle cards." These replacement cards sell for as little as $20; more complex cards combine HDD, FDD, game, serial, parallel, and other I/O controllers.

IDE controllers are capable of working with two drives; you'll need another controller if you intend to pack your PC with more drives than that. And in 1995, computer makers began using an Enhanced IDE (EIDE) specification that brings even more speed for data transfer.

The top end of controllers and hard drives for PCs use the Small Computer System Interface (SCSI) specification. The SCSI specification has been around for quite some time, appearing in minicomputers and Apple Macintosh computers before arriving on the PC. SCSI (and its faster cousin SCSI-2) offer greater speed and the ability to "daisychain" as many as seven devices inside and outside of the PC. SCSI controllers can, in theory, work with CD-ROM drives as well as hard disks and controllers, but be forewarned: there are many different flavors of SCSI, including some proprietary versions that will only work with specific devices. Make certain that any peripherals you want to attach to a SCSI chain are compatible with the version you have; check with the manufacturer of the hardware to be sure.

The difference among the various drives lies in low-level formatting, which is taken care of by special software bundled with these drives.

Hard Cards

Hard cards were an interesting moment in the development of PCs. They are not at all exotic, except in the realm of packaging: they are a small 3.5-inch hard disk bolted onto a hard drive controller and attached to a plug-in card that fits into the computer's bus.

CHAPTER 9

Among its advantages were the fact that a hard card would fit into a machine that did not have an available drive bay, and the installation was considerably easier than the process of installing a controller card and snaking data and power cables to a new drive.

The disadvantages included the fact that the card—although it only plugged into one slot—was sometimes fat enough to block access to two or even more slots on the motherboard; the hard card also drew its electrical power from the bus rather than directly from the computer's power supply, which sometimes caused problems in under-powered systems.

The cards were designed to be logically relocatable (their memory address could be adjusted) and therefore they could coexist well with a machine that already had a regular hard disk controller. Getting the hard card to function as this second drive, however, required setting and resetting jumpers because often you didn't know the existing hard drive controller's I/O and ROM addresses. The hard card must use different I/O and ROM addresses. Making sure the addresses were unique to each controller could take some exasperating experimentation.

Hard cards served a very valid purpose when the owners of the first and second generation of PCs were upgrading their machines (which often came with puny 10 MB hard drives, or none at all). They don't serve much purpose with modern machines that often start with large hard drives and include extra drive bays.

If you have an early PC with two floppy disk drives, it may make sense to remove the second, 5.25-inch floppy drive, and install an additional hard drive in its place if you can still find one available.

Drive and Controller Recommendations

Today's leading hard drive manufacturers include Conner, Fujitsu, IBM, Maxtor, Micropolis, Quantum, Seagate, Western Digital, and others. Products from any one of these companies are all comparable and there is too much change for us to make a specific recommendation of brand. There are some things you can do, though, to try to assure you buy the most reliable and current technologies:

- Read reliability surveys and reviews in current computer magazines.

- Look at the ads for major mail order computer makers, including Gateway 2000, Dell, and Compaq, to see what brand of hard drives they are currently shipping with their systems. It is not in the interests of mass market sellers to ship hard drives that have a high failure rate.

- Buy the hard disk drive that is one step down from the latest "hot" model. This will almost always save you some money and also keeps you away from any unproven technology.

There is one supposed quantification of the expected life span of a hard disk, although we do not place much stock in it. It's called MTBF, which stands for Mean Time Between Failures. A better definition might be: "Maybe True But (Often) False."

The MTBF is presented in terms of hours, and a typical disk drive might have a listing of 40,000 or even 100,000 hours. Let's think about what either of those numbers is supposed to specify: a mean (average) time between failures of something like 4.5 to 11.4 years of continuous use. If you use your machine eight hours a day, five days a week, the equivalent times are 19.2 years or 48 years.

How in the world can a manufacturer in an industry rush to market with a hot new disk drive—at most a one- or two-year research and development project—and make a claim that a device should last 11.4 years? There is obviously no way for them to put a drive in a closet and run it for that long to see when or if it fails. Instead, drive makers follow two testing tracks: one is to put drives through an intense simulation of heavy use that exercises all of their parts over a few weeks or months; the second testing regime uses a computer model that looks at every nut, bolt, chip, and platter and calculates expected lifetime based on supposedly known reliability of the parts.

If you are purchasing a new hard disk controller to go along with the drive, consult dealers as well as the drive manufacturer for their recommendation. This is less of an issue if you are attaching to the built-in IDE controller that is part of the motherboard on many modern machines; you'll only need a new controller if that one has proven to be broken or if you need to step up to a higher-performance design such as a SCSI controller.

As far as we're concerned, the MTBF ratings are interesting if true, but much more important is how well the hard drive maker stands behind its product. If a drive has a supposed MTBF of 100,000 hours but is only warranted by the manufacturer for 90 days (2,160 hours at most) we don't have reason to believe that the maker has much faith in its own product. Look for drives with two- or three-year warranties; that's a reasonable period of use for a hard drive.

And when you receive your new drive, we recommend that you examine it carefully. Look at the date of manufacture, which is usually listed on a sticker on the drive; if it's more than a year old, you should be suspicious about the quality of the drive. And in some cases, disreputable repair shops or dealers have been known to try to pass off a remanufactured or returned drive as new.

Finally, make sure that a bad track table accompanies the drive. No drive is perfect, but low-level formatting locks out the bad tracks. The percentage of bad tracks should not exceed 5 percent of the total capacity of the drive.

See Chapter 19 for more information on safeguarding your hard disk data.

Internal vs. External Hard Disk Drives

The original Winchester hard drives were huge washing machine-sized boxes that sat outside the even larger computers they served. But with the advent of the personal computer, nearly all hard disk drives moved inside the PCs they were associated with. There are some circumstances, though, where you may want to consider adding an external hard drive to your system.

First of all, your PC may have no more available hard drive bays, or the design of the PC case may make it very inconvenient to squeeze an extra device into an open bay.

Or, you may have run out of available electrical power from your PC's power supply because of a large number of internal devices and cards.

Finally, you may want to create a somewhat portable powerhouse of a hard drive subsystem. For example, how's this for a project: a four-bay storage box based on a SCSI connection. One bay holds a 270 MB Syquest cartridge drive for backup of data, a second holds a 10X CD-ROM, a third bay is used for a 2.5 GB hard drive, and the fourth is presently held open for a DVD-ROM when the prices start to settle toward earth. Each SCSI device is linked to the others by a short cable, with the a single cable snaking back to the PC. The entire subsystem can be moved from one machine to another by changing just that one connector.

IDE Drives and Adapter Cards

How IDE Works

IDE (Integrated Drive Electronics) systems put most of the brains on the hard drive itself. The adapter (also called a *paddle card*) merely sends signals from the drive across the bus. The adapter, unlike ST506 or ESDI hard disk controllers, does no data encoding or decoding; that's done in the circuit board on the drive. The drive's electronics also take responsibility for control signals for the read/write heads on the disk.

At the heart of the definition of IDE is the concept of the independence of the drive from its PC host. IDE drives use special registers for commands from the PC; the drives themselves have address-decoding logic used to match bus signals to the drive. In this way, a PC designer can locate an IDE subsystem at any port or memory address with relative ease.

Because of the rapid increase in the number and types of IDE drives and in order to maintain compatibility with older drives and ROM BIOS chips, many modern machines will not have a drive type preconfigured in the BIOS that matches the IDE drive. If you want to use all the storage space available on your IDE drive you'll have to tell the CMOS Setup program that the IDE drive is a "user definable" drive type.

Though DOS software doesn't have a problem with these user-definable drive types, some network operating systems had problems with them when they were first introduced. The problem is mostly solved, but if you're planning to use an IDE drive in your network server, discuss all the issues with your drive vendor before purchasing the hard drive.

IBM's PS/2 systems will in most cases not work with a standard IDE subsystem; IBM has developed its own slightly different flavor of the specification.

Beyond IDE

The IDE standard has become the default interface for an entire generation of modern machines, beginning about the time of the arrival of the 486 chip and continuing into the Pentium era. However, the increased capacity of new hard drives as well as the demands for speed and space of multimedia software have quickly made IDE obsolete.

The original IDE standard was intended only to support hard drives, making it necessary to have an additional SCSI or proprietary interface in order to add a CD-ROM or other storage device. IDE was also limited to a maximum of 528 MB per drive, below the capacity of the new drives and beneath the abilities of SCSI.

The accompanying table shows a summary of IDE vs. SCSI capabilities.

IDE		SCSI	
Drive Types	− Hard Drives only	+ Hard Drives, CD-ROMs, other devices	
Drive Capacity	− 528 MB with original BIOS ROMs	+ 2 GB or more	
Transfer Rate	− 2—3 MB/second	− 5 or 10 MB/second	
Cable Length	− Maximum 18"	− Up to 6 meters	
Controller Price	+ Low price	− Higher price	
Ease of Configuration	+ Very easy	− Sometimes complex and tricky	

SCSI Disadvantages

SCSI does have some limitations, principally related to the complexity of configuration. SCSI requires device drivers for each operating system, operating environment, and hardware combination. And the ultimate performance of a SCSI system is very much affected by the quality of the drive/interface combination. In certain circumstances, a SCSI system can end up slower than an IDE package.

Hardware configuration requires that each device must be assigned a device identification number, and the last device in the SCSI chain must be set up as the termination device by changing a jumper or installing a special plug.

And finally, a SCSI device is more expensive to manufacture than an IDE equivalent because of the additional logic necessary on the controller and the SCSI device.

Enhanced IDE

Enter Enhanced IDE, an extension of the original standard.

The Enhanced IDE standard deals with most of the limitations of IDE. It includes support for:

- As many as four devices from one controller, with the addition of a second connector that allows two devices on each of two channels
- CD-ROMs and nondisk devices as well as hard disk drives. EIDE supports nondisk peripherals by using a new interface called ATA Packet Interface (ATAPI), a scheme that does not require the use of device drivers
- high-capacity disk drives, up to 8.4 GB in a single volume on a hard disk
- high-speed host transfers, beyond that of the ISA bus. This allows a device to take full advantage of a VL or PCI local bus with data throughput of up to 11.1 MB per second, which compares favorably with SCSI transfer rates of 10MB/sec

And, importantly, it retains compatibility with IDE devices.

	IDE	EIDE
Drive Types	− Hard Drives only	+ Hard Drives, CD—ROMs, other devices
Drive Capacity	− 528 MB with original BIOS ROMs	+ 8.4 GB or more
Transfer Rate	− 2-3 MB/second	+ 11.1 MB/second
Ease of Configuration	+ Very easy	+ Very easy

Interface Design	Maximum Theoretical Transfer Rate
ST-506	0.625 MB/second
ESDI	2.5 MB/second
IDE	2–3 MB/second
SCSI	10 MB/second
EIDE	11.1 MB/second
SCSI-2	Up to 80 MB/second

How to Test IDE Drives and Their Adapter Cards

In general, IDE drives either work or they don't.

If the drive won't read or write, and this is a new installation (or you have just been mucking around in the computer), recheck the drive jumpers and the cables. If the drive doesn't even spin up, you may have a bad power connection or you may have put the ribbon cable on upside down so that the red stripe is away from pin #1.

A common problem in IDE installation comes when users find that their newly installed drive appears to have only a fraction of the storage capacity they were promised. The problem lies in the computer's BIOS ROM or an incorrect CMOS setup, not the IDE drive itself. The computer tries to access as many logical sectors as the CMOS says there are in the drive. If you tell the computer there are fewer sectors in this IDE drive than actually exist, it will believe you and report a smaller drive (see the installation instructions below).

If you can read and write to your IDE drive, but it won't boot, check the standard DOS headaches. Do you have clean copies of **COMMAND.COM** and the DOS hidden files on your IDE drive? If you partitioned the drive, are you trying to boot from the active partition? Did you remember to make one of the partitions active? If you have two IDE drives in the system you must boot from the master drive, not the slave.

How to Install an IDE Adapter Card

Increasingly, modern machines are arriving with IDE circuitry built into the motherboard; all that is necessary is to connect a drive to the data port on the motherboard. If there is a problem with the IDE adapter on the motherboard or if you want to upgrade to a better system, you may need to disable the adapter using a jumper or switch; consult your PC's instruction manual or the manufacturer for details.

On other machines, it is necessary to install an IDE paddle card in the system bus. The directions follow.

Remove the Old Adapter Card

If you must remove an old IDE adapter, begin by examining the cables attached to the card. Mark them with tape or a soft marker, and take notes before you disconnect them so you will be able to reinstall them properly. On many machines, don't forget to mark and remove the little two-wire cable to the remote hard drive light on the front panel of your computer case. It pulls right off the controller card and will slide back onto the equivalent pins on the new card. Remove the screw holding the card to the rear of the computer chassis and pull the IDE paddle card straight up out of the bus connector.

If you are replacing a defective IDE circuit on the motherboard, consult your instruction manual to see if it must be disabled with a switch or jumper; some systems will automatically disable built-in circuitry if a new adapter is detected in the bus.

Examine the Adapter Board

Since IDE paddle boards are so simple, you would think all adapter boards would work with all IDE drives. Unfortunately, this is not true. Buy the adapter and drive together, or check with your vendor before replacing only one half of the set.

Install 16-bit adapters and their corresponding AT-interface drives in modern machines. Extra-fast EIDE adapters sometimes are installed in PCI local bus slots.

XT-style 8-bit adapter boards with a ROM on the paddle board go in older machines to drive XT-style IDE drives.

Insert the Board in Slot

Line up the adapter board edge connector with an appropriate slot on the motherboard. Press the paddle board down, then secure it to the back of the case with a screw. Plug in the cable as described below.

How to Install the IDE Cable

IDE cables, simple straight-through 40-pin cables with three identical connectors, are hard to install incorrectly because the cable ends are keyed. In addition, most controllers (and some drives) have a "1" stenciled next to the pin #1 end of the cable connector. The cable has a red or blue stripe along one edge. Put this edge toward pin #1 on the drive and the controller. If you are attaching to an IDE circuit on the motherboard, locate the IDE connector there.

Most IDE cables have three connectors. One attaches to the IDE paddle card, and the other two are available for connection to one or two IDE drives. It doesn't matter which data connector you use for each drive; the selection of a "master" or "slave" drive is made through the use of jumpers or switches on the drives themselves.

How to Install an IDE Drive

Choose the Right IDE Drive

If you are installing a new drive and controller package, your dealer should be offering a pair that work together; be sure to ask about compatibility if you have any questions. If you are adding a second IDE drive or are planning to replace only the drive, you must do a little research.

When IDE was first introduced, not all IDE drives would work with all adapters. That problem has been mostly fixed, but it still pays to consult dealers and manufacturers about compatibility of drives, adapters, and motherboards.

And not all IDE drives function properly in a computer when a second IDE drive has been installed. Switches on the IDE drive tell the drive if it is:

- The only drive installed in this computer
- One of two drives installed, and assigned as the first drive, or master
- One of two drives installed, and assigned as the second drive, or slave

As you might imagine, if you have two identical drives or two similar drives from the same manufacturer, the chance of difficulties is less.

If you are adding a second drive to your system, discuss the situation with your drive vendor. You want to end up with compatible drives, and be able to boot off the drive of your choice—not all drives can be slaves to another drive's master, or vice versa.

Remove the Old IDE Drive If Necessary

Remove the system cover. Study the 40-wire ribbon cable at the back of the hard disk and mark it with tape or a soft marker and make notes so that you'll be able to reinstall it properly. Disconnect the ribbon cable and the 4-wire power cord from the hard disk.

CHAPTER 9

It may be necessary to remove the PC's power supply and/or other components including other drives to gain access to the bay for a new hard drive; this is especially true with "space-saver" desktop PC cases.

Most modern machines use rails screwed to the side of the hard disk that allow the disk to slide in and out of the chassis like a drawer. Some such installations hold the disk in place with clips on the front of the chassis holding the hard disk. Remove the screws holding the clips in place or squeeze the spring-loaded clips and slide the hard disk out. Other drives are held in place by one or more screws on the sides of the drive. Save any rails, clips, or screws you remove; you will need them for the new hard disk.

Set Switches

Because IDE cables are straight-through with no differentiation between drives, you must set the switches on the drive itself to distinguish the first drive (called the *master*) from the second drive (the *slave*). Look for switches, too, to tell the master drive that it is the only drive in the computer or that there is a second drive, a slave drive, installed. Consult your instruction manual or call the manufacturer of the drive for assistance if necessary.

Slide in the Drive and Connect Cables

Slide the hard disk into the chassis. Most modern machines use rails to hold the hard disk in place, but some use screws to hold the drive in place.

Connect the 40-wire ribbon cable. Be sure to connect pin #1 on the ribbon cable to pin #1 on the hard drive. If you have two IDE hard disks in your system, they will share the ribbon cable.

Plug in a 4-wire power cable from the power supply. Note that the power supply cable connectors are not rectangular. Look at one carefully; two corners have been cut off on a diagonal. Examine the socket on the hard drive carefully and be sure to install the power connector correctly.

Install any screws that hold the drive into the chassis.

Use SETUP to Tell Your Computer About the Hard Disk

When you enter the SETUP program you'll see a list of supported hard disks, complete with number of cylinders and heads. This list was stored in the BIOS ROM when it was manufactured. It is unlikely that the exact IDE drive configuration that you have will be in this hard disk list, especially if the BIOS ROM was manufactured before 1990. Until then, computer manufacturers didn't think the IDE drive would become popular, so they omitted popular IDE drive configurations from the list of drives their ROM BIOS supported.

Many IDE drives wouldn't fit into any standard drive list anyway. They may, for example, break a cardinal rule of BIOS-supported hard disks by putting more sectors on the large outer tracks than on the small-diameter inner tracks. Luckily, the CMOS drive you select doesn't have to match the physical configuration of the IDE drive, just the logical configuration. Multiply heads times cylinders times sectors per track to get the total number of cylinders on a hard disk (this is the logical size). An 84 MB IDE drive with 6 heads, 832 cylinders, and 33 sectors per track would have 164,736 sectors. If you select a hard drive type from the BIOS list that contains the same 164,736 sectors (or fewer), the drive will work. It will work even if the drive you picked has 8 heads and 624 cylinders (a different physical configuration) because the IDE drive electronics translates your computer's instructions to read a particular logical sector (in the drive the computer believes is installed) to the actual head-and-cylinder situation in the IDE drive.

If you must choose among a limited list of drive types, pick one as close as possible to your actual IDE logical size (total number of sectors), but pick one a bit smaller rather than a hair too large. Newer BIOS ROMs now support a user-definable drive with user-defined cylinder and head counts. Thus you can easily match the logical size of your IDE drive to the logical size of your user-defined drive by picking an ordinary number of heads (like 8, for example) and an ordinary number of sectors per track (17, 39, or 53 are typical values) and calculating the oddball number of cylinders you need to make the total number of sectors on the drive less than or equal to the actual number of sectors on your IDE drive.

If you don't have a reasonable size match to choose from, and you don't have (or can't use) a user-definable drive type, it makes sense to get a newer BIOS rather than wasting a quarter or a third of your IDE drive's capacity by entering too small a drive in your computer's CMOS setup.

As we have noted, though, there have been some situations where network software may not run properly on user-definable drives. Check with your LAN supplier if you have any questions.

Format the IDE Drive

IDE drives are low-level formatted at the factory. You should not attempt to reinitialize them unless you are instructed to do so by a technician at the drive manufacturer—a very rare and somewhat complex assignment of last resort.

Use the **DOS FDISK** command to partition the drive. Here's a very simple job if you take the time to be careful and thoughtful in your actions; stop, read, re-read, and think before you issue a command. The designers of this utility have also built a few "are you sure?" stop points into the procedure.

Here is a typical FDISK screen:

CHAPTER 9

```
FDISK OPTIONS

Current fixed disk drive: 1

Choose one of the following:

Create DOS partition or Logical DOS Drive
Set active partition
Delete partition or Logical DOS Drive
Display partition information

Enter choice [1]
```

Now, reading this carefully should indicate to you that option 3 is a dangerous one to choose unless you really want to delete a partition (and all of its contents), and option 4 is just for information. To set up a new disk, you want option 1.

FDISK will then present the following further options:

```
Create Primary DOS Partition
Create Extended DOS Partition
Create Logical DOS Drive
```

If you are installing a large hard drive you may want to set up one Primary and one or more Extended partitions to subdivide the drive.

For full details on using FDISK, consult your DOS manual. You should also find assistance from the maker of your hard drive.

In any case, you should always try to work with the current version of DOS. If you are using an older version of DOS, you may want to use Disk Manager to partition this disk, since DOS versions below 4.01 limit each hard disk partition to 32 MB or less, which can make life unnecessarily complex for some users.

After the disk is partitioned, format the disk with the DOS **FORMAT** command. If you intend to boot from this drive, use the /S switch or the DOS command **SYS C:** to copy **COMMAND.COM** and the DOS hidden files to the boot partition. See details on these commands in your DOS manual.

SCSI Drives and Host Adapter Cards

The SCSI (Small Computer Systems Interface) bus is completely separate from the ISA, EISA, MCA, or PCI bus on your computer's motherboard. Unlike ST506, ESDI, and IDE drives, which all rely on the computer's ROM BIOS to send read/write directives, SCSI drives are autonomous. SCSI is also used for devices including CD-ROMs, scanners, removable hard drives, and more.

When the computer boots, it checks for additional hardware ROMs (the chips that tell your computer how to interact with each piece of oddball hardware). When your computer finds that a SCSI host adapter is installed, it doesn't discover any details about the SCSI equipment attached to the SCSI host adapter. You could have as many as seven hard disks, tape drives, Iomega Bernoulli drives, optical drives, or other SCSI devices out there, but the computer doesn't have a clue. (Most modern machines are capable of interacting with multiple SCSI adapters, each with its own set of seven devices.)

The SCSI host adapter card keeps track of data flow across the SCSI bus. Each SCSI item on the bus, whether host adapter card, hard disk, optical disk, or whatever needs a unique SCSI bus address, also called *SCSI address* or *SCSI target address*. (By convention, the host adapter card is SCSI device #7.)

Any two of these SCSI devices can converse on the SCSI bus, without help from your desktop computer or its microprocessor. In fact, two SCSI devices can converse without the desktop computer's knowledge.

The Nonstandard Standard

SCSI may be a standard, but some SCSI implementations are more standard than others. There is original SCSI, and then there is SCSI-2, with both Fast and Wide variants. Devices intended for the faster SCSI-2 implementation may not work reliably with the slower original, although it is possible to go the other way most of the time. The developing SCSI-3 standard is expected to be compatible with earlier SCSI and SCSI-2 drives as well as new devices.

Then there is "proprietary SCSI," which is often used for special devices such as scanners, some CD-ROMs, and certain specialized hard drives including some removable models. There is, for example, a whole class of sound cards that include a "SCSI" adapter on the board, but closer examination will show that this adapter will only work with certain devices. Buyer beware!

In addition, many computer makers have used proprietary extensions to the SCSI standard in the past, although this is less common now. Among companies that have gone out of their way to come up with their own versions of SCSI devices are Compaq and Apple. If you are saddled with a non-standard SCSI adapter you may be able to purchase special software which fools the computer into thinking you've installed a proprietary SCSI drive if you want to substitute a lower-priced generic SCSI for "the real thing."

Two solutions that will work in many solutions are CorelSCSI from Corel and EasySCSI from Adaptec. You may find one or the other of these utilities bundled with adapters; they are also available for purchase separately.

There are other areas where they haven't worked out all of the kinks yet: very few if any dinosaur PC motherboards can work with SCSI adapters, and some older AT-style motherboards don't function properly with fast, 16-bit SCSI adapters.

Check the instruction manual for your SCSI adapter, or better yet, call the manufacturer—before you buy the card to check on the pairing of the card—with your system's motherboard and with any disk drives and other devices you want to attach to it.

Not all SCSI devices use the same SCSI software command set to communicate on the SCSI bus. If you have two SCSI devices that cannot seem to get along, you may have to speak to both of the hardware manufacturers to find a common language. In theory, the new SCSI 2-standard will take care of this problem.

The Windows 95 Solution

In theory, the combination of Windows 95 and a Plug-and-Play (PnP) motherboard should eliminate configuration problems. Be sure to include a PnP SCSI controller and hard drives that support PnP; such drives are sometimes called SCAM (SCSI Configured Automatically) devices. Is it a scam? No, but it is not perfect. You'll still need to understand the nature of your system and how its components work together.

How to Test SCSI Drives and Host Adapter Cards

You can connect as many as seven devices to a SCSI adapter. SCSI devices usually use a thick 50-wire cable.

Each SCSI device has two ports. One is used for incoming signals and the other for an outgoing cable to the next device in an electronic daisychain.

One important element of a SCSI system is that the two ends of the daisy chain have to be *terminated* to tell the adapter where the chain ends. Most devices use a special terminator plug, which fits into the SCSI output port; some units have switches or jumpers that can be set to terminate a port.

If your SCSI adapter is at the end of the chain—if only one outgoing cable is attached to it—the adapter itself must be terminated. If the adapter is in the middle of the chain, the devices at each end need to be terminated.

SCSI devices can do a bit of their own diagnostic work and report on errors using one of a set of messages sanctified by the American National Standards Institute (ANSI). That's the good news; the bad news is that, like the SCSI standard itself, not all of the codes are as standardized as they might be.

Consult the instruction manual that comes with your SCSI adapter for the details on the error codes used by your device.

Check to see that a modern machine's Setup CMOS indicates that a hard drive is not installed.

Poorly shielded SCSI cables can cause data corruption, or even prevent the computer from booting off the SCSI drive.

If the SCSI device won't read or write at all, check for proper installation, especially if you have just been working inside the computer. Perhaps you knocked a cable loose. If you have just added a new piece of equipment, make sure that it has not been given the same SCSI bus address as another device.

If you can read and write to your SCSI drive but it won't boot, check for the usual DOS problems. Do you have clean copies of **COMMAND.COM** and the DOS hidden files on your SCSI drive? If you partitioned the drive, are you trying to boot from the active partition? You did, of course, remember to make one of the partitions active?

How to Install a SCSI Host Adapter Card

CHAPTER 9

Remove an Old SCSI Adapter

If you must remove a defective SCSI adapter, begin by examining the cables attached to the card. Mark them with tape or a soft marker and take notes before you disconnect them so you will be able to reinstall them properly. On many machines, don't forget to mark and remove the little two-wire cable to the remote hard drive light on the front panel of your computer case. It pulls right off the controller card and will slide back onto the equivalent pins on the new card. Remove the screw holding the card to the rear of the computer chassis. Then pull the card straight up out of the bus connector.

Set Switches or Jumpers

The new adapter card may be set up ready to work with your system straight out of the box, but to be on the safe side read the manufacturer's installation instructions. One instance where you are certain to need a switch change is if you have another SCSI device that insists on being device #7, which is the default SCSI bus address for the host adapter card.

Check Termination

The SCSI bus must be terminated in two places: at the far ends of the SCSI cable. Each manufacturer uses its own termination technique. Read the installation booklet for your particular SCSI device or host adapter card.

Although there is no hard and fast rule, in general most SCSI adapters come with a terminator installed; this is because of an assumption that the board will be used with internal SCSI devices such as hard drives and some CD-ROMs. The host adapter (one end of the bus) is terminated, and you can terminate the last drive on the internal SCSI cable.

You can also leave the terminator in place on the adapter if you install only external SCSI devices; again, the adapter is one end of the bus and the last external device is given a terminator to end the bus there.

If you have one or more internal SCSI devices and decide to add an external device as well (a backup hard drive, CD-ROM, or scanner, perhaps) you'll have to take the terminator off the SCSI host adapter card because it is now in the middle of the bus. One terminator should be on the last internal device and the other terminator on the last external SCSI unit.

Install the SCSI Host Adapter Card

Press the card firmly down into a slot on the motherboard. Install the screw that holds the card in place. On modern machines (in general, the only type of device that can work with a SCSI bus) run the setup program, and indicate for the SCSI chain that a hard drive is not installed. If you're adding a second SCSI drive or replacing both your hard disk and controller, see "How to Install an SCSI Drive" below.

If you have an EISA computer, use the EISA configuration utility to tell your computer about the SCSI card.

How to Install the SCSI Cable

SCSI uses a straight-through 50-wire ribbon cable for SCSI devices mounted internally within a computer. External SCSI drives and the external connector on the back of a SCSI host adapter card use either a 25-pin connector that looks a lot like the parallel printer port on the back of your computer, or a 50-pin Amphenol connector that looks like a longer version of the Centronics cable connector on the back of a parallel printer. The external cables are designed so that they cannot be installed upside down or backward.

The internal SCSI cable is usually gray or multicolored. Gray cables ordinarily have a red or blue line along one edge to identify pin #1 of the cable connector; multicolored cables have a brown wire for pin #1. You must find pin #1 on your SCSI adapter, then install the cable with the #1 wire going to pin #1.

The manufacturer may have marked pin #1 on the adapter itself. You may be able to find a drawing with the location of pin #1 in the instruction manual for your SCSI adapter. If you have any doubts, call the card maker to be sure you install the cable and adapter properly. Installing the cable backward can blow a fuse in the drive or cause other damage when you turn on the power.

How to Install a SCSI Drive

Remove Old SCSI Drive if Necessary

Remove the system cover. Examine the ribbon cable on the back of the hard disk, noting the red-marked edge which should face toward pin #1 on the drive. Use tape or a soft marker to mark the cables, and take notes to help with reinstallation. Disconnect the ribbon cable and the 4-wire power cord from the hard disk.

It may be necessary to remove the PC's power supply and/or other components, including other drives, to gain access to the bay for a new hard drive; this is especially true with "space-saver" desktop PC cases.

Most modern machines use rails screwed to the side of the hard disk that allow the disk to slide in and out of the chassis like a drawer. Some such installations hold the disk in place with clips on the front of the chassis holding the hard disk. Remove the screws holding the clips in place or squeeze the spring-loaded clips and slide the hard disk out. Other drives are held in place by one or more screws on the sides of the drive. Save any rails, clips, or screws you remove; you will need them for the new hard disk.

CHAPTER 9

Set Switches or Jumpers

In some ways, the SCSI bus is like a small local area network (LAN) with many individual computers speaking to each other over a shared bus. As with LANs, each device on the SCSI bus must have its own device number (its own bus address).

Device #7 is traditionally reserved for the SCSI host adapter card. You may pick any unused address for your hard disk. Just make certain that your host adapter card hasn't reserved special relationships with particular SCSI bus address numbers. The popular Adaptec 1542, for example, treats devices 0 and 1 differently than all the rest. As a result, you might run into difficulty if you set a particular drive to device 0. Read your SCSI adapter installation manual; it will reveal the idiosyncrasies of your particular controller. Insist on installation instructions with every card you buy, and read them.

Check for Correct Termination

See the "Check termination" section in "How To Install SCSI Host Adapter Card," above.

Slide in the Drive and Connect Cables

Most modern machines use rails (flat bars screwed onto the side of the hard disk) to hold the hard disk in place. If your computer requires rails, install them on the SCSI drive and slide it back into the chassis.

Connect the ribbon cable. Be sure to connect pin #1 on each ribbon cable to pin #1 on the hard drive. Plug in a 4-wire power cable from the power supply. Note that the power supply cable connectors are not rectangular. Look at one carefully: two corners have been cut off on a diagonal. Examine the socket on the hard drive carefully and be sure to install the power connector correctly.

Install screws to hold the drive into the chassis.

Format SCSI Drive

SCSI drives are already low-level formatted at the factory, so that they do not have to be initialized like the old ST506 drives did. However, SCSI drives do have to be partitioned with the DOS **FDISK** command, then formatted with the DOS **FORMAT** command. Directions for these commands can be found in your DOS manual. (If you are using an older version of DOS, here is another place where it makes a lot of sense to upgrade to DOS 6.0 or later, since current operating systems handle large disks more gracefully.)

Dinosaur PCs: ST506 MFM and RLL Drives and Hard Disk Controller Cards

An ST506 hard drive must match the controller card. Since ST506 is not a particularly sophisticated interface, the ST506 hard disk and controller rely upon DOS for explicit "read here" or "write there" directions. Therefore, you must tell DOS how many heads and how many cylinders are in the hard drive you have installed. All these relationships (computer to controller, controller to cable, cable to hard drive, hard drive to controller, and DOS to hard drive) must be set up right, or the drive won't work.

How ST506 (MFM or RLL) Hard Drives and Controllers Work

Under the ST506 interface standard, the hard disk does none of the heavy thinking involved in data recording. The hard disk controller follows instructions from DOS to tell the drive where to move the read/write heads, when to write, and when to read. The hard disk merely follows the controller's directions.

The ST506 hard disk controller mediates between DOS and one or two hard drives. DOS decides what information should be recorded and exactly where it should go on the platters, demanding a read/write action at a particular sector and track on the hard disk. The controller translates these instructions into electrical signals to the stepper motor, which moves the heads inside the hard drive.

Many modern machines use combination floppy and hard drive controller cards. Early PCs almost always use two separate cards. In either case, the floppy and hard drive controller circuitry is independent, so that one system might fail while the other continues to work properly. The microprocessor sends an I/O write signal down the bus, along with the address that tells the memory location of the hard disk controller.

Next, DOS sends the where-to-write instruction. DOS keeps track of the information on the hard disk. It knows what file has been recorded where, which sectors are empty and available to store information, and which sectors on the hard disk are locked out because they are not suitable for safe data storage. Then DOS requests a read/write operation by track and sector number. It tells the hard disk where (to what track) to move the head assembly and what sector on the track should be used to store the upcoming data.

Finally, DOS sends the data it wants to record.

Various housekeeping bits—clock bits and error correction code bits, for example—must be added. The hard disk controller is responsible for packaging (encoding) the data before the hard disk records it. When the data is read back, everything recorded on the hard disk is sent to the hard disk controller. Data separation circuits, located on the controller, sort out this raw information, discard the housekeeping bits, and send a clean stream of stored data back to the microprocessor through the bus.

There are two popular ways to package information on ST506 hard disks: Modified Frequency Modulation (MFM) and 2,7 Run Length Limited (RLL) encoding. MFM encoding uses 17 sectors per track, and the magnetic marks on the hard disk are spaced relatively far apart. 2,7 RLL data encoding uses 26 sectors per track and packs many more magnetic marks on each track, so that an extremely precise hard disk is required. (Faster and higher-capacity drives including ESDI, SCSI, and IDE devices use newer versions of RLL encoding that compress the data tighter than 2,7 RLL does and allow far more sectors per track.)

How to Test an ST506 Hard Disk and Controller

Occasionally, a hard disk will break down and make so much noise while self-destructing that there is no doubt that the hard disk, and only the hard disk, is causing the malfunction. This noise usually starts out as a scraping, squeaking sound and eventually gets much louder. If hard disk 0 is fine, but hard disk 1 is noisy and is beginning to get louder and to exhibit read/write errors, then it makes sense to replace only hard disk 1.

Unfortunately, most troubleshooting situations are not so clear. Typically a malfunctioning hard disk fails silently. In this case, it's hard to tell whether the hard disk itself is causing the problem.

Neither hard disk nor hard disk controller can be tested alone. We test these devices by seeing how well they do their jobs, and both must be installed before either will do any work at all. Therefore, substituting a known good hard disk or a known good controller, then observing if the symptom is gone, is the ideal way to determine which part is failing. This substitution technique has some limitations. First of all, hard drives are relatively expensive and not many users have extra ones lying around on the shelf. Secondly, in some rare instances, a bad part can kill the good test part you've just swapped into the machine.

Despite these limitations, some troubleshooting suggestions follow:

- Remove the system cover. Ground your body and turn the machine on, taking care not to touch any internal part of the computer unnecessarily. First check that the hard disk platters are spinning when the power is on; put your hand on top of the hard disk to check.

- If you have any doubts about the power connection to the disk drive, you can test the connector with a voltmeter; you're looking for +5 and +12 volts. If you have any doubts about your understanding of how to use a voltmeter or about the internal parts of your machine, we suggest you leave this test to a technician.

- You can usually find one or more unused power connectors in a modern machine; you can substitute a different connector to rule out the possibility of a shorted or cut wire.

- If the power connector carries voltage but the drive does not spin up when power is applied, the drive needs to be replaced.

- If the hard disk does spin when connected to power, check the ribbon cables running between the disk and the disk controller. These cables should be connected snugly to the pins on the controller card and to the flat-edge connectors on the back of the hard drive.

- If this is a new installation, or if any other work has been conducted on the machine recently, double-check the cables, looking for a backward connection or a floppy drive cable mistakenly installed on the hard disk. If it's a new installation, you should also recheck the configuration of the jumpers on both the drive and the controller. Faulty installation, rather than bad parts, is likely to be the problem, even though the error message on your screen is an intimidating **Error Reading Fixed Disk**, **Hard Disk Failure**, or **HDD Controller Failure**.

- If the hard disk won't boot, try booting from a floppy disk instead. Check to see if you can read some or all of the data on the hard disk. If you can read data, it probably means that the hard disk and its hard disk controller are okay. A likely cause is damage to the information in the boot sector of the drive, perhaps caused by a voltage spike or other transient problem. Recopy **COMMAND.COM** and the two DOS hidden files (using the DOS command **SYS**), and then retest.

- We recommend that you install and use the most current version of DOS. Use **FDISK** to examine the drive partition setup. Did you forget to make one of the partitions active?

- If the hard disk still won't boot, or it boots but is beginning to produce read or write errors, consider using a hard disk analysis and maintenance program. We've described this type of maintenance program in Chapter 2.

If none of the suggestions discussed solves your problem, you may have to reformat the drive in order to restore it to working order. You do maintain current backups of all of your critical data, right? Before you reformat, however, read Chapter 6 carefully to make sure you haven't missed any tricks. Once you low-level format the hard disk, your data is gone.

See "Early PCs: How to Format a Hard Disk with the ST506 Interface," or "Modern Machines: How to Format a Hard Disk with the ST506 Interface," for directions on formatting.

If the computer won't format the hard disk, you'll have to replace both the hard disk and the controller. We do not recommend replacing only one unit, since a malfunctioning controller can burn out a good hard disk. It's better to replace both than to guess wrong, blow up the new disk, and end up buying two hard disks and a controller. If you absolutely need to try the cheapest solution, replace the controller first, then the hard disk.

How to Install an ST506 Hard Disk Controller

Remove the Old Controller Card If Necessary

Examine the cables connected to the card. Mark them with tape or a soft marker, and take notes so you will be able to properly reinstall them. Remove the screw holding the card to the rear of the computer chassis, and pull the card straight up out of the bus connector.

CHAPTER 9

Choose the Right Controller

Before you install a hard disk controller, you should be familiar with the differences among the various types of controllers. One major division is 8-bit versus 16-bit cards.

8-bit cards are for dinosaur PCs and have the short, single bus connector. These 8-bit controller cards usually regulate only hard disks. Typical 16-bit controller cards used in modern machines, by comparison, manage both the hard and the floppy drives. These dual-purpose controller cards are designed with two separate sets of circuits; they just share a single card and use only one card slot.

As dinosaur PC/XT computers near extinction, it may be difficult to find replacement 8-bit controller cards. If you cannot find a new card, you may have to purchase a used controller from a computer dealer; be sure to have the dealer test and certify the device before you try it in your machine.

The other major division among the various types of hard disk controllers is the data coding scheme, something that is built right into the hardware. Both 8-bit and 16-bit cards come in MFM and RLL designs, hard-wired to follow one or the other data encoding scheme. They cannot be reconfigured or adjusted to use a different data packaging technique.

The hard disk should be certified for the chosen controller's data packaging method. Whatever data encoding scheme you choose, use a matched set of hard disk and hard disk controller. Don't connect an RLL controller to an MFM-type hard disk. The combination may appear to work for the first couple of weeks, but then will rapidly start losing data.

On the other hand, an RLL-certified hard disk will work fine with an MFM controller, but the extra quality in the hard disk will be wasted because it is under utilized to record data in the MFM format.

Dinosaur PCs: Set Switches on XT Controllers

Eight-bit early controller cards have jumpers or dip switches to tell the controller and DOS what kind of hard disks are attached. Consult the controller manual to learn how to set these jumpers; on early machines there are typically about a dozen hard disk options. These include 4 heads and 306 cylinders, 4 heads and 615 cylinders, 2 heads and 612 cylinders, and so on. Use the option for your particular hard disk if it's listed. If you have a nonstandard hard disk, choose an option slightly smaller than the actual size of the hard disk. For instance, you can approximate a hard disk with 5 heads and 620 cylinders by setting the controller for 4 heads and 615 cylinders. Some of the hard disk area (the part accessed by the fifth head and the innermost tracks) won't be used, but no read/write problems will result. Of course, buying a new controller—one that's able to manage 5 heads and 640 cylinders—would allow you to have access to the full storage capacity of your hard disk. Either solution works fine technically, so it's mostly a question of economics. If you don't know how many heads and cylinders your hard disk has, call the drive vendor's technical department and ask.

Modern Machines: Run the SETUP Program

Modern machine controller cards do not have jumpers to configure them to work with different hard disks; the information is instead stored on the motherboard in the CMOS chip. Run the SETUP program once you've installed the card, and choose an appropriate hard disk type from the list in the motherboard ROM BIOS. Choose a drive type smaller than the actual hard drive if the choices in the Setup program don't match your hard disk perfectly. Newer ROM BIOS versions have more drive types to choose from, so consider upgrading your old BIOS ROM if your drive or something close isn't listed. Your computer manufacturer's technical support department will know what new BIOS versions are available and whether a new BIOS will help here.

Put the Card in the Slot

Press the card into a slot on the motherboard. Install the screw that holds the card in place.

Format the Hard Disk

Unless you have replaced a bad controller with the identical hard disk controller, you'll have to reformat the hard disk so this new controller and the hard disk can talk to each other. You will need to low-level format the drive, run **FDISK**, then high-level format the drive. This three-step process is covered in "Dinosaur PCs: How to Format a Hard Disk with the ST506 Interface," and "Modern Machines: How to Format a Hard Disk with the ST506 Interface," both above.

If you're adding a drive or replacing your present hard disk and controller, see "How to Install an MFM or RLL Hard Disk with the ST506 Interface," below, for tips about drive select jumpers and terminating resistors.

How to Install Cables for ST506 (and ESDI) Drives

A separate 20-wire ribbon data cable goes from the controller to each hard drive. The red or blue edge of the cable is for pin #1. On the controller card find the number 1 (usually stenciled next to the data cable connector pins). Hard disks have flat card-edge connectors, with a notch cut close to the pin #1 end of the connector. Put the colored edge of the data cable toward the slot when connecting the cable to the hard disk.

All the hard disks share a single controller cable. It's a wide 34-wire ribbon cable. Pay attention to the red/blue edge, so that the cable will mate correctly to pin #1 at each connection. Hard disk 0 (DOS calls it Drive C) is at the end of this controller cable. The middle connector attaches to the second hard disk (if there is one). If you have only one drive and a short, straight-through ribbon cable with only two connectors, put one connector on the hard disk and the other on the controller card, making sure you put the color-coded edge toward pin #1 at each connector.

The examples in Figures 9.10 to 9.13 should make this clear.

CHAPTER 9

On 16-bit (AT-style) controller cards in modern machines, you'll also need to attach the floppy drive controller cable. Luckily, most of these cards have "to floppy drive" stenciled on the card at the appropriate connector pins; if you have any doubt, consult the instruction manual or call the manufacturer. Since both floppy cable and hard disk controller cable have 34 wires, it is possible to mix them up. Be sure you have the floppy cable on the floppy connector and the hard disk cable on the hard disk connector.

FIGURE 9.10 Modern IDE hard drives require a power source and a data cable. Most drives are supplied set up to be the primary drive on a cable; to add a second hard drive on the same IDE chain you will most likely have to move a plug on a connecting block on the back of the drive. Study the hard drive's instruction manual and make settings before installing the drive.

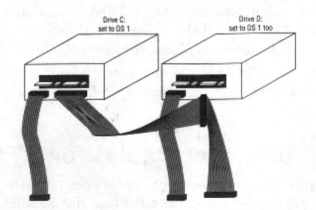

Figure 9.11 Cable routing for two ST506 (MFM or RLL) or ESDI drives. Note the cable twist at drive C. Both drives should be set to DS1. Use a separate 20-wire cable for each drive.

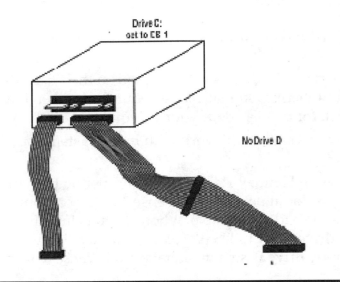

Figure 9.12 A single ST506 or ESDI hard drive with a 20-pin data cable and a 34-pin control cable. Because the control cable has a twist, set the drive to DS1.

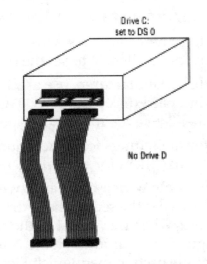

Figure 9.13 A single ST506 or ESDI drive with a 20 pin data cable and a 34-pin control cable. If the cable does not have a twist (as shown above), set the drive to DS0.

How to Install an MFM or RLL Hard Disk with the ST506 Interface (Also for ESDI Drives.)

Remove the Old Hard Disk If Necessary

Remove the system unit cover. Examine the two ribbon cables at the back of the hard disk, marking them with tape or a soft marker and taking notes for reinstallation. Then disconnect them and the four-wire power cord from the hard disk.

Remove the screws holding the hard disk to the chassis. Early PC/XT computers usually have screws threaded into the side of the hard disk. There may also be a screw or two that is accessible though holes in the bottom of the computer chassis. Many modern machines use rails screwed to the side of the hard disk, allowing the drive to slide in and out of the chassis like a drawer. To remove a 286 or 386 hard disk, look for clips on the front of the chassis. Remove the screws holding the clips in place or squeeze the clips to release them, then slide the hard disk out. On other systems you may have to remove screws. Save the rails, clips, and screws; you will need them for the new hard disk.

Set Switches/Jumpers on the New Drive

Before you install a new hard disk, you must set the *drive select* (DS) and *terminating resistor*. Hard drives have jumpers (or, occasionally, dip switches) to set the drive select number.

Some hard disk manufacturers use a 0, 1, 2, 3 numbering system for the drive select jumpers on their hard disks. In this case, the first hard disk is number 0. Others use 1, 2, 3, 4 numbering, so that the first unit is number 1, and the second is number 2. See the manual shipped with your hard disk for details about your drive.

Check also for the settings for various jumpers; the example we give here will work with many systems but not all. Be sure to customize them for your particular setup.

If you have a cable with a twist and two hard drives as shown in Figure 9.11, set the DS jumper on both drives to show that each drive is the second hard drive in the computer. This doesn't make much sense, but the computer won't confuse the drives when they're set to the same DS. The twist at the end of the cable, where it plugs into the C drive, flips the DS signals back around so the controller thinks the C drive is set to DS 0. Arcane, isn't it? However, this is the same technique used to distinguish Floppy Drive A from floppy drive B, so it must have made sense to somebody at some point.

If you have a cable with a twist and only one hard drive as shown in Figure 9.12, set the DS jumper on this drive to make it the second hard drive in the computer. The twist at the end of the cable, where it plugs into the C drive, flips the DS signals back around so the controller thinks the C drive is set to DS 0. Don't try setting the drive to 0 and using the straight-through connector in the middle of the cable. Though it sounds plausible, you'd end up with a pigtail of cable (the end with the twist) not connected to anything, which would make weird electronic echoes on the cable whenever the drive and controller tried to talk to each other.

If you have one drive and a straight-through cable as shown in Figure 9.13, things are a bit more complicated. Clone makers save money when they install a straight-through, one hard drive only, controller cable on single-drive systems. If you have this cheaper controller cable (with one connector on each end, no third connector, and no twist in the middle), set up the hard drive as if it were the first (and only) drive in the computer system. Set the drive select jumper on the first set of pins—not the second.

If you have two drives and a straight-through cable as shown in Figure 9.14, we may have a problem: such a combination is not supposed to happen. Please recheck your system. Did you mistakenly identify an IDE or SCSI cable as an ST506 or ESDI cable? If there's no mistake, set the first hard disk to DS0 (set the drive select jumper on the first set of pins—not the second). Then set the second drive to DS1 (the jumper on the second set of pins). Shrug your shoulders and go on. It's weird, but it should work fine. If it doesn't, you'll have to have a heart-to-heart talk with the maker of your drive or controller or both.

Check Terminating Resistors

The first drive (the drive at the end of the hard drive controller cable) should have a terminating resistor (see Figure 9.9 shown previously). Any second hard drive, if installed, should not have a resistor in place. Look for the terminating resistor in a socket on the bottom of the hard drive. Since very few hard disk components are socketed, it should be easy to identify a terminator.

If necessary, remove the terminating resistor from your second drive with your fingers or by sliding a small screwdriver between the resistor and the socket.

Be sure to use a terminating resistor on the drive at the end of the controller cable, but not on the drive in the middle of the controller cable.

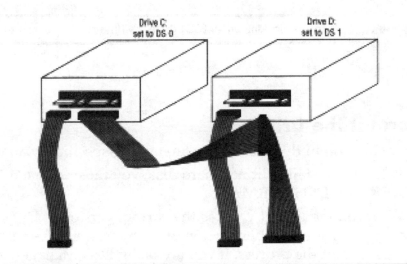

Figure 9.14 Two ST506 or ESDI hard drives connected with a 34-pin control cable with no twist at the C drive. Set Drive C to DS0 and drive D to DS1. Use separate 20-wire data control cables for each drive.

Slide in the Drive and Connect Cables

After you configure the hard disk, slide it into the chassis. Most modern machines use rails to hold the hard disk in place. If your computer requires rails, install them on the hard disk and slide it back into the chassis, following instructions in the drive's manual.

Connect the two ribbon cables to the flat edge connectors on the back of the hard disk. Be sure to connect pin number 1 on each ribbon cable to pin number 1 on the hard drive. The red (or sometimes blue) edge of the cable is the number 1 end. The gold-colored hard drive edge connectors have a notch cut into the connector on one end. The end with the notch has pin #1, so put the red edge on the ribbon cable toward the notch.

If you have two hard disks in your system, they will share the 34-wire hard disk controller cable, but each disk will have its own 20-wire data cable.

Once you've connected the ribbon cables, plug in any four-wire power cable from the power supply. Note that the power supply cable connectors are not rectangular. Look at one carefully; two corners have been cut off on a diagonal. Examine the socket on the hard drive carefully and be sure to install the power connector correctly. Then install screws to hold the drive into the chassis.

N O T E

If you're working on an ESDI drive, it's time to jump ahead to Step 5 of the ESDI formatting instructions.

Format the Drive

From here on in this section, we are talking specifically about ST506 drives.

After you install your new hard disk, you must format it. There are three steps in this process: low-level formatting, **FDISK**, and DOS **FORMAT**.

We recommend that you use the current version of DOS, which helps with the formatting process for disks of any size. If you have an older version of DOS, version 3.3 or earlier, you can use a program called Disk Manager to automate much of the process. If you are using Disk Manager, follow the directions that come with the program disk.

If you want to format your hard disk manually, read the directions in either "Early PCs: How to Format a Hard Disk with the ST506 Interface," or "Modern Machines: How to Format a Hard Disk with the ST506 Interface."

Dinosaur PCs: How to Format a Hard Disk with the ST506 Interface

How to Manually Format an XT Clone Hard Disk

Formatting a hard disk manually involves three steps: low-level formatting, **FDISK**, and high-level formatting. Remember: don't try this at home on anything but a dinosaur PC ST506 drive. The ESDI, IDE, EIDE, and SCSI drives should not ordinarily be low-level formatted by an end user.

Step 1: Low-Level Formatting

A dinosaur PC motherboard knows nothing about hard disk hardware. Modern machines, on the other hand, are engineered quite differently.

Within an XT, all hard disk physical control is supervised by the hard disk controller ROM, not the CPU or the clone's ROM BIOS. Low-level formatting examines the hard disk for bad spots, locks out the bad spots so that they cannot be written to, and writes the sector address marks on the hard disk. In other words, it is the most hardware-specific, preliminary level of hard disk preparation.

The details of low-level formatting are completely dependent on the hard disk controller. For this reason, the low-level formatting program is stored in the hard disk controller ROM. You can access the ROM format routine with the **DEBUG** command that is part of DOS. To do this, type:

```
DEBUG        <Enter>
g=c800:5     <Enter>
```

You may have to substitute a different address for the "c:800:5" in the example above; consult the instruction manual for the hard drive controller. (G=c800:5 means jump to the address c800:5 and follow the instructions at that address.)

Most hard disk controller ROMs have the low-level formatting utility at the address c800:5; but a few use other locations, including but not limited to C800:6 and c800:ccc.

A careful technician insists upon documentation whenever a new hard disk controller is presented, but one of these three addresses will usually work. You'll know right away if you have picked an incorrect address; the screen will be full of gibberish.

The instruction manual should also offer the drive's specifications and many of the answers to the questions posed by the low-level formatter.

Entering the correct address produces a screen of English language questions—not necessarily intelligible questions, just English. When faced with these controller questions, keep your wits about you. Those controllers that require answers in hexadecimal numbers will say so; don't worry, most don't. Some controllers use a 0, 1, 2, 3 numbering system for the hard disks. In this case the first hard disk (usually drive C) is number 0. Others use 1, 2, 3, 4 numbering, so the first unit is number 1 and the second is number 2.

When you're prompted to input an interleave factor, enter 3 for an early PC. You'll be prompted to enter a write precompensation cylinder factor. If you have no documentation with the drive you'll have to guess—one-half of the total number of cylinders is a reasonable rule of thumb. Both *interleave* and write *precompensation* are listed in the Glossary if you want more details.

Most Western Digital XT hard disk controllers will display a screen query asking, "Are you dynamically configuring the drive?" A "No" response means "Don't ask me any questions, just follow the jumpers on the card." A "Yes" response allows you to answer detailed questions about the hard disk design—in other words, to customize the installation. Unfortunately, some Western Digital XT controllers ask this question, then ignore your answers, and proceed to format the hard drive according to its switch and jumper settings. To ensure that your card is set up the way you want it, find out the correct jumper settings for your model of hard disk and physically configure the card correctly before you install it.

If you have to "dynamically configure" the drive, here are some hints. *Landing zone* is the track where the drive will park the head when you run a disk park program before moving the computer; this is a feature of older drives. When you're prompted for a landing zone, enter a track number equal to the number of tracks on the hard disk plus one. If absolutely no outside guidance is available about any of these questions, try using the defaults in the controller's low-level format program. They won't hurt anything and might work out well.

Often the low-level format program prompts you for a list of known-bad areas. Check the top of your hard disk for a bad track label. It is important to enter all these bad tracks. The tests done by the hard disk manufacturer are more rigorous than those done by the low-level formatting program. Some tracks that failed at the factory, after long testing, might slip through the low-level formatting program's tests, get recorded on, and eventually lose your files.

When you have answered all the questions and pressed the final carriage return, the formatting routine starts working. As the head assembly moves from cylinder to cylinder, it makes a rhythmic ticking sound. It will take a few minutes, since the entire hard disk surface area must be scanned for defects. Ten to twenty minutes is not an unusually long low-level format time for a 40 MB disk. Larger disks will, of course, take longer.

Step 2: FDISK Formatting

The second step of the hard disk formatting process uses the **FDISK** utility of DOS to prepare one or more DOS partitions (areas on the hard disk suitable for DOS files). This is a very quick process, taking about 30 seconds per partition. Up to four partitions per drive are allowed.

Unlike low-level formatting, **FDISK** is software-dependent. The low-level format program is stored inside the hard disk controller ROM, so that changing controllers changes the screen messages and low-level format process. By comparison, **FDISK** is a DOS utility. Changing DOS versions changes the **FDISK** screen messages and, to some extent the **FDISK** process, but changing the hard disk controller doesn't affect **FDISK** at all.

DOS versions below 2.0 are unable to deal with hard disks at all. A few DOS versions above 2.0 are limited to 20 MB hard disks, but DOS versions 2.0 to 3.2 can partition a hard drive as large as 32 MB. MS-DOS 3.3 can partition larger drives, but each partition is limited to a maximum size of 32 MB. MS-DOS versions 4.01 and above allow partitions of any size. Hard disk control programs like Disk Manager are designed to transcend the hard disk limitations imposed by older DOS versions.

Disk Manager provides a device driver that contains a software interface between DOS and the physical hard disk controller. When DOS looks at the device driver, it believes there is a second physical hard disk inside the computer. It addresses the hard disk, through the device driver, and receives appropriate responses from drive D.

In any case, we recommend that you upgrade to the current version of DOS, which is 6.22 (or the phantom 7.0 that lies beneath Windows 95) as this book goes to press.

Step 3: High-Level Formatting

High-level formatting (**FORMAT C:/S**) is covered in any DOS manual. Remember, if you've decided to partition your hard drive into two or more logical drives, you'll have to format each logical drive individually before writing data to it.

On DOS versions through 3.2, be sure to put the DOS system files (the two hidden files plus **COMMAND.COM**) on the first partition. That's the only place DOS looks for boot files. MS-DOS versions 3.3 and above allow you to specify an active partition, the one the computer will boot from. This active partition need not be the first partition. Of course, it must have the DOS system files installed.

High-level formatting is another slow process. Allow 3–5 minutes for a 20 MB drive; the computer must examine each track for bad sectors. A typical screen message displays cylinder number after cylinder number as each one is completed. Some DOS **FORMAT** programs then count back up through the cylinder numbers a second time before declaring the formatting complete.

How to Use Disk Manager to Format an XT Clone Hard Disk

It's not easy for the casual user to format an ST506 disk at installation, or during a recommended reformat for maintenance purposes. Even technicians who format many hard disks each week find manual formatting a big hassle. Disk Manager, a semi-automated hard disk format program, can help here.

Modern Machines: How to Format a Hard Disk with the ST506 Interface

Disk Manager, a semi-automated hard disk format program, can perform this work for you.

How to Manually Format a Modern Machine's Hard Disk with ST506 Interface

Formatting a hard disk manually involves three steps: low-level formatting, **FDISK**, and high-level formatting (**FORMAT C:/S**).

Step 1: Low-Level Formatting

Modern machines were designed in the age of hard disks; hard disk control functions were designed right into the motherboard ROM BIOS. To start a low-level format on a modern machine, use the AT diagnostics disk (the low-level format option) or the low-level format utility that's part of your computer's setup program. Choose the appropriate drive type, matching cylinders, heads, and so forth. Slower ATs should have an interleave of 2. Fast 286s, most 386s, and all 486s can use an interleave of 1.

If your drive does not match a drive type exactly, you may choose a similar, but smaller, drive and lose access to the balance of your disk.

Step 2: FDISK Formatting

Step 2 of the hard disk formatting process—**FDISK**—prepares one or more DOS partitions (areas on the hard disk suitable for DOS files). It is a very quick process, taking about 30 seconds per partition. If you're using MS-DOS version 3.3 or newer, be sure to make one of the partitions "active" if you want to boot from this hard disk.

Unlike low-level formatting, **FDISK** is software-dependent—it's a DOS utility. Changing DOS versions changes the **FDISK** screen messages and, to some extent, the **FDISK** process, but changing the hard disk or the hard disk controller doesn't affect **FDISK** at all.

We've already discussed the limitations of older DOS versions in the section above, about formatting ST506 drives on early PCs. We recommend that you upgrade to the current version of DOS, which is 6.22 as this book goes to press, or 7.0 that lies mostly hidden within Windows 95.

Step 3: High-Level Formatting (FORMAT C:/S)

High-level formatting (**FORMAT C:/S**) is covered in any DOS manual. If you have decided to partition your hard drive into two or more logical drives, remember that you will have to format each logical drive individually before writing data to it.

On DOS versions through 3.2, be sure to put the DOS system files (the two hidden files plus **COMMAND.COM**) on the first partition. That's the only place DOS looks for boot files. MS-DOS versions 3.3 and later allow you to specify an active partition, the one the computer will boot from. This active partition need not be the first partition. Of course, it must have the DOS system files installed.

High-level formatting is another slow process. Allow 35 minutes for a 20 MB drive; the computer must examine each track for bad sectors. A typical screen message displays cylinder after cylinder as each one is completed. Some DOS versions then count back up through the cylinder numbers a second time before declaring the formatting complete.

ESDI Drives and Controller Cards

How ESDI Works

ESDI is an enhanced version of the ST506 standard. Its cables and connectors are identical to ST506 cables and connectors.

ESDI drives put the data separation circuitry (the data encoding/decoding circuits) on the hard drive; ST506 puts it on the hard disk controller. ESDI drives send clean data to the ESDI controller, not the weird drive-writing signals that actually encode the data on the disk platters. Therefore, ESDI drives don't have to be as carefully synchronized with their controllers, and higher data transfer rates are possible. The ESDI interface transfers two, three, or four times as much data per second as the old ST506.

Some versions of DOS can't talk to more than 1,024 cylinders on a hard drive. To get around this limitation, many ESDI controllers allow "translation"—they lie to DOS about the physical configuration of the drive.

Theoretically, the ESDI interface can accommodate eight ESDI drives, but few controllers are designed for eight drives. If you're planning to connect more than two ESDI drives, get a special controller, then cable the drives and jumper as per the directions shipped with the controller.

We have experienced some compatibility issues in the past between certain ESDI controllers and other devices, and with Microsoft Windows. Consult the manufacturer of your adapter about any questions you may have.

How to Test an ESDI Drive and ESDI Controller

See "How to Test an ST506 Drive and Controller," above, for details. Since the interfaces are so similar, most troubleshooting techniques work for both ESDI and ST506.

How to Install an ESDI Controller Card

Remove the Old Controller Card If Necessary

Begin by examining the cables attached to the controller card. Mark them with tape or a soft marker and take notes before you disconnect them so you will be able to reinstall them properly. Don't forget the little two-wire cable to the remote hard drive light on the front panel of your computer case. It pulls right off the controller card and will slide back onto the equivalent pins on the new card. Remove the screw holding the card to the rear of the computer chassis. Then pull the ESDI card straight up out of the bus connector.

Choose the Right Controller

Not all ESDI drives and controllers work with each other. Buy them together, or check that both drive manufacturer and controller manufacturer certify that they work together. A slow ESDI drive will work with a fast controller, by the way, but a fast drive won't work with a slow controller.

Insert the Board in Slot

Line up the controller card's edge connector with an appropriate expansion slot connector on the motherboard. Press the board down, then secure it to the back of the case with a screw. Plug in the cables. Because ESDI and ST506 cables are the same, see the directions for installing ST506 cables if you can't just reinstall the cables the way they were hooked up to an original ESDI controller.

Use SETUP

Ordinarily we use **SETUP** to tell the computer what kind of drive is installed, so the computer's BIOS can issue intelligent read/write commands to the hard disk controller (which, in turn, issues its own read/write signals to the hard disk). Since ESDI hard disk controllers lie to the computer about the ESDI drive's configuration, you don't have to enter the correct number of heads and cylinders in the CMOS.

The ESDI controller does, however, require you to enter a preliminary number so the computer knows that a hard disk is installed, and the ESDI controller and the computer can start a conversation. Most ESDI controllers ask you to set the drive type to type 1 with the CMOS **SETUP** routine. To be certain your drive will work properly, read and follow your ESDI drive's installation manual.

How to Install the ESDI Cables

Physically, ESDI is a souped-up ST506 interface. ESDI uses the same cables and the same hook-up rules as ST506 (the old MFM and RLL hard drives). Read the section on ST506 cable and then return here to proceed with installation of the drive itself.

How to Install an ESDI Drive

ESDI Drives are Installed Like ST506 Drives

Follow the directions in "How to Install an MFM or RLL Hard Disk with the ST506 Interface," earlier in this chapter. *Read that section, and then come back to this section* before you format your ESDI drive.

Format the ESDI Drive

The hard drive controller will have a low-level format routine built into the ROM on the ESDI card. Follow the directions in the controller's installation manual. Remember, most ESDI drives want you to set the drive type to 1 with the CMOS **SETUP** program; read the manual to be sure.

Use the DOS **FDISK** command to partition the drive. We recommend that you upgrade to a current version of DOS. If you have an older version of DOS you may want to use Disk Manager to partition this disk, since DOS versions below 4.01 limit each hard disk partition to 32 MB or less, which may be an unnecessary complication to the user.

Format the disk with the DOS **FORMAT** command. If you intend to boot from this drive, use the **/S** switch or the DOS command **SYS C:** to copy **COMMAND.COM** and the DOS hidden files to the boot partition. Directions for **FDISK**, **FORMAT**, and **SYS** can be found in your DOS manual.

Hard Drive Troubleshooting

Problem: How do I access the CMOS System Setup to add information about the new drive?

Solution: The procedure to bring up the Setup screen varies from one ROM BIOS to another; consult your system's instruction manual. On most systems Setup is available during bootup of the system. Common instruc-

tions call for pressing **Esc** or the **F1** or **F2** function keys during bootup. Some systems allow you to access CMOS after the system has completed bootup; common instructions for such a system include **Ctrl-Alt-Esc**, **Alt-F2**, or **Ctrl-S**.

Problem: The drive will not spin up, or spins down after a few seconds.

Solution: Check to see that the drive is properly attached to a power cable from the power supply. If the power is good, this is probably a drive failure. Contact the manufacturer of the hard drive for assistance.

Problem: The drive will work as a slave, but not as a master—or as a master but not as a slave.

Solution: Check the master/slave jumpers on the hard drive; consult your instruction manual for the proper setting.

On Western Digital drives, for example, on the back of the drive between the 40-pin data connector and the 4-pin power connector, are three pairs of pins that are identified on some drives as jumper block 8. To configure a drive as the only drive in the system, there should be no jumper shunts on the three pairs of pins. To configure a drive as the master, place a jumper across pins 5 and 6, the pins closest to the 40-pin data connector. To configure a drive as the slave, place a jumper shunt on pins 3 and 4, the middle pair of pins. Pins 1 and 2, the pair closest to the power connector, are for factory use only and should not be jumpered.

Other drive manufacturers may use different jumper assignments. In some cases, mixing two drives with very different speeds or timing can cause the system not to see one of the drives. It may be necessary to swap the assignment of the two drives.

Problem: The drive has been installed and the drive parameters have been entered in the CMOS, but the drive will not boot, or the system displays the message, "HDD controller failure."

Solution: The drive must be partitioned and formatted under DOS before it can be accessed.

Problem: Can hard drives be mounted at any angle?

Solution: Consult your instruction manual or hard drive manufacturer. Most drives can be mounted right side up or on their sides without problem; it is generally not good practice to mount a drive upside down.

Hard Drive Manufacturer Support Systems

Hard Drive Manufacturer	Support Telephone Number
Conner (408) 456-4415 BBS http://www.conner.com	(800) 426-6637 voice
Fujitsu (408) 432-1318 fax, BBS http://www.fujitsu.com	(408) 894-3950 voice
Iomega (801) 778-5888 BBS http://www.iomega.com	(801) 778-1000 voice
Maxtor (303) 678-2222 BBS http://www.maxtor.com	(800) 262-9867 voice
Quantum (000) 472-9799 BBS http://www.quantum.com	(800) 826-8022 voice
Seagate (408) 438-8771 BBS http://www.seagate.com	(408) 438-8222 voice
Syquest Technology	(415) 490-7511 voice (415) 651-3338 BBS
Western Digital (714) 753-1234 BBS http://www.wdc.com	(800) 832-4778 voice

CHAPTER 9

CHAPTER 10
You Can Take It With You

We've already discussed the critical importance of backing up before you go forward. The key to truly safe computing is to have copies of current data stored at a site away from the machine.

We're not just talking about the threats from hard disk failure or a complete PC meltdown. There is also the serious problem of theft; and we need to point out that your insurance will probably cover the theft of your PC, and may even repay you for the loss of your programs, but you are very probably *not* covered for the theft of your data.

Of all of the elements of the PC, data storage has gone through the most change over the course of the evolution from dinosaur to modern machine. In this chapter we'll cover many of the most important backup devices.

Removable Hard Drives and High-Capacity Floppies

A fast and relatively inexpensive backup medium is a removable hard drive or a large-capacity floppy system. These devices are similar to standard disk drives in that information can be quickly accessed and throughput speeds approach those of an internal hard drive.

Because of their speed, some users go beyond using removable storage devices merely for archival backups. An accounting firm might, for example, keep the financial records for individual small businesses on separate Zip disks or Syquest or Bernoulli cartridges (Figure 10.1). When not in use, cartridges can be locked in a fireproof vault—important for security conscious users.

Figure 10.1 A cornucopia of large capacity removable storage media including Syquest 44MB and 270MB cartridges, a CD-R write-once read-many times disk with a capacity of more than 600 MB, an older streaming tape backup cartridge with a capacity of about 60 MB, an Iomega Jaz cartridge that can hold 1GB of information, and a relatively inexpensive and simple 100 MB Zip disk, also from Iomega.

Zip and Jaz Drives

Iomega stunned the computer industry in 1995 with the introduction of the low-cost *Zip Drive*. This portable SCSI or parallel interface drive stores 100 MB of data on a special 3.5-inch floppy disk. Although not quite as fast as a Bernoulli or Syquest drive, it won converts based on its low price—less than $200 for the drive, and about $20 per cartridge—and its ease of use. The Zip 100 has a data transfer rate of 1.4 MB/second and an access time of 29 ms.

A year later, Iomega followed up with the Jaz drive, which can store 1 GB of data on a removable cartridge and operates at a respectable 5.4 MB/second transfer rate and a 12 ms access time—just slightly slower than a typical hard drive. Some users may employ a Jaz drive as if it were a standard hard drive. The Jaz, which requires a SCSI interface, sold for about $400 in an internal model and $500 in an external version as this book went to press.

Zip and Jaz drives may end up as standard peripherals on new machines. In any case, their relative speed, ease of use, and price have set a new standard for removable drives.

Syquest Drives

Syquest offers a family of comparable systems that can store 44, 88, 105, or 200 MB on a 5.25-inch disk cartridge, or 270 MB on a high-density 3.5-inch cartridge. Syquest mechanisms are sold in subsystems offered by a number of manufacturers. The 270 MB drives for SCSI connection cost less than $400; some manufacturers offer IDE and parallel port interface versions for about the same price. Cartridges range from about $50 to $70 each, depending on capacity.

In 1996, Syquest introduced two products it hoped would compete with Iomega's Zip and Jaz devices. The EZFlyer 230, priced at about $250, can store up to 230 MB on a cartridge and is also backwards compatible with EZ135 cartridges. Available in parallel port and SCSI versions, it promises a data transfer rate of 2.4 MB/second and a 13.5 ms average seek time.

Also introduced was the SyJet 1.5 GB external drive in SCSI, IDE, and parallel port versions, priced from $400 to $500 depending on version. The SyJet delivers near hard-drive performance, including 10 ms average access time.

Bernoulli Drives

For many years, one of the leaders in the removable storage market had been Iomega with its *Bernoulli drive* technology. These are specially designed disk cartridges that connect to your PC through the parallel port or a SCSI interface. Modern versions of the Bernoulli drive have capacities of 90, 150, or 230 MB per cartridge. Drives are priced at about $400 for internal versions, $500 for an external SCSI device, and $600 for an external parallel port drive. Cartridges cost $90 to $100 each.

Though Bernoulli disk cartridges are expensive, data access time is comparable to hard disk speed. As a result, Bernoulli drives can be used as a live storage medium as well as for backup.

Bernoulli disk cartridges use a flexible disk with a metal particle coating. Unlike most other magnetic disk media, Bernoulli drives write only on the top surface of the disk, using a single read/write head. At rest, the disk curves downward, hanging below the head. This space between the head and the disk makes Bernoulli cartridges tough (Iomega says they can withstand an 8 foot drop to a hard surface without damage).

When the cartridge is installed in a Bernoulli drive, the flexible disk spins up to speed and rises close to the read/write head. If the power fails, the disk "loses lift" and falls back down, away from the head.

CHAPTER 10

CD-Recordable Devices

Recordable CD-ROM disks (also called CD-R and WORM devices) have become very popular among software developers who can create their own masters as a product is developed. The disks can also be used for low-volume publishing of database information; each disk can hold up to about 600 MB of information. As the WORM acronym testifies, these disks, priced at about $15 to $20, can be Written Once, but Read Many times. Think of them as old-style vinyl records and you'll get the idea.

We discuss CD-Rs and WORMS in Chapter 11, which covers the burgeoning multimedia world.

Tape Backups

The old reliable scheme for backups of a great deal of information is a tape drive, a technology first developed for the early days of mainframe computing. Tape drives lay down their information on a moving strip of tape held within a cartridge.

Modern tape drives are offered in internal versions and as standalone boxes with dedicated interfaces or parallel port connections. Basic units have capacities of 300 to 400 MB, with advanced units capable of storing 3 GB or more.

Tape backups are much easier to use than floppy disk drives because of the tape's capacity, but they can be painfully slow in comparison to other media. The principal reason for their slowness is the fact that tapes store information in a serial fashion, one bit after another down the length of the tape. If the information you want is located near the beginning of the tape, it can be reached fairly quickly; if it is near the end of the tape, it can be several minutes before the drive is able to fast-forward its way to that location. Think of finding a particular scene on a VCR tape and you'll get the idea.

If the drive conforms fully to the quarter-inch cartridge (QIC) standard (see the next section), you can run either the manufacturer's backup software or third-party software. This is an improvement over the past, when the manufacturers customized both the data organization on the tape and the data encoding scheme. Without standardization, if the built-in tape drive failed, the backup tapes could only be read by a drive of the identical type.

Tape backups are another area where hardware prices have dropped sharply in recent years. In 1997, an 800 MB tape storage subsystem that connects to an IDE port could be purchased for about $129; a zippy DAT drive with a 2GB capacity sold for less than $600, and an 8 GB DAT drive for less than $900. Tapes sell for about $8 to $30.

Quarter-Inch Cartridge (QIC)

Available either as DC-2000 minicartridges or full-size DC-6000 cartridges, both quarter-inch standards feature relatively inexpensive tape drives. DC-2000 systems cost about half what the DC-6000 system drives do, but they store substantially less data per tape.

Some QIC tape systems use proprietary data storage formats, while others use the QIC-40 or QIC-80 standards. A QIC-80 drive should theoretically be completely compatible with all other QIC-80 drives—they should be able to read and write to each other's tapes without difficulty. If this feature is important to you, be sure to buy a drive that is QIC-

80 certified (one that has been tested and certified by the industry's test agents), not merely a QIC-80 compatible drive. QIC tape drives record data in ordinary linear tracks laid down parallel to the edge of the tape. Most QIC-80 and QIC-40 drives use the computer's floppy drive interface to connect to the bus. Cheaper drives simply plug the unused B drive connector on your floppy drive cable into the back of the tape drive. Other QIC tape drives use an interface board to connect the tape drive cable to the bus, but again the tape drive appears to the computer to be another version (albeit a weird one) of a floppy drive. One design for an external QIC tape drive connects to the parallel port, but reroutes signals inside the computer so that the floppy drive interface signals come out through the parallel port pins. A few high-speed QIC systems use a proprietary IDE or SCSI interface.

Follow your tape drive vendor's installation and troubleshooting directions. When troubleshooting a QIC tape drive that uses the floppy drive interface, consider the common causes of floppy drive failure: incorrect drive select settings, incorrect termination, or plugging the wrong floppy drive cable connector onto the drive (for example, plugging the A drive connector to a tape drive that is supposed to be impersonating drive B). These same mistakes can choke a QIC tape drive. So can a bad floppy drive, especially if the tape drive shares cables and/or a floppy drive controller with the bad floppy drive.

Helical-Scan Drives (DAT and 8-mm)

Both 4-mm DAT drives and 8-mm helical-scan tape drives are expensive, but 4- and 8-mm tapes generally hold far more data than quarter-inch tapes. It should be no surprise that the 8-mm tape holds roughly twice as much data as the 4-mm tape and that 8-mm tape drive systems are roughly twice as expensive as 4-mm tape drive systems. Both these helical-scan standards were developed in the late 1980s for high-end audio uses, hence the name "Digital Audio Tape," or DAT.

DAT and 8-mm drives use rotating heads mounted on a slight angle to the tape. The head records a slanted magnetic trail of data at an angle to the tape, which allows much higher data densities than the ordinary lengthwise track used on quarter-inch tape media (see Figure 10.2). But the rotating heads and sophisticated tape advance mechanism used in helical-scan tape drives are expensive.

Most DAT drives are SCSI devices, often using the high-speed SCSI-2 version of the standard.

CHAPTER 10

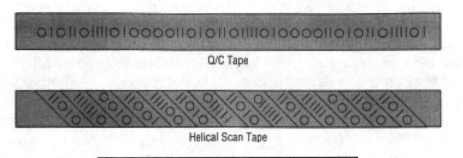

Figure 10.2 QIC tape versus Helical Scan tape.

High-End Backup Devices

Large computer installations have broken ground with other high-speed, high-capacity backup devices including CD-ROM writers, magneto-optical recorders, and transportable hard drives.

All of these have their advantages, but they come at a price. Just as we predicted in the previous edition, the price of CD-ROM writers has dropped to below $1,000, reaching as low as $500 for a basic system. CD-ROM writers are in a class called *WORM* (Write-Once, Read Many times) devices, because the disks cannot be rewritten numerous times as can a magnetic medium. CD-ROM disks have capacities of about 660 MB, and raw media costs about $20.

Magneto-optical recorders are similar to CD-ROM in their operation; they use special, high-coercivity diskettes. Coercivity is a measure of the strength of the magnetic field needed to write data; the smaller data bits of high-capacity disks demand higher coercivity.

Transportable hard drives first arose as devices for use in high-security settings, including government agencies. At the end of the day, the entire hard drive mechanism slid out of its holder and was placed in a safe. These drives are declining in popularity, although some offices use lightweight versions with parallel interfaces as a high-capacity version of a "sneaker net," picking up or delivering data to far-flung machines.

SCSI Compatibility Issues

Because SCSI hardware standards are quite detailed, SCSI hardware is very compatible. But SCSI software is not. Therefore, it makes sense to talk to your SCSI host adapter manufacturer, your Floptical drive manufacturer, and the makers of any other SCSI equipment you intend to hang onto the SCSI bus—not all adapters will work with all drives, and software drivers are not yet available for all possible combinations of SCSI devices. Do your homework before you purchase, and ask for a money-back guarantee from your vendor. In a couple of years these items will all be plug-compatible, but right now it ain't necessarily so.

Floptical Disks and Drives

Floptical brand disks look much like ordinary 3.5-inch diskettes. Like 2.88 MB floppy diskettes, Floptical diskettes are made of Mylar with a barium ferrite magnetic coating. Like ordinary 720K, 1.44 MB, and 2.88 MB 3.5-inch diskettes, Floptical diskettes store data magnetically. In fact, many Floptical drives are both read- and write-compatible with ordinary double-density (720K) and high-density (1.44 MB) 3.5-inch floppy diskettes.

Unlike ordinary 3.5-inch diskettes, Floptical disks provide optical feedback to the drive so that the drive can accurately position the read/write head over the chosen track, even if that track has become slightly eccentric. Because data-recording tracks can be much closer together than on an ordinary 3.5-inch diskette, each Floptical disk stores over 20 MB of data. Flopticals, once promising, have mostly been shoved aside by improvements in capacity and price for Syquest, Bernoulli, and new devices like the Zip drive.

How Floptical Disks and Drives Work

The Floptical disk manufacturer stamps very closely spaced concentric rings into the surface of ordinary 3.5-inch barium ferrite disks. These rings (1,250 per inch) will guide the read/write heads as they position themselves over the appropriate track on the disk. Light from an LED (light emitting diode) on the read/write head shines onto the disk, reflecting back to a photodetector which converts the light energy to electrical current. As the head moves across the disk, the light (and current) drops off over a groove and gets stronger over the flat, reflective "land" between the grooves. Therefore, the drive can distinguish one track from the next.

Using ordinary magnetic disk reading/writing technology (but using a very small read/write head suitable for the skinny tracks), the Floptical drive writes data on the flat tracks between the optical guidance grooves. Most Floptical drives are *variable mode*. Their read/write head contains both a small head to write tiny magnetic marks on Floptical diskettes and an ordinary read/write head used to read and write to ordinary 720K and 1.44 MB floppy disks.

Floptical drives are SCSI devices. They require a SCSI adapter in the computer. Since the SCSI standard allows up to seven devices chained to a single SCSI host adapter, your Floptical drive could share the adapter with a WORM or CD-ROM drive or a SCSI hard disk.

Special software redirects interrupt 13h (the interrupt the computer uses to send commands to the floppy disk) so that commands routed from the computer to the ordinary floppy drive go to the Floptical drive instead.

CHAPTER 10

CHAPTER 11
Multimedia Sound and Fury

The first PC had a silver-dollar-sized speaker capable of producing little more than annoying beeps and squawks. Today, a Modern Machine can have a symphony orchestra on board, with rich sound booming forth from tabletop speakers with powered subwoofers.

The first CD-ROM players for PCs offered little more than large-capacity platters of text, delivered at a snail's pace of 150 KB/second and requiring complex SCSI or proprietary connections to the system and sold at eye-popping prices. Today, a modern machine can have an inexpensive CD-ROM drive that runs twelve times as fast—1,800 KB/second— capable of delivering movie-like video, high-fidelity audio, and near-instant access to full encyclopedias of data.

The CD-ROM/Sound Card Connection

CD-ROMs, DVD-ROMs, and sound cards, though they are individually very different types of peripherals—the first two are storage devices and the last an electronic orchestra and sound effects generator—are very much linked in modern machines:

- CD-ROMs, DVD-ROMs and sound cards are essential elements of the burgeoning multimedia explosion
- Many sound cards are electronically linked to CD-ROMs as interfaces to the bus and as amplifiers for CD- and DVD-based audio

We'll explore CD-ROMs, move on to the developing world of DVD-ROMs, and then come back to sound cards later in this chapter. We'll also touch on game ports for advanced playing around. But first, let's look at a real-life installation project.

An Organ Transplant for a Modern Machine

Creative Labs, the "name brand" for sound cards and multimedia kits, delivered a symphony orchestra in a box to our laboratory. About two hours later, our test machine went from an anemic performer with a scratchy 8-bit sound card and a 2X CD-ROM to a wave table virtuoso and a screamer 12X CD-ROM.

The Sound Blaster Discovery CD 12X kit included a Sound Blaster 32 PnP card with a wave-table synthesizer; 1 MB of ROM containing professional-quality samples of 128 real instruments, digital effects including chorus, reverb, and pan; and a 20-voice stereo music synthesizer for compatibility with non-wave table software.

The card also includes a 4 watt per channel stereo amplifier, a joystick port, a MIDI interface for computer-controlled instruments, and microphone and stereo line-in connectors for recording sound from other sources. A built-in digital/analog mixer can blend audio information, and a volume control can adjust sources at eight levels in 2dB steps.

For high-end applications, the card can accept a SIMM RAM module for more sound samples, and as much as 32 MB of standard RAM for supported applications—an area not yet in widespread use among consumers.

The sound card plugs into an available 16-bit ISA slot and connects with an internal cable to the CD-ROM for audio. Plug and Play facilities of your modern machine, combined with a special Creative Lab utility, make it easy to assign the proper IRQ, DMA, and memory addresses to the card.

The CD-ROM, made by Mitsumi, can deliver 1,800 KB/sec data transfer with a typical access time of 150 msec. It supports DMA mode for faster transfer rates and decreased use of the CPU.

The drive slides into a standard 5.25-inch tray in a modern machine. You'll need to make two connections: a power cable from the power supply and a data cable to an EIDE connector on the motherboard of your PC, or on an EIDE paddle card in the bus. Finally, you'll need to set a pin block to identify the CD-ROM as either a master or slave unit.

Installation on our test machine went perfectly smoothly, except for a conflict between a non-Plug-and-Play network interface and the Sound Blaster card. It took an hour of experimenting with differing settings under Windows 95 Device Manager and the good services of a technical support engineer at Creative Labs to figure out a change to the CONFIG.SYS file.

Be forewarned: network cards and sound cards are often at odds, requiring management of conflicts.

The package also includes a pair of competent amplified speakers and a box full of multimedia games and an encyclopedia.

Similar packages of sound card and CD-ROM are available from other companies, and you can also purchase the various elements separately to save a few dollars. In my experience, though, there is a great deal of value to buying a package with the parts certified to work properly with each other, and to deal with a company that has an available and willing technical support staff to help you deal with technical glitches.

CD-Mania: Madonna and the Modern Machine

The first PC designers and users almost certainly never imagined that high-tech software programs would one day be stamped out on an assembly line alongside the latest Madonna album.

And yet that is the case with the increasing acceptance of CD-ROMs as a distribution medium. CD-ROMs (Compact Disc Read-Only Memory) are a computer adaptation of the CDs produced for audio systems. In fact, it was the widespread and near-total acceptance of CD players in the consumer music market that drove down the prices and pushed up the capabilities of CD-ROM machines for use with computers. The standard CD-ROM can hold about 660 MB of information on a platter that costs less than a dollar to manufacture.

CDs are coated with aluminum to reflect light and are imprinted with a pattern of pits and flat areas that denote the 0s and 1s of digital information. To read the disk, a CD-ROM player focuses a thin laser beam on a section of the spinning disk. Light reflects from the flat surfaces but doesn't reflect from the pits. Inside the CD-ROM drive, a photo detector converts these on/off light flashes to electric signals that are brought to your microprocessor across the bus.

CD-ROM players sell for as little as $100 for a basic double-speed that mounts internally, to $200-$300 for a state-of-the-art 12X-speed device. Players are available in internal and external varieties, with IDE, SCSI, and proprietary interfaces.

One class of CD-ROM drives use "caddies" to hold the disks; the caddies are slipped into an opening on the front of the drive. The caddies are intended to help stabilize the disks in the drive, and they can also help to protect the disks themselves if the disks are stored in the caddies when not in use. Extra caddies sell for about $5 each.

The other CD-ROM drive design uses a slide-out drawer like those used in most audio drives. This design is slightly less expensive to produce, and some users may find it easier to use; the sliding drawer, though, is a point of potential failure for the drive.

CHAPTER 11

Several CD-ROM makers have introduced multiple-disk caddies that allow users to load three or more disks in a single carrier for easier access. Only one disk is available at a time, but a software command can instruct the drive to swap among the available disks. Changing requires only a few seconds.

Finally, heavy users of CD-ROMs may want to consider a multiple-CD drive system. Using a SCSI adapter, as many as six drives can be installed in an external cabinet with a single connecting cable to the PC itself; a single IDE channel can support two CD-ROMs with a master and slave on the same cable.

Nearly all CD-ROM drives are read-only, but as this book went to press a new class of CD-Recordable devices had dropped below $1,000 in price. These devices use high-intensity laser beams to burn pits in special CD blanks; the resulting CD-ROMs can be read in the same machine or on a standard CD-ROM drive. Once recorded, though, the disks cannot be changed. For that reason, these machines fall within the category called WORMs (Write-Once, Read-Many) devices.

And finally, look for other new technologies for rewriteable CD-ROM drives. Panasonic has introduced its "phase-change dual-technology" (PD) that uses a laser to melt a recording medium into crystalline (reflective) or amorphous (less-reflective) pits; on playback, the laser deciphers the information in much the same way a standard CD-ROM drive works.

PD disks, which come in a sealed case similar in size to a CD-ROM caddy, have a capacity of 650 MB; they sold for about $60 each when the new system was introduced. According to Panasonic, a PD disk is good for at least 500,000 write cycles. The dual-technology part of the device's name comes from the fact that the drive can also can read standard CD-ROM disks, with quad-speed throughput.

CD-ROM, CD-Recordable (WORM), and Magnetic Optical Disk Drives

Music CDs use a pattern of pits and lands (the flat spots between pits) to record sound, and the reflected light of a laser to read the pits and lands. CD-ROM and WORM drives use similar disks to record data and similar lasers to read the CD-ROM or WORM disk.

CD-ROM disks are read-only media. CD-ROMs are very cheap to produce once an original master has been made; the first copy of a CD-ROM may cost $5,000 to make and every subsequent copy about a quarter (those prices are pretty close as this book goes to press.) Obviously, a run of 10,000 copies brings the price down very low, but they are not cost-effective for one or two copies of a block of information.

CD-Recordable drives (also called CD-R or WORM drives) by comparison, are particularly suitable for private archiving and permanent storage. WORM stands for Write Once, Read Many times, the classic role of backup media. Because WORM disks are not erasable, they provide an audit trail. You can accomplish some storage tasks better with this audit trail—for example, recording financial transactions at a bank.

MO (Magnetic-optical rewriteable) and Panasonic's PD disks are erasable; they may be erased and rewritten many times. They disks make good storage for the huge CAD and graphics image files that would otherwise fill your hard disk.

CD-ROMs, WORM disks, and Magnetic-Optical disks are sturdy, with much longer shelf life than tapes or ordinary diskettes. The data is stored optically; magnetic fields cannot erase or damage CD-ROMs, WORM disks, or MO. Because the optical pits are covered with clear plastic, accidental abrasion damage is also unlikely. Since all three optical disks remain readable more than 15 years after being written, most computer people consider them permanent storage.

How CD-ROM, WORM, and MO Drives Work

Both CD-ROM drives and WORM drives share a common disk-read technology: they shine a laser onto the disk surface and measure the reflected light level. Pits scatter the beam. The lands of the CD (that's the areas where there are no pits) reflect the beam back to the drive's photodetector. The photodetector converts the variable light levels into a variable electric current, which is, in turn, decoded into usable data.

Unlike other disk media, CD-ROMs and some WORM disks use one long spiral groove, like an LP record groove, to record data. This is called *constant linear velocity* (CLV) recording. To maintain constant linear velocity (a constant number of inches per second), CD-ROM drives and CLV WORM drives use sophisticated drive-spinning mechanisms that spin the drive slower and slower as the read/write head gets closer to the outer edge of the disk.

Other WORM drives and most magnetic-optical disks record data in multiple concentric rings (in tracks) arranged like rows of seats in a stadium rather than a single long spiral. Most other disk media (floppy disks, hard disks, Bernoulli cartridges, Floptical disks) use this track system too, recording data in concentric circles. This track-and-sector system is called *constant angular velocity* (CAV) recording.

Because the outermost edge of a CD is the hardest area to manufacture accurately and the most easily damaged, a CD-ROM data groove starts at the inside of the disk and spirals out toward the outer edge. Ordinary magnetic disk media, including hard disks and floppy disks, record on the outer tracks first, gradually working their way in toward the crowded central tracks.

WORM disks are not standardized yet—manufacturers can't even agree on CAV versus CLV recording. Many WORM disks use a thin, reflective film of metal imbedded in the CD disk. A laser "writes" to the disk by melting holes in the film, making bubbles, or otherwise disturbing the reflections from the metal film. This creates bright/dark patterns for the laser and photosensors to pick up in the read phase of the cycle.

MO disks are not standardized yet; either, but most drives use a combination of a weak magnetic field and a laser beam to record data on the disk. The medium is resistant to magnetism at ordinary temperatures. When the laser beam heats a tiny spot on the disk, though, that spot easily becomes magnetized. Unlike CD-ROM and WORM disks, the MO disk doesn't become less reflective at the lasered spots. To read the disk, the MO drive shines a gentle polarized laser beam onto the disk. When polarized light hits a magnetic field, the beam rotates very slightly. The drive photodetectors are sensitive enough to pick up the slight rotations in the laser beam bouncing off the magnetized spots on the disk.

CD-ROM, MO, and WORM drives are SCSI devices. The optical drive need not be the only SCSI device installed—a single SCSI host computer can connect as many as seven devices to the PC via its SCSI bus. Most optical drives now use generic SCSI adapters (generally the better choice), though some still require a proprietary SCSI adapter (an adapter not capable of supporting SCSI devices from another manufacturer).

CD-ROM Speed

Transfer Rate (Throughput)

Just as with a hard disk, a CD-ROM's speed is measured in several ways; the sort of demands put on a CD-ROM, though, are different from those of a hard drive.

The most important measure of speed for a CD-ROM is its data transfer rate, also referred to as *throughput*. Throughput tells you how quickly a CD-ROM drive can transfer data from a CD to the computer's data bus. While speed of access to a bit of information is very important on a hard drive where you may need to pick one small data record from a huge database, the typical use of a CD-ROM is to supply a long stream of information—audio or video for a game or other multimedia application, for example.

When CD-ROMs first arrived on the PC scene, the original data transfer rate standard was 150 KB/sec, which is considerably slower than most other data storage device. That speed was extremely limiting in multimedia applications, preventing PCs from displaying motion video well.

Several years later, a new generation of CD-ROM drives was introduced; they were capable of data transfer at 300 KB/sec, and became known as double-speed devices. The original MPC (Multimedia PC) standard developed by hardware makers set double-speed drives as a minimum requirement.

Within a few years, triple-speed (450 KB/sec) and quad-speed (600 KB/sec) drives appeared and then in short order there arrived 6X-speed (900 KB/sec), 8X-speed (1,200 KB/sec), and 10X speed (1,500 KB/sec) drives. As we go to press, the current speed demons are 12X (1,800 KB/second) devices.

The higher-speed drives achieve their throughput by spinning the CD-ROM at multiples of the original single-speed standard. The throughput pays off in smoother and larger graphics, or quicker transfer of large blocks of data.

In general, faster is better, although triple-speed drives were a technological detour—troubles with the design of that class of drive were forgotten when quad-speed devices appeared soon afterwards. We'd suggest passing up fire-sale prices on triple-speed drives. A similar situation exists with 6X-speed drives.

There is no good reason to buy a single-speed CD-ROM drive; it is not fully compatible with multimedia applications and is generally too slow for modern machines.

The vast majority of multimedia programs are optimized to work with double-speed drives; users will note only slight improvement through the use of a quad or faster drive. That doesn't mean that future multimedia products won't be intended for the faster drives. And straight data throughput for loading operating systems, programs, and database searches will always be enhanced with a faster drive.

Although double-speed devices are probably acceptable to most users, a buyer with an eye on the future will want to aim for at least a quad-speed device. The price differential between quads and 8X and even 10X drives has dwindled to just $10 or $20—go for speed.

Multi-Spin Technology

All CD-ROM drives employ CLV technology, which is sometimes claimed by manufacturers as an enhancement rather than as a standard feature.

It is all related to the design of the CD-ROM disk: think of the data recorded on a disk as a continuous string of information that runs in a tight spiral from the outside to the inside.

Here's the important issue: the circles at the outside of the disk are much larger than the circles at the center. In order to even out the flow of data, the CD-ROM drive must be capable of slowing down its rotation when its read/write heads are located at the outside of the disc. The motor spins more than 2.5 times as fast when data is being retrieved from the innermost tracks as it does when the outer tracks are being read.

Another reason for multiple spin rates for CD-ROM drives is that it is necessary on double-speed and faster drives for computer data and audio data to be read at different rates. The standard speed for audio information was set at 153.6 KB/sec (usually rounded to 150 KB/sec) when the first CDs were created; computer data was originally intended to be read at the same rate, but as CD-ROM technology advanced the reading speed of data doubled, doubled again, and is on the verge of yet another doubling. However, the standard for audio data transfer has remained unchanged; if you were to read a song at 600 KB/sec, it would sound like Alvin the Chipmunk on helium.

When a CD-ROM needs to transfer audio information, it must slow down to 150 KB/sec. When it is ready to go back to data, it speeds up.

Access Speed

Access speed is the other critical indication of the meaningful speed of a CD-ROM. This specification tells you on average how long it takes the CD-ROM mechanism to locate a particular block of information and move its read-head into position to begin data transfer.

Access speed is most important in applications where you will need to pick up a number of small blocks of data in rapid succession—for example, a database on CD-ROM. It is generally less important in multimedia games, where once a particular section has been located all the CD-ROM has to do is unload a large section of contiguous video and audio.

The lower the access speed, the faster the CD-ROM responds to requests for information. Therefore, look for the best combination of high throughput and low access speed.

Capacity

The capacity of a CD-ROM disk depends on two factors: the data encoding specification used by the publisher of the disk, and how much of the available space the publisher actually uses. The range of maximum capacities runs from about 540 MB to 682 MB.

There are two general formats for CD-ROMs, one that uses the 74-minute recording length limit of audio CDs, and a second computer-specific format that sets a 60-minute limit. If the disc maker uses an error correction encoding scheme, the maximum capacity of the audio specification is 682 MB and the computer specification 553 MB.

The nature of the material recorded on the disc can also affect its capacity. Data that is intended to be read in a continuous stream—such as audio and video—may take up slightly less space than data that is intended to be taken in many small chunks, such as database entries.

Interface

There are three common interface designs used to connect the CD-ROM to your PC: SCSI, IDE, and proprietary systems.

You will have to match your CD-ROM to any existing interface cards or ports on your system or plan to add redundant circuitry.

A SCSI subsystem typically has the highest transfer rate of available interfaces, and can be shared by as many as seven devices.

The IDE/ATAPI (Integrated Drive Electronics/AT Attachment Packet Interface) interface is an extension of the IDE adapter that is part of most modern machines and is used for controlling hard disk drives.

Some drive makers produce their own interface cards that are intended to communicate only with their drives; there are also a number of sound cards that offer a proprietary interface for a CD-ROM on board. (Some of the proprietary designs are adaptations of SCSI.)

The proprietary interfaces are rarely faster than SCSI or IDE/ATAPI, and are by design limited in expandability; they are, though, less costly to manufacture.

Start with an analysis of any interface cards you may already have in your system; you don't want to unnecessarily give up one of the relatively few available slots on the motherboard.

If you have a SCSI card in the system, you can add an internal or external CD-ROM to the SCSI chain. If you have an EIDE (Extended IDE) or IDE/ATAPI interface, you can add the CD-ROM if you are below the four-device limit.

If you have a sound card with a proprietary interface, check with the manufacturer to determine which CD-ROMs it will work with. Be sure to also find out about any necessary cables or adapters.

If you need to install a new interface, we recommend a modern SCSI controller because of its speed and ability to work with as many as seven devices including scanners, printers, and drives of all description. Other reasons to use a SCSI controller include relative ease of use with operating systems other than DOS, including OS/2, Windows NT, SCO UNIX, and NEXTSTEP. Users of a SCSI adapter can also move external CD-ROMs between a PC and a Macintosh system.

In theory, a 16-bit board will allow much greater transfer speeds than one that plugs into an 8-bit slot. However, single- and double-speed CD-ROM drives transfer data below the capability of an 8-bit board; 16-bits will only make a difference with triple-speed and faster drives.

If you plan to someday upgrade to a quad-speed drive, or if you plan to use the SCSI adapter with a hard drive or other SCSI peripheral, the extra price for the 16-bit controller is a worthwhile investment.

CHAPTER 11

By the way, if you intend to use a SCSI port that is part of a sound card, make sure that the SCSI adapter is a 16-bit model. Don't be confused by the description of the sound capabilities of the board, which may refer to the width of the board's audio channel; check the specs or call the manufacturer to determine the nature of the SCSI portion of the card.

Matching the CD-ROM to a Sound Card

If your CD-ROM and sound card were sold as a packaged set, they are sure to be set up to allow the disc to communicate both data and sound.

If you have mixed and matched a SCSI or other controller and the CD-ROM you will have to make another internal connection between the audio output of your CD to the sound card. Unfortunately, there is no single standard for the construction of the cable that runs between the two devices; consult the instruction manuals for your CD-ROM and sound card or call the manufacturers for information. Figure 11.1 is an example of card connectors on a common sound card

Data Buffer

In general, a bigger data buffer is better, assuming that the buffer is properly designed. Think of a buffer as an erasable scratch pad that the computer can refer to for some of the most commonly used information. Its value is based on the fact that most data is used more than once before it is discarded in favor of new information. Any information held in the memory chips that make up the cache can be read many times faster than data that must be found and transferred from the CD-ROM.

A properly designed cache must anticipate what to hold and what to discard. Associated with that is the size of the cache; early CD-ROMs had no cache, and then moved to 64K and then 256K memory chips. New models include 1 MB buffers.

Tray Loading vs. Caddy

Many older CD-ROM systems use a caddy, a closed plastic case that holds a CD safely away from scratches and dirt. A small metal door on the bottom slides out of the way when the caddy is inserted into the drive, permitting the readhead to come near the disk that spins within the caddy. Caddy-based CD-ROM systems also have simpler internal mechanisms.

Some users like the convenience of storing their important (and expensive) CDs in immediately available caddies instead of within the original jewel boxes. Caddies can be purchased for about $3 to $5 from computer retailers.

Later generations of CD-ROM drives accept bare disks that are placed into a tray that moves in and out of the drive. The tray systems are easier to use, but also subject to damage if the extended tray is bumped.

The newest line of CD-ROM drives include multidisk caddies that can hold several disks that can be moved in and out of position by software command. These drives still only read from one disk at a time and it takes a few seconds for the mechanism to remove one disk and replace it with another; however, for some users, this arrangement is a timesaver.

In all cases, the loading mechanism of a CD-ROM is its most fragile element.

XA Compatibility

Extended Architecture (XA) is a specification without much of a use. XA disks were supposed to permit the interleaving of audio and data information on the same track of a CD-ROM disc, permitting greater capacity and transfer speed. Such a capability would be very valuable in multimedia applications where the computer has to work very hard to be able to merge audio and video from a standard CD-ROM.

Very few XA disks were ever produced, though, and are not likely in the future. If you find one, you'll need to add a hardware decoder and software to your system. Kodak's Photo CD is a subset of the XA format, although it does not require additional hardware.

In any case, nearly all current CD-ROM drives advertise they are "XA Compatible" or "XA Ready".

Advanced Uses of CD-ROMs

Multisession Photo CDs

Kodak's Photo CD specification allows users to store and view photographs and slides. The system has been adopted by professional photographers and publishers, as well as amateurs. The photos on the CD can be manipulated and altered using advanced software.

One Photo CD can hold as many as 100 photos in standard size and resolution; very large and very high-resolution versions for professional applications take up more space.

Photo CD disks can be displayed on a special Photo CD machine that attaches to a television set. They can also be retrieved from a CD-ROM attached to a PC.

All CD-ROM devices can retrieve images from a Photo CD that is recorded in one session. But if you choose to have two or more rolls of film recorded onto a Photo CD at different times, the Kodak system will create multiple directories to those files; such a disk is called a "multisession" Photo CD. Only those later-generation CD-ROM devices that are identified as "multisession-capable" can retrieve files from images added to an original Photo CD.

In addition to multisession capability in the firmware of the CD-ROM, your interface board and software device driver must also support multisession Photo CDs.

Playing Music CDs on a Computer CD-ROM drive

Since computer CD-ROM drives were direct descendants of the audio CDs, all of the mechanical and electronic elements to play music CDs exist. What you'll need to add is a proper device driver and software program that allows selection of specific tracks.

Microsoft Windows users can play CD-ROM music tracks with the Media Player found in the Accessories Group. For more fancy options including the ability to shuffle tracks, make random selections, or to create a directory of songs by name, you can use a specialized music CD program available from software makers or as shareware. Some CD-ROMs have ways to control the movement from one track to another through buttons.

One other issue is the design of your CD-ROM. Some units have an external jack that permits direct attachment of a headphone; even more useful is a volume control for the headphone. Without these facilities, you'll have to run the output of the CD through the sound card and any attached speakers.

Installing a CD-ROM

Adding a CD-ROM to your system is very much like adding a floppy or hard disk drive. Start with an interface adapter. The most common ways to attach a CD-ROM to your computer's bus are through a SCSI board, an IDE connector, or with the use of a proprietary adapter card specific to your CD-ROM (although many of these cards are slightly altered SCSI adapters, themselves.) It is safest to purchase a CD-ROM with a matched adapter card; some packages pair a CD-ROM with a sound card that has a standard SCSI adapter or a proprietary adapter on board.

A cable connects the adapter to the CD-ROM, which can be installed in a drive bay of your PC or externally. The CD-ROM is also connected to a sound card in order to play music and multimedia effects.

Consult the instruction manual that comes with your CD-ROM for the customized installation steps for your particular device.

How to Install and Test CD-ROM, WORM, and MO Drives and Their Adapter Cards

SCSI Adapter Cards

To install or test the adapter card, use standard SCSI device troubleshooting and installation techniques.

Drive Installation

For the CD-ROM, WORM, or MO drive itself, you'll have to rely on the manufacturer's installation and troubleshooting pamphlet and on their technical support lines. Internal drives should be mounted in the computer with screws or rails, as are hard disks.

Software Considerations

Device drivers tell the computer how to interact with an oddball piece of equipment. From the computer's perspective all these optical drives are odd. Your WORM and/or MO drive will require a device driver, or a hardware interface that makes the computer think it's dealing with an ordinary hard disk rather than an optical drive. If you're installing a CD-ROM drive, don't forget to install Microsoft's MSCDEX extension drivers for CD-ROM, plus a device driver for your particular drive.

Testing the Drive

Ironically, CD-ROM and WORM technology is very sensitive to dust—not on the CD disks, but on the lenses inside the drive that guide the laser beam to the photodetector. Many new optical drives use self-cleaning lenses.

Though they're supposed to be virtually indestructible, optical disks can nevertheless go bad. If one disk won't work in your drive, but others will, the disk is likely to be bad, not the drive. Conversely, if a disk works fine in comparable drives, but won't work in your drive, better call the drive vendor for help. You'll have to take the drive in for factory service.

CD ROM caddies can become warped or damaged; try swapping the disk inside to another caddy before assuming a drive or disk failure.

Troubleshooting a CD-ROM Installation under Windows 3.1

MSCDEX.EXE Problems

Microsoft has released several updates to the MSCDEX (Microsoft CD Extensions) program. You must use a version compatible with the release DOS on your system. Microsoft DOS 6.22 contains its own version of **MSCDEX.EXE**, which is located in the DOS directory. Make sure the path to the DOS directory is properly set in your **AUTOEXEC.BAT** file.

PC Hangs Up when CD-ROM Driver is Loaded

You may have a conflict with another driver or a TSR (Terminate-and-Stay-Resident) program. Make a copy of your **CONFIG.SYS** program and re-order the device drivers to place the CD-ROM drive as the first line; this will let you test to see if the driver works properly. Check with the manufacturer of your CD-ROM and adapter to assure that you are using the latest driver for your adapter.

Examine the **CONFIG.SYS** file for a "Lastdrive" statement. If there is no such statement, and if your system is already using C, D, and E drives, add a line *before* your CD-ROM driver that reads: LASTDRIVE=Z

Examine the **AUTOEXEC.BAT** file for an **MSCDEX** line. It should be followed by an "/L:x" switch. "X" represents the drive name for the CD-ROM; make sure the specification doesn't conflict with an existing drive.

Check under the cover to see that the data cable connecting your CD-ROM with its controller is properly installed. Most cables have a red stripe on one edge; the stripe should line up with a similar marking on connectors on the CD-ROM and the controller.

Cabling Problems

If the CD-ROM drive tray opens when the system is turned on and will not work properly, you may have an improper hardware setting on the CD-ROM or adapter, or the incorrect installation of the CD-ROM's data cable. Check your instruction manual and go over installation procedures.

CD Games Pause Every 30 seconds

Actually, it's a 10.15 second pause every 30.40 seconds; those numbers are a function of the hardware design of some CD-ROMs. Edit the **AUTOEXEC.BAT** file and locate the **MSCDEX.EXE** line. Increase the buffers /M:## (/M:40) line.

Future Tech Arrives: DVD-ROM

I continue to amuse my children by referring to record albums when I should be talking about disks. The fact is, though, that compact discs very quickly turned vinyl records into audio dinosaurs. CDs won out because of their ease of use, resistance to damage, increased capacity, and most of all, the quality of sound they are capable of producing.

If we are to believe the futurists, we are all about to become outmoded once again as the CD-ROM—the computer's adaptation of the compact disc—is about to supplanted by a faster, tremendously more capacious relative called DVD. Just as with CDs, the DVD comes to the computer by way of the consumer electronics market. DVD was first envisioned as a replacement for laserdisc video and videotapes, bringing several hours of capacity for feature movies. At first the acronym stood for Digital Video Disk; as the technology moved toward use in computers, the acronym has gone away.

Initial DVD disks have a capacity of 4.7GB of data, about equal to seven CD-ROM disks. And DVD-ROM drives are backward-compatible with CD-ROMs, allowing you to use your outdated CD-ROMs. Home entertainment systems will similarly be able to play older audio CDs.

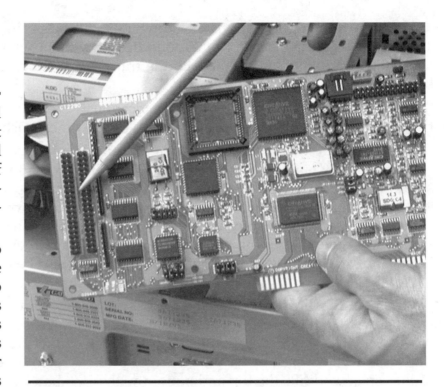

FIGURE 11.1 A basic Sound Blaster 16 from Creative Labs. Owners of older PCs may want to use one of the card's connectors to control several brands of CD-ROM drives; newer PCs typically use an onboard EIDE controller for CD-ROMs.

DVD is part of the exciting convergence of PCs and television. The laser technology and data format for DVD-ROM software and PC drives is the same as that used for DVD players intended to play movies in the family rec room.

Analysts predict that shipments of DVD-ROM drives should surpass CD-ROM drives by the year 2000, and move on to replace the older technology quickly after then. Early DVD-ROM machines are expected to cost about $500 to $750, which was about the price for early CD-ROM devices when they first arrived on the market for PCs. Once the market is fully up and running, look for a rapid decline in DVD prices even as capacity and speed increases.

There are four configurations including in the DVD specifications adopted by the industry, ranging from 4.7 GB to 17 GB. The base data transfer rate for audio and video is about 600 KB per second, which is about the speed of a 4X CD-ROM drive. For computer data, the transfer rate starts about twice that rate and is expected to move rapidly beyond that.

The Hollywood influence on the specifications was based on the typical running length of a feature film of about two hours. But the DVD specification goes beyond mere picture and sound.

With compression, a full-motion image requires about 3,500 Kbps (kilobits per second) to display; stereo surround-sound demands an additional 384 Kbps. But the international entertainment industry lobbied for three additional sound tracks for foreign language dubbing, plus four tracks of information to permit a quartet of subtitles. (Another use of the image storage space would be to offer different versions of the same film—perhaps a PG-13 and an R version, with a password protection device on the player so that parents can give their guidance.) The total space envisioned for video and audio entertainment would then require about 4,692 Kb per second; multiply that times two hours and you have space for a full motion picture with bells and whistles on one side of a DVD disk.

DVD is also set up to display movies in three different ways, depending on personal preference and the artistic judgment of the director. Widescreen yields an "anamorphic video" signal that can be used with a special widescreen television set to fill the entire screen as if it were a movie screen. A Pan and Scan version employs current methodology to fill the screen of a traditional with a specially edited version of the film that avoids cutting off parts of the image that would otherwise appear off the edges of the screen, A Letterbox mode displays the full image across the width of the screen and fills the top and bottom with black bands.

The DVD specification includes MPEG-2 compression to pack as much image information as possible on the disk. MPEG is a form of "differencing" compression; a basic frame is stored, and then subsequent bits of information describe the difference between the reference frame and subsequent frames.

The DVD-ROM drive uses a laser employing shorter-wavelength light than the standard CD-ROM drive. This allows it to retrieve information from smaller data points on a disk with tracks wound tighter together than on a CD. This brings us to the first 4.7 GB level.

Next, we come to the fact that the depth of the data layer on a DVD is half that of a CD. Designers make use of this in two ways. First, some makers will create "flippy" disks with information on both sides; users will have to stop the rotation of the DVD and turn it over to access the second side. This brings us to a potential maximum of 9.4 GB per disk, although the data is not continuously accessible. (Interestingly, there was a short life for "flippy" disks in the early days of the PC, before floppy drives were improved to have read/write heads on both sides of the recording media.)

That brings us to the next step up in the specification: multi-layer data. By varying the power of the laser beam and interposing a semitransparent filter between two layers of data, the DVD drive can read the data recorded near the surface of the disk or burrow a bit deeper to a second later. This scheme permits a bit less per layer, about 4.25 GB; multiply that times two layers and you come to 8.5 GB on one side.

Finally, designers plan to introduce DVD drives with lasers above and below the disk, permitting a total of four layers of information for a total of about 17 GB.

NOTE One potential headache: just a bit further out on the horizon are rewriteable versions of DVD drives, which may bear the name of DVD-RAMs. As this book goes to press, it appears that these devices will not be fully compatible with DVD-ROM players. This sounds like a problem that will be battled out in the marketplace: if DVD-ROMs are a big success, follow-on products are likely to be made compatible with them.

Sound Cards

A sound card gives your computer a mouth.

Music, sound effects, and speech are an essential part of the multimedia revolution. But don't think for a minute that the tiny little beeper of a speaker within a standard PC is capable of making beautiful music. In order to produce multimedia audio, you will need a capable sound card.

Windows 3.1 and Windows 95 also allow sound recording and playback from within documents.

Some of these sound boards pipe music and voice to your stereo. Others allow recording as well through the use of a microphone input, or a line input that can accept a signal from a tape recorder or CD player. Top of the line sound boards provide multiple interfaces (CD-ROM, CD player, microphone, joystick, portable speakers or AUX jack on your stereo, and MIDI).

The sound card standard is the SoundBlaster from Creative Labs. That doesn't necessarily mean that the SoundBlaster provides the best quality or the most features, although such cards have led the industry from the start. If you buy a card from another maker, be certain that it promises full SoundBlaster compatibility; without it, you cannot be sure that all multimedia software will work properly with your card.

How a Sound Board Works

When recording sound, the board feeds audio from the in jack (microphone, CD player, whatever) through an analog-to-digital converter (ADC). To play sound, the sound board converts digitized audio or digital descriptions of sounds to an analog signal that allows a speaker to reproduce sound.

Sound cards have gone through a great deal of change in the course of a few years on the scene, always in the direction of improved capabilities. The biggest points of difference are between 8- and 16-bit cards, and FM synthesis versus wave-table synthesis.

In general, 16-bit cards are capable of using more memory to describe and prepare notes, and produce better sound.

FM synthesis creates sounds by using algorithms to produce sine waves that are analogs of real instruments; depending on the capabilities of the card, the quality of output can range from Game Boy-like beeps and squawks to decent but artificial sound. Wave-table synthesis is based on the use of actual recorded samples of instruments that can be called upon and manipulated by MIDI commands.

Other features to look for include the power of the internal amplifier; many sound cards produce as little as 1 watt per channel, which is barely enough power for use with external speakers that have their own amplifiers. More modern cards generate as much as 4 watts per channel, but this is still insufficient for clean sound—they are likely to produce "noise" along with the signal. If you are a sound purist, look for a card that adds a low-level (unamplified) line-out connector that can be attached to a more generous external amplifier.

Many multimedia kits come with a pair of speakers; in our experience, the quality of these devices ranges between symphonic and spectacularly awful. Try to audition your speakers at a retail store or at a friend's setup; at the very least, buy the best pair you can afford and be prepared to send them back if they don't meet the needs of your ears.

It is generally not a good idea to use ordinary home stereo speakers directly connected to your PC for two reasons: their magnetic coils are not shielded and can cause disturbances to your monitor or damage to floppy or hard disks, and they may require greater wattage than is produced by the tiny amplifiers of sound cards. A good compromise, and a very appropriate one for users who don't want to disturb others, is the use of a good headphone instead of speakers.

Prices for sound cards, like most everything else related to computers, have come down sharply. Expect to pay about $150 to $200 for a good quality card, as little as $50 for an 8-bit clone (we suggest you don't), and as much as $400 for a top-of-the line card. If price is not an object, go for a 32-bit wave table sound card; if you need to pinch some pennies, go for the best 16-bit wave table card you can get.

How to Install and Test a Sound Board

Like many other expansion cards, sound boards use an address and an interrupt. Each device in a computer must have a unique address (the place where the microprocessor can send information for that device). Any sound card in an ISA computer (both early and modern machines) must have a unique interrupt—the signal from the device that it needs the computer's attention. EISA sound boards (which are relatively rare, by the way) use level-sensitive interrupts, so that an EISA sound board in an EISA computer could theoretically share an interrupt with another EISA device, but most sound boards are ISA and require a unique interrupt.

Use a diagnostic program to figure out what addresses and interrupts are already being used. Then set the switches and jumpers on the sound board per the manufacturer's installation instructions.

Make sure that your new sound board will work with Windows and your CD-ROM. Not all of them will. It's best to buy a CD-ROM and sound board together, but if you're adding one or the other later, talk to your CD-ROM vendor and your sound board vendor before you purchase.

Creative Labs' SoundBlaster was one of the first successful sound cards, and its capabilities have become an unofficial standard that is emulated or licensed by many other manufacturers. There is a possible difference, too; an official SoundBlaster card or a licensed card offers a very high probability of problem-free operation with software intended for SoundBlaster cards. Some emulators are less than perfect in their imitation and may cause problems.

MIDI (Musical Instrument Digital Interface) cards are a specialized form of sound card that can control the advanced sampled playback facilities of a wide range of electronically augmented musical instruments.

You'll also have to install device drivers to Windows and DOS to inform your operating system of the presence of the sound card. Consult the instruction manual for the card for details.

Most sound cards include their own diagnostic programs to test their settings and performance.

Troubleshooting a CD-ROM Installation under Windows 95

Use the Device Properties reports of Windows 95 to check for conflicts among IRQs, DMAs, and addresses that may have slipped through, despite the best efforts of the Hardware Wizard. See Chapter 21 for more details on Windows 95 troubleshooting.

Sound Drivers

If Windows 95 does not have a driver for your sound card, you can install its Windows 3.1 drivers; contact the maker of the card to see when a Windows 95 driver will be available.

Sound card drivers for Windows 3.1 products were delivered on floppy disks that accompanied the hardware. Load the disk and look for a file called **OEMSETUP.INF**. If you find it, go to Windows 95 and click the **Start** button, point to **Settings**, click **Control Panel**, and double-click the **Add New Hardware** icon. Instruct the system not to search for your new hardware; instead go to the Hardware Types box and click **Sound, Video and Game Controllers**. Click the **Have Disk** button to install the sound card driver.

If the Windows 3.1 driver disk does not include an **OEMSETUP.INF** file, use the hardware's **Setup** program to install the drivers.

Hardware Problems

If the sound from your SoundBlaster or similar card is scratchy or weak, it may be that the device's DMA setting does not match the DMA setting under Windows 95.

Click on **My Computer**, then click **Properties**. On the Device Manager tab, click **Sound, Video and Game Controllers**, then click **Remove**. Restart the computer. Once Windows 95 is up and running again, click on **Start**, point to **Settings**, click on **Control Panel**, double-click the **Add New Hardware** icon, and reinstall the sound card.

Another possible cause for poor sound performance is an attempt to mix wave file formats. For example, you cannot play a 16-bit wave file on an 8-bit sound card.

PCI Video Card Conflicts

Windows 95 display drivers do not use an IRQ. However, PCI adapters request an IRQ for full backward compatibility.

PCI devices can share PCI IRQs, but Windows 95 does not support sharing of PCI IRQs with non-PCI devices. Therefore, it is possible that a PCI video adapter may end up configured to use an IRQ already in use by another device.

To resolve this sort of problem, use Device Manager to assign a different IRQ to one of the conflicting devices.

CD-ROM Drive Letters

To change the drive letter assigned to a CD-ROM, click the **Start** button, point to **Settings**, and click on **Control Panel**. Double-click the **System** icon, then click the **Device Manager** tab. Select the CD-ROM you want to change, then click the **Properties** button and then the **Settings** tab. In the Reserved Drive Letters section, set Start Drive Letter and End Drive Letter to the drive letters you want to use. Click the **OK** button.

Restart the computer so that the change takes effect.

Game Ports

Advanced gamers will want to give their computer a hand with a joystick or other game controllers including roller balls, video game-like pads, and even specialized simulations of airplane yokes for flight simulators. All of these devices work by transmitting to the computer a set of X and Y coordinates representing a position on the screen, which itself is a display of a bitmap in memory.

In order to use one of these devices, you'll need to add a game port to your system. Some sound cards include a game port among their features; in some cases the game port performs double duty as a MIDI breakout port. You may also find a game port as part of a multi-I/O card that adds enhanced serial, parallel, and IDE ports to an older machine. Finally, you can also add an inexpensive game port card to your system. We worked with a simple ISA card from Dalco Electronics , shown in Figure 11.2, for our test machine.

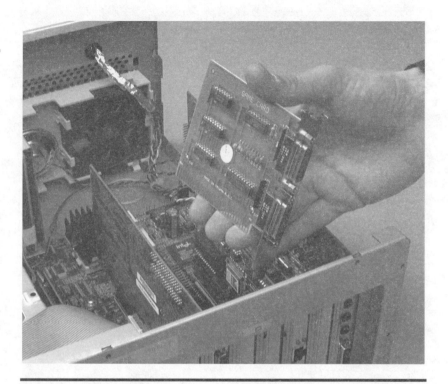

Figure 11.2 Serious gamers will want to install a game port card, like this one from Dalco, to allow use of one or two joysticks or other controllers. You can also find multifunction cards that include serial, parallel, IDE, floppy, and game ports to upgrade older machines to near state-of-the-art I/O functions.

CHAPTER 12
Video

The video monitor is your view into the computer. No matter how impressive the PC, no matter how dazzling the software, if your monitor is too fuzzy to view or too slow to keep up with your work pace, you're looking straight into frustration and aggravation.

In this chapter, we'll look at the available common video standards for modern machines, including the current state of the art, SVGA, and the previous champion, VGA. We'll also help with troubleshooting and upgrading from dinosaur standards including MDA, CGA, and EGA. And we'll also take a look at such arcane standards as 8514/A, XGA, and TIGA. We will start our exploration of video by looking at video cards, and then move on to monitors in the next chapter.

What Makes Good Video?

Let's start with a quick description of how a monitor works (we'll go into a bit more detail in Chapter 13). When we look at a computer screen, as well as at a television, we are looking through the front glass at an image that is drawn on its back side. The image is made up of hundreds of thousands or even millions of little glowing dots that are made to glow when they are struck by a moving electron beam under the control of the computer and a specialized video adapter.

Good video is a function of capabilities that reside on the video adapter, the monitor, or both:

- **Resolution**. This is a measure of the number of individually controllable dots of light on the monitor screen. The higher the stated resolution, the more information can theoretically be displayed, but this is just one part of the sharpness equation. Maximum resolution is determined by the highest capability of the video adapter and the monitor; a monitor cannot display more dots than a video adapter is capable of describing, and a video adapter cannot command a monitor to use more dots than it was designed to employ.

- **Dot pitch**. This monitor specification tells you how close together the dots are. The finer the dot pitch (the lower the number), theoretically the finer the image is. Today's better monitors have a dot pitch of 0.28 mm or less. One exception to this measurement comes from monitors that use Sony's Trinitron technology; these screens use a mask with very fine slots that affect the spacing of pixels. Specs for Trinitron devices are measured in aperture grille pitch, and .025 mm is considered quite good.

- **Refresh rate**. Also called *vertical scanning rate*, this is a measure of how often the monitor rewrites the screen. The higher the refresh rate, the more stable the image appears and the less chance of apparent flicker.

- **Image quality**. Some monitors are simply higher quality than others, using better and brighter phosphors or better electronics that can produce whiter whites and more brilliant colors. On monochrome monitors, the best displays are capable of producing a wide range of grayscale hues that improve the quality of graphics and text. Image quality is mostly in the eye of the beholder, although reviews of monitors can measure brightness and color intensity.

- **Number of colors**. The more colors that a monitor (and its associated video card) can produce, the more apparent depth and realism in an onscreen image. Think of colors as information; the ability of a display to show 30 variations of forest green, for example, permits much more detail in a wildlife scene. In order to use more colors, a display adapter needs a great deal of video memory.

- **Speed**. How fast a video adapter can construct graphic images and send them to the monitor for display becomes a very important measure as graphic programs and graphical user interfaces like Windows take over. The more colors and the greater the resolution, the harder the video adapter has to work to produce images. Modern adapters, especially those connected to the local bus of the CPU or possessed of a graphics accelerator, work much faster than earlier adapters, but there still is a tradeoff between the amount of information on screen and the speed at which scenes are constructed and displayed.

The Video Adapter

The video adapter has most of the brains of the team; the monitor mostly follows orders. The adapter controls the resolution, the scan rate, and the colors or shades of gray available on a particular monitor.

In the original design of the PC and on many modern machines, the video adapter is a card that fits into a slot on the bus (or, in a local bus design, into a slot that goes around the bus and connects more or less directly to the CPU.) Some modern machines place the video circuitry on the motherboard itself; this move typically saves a bit on cost but may reduce your flexibility when it comes to upgrades or repairs.

Nearly all modern machines make use of a PCI slot for the video adapter, helping to boost speed in a graphics-intensive world. If you have an older ISA bus machine you may find it difficult to obtain state-of-the art video cards.

NOTE Nearly all modern video cards have their own BIOS chips that extend the basic facilities of your PC. BIOS ROM is much slower than the RAM in your system memory, and many video card makers offer utilities that allow you to relocate the contents of the video BIOS into system memory; these often involve programs that are added to your **AUTOEXEC.BAT** file to perform the relocation of the BIOS at bootup. Check your instruction manual for details.

Video adapters also often require the use of device drivers which are added to your operating system to let DOS or Windows know about the capabilities of the card. The instruction manual for the card should give details on installation of the drivers.

It is a good idea to keep in touch with the maker of your video adapter, especially if you have purchased a state of-the-art device or if there are significant changes to the operating system. Most video adapter makers regularly post updated or improved versions of their video device drivers on their bulletin board systems or will send them to registered users. Newer drivers can improve speed, add features, or fix bugs in previous releases.

In any case, it pays to have a fully capable video adapter and as good a monitor as you can justify buying. If you're upgrading in stages, buy the video adapter first; if the monitor's capabilities are greater than those of the adapter you won't be able to use them.

It is also important to realize that many PCs cannot be upgraded to VGA and SVGA because of limitations in their ROM BIOS. Check with the PC manufacturer or the maker of the video adapter for details. In some cases, you may be able to upgrade the BIOS of an old machine.

Figure 12.1 One example of a current video card is this ATI 3D Xpression adapter, shown being installed in a PCI slot. This video card includes a graphics accelerator and 3-D functions based on Microsoft's Direct 3D extensions to Windows 95.

Figure 12.2 This TV tuner and video input card from ATI is an example of a video daughtercard; it attaches to an onboard connector on many current ATI graphics cards to allow users to watch TV or videos on a computer monitor and to capture still frames and movie clips from the video feed. The card can also perform advanced functions, including creating transcripts based on closed-captioned broadcasts.

Video Memory

Video cards define how many colors your monitor can employ to display an image. The more colors used by the card, the more bits of information are necessary to describe each one; cards are sometimes categorized according to their *color depth* as 8-bit (capable of describing as many as 256 colors), 16-bit (65,536 or 65K), or 24-bit (16,777,216, or 16.7 million.)

The price of RAM has dropped sharply over the past year, but memory continues to be one of the most expensive elements of a graphics card, especially since advanced cards seek to squeeze out every possible drop of speed by using new types of RAM such as EDO, VRAM and WRAM.

How much memory do you need? High-end graphics cards can benefit from huge banks of memory—some come equipped with as much as 32 MB of RAM—but consumer-grade cards for gaming will typically work fine with 2 MB of RAM, with 4 MB allowing higher resolution and more colors.

RAM needs are a function of the resolution of the image and the number of colors available to the RAMDAC before it converts the image to an analog signal.

Here's the math: multiply horizontal resolution times vertical resolution to give you the total number of pixels, and then multiply the result by the number of bytes of color (1 byte equals 8 bits or 256 possible colors, 2 bytes equals 16 bits or 65,536 colors, 3 bytes equal 24 bits or 16.7 million colors, and so on).

It works out like this: a commonly used 640x480 resolution requires about 600K of RAM at 16 bits and just under 1 MB of RAM at 24 bit color. If you're working with a larger monitor and want to use the higher 800x600 resolution, you'll need about 1 MB for 16-bit color and 1.44 MB for 24 bits of color depth.

The amount of RAM on the card is directly related to the resolution and number of colors it can work with. For a modern machine running Windows, we recommend a minimum of 1 MB of RAM; consider 2 MB if you work at highest resolutions and number of colors, and 4 MB of RAM for the most spectacular multimedia games, especially if you are using a new class of SVGA cards offering 3D image construction. Professional graphic artists and designers typically start at 4 MB of RAM and go on up from there. The good news is that the plummeting price of RAM has made video memory very inexpensive; as this book went to press, video card makers were charging about $10 to $20 per MB of DRAM.

Basic video memory is called *DRAM* (Dynamic RAM) and is similar to the devices used in system memory. DRAM provides access either to the digital to analog converter (called a *RAMDAC*) or to the graphics controller.

A faster alternative is *VRAM* (Video RAM) which is dual-ported, meaning it has two exits for information and can react more quickly to demands from either end of its pipeline. VRAM offers a second output port specifically for the

use of the RAMDAC, permitting higher refresh rates. VRAM is probably worth the extra cost—about $50 per MB to a video card at 1997 prices—if you work at resolutions of above 800x600 and 65,535 colors or more.

Next up the line are memory technologies called EDO DRAM, EDO VRAM, and WRAM.

EDO stands for Extended Data Out, an indication of an expanded bandwidth for its data. DRAM and VRAM versions of EDO chips are said to be about 25 percent faster than equivalent standard chips. EDO memory improves speed by allowing the next cycle of memory to begin before the previous cycle finishes its job. EDO is popular because it is very similar to existing RAM in its demands and therefore can be easily integrated into existing designs. EDO is becoming the typical specification for system memory, and some video makers were offering EDO DRAM or EDO VRAM at the same prices as standard DRAM or VRAM. EDO RAM will begin to cause slowdowns, though, any time color depths of more than 8 bits per pixel are used.

Another improvement—but more difficult to implement—is *WRAM* (Window RAM), which is specifically intended for use in systems running GUIs.

Video Resolution

The more individually controllable dots of light on the monitor screen, the crisper the image. Resolution is indicated as *horizontal dots* x *vertical dots* on the screen.

Whatever the capability of the monitor, it is still up to the video display adapter to produce the signal that drives it. All of the video modes are the result of a partnership between the video card and the monitor.

As this book goes to press, nearly every PC uses the SVGA standard in one or another of its advanced modes. Table 12.1 shows many of the video modes available over the history of the PC.

Table 12.1 Video Standards

Resolution	Colors	Mode	Char. Box	Vertical Freq. (Hz)	Horiz. Freq.	Hardware Compatible
MDA Monochrome Display Adapter (1981)						
720 x 350	1	Text	9 x 14	50	18.43	None
CGA Color Graphics Adapter (1981)						
640 x 200	16	Text	8 x 8	60	15.75	None
320 x 200	16	Text	8 x 8	60	15.75	None
160 x 200	16	Graphics	None	60	15.75	None
320 x 200	4	Graphics	None	60	15.75	None
640 x 200	2	Graphics	None	60	15.75	None

Table 12.1 Video Standards (continued)

Resolution	Colors	Mode	Char. Box	Vertical Freq. (Hz)	Horiz. Freq.	Hardware Compatible
HGC Hercules Graphics Card (1982)						
720 x 350	1	Text	9 x 14	50	18.1	MDA
720 x 348	2	Graphics	None	50	18.1	MDA
EGA Enhanced Graphics Adapter (1984)						
640 x 350	16	Text	8 x 14	60	21.85	CGA, MDA
720 x 350	4	Text	9 x 14	60	21.85	CGA, MDA
640 x 350	16	Graphics	None	60	21.85	CGA, MDA
320 x 200	16	Graphics	None	60	21.85	CGA, MDA
640 x 200	16	Graphics	None	60	21.85	CGA, MDA
640 x 350	16	Graphics	None	60	21.85	CGA, MDA
PGA Professional Graphics Adapter (1984)						
640 x 480	256	Graphics	None	60	30.5	CGA
VGA Video Graphics Array (1987)						
720 x 400	16	Text	9 x 16	70	31.5	CGA, EGA
360 x 400	16	Text	9 x 16	70	31.5	CGA, EGA
640 x 480	2, 16	Graphics	None	60	31.5	CGA, EGA
320 x 200	256	Graphics	None	70	31.5	CGA, EGA
MCGA Memory Controller Gate Array (1987)						
320 x 400	4	Text	8 x 16	70	31.5	CGA, EGA
640 x 400	2	Text	8 x 16	70	31.5	CGA, EGA
640 x 480	2	Graphics	None	60	31.5	CGA, EGA
320 x 200	256	Graphics	None	70	31.5	CGA, EGA
8514/A (1987)						
1024 x 768	16, 256	Graphics	None	43.48	35.52	VGA passthrough
640 x 480	256	Graphics	None	43.48	35.52	VGA passthrough
SVGA Super VGA or VESA Specification (1989 and subsequent expansions)						
640 x 480	256–16.7M	Graphics	None	50–120	24–86	VGA, CGA, EGA
800 x 600	16–16.7M	Graphics	None	50–120	25–86	
1024 x 768	16–16.7M	Graphics	None	76–100	24–86	
1280 x 1024	16–16.7M	Graphics	None	76–100	24–86	
1600 x 1280	16–256	Graphics	None	76–150	24–86	

Table 12.1 Video Standards (continued)

Resolution	Colors	Mode	Char. Box	Vertical Freq. (Hz)	Horiz. Freq.	Hardware Compatible
XGA Extended Graphics Array (1990)						
640 x 480	256	Graphics	None	43.48	35.52	VGA
1024 x 768	256	Graphics	None	43.48	35.52	VGA
640 x 480	65K	Graphics	None	43.48	35.52	VGA
1056 x 400	16	Text	8 x 16	43.48	35.52	VGA

Each step along the way from CGA to today's amazing SVGA adapters brought dramatic change. It is almost comical to compare how crude and unimpressive a CGA screen looks in comparison to a multimedia screen from SVGA today. Everything has changed: resolution, number of colors, and speed.

Resolving Resolution Issues

Using a monitor at 1280x1024 resolution gives you four times as much viewable information as can be presented at a standard 640x480 setting—four times as many cells in a spreadsheet or four windows with four word processing documents or any other widescreen or ultra-sharp use you can conjure. That's the good news. The bad news is that individual elements on the screen are one-fourth as large.

Although high resolution may be essential in certain applications such as desktop publishing and graphic arts work, for many users text is simply too small for comfortable writing and editing.

One solution is to use a "zoom" feature that may be an element of the driver for your particular graphics adapter or available as a separate graphics utility software package. Zooms are a compromise, adding some extra keystrokes or mouse clicks to views of the screen and giving up some of the advantage of high resolution in the first place.

For many users, the higher resolutions of modern graphic adapters has been accompanied by an increase in the size of the monitor on their desk. Where once a 13-inch monitor was considered large, today a 14-inch screen is considered hopelessly small; serious computers seem to begin with 15-inch screens and move quickly to 17-inch models. (Monitors are measured along the diagonal from one upper corner of the screen to a lower opposite corner.)

Super VGA Cards

The current state of the consumer-level art in graphics cards is the Super VGA, an extension of the VGA standard developed by third-party manufacturers and in common use on nearly every modern machine. IBM's XGA was intended as its own improvement on the standard but has not migrated to AT-bus machines.

SVGA was originally defined as a small improvement over standard VGA, with resolution of as much as 800x600. As it turned out, that particular resolution level is very infrequently used, and the SVGA definition has expanded and improved to include specifications of 1024x768 and 1280x1,024 and higher. And SVGA also extends downward, including within it a superset of all of the modes and specifications of VGA, which itself included most of the earlier EGA and CGA modes.

The downside to this somewhat soft standard has been the necessity for customized video device drivers for each SVGA card so that the operating system can know exactly what kind of standard "standard" is in use.

In any case, you will need a SVGA video adapter and an SVGA-capable monitor in order to use nearly all current multimedia games and business applications. You should be able to get along with VGA 640x480 resolution for basic tasks like word processing, spreadsheets, and databases. Anything less is going to be a problem, sooner or later.

3-D Graphics Adapters

Are you ready to enter the PC third dimension? Hot and flashy 3-D graphics accelerators are now available as part of new systems and as upgrades to existing computers. They are yet another extension to the flexible SVGA standard.

All of the new cards offer impressive gains in speed and visual quality on 3-D software. And it is also reasonable to expect speed improvements of 25 percent or more over 2-D graphics accelerators running equivalent applications.

But it is important to understand one thing right up front: what you'll see on screen is not really 3-D, at least not in the "Special Glasses Reach Out and Touch the Butterfly Hovering in Front of Your Nose" kind of way.

Instead, think of the 3-D video graphics as the difference between an old Road Runner cartoon and the modern state-of-cartoon-art seen in *Toy Story*.

When designers and marketers speak of 3-D today they are talking about the ability of a graphics card to produce and manipulate 3-D pixels, which are tiny points of light based on the mathematical representations of width, height, and depth of a shape. It is the addition of depth that opens the door to the next great thing in graphics.

Add this new term to your PC lexicon: *texels*, which are pixels (dots of color and brightness that make up the Picture Elements of an image) with a third layer of information defining the pixel's texture.

What are 3-D Graphics?

3-D cards bring together a combination of specialized graphics processing, high-speed dedicated memory, and advanced software schemes. It all comes down to the addition of "depth" to video images.

In mathematical terms, width and height are called X and Y dimensions, while depth is the sought-after Z dimension.

On the software side, there are half a dozen impressive extensions to the graphics capabilities of the PC. At the heart of the improvements are texture mapping, Gouraud shading, and Z-buffering. The first two are ways to use the computer to apply realistic textures and color and light shadings to the basic shapes that make up images; the effect is to allow for complex simulation of perspective and shadow.

It is texture mapping that gives the most eye-popping effects. Textures, with variation for perspective and changing atmospheric conditions, are applied to a shape and modified as action demands. Texture mapping is much slower to produce and manage than flat or Gouraud shading because it adds one full additional level of information to be generated, manipulated, and stored in a new block of memory called the Z-buffer.

Gouraud shading is a step up from flat shading, which assigns a single shade and intensity to fill the interior of a computer-generated shape. Although flat shading is very fast, it robs an image of the variations that give the appearance of depth and reality.

Z-buffering is a scheme that assigns the computer to keep track of the depth of each shape including hidden surfaces that cannot be seen in the current view, and to manage their appearance as the view changes. Most of the graphics chips use information in the Z-buffer to determine whether pixels in an object are in front of (and thus displayed) or behind (and thus hidden) another object.

In a three-dimensional world, the entire database representing the modeled "world" is processed for every frame displayed, with the relative position and orientation of every object recalculated in every frame. Just as in the real world, we may be looking at only the portion of an object that is in direct view, but the rest of the object—its depth and mass—exists nevertheless.

How a 3-D Graphics Card Works

3-D images are created in what designers call the 3-D graphics pipeline, a connection that starts at the computer's CPU and passes through the graphics adapter en route to your monitor.

Despite the impressive raw power of a Pentium-class CPU, most users would not be at all satisfied with the slow-down in image creation that would result if the CPU was all alone in rendering advanced 3-D graphics.

To accomplish their magic without bringing your PC to a halt, most of the new 3-D graphics cards offload some of the intensive number-crunching assignments from the computer's CPU to a specialized chip on the graphics card itself. Not only does this reduce the load on the CPU, it also allows tasks to take place simultaneously. While the rendering engine produces the current frame on the dedicated processor on the 3-D card, the Pentium's CPU is calculating the geometries of the next frame.

The operating system is the highest level control for your PC, controlling the disk and system memory operations of your computer. An API (Application Programming Interface) stands between your operating system and your 3-D graphics accelerator to translate specific demands of the software to the capabilities of your graphics hardware.

The next step is the geometry engine, which translates descriptions of an image into smaller polygons—triangles and other vector graphics (geometric forms that are drawn from point to point, much like you would draw a triangle on a piece of paper).

Generating the polygons and rotating them in a scene to support the 30-frames-per-second imagery of an advanced game is a very calculation-intensive assignment. This is a task that is very well suited to the floating point juggernaut known as a Pentium CPU.

The third element is the rendering engine, which has the assignment of pixel processing. This includes rendering of polygons with shading, the attachment of textures, overlaying atmospheric effects like fog or lighting, perspective correction, and hidden surface removal. The end result is a pixel-by-pixel description for an image, ready to be transmitted to the monitor.

Each board works with a driver that stands between the operating system and the card, directing appropriate calls from the operating system directly to the hardware. The controller converts information into a pixel-by-pixel description of the image.

From the controller, the graphics information is sent to the memory on the card itself, a so-called frame buffer that prepares the image as a grid. Finally, a chip or chip set called the RAMDAC (Random Access Memory Digital-Analog Converter) changes the digital pixels to the analog signal required by nearly all monitors.

AGP: Even Faster Graphics to Come

Even as the first wave of 3-D graphics cards arrives, another very promising technology is taking shape. New motherboards incorporating Intel's Accelerated Graphics Port (AGP) were expected in mid-1997.

The AGP design allows main system memory to be allocated to support 3-D facilities, permitting very high speed creation and transport of images. This adds a functionality to PCs that has been available to workstations for some time.

AGP will allow 3D textures to be stored in the computer's memory and transferred to the graphics accelerator at high speed. Because memory in the PC itself can be used to supplement onboard graphics memory, the cost of graphics required to run 3-D and other video intensive applications may be reduced.

The AGP will be able to run at speeds of up to 133 MHz and transfer data at up to 500 MB per second; compare this to cards plugged into a PCI bus with a current speed limit of 33 MHz and maximum throughput of 132 MB per second.

Video Graphics Array (VGA)

VGA is another IBM-developed standard, originally included as part of the early Micro Channel PS/2s. In many ways, the arrival of the VGA defined the birth of the video portion of the modern machine; today's SVGA is a built upon its foundation.

VGA gains its name from the VLSI (very large-scale integration) chip which is its engine; the processor was called the *Video Graphics Array*. A VGA card produces a high-resolution, multicolor video display. Screen images are crisp, and as many as 256 different colors can be displayed on the screen at once. The VGA card uses *analog* (variable voltage) rather than *TTL* (simple on/off) signals; therefore, VGA-compatible monitors must also be analog. VGA cards and monitors use a 15-pin DB15 video cable connector instead of the standard 9-pin DB9 you expect on monochrome, CGA, or EGA monitors.

How a VGA Card Works

When IBM introduced VGA on its 1987 crop of PS/2 computers, VGA was a premium product; by today, though, the basic electronics for a VGA adapter and its more capable SVGA cousin have dropped well below $100 plus the cost of video RAM.

If you are willing to limit yourself to 640 x 480 pixel VGA resolution, an inexpensive single-frequency VGA monitor will do. But you'll need a multiscanning monitor to run the higher VGA resolutions. Keep this in mind when swapping monitors to test a suspect computer or monitor.

Most modern software is written to work with a VGA at 640 x 480 resolution; if you want to use the higher VGA resolutions, you'll need a *software driver* (a piece of software that tells your video card how to reinterpret the video instructions your software is sending to the card). Most video cards come with drivers for major applications, and you can usually obtain more drivers through on-line bulletin board systems maintained by manufacturers. Programs that run under Microsoft Windows will work with whatever drivers are installed for Windows itself.

A well-written video card driver will increase the response speed of your monitor. Screens will scroll quicker, graphics will redraw faster, and you won't go gray watching the Windows hourglass. The popular computer magazines regularly bench test video cards and drivers. A video card maker saddled with slow drivers will quickly rewrite their drivers to improve their card's performance. Be sure to install these new drivers when your video card maker issues them. You'll have to ask for the latest driver; video card owners are not automatically notified of updates.

Since the monitor is a servant of the video adapter, it turns a pixel on or passes over it and leaves it blank at the explicit pixel-by-pixel direction of the video adapter card. The VGA card provides an analog signal to each of the three electron guns for each of the 307,200 (640x480) pixels, 480,000 (800x600) pixels, 786,432 (1024x768), or 1,310,720 (1280x1024) pixels on the screen.

Ordinary VGA cards can produce 262,144 (256K) different colors. But a basic VGA video card typically doesn't have enough memory to store 262,144 different colors, and instead the card is run in 16-color mode (16 different colors displayed simultaneously) or in 256-color mode (256 different colors displayed at the same time).

But even in 16-color mode, your VGA card gives you a lot of color choices. You are allowed a maximum of 16 different colors, but these 16 colors can be chosen from the full palette of 262,144 colors that the VGA card knows how to create. Think of software programs you have installed recently, the ones with a choice of subtle color schemes. When you choose the "Desert Mist" or "Presidential Pomp" color scheme, you're choosing one particular 16-color palette or another from the full 262,144 colors available.

High resolutions use up lots of video memory; remember that the specifications for each pixel are stored in the VGA card's memory, and these high resolutions have lots of pixels. Color uses up video memory, too. Sixteen-color modes require half as much memory as 256-color modes. If your VGA card has only 256K of memory on board, you're going to be stuck with 640x480 or 800x600 resolution and only 16 colors. 512K of video memory allows the highest resolution *or* 256 colors, but not both. 1 MB of memory on the video card gives you both.

Let's assume your VGA card has enough video memory to store instructions for the 307,200 or 480,000 or 786,432 pixels displayed on your monitor. It's time to redraw the monitor screen. How can the computer move that much information into the card fast enough to satisfy you?

Ordinary frame-buffer video cards don't give the computer's CPU any help. A 16-bit VGA card allows the CPU to shovel in more bits per microsecond than an 8-bit card does, but because these VGA cards sit passively, video response

is primarily a function of CPU speed. In addition, the CPU must figure out how each pixel should be displayed—which takes a lot of CPU time that could be better spent on other tasks.

By comparison, accelerator cards and coprocessor cards take over routine video tasks from the CPU. These VGA cards cost more, but they have the brains to recalculate what pixels should be lit as text or graphics scroll up the screen, to draw a shape on the screen by themselves, or to fill a shape with color. And they are much faster than the CPU. If you are routinely redrawing the whole screen (using Windows, scrolling WYSIWYG text, using draw and paint programs) you will be surprised by how much faster an accelerated or coprocessed VGA card responds.

Troubleshooting a VGA or SVGA Card and Monitor

Before You Do Anything Else

Before you do anything else, make sure that the video adapter is properly seated in the PC's bus and that it is properly connected by cable to the monitor. Then check that the monitor is plugged into a source of wall current—it may be plugged into a special outlet on the back panel of some dinosaur machines, or it may connect directly to the wall outlet. Finally, make sure that the monitor is turned on.

Do you see an indicator light on the monitor? If not, check to see if there is a fuse on the monitor, and that the wall outlet is live.

Finally, check that the contrast and brightness settings on the monitor are not turned off all the way.

Where to Find a VGA or SVGA Card

To locate the VGA card, you must first remove the cover from the computer system unit. Many computer manufacturers put video circuitry on the motherboard, so you may not have a separate video card. Since the monitor is attached to the video adapter card, look on the back of the system unit to find the 15-pin female connector that your monitor data cable plugs into. The 15-pin connector, called a *DB15*, is the video port on the video card or on the motherboard.

How to Test an SVGA or VGA Card

Many SVGA or VGA cards come packaged with diagnostic software. This software is helpful if the video is working, but not 100 percent correctly. QA Plus and CheckIt will also test a mostly-working card for subtle malfunctions.

When the computer has no video, first check the switches and cables. Make sure that the computer and monitor are both plugged in and turned on. Check the video data cable from the card to the monitor. It must be plugged in tightly and screwed down at the video card end. You should also check the brightness and contrast controls on the monitor, but don't adjust these controls and then accidentally leave them in the dim position. In general, the monitor is brightest when the knob is as far clockwise as possible.

A **No video** error can be produced by the card, the monitor, or a multitude of problems in the computer system unit. The troubleshooting charts in Section 3 provide a plan to help you identify the culprit. Before jumping into the troubleshooting charts, though, try a couple of quick swaps if you have duplicate monitors or SVGA- or VGA-equipped computers available. Attach the suspect monitor to a known good computer. If the monitor works on another SVGA- or VGA-equipped computer, the problem is clearly the system unit or the card. Recheck the DIP switches and jumpers on both the video adapter and the computer motherboard. Consult the computer and card manuals for switch and jumper settings.

Try installing your suspect video card into a known good computer that is configured for the same type of card. The best test equipment is an identical working version of your dead machine. Swap the parts of the dead machine one by one into the working machine. When the symptom finally jumps from the dead computer to the good one, you know that the last part you swapped is the culprit.

If you have one or two incorrect characters in an otherwise good screen, the video memory located on the video card is at fault. Replace the card.

A good practice is to use a capable diagnostic software package like CheckIt or QA Plus to test the video memory before you replace the card.

How to Remove and Install a Video Card

Before you remove a video card, you must turn off the computer and the monitor. Disconnect the data cable (it runs from the video card to the monitor) at the video card end. You will probably have to remove two small screws that are used to hold the cable connector tight to the card. Remove the system unit cover. The card itself is secured to the back wall of the system unit chassis with a single screw. Remove and save the screw. Remove the card. Lift the card straight up; it should require only moderate force.

Installation is the reverse of removal. Most video cards are 16-bit cards now, though 8-bit cards are still available. Look for a vacant double-length 16-bit slot on your motherboard. As we have noted, nearly all new SVGA cards are designed to plug into a PCI slot; you may have difficulty finding a state-of-the-art card for an ISA slot although older models may be offered at a full-line dealer or mail order house.

Line up the slot connector on the card with the slot on the motherboard, then press down firmly. When the card is in place, the screw hole on the card will line up with the screw hole in the back of the chassis. Reinstall the screw and test the machine.

If you are installing a different type of video card—if, for example, you're replacing the original VGA card with a new SVGA card—be sure to consult your PC's instruction manual to see if there are any switches or jumpers on the motherboard that need to be set to reflect the new video adapter. If you have a modern machine, you may need to run the Setup program in order to store the new hardware information in CMOS on the motherboard. And as we have also noted, check with the maker of your motherboard or system to determine if you need to upgrade the system BIOS.

Dinosaur Video Standards

Color Graphics Video Adapter (CGA) Card

The Color Graphics Adapter (CGA) was the first bitmapped display adapter for the PC, and dates to the early days of the dinosaur.

A CGA adapter drives an *RGB* monitor, which draws its name from the fact that it receives separate red, green, and blue signals for the corresponding color phosphors painted on the inside surface of the picture tube.

A CGA adapter is not compatible with a current SVGA or VGA monitor, and most current monitors will not work with an outdated CGA adapter.

The CGA card was the first IBM PC video card capable of two new features: 16-color display, and the pixel-by-pixel screen control necessary to display graphics. CGA adapters treat the screen as a grid that is 200 pixels (picture elements) tall and 320 pixels wide. When working in the 320 x 200 pixel mode, the video card is able to display 4 of the 16 available colors on the screen at any one time. Since it has relatively few pixels—and these pixels are quite large—

a CGA card has much poorer resolution than a monochrome card. Nevertheless, color display and the potential to draw pictures or graphs dot-by-dot on the screen made the CGA very popular.

CGA cards also offer a special high-resolution mode that provides two colors (for example, black and white) on the screen at a time. The two-color mode uses a 640x200 pixel grid, permitting reasonably sharp display of text, although it is still coarser than the 720x348 resolution available with a Hercules Graphics card, and well below the capabilities of a modern adapter.

How a CGA Card Works

A CGA board contains enough memory (16K) to store information for each pixel on the color monitor screen. (For comparison's sake, consider that modern machines typically sport SVGA cards with 1 MB, 2 MB or even 4 MB of video RAM.) All video data, whether text or graphics, is stored pixel-by-pixel in the video memory. The monitor reads the video memory 60 times per second and places its contents on the screen. To display a simple letter—for instance, a capital *T*—the electron beam in the monitor excites one horizontal row of pixels and one vertical column of pixels.

A program can display text either by creating the text font from individual pixels or by asking the BIOS ROM to display text using its standard font. In the first case, the text is stored in the video memory as a collection of dots, not as a complete character.

To display a graphic (a picture composed of many little dots of color), the individual pixels are excited. As we have noted, only four colors can be used on the screen at any one time, but there are always two palettes of four colors available and ready to be switched into place. Three of the four colors in a given palette are predetermined by the video adapter circuitry. Any of the 13 other colors in the basic set of 16 can be chosen as the fourth color in either palette.

How to Test a CGA Card

See "Before You Do Anything Else" above to test the electrical and signal connectors of the card and the monitor.

To locate the CGA card, you must first remove the cover from the computer system unit. On a dinosaur, the video card is often (but not always) on the far left, as far away from the disk drives and power supply as possible. Since the monitor is attached to the video adapter card, look on the back of the system unit to find the 9-pin female connector that your monitor data cable plugs into.

Many diagnostic disks provide video troubleshooting help. CheckIt, QA Plus, and IBM Diagnostics provide test programs to demonstrate all 16 colors and both palettes. These disks will only work, however, if you have readable video.

If the problem is that you have no video at all, check for an incorrect match between the monitor and the video card. Don't use CGA cards with monochrome text monitors. That mismatch causes snow on the monitor, since the video data transmitted for a line of color text is gibberish to a monochrome text monitor.

If you have a dinosaur XT clone, check for proper DIP switch settings on the motherboard. Modern machines need to have the video type set correctly in their CMOS setup memory chip, but these machines are able to display an initial error message, such as **Incorrect setup. Wrong video adapter.**

If you have one or two incorrect characters in an otherwise good screen, the video memory located on the video card is likely at fault. You can use QAPlus or CheckIt diagnostic software to test the video memory before you address the issue of getting a new card.

You may have a hard time finding a replacement CGA card, although you may have luck obtaining a used relic from a computer repair shop. Check with the manufacturer of your computer or the maker of the ROM BIOS to see if the machine is capable of working with a more advanced graphics card such as a VGA.

How to Remove and Install a CGA Card

Before you remove the CGA card, you must turn off the computer and the monitor. Disconnect the data cable from the video card to the monitor at the video card end. You will probably have to remove two small screws that are installed to hold the cable connector tight to the card.

The card itself is secured to the back wall of the system unit chassis with a single screw. Remove and save that screw. Lift the card straight up; it shouldn't require great force.

Installation is the reverse of removal. Because CGA video cards are 8-bit cards, any bus connector in any of the clones is appropriate, although some systems suggest keeping the video card as far away from the power supply as possible. Carefully line up the card edge connector with the slot on the motherboard, then press down firmly. When the card is in place, the screw hole on the card will line up with the screw hole in the back of the chassis. Reinstall the screw, reattach the video cable, and test the machine.

If you are installing a different type of video card, be sure to set any switches and/or jumpers on the motherboard to reflect the new video adapter. See your motherboard manual and the section of this chapter that covers your new video card for more details.

Monochrome Display Adapter (MDA)

Even older than the CGA card by a few months, this text-only monochrome card is officially known as the Monochrome Display and Parallel Printer Adapter.

The MDA was the original display adapter that was offered with IBM's very first computer, the IBM PC. It was intended to work with IBM's own text-only monochrome monitor. Only a handful of early clone makers bothered to adopt the MDA, and only a few monitor makers emulated IBM's design for the monitor.

Soon after the introduction of the IBM PC, the Color Graphics Adapter (with lower resolution but the ability to draw graphics—primitive by today's standards, but graphics nevertheless—and able to use color) arrived. The first major third-party adapter was the Hercules Graphics Adapter, which sat between the two cards: it was a high-resolution monochrome text card that could also display monochrome graphics.

MDA is all but abandoned by most modern software; as a starter, Microsoft Windows will not work with MGA at all because the adapter cannot display bitmapped graphics. You will probably be able to continue to perform such text-oriented applications as word processing and some database work, but not much else.

If you have an MDA adapter, check with the manufacturer of your PC if it is still in business or with a ROM BIOS maker to see if the ROMs can be upgraded to work with a VGA adapter. If not, the only solution to improving your computing capabilities is to put Old Faithful in the closet; none of the adapter cards and the monochrome monitor can likely be used with a modern machine.

If your MDA adapter has failed, you may find it very difficult to find a replacement that will work with your ROM BIOS and system; it may be possible to obtain a used part from a computer shop. You may also be able to obtain a Hercules Graphics card or one that emulates that mode.

The monochrome text-only video adapter card is technically considered a *character-mapped* system, capable only of displaying 256 preformed characters (called the IBM PC character set) in standard positions on the screen. The card cannot draw free-form graphics images on the screen because it is not capable of pixel-by-pixel (dot-by-dot) control of the monitor screen. It is capable of driving only a monochrome monitor. Hooking it to an RGB color monitor will produce only snow on the screen, and may damage the monitor or the card (or both).

The card treats the monitor screen as if it were a grid of 80 columns of characters by 25 rows. Each of these positions may contain one of the preformed characters, nothing else. This text-only card is also capable of a 40-character-wide by 25-row format. Programmers rarely used this alternative format, but you'll occasionally see it in old programs and games that somehow managed to coax a bit of a picture out of some of the symbols in the IBM character set.

How a Monochrome Text-Only Video Adapter Card Works

The video card contains enough memory to store information for each character position on the screen. The monitor is continuously placing data from the video memory on the screen. A monochrome monitor will read the video memory and write it on the screen approximately 50 times per second.

When a program needs to write characters to the video screen, it may put data directly into video memory or it may ask the ROM to write the characters on the screen and rely on the ROM to put the necessary data in video memory. In either case, the video memory holds a record of the character (including the null character for blanks) to be displayed at each position on the video screen.

How to Test a Monochrome Text-Only Video Adapter Card

First, test the card and the monitor as discussed in "Before You Do Anything Else" earlier in this chapter.

Many diagnostic disks provide video troubleshooting help. CheckIt and QA Plus, for example, include video test programs. Of course, you'll have to be able to see some video on the screen to use them.

If you have no video at all and have made any changes under the covers of the computer since the last time the monitor worked, check for an incorrect match between the monitor and the video card. Check for proper switch settings on the motherboard of a dinosaur PC. On modern machines, the BIOS checks to see that the video type is set correctly in their CMOS setup memory chip. Modern machines are able to display an initial error message, such as **Incorrect setup. Wrong video adapter**.

One indication of the failure of a MDA is when characters change on the monitor all by themselves; a Greek character, or a face, or a punctuation mark suddenly appears on the monitor in the midst of text, replacing the original letter of the alphabet. If you reload the text from the PC, the screen may be fine or the problem characters may appear somewhere else.

A misdisplay of characters is an indication of a problem with the memory on the video adapter card, causing an unwanted change in the stored information.

If you suspect that your monitor is malfunctioning, try connecting it to another known good MDA if you can find one; or connect a known good monitor to your MDA.

How to Remove and Install a Monochrome Text-Only Video Adapter Card

To locate the card, you must first remove the cover from the computer system unit. The video expansion card is often but not always on the far left, as far away from the disk drives and the power supply as possible. The monitor is attached to the video adapter card, so look on the back of the system unit to find the 9-pin female connector that your monitor plugs into. That 9-pin connector, called a DB9, is on the video card.

To remove the monotext card, first turn off the computer and monitor. Disconnect the data cable that runs from the video card to the monitor at the video card end. You will probably have to remove the two small screws that hold the cable connector tight. The card itself is secured to the back wall of the system unit chassis with a single screw. Remove and save this screw. The card should be lifted straight up, which shouldn't require much force.

Installation is the reverse of removal. Because MDA video cards are 8-bit cards, any bus connector in any of the clones is appropriate although a slot as far as possible from the power supply is suggested. Line up the slot connector (card edge connector) on the card with the slot on the motherboard carefully and press down firmly. When the card is in place, the screw hole on the card will line up with the screw hole in the back of the chassis. Reinstall the screw, reattach the monitor cable, and test the machine.

If you are installing a different type of video card, be sure to set any switches or jumpers on the motherboard to reflect the new video adapter. See your motherboard manual and the section of this chapter dedicated to your new video card for more details.

Hercules Graphics Card (HGC) or Monochrome Graphics Video Adapter (MGA) Card

Hercules Graphics introduced its graphics and text hybrid about a year after the birth of the dinosaur IBM PC. The HGC (its non-Hercules clone of the MGA) and a version that includes a parallel port, the MGP, combines the best aspects of both monochrome text and color video adapters: well-defined, crisp characters as well as pixel by pixel control of the monitor display.

How the MGA or MGP Card Works

HGC and compatible cards produce two video modes: text and graphics. In text mode the cards display clear, crisp, predrawn characters. This mode uses an 80 x 25 character grid on the display screen. There is sufficient video memory on the MGA board to store a character for each of the 80 positions per line and for all 25 lines on the screen. The monitor reads data from the video memory and writes it to the screen 50 times per second.

When a program needs to write characters to the video screen in text mode, it can put data directly into video memory or it can ask the ROM to write the characters on the screen and rely on the ROM to put the necessary data in video memory. In either case, the video memory holds a record of the character—including the null character for blanks—to be displayed at each position on the screen.

The card includes 64K of video memory, enough to store up to 16 text pages, or in graphics mode, enough for two full-screen pages of monochrome graphics. The additional stored pages in text mode can be used to predraw that many succeeding screens of data. This technique provides extremely quick page-down capability, since the information for succeeding pages is already in memory and ready to be displayed instantly. Some monochrome software uses this feature, but quick screen changes are not generally a high priority for monochrome applications.

In graphics mode, the HGC/MGA controls each pixel on the display screen individually. The screen is divided into 720 pixels horizontally and 348 pixels vertically.

Compare this to the CGA. CGA boards can show only half that resolution, having 320 pixels x 200 pixels. But CGA video cards store color information for each individual pixel in the video card's memory, and color uses up more space than monochrome information.

Characters can be displayed when the MGA or MGP card is in the graphics mode, but they are individually drawn onto the screen pixel by pixel. Pictures are also drawn pixel by pixel.

How to Test an HGC, MGA or MGP Card

Check the card and the monitor as discussed in "Before You Do Anything Else" earlier in this chapter.

To locate the MGP card, first remove the cover from the computer system unit. The video expansion card is often, but not always, on the far left, as far away from the disk drives and the power supply as possible. Because the monitor is attached to the video adapter card, look on the back of the system unit to find the 9-pin female connector that your monitor plugs into.

Many diagnostic disks provide video troubleshooting help. QA Plus and CheckIt, for example, contain video test programs.

If you have no video at all, check for an incorrect match between the monitor and the video card. Don't attach MGA and MGP cards to color monitors. Mismatches between the video card and the monitor usually cause snow on the monitor screen.

If you have an early PC, check the DIP switch settings on the motherboard. DIP switches control the video address that the motherboard is trying to use. Incorrect DIP switch settings usually produce a flashing cursor with no additional video display. Modern machines need to have the video type set correctly in their CMOS setup memory chip, but these machines are able to display an initial error message such as **Incorrect setup. Wrong video adapter.**

If you have one or two incorrect characters in an otherwise good screen, the video memory located on the video card is most likely at fault. You can use a diagnostic program to test the video RAM before you buy a new card.

How to Remove and Install an HGC, MGA, or MGP Card

Before you remove the MGA or MGP card, turn off the computer and monitor. Disconnect the data cable from the video card to the monitor at the video card end. You will probably have to remove two small screws that hold the cable connector tight to the card. Remove the system unit cover.

The card itself is secured to the back wall of the system unit chassis with a single screw. Remove and save the screw. Lift the card straight up; it shouldn't require extreme force.

Installation is the reverse of removal. Because HGC/MGA video cards are 8-bit cards, any bus connector in any of the clones is appropriate. If you are replacing the card with another type, you may have to use a 16-bit slot on a modern machine. Carefully line up the card edge connector with the slot on the motherboard, then press down firmly. When the card is in place, the screw hole on the card will line up with the screw hole in the back of the chassis. Reinstall the screw, attach the monitor cable, and test the machine.

If you are installing a different type of video card—if you're replacing your old card with a VGA or a color card, for example—be sure to set any switches or jumpers on the motherboard to reflect the new video adapter. See your motherboard manual for more details.

Enhanced Graphics Adapter (EGA) Card

The EGA card is a footnote to history, an advanced graphics and text card that stood between the popular CGA and the pervasive VGA standards. It failed to deliver the huge palette of colors that the coming multimedia revolution would demand, and today it is almost forgotten.

This card provides medium- and high-resolution color or monochrome video display. It operates in either text mode (for word processing) or graphics mode (where charts and pictures can be drawn on the screen dot by dot). It is capable of producing 256 different colors when teamed with an EGA monitor, but the EGA card can display only 16 of those colors on the screen at one time.

A data cable connects an EGA monitor to the EGA card, using a 9-pin (DB9) socket on the card.

How an EGA Card Works

An EGA video card is capable of multiple video modes. One mode, EGA monochrome, treats the screen as a 720x350 pixel grid. The grid has 720 pixels per horizontal line, and 350 lines per screen. In this monochrome mode, the EGA card drives a simple monochrome monitor to replicate the features of a Hercules Graphics Card. Many color modes

are possible, ranging from 320x200 pixels (emulating a CGA video adapter) to 640x350 pixel screens with 16 different colors on-screen simultaneously. Extended EGA cards have two new video modes, both with 16-color VGA-quality resolution. Most color modes will work either with an EGA color monitor or with a multiscanning monitor, but Extended EGA *requires* a multiscanning monitor.

The monitor is a servant of the video adapter; it turns a pixel on or passes over it and leaves it blank at the explicit pixel-by-pixel direction of the EGA card. EGA cards provide two on/off signals to each of the three electron guns. One signal is high intensity (bright) and one is low intensity. There are 256 different possible combinations of these six signals, thus 256 possible colors. At 640x350 resolution, the screen contains over 200,000 pixels. All this video information must be stored somewhere, so EGA cards have as much as 256K of video memory on the card. (Original IBM EGA cards had only 64K, but performance was limited, so 256K soon became the standard.)

The computer sends data to the video card. When the card is in text mode, the computer sends alphanumeric characters which are stored in video memory. The video card character generator changes each text character into a pattern of pixels and sends that data to the monitor pixel by pixel.

In graphics mode, the computer sends pixel-by-pixel instructions directly to the video card memory. The card then transmits that information to the monitor, which displays and redisplays the contents of video memory. The monitor refreshes the screen (re-energizes the pixels) 60 times per second, which provides a fairly stable image.

How to Test an EGA Card

To locate the EGA card, first remove the cover from the computer system unit. Because the monitor is attached to the video adapter card, look on the back of the system unit to find the 9-pin female connector that your monitor data cable plugs into.

EGA adapters and EGA monitors use DB9 connectors. Monochrome (MDA, MGA, and MGP) video cards and color (CGA) video cards also are equipped with a DB9 connector. Therefore, it is not easy to tell any of these video cards apart by looking at the outside of the computer. If you have doubts about your video card's identity, it's best to take off the system unit cover and look at the video card. Most EGA boards have DIP switches to set the various possible EGA video modes. In addition, most EGA board manufacturers provide a prominent decal or other label on the EGA card.

Whenever you install a new EGA card or have doubts about an old one, you should test the separate EGA modes, both monochrome and color. Luckily, EGA cards are usually sold with diagnostic software to make this testing easy.

But suppose you have no video display at all, or the screen is displaying snow or other gibberish. There are many possible causes for this type of problem. See "How to Test a Monitor" in Chapter 13. Usually you will find the problem there. If not, here are some other ideas.

EGA cards have many modes, with the initial bootup mode usually controlled by DIP switches or jumpers. Make sure that the motherboard setting of these switches or jumpers matches the EGA card setting. Remember that many 286 and 386 PCs, and some older 486 computers, have a jumper on the motherboard for color versus monochrome video; you'll also have to make changes to the setup information in the CMOS chip.

Finally, make sure that the EGA card is set to work with the monitor you're using. Check your EGA card and computer motherboard manuals for the correct switch settings.

With more advanced video cards, it becomes more valuable to have a good diagnostics program to test its various modes. As with any other video card, the most likely culprit for many display problems is a failure in video memory on the card. Run diagnostics before considering replacing the memory—held in sockets on many EGA cards—or the more expensive card itself.

How to Remove and Install an EGA Card

Before you remove the EGA card, turn off the computer and the monitor. Disconnect the data cable from the video card to the monitor at the video card end. You will probably have to remove two small screws used to hold the cable connector tight to the card. Remove the system unit cover. The card itself is secured to the back wall of the system unit chassis with a single screw. Remove and save that screw. Lift the card straight up; it shouldn't require great force.

Before you install an EGA card, read the manual and set the DIP switches as necessary. The motherboard DIP switches may also need to be reset if you are changing from monochrome or from RGB color video to EGA.

Installation is the reverse of removal. Because EGA video cards are 8-bit cards, any bus connector in any of the clones is appropriate. When the card is in place, the screw hole on the card will line up with the screw hole in the back of the chassis. Reinstall the screw and test the machine.

If you are installing a different type of video card—if, for example, you're replacing the original CGA card with an EGA or a VGA card—be sure to set any switches or jumpers on the motherboard to reflect the new video adapter. See your motherboard manual for further instructions.

You may find it difficult to find a replacement EGA card, since that standard has been abandoned by card makers. You may have luck locating a used card at a computer repair shop. And some but not all ROM BIOS chips on early PCs and older modern machines may be able to accommodate a VGA adapter; check with the manufacturer of your PC or a BIOS maker.

Exotic Video Cards

Extended Graphics Array (XGA) Card

IBM introduced XGA as a follow-on to its 8514/A standard with its advanced 486 PS/2 computers in 1990. The XGA standard requires a Micro Channel Architecture (MCA) computer used only on high-level PS/2s and a tiny handful of clones.

XGA cards provide very high resolution (1024x768 pixels per monitor screen) and the potential to display 65,536 colors onscreen simultaneously if you choose 640x480 pixel (standard VGA) resolution. In addition, XGA cards can be switched to emulate an ordinary VGA card with 16 colors and 640x480 pixel resolution. XGA cards use a micro-processor on the card to do most of the routine work associated with screen redraws. 8514/A, TIGA cards, and VGA cards with accelerators also use video card microprocessors for fast video response.

How an XGA Card Works

XGA cards use the 32-bit MCA bus and MCA bus mastering (the card can take over the bus to speed up data transfer into the card). Therefore, they are surprisingly fast, but limited to the PS/2 family.

Each pixel of an XGA-compatible color monitor is really a trio of phosphor dots. When excited by an electron beam, each dot glows red, green, or blue. Inside the monitor, three separate electron beams scan across the CRT screen. Each beam is responsible for exciting a single color of phosphor in each pixel.

The XGA card provides an analog signal to each of the three electron guns for each of the 307,200 (640x480) pixels or 786,432 (1024x768) pixels on the screen.

High-resolution monitors use up lots of video memory—remember that the specifications for each pixel are stored in the XGA card's memory, and these high resolutions have lots of pixels. Color uses up video memory too. Sixteen-color modes require half as much memory as 256-color modes. Remember that we are talking about dedicated *video memory* here (memory chips on the video card, or in the sockets on the motherboard dedicated to video memory if the XGA card is built right into the motherboard), not *system memory* (ordinary memory chips on the motherboard or on a memory expansion card).

How to Test an XGA Card

Some PS/2s feature XGA integrated on the motherboard, while others use a separate XGA card. (And many mid-level or low-priced PS/2s feature VGA video, so don't jump to the conclusion that your PS/2 has XGA merely because it's a PS/2.)

Remove the cover from the computer system unit. Because the monitor is attached to the video adapter card or to the video connector on the motherboard, look on the back of the system unit to find the 15-pin female connector that your monitor data cable plugs into.

PS/2 computers come with diagnostic software. Use this to check your XGA card and monitor.

Replacement XGA adapters can be obtained from IBM; you should also be able to install a VGA or SVGA card in its place. Check with IBM if you have any questions. If the XGA adapter is part of the motherboard of your PC, you should be able to disable it with a jumper setting and have the computer recognize a card installed in the bus instead.

8514/A Video Card

IBM introduced 8514/A in 1987 on PS/2 computers with the Micro Channel Architecture. The original IBM standard provided 1024x768 pixel resolution, but used an interlaced monitor. *Interlacing* (painting the monitor screen in two passes of the electron gun rather than all at once) allows high-resolution graphics on a moderately priced monitor, but interlaced video tends to flicker.

The Video Electronics Standards Association (VESA) 8514/A adaptation of the 8514/A standard calls for noninterlaced monitors and a vertical scan rate of at least 70 screen refreshes per second. Many 8514/A video cards provide 72 or 76 Hz scan rates for crisp, flicker-free pictures on large monitors.

How an 8514/A Video Card Works

8514/A uses the same monitor-to-video-card interface as Super VGA and Extended VGA. In other words, a multi-scanning VGA monitor that works fine with a high-resolution VGA card will work fine with an 8514/A card. But your computer communicates with an 8514/A card quite differently than with a VGA card.

Your computer tells the 8514/A card "Please draw me a box" or "Rotate this box." This is known as *vector graphics*. The CPU issues a very high-level command and the 8514/A video card figures out how to execute it. By comparison, monochrome graphics, CGA, EGA, and frame-buffer VGA cards use *raster graphics* and rely on the computer's main CPU for most video processing. In raster graphics the computer's CPU figures out pixel by pixel what should be on the monitor screen.

8514/A cards are much faster than raster graphics video cards, especially when running Windows and CAD software. TIGA cards also use vector graphics, but TIGA cards are built around a microprocessor from the Texas Instruments 34010 and 34020 family of video chips. TIGA is particularly fast for CAD applications. IBM's XGA video standard was designed particularly for the Microsoft Windows market. But any of these coprocessed video cards (8514/A, TIGA, and XGA) will be dramatically faster running Windows than will the ordinary raster graphics VGA card.

How to Test an 8514/A Card

Remove the cover from the computer system unit. Because the monitor is attached to the video adapter card or to the video connector on the motherboard, look on the back of the system unit to find the 15-pin female connector that your monitor data cable plugs into.

If the computer has no video at all, first check the switches and cables. Make sure that the computer and monitor are both plugged in and turned on. Check the video data cable from the 8514/A card to the monitor. It must be plugged in tightly and screwed down at the video card end. You should also check the brightness and contrast controls on the monitor, but don't adjust these controls and then accidentally leave them in the dim position. The monitor is usually brightest when the knob is as far clockwise as possible.

Some 8514/A cards have VGA support built in. Other 8514/A cards are designed for a computer with a separate VGA card or with VGA on the motherboard. In either case, the computer runs in VGA mode while booting, then switches over to 8514/A mode. Do you have a VGA card installed? Does your 8514/A card require a separate VGA card? Does the VGA card work?

Memory Controller Gate Array (MCGA)

This adapter was a hybrid of a hybrid, and is all but forgotten in the history of PC video except by those owners of a small group of low-end IBM PS/2 models that used it. The adapter offered a mix of VGA, MDA, and CGA. There are two text modes, one mode close to the CGA standard and the other somewhat like VGA. For graphics, there are several CGA-like modes as well as a pair of severely limited VGA modes hamstrung by the 64K total RAM associated with the adapter.

An MCGA-based system uses VGA-style connectors, and can be used with standard VGA displays. The system is capable of detecting color or monochrome monitors and can reset its mode automatically.

How to Test and Upgrade an MCGA

Use IBM's supplied diagnostics to test the MCGA circuitry. Be sure that the monitor is attached, turned on, and properly adjusted before concluding that the problem lies with the adapter.

The MCGA is integrated into the motherboard of the PS/2; therefore, it cannot be repaired or upgraded. Instead, it can be bypassed completely by plugging a PS/2 VGA adapter into the system bus; the MCGA will be automatically disabled.

Texas Instruments Graphics Architecture (TIGA) Card

Texas Instruments launched its own graphics interface, called TIGA (Texas Instruments Graphics Adapter.) These TIGA video cards use a Texas Instruments 34010 or 34020 video microprocessor chip and vector graphics.

Many of the early users of TIGA card were design professionals who needed 24-bit photo-quality color; most of the standard's advantages have been adopted by Super VGA cards. TIGA cards provide very high resolution (1024x768 pixels per monitor screen or better) and improved speed.

How a TIGA Card Works

TIGA cards use a very high speed VGA-style analog monitor. The monitor turns a pixel on or passes over it and leaves it blank at the explicit pixel-by-pixel direction of the video adapter card. The TIGA card provides an analog signal to each of the three electron guns for each of 786,432 (1024x768) pixels on the screen. 1280x1024 pixel resolution has 1.3 million pixels, almost twice as many.

Though TIGA uses the same monitor-to-video-card interface as Super VGA and Extended VGA, your computer communicates with a TIGA card quite differently than with a VGA card. Your computer tells the TIGA card "Please draw me a box" or "Rotate this box." This is termed *vector graphics*. Most other video cards use a pixel-by-pixel technique; the computer says "Please turn on this pixel"—a technique called *raster graphics*. Frame buffer VGA cards (ordinary VGA cards without an accelerator), EGA cards, MGP cards, and RGB cards use raster graphics.

Because most TIGA cards come with Windows drivers, any program you will be running from within Microsoft Windows should be able to use the TIGA card's fast video microprocessor. But other DOS-based software may not have a TIGA driver.

How to Test a TIGA Card

Remove the cover from the computer system unit. Because the monitor is attached to the video adapter card or to the video connector on the motherboard, look on the back of the system unit to find the 15-pin female connector that your monitor data cable plugs into.

Check the card and the monitor as discussed in "Before You Do Anything Else" earlier in this chapter. If the computer has no video at all, first check the switches and cables. Make sure that the computer and monitor are both plugged in and turned on. Check the video data cable from the TIGA card to the monitor. It must be plugged in tight and screwed down at the video card end. You should also check the brightness and contrast controls on the monitor, but don't adjust these controls and then accidentally leave them in the dim position. In general, the monitor is brightest with the knob turned clockwise.

Some TIGA cards have VGA support built in; others are designed for a computer with a separate VGA card or with VGA on the motherboard. In either case, the computer runs in VGA mode while booting, then switches over to TIGA mode. Do you have a VGA card installed? Do you need one? Does it work?

Video Troubleshooting

Problem: I have no video at all.

Solution:

- Start with the monitor: is it plugged in, turned on, and properly attached to the video adapter with a cable? Check to see that the brightness and contrast settings on the monitor are proper. Once those elements are established, turn off the power, unplug the PC, and remove its covers. Is the video card seated properly?

- Have you removed the card to make changes to its settings? If so, check any jumpers or switches to see that they are set correctly.

- If everything checks out properly, try installing the suspect video card in another system to see if it works, or install a known good video card in your system to see if it works with your monitor.

Problem: My screen is showing incorrect colors, dots, or streaks in DOS games or applications.

Solution:

- This may be caused by a system bus running out of synch with your video card. Consult your video card maker or PC maker to see whether "wait states" need to be added to the bus.

Problem: I see random characters on screen during the running of a graphics program.

Solution:

- There may be a memory conflict for the video adapter. For most adapters (consult your instruction manual) you'll need to exclude from the control of **EMM386.EXE** the memory address occupied by the video adapter. To do so, edit the **CONFIG.SYS** file and locate **EMM386.EXE** as follows:

```
EMM386.EXE X=A000-C7FF
```

If **HIGHSCAN** appears on that line, it must be removed.

- Some video cards require that the BIOS "Video Shadow" or "Video Cache" RAM be disabled. Check the instruction manual and consult with the video adapter manufacturer if necessary.

Problem: When I disabled video shadow, my 486 25MHz PC produces occasional DMA errors.

Solution:

- Some of the early versions of the 486 25MHz chip, the "B Step" version, had a problem in this regard. To get around this, enable the "Video Shadow", but disable "Video Cache" and "Adapter Shadow." Later 486 CPUs do not have this problem.

CHAPTER 13
Monitors

You may not know much about the electronics of video monitors, but you'll know what you like. The newest and highest-tech of modern machine video displays are Rembrandts compared to the cave scrawls of dinosaur systems.

The current state of the art for consumer PCs are SVGA monitors. Most modern machines can work with them, although early PCs may require new video display adapters and, possibly, upgrades to ROM BIOS chips. The oldest of the dinosaurs may not have BIOS fixes or motherboard circuitry to work with advanced video systems.

And though 14-inch monitors are still on the market at the low end of the price scale, most PC buyers would today consider a 15-inch monitor the minimum acceptable size for graphics-intensive computing such as Windows 95 applications, with 17-inch devices increasingly popular.

For our purposes in this book, monitors are *not* repairable—at least not by anyone other than a highly skilled technician. That's the bad news; the good news is that monitors are generally very reliable. (The best thing you can do to protect the life of your monitor is make sure it is plugged into a good-quality surge protector. The second best thing you can do is to make sure that the cable between the monitor and the video card is firmly attached at each end and not crimped or pinched.)

If you intend to use high-resolution settings on your monitor, make sure that the display device and your graphics adapter are a good match for each other. You cannot view more pixels than your monitor can display, and you cannot ask a graphics adapter to address more pixels than it is capable of rendering in memory.

Another issue for some users is the physical size of the monitor itself. In rough terms, the depth of a monitor in its case is about equal to the diagonal measurement of the tube; a 21-inch monitor will take up a lot of space on a typical 30-inch-deep desktop. And monitor weight also increases with size, with some monsters weighing in at 75 pounds or more.

How a Monitor Works

A monitor is, at heart, a very high-quality television set that is tuned to just one channel: the signal coming out of the PC's video adapter. The other side of the glass front of the monitor is coated with phosphor compounds that glow whenever an electron beam strikes them. The monitor's electronics view the screen as a grid of dots to be painted with light. Each of the group of red, green, and blue dots is called a *pixel*, which stands for picture element.

There are three ways to draw an image or a character on the screen:

- One way uses simple instructions from the CPU that tells the video card and the monitor to display the letter "J" at position 12,180. The card needs to have a definition for each letter and a particular style for that letter; the description is then communicated to the monitor in the form of instructions about which individual dots to illuminate. The original monochrome display adapter used such a scheme, and all subsequent improvements to graphics modes maintain this basic text ability.

- Another means of drawing images uses a video display adapter that maintains a library of shapes and colors which are then communicated to the monitor.

- Modern graphical user interfaces (GUIs) like Windows and OS/2 Warp produce the entire screen as a bitmap in memory, drawing all characters and graphics; this bitmap is then transferred by the video card to the monitor for display as a series of illuminated dots. Bitmaps are not nearly as fast as direct display of characters, but offer other significant advantages, such as the ability to draw any type of imaginable image and use an unlimited number of type styles and sizes.

Types of Monitors

Inexpensive monochrome monitors, the kind that were standard on PCs through the 1980s, are capable of displaying only one color: usually white, green, or amber against a black background.

There are also some very capable monochrome displays for modern machines. Higher-priced monochrome monitors—for example, VGA monochrome monitors—are available with very high resolution and multiple shades of gray.

Ultra-high-resolution, monochrome monitors with proprietary video systems intended for desktop publishing and computer-aided design usually have extra-large screens, often designed to show two facing pages, or a vertical page in true proportions.

But high-resolution color video has really taken off in the 1990s. SVGA color monitors are now standard equipment on PCs, with resolutions of up to 1280x1024 on home machines.

Microsoft Windows, large spreadsheet, and desktop publishing users appreciate a full-page view of their work. In addition, high-level graphics users are choosing to manipulate photos, video, and animation with 24-bit color video cards capable of displaying millions of subtle color shades.

About Monitor Size

What exactly do they mean by a "15-inch" monitor? In theory, screen size is measured as the diagonal distance (top left to bottom right, or top right to bottom left corner). However, not all screens are shaped the same, and in any case the plastic frame around the screen (called a "bezel") can crop as much as an inch on all sides of the tube.

Partly as the result of some consumer lawsuits, monitor makers now are a bit more careful in their claims. Look for the manufacturer's specification of "maximum viewable image size." You'll often find that a 15-inch screen has viewable sizes in the range of 13.5 to 13.9 inches; 17-inch screens are usually in the range of 15.5 to 16 inches.

Probably more important is to consider the differences in square inches of screen real estate offered by monitors of various sizes. Going from a 14-inch monitor to a 15-inch box yields a 25 percent boost in size, from 72 square inches to 90 square inches. Going from a 15 inch monitor to a 21-inch behemoth more than doubles the view, from about 90 square inches to about 185 square inches.

But we're not yet finished with cutting your image down to size: consider the fact that very few monitors actually send electrons all the way to the edges of the tube. And those that are capable of doing so may deliver a distorted picture at the edges. You'll want to adjust the picture to deliver the best view, usually resulting in a frame of about a quarter inch on all sides.

(It is also worth noting that on some monitors, each time you adjust the resolution, the side-to-side and diagonal measurements of the image may change.)

As I write these words, I am looking at a 17-inch monitor that delivers a diagonal viewable image size of about 16.2 inches; at 640x480 resolution, the image itself measures about 15.5 inches on the diagonal.

Monitor Size	Typical Viewable Image Size	Typical Square Inches	Real Estate Index*	Typical Maximum Resolution
14-inch	13.2 inches	72 inches	100	1024x768
15-inch	13.7 inches	90 inches	125	1024x768
17-inch	15.7 inches	115 inches	160	1280x1024
20-inch	19 inches	168 inches	187	1280x1024 to 1600x1280
21-inch	19.8 inches	185 inches	260	1280x1024 to 1600x1280

[Sandler's Real Estate Index: Square inch measurement of viewable image size are compared to 14-inch monitor. For example, the 21-inch monitor listed here is approximately 2.6 times larger than a 14-inch screen.]

The Elements of a High-Quality Display

Dot Pitch

The first thing on which most monitor buyers concentrate is the *dot pitch*, a measurement of how close together the dots of phosphor are that make up a video monitor's image. The finer the dot pitch (the lower the number), the finer the image is theoretically. Today's better monitors have a dot pitch of 0.28 mm or less.

On traditional monitors using dot masks, dot pitch is measured as the diagonal or vertical distance between two dots of the same color. The smaller the dot pitch the finer the image; look for a dot pitch of .28mm or less for a desktop 15-inch monitor and .31 or less for a larger 20- or 21-inch monitor.

Trinitron and similar tubes are measured by stripe pitch; NEC CromaClear and Panasonic Pure Flat tubes present measurements of mask pitch. Both represent the horizontal distance between two stripes of the same color. Look for pitches of .25mm or less for desktop monitors and .30mm for 20- and 21-inch models.

One developing class of monitors are large presentation devices used in instructional settings and as part of a family room PC/entertainment center system. These monitors, which are big even by television standards—up to 42 or 48 inches in size—are intended to be viewed at some distance from the screen. Typical dot pitches for these room-size monitors can be in the range from .75mm to .90mm and larger; one design uses a smaller dot pitch at the center and a larger dot pitch at the corners where information is presumably less important.

Refresh or Scan Rate

Refresh rate, also called *vertical frequency* or *vertical scan rate*, tells you how many times per second the monitor redraws the image on screen. Most current users find that refresh rates below 75Hz cause visible and annoying flicker. Slow scan rates produce flicker because of the decay of illumination of the phosphor between passes of the beam. High scan rates produce a rock-solid image, but monitors capable of high scan rates are more expensive. A scan rate that is adequate on a 14-inch monitor will seem flickery on a big 17-or 20-inch monitor, because the high-resolution video modes often used on these large monitors need a higher scan rate.

For most monitors, the refresh rate declines as the resolution increases; in other words, a monitor may be capable of 100 to 150 Hz at 640x480 resolution, but only 75 to 85 Hz at the 1280x1024 setting. Put another way, when you see a high refresh rate advertised for a monitor, this is almost always referring to the display's capability at its lowest resolution; pay attention to its specifications at the resolution you intend to use most often.

The original IBM PC's monochrome card rewrote the monitor screen 50 times per second. A vertical scan rate of 50 Hz is too slow for most peoples' eyes, so IBM specified long-persistence phosphor compounds on the monitor screen. Once excited, these phosphors continue to glow for a while even after the electron beam has moved on to another part of the screen. This cures the flickering, but the monitor displays annoying ghosts when the user scrolls text.

An RGB color monitor (the color monitor paired with the CGA video card on the early IBM PC) refreshes the screen 60 times per second. High-resolution VGA and multiscanning monitors refresh at rates as high as 80 times per second.

Do you see a pattern in these numbers? A high vertical scan rate is better. Monitors that can handle super VGA (800x600) screen resolutions at 70 or 72 refreshes per second look good. The same super VGA resolution on a lower-quality "super VGA" monitor that refreshes the screen 56 times per second will look jumpy and flickery. That's why VESA, the Video Equipment Standards Association, has increased the vertical scan rate for super VGA video cards and monitors from 56 Hz to 72 Hz.

In electronics, by the way, the number of times per second an operation is performed is measured in *hertz* (Hz), named after Heinrich Hertz, the nineteenth-century German physicist who made breakthrough discoveries about electromagnetic waves. A monitor with a vertical screen refresh rate of 72 times per second will be listed at 72 Hz. When an operation takes place thousands of times per second, it is measured in *kilohertz*, written as KHz. Very fast operations, including clock cycles, are counted in *megahertz* (MHz) for millions of operations per second.

Horizontal frequency is a measure of the time it takes to draw one line across the width of the screen. This snippet of activity is measured in kilohertz, or KHz. Horizontal frequency is an element of a monitor's refresh rate, since the electron beam must move across the screen in order to work its way from upper left to bottom right in creation of a complete image.

Interlaced vs. Noninterlaced Monitors

In the high-tech equivalent of the search for a free lunch, monitor designers came up with *interlaced* monitors, displays that refresh only the odd-numbered row of pixels in one pass, then refresh the even numbered rows of pixels in a second pass. Interlaced monitors can display high-resolution video (many rows of pixels on the screen), yet they cost much less than noninterlaced monitors.

It's a subjective decision, with some viewers not minding the flicker that is inherent in the design; others can't abide interlaced monitors, especially if they spend many hours in front of the screen.

Screen Shape

The sheet of paper in the book you are reading is more or less flat. Monitors, on the other hand, are more or less curved. The curved edges of the video display tubes are a holdover from the original design for television sets, which had to find a way to deal with the fact that the edges of the screen were farther away from the electron gun than the center of the screen. Some of that problem of physics has been solved by modern electronics, but nearly all tubes still have a bit of curve today.

Tube designs are spherical, cylindrical, and "flat".

Spherical tubes present a face like a slice of a ball, with curves at the top, bottom, and sides. They are generally the least expensive, but often the least pleasing to critical eyes. They are usually seen on 14-inch models; some 20-inch monitors use spherical tubes to present a lower-cost alternative to 21-inch behemoths.

Cylindrical screens are like a slice taken from the front of a large barrel, resulting in a nearly flat vertical and a slightly curved horizontal shape. Cylindrical tubes are well suited to Trinitron designs (Sony's original design has since been licensed and adapted by Mitsubishi and other makes).

Most "flat" screens are close enough to claim the name, but still deserving of quote marks. These designs are a slice of a very large sphere, so large that the curves are barely perceptible. Some of these designs sacrifice a bit of sharpness at the edges.

In 1996, Panasonic introduced the Pure Flat CRT design, which is, as the name suggests, truly level in all dimensions. This design uses a slot mask held flat by tension.

Color and Gray Shades

The number of colors offered on a monitor is determined by the capabilities of the video adapter. More color does not make the monitor display any sharper, but it does make it easier to read or easier to pick out details in an image, which may make additional colors the functional equivalent of sharpness.

Sixteen colors are sufficient for text work and simple graphics. 256 colors are the current minimum for multimedia work, with settings of 65K and 16.7 million colors common. And if you perform any graphics editing, including retouching and manipulation of photographs, you'll need a high-resolution video card and monitor.

Higher color counts come at a price, though, and we're not merely referring to purchase cost. The more colors the system has to draw with and transfer, the slower the screen redraws and general video response.

A high number of colors place a great demand on video display adapters. Many modern machine graphics adapters usually come with 1 MB of DRAM (Dynamic RAM), and can be upgraded to 2 MB to add more colors at higher resolutions. To pick up a bit of speed, you can use an adapter with VRAM (Video RAM), or WRAM (Windows RAM) (see Chapter 12).

The best buying decision is probably to buy no more capability than you need, but to have a video adapter that can be upgraded if necessary.

A side area in the use of color involves gray shades on a monochrome monitor. Gray shades can make the display seem much sharper, even though you are still working with the original number of pixels per screen. Clever font designers use gray shades strategically on the edges of characters to fool the eye, a technique called *anti-aliasing*. The user perceives noticeably crisper fonts with cleaner, smoother curves.

Antiglare

One not-minor issue for monitor owners is dealing with glare from office lighting and open windows. The cheapest monitors can be so shiny you could comb your hair in the reflected glare.

There are several things that can be done to reduce interference from outside light sources. The first issue is often to deal with the lighting situation at your workplace. Some users find a good solution in turning off overhead lights and replacing them with smaller, focused "task" lights on your desk or alongside. You can also install light-filtering shades or curtains to reduce glare from outside sources.

Monitor makers can mount their devices on a tilt-and-pivot stand that allows adjustment.

The lowest level of glare protection is a coating that is sprayed onto the outside or inside of the glass that faces the user. Newer techniques called *spin coating* can apply a very thin, optically clear protection.

The current high-tech solution was introduced by Toshiba and is called the "microfilter" CRT. In this scheme there is a tiny colored filter over each phosphor dot; the filter absorbs light bouncing off the filter. An added plus for this design is that the tubes can be made of clear instead of tinted glass, allowing the monitors to be slightly brighter than standard devices.

The Importance of Maintaining Control

There is an almost irresistible urge to fall under the spell of a dummy of a monitor, a device that has only an on-off switch. But in truth, that is not a wise decision. No two offices or rec rooms have the same lighting conditions; your eyes may be different from mine; indeed, two models of the same monitor may have different brightness, contrast, or color levels. Finally, everything is subject to change over time.

Therefore, we recommend buying a monitor with a full set of controls. The best location for these controls is on the front side of the monitor; you will want to be looking at the screen at a standard reading distance as you make adjustments.

The original design for computer monitors used knobs or wheels to make analog adjustments; lower-priced (and mostly outdated) models still offer these controls. The problem with knobs is that settings made with them affect only the current resolution; any time you change resolution—which includes bouncing out of Windows to DOS—the image size, centering, brightness, contrast, and other settings may bounce around.

Modern monitors use digital controls with digital memories that store the settings you make for each resolution or graphics mode; the monitor will sense changes and use stored settings automatically.

Other advanced features include on-screen menus that allow you to use the monitor itself to display instructions on making settings, and in some cases produce test patterns for the purpose.

The monitor should at least include controls for brightness, contrast, vertical size, horizontal size, and position. Some less-expensive monitors may offer a switch to turn on or off "overscan," which expands the image vertically and horizontally; this gives you less flexibility than separate controls and may result in a situation where text is placed off the displayable face of the monitor.

Better monitors include a degaussing circuit that clears up color and convergence problems caused by magnetic fields; the process can take place automatically each time the monitor is turned on, or it can be initiated by pressing a button among the controls.

An advanced color adjustment, offered in addition to color level, allows setting a monitor's white balance; photographers sometimes refer to this sort of adjustment as *color temperature*. A white balance setting can add a slight pink (warm) tint or a slight blue (cool) tint to what might otherwise be pure white. This sort of feature is valuable if the particular monitor has a warm or cool tint as delivered.

Other advanced image controls are intended to compensate for distortions such as pincushioning in which vertical lines bow outward, or barrel distortion in which the lines bow inward. A trapezoid control can improve trapezoidal distortion which gives an image varying widths at top and bottom.

Why Bad Things Happen to Good Monitors

Why does the monitor that got good reviews in a computer magazine, or the one that shone with uncommon excellence on the shelf at the dealer, look like a 1956 Philco when you plug it in at home or at your office?

The fact is that monitors are subject to variations in assembly, and are also vulnerable to problems brought about by mishandling in shipping or setup. Much of the problem is related to the fact that there is still a bit of hand work in finishing of display tubes and in the placement and adjustment of the electromagnets that aim electrons at the screen. A minor misplacement or a shift in location after a monitor leaves the factory can throw a monitor out of focus, shift its image off center, or otherwise affect image quality.

Over time, power supplies will age and change characteristics, and the stress and strain a monitor undergoes as it is turned on and off can have an effect.

Be sure to test your monitor meticulously when you first plug it in. And don't be afraid to reject a monitor that doesn't live up to your expectations. For that reason, be sure to buy the screen from a reputable dealer willing to give you a money-back guarantee that will be in effect for a reasonable period of time after purchase. Compare the potential savings you may obtain from a mail order house to the cost of returning a bad display if necessary.

Testing Your Monitor

Most diagnostic programs include a set of test screens that allow you to explore the capabilities of your monitor and video card; some card or monitor makers include a few specialized demo programs with their products. But for the ultimate in custom adjustment and testing of your monitor and card, I'd recommend you try one of the DisplayMate products from SONERA Technologies, available from the maker at (800) 932-6323.

DisplayMate for Windows is an end-user video utility designed to set up and tune a monitor for optimum image and picture quality. The program will walk you through more than a dozen detailed exercises using the monitor's adjustments to display as much detail in as sharp a presentation as possible.

The program supports modes from 16 colors to 24-bit 16.7 million colors; all resolutions up to 4096x4096; all screen shapes and aspect ratios including landscape, portrait, and HDTV; and runs under any video board and monitor supported by Windows.

The program's all-purpose diagnostic screen can be used as your Windows opening screen for a daily checkup (see Figure 13.1).

The next step up are DisplayMate and DisplayMate Professional, comprehensive video system hardware diagnostics that test every aspect of a computer's video system including monitor,

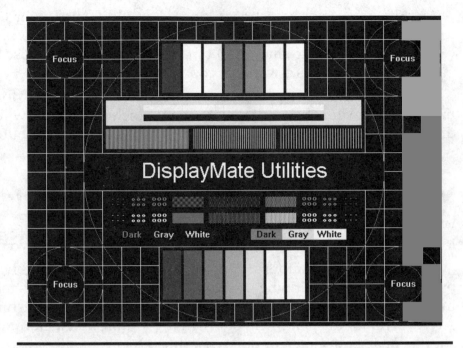

Figure 13.1 Display screen from *DisplayMate for Windows*, a diagnostic program for monitors.

video board hardware and registers, video BIOS, and video data area. It includes more than 200 test patterns and 200 diagnostic tests. The program can check accurate timing and frequency measurements for all monitor scanning parameters.

Green Monitors

Green monitors can display hundreds of colors, not just the color of the forests or money. The term *green* refers to a standard that is intended to reduce electrical usage by devices; these monitors have their own internal hardware that will reduce power draw or even shut down the device entirely if there is no user activity for a particular period of time. Green monitors often also work with software and BIOS-based controls.

Look for compliance with the Energy Star standards for consumption in sleep modes and the Display Power Management Signaling (DPMS) standard which allows a DPMS-compliant graphics card to initiate sleep modes. Some monitors support the Swedish Nutek standards, which are even more stringent in power consumption controls.

If you are concerned about electromagnetic emissions from monitors, look for compliance with the current MPR-II specifications, or the even more stringent TCO standard. (Your best defense against electromagnetic emissions is to sit at a proper distance from your monitor, generally about an arm's length, and never to operate a monitor with its cover off or with a crack or other opening in the shielding.)

Plug-and-Play Monitors

With the arrival of Windows 95 and the Plug-and-Play standard came monitors that are capable of communicating with the PC when they are plugged in.

The new monitors use an adaptation of the common DB-15 VGA cable and connector to send information about the monitor's capabilities to the graphics adapter in the PC, and vice versa. The biggest problem addressed by this new intelligent connection is avoiding refresh rate mismatches between monitor and adapter.

The cables use four rarely used data lines in the cable for this purpose; the monitor and adapter must subscribe to the Display Data Channel (DDC) protocol put into place by the Video Electronics Standards Association (VESA). Some monitors indicate compliance with DDC by coloring their cable connectors bright blue.

Just to make things confusing, there are already several flavors of the DDC standard that are more or less compatible. DDC1 has PnP monitors continuously sending information back up the wire to the graphics adapter; the more advanced DDC2B specification has the monitor send information to the PC only when it is requested to do so by the graphics adapter. Monitors must support both DDC versions 1 and 2B, while the adapter can support either specification.

By the way, a DDC monitor will work without problem on a PC without Plug-and-Play capabilities, and with an adapter that does not support DDC. The system will simply be as dumb as it always was before the new specification.

Future Connections

Even further advanced is the DDC2AB specification that allows software control of monitor features including color settings and size and distortion adjustments. The DDC2AB specification is not expected to be widely used; instead, it will be supplanted by the upcoming Universal Serial Bus that will offer the same facilities.

The Universal Serial Bus is intended to allow daisychaining of peripherals including mice, keyboards, and printers. Some monitor makers may produce displays intended to serve as USB hubs for various devices.

Yet another piece of future tech is EVC, a Swiss Army Knife of a specification designed to replace the 15-pin VGA connector with a connector that combines support for audio, DDC, USB, and the FireWire high-speed serial interface. As this book goes to press, no consumer-level EVC monitors have been produced and there is no certainty they ever will be.

The Search for Better Resolution: A Monitor's-Eye View

When IBM introduced the PC in 1981, a monochrome text-only video card, the Monochrome Display Adapter (MDA) board, and a monochrome monitor were standard. The MDA video system could produce 25 lines of text with 80 characters per line. This is still a readable display, even in the standard green and black.

IBM simultaneously introduced the CGA video card, a much coarser, grainier display that bleared a lot of eyes. Users liked the color and crude graphics and put up with the lower resolution.

Improvements in monochrome video cards began almost immediately. The Hercules card, also called a Monochrome Graphics Adapter (MGA) or Monochrome Graphics Adapter with Printer Port (MGP) card, provided monochrome graphics on a simple monochrome MDA-style monitor because it allowed pixel-by-pixel (dot-by-dot) as well as character-by-character control of the display. The Hercules design permitted the board to display Lotus 1-2-3 graphics while still allowing a high-resolution text display.

The next improvement was IBM's EGA in 1985, which proved to be a short-lived halfway measure. EGA features both color and monochrome modes, with pixel-by-pixel video control. EGA color was very popular, but hardly any software was written for EGA monochrome.

These three video adapter cards—MDA, MGA, and EGA (in monochrome mode) use a horizontal scan rate of 18.43 MHz and a vertical scan rate of 50 Hz (50 refreshes per second).

MDA, MGA, and EGA monochrome resolution is 720x348 pixels (MGA) or 720x350 pixels (MDA and EGA). For an 80-character, 25-line screen of data, that means each character is allocated an area with dimensions of 9x14 pixels. Spacing between lines and between characters eats up some of these pixels, so the actual character is formed out of a 7x9 pixel rectangle (with two more rows of pixels available for letters with descenders (tails below the line), like *p* and *q*).

Beyond MDA, MGA, and EGA, the next higher monochrome resolution is VGA monochrome, which requires both a VGA card and a higher-priced VGA monochrome monitor. VGA provides 720x400 pixel resolution in text mode. That adds two horizontal rows of dots per character. In graphics mode, VGA works with a 640x480 pixel grid, which provides significantly more pixels per screen than the 720x348 pixels available with an MGA (Hercules) card. The distinguishing feature of VGA monochrome monitors, though, is their gray scales. These multiple shades of gray are displayed by an analog monitor with a 15-pin video data cable connecting the monitor to the computer system unit. VGA monitors use a horizontal scan rate of 31.5 KHz, well outside the operating range of simple MDA monochrome monitors.

Computers dedicated to desktop publishing can be equipped with ultra-high-resolution monochrome monitors that allow you to view two complete pages of text side by side. Many of these sophisticated monitors require a proprietary video card and special video drivers.

The imprecise big-pixel color monitors, first found on IBM PCs in 1981, had 200 scan lines across the screen. These RGB color monitors, driven by CGA video cards, had a resolution of 320x200 pixels, which ain't so hot. Higher-priced color video systems (such as EGA, VGA, XGA, and 8514) have many tiny pixels on the screen, so subtle curves seem smooth and individual pixels are unnoticeable. CGA video cards and the RGB monitor did introduce graphics to the PC world. CGA cards allow pixel-by-pixel control of the monitor screen. The PC's original monochrome display, by contrast, could display only preformatted characters in an 80- column x 25 row grid.

In 1985, IBM introduced EGA color with more pixels per scan line and more scan lines per screen than RGB monitors used. The highest resolution color EGA mode treats the screen as a 640x350 pixel grid.

IBM's 1987 VGA video standard had a maximum resolution of 640x480 pixels. The VGA standard has four video modes, all with a horizontal scan rate of 31.5 KHz. Two different vertical scan rates are required though, so VGA monitors must be capable of either 60 or 70 Hz (60 or 70 complete raster refreshes per second).

The general pattern is more pixels per screen and more screen refreshes per second—in other words, we keep asking for faster monitors capable of displaying more pixels per second. In the early CGA/EGA/VGA days, people were content to buy a new monitor when they upgraded to a new video standard. Each new video standard used dramatically different technology; for example, different wires in the monitor-to-video-card cable, and different signals carried on those wires.

The improvement from VGA to Super VGA was different. Super VGA is hard to define precisely since it is has a virtually unlimited upside. It was originally an industry specification for 800x600 displays, but has zoomed well past that.

Super VGA monitors are simply capable of processing the video card's instructions faster (refreshing the screen more often and displaying more individual pixels on each screen). Therefore, multiscanning monitors compatible with multiple video standards became attractive to buyers who didn't want to lock themselves into a particular video standard when they bought a monitor.

IBM's 8514/A (1987) and XGA (1990) video standards are optimized for CAD and Windows, respectively. But 8514/A and XGA do not demand a qualitatively different monitor. They both run on high-end VGA-compatible multiscanning monitors.

The VGA monitor design has been durable and flexible. We expect revolutionary improvements in the next few years in the video cards that drive this VGA family of monitors, but we suspect the monitors themselves will become faster without revolutionary changes in design.

Under the Covers

How a Monochrome Monitor Works

Inside a monitor, an electron beam is aimed toward a phosphor-coated screen. The phosphor glows whenever the electrons hit it, producing lighted images on the screen (see Figure 15.1). When the monitor is plugged into a video adapter card, it receives a signal called the *scan frequency*. The monitor must lock in on the scan signal; in other words, the electron beam must cross the screen in synchronization with the scan signal.

The electron beam starts at the top left of the screen. It scans across the screen from left to right, exciting some dots of phosphor and passing by others. When the beam reaches the right side of the screen, it quickly returns to the left and scans another line directly beneath the first one. An ordinary monochrome monitor has 350 of these scan lines per screen.

When the electron beam reaches the bottom right of the screen, it leaps up to the top left corner and proceeds to trace the 350 scan lines from the top again. This set of 350 scan lines—which is often visible when the brightness control is turned up too high—is called the *raster pattern* (or *raster*).

An ordinary monochrome monitor *refreshes* (rescans the complete raster) the screen 50 times a second. The vertical scan rate is, therefore, 50 Hz. By comparison, the horizontal scan rate is 18,432 times per second (18.432 KHz). As the electron beam flies across the screen (18,432 times per second) it passes 720 pixels (dots of phosphor) per line. The video adapter card, located in the computer system unit, provides explicit directions to the electron gun in the monitor. As the electron beam scans across the screen, the video card calls for a burst of electrons here to excite this pixel, or a burst of electrons there to excite that pixel.

How a Color Monitor Works

A color monitor creates color display by combining the three primary colors of light: red, green, and blue. Black is the absence of any color. Yellow is created by combining green light and blue light. White is created by combining all three light sources.

We discuss four types of color monitors in this section. An RGB monitor is the cheapest and provides the lowest picture quality. EGA, VGA/SVGA, and multiscanning monitors are progressively more expensive, but each price jump provides a sharper picture (better resolution) and more colors. Each monitor must be paired with an appropriate video display adapter card (located in the computer system unit).

The cheapest color monitor, called an *RGB monitor*, has low resolution; the image is not very crisp. RGB color monitors have relatively few pixels. These pixels are also relatively large, and each contains a trio of phosphor dots: one red, one green, and one blue. There are three separate electron beams, each dedicated to stimulating a single color of phosphor. As we mentioned earlier, other colors are made by mixing red, green, and blue light in the appropriate proportions. Red is displayed by exciting only the red phosphor portion of the pixel. Purple (or magenta) is produced when both blue and red dots are glowing. When all three phosphor dots in a pixel are excited, the three colors of light combine to show white on the screen.

To display a simple letter, for example, a capital *T*, the electron beam excites one horizontal row and one vertical column of pixels. *Resolution* (crispness of image) is not very good on an RGB color monitor; if you look closely you can see the individual pixels.

The three primary colors of light are controlled by simple TTL (on/off) signals; therefore, subtle color shadings are not available. RGB monitors can produce 16 colors. The monitor has a 9-pin connector on the cable running from the monitor to the video card, and it is compatible with the CGA video card.

EGA monitors also have a 9-pin cable carrying data from the video card to the monitor, but they must be paired with an EGA video card in order to work. EGA monitors are capable of substantially better resolution than RGB monitors, and they have two *intensity* (brightness) signal levels available for each primary-color light source. These intensity variables allow more color selections; EGA monitors can produce 64 colors.

You can readily distinguish VGA monitors from CGA and EGA monitors because VGA monitors have a 15-pin video data cable. These monitors use an analog signal, which can be adjusted anywhere in a voltage range. If CGA and EGA monitors use simple binary (on/off) signals, analog monitors use a continuously variable signal (like a dimmer switch). This analog signal allows precise brightness control at each of the three primary-color light sources, yielding many delicate color shadings. A VGA monitor can display millions of colors, but few video cards can push the monitor that far.

VGA, CGA, and EGA monitors are not interchangeable. A VGA monitor will not even plug into a CGA or EGA card, much less work properly with it. An SVGA monitor is not intended to work with a VGA adapter—it uses a 15-pin connector instead of VGA's 9-pin standard—but there are adapters available that allow SVGAs to work at lower resolution with a VGA controller.

How a Multiscanning/Multisynch Monitor Works

Multiscanning monitors can lock onto multiple vertical and horizontal scanning frequencies, so a single multiscanning monitor is compatible with many different video cards.

Multiscanning monitors are continuously improving. The original version, the NEC MultiSynch, was compatible with monochrome, CGA, EGA, and PGA (IBM Professional Graphic Adapter, a video standard that never caught on). Some newer multiscanning monitors can operate with all these standards and VGA, super VGA, (800x600) and Extended VGA (1024x768), which means they are also compatible with 8514 cards and TIGA cards. Most can deal with either 60 or 70 Hz vertical frequency (VGA family). Some of them can handle 50 Hz, so they're compatible with the IBM PC's original monochrome display adapters and EGA monochrome. The best ones can refresh a high-resolution 1024x768 display at 72 Hz (72 times per second).

Most multiscanning monitors are shipped with both 9-pin and 15-pin cables, so you can easily hook them to any standard video card.

Monitor Prices

As this book goes to press, prices for monitors had stabilized after a few years of dropping. The monitor of choice is currently the 15-inch device. Here is the price range from discount sources for a randomly selected group of noninterlaced monitors, updated in early 1997:

14-inch SVGA, .28mm DP	$200-$250
15-inch SVGA, .28mm DP	$300-$400
15-inch SVGA, .25mm Trinitron aperture	$400-$475
17-inch SVGA, .28mm DP	$600-$900
17-inch SVGA, .25mm Trinitron aperture	$880-$1,000

20-inch SVGA, .28mm DP	$1,300
20-inch SVGA, .30mm Trinitron aperture	$1,700
21-inch SVGA, .28mm DP	$1,600-$1,800

How to Test a Monitor

If your monitor has no video, it's best to start with a quick switch and cable check. Are both the computer and the monitor plugged in and turned on? Look for an indicator light to tell you the monitor is receiving power. (For a cruder but interesting way to see if your monitor is powering up, you can try the following manual test. Monitors develop a big electrostatic field in the first couple of seconds after they are turned on; turn off the power to the monitor, then hold the back of your hand to the monitor screen and power it back on. The hair on the back of your hand will stand up as the electrostatic field develops.)

Check the video data cable from the video card to the monitor. It must be plugged in tight and screwed down at the video card end.

The next things to check are the brightness and contrast controls on the monitor. Many (but not all) monochrome monitors show a raster pattern when they are powered on and the brightness knob is turned all the way up, whether the monitor is connected to a computer or not. Don't adjust these controls and then accidentally leave them in the dim position; we've all done this. It can be very frustrating to finally fix a video problem without realizing you have fixed it because the monitor brightness is adjusted so low that no characters are visible. In general, full-stop clockwise is the brightest position.

An absence of video can be caused by the video card, the monitor, or a multitude of problems in the computer system unit. The troubleshooting charts in Section 3 provide a plan to help you identify the culprit. Before jumping into the troubleshooting charts, try a couple of quick swaps if you have duplicate monitors or comparably equipped computers available. Try attaching the suspect monitor to a computer that you know works. If the monitor works on the comparable computer (one that has the same video adapter card), then test the suspect computer and the video card. For testing ideas, check the section of this chapter dedicated to your particular video card and the troubleshooting charts in the Appendix of this book.

If you have *snow* (a fuzzy, random-dot effect) on your monitor, the most likely problem is an incompatible video card. The card is sending signals, but signals from a CGA card with a 15.75 KHz scan rate are gibberish to an MDA monitor with a scan rate of 18.43 KHz. Make sure you've hooked up your monitor to a compatible card.

If you have a dinosaur using an 8088 or 8086 CPU chip and you have a flashing cursor and no other video, check the DIP switch settings on the motherboard. DIP switches control the video address the motherboard is trying to use. The monitor is usually smart enough to put a cursor on the screen—even without any direction from the computer—but incorrect DIP switch settings send the data to the wrong place in video memory (for example, to the nonexistent color video adapter). As a result, the actual video card gets absolutely no information from the computer and puts nothing besides the cursor on the video display screen. 286, 386, and 486 computers also need to have the video type set correctly in their CMOS setup memory chip, but these machines are smart enough to switch to the monitor's display mode long enough to display an initial error message, such as **Incorrect setup. Wrong video adapter**.

If your problem is one or two incorrect characters in an otherwise good screen, the video memory located on the video card is at fault. Replace the card. If you feel like double-checking before buying a new video card, use diagnostic software to test the video RAM (video memory).

Sometimes the screen will roll upward or downward. This is caused by an incorrect vertical sync adjustment. Most monochrome monitors have an external vertical sync knob. When you adjust it, first change the misadjustment to a slow upward roll, then try to stop the roll completely. If you go too far and the screen starts to roll downward, try to slow and then stop the downward roll.

Horizontal misalignment is usually slight, but occasionally it is so severe that the screen message appears to have rolled entirely around so that it is displayed as a mirror image of itself. If your computer has an external horizontal sync knob, use this knob to correct the problem.

Monitors are very similar to television sets. If you have a horizontal or vertical sync problem that seems too intimidating, or if the bottom line of letters is much larger than the top line (a sign of poor linearity adjustment), a good computer repair shop—or possibly a TV repair shop—should be able to correct the problem. Monochrome monitors tend to be inexpensive, so more than an hour of repair work is not likely to be cost-effective.

Color monitors are also susceptible to convergence problems. Each pixel is really a trio of phosphor dots. It is important to have these dots bunched closely together or the display will be fuzzy, with one or more colors bleeding off the edges of white text. Television shops can adjust the convergence by slightly altering the angle of the three electron beams to bunch the trio of dots in each pixel closer together.

How to Remove and Install a Monitor

Turn off the monitor and the computer. It is not good practice to attach a cable to a computer that is powered up; a slight misalignment of the plug could result in a short that could damage the video adapter, the monitor, the motherboard, or all three.

Unscrew the two tiny screws holding the monitor data cable to the video card. Disconnect the video cable and power cables, then replace the malfunctioning monitor with an equivalent good one.

If you are replacing both the monitor and the video card, refer to the section that covers your particular video card for card installation hints. Remember, both the motherboard and the video card DIP switches and/or jumpers may need to be reset if you are changing the video display type from monochrome to color or from MDA monochrome to EGA or VGA monochrome. Check your video card manual and your motherboard/computer owner's manual for details.

CHAPTER 14

The Serial Connection

It's the morning commute, and thousands of cars, trucks, and buses speed along in a thick river on an eight-lane limited access superhighway.

And then the entire column comes to a single tollbooth with a gate in front of a single-lane tunnel. That's pretty close to the situation inside your computer when data is forced to switch over from the 8-, 16-, or 32-bit wide superhighway that connects the CPU, memory, and most internal devices to the local road that exits to most modems and some other external peripherals.

The single-lane roads are called *serial lines*, because the data is forced to march one bit behind the other. The computer adds marker signals to indicate the beginning and end of each word of data, and in many cases, also adds error-detecting codes so that there is a reasonable chance at correcting errors in transmission.

A serial port provides a single-file two-way channel for data. Information flows either from the computer to an external device or from the device back to the computer.

Serial connections are a holdover from the early days of computerdom, when the massive room-sized machines were relatively slow so that forcing data into a single line didn't have that much of an effect on overall speed. Many early PC printers used a serial line; today almost all modern machine printers use the faster and much simpler to configure parallel port.

Because serial cables can reliably run 200 feet between devices (compared to the 15–25 foot maximum for unamplified parallel cables), they are often still used for remote printers.

One area where serial connections are still an essential part of PCs is modem-to-modem communication. A computer modem uses the telephone wire to send and receive information; a telephone connection is made up

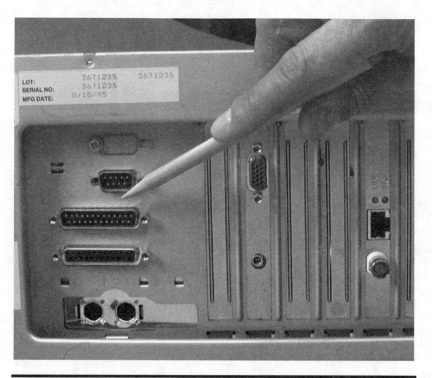

Figure 14.1 Serial connectors COM1 and COM2 on the back panel of a PC.

of a single pair of thin wires, with information sent down only one of the wires. Serial ports are also commonly used to communicate with devices such as mice, which don't need to send a tremendous amount of information at one time. And then finally, serial ports are used with devices that have particularly unusual communication requirements. As we've noted, serial communication is sometimes difficult to set up, but it is much more flexible in configuration (see Figure 14.1).

How a Serial Port Works

An 8-bit byte of information is carried in parallel form on the computer bus; in other words, all 8 bits are transmitted from place to place simultaneously across eight side-by-side wires.

To send this information out a serial port, it must be repackaged. The byte is broken into 8 separate data bits which follow one behind the other; the byte is preceded and followed by one or two stop/start bits that bracket the package of information, and usually followed by a parity checking bit that helps with error detection.

The hard work of chopping up parallel data bytes and sending them out in a serial stream (and going the other way) is performed by a device called a *UART* (Universal Asynchronous Receiver/Transmitter). Nearly every PC uses one of four UART chips; they will all work with basic communications software, but the older, slower chips will not support high-speed modems.

The original PC used a chip labeled the 8250; this device is not reliable for modem speeds beyond 9,600 bps. A greatly improved chip was the 16450, which should accommodate 14,400 bps modems.

The current rulers of the serial world are the 16550 and its improved cousin the 16550A. These chips improve on the earlier UARTs with the addition of a 16-byte first-in, first-out buffer which is just enough to keep the serial port busy in a multitasking environment. In other words, your modern machine's CPU may be working on several tasks under Microsoft Windows and be dividing its attention from one device to another; the buffer on the 16550 and 16550A is big enough in most instances to allow it to continue work without interruption.

NOTE

The buffer in the 16550 and 16550A must be turned on by communications software, and some older programs were not written with this in mind and cannot do so.

To find out what kind of UART is in your system, you can use one of a number of diagnostic programs that examines the capabilities of your serial port. One such diagnostic, MSD (Microsoft Diagnostics), is shipped along with DOS 6.x and Windows 3.1; you should find it in your DOS or Windows subdirectory. Go to the DOS prompt and type **MSD** and press the **Enter** key to launch the diagnostic program. Then go to **COM PORTS** and examine the last line of the report you find there; it will tell you the type of UART in use in your system.

The 8250, 16450, 16550, and 16550A chips are pin-for-pin compatible with each other and it is easy to upgrade from an earlier UART to a state-of-the-art chip *if the UART is mounted in a socket.* If the UART is soldered into place, it cannot be directly upgraded (see Figure 14.2).

Some modern machines use VLSI (Very Large Scale Integration) or ASIC (Application-Specific Integrated Circuits) chips that combine a number of functions. Some of these devices emulate a 16450 or 16550 UART as part of a package that includes circuitry for a parallel port and game port. If your system has a VLSI or ASIC chipset, the UART cannot be directly upgraded either.

The solution for systems where the UART chip cannot be simply removed and replaced is to install a high-speed serial communications card. These devices can add one, two, or even four serial ports; combination cards can also add a bi-directional parallel port.

If you add one of these special I/O cards, you will probably have to disable one or more of the serial ports

Figure 14.2 In some systems you can remove a socketed 16450 UART and replace it with a bare 16550 UART chip to allow use of high-speed modems and other devices. (Dalco Electronics)

CHAPTER 14

on your PC. I/O cards are priced from about $25 to $100; be sure that you are getting a 16550 or 16550A for your money—there is no reason to put in a new 8250 or 16450.

Working Around an Old 8250 UART

One back door to upgrading your 8250- or 16450-based system to work with a modern 33.6 Kbps or faster modem is to completely go around the serial ports of your system and instead use an internal modem.

Internal modems have two parts: a dedicated serial port of their own, and a telecommunications section. Nearly every high-speed modem is based on a 16550 or 16550A UART. Another advantage of an internal modem is that it can usually be set to be COM3 or COM4, and therefore not be in conflict with existing serial ports. (The disadvantages of internal modems include the fact that they use a bus slot, draw internal power, lack visible status indicators like those on an external unit, and don't offer an on/off or reset switch—on most internal modems, the only way to clear an unusual condition is to turn off the power to the PC itself. For these reasons we generally prefer external modems, with the exception of situations like the one outlined above where we need to go around or replace an 8250 UART.)

Parameters

The role of the UART is made complicated by the many different package designs for computer words. These are called *parameters* or *protocols*.

Modern PC serial communication can use either 7 or 8 data bits, with either 1 or 2 stop bits appended. The serial device may use either even or odd parity, or use no parity checking at all. In addition, many different transmission speeds—ranging from 110 bits/second to a hardware maximum of 115,200 bits per second—are allowed.

Before any two serial devices can communicate, the parameters must be set and agreed upon by the devices at both ends of the connection. Many serial port problems can be traced to incorrect parameter setup. At the computer end, parameters are set with software, using communications software for a modem or occasionally through the facilities of the DOS MODE command.

A modem device is usually pretty flexible in working with whatever parameters are sent its way by the modem; serial printers and some other device may be more hidebound. You may have to change DIP switches on a printer, or exactly match the capabilities of the printer with your communications settings. See Figure 14.3.

Serial Cables

Although there are 25 pins on the DB-25 connector originally used for serial communications, in almost every use of a serial connection on a PC only 9 pins are ever used, and most implementations use less than that.

Most modern serial devices use standard cables that can be purchased off the shelf or from mail order houses. You should also be able to rely on the recommendation of the dealer who sold you the printer, modem, or other device you are connecting to.

Your computer may have a 25-pin male, 9-pin male, or a 25-pin female serial port. When we have to, we patch the mismatches with gender menders and 9- to 25-pin pigtails, leaving interesting tangles hanging out the back of the machine.

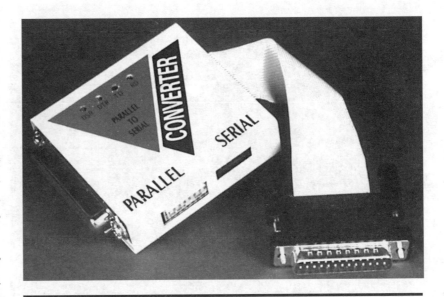

Figure 14.3 An interface converter can change a serial signal to parallel, or the other way around. (Dalco Electronics)

We found a mind-boggling array of cables and connectors in the Dalco Electronics Catalog; you'll also find offerings from specialty hardware vendors in publications like Computer Shopper magazine.

If necessary, most computer shops will make a custom serial cable for you, although the price can be prohibitive. A better solution is the use of a configurable cable, such as Smart Cable from IQ Technologies (Figure 14.4).

The simplest solution to using a serial port is to purchase a device that comes packaged with its own serial cable. In this case, all you have to do is plug it in.

Black Magic

In the early PC days, a serial cable was a concept, not a definition. All serial cables were based on the idea of bits of data moving one behind the other down the length of a wire, but the choice of which wire was used for which purpose was often inconsistent from device to device.

Figure 14.4 A Smart Cable from IQ Technologies performs an electronic balancing act, matching the wires on one side of a serial cable with the needs of the wires on the other side.

It was very common in the early days to have to buy a "Hayes" cable for a particular class of modems, an "HP" cable for a group of plotters, an "Epson" cable for certain printers, and so on. The closets of our labs are filled with these orphan cables.

Most of these problems are gone for modern machine peripherals. Nearly all printers today use the standardized parallel interface; most modems and specialized serial devices use "straight-through" cables, with Pin 1 at one end directly connected to Pin 1 at the other end, and so on. (An exception to this scheme are "null modem" cables used to directly connect one PC to another and used by software programs such as LapLink; these cables connect the *receive* wires to *send* wires so that each of the two machines can communicate.)

Nevertheless, there are still some situations where you will need an unusual serial cable connection. One example, of special interest to readers of this book, may come if you want to match a dinosaur-era device to a modern machine, or if an old dinosaur-era cable fails.

One extremely interesting solution to serial cable connections is the SmartCable, a bit of electronic magic that is able to look to its left and to its right and help you figure out which wires need to be connected to each other with the flick of two switches, following the simple logic of the LED lights on the SmartCable. SmartCables, which cost only slightly more than a standard cable, can be used to temporarily link two devices until a custom cable is constructed, or can be left in place. We keep a 9-pin and 25-pin SmartCable on the shelf in our lab at all times. You can use a solderless jumpbox, like the one shown in figure 14.5, to create and test serial cable configurations.

Serial Port Address

We have covered parameters and cables, which are two tricky parts of the serial port setup. The last consideration is the serial port address. Early DOS versions allowed two serial ports, called COM1 and COM2, each at a different address.

Under current versions of DOS, users can have two additional ports, called COM3 and COM4. Each of these DOS serial ports has an associated physical address (a place where DOS will send data that it's trying to shove out the serial port). Use switches or jumpers on the serial card or modem to set up the card to use a particular physical address. Once the port address (the physical address) is set, use the **MODE** command to tell DOS where to send serial output. It makes sense to set the first serial port in a computer to **COM1**, since that's the default setting for the DOS **MODE** command.

Each serial port must have a different address. If you don't do this, your modem software will try to send dialing instructions to your mouse. Each physical port also has a corresponding interrupt number. Appendix D, the list of standard I/O addresses and their associated interrupts, will help you choose the interrupt that matches the physical address you selected. Serial cards, modems, and other serial devices are shipped with installation manuals. Read them.

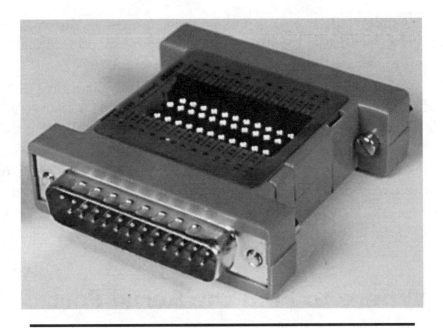

Figure 14.5 A solderless jumpbox can be used to make custom serial cables; insert a pre-stripped wire into sockets to connect pins. (Dalco Electronics)

Serial Port Connectors

Most PCs include two serial ports. On dinosaur machines, the ports were typically a part of an I/O (input/output) or multifunction card. On modern machines, the ports are usually part of the motherboard itself.

The official description for serial ports, called the *RS-232C specification,* was at the time of the launch of the original PC most commonly used with a DB-25 connector—a D-shaped device with 25 pins on the port and 25 pinholes on the cable. The parallel connection on the PC also used a DB-25, with a female connector on the port and a male connector on the cable.

As we've discussed, a serial connection comes down to just a single wire for the transmission of data; a computer serial port uses a total of nine wires for most communication with devices such as printers and modems—the extra wires are used to control the port or machine.

As the PC began to grow in popularity and capability, designers began to run into problems fitting two or three DB-25 connectors on an expansion card. IBM made a change with the introduction of its PC-AT machine, substituting a 9-pin D connector (the DB-9) for the use of the serial port.

Many older machines used a DB-9 for the first serial port and a DB-25 for the second port; other machines offered both DB-9 and DB-25 connectors for both ports. And cable manufacturers also offered converters that allow a 25-pin cable to connect with a 9-pin port, or the other way around.

In this chapter, we'll describe the serial connection and the problems that arise when add-on devices (*peripherals*) are attached to the computer via the serial port. We'll also show you how to test the serial connection.

Where to Find the Serial Port

There are three styles of serial port connectors: the original DB25 male connector with 25 pins as shipped with dinosaur PCs; the modern machine's 9-pin serial connector fitted with a DB9 connector, and—just for confusion's sake—a 25-pin female serial port connector shipped with several but not all IBM PS/2 models.

The DB9 socket on a modern machine has a female DB9 connector with nine holes; it is intended to mate with a cable with a male DB9 connector. If your machine has a VGA card, it will also have a male DB9 socket intended to mate with a female socket on a video cable.

If you don't find a 9-pin serial port, look for a 25-pin male connector with protruding pins in the rear of the computer. Once again, a reminder: if you find a female DB25 connector on the back of the computer, it's most likely the socket for a parallel port. If you have any doubts about ports, consult the instruction manual for your PC and any add-in cards in the system. It's a good idea to label your ports with a marker or tape once you have confirmed their identity.

How to Test a Serial Connection

The first step in testing a serial connection is to check how many serial ports the computer believes it has. If you have two physical serial ports, but a diagnostic program shows only one, then clearly the device-addressing switches on one or the other are not set right.

When a diagnostic program checks the serial ports, it reads the equipment list, a file the BIOS assembles as it boots the computer. The BIOS checks serial port addresses, but doesn't compare each physical card with its address; it is possible to set up two serial ports so they have the same address (both set to COM1, for instance). The BIOS will never catch this.

It is also possible to accidentally set the switches on a serial port so that its I/O address is one that DOS cannot recognize. Because the BIOS doesn't see this serial port, it doesn't include it in the equipment list.

Next, rethink the links between physical address, interrupt, DOS **MODE** command, software setup, and other parameters. Make sure you're not trying something illogical like sending data to COM1 when the printer cable is connected to COM2. It's also a common mistake to send modem commands to the port used by the mouse.

The BIOS can only talk to two serial ports: COM1 and COM2. However, some software can bypass the BIOS and address two more communications ports directly; some internal modems are routinely set to COM3 or COM4. If you are mixing and matching hardware and software, be sure your software allows you to set the serial card to one of these nonstandard addresses.

Serial cards are packaged with instruction manuals that give suggested address switch (or jumper) settings. Remember, when you install a serial port you must give it a unique I/O address. On the card you just installed, the I/O address is a physical address set by switches or jumpers. DOS simplifies things for you at this point by dealing with the logical address: COM1, COM2, COM3, etc.

Some serial port manuals refer to hexadecimal addresses instead of the DOS COMx names. COM1, for example, is the physical I/O address 03F8 and is paired with interrupt 4. COM2 is the I/O address 02F8 and is paired with interrupt 3.

Be sure you receive and hold on to all the instruction manuals for the parts of a computer when you take delivery. If you've got a system with an add-on serial port or a multifunction card, they're probably accompanied by minimal documentation—these devices are commodities imported from the lowest bidder. We have run into situations where the addresses printed on the card and in the manual were both different and were both wrong. Check the jumpers on the serial card or the modem against the manual to find out what address it has been set to.

If these steps do not reveal an obvious problem, use a serial test program with wrap (loopback) plug capability. CheckIt and QA Plus both have a test program that sends data out the "transmit data" (TX) line and checks to see that it has been properly received on the "receive data" (RX) line.

These tests require a wrap plug which is sometimes provided with the diagnostics software. You can also purchase one from an electronics supply house. If you feel like making your own, you can construct one out of a female RS232 plug or a female DB9 plug. You will have to make three soldered connections. Table 14.1 tells you which signal pins must be soldered to other signal pins. Use short jumper wires or clean solder bridges to connect the pins together electrically.

Table 14.1 To Make a Serial Port Wrap (Loopback) Plug, Solder These Connections

Solder this signal . . .	. . . to this signal	. . .and this signal
TXD	RXD	
RTS	CTS	CD
DTR	DSR	RI

See Table 14.3 for explanations of each abbreviation.

If a serial port passes the wrap plug test, there's a 99 percent chance it's good. Look again for mismatched COM port and interrupt, or for an incorrect **MODE** command. The troubleshooting charts in Section 3 will lead you, step-by-step, through our serial port diagnostic/repair procedures.

Table 14.2 is a pinout diagram for DB25 serial ports showing which pin carries which signal. Table 14.3 is the pinout diagram for the most common (modern) DB9 serial ports. There were a few nonstandard 9-pin designs in the early 1980s, but they are not currently manufactured.

Table 14.2 25-Pin Serial Port Pinouts, Male or Female

Pin	Name	Protocol Code	
1	Chassis ground		
2	Transmit data	TXD	
3	Receive data	RXD	
4	Request to send	RTS	
5	Clear to send	CTS	
6	Data set ready	DSR	
7	Signal ground		SG
8	Carrier detect		CD
9	Transmit current loop return (obsolete IBM Asynch Adapter)		
11	Transmit current loop data (obsolete IBM Asynch Adapter)		
18	Receive current loop data (obsolete IBM Asynch Adapter)		

Table 14.2 25-Pin Serial Port Pinouts, Male or Female (continued)

Pin	Name	Protocol Code	
20	Data terminal ready		DTR
22	Ring indicator		RI
25	Receive current loop return (obsolete IBM Asynch Adapter)		

Table 14.3 9-Pin Serial Port Pinouts, Male

Pin	Name	Protocol Code
1	Carrier detect	CD
2	Receive data	RXD
3	Transmit data	TXD
4	Data terminal ready	DTR
5	Signal ground	GND
6	Data set ready	DSR
7	Request to send	RTS
8	Clear to send	CTS
9	Ring indicator	RI

Null Modems

A *null modem* is not a modem but actually a special cable that can be used to directly connect two serial ports as if there had been a pair of modems between them. The special cable is necessary because a serial port is designed so that the transmitted data coming out of one machine is switched over to the received data input on the other. Actually, because serial communication is two-way, both transmit and receive lines are crossed within the cable.

Null modems are used in many simple network and data transfer programs, including the popular LapLink application widely used for temporary connections between two computers.. LapLink and many other such programs are shipped with a null modem, but in some cases you may need to order one; you'll find a collection of cables in the Dalco Electronics catalog and among the offerings of other electronic hardware specialists.

You can also build your own. The details of the pin-to-pin connections of a null modem can be found in Table 14.4. You might find it easiest to sacrifice an existing serial cable and cross some of its wires rather than starting from scratch.

Table 14.4 Null Modem

25-Pin Number Connector "A"	25-Pin Number Connector "B"
1	1
2	3
3	2
4	5
5	4
6 and 8	20
20	6 and 8
7	7

How to Remove and Install a Serial Port

If you have a serial port on the motherboard, you may have to disable it by setting a jumper or switch before you attach a new I/O card in the bus. The following instructions apply to removal and installation of add-in cards with I/O functions.

1. Remove the cables and computer cover. Disconnect the serial cable (if installed), and remove the system unit cover.

2. Remove the old card. Remove the single screw holding the card to the back of the system unit chassis and save it. Pull the old serial card straight up out of its slot.

3. Set switches and jumpers. Before you install a serial card, read the instruction manual that comes with the card. If you have any questions, reread "How a Serial Port Works" earlier in this chapter.

4. Install the new card. An old-style serial card is an 8-bit device, so it will fit in any slot. Line the card up with the expansion slot connector, then press it down firmly. When the card has settled into the bus connector on the motherboard and the screw hole lines up with the hole on the top or back of the chassis, reinstall the screw.

5. Test the new serial card. Test the machine with the cover off first—just be careful not to touch anything inside the machine while the computer is on. If the computer tests well, reinstall the cover and screws. It's not unusual to find that you have not set the switches exactly right on the first try. If you have problems getting the new card to work properly, the troubleshooting charts in Section 3 should help.

Future Tech: FireWire

The 1394 high-speed serial bus is based on a specification that allows connection of as many as 64 devices (63 peripherals and a host computer) through a single port. The initial implementation brings a speedy throughput of 200 Mbps (equivalent to 25 MBps); future versions are expected to approach or reach a theoretical limit of 1.6Gbps (200 MBps.)

The bus, which bears the zippy name of FireWire in Apple's marketing push, is due to pop up on new and replacement motherboards in 1997. The first devices to support the 1394 specification are expected to be video and multimedia products including digital video cameras; later uses are expected to include printers, scanners, hard drives, and network interface cards.

Adaptec was the first manufacturer to market with boards for existing systems with its AHA-8940 FireWire-to-PCI host adapter in late 1996.

CHAPTER 15
Modems

Modems are your entrance ramp to the global information superhighway. Their purpose is to **MO**dulate the digital signals of your PC so that they can be sent in analog fashion over a telephone wire; incoming analog signals are **DEM**odulated to become digital.

Here's what that means: your computer is storing information in the form of 0s and 1s. That stream of digits is assembled into a stream of information by the PC's UART (Universal Asynchronous Receiver/Transmitter) and sent as a serial signal to a modem. There the electronics of the modem changes the bits into a warbling sound wave that indicates 1s with its peaks and 0s with its valleys; this signal is an "analog" of changes in values between the bits. At the other end of the connection, another modem receives the wave and converts the peaks and valleys back into 1s and 0s for the recipient.

Modems come as internal cards that attach to the bus, or as external devices that connect through the PC's serial port. Each style has some significant benefits.

How to Buy a Modem

Although there are literally dozens of modems on the market, each making loud claims about how they are unique and special, the fact is that nearly every one of them has to go through the same computer gateway and none of them can perform better than the capabilities of the UART employed within an internal modem, or on the serial port of the system to which an external modem is attached. We discussed UARTs in detail in Chapter

14; be sure to know the capabilities of your system before you purchase an external modem that is beyond the capabilities of your PC.

There are also only a limited number of primary manufacturer of chip sets in use in the most modern of modems; the brain of nearly every modem comes from Rockwell International, Texas Instruments, Motorola, Lucent, or IBM. There are literally dozens of modems on the market, with tremendous change from month to month in price and capabilities. (Not to worry: the trend, from the start, has been for falling prices and increasing functionality.)

The state of the art in terms of speed and capability today are 33.6 Kbps devices and the developing 56 Kbps specification (Figure 15.1). We'll discuss real and potential speed later in this chapter. In a nutshell, though, our advice is this: look for a good price on a top-of-the-line modem rather than a cheap price on a cheap modem; you can very quickly pay yourself back for the cost of a speedy modem in lower telephone charges and increased productivity.

FIGURE 15.1 A 33.6 Kbps internal modem card from Cardinal Technologies; the manufacturer promises the card can be upgraded to 56K later.

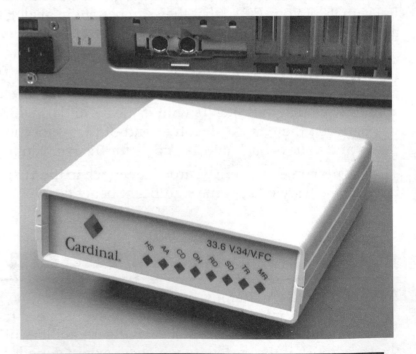

FIGURE 15.2 An external modem, like this 33.6 Kbps device from Cardinal Technologies, connects to a serial port and does not occupy an internal slot. Dinosaurs and some older modern machines lack the necessary 16550 UART serial controller for high-speed communication.

Modem Quality

In our opinion, there are three classes of modems: commodity, consumer quality, and high-end.

Commodity modems are the least expensive models. They often employ older technologies or cut corners by using off-the-shelf components instead of custom-designed devices. That's not to say that they won't work—in fact, one of the most reliable modems in the Word Association laboratories is a no-name metal box that is able to hold onto the sometimes-weak phone lines in our remote location better than a few of the more expensive brand-name devices.

In general, though, we have better luck with brand-name *consumer-quality* devices. These devices are usually more flexible in configuration and employ more current technologies. And these makers of the modems are more likely to be in business a year or so down the road when the next revolution in technologies comes along; with luck, you'll be able to upgrade your modem to keep current. (In fact, a good feature in a modem is the presence of "flash memory" that can be updated from a disk or even over the phone lines.) Consumer-quality devices usually cost about $25 to $50 more than no-name machines. A few of the trusted brand names for modems includes AT&T, Boca, Cardinal, Hayes, Microcom, Motorola, Practical Peripherals, Supra, U.S. Robotics, and Zoom.

The third class of modems are *high-end* devices. These are mostly intended for use with network servers or with mission-critical systems. Some such units offer special features including Caller ID recognition, password, and call-back security.

One unusual class is lead by Microcom, which offers a line of modems that connect to the parallel port of your PC; in doing so, they neatly skirt problems with outmoded UART chips and may offer other advantages in certain circumstances.

Support for 33.6 Kbps modems is just beginning, and widespread use of 56 Kbps devices is still on the horizon; you may have to wait a while before your Internet provider or a national on-line service offers local service at these rates— consider the fact that they will have to replace hundred or thousands of perfectly good modems to upgrade.

There is, however, no good reason to purchase a 14.4 modem, and little reason to save a few dollars by buying a 28.8 unit instead of a 33.6 Kbps modem; in either case, the small amount of money you would save would quickly be eaten up in telephone charges and lost productivity.

The fastest of consumer-quality modems sell for about $150 to $200 as this book goes to print. If your long-distance phone charges are 15 cents per minute, you will break even on the purchase of a new 28.8 Kbps modem after less than 22 hours of use (less than half an hour a week over the course of a year). Add to the equation the fact that you may also be paying a per-minute rate for an on-line services; the faster your modem, the faster you should be able to get in and out of the service with the information or files you want.

Similarly, you should expect fax facilities to be included with any modem; don't accept a slower and outmoded 9600 bps fax component on the modem-a few dozen fax calls at 14.4 Kbps will make up any difference. If you have only a single telephone line in your home or small office, you might want to look for a modem that includes support for distinctive-ring services offered by most telephone companies. With such a setup, you can obtain a second telephone number for the same single line and devote that number to incoming faxes or telecommunications; the second number, which costs less to install and use than a separate phone line, has a different sound or pattern to its ring, and a sophisticated modem can be instructed to automatically answer calls to the second number only.

External vs. Internal Modems

External modems have LEDs or other indicators making it easier to diagnose problems, and external modems can be turned off to reset them without shutting down the computer. They also do not draw power from the PC bus or produce heat under the covers and do not use one of the computer's limited bus slots.

Internal modems are usually a bit less expensive because they do not require a case, power supply, and cable. And though they use one of the internal slots, they don't necessarily use up one of the PC's two standard COM ports—they can be set to COM3 or COM4 with the proper software. Table 15.1 discusses the pluses and minuses associated with external and internal modems.

Table 15.1 External versus Internal Modems

	External Modems	Internal Modems
Slots	+ Do not occupy an internal slot	- Occupy an internal slot
Ports	- Uses a serial port	+ Usually supplies own port
Power, Heat	+ Does not draw on PC's power supply, does not add to internal heat. Can be turned off	-Draws power from internal power supply and adds some heat within case Generally cannot be turned off.
Indicators	+ Usually offers range of indicator lights to show	- Some models offer windows display of progression of session progress of session
High-speed with old UART?	- No Requires changing UART or addition of a serial adapter which occupies slot in bus	+ Provides own high-speed UART
Reset	+ Can be reset by turning off power switch or unplugging	- In some situations, lock-up of modem can only be cured by resetting entire computer
Price	- Slightly higher because of case, power supply, cable	+ Slightly less expensive

One exception to the UART problem comes with the use of a parallel port modem, like ones in the MicroCom DeskPorte parallel family. These devices use a special device driver that redirects communications to the parallel port, and generally operate at or above an equivalent serial port device.

Although modems are increasingly standardized, it is sometimes necessary to communicate with another modem of the same type, and perhaps the same brand. If the modem uses an optional data-compression standard such as MNP, you need another MNP modem to get the benefits of the data compression. Some very fast proprietary modems will only speak to another identical model.

In our laboratory upgrade projects for this book, we worked with a pair of capable high-speed fax modems from Cardinal. One, the Cardinal MVPV341, was a 33.6 Kbps internal V.34 fax modem that plugged into an ISA-bus slot and provided Windows 95 Plug-and-Play compatibility. As an internal card, it included its own 16550 UART, providing high-speed communication in any modern machine and many dinosaurs. The firmware for the modem is stored in FlashROM that can be updated by downloading new versions from the Cardinal website or BBS. The modem also includes a promise from Cardinal that it is "uptradable" to 56K X2 compatibility in the future.

The second device was the Cardinal MVP34XF, a 33.6 Kbps External V.34 Fax modem, which also featured Windows 95 Plug-and-Play compatibility, an updateable FlashROM and uptradability to 56K X2 compatibility. I couldn't use the external modem, though, on a venerable 486 DX/2 machine in the laboratory since that computer did not have a 16550 UART controlling its internal serial port.

Fax Modems

Nearly all modern internal modems and external modems now include fax capabilities. Using a capable piece of software, you can send anything you see on screen over a telephone line to a fax machine or another fax modem.

If you want to send a copy of piece of paper, you'll need to add a scanner to the mix; scan whatever you want to send and save it as a graphics file and then use your fax software to send it over the phone lines to another fax, or send the graphics file as a stream of data to a standard modem and then print out the image using the facilities of a word processor and its attached printer.

To use your fax modem to receive incoming faxes, you'll have to leave the modem and PC on all the time, with the modem set to **Auto Answer**. This may represent a hardship if your PC uses a voice phone line for communication.

You can use an attached printer to make hard copies of any received faxes.

Despite these shortcomings, a fax modem is a very valuable addition to your system if you want to quickly send hard copy notes anywhere in the world. In the Word Association offices, we use the fax modem for outgoing faxes and a regular facsimile machine for all incoming messages.

The biggest problem with these cards, as with any add-ons, is setting up the I/O addresses. You set the addresses with jumpers. Because there are always alternative settings, it's important to make sure that the fax card you buy has documentation.

When you first run the card's setup program, you tell the software how you have set the jumper selection, but these I/O addresses can conflict with other hardware in your computer. If your computer won't work now, or the add-on board seems to be dead, you may have such a conflict. In severe cases, you may even lose your setup program. Take out the offending card, consult its documentation, set the jumpers to another selection, and try again. We remind you to use a diagnostics program to map the available I/O addresses.

Modern Modem Standards

The Consultative Committee for International Telephone and Telegraph (CCITT) is an international association that establishes and oversees worldwide communications standards. CCITT standards begin with a "V" and are followed by a numeric code.

The original American standards were developed by Bell Labs in the 1960s and 1970s. The newer CCITT standards generally cover the same protocols. The developing 56 Kbps modem, which we'll discuss in a moment, does not yet have an officially recognized standard.

Among modern standards are:

- **V.22**. 1,200 bps. Synchronous or asynchronous data transmission, with full-duplex operations over 2-wire leased or dial-up lines. Comparable to Bell 212A.
- **V.22 bis**. 2,400 bps.
- **V.32**. 9,600 bps, fallback to 4,800 bps. The first universal standard for 9600-bps modems on dial-up or leased lines.
- **V.32 bis.** 14,400 bps. Includes the ability to "retrain" connected modems to reduce transmission speed to deal with line noise if necessary.

- V.34. 28,800 to 33,600 bps. This is the state-of-the-communications-art, at least as far as formally recognized international standards. In 1996, firmware improvements allowed modems to eke out a bit of extra speed, moving from 28.8 Kbps to 33.6 Kbps in good conditions.

> For a short period of time prior to the completion of the V.34 specification, there were a handful of modem makers with devices that worked at 28.8 Kbps; they were grouped under the V.fc interim label; we recommend against purchasing this orphaned technology, although V.fc devices are supposed to be able to work with V.34 modems.

Error Correction and Data Compression

Once the speed of transmission of information bits has been set, you can add protocols that help assure error-free transmission of data or that compress data so that the effective rate of transmission is even greater. You must have the same protocols installed at both ends of the modem connection in order for the information to be properly encoded and decoded.

Among current protocols are:

- **NP Levels 1–4**. The Microcom Networking Protocols permit error-free asynchronous transmission of data.
- **MNP Level 5**. This protocol adds a data compression algorithm to the error-correction code. Data is compressed by a factor of about 2:1.
- **V.42, V.42 bis**. The CCITT definition for a protocol that is comparable to MNP Level 5.

The 56K Holy Grail

At the start of 1997, what had once been declared as impossible became possible-but not assured.

We're talking about the 56 Kbps modem, an astounding speed for telecommunication over standard telephone lines. Over recent years, modem designers had succeeded in pushing communication in exciting but relatively small increments: from 300 bps when the IBM PC first arrived to 1,200, then 2,400, 4,800, 9,600, and finally 14,400. When modem makers figured out a way to double communications speed to 28,800 bps (28.8 Kbps) 1993, they did so with a warning that technology was reaching very close to the speed limit. That seemed to be proving true in 1996 when modem makers came out with a very small, incremental increase to 33.6 Kbps.

As this book went to press, there was no final agreement on a standard for the high-speed technology; among marketing names for the technology are V.56 and V2X.

In fact, 33.6 Kbps may well prove to be as fast as many of us can push data over the pair of copper wires that run from our home or office, despite the major news of the introduction of 56 Kbps modems at the start of 1997.

First of all, the new communications devices are not modems in the same way that 33.6 Kbps modems are. The older devices were intended to produce a modulated analog signal that represents the digital original. And secondly, the potential top speed of 56 Kbps is one-way from the source to your computer; going the other way, your requests for information and other data are sent at up to 33.6 Kbps. This design element will work well in an Internet environment.

The new 56 Kbps devices operate as analog modems from your office or home to the central office of your telephone company—a distance that could be very near in a large city and relatively far away in rural areas. At the local central office, the system expects to find a compatible 56 Kbps modem and a totally digital link that goes directly to the service provider you have connected to. If the number you have dialed is itself connected to a distant central office by an analog phone line, the best you can hope for is a 33.6 Kbps session.

You will not be able to connect at 56.6 Kbps between two compatible modems if they are each connected to the central office by an analog line.

Among manufacturers of chipsets for the new technology are Texas Instruments (supplying U.S. Robotics among others), Rockwell Semiconductor Systems (supplying Hayes and Microcom), Lucent, and Motorola. Some modem makers released 33.6 Kbps models in early 1997 that they promised could be upgraded to 55.6 Kbps speed later on.

Among service providers announcing support of the high-speed connection were America Online, CompuServe, Prodigy, and MCI Internet.

If a 56 Kbps modem cannot establish a top-speed connection all the way to the receiving end, the two devices negotiate back and forth until they find a speed that will work.

Troubleshooting an External Modem

When it comes to troubleshooting an external modem, you should test the separate components. Test the port using a diagnostic program, as outlined earlier in this chapter.

Do the modem lights turn on when power is applied? (Some modems have a self-test that should generate an **OK** or other message after the device is turned on.) Next check the settings in your software program: is it set to use the proper COM port? Next check the cable running from the serial port to the modem by substituting a known good replacement cable.

Test the connection from the computer to the modem by going into the Terminal section of your software program. Type **AT** and press the **Enter** key. If your modem is working and is properly attached to a working serial port through a working cable, the software program should report back an **OK** message on screen.

The last element to check is the quality of the phone line itself. Is the modem plugged into a phone jack properly? Swap a known good phone cable for the one in use. Try plugging a telephone into the jack to confirm that there is a dial tone on the line. If the jack itself is dead you may have to troubleshoot the phone line within your home or office; if the problem lies at the Network Interface between your building and the phone company's incoming line, it's time to call the phone repairman.

Troubleshooting an Internal Modem

When you install an internal modem, be sure to set the *IRQ* (interrupt jumpers) and the I/O address jumpers correctly. Test the machine before reinstalling the cover, since it's easy to make a mistake here. The I/O address must be unique—it must not interfere with another serial device already installed in the machine.

If your telecommunications software supports COM3 and/or COM4, set the modem to COM3—you are unlikely to have another serial device set to COM3. Be sure to set the IRQ for the I/O address you are using. Each I/O address is paired, by tradition, with a particular interrupt. See Appendix D for a list of common I/O addresses and their associated interrupts.

Then check the phone line. Is the modem plugged into a phone jack properly? Swap a known good phone cable for the one in use. Try plugging a telephone into the jack to confirm that there is a dial tone on the line. If the jack itself is dead you may have to troubleshoot the phone line within your home or office; if the problem lies at the Network Interface between your building and the phone company's incoming line, it's time to call the phone repairman.

Telecom Software Problems

Whether you use an external or internal modem, your telecommunications software must be set up correctly. A minor baud rate error or the incorrect I/O address will make your perfectly good modem appear to be stone-cold dead (modems are that way; they either work fine or they won't work at all). Some pieces of communications software are very picky about the brand of telecommunications hardware in your system.

The Call-Waiting Headache

Many home and office telephones are equipped with a phone company service called "Call Waiting," which notifies you when a second phone call is coming in on a line. You can place the first caller on hold to answer the second caller. You'll hear a tone at your end of the connection, and the first caller will hear a click.

Unfortunately, the Call Waiting signal can be interpreted by some modems as a drop in the phone line; this can result in the loss of the line or a loss of characters.

If your phone line has Call Waiting, you can avoid disruptions for outgoing calls. You can manually enter *70 from the dialing pad of a telephone before a call is placed; then dial the number you want to communicate with from the telephone or your telecommunications program. Call Waiting will be disabled for the duration of the current call. As soon as you hang up, though, it will be back in effect.

Another way to accomplish the same thing is to have your telecommunications program automatically include the disable signal before any call is dialed. Some programs have features that allow you to specify this. On other pieces of software, put *70, (include the comma) at the end of the dialing prefix.

The only way to avoid interruptions on *incoming calls* is to remove Call Waiting from your telephone line. The only way to avoid interruptions at the other end is to advise your callers to disable or remove Call Waiting on their phone service.

The Parallel Interface

Printers and parallel ports are tied together like a light bulb and a power line. As we have discussed, a parallel port is a continuation of the computer data bus that can carry eight bits of information (one byte) alongside each. In theory, a parallel port is eight times as fast in delivering information as a serial port, which sends those same eight bits one after another down a single wire.

Going Parallel

The original PC parallel port had a single function: to send data in one direction, from computer to printer. An adapter called a *parallel card* collected data from the computer bus and sent them it 8 bits at a time to the printer (Figure 16.1).

For years the parallel port was called the printer port; few other parallel devices existed. As a one-way communication device, it was subject to occasional roadblocks. For example, if the computer

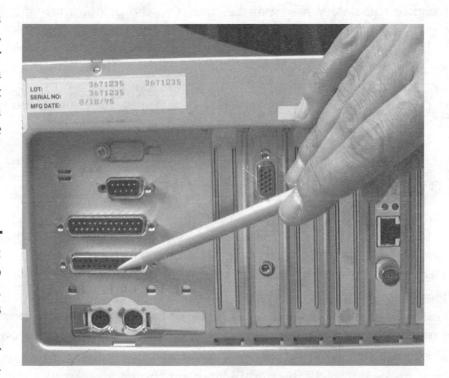

Figure 16.1 A parallel connector on the back panel of a PC.

received an **out-of-paper** or **printer-busy** signal from the printer, that signal held up data transmission.

Newer, modern machines have two-way parallel ports (*Enhanced Parallel Port* or *EPP*) so that data can flow freely into and out of the computer. The two-way parallel port has spawned a whole raft of parallel-interface peripherals. You can now buy modems, network adapters, CD-ROM drives, Bernoulli boxes, even external hard disks and tape backup units that communicate with the host computer through a parallel port (see Figure 16.2).

Despite the flashy new parallel peripherals, printers are still the most common peripheral on a parallel port. Most printers sold in the last five years have been parallel printers. However, since printers come in two forms (serial and parallel), you can't assume that the printer cable is a parallel device. If you don't know whether your printer is serial or parallel, we'll help you sort out the cables and connectors in the next few paragraphs.

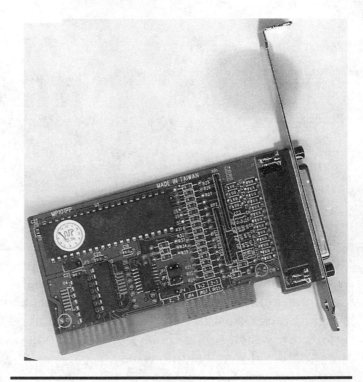

Figure 16.2 You can add an Enhanced Parallel Port card to an older machine to get the benefits of bi-directional parallel communication. (Dalco Electronics.)

How a Parallel Port Works

Because computers store information in 8-bit bytes, the simplest way to send a byte of information to a printer is to use eight separate wires from computer to printer. Each of the 8 bits is sent on its own wire, parallel to other wires within the cable.

Three signal lines on early parallel ports were assigned to the printer to send **out-of-paper**, **printer-busy**, and **data-acknowledgement** signals back to the computer. The parallel port could transmit signals on the eight data lines, but not receive them. New parallel ports can either send or receive on all lines.

A standard parallel printer cable—sometimes called a *Centronics cable* for the 36-pin Centronics connector at the printer end—connects the parallel card to the printer. Unlike serial ports, all parallel ports send the same signals on each particular pin, so no custom parallel cables are needed. (For those who must know, in Table 16.1 you'll find a listing of the pin assignments for a standard parallel cable.)

Table 16.1 Signals on a 25-Pin Parallel Port Connector

Pin	Name
1	Strobe
2	Data bit 0
3	Data bit 1
4	Data bit 2
5	Data bit 3
6	Data bit 4
7	Data bit 5
8	Data bit 6
9	Data bit 7
10	Acknowledge
11	Busy
12	Paper Out
13	Select
14	Auto line feed
15	Error
16	Initialize printer
17	Select input
18	Ground
19	Ground
20	Ground
21	Ground
22	Ground
23	Ground
24	Ground
25	Ground

Unfortunately, parallel cables are only guaranteed to be accurate for runs of 12 to 15 feet, though users sometimes successfully employ cables as long as 25 feet. Each case is different. If it works, it works. If a longer run does not function reliably, there are several solutions. One involves the use of a *parallel line booster*, a specialized amplifier that can extend the useful transmission distance of a parallel signal as much as 2,000 feet; these relatively inexpensive devices (less than $100 from mail order sources) essentially convert the parallel signal into a specialized high-speed serial signal and sends them over a standard telephone cable to a receiver where the signal is changed back to a parallel signal.

CHAPTER 16

Where to Find the Parallel Port

Look at the back of your computer. If you have a printer, follow the printer cable back to the computer and examine that connector first. Parallel ports use 25-pin connectors (called *DB25 connectors*). Male DB25 connectors have protruding pins; female DB25 connectors have openings to accept the pins. The parallel port on the computer system is a female DB-25 socket. The cable to the printer has a male DB25 connector.

Just to make things interesting, serial ports can also use a DB25 connector. On the oldest PCs, there was often serious confusion because some serial ports used female DB25 sockets identical to the parallel port socket. All modern machines and most PCs after that period of initial confusion use male connectors for serial ports; most makers have changed over from 25-pin DB25 sockets to the smaller but still capable 9-pin male DB9 connector.

IBM—which has almost always marched to its own drummer—reintroduced the confusion with some of its PS/2 computers in the early 1990s. If you're lucky, your machine will have labels identifying the nature of all connectors on the back panel; in any case, consult the PC's instruction manual if there is any question.

A computer can have as many as three parallel ports, although systems with more than two are rare. Parallel ports can be found on the video cards of some early PCs, on multifunction cards of old machines, on separate I/O (input/output) cards, and, on modern machines, often on connectors that attach directly to the motherboard and poke out of the back of the PC.

How to Test a Parallel Port

Parallel ports do not often fail; it is more likely that the cable has worked loose, been crimped, and shorted out, or that a change to a software setting or a driver has caused it to stop responding. In our experience, the most likely cause is a failed cable. We recommend keeping a replacement parallel and serial cable in your supply cabinet.

Some logical steps to troubleshoot parallel port problems follow.

Start by checking the power cable to the printer. Most printers have a self-test capability; check the instruction manual to do so. If the self-test does not work, your printer has a problem.

Next, check the data cable connections between the parallel port and the printer. Is it firmly attached at both ends? Try using your new or known good spare cable. If changing the cable fixes the problem, throw away the old cable.

Next (if possible) take the printer and the cable to another machine that has a working parallel port. If the printer and the cable work, then you can assume that the parallel port on the original PC has either failed or has an improper setting.

The troubleshooting charts in Section 3 give more hints.

If both the printer and the cable are good, use a diagnostic disk to see what parallel ports the computer thinks are installed. If you have two physical parallel ports, but Norton's System Information program, CheckIt, or QA Plus shows only one, the switches and interrupts on one of the ports are probably not set correctly.

Some of the earliest video-with-parallel port cards have a port enable/disable jumper. Check the manual for such a jumper. In addition, the physical port address and the interrupt assigned to the card are set with jumpers on some parallel cards. Again, check the manual.

As with serial ports, you must be careful to give each parallel port its own unique hardware address. DOS refers to these different addresses as *LPT1*, *LPT2*, and *LPT3*. Be sure that your software is set up correctly to send information to the appropriate parallel port. The printer cabled up to LPT1 won't print your document if the word processor is sending the text to LPT2.

If you find no obvious problems, investigate the parallel port further. Try the CheckIt or QA Plus printer port tests. They require a *wrap* plug (also called a *loopback* plug), which sometimes comes with the software or can be purchased from an electronics house. Or you can construct out of a spare male RS232 plug (available at electronic parts supply houses).

If you want to make your own wrap plug, you can short out the pins of a DB25 connector with solder or connect together wires in a short parallel cable. Use short jumper wires or clean solder bridges to connect the pins together electrically. You must make five solder connections. The details can be found in Table 16.2.

Table 16.2 Parallel Loopback Plug: To Make a Wrap or Loopback Plug for a Parallel Port, Solder These Pins Together on a DB25 Male Connector

Solder pin	To pin
2	15
3	13
4	12
5	10
6	11

If the parallel port passes the wrap plug test, the port is probably good. Check again for a mismatched LPT port and interrupt, or for mismatched word processor output parameters. If you still can't find the problem, try the troubleshooting charts. They have complete, step-by-step, parallel port diagnostic/repair procedures.

How to Remove and Install a Parallel Port

Many modern machines have serial and parallel circuitry built into the motherboard; the ports extend out of the back of the chassis. If there is a problem with the parallel adapter on the motherboard or if you want to upgrade to a better system, you may need to disable the adapter using a jumper or switch; consult your PC's instruction manual or the manufacturer for details.

The instructions that follow apply to parallel ports that are on an add-in card plugged into the bus.

1. Remove the cables and computer cover. Before you remove a parallel port, turn off the computer and unplug it from the wall. Disconnect the printer cable (the cable from computer to printer) at the parallel port end. The cable may have two long, threaded knobs on the card end or a pair of narrow thin screws to hold the cable connector tight to the card; unscrew the knobs or screws by turning them counterclockwise. If the parallel port is part of the video card (a very early-era design), remove the video cable too. Once you've disconnected the cables, remove the system cover.

2. Remove the old card. The card itself is secured to the back wall of the system unit chassis with a single screw. Remove that screw and save it. Lift the card straight up; it shouldn't require too much force.

3. Install new card. Installation is the reverse of removal. Old-style parallel, video-with-parallel, and multifunction cards are 8-bit cards, and any bus connector is appropriate. Carefully line up the edge connector on the card with the slot on the motherboard and press down firmly. When the card is in place, the screw hole on the card will line up with the screw hole in the back of the chassis. Reinstall the screw and test the machine.

CHAPTER 17
Hard Copy

In the early days of computers, printers were expensive, large, slow, loud mechanical devices somewhere between a lawnmower and a Smith Corona typewriter. They generally used a mechanism with a spinning daisy-wheel with typewriterlike molds for each character (or IBM's variant, the Selectric ball); a hammer would strike the character through a ribbon and onto the paper. They were called *character printers*.

Large printers used with computer mainframes would have a set of wheels a full page wide so that they could print a line at a time; they were called *line printers*. That name lives on in the official name for the parallel port on PCs, LPT1.

The important thing to understand about these devices is that they were character-oriented. The computer would send a signal that would tell the printer to hit the letter "J" mold against the ribbon. If you wanted to type an italic *J*, you had to change the type wheel or ball to one that had an italic *J*.

Soon after personal computers arrived on the scene, printer manufacturers introduced a whole new type of design. All of these devices fit into a category called *dot matrix printers*. Nearly every printer now sold for use with PCs uses this technology, which is cheaper, smaller, faster, and quieter than character printers.

Dot matrix printers draw characters by making tiny dots that appear to the eye to merge into a continuous line. The same principle is used to draw an image on a television screen or monitor, or to produce a printed photograph in a book or newspaper. A dot matrix printer can be made to create a character of any design, limited only by the fineness of the dots and with it the number of dots that could be fit in a particular area. The dots can be used to make pictures and other graphics.

The work that is involved in producing the images of characters can be performed at the printer, or it can be produced in the form of a page-sized bit map at the computer. Bit maps are particularly appropriate when you are producing an image is derived from Microsoft Windows or another graphical user interface.

Solving Printer Problems

In this Fourth Edition, we have dropped detailed troubleshooting for daisywheel printers; they are generally not worth repairing if they break down. If you do have a problem with a daisywheel, spend a few minutes to check the following: is the printer plugged into a powered outlet? Has the printer blown a fuse on its back panel? Is the printer properly connected to the computer with a data cable? (Try substituting a known good cable.) Do your applications programs have a proper printer driver or description to work with the daisywheel device? One quick way to test a daisywheel is to go to the DOS prompt and ask for the display of a **DIR**ectory of the current disk; then press the **Print Screen** key (or **Shift-Print Screen**) on your keyboard. If the printer is functioning and properly cabled to the computer, it should print a copy of the directory.

Figure 17.1 Data switches, like this A/B device allow one computer to work with several devices vying for the attention of a single serial or parallel port, or allow several computers to share a single device. Automatic data switches are able to automatically open the door on command from the PC. (Dalco Electronics.)

Types of Printers

For modern machines, there are three major types of printers: *dot matrix* or *impact*, *ink jet*, and *laser*. Despite the distinction, all three are dot matrix printers.

When you set about to purchase a printer, remember that the quality of your printed output is the principal way by which most others will view your work. It may not make a lot of sense to spend thousands of dollars on a nifty computer system and then scrimp on a cheap and unimpressive printer.

For most modern users, the machines of choice are laser printers and their close cousins, ink jet printers. We'll discuss both in this chapter.

Increasingly, many computer users are exploring the use of color output. Relatively inexpensive color ink jet and dot matrix ribbon or wax transfer printers are available; color laser printers are still well beyond the budget for most personal computer shoppers.

Dot Matrix Printers

Dot matrix printers today make up the low end of the printer spectrum, with prices as low as $100 for basic models. The major distinction among these devices is the number of pins that are used to draw the dots for each letter; a 24-pin printer is capable of drawing much finer characters and graphics than a 9-pin device.

The other distinction involves which printer specification they most closely emulate. The most common printer designs are Epson devices and IBM Proprinter machines; there are very few dot matrix printers offered that are not capable of acting like one or the other of these devices. We'd stay away from an oddball printer unless its manufacturer can convince you of a really good reason to use it, and will provide drivers to work with the software you use.

Ink Jet Printers

Ink jet printers squirt tiny droplets of ink in programmable patterns. They are very similar to dot matrix impact printers, except that they replace hammers and pins with ink nozzles; characters are made up of dots.

The first ink jet printers required a special coated paper and were rather expensive; current models can work with any smooth paper and have dropped in price to a few hundred dollars.

Ink jet printers are every bit as impressive as a low-end laser printer—with the same 300 dot per inch resolution—at least when they are first taken out of the box. Quality can fall off slightly if the nozzles are not kept clean, if poor quality paper is used, or in extremely humid conditions.

As with dot matrix printers, there are a few common designs that most machines can emulate; look for Hewlett-Packard Ink Jet or Canon emulation to be sure of compatibility with a wide range of software packages. And before you buy an ink jet printer, check on the price and availability of ink cartridges for the printer. You should also attempt to compare per-page cost for ink jet devices; the specifications for printers should give you the information you need.

Laser Printers

Laser printers are as commonplace in the American office as copy machines. The differences between the two are not as great as you might think. You can think of a laser printer as a computerized copy machine, requiring the same kind of care.

Laser printers should be able to emulate a Hewlett-Packard Laserjet device in order to work with all sorts of software, including Microsoft Windows.

The important specifications for a printer are: resolution (with 300 dots per inch the current minimum, and 600 dpi increasingly common), pages-per-minute (based on the output of simple text pages, and usually starting about 4 or 6 ppm), and printer memory (1 MB is a minimum, but 2 MB is more realistic if you are going to print out graphics of any complexity.)

Bear in mind that the page-per-minute rating is based on plain text pages; it can take quite a while—sometimes several minutes—for the computer to compose a complex bit map and send it to your printer for output. In such a case, a 4 ppm printer is just as fast as a 20 ppm device—they'll both put out only a single page at a time.

Another critical difference between laser printers involves the quality of construction and the cost of consumables. You can often gauge the quality of construction by looking at the length of warranty offered by the manufacturer; read reviews in PC magazines, too.

Some printers, including most Hewlett Packard models, put a lot of the mechanical elements in a removable cartridge that also contains a supply of toner; the cartridge is replaced after a certain number of pages have been produced. In the case of the HP printer, the cartridges sell for between $75 to $100, depending on model. Another sort of design—used by Okidata and others uses inexpensive toner cartridges priced at $20 or below; an image drum, priced at about $200, is replaced every dozen or so toner cartridges.

Both schemes work, and in many cases work out to about the same cost per page. One advantage of the HP design is that it has spawned a fairly busy industry of cartridge refillers; each unit can usually be restocked with toner three or four times at a savings of about 50 percent over new cartridges.

Determining the Source of a Printer Problem

A parallel or serial printer port rarely breaks; the most common sources of problems for hard copy output are cables, switches, and the printers themselves.

Here are some steps that can help identify the source of a problem:

- Run the printer's self-test. Consult your instruction manual or call the manufacturer to learn how to test the machine. If the self-test fails, your printer needs servicing.

- If the self-test works, move on to test your printer and cable. Turn on the printer. Go to DOS and display the **DIR**ectory of the current directory. Now press the **Print Screen** (or **Shift-Print Screen**) button on the keyboard. The directory should be produced on the printer; some devices may require you to turn the printer from On Line to Off Line and then press **Form Feed** in order to manually eject a page from the printer.

  If the printer works in this test, your problem is related to a software setting in your application or operating system.

- If the printer fails the test, try substituting a known good data cable and running the same test. If the printer now works, the original cable has failed and should be replaced.

- If the cable is not the problem, try hooking the printer to another computer. Try the printer from an application and from DOS, as described above. If the printer doesn't work, it should be taken in for service; if it does work properly, your problem lies with the original computer.

Test the serial or parallel port of your computer as appropriate, using a diagnostic software program.

If you have a very old printer, you may have a nonstandard serial cable; consult the instruction manual for details. In Chapter 14, we discussed one almost-foolproof solution to serial cable problems, a magical device called the SmartCable, sold by IQ Technologies. The SmartCable can adjust to match the needs of either end of the connection.

See Chapter 14 for more serial connection troubleshooting tips.

Hardware Checks

Is the printer turned on and connected by cable to the parallel port of your PC?

Start by making sure the printer itself is functioning by performing a self-test. Each printer has its own way to produce a test page; consult your instruction manual.

Next check the connection from your PC to the printer by sending a simple file from DOS. (You can branch to the DOS prompt from within Windows 95, or exit Windows 95 to the prompt.) Type the following and then press **Enter** to send it to the printer:

```
COPY C:\AUTOEXEC.BAT LPT1<Enter>
```

(If C: is not your boot drive, or if your printer is not connected to LPT1—the standard parallel port designation—you will have to make appropriate changes in the command.)

You may need to manually eject a page from your printer to see the results. On most devices, press the **Off Line** button and then **Form Feed**.

If the printer produces a copy of your **AUTOEXEC.BAT** file, you have established that the printer, its cable, and the PC's parallel port are all functioning properly.

Next, eliminate problems with any advanced text processing application. If you are running Windows 95, click the **Start** button, point to **Programs**, then to **Accessories**, and finally select either **Notepad** or **WordPad**. Type some text on the screen, and then attempt to print.

If you cannot print from either of the accessories, check the settings for the printer port using Device Manager. Open the **Properties for Ports (COM & LPT)** and then double-click on the port for your printer—usually **Printer Port (LPT1)**.

Click the **Resources** tab and check that the conflicting devices list does not indicate a conflict. Examine the settings for the port. The usual input/output range for a standard LPT1 port is 0378-037A; if there is a second parallel port installed, LPT2 is ordinarily assigned to 0278.

If there appears to be a conflict, or if the port settings are incorrect, use Device Manager to remove the printer port from the system and then restart the computer. When Windows 95 is running again, click **Start**, point to **Settings**, then click on **Control Panel** and double-click on **Add New Hardware** to allow Windows to detect the hardware again.

Printer-Software Issues

If you can print from a DOS command prompt but not from within Windows-based programs and you have already examined port settings, there may be a problem with spool settings or bi-directional communication. A *print spool* holds information prepared by the PC for printing; copying information to the spooler allows the computer to get back to other tasks and leave output as a background function.

Experiment to see if the problem lies in the spool settings. Click the **Start** button, point to **Settings**, and the click on **Printers**. Bring the mouse pointer to the printer you are attempting to use, and then click the right mouse button to bring up a submenu; click on **Properties**. Then click on **Details** and the **Spool Settings** button. Finally, click the **Print Directly to the Printer** option button to turn off spooling.

If the **Details** tab indicates that the printer is set up to support bi-directional communication, try turning off that advanced facility. Click the **Disable bi-directional support for this printer** option button.

Click on **OK**, and then try to print from Notepad or WordPad. If the printer now functions properly, experiment with other settings for the spooler and experiment with them in combination with the bi-directional printing option.

Bi-directional printing requires an improved parallel printer cable, one that conforms to the IEEE 1284 specification; you may need to replace your printer cable to use its facilities. Bi-directional printing may also fail if the cable is too long. And you may lose bidirectionality if the parallel cable goes through a switch box or line extender.

Printer Drivers

Printers vary in the way they handle carriage returns and line feeds and the way they interpret escape codes for fonts and print size. To accommodate these differences, you must install a software program called a *printer driver*. Modern word processing software is delivered on ten or more disks, due to the amazing number of printer drivers the software must provide.

The most common reason for printer problems is an incorrect printer driver installation. This doesn't mean that you've installed the printer incorrectly, but that you've installed the wrong printer driver while setting up the software. The result can be some truly odd characters that appear when you print bold or underlined words. When you first use the software, you must select the correct printer driver to copy into the program. If you don't see the exact model number and guess wrong, or if you inadvertently type the wrong choice, you will install the wrong printer driver.

Application Settings

There are too many applications and too many combinations of problems to deal with here. However, there are a few basic areas to explore before you call the maker of the software.

First, determine the nature of the printing problem. Are you able to produce text but not graphics? Will text print but not produce proper fonts? Does the problem only occur in one document?

One interesting test is to attempt to print a blank page to the printer; if this works, there may be a problem with memory or fonts.

It may be necessary to reinstall the applications or there may be a problem with the System Registry (used for 32-bit applications) or an **.INI** file (for a 16-bit program). Some older Windows 3.X applications may need modification of their **.INI** files to run properly under Windows 95. Contact the maker of your application.

Finally, there may be a problem with the printer driver for your hardware. Windows 95 supports more than 800 printers directly and can work with most Windows 3.1 and 3.11 printer drivers. At installation, if a Windows 95 printer driver is available, it will be used. Contact the maker of the printer to see if an updated driver is available.

Printer Speed

Printers, like hard disk drives and CPUs, sometimes exist in an Alice in Wonderland world when it comes to measures of speed. A dot matrix may in fact be capable of zipping along at 192 characters per second on a small-sized font, but may slow to 160 cps on a larger font. And dot matrix printers usually make a distinction between draft and letter quality printing; the difference in characters per second can be very significant: the same printer in the above example may be able to produce its best type at a relatively slow 45 cps. A truer measure would be number of hammer strikes per second, but that by itself wouldn't tell you how long your resume will take to exit the printer. And neither specification will easily inform you how long it will take to print out a graphic.

Here's a real-world appraisal: a typical single-spaced page of manuscript for this book contains 381 words or 1,762 characters (in the English language, the average word length is about 5 characters). At 192 cps, a dot matrix printer would require about 9.2 seconds to spit out a draft-quality copy of the page; at the (near) letter-quality speed of 45 cps, the page would require a fairly slow 39 seconds.

Similarly, a laser printer may be advertised as an 8 ppm (page per minute) device. But laser printers are page printers in that they form the entire page in their internal memory (or in some designs, in the memory of the PC) and then produce the page in a single pass. The 8 ppm specification refers to the speed of continuous pieces of paper through the printer after the pages have been formed in memory—each page requires 7.5 seconds, which works out to something like 235 cps. However, creating the first page of a text document typically requires 20 to 30 seconds; a more reasonable ppm rating for an 8-page document is about 6.6. Remember, though, that a laser printer is always producing letter-quality pages—there's no need for an adjective like "near."

Creating a complex graphic image can slow a laser printer to a crawl, sometimes requiring a minute or more to create the page; once that page is completed, it will be spit out at the ppm rate—7.5 seconds in the example of our supposed "8 ppm" example.

What can you do to improve printer speed? A laser printer will benefit from the addition of RAM; the memory will either speed the creation of the page being printed or allow creation of the next page in the background as the current one is being produced.

One device that improves your computing environment is a hardware printer cache or a software printer buffer; either one will allow you to move on to new tasks while pages are created and stored in the background. Neither solution speeds up the production of the pages themselves, but they do improve your personal productivity.

Printing Speed Under Windows 95

There are two elements to printing speed under Windows 95:

- **Printer "Drop" Speed:** The amount of time from when a print job is sent to the printer until when the job is complete.
- **Return to Application (RTA) Speed:** The amount of time from when a print job is sent to the printer until you regain control of the system.

Each of these times can be affected by settings to the print spooler of Windows 95.

Click on **Start**, point to **Settings**, and then click **Printers**. Identify the printer you want to use, and then use the right mouse button to select it. Click on **Properties**, the **Details** tab, and finally click the **Spool Settings** button.

To adjust RTA speed, click **Start printing after first page is spooled.** For most printers, use EMF as the spool data format. (PostScript printers must use the RAW spool data format.)

To adjust Printer Drop Speed, click the **Print Directly to the Printer** option button or click **Start Printing after last page is spooled.**

CHAPTER 18
Your Computer's Hands and Eyes

Your fabulously capable, high-speed personal computer would be no better than a high-tech boat anchor were it not for its ability to communicate with the outside world. We make use of PCs by printing out their product, sending them over a telephone wire, or using a network connection.

And your PC would not be all that impressive if it could not respond to input it receives from that outside world through keyboards, mice, scanners, laboratory control devices, and more.

In this section, we'll discuss two important input devices, a hand and eye for the computer: the mouse and the scanner.

Mice

A mouse gives your computer a hand.

This electronic rodent changes small hand motions into cursor motion on-screen. Although the general concept has been around for many years, it was with the arrival and acceptance of graphical user interfaces like Microsoft Windows that mice went from an option to a necessity on most modern machines (see Figure 18.1).

There are two ways for a mouse to communicate with the computer. Serial mice (Figure 18.2) use a standard serial port. Bus mice, on the other hand (Figure 18.3), have a unique address of their own and a dedicated bus mouse controller card—they are still serial devices, but they don't use the serial port, its address, or its interrupt.

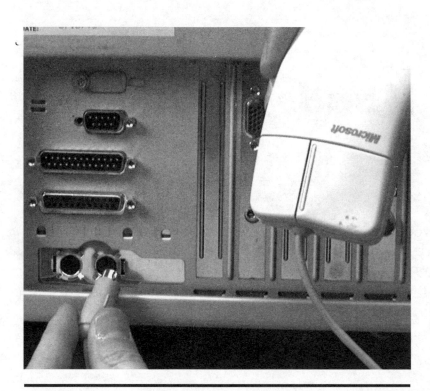

Figure 18.1 A PS/2-style mouse connector on the back panel of a PC.

Figure 18.2 This serial mouse connects to a standard serial port on a PC.

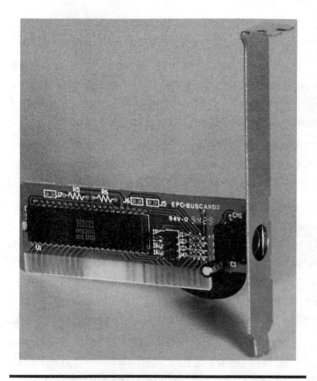

Figure 18.3 Installing a Bus Mouse card allows use of mice with 9-pin connectors and saves you from giving up one of your two standard serial ports for the purpose. (Dalco Electronics.)

How a Mouse Works

When you slide a mouse across the desktop or a special mouse pad, the mouse detects this motion, in both horizontal and vertical directions. The mouse sends this information to the computer, typically along a cable to a serial port or to a dedicated mouse card installed in an expansion card slot. A few cordless models use infrared or radio signals to communicate between mouse and computer. Inside the computer, a *device driver* (a software program designed to interface the mouse to the computer) translates the mouse signal into instructions the computer can read.

There are many ways for mice to detect hand motion. Most mice use a track ball, which rolls as your hand slides the mouse across a flat surface.

In all, there are four types of mice, and two related devices worth considering:

- Mechanical mice
- Optical mice
- Optomechanical mice
- Wheel mice
- Trackballs
- Joysticks

Mechanical mice have a hard rubber ball inside that rests loosely in a chamber surrounded by sensing rollers. As the mouse is moved along a desktop or a mouse pad, the ball contacts the rollers (Microsoft calls its internal parts *shafts*), which cause copper contacts or brushes to sweep across a segmented conductor. In function, the arrangement is somewhat like the brushes of an electric motor, except that the rotating contacts within the mouse are circuit-board "lands."

The conducting strips are attached to a circular board in a spokelike arrangement. The conducting wheel is called an *encoder*. As the moving conductor goes across the segmented contacts, electrical impulses are generated; the signals are counted in the attached electronic circuitry.

CHAPTER 18

The impulses can be either negative or positive, depending on the direction of rotation. The polarity of the pulses tells the electronics the direction the mouse is moving, and the speed of the pulses shows how fast the mouse is moving.

The two rollers inside the mouse ball cavity are opposed at 90° to each other, allowing them to differentiate between horizontal and vertical movement. If both rollers turn, the movement is interpreted as oblique and the electronics of the mouse interpret the relative speed and polarity of the pulses to compute a precise direction of movement.

Common to all mouse designs are one or more micro switches that lie beneath the buttons on the mice. Pressing the button closes the switch and send a signal (a *click*). The mouse software is in charge of interpreting the signals to determine if buttons have been double-clicked.

Optical mice have no moving parts and offer very high resolution; they are used in applications where very fine motions must be picked up, such as in certain art and graphics programs. Optical mice use a special grid pad with a reflective surface. When the mouse is moved on this surface, a light-emitting diode (LED) shines light onto the pad; photosensors in the mouse detect motion from the streaks of light reflected back from the grid. Once the pulses are received and counted, the optical mouse functions as do mechanical and optomechanical designs. However, because there is no mechanical component as you move the optical mouse, it will feel very different from a mechanical device.

Optomechanical mice are a hybrid design that lie between mechanical and optical devices. With this device, the movement of the ball is translated into an electrical signal by an optical device. The mechanical ball turns rollers, just as with a mechanical mouse, but instead of using mechanical electrical contacts, the optomechanical design rotates slotted or perforated wheels. An LED shines through the openings on the wheel; optical sensors on the other side count the resulting pulses.

Wheel mice, a rarely seen alternative, use two wheels at right angles—one to measure horizontal movement, the other to measure vertical movement.

Trackballs are upside-down mechanical mice. The ball rests loosely in a cavity, with sensors that track horizontal and vertical movement. Instead of moving the hardware across the desk, you use your hand to spin the ball in place.

There are two advantages to trackballs: the first is that it can be laid on a desktop and take up just a small amount of valuable real estate. The second way to use a trackball is to incorporate it into a keyboard.

A specialized version of the trackball is a small button that is integrated into some keyboards of portable PCs. One brand name for the pointer is *Trackpoint*. These pointers work by interpreting gentle pushes up, down, left, or right and converting them to mouse movements.

Joysticks work in a manner similar to the Trackpoint devices. Instead of rollers, joysticks use pressure-sensitive electronics or mechanical potentiometers, which vary voltage by changing resistance in an electronic circuit.

CHAPTER 18

Microsoft's IntelliMouse

As is often the case, when Microsoft speaks, the entire industry listens. When Microsoft entered the market with its own elegant and sturdy design, it immediately became the model against which other mice were judged.

In early 1997, Microsoft introduced an updated design with some new features. The IntelliMouse is a hardware/software combination that, when combined with new drivers, provides some extended features. As you would imagine, one of the first users of the new design was Microsoft itself, which included new features in its Office 97 product.

The IntelliMouse is slightly larger than a standard mouse and adds a small wheel between the left and right buttons.

With the IntelliMouse you don't need to use scroll bars to scroll, pan and zoom. For example, to move a display up or down you can use the vertical scroll bars at the right of the screen, or you can simply move the IntelliMouse wheel forward or back. The wheel also includes a microswitch similar to the standard left and right mouse buttons. If you press down on the wheel and roll the mouse, your display pans left or right. You can also control the speed of the pan: the further you move the mouse, the faster the pan. And, if you press the **Ctrl** key while you roll the wheel, you can zoom your display, while a **Shift** plus wheel roll shifts into DataZoom (outlining) mode.

Of course, once you install the IntelliMouse, you can use it like a standard mouse with applications that don't support its extended features.

Mouse Tracking Resolution

Mice and other pointing devices can differ in their ability to read very small movements. Older mice were usually able to discern differences in location as small as 1/200th of an inch; this ability is called *resolution*. High-resolution models send more motion signals to the computer per inch of hand motion, with resolution as great as 1/1200 inch.

With an optical mouse, resolution is determined by the spacing between the horizontal and vertical gridlines and the ability of the mouse electronics to read the grid. With a mechanical or optomechanical mouse, higher resolution requires more holes in the light wheel or more physical segments for the mechanical brush to pass over.

Some designers improve effective resolution by sophisticated software routines. By counting the actual pulses and then interpolating what would fall between the physical pulses, higher resolution performance can be simulated.

For most desktop applications, including moving the on-screen pointer under Microsoft Windows, the difference between 200 points per inch (ppi) and 400 or 1200 ppi may not matter enough to be worth the extra expense. If you are using the mouse for drawing or other fine graphics manipulation, though, higher resolution may be worthwhile.

CHAPTER 18

One other difference between high- and low-resolution pointing devices is the speed of on-screen movement. Most high-resolution devices seem much quicker.

Many input devices allow you to vary the *sensitivity*—the relationship between the distance moved on the desktop and the distance moved on the screen. Similarly, acceleration can often be controlled by software setting; *acceleration* is the relationship between the speed and distance of mouse movement and the speed and distance of cursor movement. As you move the physical mouse faster, the on-screen pointer or cursor picks up speed.

Connecting the Mouse

Serial mice require a unique serial port address and a unique interrupt number; your mouse manual should help you set these parameters. A serial mouse requires a unique address because it gets control signals from the bus. The microprocessor speaks to a device by sending an address down the bus. All the devices are looking at the bus, waiting for their distinctive address. When a device recognizes its own address on the bus, it pays attention to the subsequent data signals. In order to receive these signals, a mouse must have its own address.

Most of the time, the mouse is trying to send, not receive, information. When a mouse is ready to transmit data it sends an interrupt to the microprocessor. The microprocessor looks up the interrupt number in the interrupt vector table, which tells the microprocessor to start using mouse-specific routines to accept the incoming data. The mouse and a modem cannot share an interrupt number. If they did, the microprocessor would be trying to interface with the mouse as if it were receiving telephone data communications via the modem.

Bus mice also need a unique address and a unique interrupt. Because they do not use a serial port, though, there is no possible interference with a serial device such as a modem or a serial printer. Bus mice, therefore, do not get assigned a COM port. The way bus mice communicate varies from manufacturer to manufacturer. Each makes a bus mouse controller card with a proprietary chip responsible for communications between the mouse and the CPU. The mouse card requires its own interrupt, and interrupt interference is the only place where mouse cards might conflict with the other hardware installed in the computer. If you need to add a mouse to your system, you might want to consider using a bus mouse in order to avoid giving up one of your two standard serial ports.

IBM has seen to it that most IBM PS/2s come with a built–in mouse port, and some other makers of modern machines have done so, too. These mouse ports use serial mice with a funky, nonstandard serial connector.

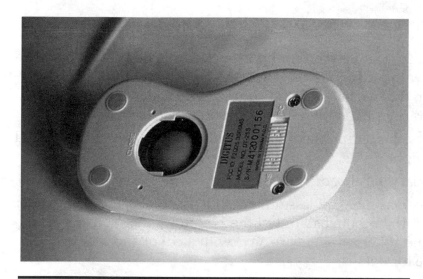

Figure 18.4 If your mouse finds the going a bit sticky, it may be worthwhile to replace the mouse roller; most standard mice user either 1-inch or 7/8th-inch balls. In most designs, a simple release mechanism on the bottom of the mouse will free the ball. (Dalco Electronics.)

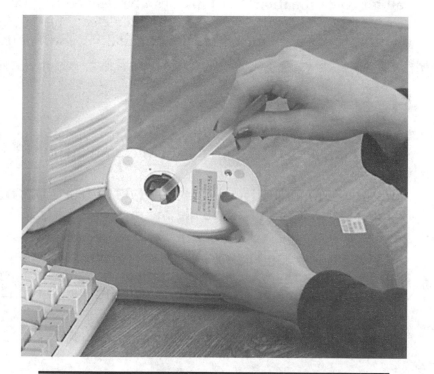

Figure 18.5 To be truly fastidious about your mouse's personal hygiene, you can use a cleaning kit with specialized fluid and a roller brush. (Dalco Electronics.)

CHAPTER 18

How to Test a Mouse

If you have trouble with a mouse attached to a serial port, try testing the serial port alone first. See "How to Test a Serial Port" for testing suggestions. If you find no problem with the serial port, check the mouse setup (address, interrupts, driver, etc.) to make sure that another serial device in the machine doesn't conflict with the mouse. If you suspect a conflict, test the mouse with the other device temporarily pulled out of the computer.

If you are having trouble with a bus mouse, double-check the setup. Make sure that the mouse driver is installed in the **CONFIG.SYS** or **AUTOEXEC.BAT** file, that it's the right driver, and that the interrupt is correct.

An optical mouse will not work properly without the special optical pad. The pad must be correctly oriented as well.

If an optomechanical or a mechanical mouse works but seems jerky and less fluid than it should be, check the roller ball for contamination. Most mice can be cleaned (Figure 18.4). Pop the ball out of the bottom of the mouse; it's usually held in with a snap ring. You can then clean the ball (and rollers, if there are any) with alcohol and a lint-free rag (Figure 18.5). Check the instruction manual for your mouse for details.

How to Install a Mouse

Mice come packaged with mouse device drivers and test software. Be sure that you are using the correct mouse driver. A Microsoft mouse must have a Microsoft mouse driver; it probably won't work with Logitech mouse drivers, for example.

Install the mouse driver in the **CONFIG.SYS** or **AUTOEXEC.BAT** file. Most mice are shipped with two drivers, one suitable for the **CONFIG.SYS** file and one for the **AUTOEXEC.BAT** file. You can use either. Read the installation manual for your mouse.

If you are running Microsoft Windows—one of the main reasons to use a mouse—the operating system comes with a driver that works with most pointing devices; if you have an unusual device, you should expect to receive a custom driver from the manufacturer, along with instructions on how to install it in Windows.

Scanners: Giving a PC a View

A scanner gives your computer eyes.

You can use a scanner to capture drawings and photographs that can be used as part of your printed or on-screen work. A scanner can also work in conjunction with an optical character recognition (OCR) program to convert typed or printed text into computer files that can be edited and changed.

How a Scanner Works

Scanners bounce light off a target—either a picture or text—and measure the amount of reflected light. Most of this light is reflected from white paper, less from halftones in a photograph, and almost none from black text characters. The scanner sends this information to a scanner interface card in the computer, where either OCR or graphics software takes over. The software processes the light level measurements. The resulting file can then be saved as a standard bitmap file for further manipulation by the computer.

Color scanners shine three separate lights (red, green, and blue) on the image, or use a single light with a set of red, green, and blue filters.

Scanners and OCRs will work with any computer, although both make very heavy demands upon the microprocessor, video, and hard disk systems; this is not the sort of work you would want to perform using an early PC.

OCR software converts light gray shades to white and dark gray to black. Then, using this two-color image, the OCR software tries to identify the letter written on the paper. Character recognition software uses one of two techniques: font matching and feature recognition. *Font matching* compares the character against all memorized fonts, similar to using tracing paper to match an unknown shape against stored standard patterns. *Feature recognition* uses logic and piece-by-piece analysis of a character to deduce what letter it really is. Feature recognition relies on questions such as "Is there an extender protruding below the line of type?" (*p, q, g, y,* and *j* all share this characteristic feature). By asking itself successive questions, the software is able systematically to eliminate characters. Pattern recognition software is more flexible, since proportional spacing and new fonts are less likely to throw it off stride. It is also more expensive.

Graphics software retains the middle range of signal values, the ones that represent gray tones in an image. Some scanners convert the intermediate gray tones to dithered patterns (prepared patterns of black and white dots that match the approximate light/dark ratio of the gray tone). Other scanners retain up to 64 levels of gray tones in the stored image (this is called *gray scaling*). Gray scaling is more expensive, and requires a lot of memory to store an image.

CHAPTER 18

How to Install and Test a Scanner

1. Install the scanner interface card. There are two interface connections commonly used by consumer-level scanning devices. One uses a high-speed SCSI card, with the scanner capable of being one of seven devices in a chain. The other means of connection uses a proprietary interface card specific to the scanner; in many cases, the card is an adaptation of SCSI, but other devices cannot usually be used with the specialized card. A third method uses the PC's parallel port.

   The scanner itself is external to the PC, whether it is handheld or desktop in design.

   A scanner interface card is similar to other expansion cards. It is held firmly into the computer with a machine screw. If you need to remove an old scanner card, remove the screw and pull the card straight up out of the bus connector on the motherboard.

2. Set switches and jumpers on the scanner interface card. If you are attaching to a standard SCSI host adapter card, you will have to assign the scanning device an address code and may have to make other adjustments to the adapter card; see the sections about SCSI adapters in Chapter 9. If you are using a proprietary interface card, consider possible interference from the equipment already in the computer before you install it. The interface board must have a unique interrupt number and a unique address. Unfortunately, many scanners use the interrupts assigned to parallel or serial ports. Most of these interface boards allow you to choose among a number of possible interrupts and a number of addresses. Nevertheless, careful planning, with scanner manual in hand, is required.

   Diagnostic software (we discuss a number of brands in Chapter 20) can scan the peripheral equipment in your computer, then report what address and interrupt each peripheral is using. This is information that can really help.

3. Install the card. Select a suitable expansion slot. Line up the card with the expansion slot connector and press down firmly. The card should slip into the connector. Reinstall the screw so that the card is snug in the computer case.

4. Plug in the scanner and test it. The installation manual tells you how to set the scanner switches and how to hook up the cables. The scanner manufacturer will give you test software or troubleshooting information customized for your particular scanner.

CHAPTER 19

Living the Good Life:
Back Up Regularly

One definition of a conservative lifestyle: wearing a belt *and* suspenders. That's our general philosophy of computer life: we want to get as close to a fail-safe world as we can, where a hardware failure, a software error, or a slip of the fingers at the keyboard is a mere annoyance and not a job-threatening disaster.

And there's an important rule to keep in mind: your hard drive will fail someday. It may be tomorrow, or it may be in ten years, but it *will* fail. It's up to you to be prepared for the hereafter.

But first, some horror stories we have seen: a writer who lost the only copy of her forthcoming book (a friend accidentally formatted the hard disk, and there were no backups), an engineering company that lost $100,000 of work on a hard drive that everyone thought someone else was backing up, and a law student who owned just three floppy disks and was unable to retrieve a semester's worth of work from a worn-down circle of Mylar.

Before you begin to feel ill, consider that all these horror stories could have had a happy ending with the use of backup software, data recovery utilities, and a bit of common sense.

In this chapter we'll explore the best methods for protecting and recovering data. You can often rebuild and retrieve lost files, but it's easier to protect your data *before* there's a problem.

We will start by discussing software programs that can perform automated backups of data to other media, move on to software that can help you monitor the health of your hard drive and make some repairs to its data structure, and then conclude with a survey of backup hardware including tape drives, removable hard disks, and super-floppies.

Because DOS writes to hard and floppy disks in basically the same way, the procedures for guarding and recovering data from these two types of disks are similar.

An Emergency Life Saving Disk

One very valuable weapon in the PC user's arsenal is an emergency boot disk. Some of the diagnostic and repair utilities we've mentioned in this book will do this for you as part of their preparation.

To make one for yourself, format a fresh diskette being sure to add the system tracks. The command is:

```
FORMAT A: /S<Enter>
```

Substitute the drive letter for your boot drive if necessary.

Then copy over your AUTOEXEC.BAT and CONFIG.SYS files to the floppy. Use an editing program to change drive specifications and subdirectory names on the floppy copies of these files so that they all refer to the root directory of the floppy.

Finally, copy to the floppy disk all utilities and device drivers referred to in the AUTOEXEC and CONFIG files.

Label the disk and put it aside in a safe location. If the boot tracks for your hard drive are ever damaged, you can use the emergency disk to bring the system back to life and copy the system tracks back to the hard drive, if needed.

If you upgrade to a new version of DOS, be sure to make a new version of the emergency floppy.

A number of PC utility programs including Symantec's Norton Utilities automate the process of making an emergency or "rescue" disk for the same purpose. Some antivirus programs, including McAfee Antivirus also create emergency disks with the added protection of sweeping your files for infections beforehand.

CHAPTER 19

A Quick Primer on Data Structure

Before we discuss backup procedures, let's take a quick review of some of the basics of hard and floppy disk structures.

Both hard disks and floppies record the following information in the first (boot) section on track 0: media type, DOS version, and—if it's a bootable disk—instructions telling the computer to read the system files. Both floppy disks and hard disks are also formatted with the File Allocation Tables (FATs) starting at the beginning of the second sector on track 0. The FATs vary in length, depending on the version of DOS used to format a particular disk. Typical hard disk clusters are 2K. Remember, though, that cluster size is not fixed on either hard or floppy disks. In fact, hard disk programs like Disk Manager use the variable cluster size to finesse the 32 MB hard disk size barrier in older versions of DOS.

One difference between hard and floppy disks is the fact that a hard disk can be partitioned into different sections (one for DOS and one for UNIX, for example). Floppies, on the other hand, can accommodate only one operating system per disk. If you want to boot from your hard disk—and most users do—you'll need to record the address of the system files that start the boot process in the boot sector on track 0.

Despite these differences, the data itself is laid down in much the same way on both floppy and hard disks, with surprisingly few adaptations necessary for the large size and increased speed of a hard disk.

Start Out by Backing Up

Most data loss can be prevented with good backup habits. If you keep copies of your data that are only a few hours old, the worst thing that can happen to you due to the failure of your computer or one of its disk drives is the loss of a few hours' worth of work.

There are three levels of backup:

- The first level is *current document backup*, which is a feature that is common in many advanced application programs. For example, this fourth edition of *Fix Your Own PC* was written using Microsoft Word for Windows. That program—and most other major word processors, including Novell's WordPerfect for Windows—allows you to turn on **Automatic Save** (Microsoft Word) or **Timed Document Backup** (WordPerfect) which, at specified time intervals, makes a copy in a separate backup directory of whatever documents you have open. On our speedy system, we ask Word to update its temporary backup file every three minutes. In this way, if Word, Windows, the operating system, or a piece of hardware causes the PC to seize up, we have a copy of the file that is no more than three minutes old and usually younger.

- The second type of backup we'll call *version backup*. Under Word there is an option to **Always Create Backup Copy**; WordPerfect calls the option **Original Document Backup**. In either of these schemes, any time you save a file, the program makes a copy of the previous version of the file. (The standard filename for the backup under Word is Backup of {filename}.WBK. Under WordPerfect the format is FILENAME.BK!.) Under this system, if you decide that the changes or additions you have made to the current version are not what you want to keep, you can revert to the previous version.

- Finally, and most importantly, there are backups we'll call *off-site backups*. These are copies of all your important data files that are maintained on some sort of removable media that can be kept on a shelf or in a fireproof safe or in a safe deposit box inside a bank's fireproof safe. Removable media include standard floppy disks, specialized high-capacity floppy disks, optical disks, portable hard disks, removable hard disk cartridges, tape backups, and recordable CD-ROMs.

CHAPTER 19

After you have addressed the issue of protecting against total loss of data, you should install a data-recovery program.

You may have noticed that we have only discussed backups for data. In theory, you should not have to maintain backups of application programs if you take care to keep their original installation diskettes or CD-ROMs in good condition.

Microsoft Utilities Included in MS-DOS

MS-DOS includes a pair of backup utilities, Microsoft Backup for MS-DOS and Microsoft Backup for Windows, along with their companion programs, Microsoft Restore for MS-DOS and Microsoft Restore for Windows. When you install MS-DOS you'll be given the option of installing the DOS or Windows version of the programs; you probably won't need both. (These programs were adapted by Microsoft from versions created by Symantec.) Similar versions of these utilities are a part of Microsoft's Windows 95 product.

These programs permit you to back up single files or entire directories on command; they can distinguish between files that have never been backed up (or *archived*, as DOS refers to the practice), those that have changed since the last archive was performed, and those that are unchanged; and the programs can be set to perform many tasks automatically, helping you establish and maintain a rational schedule for backups.

You can obtain full information about the programs from your DOS or Windows manuals; a quick help screen is available from the DOS prompt by typing **BACKUP /H<Enter>**. (Information on all DOS commands is available in this way in current versions of the operating system.)

Microsoft Backup is intended to back up files from one disk to another. You can back up all files on a disk or only files that have changed since your last backup, schedule backups so that they are done automatically on a regular basis, and restore files that you have backed up.

Microsoft Restore restores files that were backed up by using any version of Backup from MS-DOS versions 2.0 through 5.0. If you are restoring files that were backed up using the **MSBACKUP** program in MS-DOS 6 or later, use that version of the **MSBACKUP** program to restore those files.

Third-Party Backup Utilities

Specialized backup products are more convenient than the MS-DOS Backup and Restore programs. They use compression and speed-up routines and estimate in advance the number of disks you'll need. They also read the data straight through the DMA (Direct Memory Access) chip, thus speeding up the process dramatically.

A complete hard drive backup is only necessary occasionally: to have a full record of the contents before you make a major change and when you need to reformat. This could be as a result of upgrading your DOS, or when you're warned to do an immediate backup by a disk repair utility.

After the initial backup, the only items you really need to back up are important data files and some system-setting files—it's always worthwhile to maintain a full set of **AUTOEXEC** and **CONFIG** files, for example.

The leading utilities (and a number of public domain and shareware programs) provide a user-friendly shell for file manipulation. You can mark as many files as you wish, then copy them all to a backup disk with a single command. This eases the pain of typing in the names of a dozen files, which is the usual reason that users put off making backups.

Consult the utilities section of your computer retailer or mail order catalog for the latest and greatest backup programs. Among our favorites are *Cheyenne BackUp for Windows 95* and Seagate Software's sophisticated *Backup Exec for Windows 95*. Make sure any backup software you purchase matches your hardware; if you are going to back up to a Zip drive or a Syquest cartridge, make sure each is supported.

How Often Should You Back Up?

How often is enough? Answer us immediately after the next time your hard drive dies.

Every user can come up with his or her best answer. We perform backups Mondays, Wednesdays, and Fridays at the end of the day, and we do an extra backup any time we've been working on an especially important project. Some users make a backup an essential part of the end of every day.

And I have one special backup task: if I am going to be out of the office on a long trip, I make a complete image of my document subdirectory on a 270 MB Syquest drive and throw it in my briefcase. This is a protection against a catastrophe while I am away and an (as-yet unused) emergency disk in case I absolutely must get into one of my files while I am on the road. Sometimes I also copy over a complete subdirectory of files to my laptop computer for the same reason.

Good practice calls for having at least an "A" and a "B" tape; better yet, five tapes labeled Monday through Friday. In this way, you protect yourself against accidentally damaging your only backup copy of some files.

Also remember that backup media will eventually fail, just like any floppy disk or hard drive. Plan on retiring backup tapes or disks at least once a year.

CHAPTER 19

The Hard Side of Backups

Making off-site backups of your valuable data presents a logical and procedural dilemma for most users. The whole goal is to make copies that are as current as possible and yet are physically separated from your main computer so that a failure (or theft) will not take away irreplaceable information.

Your style of backing up data will vary, based on the types and sizes of files you create.

Floppy Disk Backups

If you are working in a character-based environment—word processing, spreadsheets, and simple databases—you may be able to use floppy disks to store backup copies of your files. Using a disk-doubling utility, you can store as much as 2.88 MB of information on a single floppy. However, a floppy disk is relatively slow, and once it is filled you will run into a logistical headache keeping track of the location of the latest versions of files.

Where Should You Back Up?

As we have noted, if you have only a few files that you need to protect, you may be able to get away with using floppy disks as a backup medium.

However, you are certain to find that you quickly run out of space. You should consider using one of a number of removable high-capacity backup systems, including tape, disk cartridges, and other technologies. We discuss each in detail in Chapter 10.

Oops! How to Recover from an Accidental Deletion or Format

Deleting a file or reformatting a disk full of data sounds like capital punishment, but in the world of personal computing there are reprieves available. However, the reprieves only work if you act quickly after performing the offending act. In this section, we'll explore some critical lifesaving utilities.

Undeleting

When you erase or delete a file, DOS doesn't actually remove the file from the disk. Instead, it first changes the name of the file in the directory by writing hex code E5 (written E5H in computerspeak) over its first character. The old file and the details of its size and date and time of creation are still on the disk, but the DOS **DIR** command doesn't display this information because it has been programmed to ignore any filename that begins with **E5H**.

After completing this first step, DOS zeros out the FAT entries to indicate to the system that the physical space on the disk where the deleted file was stored is available for a new file. When DOS examines the FAT, it will now see the zeroed-out clusters as vacant space where it can write new data.

If you catch your mistake soon enough, you can use a diagnostic program with an **undelete** option—Microsoft Undelete (part of current DOS), PC Tools, or Norton Utilities, for example—to display any files with an E5H as the first character. You can then change the first character of the filename back to the proper character; the undelete program then automatically fixes the FAT entries.

The most recent version of each of these tools also installs an automatic guardian that further protects you against accidental deletion. They can install a small program (a *TSR*, or terminate-and-stay-resident program) that constantly monitors your system activity. Any time a file is deleted, it is actually moved into a special undelete or "trash can" directory; depending on the settings you make when you install the undelete program, these files are kept intact for a specified number of days or until the amount of space they occupy reaches a preset limit. At that time, the oldest files are actually removed.

Read the instruction manuals carefully for this type of software and be sure to use these programs on any mission-critical disks in your system. Depending on how you do your work, you may not need to turn on the deletion guards for floppy disks.

With delete tracking, undeleting an accidental delete is almost painless, as long as you recover the file before DOS writes over the sector. When will that be? It depends on how much work you're doing that writes to the disk. If you wait several days or do substantial writing to the disk, your chances for recovery diminish.

Under some of these programs, you should avoid running COMPRESS or Norton Speed Disk if you need to recover a deleted file, at least until you've recovered the file. When you run defragmenting programs such as these, the files on your hard disk are moved around, so the cluster chains stored in the deleted-file database are no longer valid.

Finally, you can try to undelete a file even if DOS has overwritten part of its contents. Most undelete utilities run into trouble when confronted with fragmented files. When DOS deletes a file, as we mentioned earlier, it takes two actions: it writes hex E5 in place of the first letter in the filename, and it puts a null (hex 00) in every cluster record in the FAT table attached to that file. Once the FAT is zeroed, the linking information for that file is gone. In this case, an undelete utility can look at the total original file length in the directory, but it can't determine the exact clusters on which the file was recorded; it can only assume that the file was contiguous and link a row of clusters that equal the file's original size. You have a better chance of recovering accidentally deleted files if the files are contiguous. For this reason, using defragmenting utilities regularly to compress your files is a good practice.

CHAPTER 19

Recovering from Accidental Reformatting

When you format a disk you are doing two things: establishing (or reestablishing) the magnetic markers that divide the disk into logical sectors and deleting any files that are already present on the disk. Actually, though, the deletion follows the same procedure we've already explored for individual files—the filenames are changed to begin with E5H and the FAT table is zeroed out. This means that even a reformatted disk can be recovered if you act before new data is written to the disk.

Until the arrival of DOS 6.*x*, reformatted floppy disks were generally beyond recovery; current DOS has extended protection to all standard-format disks.

There is a "gotcha" here, and a big one. Under the current version of DOS, a standard reformat of the disk will automatically make a "mirror" or *image* file that contains the old FAT in a different part of the disk. In this way, the disk structure can be reconstructed if necessary; if new files have been recorded over the locations of the former files, of course, the data will be destroyed and the index will be useless. Under DOS 6.*x* there are three kinds of formats for floppy disks:

- **Unconditional Format**. This is a physical formatting of the disk, followed by a logical format. All the data is destroyed and the disk cannot be unformatted. The command is: **FORMAT A: /U** for the A drive. Note that you cannot perform an unconditional format on a hard drive because DOS does not physically format those devices; low-level formatting of hard drives requires special utilities specific to each drive and is usually done at the factory. You should use an unconditional format if you have been experiencing sector errors on a disk; copy any retrievable data from the disk to another storage device before performing the format.

- **Quick Format**. DOS will store a copy of the FAT as a mirror file and rework the disk's logical format but will not check the sectors for reliability. This is the quickest way to clear a disk for new files, but this method is not advised if the disk has been causing problems. The command is: **FORMAT A: /Q** for the A drive.

- **Safe Format**. This is the same as a quick format, but it includes a check of sectors for validity, finding and blocking out clusters that can cause errors. It is not as thorough a process as an unconditional format, but the disk can be unformatted. The command is: **FORMAT A:** for the A drive.

We recommend that you perform safe formats most of the time, reserving quick formats for those situations where you are certain that the disk is in good condition. Use unconditional formats when you want to try to resurrect a disk that has been causing difficulties. Don't work too hard to reuse a problematic floppy disk, though; it makes sense to throw away a 30-cent disk before it causes a thousand-dollar headache by causing you to lose important data.

Read your DOS manual for full details on how to use the **Unformat** command. As **Unformat** rebuilds the disk, it will display how many subdirectories it has found; if you use the /L switch, it also shows you all the files in each subdirectory.

If **Unformat** finds a file that appears to be fragmented across several locations on the disk, it will be unable to fully recover the file and will truncate the file at the end of the first part.

To determine whether **Unformat** can restore a formatted disk in drive A, enter the following command:

UNFORMAT A: /TEST<Enter>

Third-Party Programs

Unformatting should not be something that you have to perform often, if ever. But if you want to have a belt-and-suspenders operation, you should invest in a more capable unformatting program, such as those offered by Norton/Symantec or other third-party vendors. In addition to a more elegant and complete interface, these programs may be able to restore files that are fragmented and to get around other limitations of Microsoft's programs. Most of the data-loss-prevention programs designed for hard drives are made up of two parts. The first part makes copies of the FAT and root directory. If your FAT or root directory gets corrupted, the second part of the program uses these copies to recover data from the disk. Two protection/recovery systems that perform well are the PC Tools Mirror/Diskfix combination and the Norton Utilities Image/Disk Doctor team. These programs can be used to reconstruct either hard or floppy disks. Most users load only the preventive half of the program on their hard disk, preferring to take their chances on data loss with a floppy disk.

The programs work by keeping a backup copy of the FAT and root directory in a special hidden file. When something goes wrong, you can run the corresponding disk repair program, which restores the disk to its original condition. If you haven't run **Mirror** or **Image** before, the disk repair component will attempt to reconstruct the data but may not be able to reconstruct all files in their entirety. The programs also offer a **Delete Tracking** option that keeps a record of all deletes and permits quick and easy retrieval of deleted files.

Using Compression or Defragmenting Utilities

When you store a file on disk, the operating system puts the file in an available space on the disk. On a freshly formatted disk, the file will be stored in a contiguous fashion, one sector after another from the beginning to the end. When you store your next file, it may well begin right at the end of the previous file and continue from there.

Fragmentation occurs when you reopen an existing file and expand it; the operating system may not be able to place the additional sectors of the file immediately after the end of the original file. In fact, for files that are opened and changed regularly—and most data files are altered many times between creation and completion—the data may be scattered across several places on the disk.

The File Allocation Table keeps track of where the files are and directs the hard drive on how to attach the pieces together when you ask it to read the file.

However, fragmented files take a bit longer for the hard drive to read and present a danger if the FAT is ever damaged. The solution is to defragment, or *compress*, files from time to time as part of your regular maintenance duties.

Current versions of DOS include a utility called **DEFRAG** that will automatically reorganize your disk by pulling scattered pieces of your files into contiguous clusters. Third-party versions include Norton's Speed Disk and PC Tools Compress.

Undeleting and unformatting is much easier when the utility doesn't have to jump all over the disk, tracing a web of pointers. In fact, if you run a compression program regularly, it is possible to ensure 100% data recovery from accidental file deletions (and substantial recovery from an accidental format), even if you haven't run **Mirror** or **Image** regularly.

Surface Analyzers

Surface analysis programs analyze your hard drive by performing a read/write test to see if the entire surface can reliably hold data. Using ingenious data-repair algorithms, they reconstruct the data in the suspect areas that DOS can't read.

From the start, DOS has included a limited-capability surface analyzer called **CHKDSK**; beginning with DOS 6.2, users were also given a much more capable utility called **SCANDISK**.

SCANDISK performs a surface analysis of your disk, gives you a report on fragmented files, and searches for—and usually repairs—lost clusters and cross-linked files in the FAT. Consult your MS-DOS instruction manual for full details, and use the utility at least once a month—more often if you are a heavy user or if you have any reason to worry about the integrity of your hard disk.

Third-party surface analyzers include more complex and thorough tests. Such products include SpinRite 4.0, which is so thorough in some of its actions that it can take all night long to analyze a drive; similar programs include Norton Utilities.

Any of these programs can be counted on to find bad spots, move the data to a safe part of the disk, and mark the bad spots so that they won't be reused. These programs are easy to use and take less than an hour to run on an average-size drive. Their value is in catching bad spots before you lose data. We recommend running one of these programs at least once a week.

 Some disk analysis programs will overwrite the bad track table that is placed on every disk when it is first tested at the factory, something we're not very happy to see. The naked truth is that nearly every hard disk has a few bad tracks when new, and they are locked out during the low-level formatting of the disk; we recommend that you don't purchase a hard drive that arrives with more than 1 or 2% not working; you should find a label on the outside of the disk listing the bad areas.

The CHKDSK Conundrum

One of the strengths—and weaknesses—of MS-DOS is the fact that it is supposed to be "downwardly compatible" with all previous versions of the operating system. In other words, if you have a piece of software that was written for features available in DOS 3.3, 4.0, or even 1.1, the current version of DOS should be able to support the program. The bad news is that there are more than a few compromises or outdated features still hanging around from the old days.

One example is the **CHKDSK** utility, a diagnostic and limited repair facility. It will still work in that way, although it is not in the same league as **SCANDISK**, which replaced it, and it is much less capable than a third-party disk repair utility.

If you have no other error-correction utilities and you must make an immediate repair, DOS **CHKDSK** is better than nothing. You won't have a second chance to repair the file, though, so don't use **CHKDSK** on really valuable data disks. If you must use **CHKDSK** because you have access to nothing else, here are some suggestions:

- Try to read or boot the floppy disk, then run **CHKDSK**. The command is: **CHKDSK<Enter>**.

  CHKDSK analyzes both FATs (both copies of the FAT table stored on the disk) and reads the disk directory, looking for the most obvious data storage errors. This quick check reveals lost clusters and cross-linked file problems.

A cross-linked file has some portion of the data area shared by two files. It's smart to copy both of the cross-linked files to different disks and then to examine them to see which file is correct and which is saddled with an inappropriate tail-end of alien data. If you save both files before running **CHKDSK/F**, you will have more options (more copies to play around with) while you're trying to recover some usable data.

Now run **CHKDSK** with the /F switch. The command is: **CHKDSK /F<Enter>**.

This message comes up on the monitor: xx Lost Clusters Found in yy chains. Convert Lost Clusters to Files (Y/N)?

- Press **Y** for yes, then look in the root directory for files named **FILE0000.CHK**, **FILE0001.CHK**, and so on. Examine these files using a text editor. Save anything that looks useful, and delete anything that is clearly trash.

Most of the time, the files created by **CHKDSK** are useless. DOS just left an extra bit lying around in the FAT table while it was erasing files. **CHKDSK** finds this extra bit and sounds the alarm.

A few lost clusters every few months is not unusual, especially if you turn the computer off while running Microsoft Windows. If you run into this sort of problem often, it is time to consider a possible problem with the disk controller or disk drive.

Saving Your Data from a Faltering Disk

If your drive begins to mislay files or report impossible-looking file sizes, assume that the problem is in the FAT.

If **SCANDISK** cannot fix the trouble automatically, you may need to use the advanced techniques available within the Norton or PC Tools packages. The Norton Utilities, for example, includes a full set of manual steps that show you how to fix a bad track 0, fix bad directory entries, recover subdirectories from a bad directory, edit the boot record, and edit the partition table.

If you don't have the time, skills, or stomach to perform brain surgery, you can send ailing disks to a commercial data-recovery service. You'll find listings of such companies in the back pages of many of the major computer magazines.

If you think the problem is so severe that you will need the help of a data recovery company, you should probably leave the disk untouched by recovery software so that you do not make a bad situation worse.

We particularly recommend using a commercial data recovery service if the disk has been damaged by fire or water or if the disk surface has been damaged by the actual crash of the read/write head into the surface.

Aside from physical damage to a disk, probably the trickiest data recovery problem is a bad sector in the middle of a long file. If the sector is, in fact, totally unreadable, all the rest of the file may be lost. For example, a tiny error equivalent to an inkblot covering two bad characters on page 13 could make the hard disk lose the rest of this book. DOS can correct small errors—the equivalent of one bad character—itself. But no program can correct more than 11 bad bits (that's about one-and-a-half 8-bit characters).

Some programs can read through the bad place just as you can skip over an inkblot on the page of a book. But you, the brains behind this file, will have to manually go into the file and reconstruct the missing information under the inkblot. This is practical with text, marginally practical with database and spreadsheet files, and all-but-impossible if you're dealing with a program file like WordPerfect. But you can probably reload your program files from backup disks, so it's not a big problem.

Reformatting the Hard Disk

If you regularly use a disk analysis program to detect bad clusters, you shouldn't have to worry about reformatting the drive until the number of reported errors begins to increase.

If you're not using a disk analysis program, be prepared to reformat your hard disk at least once a year. Over time, the hard-drive head assembly drifts out of alignment with the tracks it originally laid down on the platters. As the misalignment increases, the heads begin to read and write data less accurately. When you reformat the disk, the heads are aligned with the new tracks it lays down and, although it's not quite the same as on a new drive, the alignment is internally consistent.

SpinRite 4.0, Norton's Calibrate (part of the Norton Utilities), or some other utilities tools can nondestructively low-level format the drive—no tedious backup and restore necessary!

Older hard drives were based on stepper motors, which depend on mechanical parts to keep the heads in the right place over the tracks. Stepper motor drives may need to be reformatted as often as once a year. (Remember to make copies of the data on a drive before you reformat.)

More modern drives uses voice coil mechanisms, which use electronics to determine when the heads are in the right place. Because a voice coil drive cannot go out of alignment, it never needs reformatting.

Summary of Data Protection Measures

Here's a summary of the measures you can take to protect your data on floppy and hard disks.

Protecting Your Data on Floppies

1. Make backup copies of important data.
2. Buy good-quality disks. Some manufacturers offer lifetime guarantee disks; if something happens to track 0 (where the directory and FAT are stored) you can send the disk back to the manufacturer to reconstruct the data.
3. Learn how to use quality undelete utilities to rescue you when the inevitable mistake happens.
4. Perform step 1 regularly.

Protecting Your Data on Hard Disks

1. Make backups.
2. Run PC Tools **Mirror** or Norton's **Image** every time the machine boots. If you are working with a DOS system, start all application programs from batch files that run **Mirror** or **Image** as the last step before returning to the root directory.
3. Run PC Tools or Norton's **UNFORMAT** if you mistakenly format your hard disk.
4. Run defragmenting (compression) utilities regularly.
5. Run surface analyzers regularly.
6. If your hard disk uses a stepper motor, reformat it once a year.
7. Perform step 1 regularly.

CHAPTER 20

Diagnostic and Reporting Programs

What's Going On?

When the ship's doctor of a Federation Starship needs to find out what's going on inside an injured or ill Star Trek crew member, he or she waves a tricorder over the patient's body. When you're on your own trek to figure out what ails your PC, the nearest we've got is a good diagnostic program.

In this chapter, we'll look at the various types of diagnostic programs available, plus configuration utilities used to prevent hardware conflicts when installing new boards.

Let's start with one unfortunate fact: your PC has to be able to start up and boot from a floppy or hard disk in order to run a software-based diagnostic program. If all you hear when you flick the switch is a stony silence, you're going to have to figure out what is wrong by yourself (with the help of this book, of course.)

Some diagnostic programs are also dependent on the presence of a working copy of DOS or Windows; others are capable of running off their own limited equivalent to DOS or with the assistance of an emergency boot disk you will be asked to create when you first install the diagnostic.

Another unfortunate fact: even the very best diagnostic program still requires a capable supercomputer to interpret its findings. That supercomputer is your brain.

Diagnostic Fallacies

No matter how good the diagnostic programs, none are able to test every last modular element of your PC. Here are a few examples of real-world problems that were beneath a diagnostic program's radar:

Diagnostics programs cannot check on the health and performance of your power supply. We've heard the story of one inexperienced technician who replaced four or five hard drives in a row because his diagnostic disk kept reporting sector read/write errors on the drive. A new drive would function well when first installed, then report increasing errors during all-night read/write testing to confirm that the repair was done correctly. Each morning he examined the error log, saw the new read/write errors, and assumed that the hard disk he had replaced the previous day was defective. Many hard drives later, the true cause was discovered: a bad power supply.

Figure 20.1 Advanced troubleshooters can install a specialized card like this Discovery Card device from AllMicro in the bus to report on IRQ and DMA usage. Other such cards include Post Probe, a universal Power-On Self-Test card that promises to debug even a "dead" PC.

Diagnostic programs sometimes are not very good at spotting intermittent problems—a transitory short in a card that only happens when the system is hot, for example. (One way to deal with that situation is to put the diagnostic program into a repetitive loop and run the machine all night.)

Or the program may not be able to spot an interrupt or memory conflict for a device that appears to be turned off.

And many diagnostic programs seem to specialize in rounding up all the usual suspects for a problem, sometimes overlooking more obscure problems. Another real story: A PC owner with printer problems tested her machine with a general-purpose diagnostic disk and was told the system was operating properly; therefore she assumed the printer was bad. A second check, with a more sophisticated diagnostic program, showed that the parallel port was failing.

HArdware testers, like the Discovery card shown in Figure 20.1, can report on the health of a PC system even if the software does nit run. A modular tester like the one in Figure 20.3, can check the continuity of a wire in a nettwork cable and indicate whether it is carring a singal.

And even the best diagnostic programs are not likely to spot a problem in an external cable. In the above example, the port could check out fine, the printer could perform perfectly, but the cable could be dead.

Whole Machine, Disk/Data Diagnostics, and System Snoopers

I'm going to divide the world of diagnostic disks into three categories:

- **Whole Machine Diagnostic** products attempt to test the entire machine. They test memory, the microprocessor, the DMA chips, the numeric coprocessor, the floppy and hard drives, the serial and parallel ports, the video, the mouse, and the keyboard. They also provide full system configuration information (including the interrupt and memory addresses used by each piece of hardware).

- **Disk/Data Diagnostics** concentrate on the disk drives and the data structures of the hard disk and/or the floppy disk, painstakingly reading each sector in search of corrupted data. These programs usually include some very sophisticated data recovery utilities. A typical disk/data diagnostic disk provides intensive testing routines, bad sector lock-out, file-moving utilities, and a sector-by-sector hard disk editor.

- **System Snoopers** report on the hardware and software installed in the computer plus the interrupts and addresses used by that hardware, but don't attempt to test it. You must know which interrupts and memory are in use when installing new cards, especially network, MIDI, fax, and other exotic hardware items. Each expansion card needs its own interrupt and a memory address area all to itself. Products in this class sometimes call themselves *configuration utilities* or *system information utilities*.

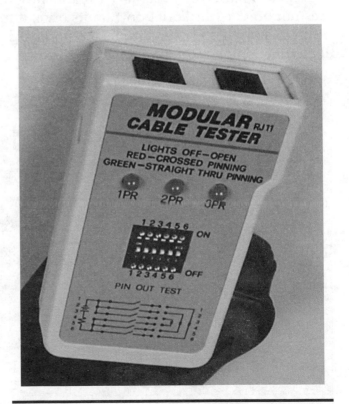

Figure 20.2 A modular tester can check wiring status and continuity on a network cable. (Dalco catalog.)

CHAPTER 20

How Diagnostic Programs Work

Imagine that your computer is a patient in the hospital. Diagnostic disks are excellent at testing one limb at a time (the serial port, extended memory, or keyboard, for example). The patient must be conscious, though, to report to the doctor, or the tests are useless.

Let's use CheckIt and its partner WinCheckIt/Pro as an example. The program runs the serial port through some pretty fancy hoops, sending data out on the TX (transmit data) line, checking for correct reception on the RX (receive data) line, and testing for correct signals on the RTS, CD, and DTR lines. Don't panic about all this TX, RX, and RTS stuff—we're not building a serial port, we're just testing it. Let the diagnostic program do the work.

CheckIt (Figure 20.3) is a very capable program and one of the favorites in our office. The problem is that CheckIt does not operate the serial port on its own; it must instead ask the CPU to operate the serial port. For this serial test to run reliably, the power supply, motherboard, CPU, BIOS ROM, minimal RAM memory, video, and keyboard must all be functioning moderately well. Some parts, like the CPU, the memory, and the power supply, must be just about perfect or the serial port test will fail, whether or not the serial port itself is bad.

Since almost all the diagnostic tests require a living, breathing patient (a functioning computer) to run the test and to communicate with the diagnostic software, this sort of software is ideal for torture-testing a running computer. If you must certify that a particular computer is good, you can't beat a good diagnostic program that can be set to test all day or all night without any supervision.

But there is also a flaw even with this sort of extensive automated checkup. The diagnostics programs can test the machine longer, in greater depth, and more creatively than any of us users ever could—except by using the machine—and therein lies the potential problem. Many technicians run 72 hours of sophisticated diagnostics on a particular machine, then hand the machine to the user, swearing that everything is perfect. Within five minutes of normal use, the

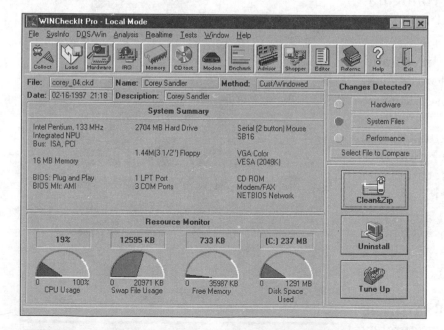

Figure 20.3 WinCheckIt Pro is an example of a capable Whole Machine Diagnostic program.

machine breaks and the technician looks like a fool. There was nothing wrong with the diagnostic disk, nothing wrong with the technician, and nothing wrong with the user. It's just that the user may be asking the computer to do something that the diagnostic program didn't check.

Limitations Inherent in the Testing Process

Suppose your diagnostic disk tells you that something in a particular system—let's use the floppy drive as an example—is malfunctioning.

Is this true? Maybe.

One thing you can be sure of is that something is wrong. It just may not be exactly what the diagnostic program is reporting. Diagnostics often don't tell us which part is bad, only that a particular subsystem is bad. Because any one of several components may cause a given symptom, it is often impossible to know from the diagnostic report exactly which component is to blame. Instead, use the report as your starting point in exploring the system using the techniques described in this book and in the troubleshooting flowcharts.

Low Memory

There are some parts of the computer that diagnostic programs cannot always reliably test. Think of them when you get stumped, when the likely suspect is clearly not the right one.

Memory test programs have difficulty writing patterns to low memory and reading the patterns back. The reason for this is that low memory contains the interrupt vector table, the stack, and various system files (these terms are defined in the glossary). In other words, this is the autonomic nervous system of the computer. If the diagnostic software improperly disturbs the contents of low memory, the patient is as good as dead—you can hardly test its reflexes.

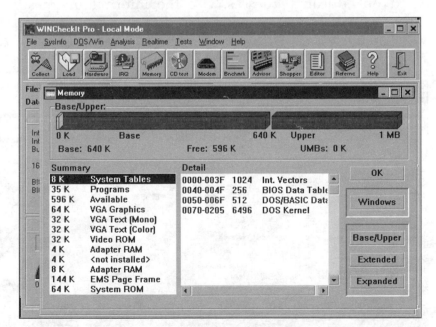

Figure 20.4 Part of the Memory report from WinCheckIt Pro.

Some diagnostics programs—including newer versions of QA Plus—are able to move what they can out of low memory before testing, then turn off the interrupts and test the bottom 16K of RAM. We would still suggest you consider low memory *terra semi-incognita*, at least as far as the contents of low memory is concerned.

A Sampling of Diagnostic Programs

Diagnostic program error messages, your computer's BIOS ROM error messages, and DOS error messages are all based on educated guesses. Use the information these

Figure 20.5 The hardware report of WinCheckIt Pro.

error messages give you, but remember that they are not infallible. We list common error messages in the appendices and suggest approaches to try if one of these messages appears on your screen.

This section describes several of the diagnostic programs that are currently on the market.

Whole System Utilities

Symantec's Norton Utilities

Peter Norton began his empire selling a rather simple "unerase" utility to computer enthusiasts and clubs when the IBM PC was first introduced. He went on to form his

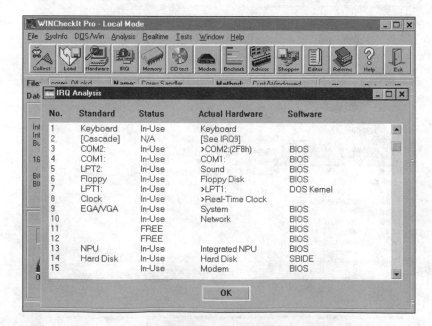

FIGURE 20.6 The IRQ analysis screen of WinCheckIt Pro.

own company and launch a series of successful books about the innards of the PC. Eventually Peter Norton Computing was purchased by the other major utility player, Symantec.

Other products may have some individual elements that are better, or offer some specific bells and whistles that may hold special appeal; overall, though, Symantec's Norton Utilities offers a pretty complete and well-polished package.

At the heart of the package is Norton Disk Doctor, which operates in the background to search out disk and system problems and can launch utilities to make repairs to many problems. System Watch monitors system resources under Windows and alerts you to potential and real problems.

Other Windows-specific elements include INI Tuner, INI Tracker, INI Editor, and INI Advisor, which help you manage your system's initialization files.

There is, of course, the latest version of the venerable UnErase file recovery, along with UnFormat and File Fix, which can bail you out of some sticky problems.

Symantec Norton Utilities

Symantec Corporation

10201 Torre Avenue

Cupertino, CA 95014

(800) 441-7234

(541) 334-6054

http://www.symantec.com

Symantec Norton Utilities for Windows 95

As befits a product that has its roots back in the very earliest days of MS-DOS, Norton Utilities was the first to market with tools for the Windows 95 user. The suite of utilities in the package contains mostly optimized versions of Norton's best-selling Windows 3.1 tools, including Norton Disk Doctor, Speed Disk, UnErase, Image, and System Information.

New for the Windows 95 package is a Pre-Installation Tune-up product that helps diagnose problems, make repairs, and tune-up your Windows 3.x system to prepare it for the installation of the new operating system. Also new is Norton System Doctor, which runs in the background of Windows 95 to monitor system resources and to automatically launch appropriate utilities to correct problems it detects. The Space Wizard utility locates duplicate, outdated, and unnecessary files, helping to free disk space before and after the installation of Windows 95.

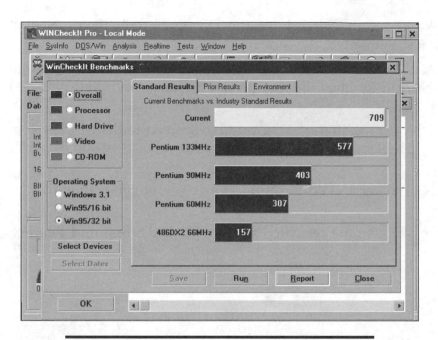

Figure 20.7 A Benchmark screen from WinCheckIt Pro.

CheckIt/WinCheckIt

TouchStone Software Corp.

2124 Main St.

Huntington Beach, CA

(800) 531-0450

(714)969-7746

http://www.checkit.com

Diagnostic and Data Recovery Utilities

Hard disk diagnosis and data recovery are closely allied. You may choose to buy separate programs to perform each function or you can look for products that combine all features. Descriptions of some of the best follow; be sure to check the utilities shelf of your computer retailer or a mail order catalog for the latest and greatest.

CheckIt and WinCheckIt

The heart of this product is its extensive reporting ability that sends a snoop to every corner of your machine and comes back from its expedition with notes on everything it finds.

Also included in the package are diagnostic and cleanup facilities with an uninstall program that can find orphaned shortcuts, desktop, and Start Menu items as well as abandoned parts of Windows programs.

QA Plus

QAPlus is one of the leading PC diagnostic software packages, bundled with several million PC systems from manufacturers such as Intel, DEC, NEC, and Gateway 2000. It is also available for purchase as a standalone. The program is offered in three options: QAPlus, QAPlus/FE, and QAPlus/Win.

QAPlus offers diagnostic programs for the system board, RAM, video adapter, floppy and hard drives, parallel and serial ports, keyboard, joystick, CD-ROM, printer, mouse, and speaker.

System and performance information is provided for hardware configuration, including detailed information about drives, memory, video, ports, BIOS, CPU and more. You'll be given a report on interrupts, device drivers, the DOS environment, and the DOS Memory Map. System utilities included in the package include a CMOS Editor, COM Port Debugger, File Editor and Comparer, Bad RAM Locator, Hard Disk Park, and an MFM Hard Drive Low-Level Formatter. And the package is bundled with Cosession communications software that enables your PC and QAPlus to be operated over a modem by service and support personnel with the same Cosession software.

One step up is QAPlus/FE, which is aimed at service technicians. It includes the same suite of tests and reports as QAPlus, adding SCSI tests and utilities and the ability to set up a custom set of tests that can be run multiple times or across multiple machines. The package includes loopback plugs for the serial and parallel ports.

QAPlus/Win is a Windows-specific program that includes access to the Electronic Technical Support Center. Using an attached modem, you can click on a button and dial ETSC where a technician will be able to look at your system configuration and run tests over the phone line; use of ETSC is on a fee basis.

QAPlus, QAPlus/FE, QAPlus/Win

DiagSoft, Inc.

5615 Scotts Valley Drive, Suite 140

Scotts Valley, CA 95066

(800) 342-4763

(408)438-8247

http://www.diagsoft.com

Rescue

S.O.S.: your hard drive has crashed, taking with it your DOS boot tracks. Or, your computer can no longer find essential data or program files on a floppy disk.

One easy, automatic solution to most data problems is Rescue. The program can recover data from most standard floppy drives, and from MFM, RLL, IDE, ESDI, and SCSI hard drives. It will also work with most compressed drives.

Among the strengths of Rescue is the fact that the program disk includes its own operating system, allowing it to go directly to the hardware disk controller. This design allows Rescue to get past possible damage in Sector 0 on a disk, allowing the program to read the data without having to deal with a damaged boot sector.

Rescue can recover files even if one or both of the File Allocation Tables are damaged. If one FAT cannot be used, Rescue will locate and use the second copy; if both are trashed, Rescue can still read the files, but will not do so automatically; you'll have to work with the program to manually mark and save specific sectors of data. This emergency repair process is best suited to such ASCII text as word processing files; programs can be recovered from original copies and reinstalled once the drive has been reformatted.

Rescue is also able to recover data from a drive with a bad or missing primary disk partition; if there are more than one damaged partitions, AllMicro also offers an advanced version of the product called Rescue Professional.

Rescue will work with any DOS formatted drive; it is not compatible with Windows NT.

Rescue

AllMicro, Inc.

18820 US Hwy. 19 N. #215

Clearwater, FL 34624

800-653-4933

813-531-0200 fax

Hurricane

Is a storm raging beneath your Windows installation? Hurricane is a suite of utilities that will explore Windows while it is running and offer speedups and tuneups.

The utilities include:

- Discover for Windows, a graphical report and analysis with extensive detail on Windows resources and memory allocation, all sorts of memory, and the CPU, video, and disk drives. In fact, we learned things about our disk drives and printer drivers we have never seen reported in any other system report.

- WinGauge, a real-time performance monitor for Windows. In addition to helping you monitor the status of your system, it has a set of dashboard warning lights to alert you to potential memory and resource error conditions before they occur.

- Hurricane Tools, a set of automatically configured utilities including Heap Expander, which automatically compacts and frees resources and dumps system-cluttering application "leftovers" when programs are exited; Screen Accelerator, a video display speedup; Virtual Cache, an extension to 32-bit file access that adjusts itself to allocate memory only as needed, with a print cache; Global DOS Manager, which manages Windows' use of DOS memory and also permits Windows to use parts of upper memory (between 640K and 1 MB) that are not ordinarily available to it.

Hurricane also integrates well with Helix Software's Multimedia Cloaking, a separate product that blasts open space in DOS memory for the use of DOS programs. Cloaked utilities use almost no conventional or upper memory and instead reside in extended memory, and run faster and more reliably in most instances. Included utilities cloak the Microsoft CD-ROM extensions (MSCDEX), a mouse driver, and a disk cache. On most systems, cloaking will open up at least 50K of RAM for the use of programs.

Hurricane

Helix Software Co.

47-09 30th St.

Long Island City, NY 11101

(800) 392-3100

The Troubleshooter

The Troubleshooter is a fully capable diagnostics program that exercises just about every part of the motherboard, nearly all types of memory, and all attached peripherals including multimedia devices such as sound cards and CD-ROMs. It also can query attached SCSI devices.

One unusual feature of The Troubleshooter is its ability to self-boot using its own non-DOS operating system; this allows you to test the basic functions of your machine and peripherals independent of DOS and its settings. This also means the product will work with any installed operating system, including DOS, UNIX, OS/2, and others; however, running the program from the self-boot tracks does not permit full testing of some elements of the system such as mice, sound cards, and other devices that load through the use of device drivers.

The program can also be copied to the hard disk and run from the DOS prompt. This procedure gives full access to all of the tests. You can also run many of the tests with "beep" codes so that you can troubleshoot elements of a machine that does not send usable video.

The System Information screen includes full information on the machine type, BIOS, memory, and attached devices.

Troubleshooter tests include:

- **Motherboard**. CPU (180 test points), Co-Processor (258 test points), DMA controller, CMOS settings, CMOS RAM, real time clock, system timers, interrupt controller, keyboard controller.
- **Memory**. Base memory, extended memory (up to 4 GB), external cache (up to 2 MB), memory refresh and address lines, walking bits, pseudo random, checkerboard.
- **Floppy and Hard Disk Drives**. Controller diagnostics, seek test, read/write test analysis, low-level formatting.
- **Serial Port Tests**. Handshake signals, loop-back controller, interrupt generation.
- **Parallel Port Tests**. Controller diagnostics, status port test, interrupt generation, printer output.
- **Video Adapter Tests**. Monitor alignment and linearity, color palettes (CGA, EGA, VGA, and SVGA), character set and attributes. Includes Super VGA memory testing (up to 4 MB) for VESA cards.
- **Keyboard Tests**. Keyboard controller signals, keyboard scan codes, LED and key operation, keyboard clock, data line and ASCII Codes.
- **Mouse Tests**. Operation, buttons, text and graphics modes.
- **Multimedia Tests**. CD-ROM tests: transfer, random seek, audio disc player. Sound card tests: PC speakers, FM synthesizer, and PCM sample.
- **SCSI Utilities**. Identify SCSI devices; low-level format.

Also included is a program to perform a low-level format on IDE drives. Tests can be set up in batched and timed cycles that permit burn-in and soak testing that can extend for several days.

The Troubleshooter

AllMicro, Inc.

18820 U.S. Hwy. 19 N. #215

Clearwater, FL 34624

800-653-4933

813-531-0200 fax

RAMExam

RAMExam, made by Qualitas, detects classes of memory errors not ordinarily found by the basic POST test.

A full suite of tests is executed every time the program is run; users can view a basic scorecard or an advanced screen with full details.

The program can be run manually, or it can be added to your system files and automatically run in the "quick" mode each time you boot up your system.

RAMExam employs six different tests, each targeted at specific types of memory failure:

- **Stuck-At Fault**. This fault occurs when one or more bits retain the value that exists in the memory when the system boots, regardless of attempts to write new values into the memory.
- **Transition Fault**. A transition fault is similar to a stuck-at fault with the exception that the value of the defective bit changes one time before it assumes a "stuck" state.
- **Coupling Faults**. A coupling fault occurs when a change to one or more bits causes an error in one more other bits. Coupling faults fall into two categories:
  - **Inversion Fault**. This type of error occurs when a change to one bit causes an unwanted change to another bit.
  - **Idempotent Fault**. This type of error occurs when a change in one bit forces another bit into a "stuck" state.

  Additionally, multiple coupling errors can occur simultaneously. These are either "linked" or "unlinked" faults:
- **Linked**. There are common bits involved in multiple errors. For example, changing either of two bits erroneously cause a third bit to change.
- **Unlinked**. Multiple, independent errors.

RAMexam

Qualitas, Inc.

8601 Georgia Avenue,

Suite 908

Silver Spring, MD 20910

301-578-8400,

800-733-1377

First Aid 97

CHAPTER 20

CyberMedia's First Aid 97 is an ambitious product that purports to automatically fix Windows problems. Even more important in some ways is the program's ability to intercede between a crash and the shutdown of Windows 95. In most cases, First Aid will give you the necessary time to fix the problem without losing your work in progress.

First Aid 97

CyberMedia Inc.

3000 Ocean Park Blvd., Suite 2001

Santa Monica, CA 90405

(800) 721-7824, (310) 581-4700

http://www.cybermedia.com

PC Care 95

Not surprisingly, American Megatrends Inc., maker of the AMI BIOS, offers a utility that is very capable in diagnostic and reporting facilities.

PC Care 95

American Megatrends Inc.

Norcross, GA;

(800) 892-6627

(770) 246-8600

http://www.megatrends.com

Win Sleuth Gold Plus

Win Sleuth Gold Plus is a particularly elegant package of diagnostics for Microsoft Windows users. As befits a Windows application, it includes graphical representations of memory, peripherals, and other hardware elements as well as colorful reports on memory usage, interrupts, and other parts of the environment.

One of the more unusual—and useful—features of this program is the Installation Assistant, which includes Conflict Finder, a utility that checks your system for conflicts in DMA, IRQ, and I/O port addresses. The program directs you to create a special boot disk for your system which is then used to examine all the settings of device drivers and settings on peripherals installed in the machine at boot-up. (The processor is put into Virtual 86 mode and then the Conflict Finder watches each device driver as it loads; after all have been loaded, the program will prepare an extensive report on any conflicts it finds.)

The iniExpert facility allows you to examine and modify your Windows environment based on recommendations made by Win Sleuth Gold Plus. The files that are checked by the program include **WIN.INI** (the listing of general preferences for the Windows environment); **SYSTEM.INI** (information used by Windows to communicate with your system hardware); **PROGRAM.INI** (the home of preferences for the Program Manager Windows shell); **CONTROL.INI** (where Windows stores the information about color schemes for its interface and information about printers and installable drivers), and **WINFILE.INI** (where preferences for the File Manager are held.)

The Conventional Memory report of Win Sleuth Gold Plus is one of its most detailed; conventional memory is nominally the first 640 KB of RAM and is the landscape available to DOS programs without the use of extended memory managers.

As pretty as the graphic displays are, some of the information on the memory report may not make absolute sense if you are using an advanced memory manager such as QEMM or device "cloaking" utilities that allow you to put the equivalent of ten pounds of programs in a five-pound bag.

The suite of Win Sleuth Gold Plus tests and reports include:

- Hardware Configuration
    BIOS information
    CMOS settings
    Network information
- Environment
    Operating system
    Disk cache
    Tasks and modules
    TSRs and drivers
    Windows settings
    Open files
- Interrupts
- CPU test and benchmarks
- Speaker test

- Keyboard test
- Disk drives
  Disk information
  BIOS
  Utilization
  Benchmarks
  Disk tests
- Video
  Hardware information
  Device capabilities
  Benchmarks
  Hardware testing
- Memory
  Conventional memory
  Upper memory blocks, EMS, XMS
  Benchmark
  Chip test
- Ports
  Parallel port tests
  Serial port tests
  Multimedia tests
- Installation Assistant
  Processor ports
  DMA/IRQ map
  Conflict Finder
- iniEXPERT
  Initialization file checker

Win Sleuth Gold Plus v. 2.0

Dariana Software

5241 Lincoln Ave., Ste. B5

Cypress, CA 90630

(714) 236-1380

236-1390 fax

DiskMapper

Think of this reporting utility as a road map for your hard disk. It churns away for a while and then returns with a graphical representation of the contents of your drive. You can zoom in on any directory or sub-directory, remove or archive a file, and even launch files from the display.

DiskMapper

MicroLogic Inc.

89 Leuning St., P.O. Box 70

Hackensack, NJ 07602

(800) 342-5930

(201) 342-5930

http://www.miclog.com

CHAPTER 20

The Discovery Card: A Hardware Sherlock

This is either the smartest or dumbest tool you could ever use in your PC. Either way, it's a nifty solution to uncovering IRQ and DMA conflicts.

Among the problems the card fixes are these: adapters that are set improperly, adapters that claim to use a particular interrupt or DMA but actually don't, and adapters for which instruction manuals have long ago disappeared.

The Discovery Card is an adapter card that plugs into the computer bus. You leave the cover off the machine and then turn on the PC and watch the 18 red indicator lights on the card; any time one of the 11 interrupts or 7 DMA channels is accessed by any part of the computer, the appropriate light will turn on and stay on.

One green LED is reserved for the CPU. There are red indicators for DMAs 0 through 3 and 5 through 7; red LEDs also await to signal use of IRQs 2 through 7, 10 through 12, and 14 and 15. IRQ is labeled as 2/9, since IRQ 2 passes through to IRQ 9 on modern machines. IRQs 0, 1, 8, and 13 are reserved for the system itself and do not pass signals across adapter slot lines and therefore are not on the card.

After you've booted up the operating system, you next call up each of your attached devices and exercise each of your pieces of software. For example, if you send a command to your sound card and DMA 7 lights up, you know how that card is configured. If you reset your machine and then find that your scanning software also causes DMA 7 to light up, you'll have before your eyes the evidence of a conflict.

The card, which sells for about $300, is a very appropriate tool for a computer repair shop or for anyone who regularly has to unravel hardware problems.

The Discovery Card

AllMicro, Inc.

18820 US Hwy. 19 N. #215

Clearwater, FL 34624

800-653-4933

Summary

Diagnostic disks can't tell you everything, but they are very useful. You should consider buying one of the whole-machine diagnostics if you need to test or repair your computer. You'll also need a configuration utility to figure out how to set the switches and jumpers on new expansion cards.

Because each of these diagnostic programs uncovers slightly different types of problems, you'll probably be best off investing in one of the disk/data diagnostic programs as well as a whole-machine diagnostic. These diagnostic programs are good. But always remember that your brain, especially if you are an experienced technician, is better. And nothing beats the eyeball when troubleshooting misinstallation problems such as cables, switches, and jumpers. Use the diagnostics and consider their repair recommendations, but don't follow them blindly.

CHAPTER 21

Troubleshooting Under Windows 95

Windows 95 goes a long way toward the elusive goal of the Plug-and-Play computer. It includes a capable utility called the Device Manager that allows you to assign and monitor the IRQ interrupts, DMA assignments, and memory addresses for most devices. And the most modern of modern machines now come equipped with an updated BIOS that includes so-called Plug-and-Play facilities.

The Plug-and-Play (PnP) specification that was introduced with Windows 95 is intended to allow the PC, add-in hardware devices, drivers, and the operating system to configure themselves automatically without user intervention. In theory, under PnP, when you plug a new sound card or internal modem or hard drive or other device into your PC, the system would be capable of recognizing your action and setting IRQs, DMAs, memory addresses, and other instructions to avoid conflicts

Plug-and-Play is consists of three parts: a PnP-aware operating system, a PnP-enabled ROM BIOS, and hardware specifically designed to work with the specification. You can obtain some benefit with any of the three parts, but you'll need all of the elements for full automation.

The PnP specification will be widely used in add-in cards, including video adapters, network interfaces, internal modems, and the like. Many external devices will also be able to communicate with the BIOS. As this book goes to press we have already seen PnP external modems, Uninterruptible Power Supplies, and monitors.

If you use Windows 95 with older, "legacy" hardware, you can use the Device Wizard to detect, identify, and configure those devices that will respond to software commands. It may be necessary to change jumper settings and switches on older cards.

In theory, with all three elements in place and a PC stuffed with PnP devices, you should be able to add or remove elements at will, with the system making adjustments automatically. In reality, it will likely be some time before all of the add-in cards and devices in a modern machine are fully PnP, and we can also count on manufacturers to stray from the official specifications for a PnP device for technological or marketing purposes. You'll still need to become involved in resolving the inevitable conflicts between the things we stick into or attach to our PCs.

Using Device Manager to Fix Conflicts

The Device Manager facility of Windows 95 can be used to examine and make changes to software-configurable devices. Older devices that use jumpers or switches for configuration must be configured manually, although Device Manager can still be of assistance in determining settings.

To get to the Device Manager, click the **Start** button, point to **Settings**, and then click on **Control Panel**. Finally, click on **System** (see Figure 21.1–21.4).

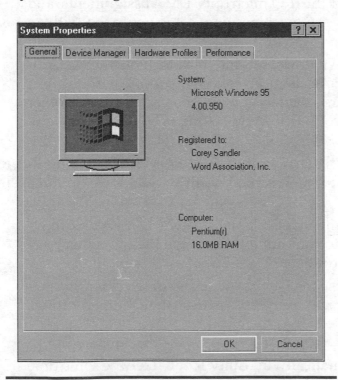

Figure 21.1 The front page of the System Properties display under Windows 95.

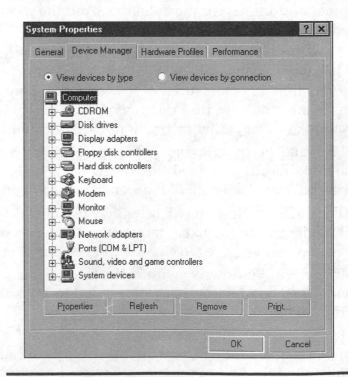

Figure 21.2 The Device Manager with devices sorted by type.

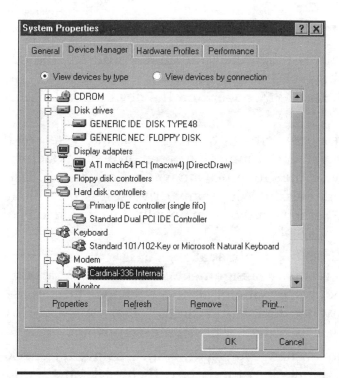

Figure 21.3 Click on the **+** mark to expand the tree of Device Manager and examine a specific piece of hardware.

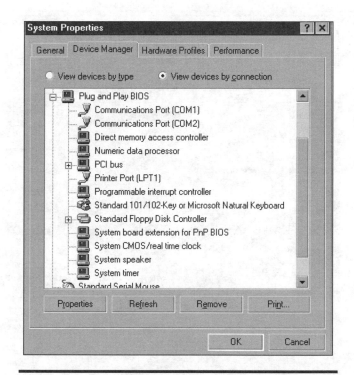

Figure 21.4 Click on **View Devices by Connection** to delve into the organization of the hardware in your PC. Note that the Device Manager will report the presence of a Plug-and-Play BIOS if it finds one.

Check the hardware tree list under **Computer** for devices with a problem. An exclamation point in a yellow circle indicates a potential conflict; an **X** in a red circle tells you that an ill-behaved device has been disabled.

You can move on to the specific device in Device Manager and look at its properties. Double click on a device to check its properties (Figure 21.5); Device Manager will tell you a bit about the hardware itself and whether it appears to be working properly. Actually, the report will only tell you if the device is communicating clearly with the system.

Under the **Resources** tab (Figure 21.6) you will see a window indicating which resources are available for the selected device. The scroll box at the bottom of the page shows a Conflicting Device list. With the information in the two windows you should be able to figure out the source of the conflict and a solution.

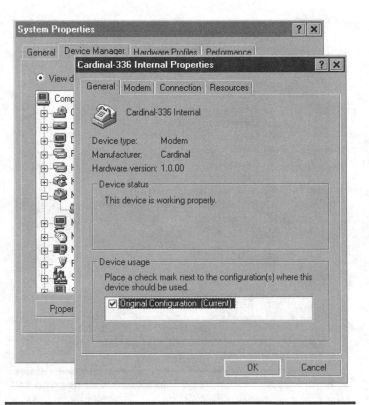

Figure 21.5 Clicking on a device brings up its Properties folder. Here in the General tab you'll learn whether the hardware appears to be working properly.

Automatic Settings

If Windows 95 successfully detects an attached device, the Use Automatic Settings check box should be checked on the Properties tab of Device Manager and the device should function properly.

However, if resource settings have been manually set, or if Windows 95 is making an assumption based on default (factory) settings for a device, the Properties tab will indicate use of Basic Configuration 0 through 9. With many drivers, it is possible to click the Change Settings button to manually adjust elements of the resource settings.

If the automatic setting is not available, or if you turn it off in order to make a manual reassignment of an interrupt or other assignment, Windows 95 will not be able to change the settings by itself and may not be able to readjust other Plug-and-Play devices across their full range of possible assignments.

To make a manual change to a setting, first remove the checkmark from the Automatic Settings box; then click on **Change Settings**. You can scroll through available interrupts or memory addresses using the arrow keys. Pay attention to the report of possible conflicts with other hardware (see Figure 21.7).

If you believe a problem lies with an incorrect or corrupted device driver, restart Windows 95 in Safe Mode and remove the conflicting drivers under Device Manager. Then restart Windows 95 normally and start the Add New Hardware Wizard from the Control Panel. To completely disable a device in Device Manager but leave it in place in the system—one step in an advanced troubleshooting process—click the **Original Configuration (Current)** check box on the General tab to clear it. You can later enable the check box, once the conflict has been resolved.

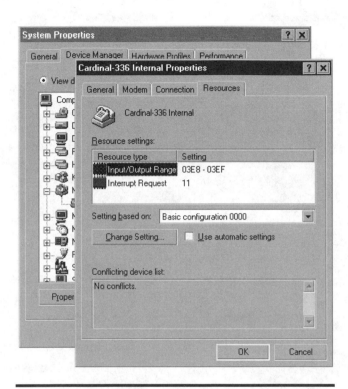

Figure 21.6 The Resources tab reports on the I/O range, Interrupt, DMA (if used) and other information for a particular piece of hardware. Look in the lower section to see if Windows 95 reports that the device is conflicting with the resources used by another device.

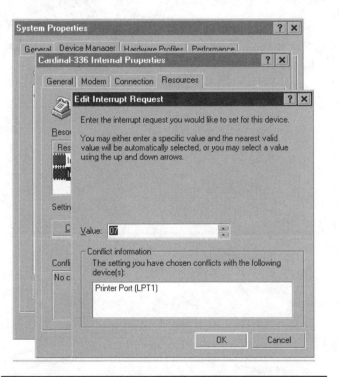

Figure 21.7 The Edit Interrupt Request screen will warn if your selection is in conflict with the resources of another piece of hardware.

CHAPTER 22

Common Sense Solutions to Common Problems

Your computer was working fine yesterday. Today when you turned it on, it sat there like a big expensive piece of dead plastic, silicon, and sheet metal.

Maybe if you're lucky, you hear some sounds or see a cryptic error message on the monitor. Or the computer works fine but the printer won't print, or the scanner won't scan, or the keyboard won't respond to your fingers.

Throughout this book, we've discussed all sorts of general troubleshooting procedures intended to narrow down the problem and solve the mystery.

We're near the end now. In this section we'll start with a fixer-upper tour of PC hardware that builds on the explanations of the rest of the book, and then we'll take a look at a few very common problems and offer specific solutions for them—if you're lucky, you'll find a quick and easy solution to your problem here.

Hardware Starting Points

There is hardware and there is hardware: the lack of a simple machine screw—about a penny's worth of metal—can cause an adapter card to not seat properly in the system bus and cause your $2,000 PC to resemble an electric paperweight. Or, a sudden spike in electricity—caused by an lightning storm or your kid opening the refrigerator—can fry a $100 power supply or a $500 CPU in an instant.

A simple screw or even a power supply are relatively inexpensive and simple to install; a cooked motherboard is a lot of work to replace and may not be cost-effective.

Floppy Drives

Floppy disk drives are cheaper, smaller, and more reliable than they ever used to be. They're also used a lot less now than in the early pre-hard disk days of PCs.

Therefore, floppy disk alignment problems and outright failures are very uncommon now. When one occurs, it generally makes much more sense to replace the drive—about a 15-minute and $30 to $50 investment—than to attempt to make a repair.

The most common problems with floppy drives are failures of mechanical parts like latches and springs. We've also lost a few drives to human failure: an insistent shove of a 3.5-inch floppy disk into a 5.25-inch slot will chew up a drive.

You can check on drive alignment with a special diagnostic program that includes a factory-formatted floppy test disk that is certified as "correct." QA Plus offers a special diagnostic package with such a disk, as does Landmark with its AlignIt package. If the floppy drive does have an alignment problem, though, it will require special shop equipment to fix it and that doesn't make a lot of sense in most situations.

More likely, though, you'll figure out your floppy disk drive is causing problems all by itself. Create a disk on a machine you believe to be working properly, and one on the suspect floppy drive. Move the floppy disks from one machine to another. If some but not all drives can read it, one of the drives is out of alignment or working improperly.

Power Supply

Your computer, depending on the design of its power supply, has the right to expect a steady and reliable source of electricity in the range of 110-120 volts at 50 to 60 cycles per second. (Your power supply may also be able to switch to work with foreign current sources of 240 volts.)

Modern machine power supplies are pretty good at dealing with current that dips slightly below that range momentarily or that surge a bit above the top end. But power supplies are not designed to work with long-term overvoltage or undervoltage situations. Severe spikes can pass through some power supplies and travel through the 12- and 5-volt DC lines to the chips. Long-term overvoltage conditions stress every motor and every chip in the computer.

Chronic undervoltage produces its own set of symptoms. A hard disk that is getting less than 12 volts, for example, may not come up to speed the first three times you turn on the computer in the morning. The fourth time, though, it may work fine and seem okay all day. Low voltage can also cause mysterious intermittent computer lockups.

If you are constantly replacing parts, we'd suggest you start by buying or borrowing a voltmeter or other line voltage testing device and plugging into your wall socket. If the meter reads outside the standard range for no good reason, you may want to call the electric company or an electrician.

What can cause power fluctuations? The reasons run from the ordinary—a "brownout" on the hottest day of the summer or power line interference by major appliances—to just plain bad electrical service.

When an air conditioner or a refrigerator turns on, the draw caused by its motor may well produce a momentary dip in the line voltage, followed by a spike as the power comes back up. Thunderstorms are also notorious for the voltage spikes they cause.

A momentary dip in current will cause the voltage to drop so low that the memory chips start to forget things. When this happens, the computer locks up. Perhaps you didn't see the lights brown out for an instant during the voltage drop. It doesn't matter. A voltage drop lasting only a thousandth of a second can lock up the computer.

Similarly, a momentary voltage spike to the hard disk head may write gibberish in the middle of a file, or much worse, to the boot sector or the FAT (File Allocation Table). You will not notice this problem until you go back and try to read the file or boot from the hard disk. This is where routine use of disk maintenance programs can pay off. Run a disk utility such as Norton Utilities on a regular basis so it can catch and repair these problems. If the boot sector is trashed, try SpinRite, Disk Doctor, or DiskFix. They might be able to repair the boot sector, and if not, may be able to trick DOS into working properly anyway.

I happen to live on a somewhat remote island off the coast of Massachusetts which used to be served by an antique and notoriously unreliable diesel power generator. Voltages would drop below 100 or rise above 130 regularly, and outages were sometimes a weekly occurrence. Now we have a 30-mile-long electrical cable to the mainland . . . and a set of still-antique wires on poles. All of the computers in my office are plugged into UPS boxes and every other major device is protected by major spike protectors or line conditioners.

Every system in any home or office should, at the very least, be plugged into a *spike protector*. These units, which sell for $10 to $50, are electronic sacrificial lambs—they are intended to blow a fuse or even blow up themselves but shut down the line to your computer if there is a dangerous spike headed its way.

A *line conditioner* is a device (priced less than $100) that boosts the power during momentary drops and acts as a surge protector as well.

Uninterruptible Power Supply (UPS) systems are electronic guarantors of a reliable source of power in brownouts, overvoltage situations, and even power failures. They generally include line conditioning circuitry as well as a large internal battery and a regulator. UPSes come in two designs, a "standby" style that includes a very fast switch that can jump into the fray to substitute the battery power for line current in an emergency, and a true "uninterruptible"

style that constantly feeds your computer from its battery at the same time as it uses line current to keep the battery charged. UPS systems sell for between $150 to $300 for units intended to work with single PCs.

If you have checked your line current and are satisfied it is within the proper range, or have dealt with any problems through the use of a line conditioner or a UPS, you can use your voltmeter to check the DC output of the power supply within the computer. We discuss this in more detail in Chapter 8.

Hard Disk or Hard Disk Controller Problem?

Another area where a diagnostic program can be less than precise is in the distinction between a failure of the hard disk and a problem with its hard disk controller. A diagnostic program can test for accurate data storage and recovery, and many programs have very sophisticated in-depth hard disk testing routines.

Unfortunately, there is no way to eavesdrop on the hard disk controller and the hard disk as they attempt to read or write data. If a bad controller is sending incorrect control signals to the hard disk, you'll have a data storage failure. If the controller is good, but the hard disk doesn't correctly follow the controller's directions, you'll also get data storage failure. Even a bad cable can cause intermittent failures. Refer to Chapter 11 for some troubleshooting ideas if you think your hard disk is failing.

Solving Printer Problems

Check the Cables First

Before you think we're trying to embarrass you with a problem we haven't had ourselves, let us assure you that sooner or later every computer owner has a moment of sheer panic caused by something as simple as an unplugged PC or monitor or a blown fuse down in the basement that was caused by a disagreement between the vacuum cleaner and your color TV.

Always check the electrical connection first if your computer appears to be dead. Is the PC plugged in to the wall, and is the other end of the power cable properly attached to the PC itself? Check the power outlet by plugging a lamp or radio into the socket. If your computer is plugged into a spike protector, line conditioner, or UPS (something we highly recommend), check that one of these protective devices hasn't blown a fuse.

The next thing to check is the jumble of cables worming out of the back of the computer; it's easy for one of them to get unplugged by a vacuum cleaner, your cat, or a tug from the other end of the cable.

Check all the connections to make sure they are firmly seated on their sockets; screw cables into connectors where possible, making certain that the plugs go into place evenly without one side off-center.

A loosely connected video cable, for example, will sometimes cause blurred characters or a color shift. A wobbly printer cable can make "Now is the time for all good men to come to the aid of the party" come out as "Mpe od yjr yo,r gpt s;; hppf ,rm yp vp,r yp yje sof pg yjr [sryu."

If the cable connections are okay, follow the suggestions in the rest of this chapter. If the quick fixes in this chapter don't get you up and running, consult the troubleshooting charts in Section 3. Follow the chart's questions and answers to point you to another troubleshooting chart that will suggest a solution.

Coaxing a Printer to Speak to You

The causes of a printer malfunction can range from a broken or disconnected cable (most likely) to a bad printer port (the least likely). The switch boxes or the printer itself are also potential culprits.

Test the possible causes, in this order:

- Software configuration
- Cable
- Switch box (if there is one)
- Printer
- Parallel port

Software Configuration

Before you break out your screwdriver, take a moment to check whether your computer has done anything to disable or redirect the parallel port. Have you installed a new operating system, utility, or application since the last time the program worked? Examine your **AUTOEXEC.BAT** file for any **MODE** commands; were they there before the last installation of software? Try removing them temporarily to see if this solves the problem.

Go to the DOS prompt (exit from Windows if it is running), and type the following command:

MODE LPT1:<Enter>

The system should report that the LPT1: port, your first parallel port, is not redirected. In some unusual situations, a software program may redirect the output headed to the parallel port to the serial port instead. This command will clear that situation. Make sure your printer is turned on and attached to the PC. Now type the following command:

DIR > LPT1:<Enter>

This command will send a copy of the filenames of the current directory to LPT1, your parallel port. The directory should spit out of your printer; on some devices, including laser and other page printers you may have to press the **Off Line** switch and then **Form Feed** to eject the page from the printer.

If you receive a printed copy of your directory, then you know that your printer, printer cable, and parallel port are functioning properly; the problem must therefore lie in a software setting of DOS, Windows, or an application program.

Cable

Test the cable by substituting a known good one.

Switch Box

Test a switch box, if it is in use, by removing it from the circuit and attaching the cable directly to the computer and printer. If the printer works now, you either have a failed switch or a problem with one of the extension cables used with the box.

Printer

Run your printer's self-test to check on the mechanism. If it appears to be working properly, test the printer by hooking it up to another computer in your office or take it to a friend's setup. If you purchased the printer from a retail store, you may be able to bring the device to the shop to test it there. That may or may not be possible if you bought the printer or your computer from an electronics superstore.

Parallel Port

To test the parallel port, use a diagnostics software package; the best utilities require use of a loopback plug that attaches to the port and simulates an attached device for the purposes of the test. If you have eliminated the printer and cable as the reasons for the failure, use the loopback to test the port fully.

Soothing Balky Floppy Disk Drives

I don't recommend the repair of broken floppy disk drives, because they are so inexpensive to replace. But there are some things you can do to maintain drives that are exhibiting problems but still working.

The first thing to do is keep the disk drives clean. Use a vacuum cleaner to suck out the dust that may work its way into the drives.

Buy a disk cleaning kit to treat dirty drive heads. Follow the manufacturer's directions carefully and be sure not to overdo the amount of solution or frequency of cleanings.

By the way, noise is not always an indicator of trouble. A noisy floppy drive may have been born that way; run a full set of diagnostics.

Occasionally, a floppy drive malfunctions because its cable is loose and must be pressed back in place. To correct this problem, turn off and unplug the computer, open the computer case, trace the cable to its attachment, and press it firmly.

If these fixes don't solve your problem, see Chapter 8 for instructions on replacing your floppy drive, a simple fix with a price tag of less than $50.

CHAPTER 22

Reviving Failed Hard Disks

The primary cause of hard disk failure at bootup is a loose cable or a dislodged controller card. Turn off and unplug the computer, open the computer case, and press the card or cable back in place.

Other sources of problems are a damaged boot track, system files, or a failure of the disk mechanism itself. We cover those possibilities in Chapter 9.

Flaky Power Supplies

Another cause of hard disk failure—as well as problems with CMOS—is a malfunctioning power supply. A symptom of this problem is a disk that boots properly but then dies as the machine gets hot. The message that appears on your screen is something like **Seek error. Abort, Retry, Fail?**.

What may be happening is that the power supply is putting out 8 or 10 volts instead of the proper 5 volts to the motor. The motor therefore runs too fast and gets too hot; it ends up being unable to read or write properly. Not all drives choke on a malfunctioning power supply, but less expensive drives often do.

You can check for this sort of problem by substituting a known good power supply with the existing hard disk and controller.

Did Your Computer Lose Its Setup on the Bedpost Overnight?

On modern machines, a common bootup error message **is Invalid Configuration Information** followed by **Hard Disk Failure**. The problem may be as simple as dead batteries.

Open the case, replace the batteries with fresh ones, and run the **Setup** program. (On older PC-AT class machines, you may have to use a boot disk with the **Setup** program on it; be sure to keep a copy at hand.) 80386 and later machines have the **Setup** program stored in ROM, so you don't have to keep track of the disk.

Some early name-brand 286 machines had the batteries soldered to the motherboard. The batteries were supposed to last five years, but they expired prematurely and the unfortunate owners were informed that they had to buy new motherboards—an expensive proposition. More than one of these owners bought clones as replacements for their name-brand computers. Why? Because clones had plain old AA batteries that are easy to replace. There's a lesson here: if you're considering buying a name-brand computer, be sure to ask about the compatibility and price of replacement parts.

Recovering Memory Failures

Memory problems often reveal themselves with an obnoxious nonmaskable interrupt (NMI) error message on your monitor.

If you have a Dinosaur XT or a 286-based machine, the most common cause of memory failures is a popped memory chip. You can easily fix this by turning off and unplugging the computer, opening the case, and pressing down on the chips with your thumb.

If you have a 386 or 486 machine with SIMM strips, make sure the strips are tilted and snapped into place properly. More subtle memory problems can show up as intermittent malfunctions in almost any component, such as the hard disk.

It's best to discharge static electricity by touching a grounded piece of metal before you begin working inside your computer; one good ground in most offices and homes is the center screw on an electrical outlet.

Missing Device Drivers

The symptoms of a missing device driver are usually something like this: your computer boots but drive D has disappeared, the scanner has stopped scanning, or you can't get back on the network.

If you are working under DOS or Windows 3.1, you should first direct your attention to the CONFIG.SYS and AUTOEXEC.BAT files to see if there is problem with driver references there. Have drivers been removed, renamed, or moved? If you are working under Windows 95, go the Device Manager (discussed in Chapter 21) and check for the presence of proper drivers for your devices.

When you check your **CONFIG.SYS** file, see that it includes all the DEVICE= statements required to load all your device drivers.

Add-on peripherals and boards are often shipped with installation disks that contain alterations to the **AUTOEXEC.BAT** and **CONFIG.SYS** files. Before you install an add-on, copy your files to **AUTOEXEC.OLD** and **CONFIG.OLD**, then rewrite the originals to add the necessary DEVICE= statements. The lines required by the device driver will now be in your **CONFIG.SYS** file, and you'll have the backup files in case something goes wrong and you want to look at the old instructions.

A corresponding problem crops up with Windows. The **WIN.INI** file of Windows 3.1 contains specific instructions to the computer about the Windows setup. New software writes additional lines into **WIN.INI**; the well-mannered software makes a copy of the old file and keeps it for you, in case you uninstall or need to make other changes. If you get strange symptoms, something may have zapped your **WIN.INI** file.

CHAPTER 22

Nonworking Color Monitor

Make sure your monitor is properly connected to the video adapter of the PC and plugged into a working wall circuit. Check the brightness and contrast settings on the monitor; an accidental turn of a knob may make the screen dark and unreadable. It can easily be brought back to normal by readjusting the knob.

Some monitors have an external fuse; unplug the unit and remove the fuse. Examine it carefully and replace it if it has blown; if it appears to be good, the fuse may have come unseated because of heat or vibration.

Do not attempt to make internal repairs to a color monitor; the video circuitry uses very high voltage, and any adjustments require specialized training and equipment.

SCSI Driver Problems

There are two elements of the configuration of a SCSI adapter and its attached devices.

First is the configuration of the SCSI bus itself. This includes terminating both ends of the SCSI bus, setting each device's Logical Unit Number (LUN), and setting the device IDs. The LUN is used to differentiate among multiple SCSI adapters in one system. The SCSI device ID is used to designate the various devices attached to a single adapter.

Second is the configuration of the SCSI host adapter, including assignment of nonconflicting IRQ line, DMA channel, and memory address.

Here are some troubleshooting steps:

1. Double-check that the SCSI bus is terminated at each end. A SCSI adapter can be at one end of a chain with a peripheral at the other end, in which case one termination point is the adapter and the other is the peripheral. Or, the adapter can sit in the middle of the chain, in which case the termination points are on the peripherals at each end of the SCSI bus.

2. Many cards that adhere to the ASPI standard, a common modern definition for SCSI adapters, can be set up to allow the PC to boot from the SCSI adapter, although this is not the way most PCs are set up. It is good practice to disable an onboard boot ROM BIOS if the SCSI adapter is being used as a secondary disk subsystem.

3. The Windows 95 SCSI drivers support only the switches and parameters supported by the real-mode drivers provided by the maker of the SCSI adapter. If the SCSI card works under MS-DOS but does not work fully under Windows 95 using a protected mode driver, check the parameters in the real-mode driver line in the **CONFIG.SYS** file, and modify the switches or parameters in the **Settings** tab of Device Manager. Better yet, call the maker of your SCSI adapter or Microsoft for help here.

Liquid on the Keyboard

If a can of cola or a cup of coffee has spilled on your keyboard, you may be out of luck—replacement keyboards sell for as little as $30 for a cheap model to about $125 for deluxe replacements.

If you are very daring or cheap, you can try this: unplug the keyboard and remove any batteries it may contain. Rinse the keyboard under running water and then let it drain and dry out for several days. When it is completely dry, plug it in and try it again. It just may work.

PS/2 Password Predicaments

Most PS/2 machines include one or both of a set of password protections. For most users, the passwords can be important safeguards in environments where computers are accessible to unauthorized visitors. They can also be the cause of problems if passwords are lost or if the memory holding them is somehow corrupted or disabled.

The basic password protection is the *power-on password*, which is set as part of the configuration program. The system will ask the user to enter the password before the Power-On Self-Test is completed and the operating system is booted.

The power-on password is stored in a section of battery-backed setup memory.

If you forget the power-on password, or if the battery-backed memory loses its contents or is corrupted, you can erase the password by removing the covers of the system and moving the power-on password jumper on the system board; full instructions and the location of the jumper can be found in the manuals for your PS/2 system.

A more serious level of electronic lock and key is provided by the *privileged-access password*. This code allows you to lock away access to the system programs or to make modifications to the configuration files for computer hardware.

When a privileged-access password is set, it is recorded in a special section of nonvolatile memory. If you forget the password, the entire motherboard will have to be serviced by the computer maker or replaced.

There is a privileged-access jumper on the motherboard that is used to disable or enable the setting of the password itself; this jumper will not get you out of a problem with a lost password—you must know the code in order to disable it, even with the jumper.

CHAPTER 22

Windows 3.1 Troubleshooting

This book concentrates on the hardware side of the computer equation, but it is a basic fact of PC operation that the hardware and software are inextricably intertwined; each can cause the other trouble, and determining the source of the problem is sometimes as easy as herding cats.

In this section we'll look at a few of the software settings that can cause problems for your hardware. For a more detailed examination of Windows configuration issues, we suggest you read *teach yourself...Windows 95* by Al Stevens (MIS:Press, 1996). For more information on specific troubleshooting information, *IRQ, DMA, and I/O* by Jim Aspinwall (MIS:Press, 1995) covers in detail a number of problems device conflicts may cause.

The most common troublemakers are conflicting assignments for memory, IRQs, DMAs, and incorrect **.INI** file and driver settings.

Situation: System Boots but Windows Will Not Load

This is almost certainly a software problem. Here are some possible blocks to loading:

- **Fastdisk Failure**. Your hard disk controller may not be compatible with the Fastdisk utility; in order to use Fastdisk, the controller must be completely compatible with the WD1003 chip. Check with the manufacturer of your controller if you have any doubts. To disable Fastdisk, edit your **SYSTEM.INI** file and place a semi-colon at the start of these two lines to turn them off, as follows:

```
;DEVICE=*INT13
;DEVICE=*WDCTRL
```

- **EMM386 Exception Error** *xx*. Check the error code number in search of a possible memory problem. Other hardware-related problems that could generate this message include an improper CPU or bus speed caused by pressing the **Turbo** button on some PCs, or through an inappropriate **CMOS Setup** including wrong memory interleave or register-level settings. Consult your PC's instruction manual or the manufacturer for assistance.

- **Windows Lockups without Error Messages**. From the DOS prompt, try loading Windows by typing:

```
WIN /B<Enter>
```

This will create a file called **BOOTLOG.TXT** in the Windows directory that records start-up status information; if Windows does not start, you will be able to see at which point the failure came. A good Windows configuration guide may help you here, or you may need to call Microsoft or your system manufacturer and discuss your findings in search of a solution.

If loading proceeds as far as the Windows logo and then stops, two likely suspects are the video display driver or system fonts. Try reinstalling the video driver through Windows **Setup**; when you are asked whether you want to use the currently installed driver, choose to install a new copy instead. If the new video driver does not solve the problem, install the standard Windows VGA driver. Contact the maker of your video board to see if there is an updated driver available.

General Windows 3.1 Troubleshooting Steps

Test your Windows installation in small increments by starting with a Standard Mode load instead of the usual 386 Enhanced Mode.

Standard Mode Test

Standard Mode is a reduced version of Windows that is supposed to be able to run on 80286 processors. This version is not of much use to modern machines with multitasking applications, but it is a valuable tool in troubleshooting, since it will in many cases allow you to get past hardware compatibility problems long enough to identify and fix them.

From the DOS prompt, type

WIN /S<Enter>

to start Windows in Standard Mode. If it doesn't load, you'll have to reinstall the Windows drivers or the entire Windows system; change to the Windows subdirectory and run **Setup**.

Minimal Windows Test

Another important troubleshooting technique involves starting your system and then Windows with the minimal number of special programs and assignments and then adding them back in one at a time until Windows chokes.

Create a DOS boot disk that loads your system files, memory manager (EMM386, QEMM, or similar), mouse driver, and any other Windows-specific files and then boot the system. Or, you can press **F8** when your system beeps during bootup and then answer **Y** or **N** to each of the lines of your **CONFIG.SYS** and **AUTOEXEC.BAT** file as you are queried about them. Under either method, stop short of loading Windows itself.

Use an editor and load **WIN.INI** from your Windows subdirectory. Temporarily disable any applications automatically loaded at Windows startup by placing a semicolon in front of the commands; look for any line in the [windows] section of **WIN.INI** that begins

```
Load=
    or
Run=
```

Save the **WIN.INI** file and then type **WIN** and press **Enter** to load Windows; press and hold down the **Shift** key while Windows is starting. Holding that key will instruct Windows to bypass your StartUp group and not load any applications included there.

If Windows starts, click on the **StartUp** group to open it and then drag any Program Items you find within it to a different group. Then delete the StartUp group (highlight the menu bar for **StartUp** and click on **File** and **Delete**, or press the **Delete** key). Then create a new StartUp group, using the same name (click on **File** and **New** and select **Program Group**).

Reboot in your ordinary method; if Windows still doesn't start, the steps we have gone through indicate you probably have a problem with some of the elements of the **SYSTEM.INI** or **WIN.INI** files. If you're a careful Windows user, you will have recent backups of the files; back up the suspect files under a different name and then copy your older versions of the files into your Windows directory. Restart Windows; if it works now, you can examine the differences between the faulty files and the ones that worked in search of the source of the problem and its solution.

Starting Again: Reinstalling Windows

If you've got the room on your hard drive, one good test effort is to reinstall a new copy of Windows into a new directory with a different directory name. Instruct Microsoft's installation program to ignore the fact that it has found a second copy of Windows on your drive.

Load the new installation of Windows. If it seems to be working properly, move over *copies* of parts of the old Window installation. Start by bringing over copies of the old **SYSTEM.INI** and **WINDOWS.INI**. Test the new Windows installation.

Now bring over copies of all of the old ***.GRP** files and try Windows again.

Your goal is to either rebuild a new working version of Windows with as many of the old elements as needed or to incrementally add pieces of the old installation to the new one until it fails and reveals the source of the problem.

If you don't have room to make a complete reinstallation of Windows on your hard drive, you can make copies of your essential files including ***.INI** and ***.GRP** in a temporary directory.

Be sure to make copies in another place of all document files for all the applications stored within the Windows directory and subdirectories.

WARNING

Make copies of the applications themselves unless you are willing to reinstall them all from their original disks. When you've copied all the items you don't want to lose, stop and think again: is there anything in the Windows directory you've missed? Once you are certain all is well, delete the contents of the Windows directory and reinstall Windows.

If your new Windows installation works, bring back your **.INI** and **.GRP** files one at a time, checking to see that Windows still functions. Then bring back your applications and document files.

Windows 3.1 Memory Conflicts

The first indication of memory conflicts—an attempt by hardware or software to use a single location in memory for more than one purpose—often comes in DOS before Windows starts. Most problems lie in the Upper Memory Area from 640KB to 1MB.

Memory errors can cause error messages from EMM386 (or QEMM or similar programs) at bootup. You may also receive warnings from device drivers for particular pieces of hardware, or the device itself may stop working.

If you have just installed a new piece of hardware, you most likely have a memory, IRQ, or DMA conflict. Remove the device and restart your system; if the problem goes away, you know that you will have to adjust IRQ or DMA settings on the new device. (You could also leave the new device as it is and seek to make changes on older elements of your system, but to do so is to add a whole new level of complexity to your efforts.)

Memory conflicts arise when two devices attempt to use the same address or overlap parts of their data. The problem can also come if DOS does not recognize that a particular device plans to use a specific memory range; DOS may load device drivers or TSRs into that location at bootup.

Fixing UMA Assignments

A careful user will maintain a listing of all UMA assignments as each new piece of hardware or software is installed; a good place to keep this is on a page of your PC's instruction manual. While you're at it, keep a listing of all IRQ and DMA listings and serial numbers and dates of purchase for all hardware and software. (Why use paper and pencil when you've got a perfectly wonderful computer? Well, sometimes the computer won't start, which is why we're here.)

Exclude from the use of any memory manager (EMM386, QEMM, and similar products) any UMA ranges that are under claim by adapters. Consult the instruction manual for your memory manager (EMM386 is covered in the documentation for DOS).

CHAPTER 22

As an example, to exclude a section of UMA under **EMM386.EXE**, you must add an X (for exclude) switch to the command line. To block off the use of C000-CBFF (the home of many VGA adapters) and D000-D3FF (used by many network adapters), use

```
C:\DOS\EMM386.EXE NOEMS X=C000-CBFF X=D000-D3FF
```

Make changes to the memory manager listing in **CONFIG.SYS** and reboot the system to see if the problem has been solved.

Blocking Windows out of UMA

If the problems persist, Windows may not be recognizing that a particular memory range is intended to be set aside for the use of a device.

You can set up a temporary roadblock around such problems by loading Windows with a /**D** switch; this instructs Windows to exclude from its use all memory from A000-FFFF, the entire Upper Memory Area.

The command is:

WIN /D<Enter>

If Windows works properly, you can assume that the problem lies in the allocation of the UMA. You can then attempt a trial-and-error adjustment of the exclusion area in search of the problem.

Other Conflicts

We've already discussed IRQ and DMA conflicts in Chapter XX. Make certain that any new device does not lay claim to an interrupt or DMA channel already in regular or intermittent use by other pieces of hardware.

Many devices also require an I/O base address, the memory location where it ties into DOS. Again, these must be unique for each device.

Remove any new device and check its setting before reinstallation.

Out of Memory

One of the great mysteries—and huge annoyances—of Windows 3.1 is the Not Enough Memory message nearly every user sees from time to time. It doesn't matter whether your system has the minimum base of 4MB of RAM or is a super system with 16 or even 32MB of memory.

The cause of the problem is not a lack of RAM but rather an overuse of one or the other of a pair of tiny 64KB areas of memory called the Graphics Device Interface (GDI) heap and the User heap. Collectively, they are called *Windows resources*.

The *GDI heap* is used for management of graphics, including output to video displays and printers; the *User heap* oversees I/O, the Windows timer, and management of the on-screen elements of the Windows program itself.

As you've already discovered, you can run out of resources even with a huge amount of unused RAM. In fact, any time your system drops much below about 50% resources, your Windows installation may begin to slow down, act unpredictably, or even freeze.

You can check on how much available resources you have remaining from the Program Manager or File Manager by clicking on **Help** and then **About Program Manager** or **About File Manager**. You'll see a percentage reading for Resources; this is a report of the amount of space remaining in the smaller of the two heaps.

To keep your Resources available, try to reduce the number of programs you have open at one time. Yes, we know that the ability to switch from application to application is one of the reasons many people use Windows in the first place, but you should realize that all good things seem to have their price.

You can also save resources by limiting the number of open document windows within a single open application; for example, keeping six separate word processing files open at the same time can eat up a lot of your precious resource space. Removing any unnecessary icons from a program's tool bar will also help.

Reduce the number of open program group windows in the Program Manager, too.

CHAPTER 22

Intoduction to Troubleshooting Charts

Welcome to the Troubleshooting Charts. These charts illustrate the pattern of thought to follow as you diagnose a non-working computer. Even an inexperienced non-technical computer owner can follow this simple, step-by-step technique. This is the same reasoning process taught to many new technicians who are learning on the job or attending computer repair classes.

This technique was developed in a computer store where replacement parts are always available. If you're using the charts at home, without any duplicate parts to swap in, see if you can use a friend or colleague's computer to test your malfunctioning printer, monitor, or keyboard. If you are repairing machines at work, do you have access to parts you know are working from equivilant machines in the office? If no loaner is available, you'll just have to put in a new card or disk when you get to a point in the troubleshooting charts where we suggest swapping on one of these parts. If the new part doesn't fix the problem, don't give up in despair. Even in repair shops, the technician has to bit the bullet and replace the most likely part. One of the things you par for (at $50 or $100 an hour) is the right to rent the repair shop's parts for diagnostic purposes.

Despite buying an occasional extra drive or card, you'll still save a lot of hassle and a lot of money doing your own simple repairs. Some of you may not want to actually perform the repairs, preferring instead to establish the most likely bad part by reading the troubleshooting charts and then take the computer to the repair shop for the actual computer surgery.

Take the following precautions before you work through the charts:

1. Always turn off the computer before installing or removing any components.

2. Always back up your hard disk before you do anything, even fixing a serial port. At the computer store, we strongly recommend backing up the hard disk before a computer comes in for any repair and make each prospective customer sign a release accepting full responsibility for their own data.

3. When a professional technician repairs a computer with multiple problems, they start with one problem, fix it, and then tackle the next. You may have to loop through these troubleshooting charts a second or third time to catch all the bad parts in a particularly sick computer.

4. Always deal with screen error messages first, before trying to diagnose any additional problems. Appendices A, B, and C list these screen error messages and our recommended fix for each problem. Appendices A and B cover error messages printed on your monitor, with the IGM-style numeric messages (e.g., "1701") covered in Appendix A and the English-like text messages (e.g., "Disk Driver 1 Seek Failure") in Appendix B.

5. Note where and how cables and wire connectors are attached before you begin disassembling your computer. You will be astonished by the poor documentation in this industry. If you don't write the details down while tearing apart the computer, you may well have to re-engineer the computer yourself during reassembly.

6. If at any point you think the monitor and/or keyboard you are using to test your computer might be bad, check them by connecting them to a known-good computer.

7. Before attempting major repairs, consider the cost of replacing this computer. Ask yourself whether it's worthwhile to repair the beast. Remember, you can buy twice as much computing power for half the money you had to spend two or three years ago.

With these points in mind, turn to the Start Chart. Follow each step carefully and you should easily discover what's wrong.

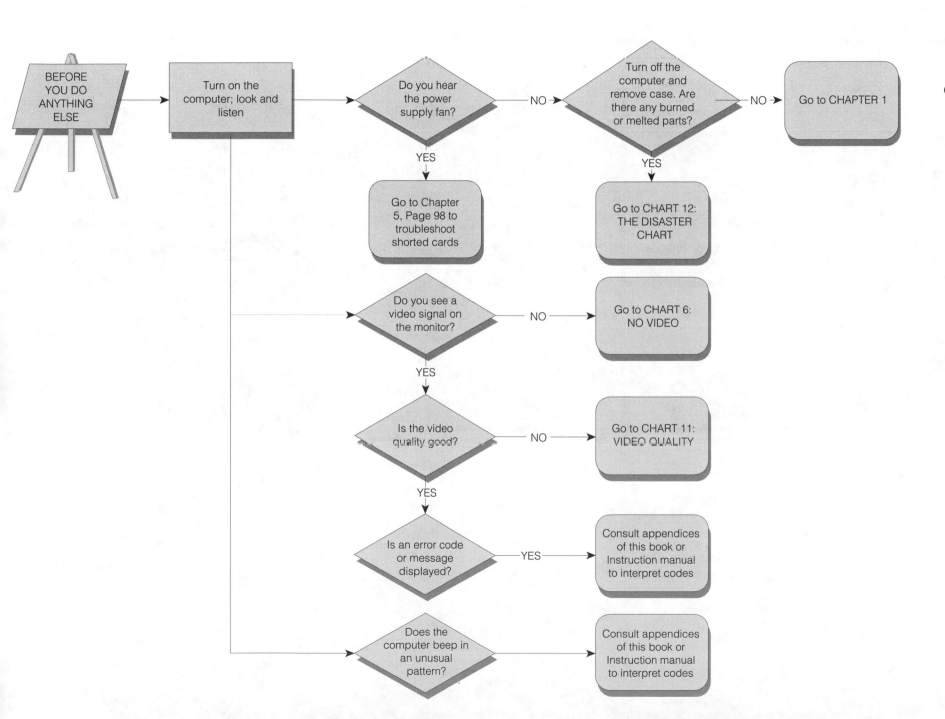

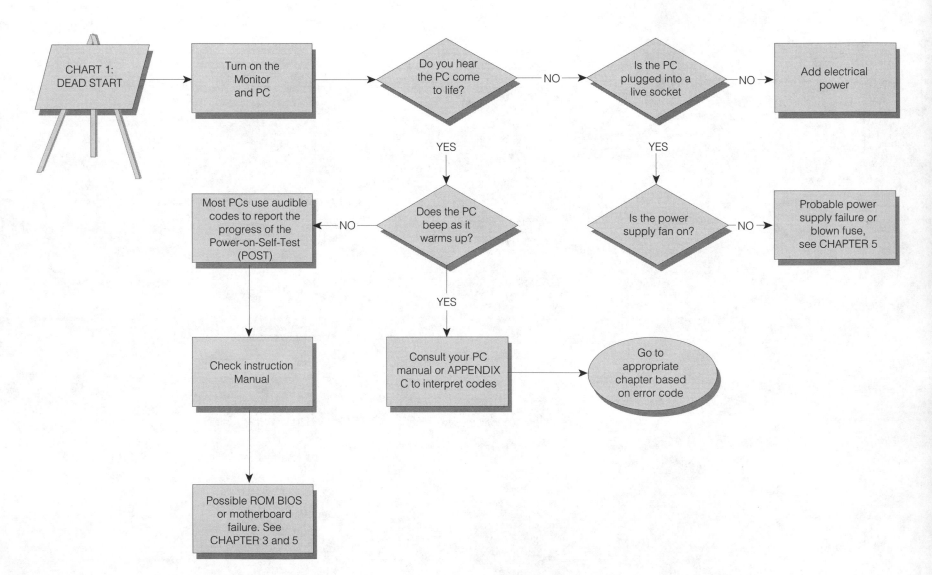

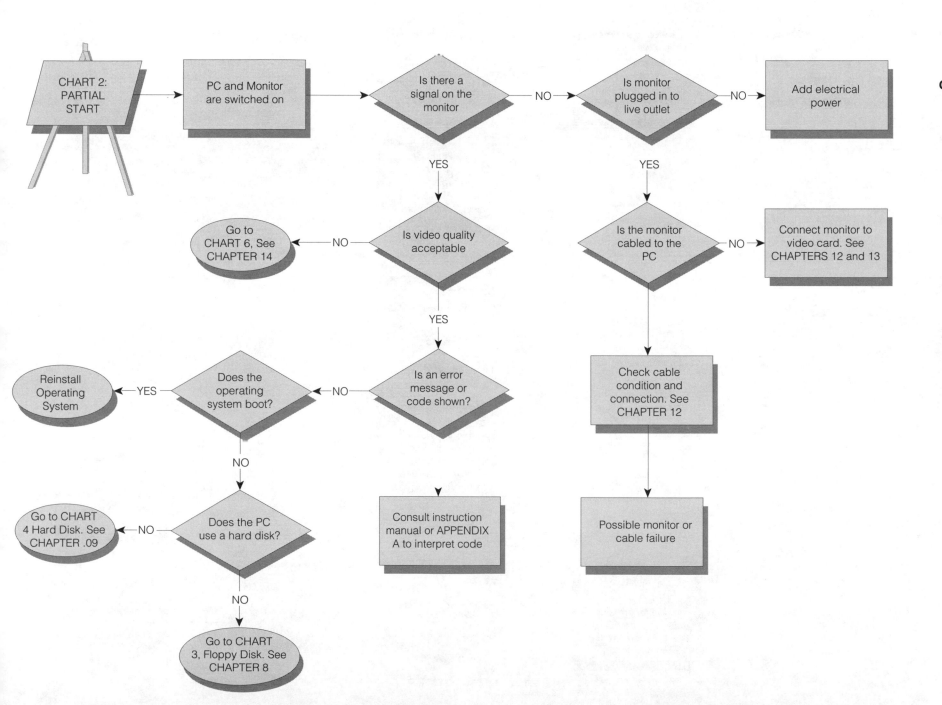

CHART 2: PARTIAL START

PC and Monitor are switched on

Is there a signal on the monitor — NO → Is monitor plugged in to live outlet — NO → Add electrical power

YES

Is video quality acceptable — NO → Go to CHART 6, See CHAPTER 14

YES

Is an error message or code shown? — NO → Does the operating system boot? — YES → Reinstall Operating System

NO

Does the PC use a hard disk? — NO → Go to CHART 4 Hard Disk. See CHAPTER .09

NO

Go to CHART 3, Floppy Disk. See CHAPTER 8

Consult instruction manual or APPENDIX A to interpret code

YES

Is the monitor cabled to the PC — NO → Connect monitor to video card. See CHAPTERS 12 and 13

Check cable condition and connection. See CHAPTER 12

Possible monitor or cable failure

CHARTS

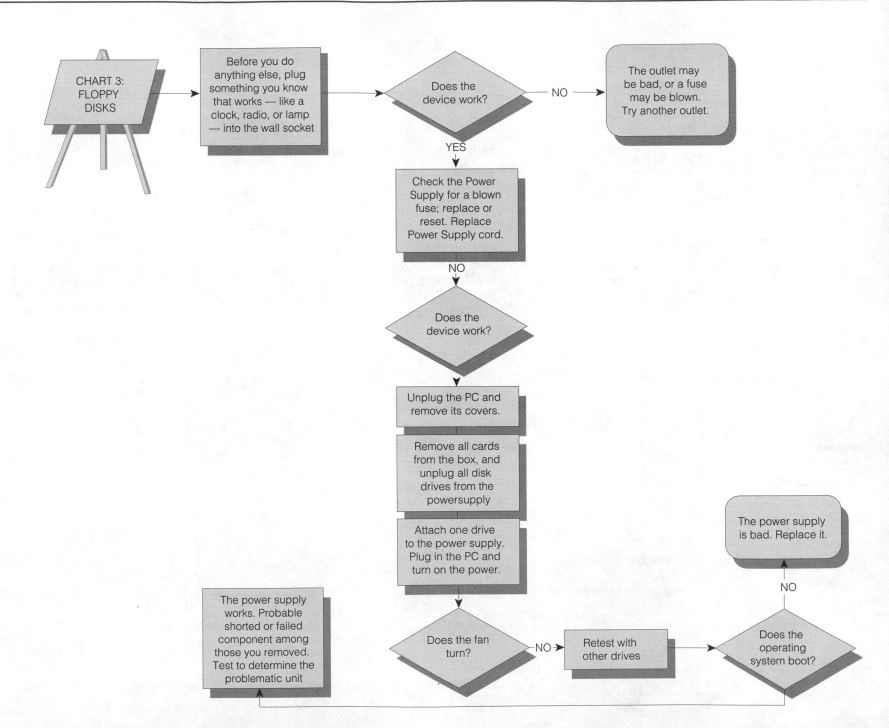

CHART 3:
FLOPPY
DISKS

Before you do anything else, plug something you know that works — like a clock, radio, or lamp — into the wall socket

Does the device work?

NO → The outlet may be bad, or a fuse may be blown. Try another outlet.

YES

Check the Power Supply for a blown fuse; replace or reset. Replace Power Supply cord.

NO

Does the device work?

Unplug the PC and remove its covers.

Remove all cards from the box, and unplug all disk drives from the powersupply

Attach one drive to the power supply. Plug in the PC and turn on the power.

Does the fan turn?

NO → Retest with other drives

Does the operating system boot?

NO → The power supply is bad. Replace it.

The power supply works. Probable shorted or failed component among those you removed. Test to determine the problematic unit

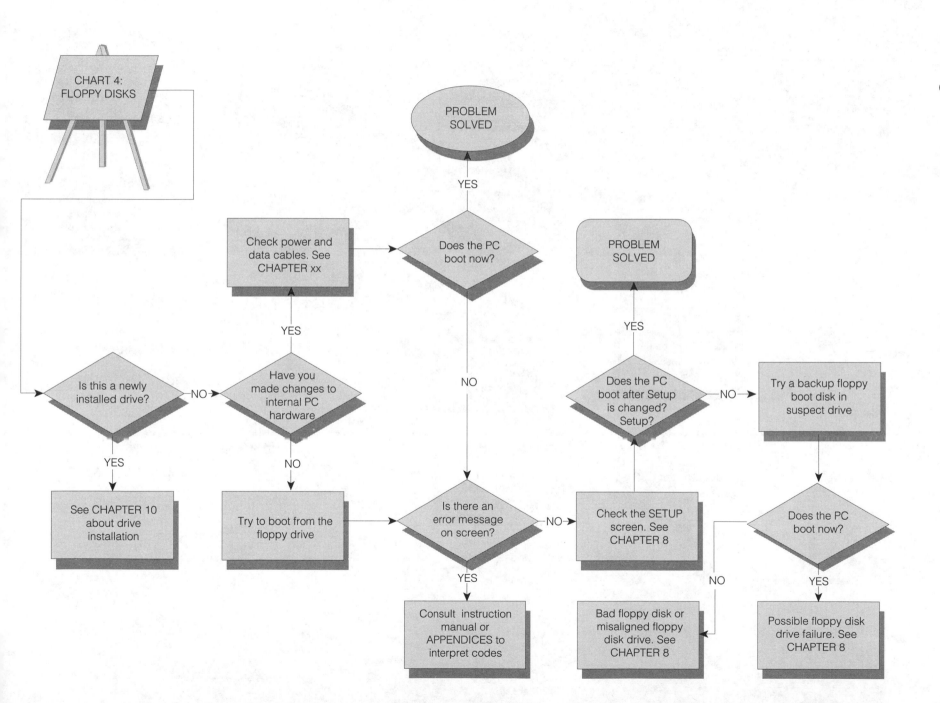

CHART 4:
FLOPPY DISKS

PROBLEM
SOLVED

↑ YES

Check power and
data cables. See
CHAPTER xx → Does the PC
boot now?

↑ YES

PROBLEM
SOLVED

↑ YES

Is this a newly
installed drive? —NO→ Have you
made changes to
internal PC
hardware → Does the PC
boot after Setup
is changed?
Setup? —NO→ Try a backup floppy
boot disk in
suspect drive

↓ YES ↓ NO ↓ NO

See CHAPTER 10
about drive
installation

Try to boot from the
floppy drive → Is there an
error message
on screen? —NO→ Check the SETUP
screen. See
CHAPTER 8 Does the PC
boot now?

↓ YES ↓ NO ↓ YES

Consult instruction
manual or
APPENDICES to
interpret codes

Bad floppy disk or
misaligned floppy
disk drive. See
CHAPTER 8

Possible floppy disk
drive failure. See
CHAPTER 8

CHARTS

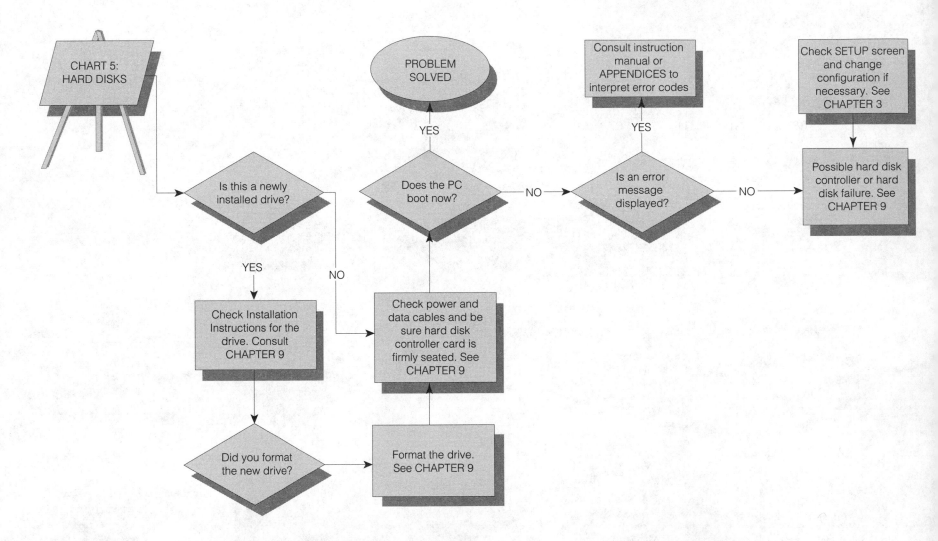

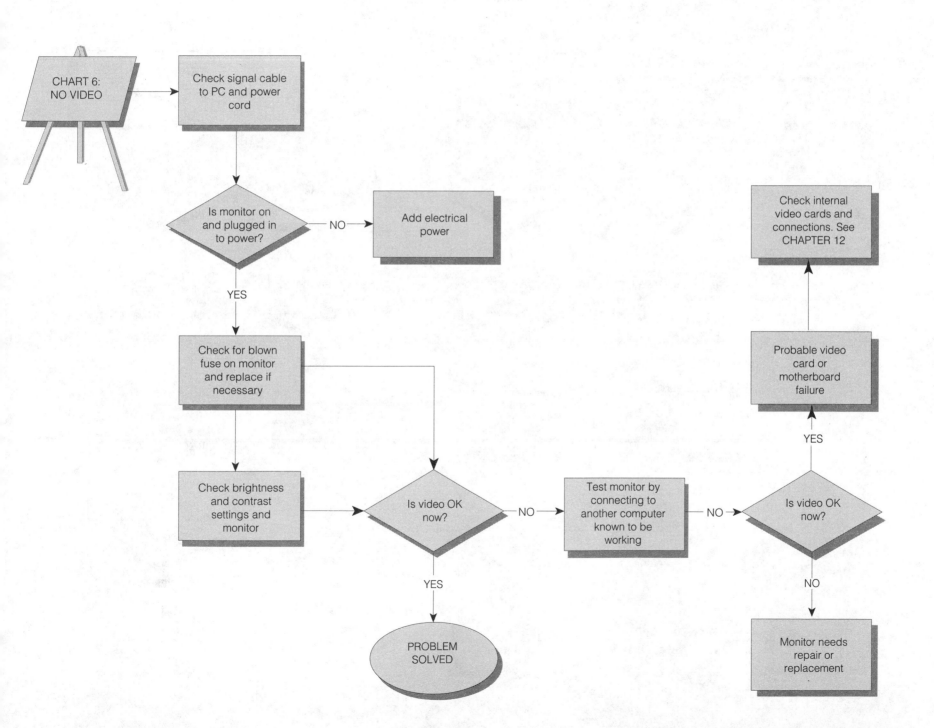

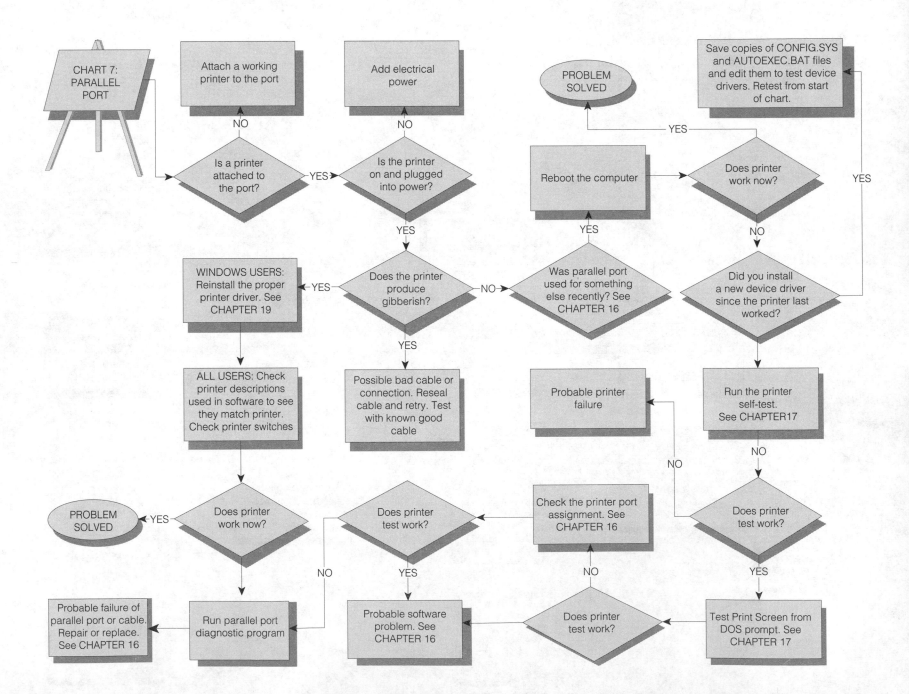

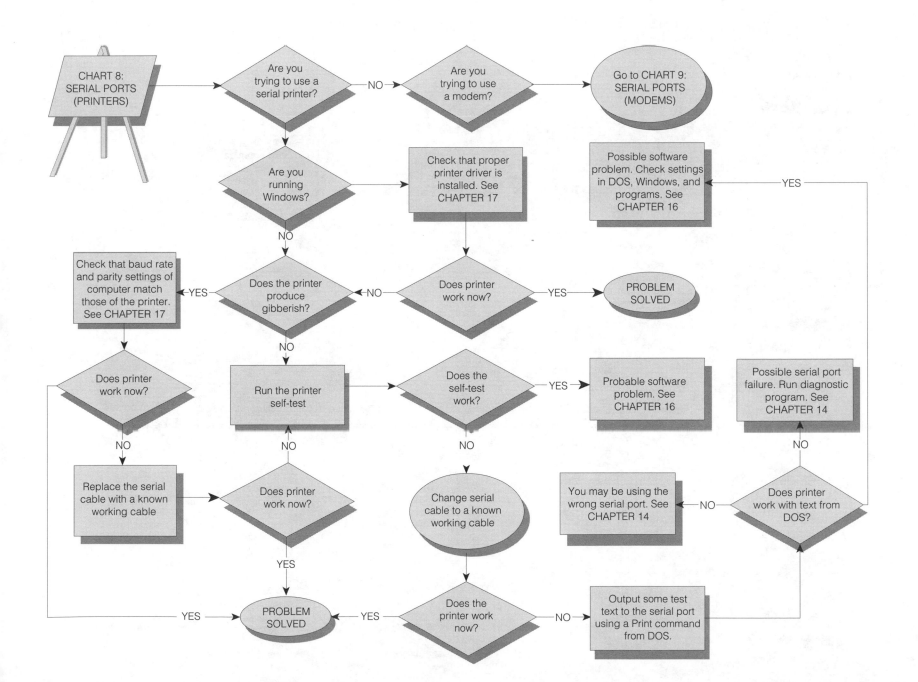

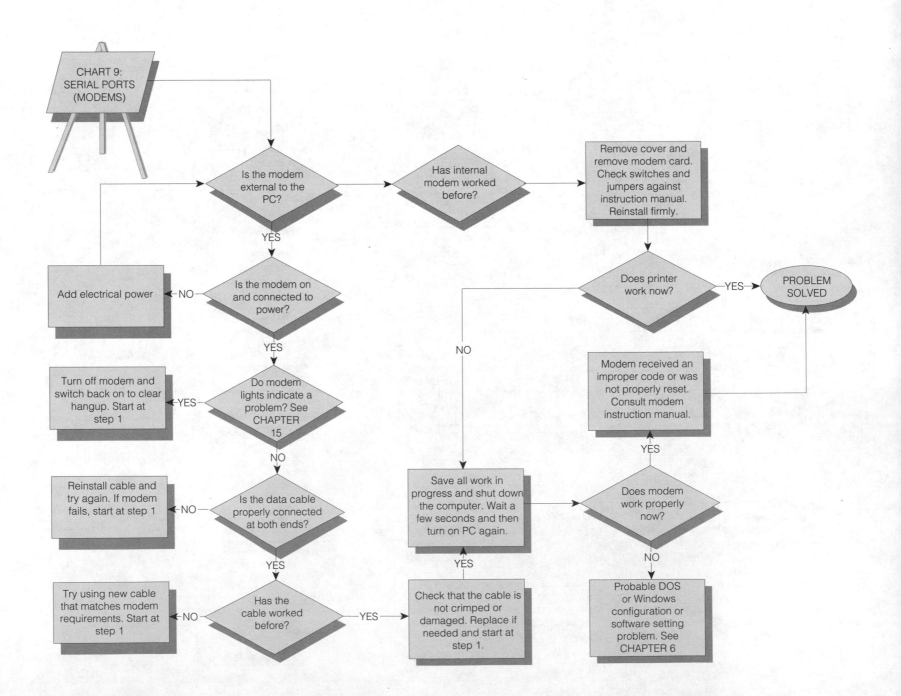

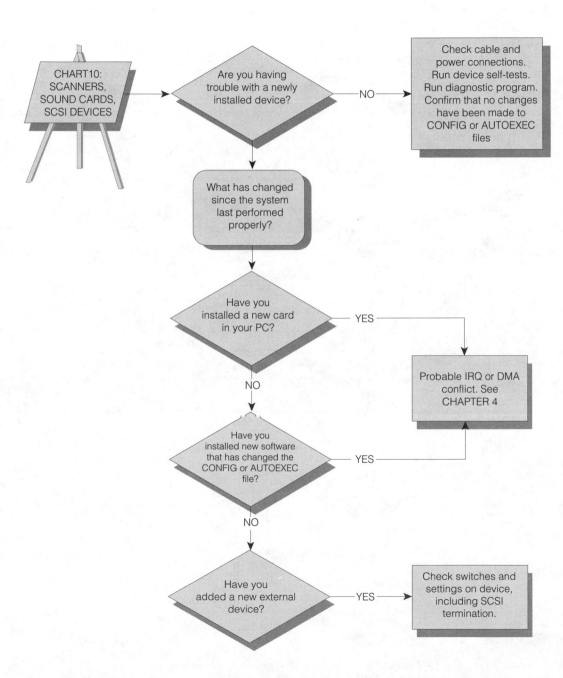

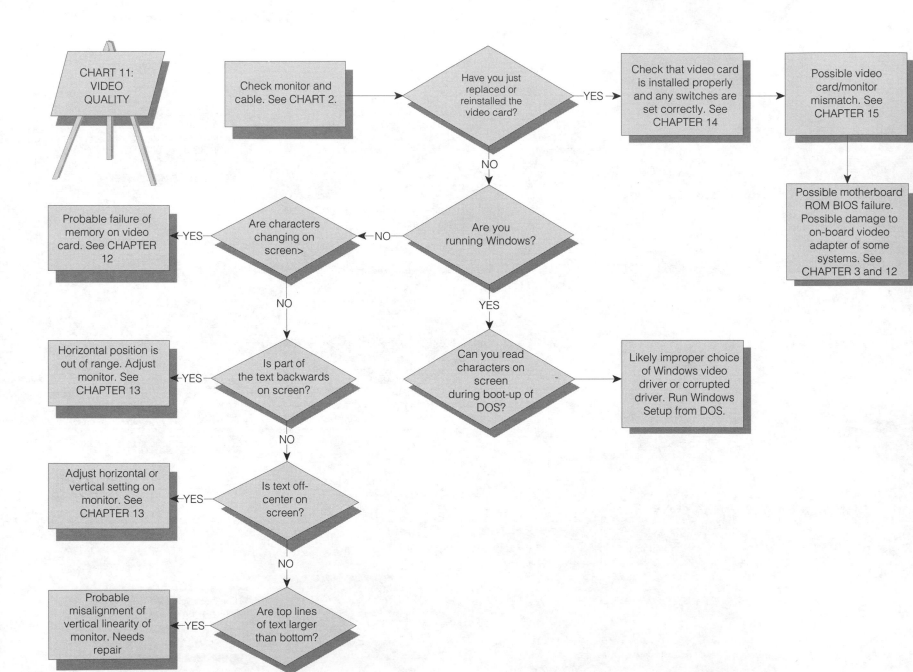

CHART 11: VIDEO QUALITY

Check monitor and cable. See CHART 2.

Have you just replaced or reinstalled the video card? — YES → Check that video card is installed properly and any switches are set correctly. See CHAPTER 14 → Possible video card/monitor mismatch. See CHAPTER 15 → Possible motherboard ROM BIOS failure. Possible damage to on-board viodeo adapter of some systems. See CHAPTER 3 and 12

NO ↓

Are you running Windows? — NO → Are characters changing on screen> — YES → Probable failure of memory on video card. See CHAPTER 12

Are characters changing on screen — NO → Is part of the text backwards on screen? — YES → Horizontal position is out of range. Adjust monitor. See CHAPTER 13

Is part of the text backwards on screen? — NO → Is text off-center on screen? — YES → Adjust horizontal or vertical setting on monitor. See CHAPTER 13

Is text off-center on screen? — NO → Are top lines of text larger than bottom? — YES → Probable misalignment of vertical linearity of monitor. Needs repair

Are you running Windows? — YES → Can you read characters on screen during boot-up of DOS? → Likely improper choice of Windows video driver or corrupted driver. Run Windows Setup from DOS.

CHARTS

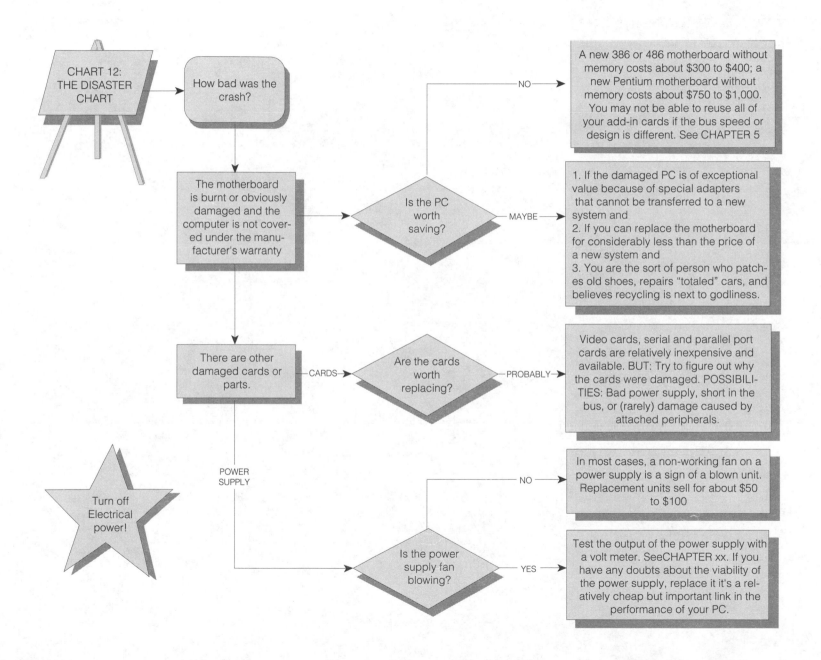

CHART 12:
THE DISASTER
CHART

How bad was the crash?

The motherboard is burnt or obviously damaged and the computer is not covered under the manufacturer's warranty

Is the PC worth saving?

NO → A new 386 or 486 motherboard without memory costs about $300 to $400; a new Pentium motherboard without memory costs about $750 to $1,000. You may not be able to reuse all of your add-in cards if the bus speed or design is different. See CHAPTER 5

MAYBE → 1. If the damaged PC is of exceptional value because of special adapters that cannot be transferred to a new system and
2. If you can replace the motherboard for considerably less than the price of a new system and
3. You are the sort of person who patches old shoes, repairs "totaled" cars, and believes recycling is next to godliness.

There are other damaged cards or parts.

CARDS → Are the cards worth replacing?

PROBABLY → Video cards, serial and parallel port cards are relatively inexpensive and available. BUT: Try to figure out why the cards were damaged. POSSIBILITIES: Bad power supply, short in the bus, or (rarely) damage caused by attached peripherals.

POWER SUPPLY

Turn off Electrical power!

Is the power supply fan blowing?

NO → In most cases, a non-working fan on a power supply is a sign of a blown unit. Replacement units sell for about $50 to $100

YES → Test the output of the power supply with a volt meter. SeeCHAPTER xx. If you have any doubts about the viability of the power supply, replace it it's a relatively cheap but important link in the performance of your PC.

APPENDIX A

Numeric Codes/Text Messages

Motherboard Failures (101–109)

101-System Interrupt Failed

On dinosaur PCs based on 8008 or 8086 CPU chips, this error code indicates a failure of the motherboard. If you're lucky, this could be a transitory problem—related to an unusual condition, cold or warm temperatures that can make electrical contacts shrink away from each other or expand to short out a trace, or loose wires in one of the many connections to the board. The problem may go away the next time you boot the system, or you may be able to fix the problem by removing the cover and reseating connecting cables and pressing down on CPU, memory, BIOS, and other socketed chips.

If you cannot get past a 101 code, though, you will have to replace the motherboard; on true Dinosaurs it may be time to retire the entire system because it is not cost-effective to buy a new motherboard.

If you have a computer based on a later CPU, this error code reports an unusual condition where a failed motherboard or an add-in board is interfering with the interrupt controller chip. Once again, you will have to replace the motherboard if the error seems permanent.

102-System Timer Failed

There is a bad timer chip on the motherboard; you may have to replace the motherboard if the error seems permanent.

103-System Timer Interrupt Failed

The timer chip cannot get the interrupt controller chip to send interrupt zero (the timer interrupt). Once again, if the error persists, the motherboard is bad and must be replaced.

104-Protected Mode Operation Failed

This error code applies to the AT only. The computer must switch into protected mode to count and check the extended memory in an AT, even if there is no extended memory (it must check and see that there are zero kilobytes of extended memory). A bad motherboard can cause a failure to switch into protected mode.

Another possible source of this problem is a failing keyboard which can direct its internal 8042 controller chip to keep sending signals on address line 20 to the processor. The processor needs to use address line 20 as a regular address line when it is in protected mode, but the 8042 chip will not get off the line. Eventually the BIOS ROM sends the error message. A Phoenix BIOS sends a similar error, **Gate A20 failure,** to complain about a continuously busy address line 20.

Check the keyboard switches to see if they are misset, and be sure that the keyboard cable is properly connected. Next, try a new keyboard. If you cannot make the error go away you will have to install a new motherboard.

105-8042 Command Not Accepted. Keyboard Communication Failure

You have a bad 8042 keyboard controller chip, or a bad keyboard. Try another keyboard known to be good. If the new keyboard does not work, this indicates a probable failure of the 8042 chip on the motherboard; if it is socketed, it can be replaced, although you should consider the fact that new keyboards are available for as little as $20. If not, or if the replacement does not fix the problem, the motherboard must be replaced.

106-Post Logic Test Problem

Logic Test Failure

This is a catch-all error code, covering any problem found during the Power-On Self-Test (POST) that doesn't fit into any of the other categories, but is believed to be caused by a bad system motherboard. Other factors, like faulty cards, can also cause this error.

Turn off the computer, pull all the cards out of the machine except the video card, then turn the computer back on. If the error has gone away, try replacing one card at a time and retesting until the bad card is isolated. Don't worry about additional error messages that appear when your cards are removed. If the 106 error message doesn't go away when only the video card is installed, then you'll probably have to replace the motherboard. There is a slight chance, though, that the video card is the culprit. To check this, try installing a known good video card; if the error is still present, the motherboard must be replaced.

107 NMI Test Failed

A "nonmaskable interrupt" test of the microprocessor failed; an NMI is an interrupt that cannot be disabled by another interrupt. If this error persists, the microprocessor must be replaced. Motherboards with sockets for the CPUs allow users to swap the CPU; those that have the microprocessor soldered into place will require a service call or replacement of the motherboard. Be sure to compare the cost of an new motherboard to the price for a single CPU chip.

108 Failed System Timer Test

The timer chip on the motherboard is not working. On some motherboards the chip can be replaced; otherwise the motherboard will have to be replaced.

109 Problem with First 64K RAM

DMA Test Error

This code indicates a problem within the first 64K of RAM, which in the original PC was the entire capacity of the motherboard. You will have to track down and replace the faulty chip or chips, or replace the motherboard.

Some older PCs have the first block of memory soldered to the motherboard and the chips cannot be replaced by the user; more contemporary computers have all memory in sockets and the chips can be easily replaced.

On old 8088-based motherboards, a 109 code indicates than one or more chips in the first row of nine—marked Bank 0—is bad. Locate and replace these nine chips.

If you have an 80286 or 8086-based motherboard, the code indicates that one or more of the chips in the first two rows of nine are bad; locate and replace these 18 chips.

If you have a 386 or an older 486-based motherboard, the 109 code indicates that any of the first 36 memory chips could be bad. Consult your PC's instruction manual to locate and replace the proper chips.

Modern machines with 486 and Pentium processors use SIMMs or DIMMs to hold large blocks of memory; these strips can easily be replaced. One way to isolate the problem is to swap SIMMs from higher blocks (Block 1, 2, or 3) for the lowest range of memory held in Block 0. If the problem goes away you can assume that the SIMM originally in Block 0 is the source of the problem.

PS/2 Error Codes

Consult your instruction manual for more information. Some clone makers also make use of the same code numbers and messages.

110-PS/2 System Board Error. Parity check.

111-PS/2 Memory Adapter error.

112-PS/2 MicroChannel arbitration error, system board.

113-PS/2 MicroChannel arbitration error, system board.

165-PS/2 System options not set.

166-PS/2 MicroChannel adapter timeout error.

199-Configuration not correct. Check Setup.

IBM Error Codes

Codes used by some IBM machines and some clones that have adopted the same set. Consult your instruction manual for more information.

115-System board, CPU error.

118-System board memory error.

119-2.88 MB diskette drive installed but not supported.

120-System board processor, cache error.

121-Unexpected hardware interrupts occurred.

130-POST—no operating system, check diskettes, configuration.

131-Cassette interface test failed, PS/2 system board.

132-DMA extended registers error. Run diagnostics.

133-DMA error. Run diagnostics.

134-DMA error. Run diagnostics.

General Error Codes

161-System Option Not Set, or Possible Bad Battery.

162-System Option Not Set, or Invalid Checksum, or Configuration Incorrect.

163-Time and Date Not Set.

The CMOS memory has forgotten the PC's setup configuration. This can be caused by the failure of backup memory for the CMOS, a short in the motherboard (rare), or an unusual software condition.

Try first to reset the CMOS to its proper settings; consult your instruction manual and your printed backup listing of correct settings (you do have one ready at all times, right?)

The next step is to replace the battery and rerun the Setup program. If replacing the battery does not fix the problem, you may have a faulty power supply. Another possibility is a failed RTC-CMOS chip, which can be replaced if it is in a socket on the motherboard; if it is soldered into place, the motherboard will have to be replaced.

164-Memory Size Error

Another indicator of a problem with your battery-backed CMOS memory, which stores your system configuration.

Run your setup program and retest; if the error is still there, remove the covers of the PC, replace the battery, and run your setup program again.

If you still have the error, turn off the computer, open the case, and press down on all of the memory chips or the SIMM or SIPP chip carriers to make sure they are all firmly seated into their sockets. Then turn on the computer and retest. If the error continues, you may want to remove all of the memory chips or carriers and bring them to a repair shop equipped with a memory testing device; replace any chips that fail the test and reinstall them in the machine.

If no RAM chips fail in the memory tester, the problem may lie in a faulty power supply. Replace it with a known good unit. If this doesn't solve the problem, you may have an unusual and rare problem with your motherboard.

201-Memory Error

For an XT (8008 or 8086 CPU chips), this error code means that something is wrong with the RAM on the motherboard. No further details are available from the computer's self-tests; you'll have to manually test the RAM chips, replacing memory as necessary. A worst-case scenario is a failure of the memory addressing chips on the motherboard, which means that the motherboard must be replaced.

If you have an AT-class machine (80286 and above), this error code means that there are one or more bad memory chips. Turn off the computer, open the case, and press down on all the memory chips. Make sure they are firmly seated in their sockets, then close the case and turn on the computer to retest the memory. If the error is still there, remove all the memory chips and take them to a repair shop equipped with a memory-testing device; replace any chips that fail the test and reinstall them in the machine.

Some machines, including original IBMs and some earlier Compaqs, have at least the first 64K or 256K soldered in place on the motherboard. With such machines, test any socketed RAM first in hopes that you will find the problem there; otherwise, you may have to have to replace the motherboard or (if it makes economic sense) professionally repaired.

202-Memory Address Error Lines 0–15

203-Memory Address Error Lines 16–23

An indication of one or more bad memory chips. Turn off the computer, open the case, and press down on all the memory chips to make sure they are firmly seated in their sockets. Close the case, turn on the computer, and retest it. If the error is still present, remove all the memory chips and take them to a repair shop equipped with a memory testing device; replace any chips that fail the test and reinstall them in the machine.

Some machines, including original IBMs and some earlier Compaqs, have at least the first 64K or 256K soldered in place on the motherboard. With such machines, test any socketed RAM first in hopes that you will find the problem there; otherwise, you may have to replace the motherboard or (if it makes economic sense) professionally repaired.

301-Keyboard Error

Make sure that the keyboard is connected properly; check that the cable is plugged in at both ends and there are no cuts or crimps in the wire. Check to see if any keys are stuck, or if books or other objects are resting on the keyboard. Turn off the computer and turn it back on again. If the error is still there, test the PC with a known good keyboard before you replace a possibly failing unit.

302-System Unit Keylock Is Locked

The key lock on the front of modern PCs may be locked in the off position, grounding out the keyboard to motherboard circuit. Turn the key to the on position. (If you don't use the key lock, store the system keys with your system documentation so that your PC does not become accidentally disabled.)

Or, you may have accidentally disconnected the jumper wires from the keyboard lock to the motherboard while installing a new hard disk or internal card.

Another possibility is a faulty keylock switch, or a keyboard key stuck down.

303-Keyboard or System Unit Error

304-Keyboard or System Unit Error, Keyboard Clockline Error

The keyboard controller chip tests the keyboard during the Power-On Self Test. Error codes 303 and 304 indicate that the keyboard is not sending the right replies to the POST queries. Check for stuck keys. The keyboard cord or the keyboard itself may be bad.

Check also that the XT/AT switch on the bottom of many keyboards is in the proper position.

401-CRT Error #1

501-CRT Error #2

An XT code indicating that a monochrome display adapter (Code 401) or the color graphic adapter (Code 501) is malfunctioning. Check to see that the card is properly seated in its bus slot. If the error continues, replace the card.

601-Disk Error

A broad description of disk problems, it can be caused if the computer is looking for a nonexistent floppy drive. This can occur if Setup contains information about a drive that has been removed from the machine or unplugged. A bad floppy disk can also cause the problem.

More serious causes are failed disk drives or controllers; check first that cards are properly seated in their bus slots and that power and data cables are attached correctly. The devices can also be tested by swapping known good units.

602-Disk Boot Record Error

Another vague but threatening message that can be caused by a number of problems, from a bad floppy disk to a bad floppy disk controller.

Try using a new known good floppy disk boot disk. (Test the boot disk in another PC.)

If you have recently been working inside the computer case, chances are good that you have knocked a cable loose or installed a drive cable improperly.

If the problem continues, the most likely cause is a bad floppy drive; try swapping a known good floppy drive. If the machine still doesn't boot, replace the controller.

1701-Hard Disk Failure

Somewhere between a headache and a nightmare, this is an indication that the hard disk controller has not received the response from the hard disk that it expected.

Possible causes include: (1) the power cable may not be properly connected to the hard disk; (2) the data cables connecting the hard disk to the controller may be installed incorrectly; (3) the drive-select jumper on the hard disk may be set wrong; (4) the hard disk may be deadl or (5) the hard disk controller may be dead. The first three possibilities are more likely if you have recently been working under the cover of the PC.

After you have checked all cables and jumpers, try swapping a known good controller to see if it solves the problem. If nothing else solves the problem, suspect a failed hard drive. Although in most cases it does not pay to repair a hard disk, there are companies that specialize in retrieving data stored on failed drives; you'll find their names advertised in PC magazines.

Note that 1701 is an error message programmed into the BIOS of the hard disk controller card, and therefore can vary from system to system. Some messages are more specific about the source of the problem; consult your hard disk and controller instruction manuals or call the manufacturers for more information.

1780-Disk 0 Failure

1790-Disk 0 Error

1781-Disk 1 Failure

1791-Disk 1 Error

The hard disk controller has not received the response from hard disk 0 or 1 that it expected. Possible causes include:

- the power cord may not be connected to the hard disk,
- the cables connecting the hard disk and its controller may be installed incorrectly,
- the drive select jumper on the hard disk may be set wrong,
- the hard disk may be dead
- the hard disk controller may be dead.

The first three possibilities are more likely if you have recently been working under the covers of the PC.

Check that the controller and power and data cables are properly attached and examine the settings on the controller. Swap a known good controller and see if the problem is solved. If all else fails, suspect a bad hard drive.

Hard disk 0, the first physical hard disk, is always named logical drive C; Hard disk 1, the second physical hard disk, is usually named logical drive D.

Sometimes the hard disk is split into more than one logical drive (in other words, treated by the computer as if there were two or more separate drives, each with its own directory tree and its own physical space.)

Error codes 1780 and 1790 do not refer to any particular logical drive, though, just to the first physical hard disk assembly, whether mounted inside the computer case or attached externally via a cable to a hard disk controller card inside the computer. Similarly, error codes 1781 and 1791 do not refer to any particular logical drive, but merely to the second physical hard disk assembly.

1782-Disk Controller Failure

The hard disk controller may be bad. Some controllers will report this error if hard disk cables are improperly installed. Another possibility arises if you have installed a new card in your PC which has its ROM BIOS at the same memory address area as the hard disk controller card's ROM. Remove the new card to see if the controller will work; if that solves the problem, consult with the maker of the new card to see if you can set the BIOS to a new location.

Text Error Messages

On modern machines, text error messages are more common than the original IBM-style numeric error codes. This appendix lists some sample Phoenix BIOS ROM error messages and American Megatrends, Inc. AMIBIOS messages. Some other makers of BIOS chips use similar error messages.

Because DOS also displays a number of error messages that imply hardware failure, we have included a selection of DOS errors in this appendix as well. Each version of DOS has characteristic error message wording; don't be concerned if your error messages do not match our MS-DOS, AMIBIOS, or Phoenix BIOS examples word for word.

Each entry includes the error message displayed on the screen, followed by a description of the possible causes of the error and our recommendations on how to correct it. We list error messages that start with a variable number—for example, "*xx*=scancode, check keyboard"—under the first word in the message (in this case "Scancode"). Messages that start with a fixed number—for example, "128 not OK, Parity Disabled"—appear at the beginning of the list, in numeric order.

If you have a numeric error message (numbers only, or numbers plus a short phrase), refer to Appendix A, where we have listed the IBM-style numeric ROM error messages. In Appendix C, we catalog computer beep error codes.

128K NOT OK, PARITY DISABLED

The first 128K of RAM has failed the Power-On Self Test. Turn off the computer, then turn it back on and reboot. If the error message repeats, there is a problem with the RAM.

For some reason, the first 128K of RAM is not responding to the CPU. The memory chips may be bad. Remove the first 128K and take the chips to a computer repair shop to be tested. Or, you can try switching the high and low memory on your motherboard. In 8086 and 8088 machines the first bank of memory contains the first 64K (or the first 256K if the computer is using 256K chips), so that switching the first and second banks (or the third and fourth banks) may solve the problem. Read your PC's instruction manual to find out which is the first bank on your particular motherboard.

A bad motherboard can also cause this problem. If the memory chips all test to be good, you will have to replace the motherboard itself.

8042 GATE-A20 ERROR

Usually caused by a bad keyboard. See the discussion of "Gate A20 Failure" errors in Appendix A.

8087 NMI AT *XXXX:XXXX*. TYPE (S)HUT OFF NMI, (R)EBOOT, OTHER KEYS TO CONTINUE

The 8087 math coprocessor chip (an add-on chip in some systems) has generated a nonmaskable interrupt (NMI) error. The 8087 chip must be tested thoroughly and replaced if it has failed. Before you turn off the system, you should attempt to save the data you were working on when you received this error message. Type **S** to shut off the NMI message and you will be able to proceed with your work temporarily; perform an orderly shutdown of your task, and then test the 8087 using a specialized math coprocessor test program.

ACCESS DENIED

You tried to replace a write-protected, read-only, or locked file.

If this error occurs because a particular file is write-protected or read-only, you can use the DOS **ATTRIB** command or a utility to change the file's attributes if you need to.

You may also receive this error if you try to access a directory name as if it were a file.

Check to see if the disk is write-protected. Sometimes the part of the floppy drive responsible for detecting the write-enable notch (on a 5.25-inch disk) or the covered write-enable slide (on a 3.5-inch disk) is broken. If so, the drive will assume all disks are write-protected. Floppy disk drives are not easily or efficiently repaired; replacement units sell for $50 or less.

ADDRESS LINE SHORT!

Notice that exclamation point! This could be a problem with memory chips; reseat the chips and test again. If the problem continues, you can try to replace the memory with new or known good chips, but you're probably dealing with a faulty motherboard here that must be replaced.

ALLOCATION ERROR, SIZE ADJUSTED

CHKDSK compared the apparent physical file size on this disk to the allocated size in the disk directory and the two didn't match. If the physical file seemed too long, CHKDSK truncated the file (cut off the tail end of the cluster chain) to match the size allocated in the directory. If the physical file seemed too short, CHKDSK changed the directory entry to reflect the real file size.

This error can happen to any user on rare occasions. If you get this error more than once in a six-month period, you should be concerned that your hard disk drive is starting to act up. Read the information about the "Hard Disk Read Failure" message in this section and take steps to safeguard your data. Back everything up, run a hard disk diagnostic/repair utility, and keep alert to possible new symptoms.

Next time, use **SCANDISK** (available in DOS 6.2 and later) or PC Tools **DISKFIX** or Norton's **Disk Doctor** rather than **CHKDSK** because they are capable of saving more of your data rather than arbitrarily truncating the file.

ATTEMPTED WRITE-PROTECT VIOLATION

You tried to format a write-protected floppy disk. See "ACCESS DENIED" for a discussion of possible hardware problems with the floppy disk drive that may cause this error.

BAD DMA PORT = xx

The DMA (Direct Memory Access) controller chip has failed the POST. The motherboard will probably have to be replaced because the DMA chip is soldered into place.

BAD OR MISSING COMMAND INTERPRETER

Your computer cannot find the essential **COMMAND.COM** file of DOS.

This message will appear if you are attempting to boot from a floppy disk that does not have system tracks; this is a common occurrence if you leave a data disk in the drive when you turn on your machine.

The error can also be generated if you somehow have altered the correct path to the location of **COMMAND.COM** in the root directory of your hard disk. Another possibility can arise if you are using a "shell" program and have the wrong path listed in **CONFIG.SYS**.

BAD PARTITION TABLE

ERROR READING/WRITING THE PARTITION TABLE

You should only see this error message as part of the process to format the hard disk; it means you ran the FDISK program improperly. Rerun FDISK and then try to format the disk again. If you receive the message again, you may have low-level formatted the drive improperly. Go back to the beginning of the format instructions for your machine listed in Chapter 11. Read the instructions carefully, and try the entire format sequence again. You can also use an automated formatting utility such as Disk Manager.

Another possibility is that your PC has picked up a computer virus. Run a virus checker and follow the program's instructions to isolate and remove the virus if one is found.

If you are certain you have low-level formatted and run **FDISK** and **FORMAT** correctly and tried the other fixes listed in this section, there is a remote possibility of a hard disk controller error. Try substituting a known good controller to see if it fixes the problem.

Otherwise, you most likely have a bad hard disk that will have to be replaced because it is incapable of recording a readable partition table.

nnnK Base Memory

BASE MEMORY SIZE=*nnK*

These are not error messages. They are informational messages from your computer at boot-up, reporting that it has successfully tested *nnn* kilobytes of base (system) memory.

BUS TIMEOUT NMI AT SLOT X

This is an EISA bus error. Run the EISA configuration utility, making certain you have correctly configured the EISA boards in your computer. If that doesn't fix the problem, consult the maker of the card installed in slot X. A faulty card is more likely than a failed motherboard, although both are possible.

C: DRIVE ERROR

D: DRIVE ERROR

The hard disk C:, the first hard disk in your machine, is not set up properly in CMOS. Or, the second hard disk, drive D:, is not set up properly in CMOS.

Run the CMOS Setup program. See also, "Hard Disk Configuration Error."

C: DRIVE FAILURE

"D: DRIVE FAILURE"

See "Hard Disk Failure."

CACHE MEMORY BAD, DO NOT ENABLE CACHE!

The cache memory on the motherboard is malfunctioning; consult your instruction manual to find the location of the cache chips. Reseat the cache memory chips and try again.

This is an AMIBIOS error message; run AMIDiag if it's available. If not, try replacing the cache memory. Though the cache controller chip on the motherboard could also cause this problem, it's not likely; replace the motherboard only as a last resort.

CANNOT CHDIR TO (pathname). TREE PAST THIS POINT NOT PROCESSED

One of your directory files has been trashed.

CANNOT CHDIR TO ROOT

Your root directory file has been trashed.

CANNOT RECOVER (.) ENTRY PROCESSING CONTINUE

The entry (working directory) has been trashed.

CANNOT RECOVER (..) ENTRY PROCESSING CONTINUED

CANNOT RECOVER (..) ENTRY, ENTRY HAS A BAD ATTRIBUTE (OR LINK SIZE)

CHDIR (..) FAILED, TRYING ALTERNATE METHOD

The entry (parent directory) has been trashed.

A third-party utility such as the Norton Utilities should be able to correct any of these problems.

APPENDIX B

Read the information about the "Hard Disk Read Failure" message, too. Directory files should not fail; this is an early warning of possible hard disk troubles. Back up your data, run hard disk diagnostic/repair utilities, and watch for possible new symptoms.

CH-2 TIMER ERROR

The timer chip 2 or interrupt controller logic on the motherboard is malfunctioning. Replace the motherboard.

CMOS BATTERY STATE LOW

Replace the clock/CMOS battery.

CMOS CHECKSUM FAILURE

The checksum error correction method used to check the CMOS setup chip's data integrity shows the CMOS data is corrupted. Replace your clock/CMOS battery and run Setup. If you still receive the error, the CMOS chip must be bad and the motherboard will have to be replaced.

CMOS DISPLAY TYPE MISMATCH

The CMOS chip thinks you have a monochrome video card installed, but you actually have CGA or VGA, or vice versa. Run Setup so that the CMOS information matches the actual video card installed.

CMOS MEMORY SIZE MISMATCH

The CMOS chip thinks you have more or less memory installed than you actually have. Run Setup.

Poorly seated memory chips or SIMM memory modules might not show up when the computer examines its physical memory during the boot process. If you know for sure how much memory is in the computer, and you know for sure that you gave the proper information to the CMOS chip during Setup, better turn off the computer and carefully examine each memory chip and SIMM strip. One is probably loose. See also the error message, "Errors Found; Incorrect Configuration Information, Memory Size Miscompare."

CMOS SYSTEM OPTIONS NOT SET

CMOS TIME & DATE NOT SET

The CMOS setup chip's data is corrupted. Run Setup. You must use the correct Setup program for your computer, not any old setup diskette lying around. Most new computer have Setup in ROM BIOS (you'll see a message such as "Hit <DEL> if you want to run Setup" or "Press <DEL> if you want to run Setup or Diags" whenever your boot the computer. Older computers used customized setup disks, which often malfunctioned if used in a different brand of computer.

COM PORT DOES NOT EXIST

You are attempting to use an invalid COM port. Check all the COM ports in your machine using diagnostic utilities like CheckIt, QA Plus, or Norton Utilities, to make sure your computer recognizes the COM port you are trying to use. For example, you will get this error on a machine with two physical serial ports with both set to COM1 if you try to send printer output through COM2. For more information about serial port setup, see Chapter 16.

CONFIGURATION ERROR FOR SLOT *n*

You have just added an EISA card and haven't configured it, you unplugged your CMOS backup battery, or the battery power is low.

In all cases you must run the ECU (EISA configuration utility). If the battery is bad, replace it first, and then run the ECU.

CONVERT DIRECTORY TO FILE?

Stop! Tell CHKDSK "No" or you will lose the entire directory with all of its files. Instead, use PC Tools DISKFIX, Norton's Disk Doctor, or another disk repair utility to save the directory and its files.

CONVERT LOST CHAINS TO FILES (Y/N)?

ERRORS FOUND, F PARAMETER NOT SPECIFIED. CORRECTIONS WILL NOT BE WRITTEN TO DISK

X LOST CLUSTER(S) FOUND IN Y CHAINS. CONVERT LOST CHAINS TO FILES (Y/N)?

You will receive these error messages if CHKDSK finds lost chains while inspecting a disk; a similar message comes from the more capable **SCANDISK** program that is a part of DOS 6.2 and later. A lost chain is a group of clusters that is not connected to any known file. None of the files in the disk directory contains the chains of clusters; CHKDSK has found a chain in the File Allocation Table (FAT), but has no clue as to its meaning.

In most instances, lost chains are not significant. When you delete a number of files, the delete process may miss a link in the file chain. (Another possible cause: a power dip or surge during an operation may cause the computer to write a tiny blip of trash information to the FAT.)

Run **CHKDSK/F** or answer "Yes" to SCANDISK's query to fix the problem.

You should not receive this sort of error message very often; regular FAT problems are early indicators of hard disk controller or hard disk drive problems.

DATA ERROR READING DRIVE X:

DISK ERROR READING (OR WRITING) DRIVE X:

Most disk drives eventually begin to go out of alignment and cause the generation of one of these errors. Disk utilities such as PC Tools DISKFIX, SpinRite II, Norton's Disk Doctor, QA/WIN, and QA Plus can read the data and allow the rewriting of the data using the current alignment of the read/write heads.

DECREASING AVAILABLE MEMORY

This informational message usually appears together with a memory or CMOS memory configuration error. Read the error message to determine the problem.

DISK BAD

Some part of the hard disk system is bad. As usual, you should check the cheapest possibilities first. Check the hard drive cables inside the computer. If you have recently been working inside the computer, you may have knocked one of the hard drive cables loose.

Next, check to see if the hard disk is spinning. You can feel a slight vibration or hear a low whine when the hard disk is on. Try unplugging the four-wire power connector at the hard disk, then plugging it back in—this makes it easy to distinguish the hard disk noise from other computer sounds.

If the hard disk is not spinning, try plugging in a different power cable from the power supply (all of the four-wire cables are identical). Still no spin: you have a bad hard disk.

We recommend replacing both the hard disk and the hard disk controller together. See Chapter 9.

If the hard disk is spinning, then you may be able to get away with replacing only the hard disk controller, but we still suggest replacing both elements.

DISK BOOT ERROR, REPLACE AND STRIKE KEY TO RETRY

The computer is attempting to boot but cannot find a system disk. Check to make sure there's a known good system disk in Drive A.

You can also receive this message if you have no disk in drive A and are trying to boot from the hard disk if the DOS system files are missing or have been damaged. System tracks can be reinstalled to a hard drive without reformatting the disk. See Chapter 9 for directions on installing hard disks and Chapter 19 to learn how to recover hard disk data.

DISK CONFIGURATION ERROR

HARD DISK CONFIGURATION ERROR

The CMOS chip, which holds the hardware configuration information for 286 through Pentium computers, is reporting an improper code stored within. The BIOS ROM on the system motherboard must read the information inside the CMOS chip each time the computer boots up.

One example of how this sort of an error could be generated is if you have installed a 1.44 MB 3.5-inch floppy drive in an old 286 machine, a computer built before such high-density drives existed. When the old ROM consults the information stored in the CMOS chip, it runs into a code it doesn't recognize.

Older PCs were developed before the wide range of hard disk choices now available, and the ROM may refuse to work with a high-capacity or high-speed design of today.

You may be able to update the ROM on your motherboard to fix such a problem.

DISK DRIVE 0 SEEK FAILURE

DISK DRIVE 1 SEEK FAILURE

Check the A drive cables (Drive 0) or the B drive cables (Drive 1) first. Most manuals say this error is caused by a bad disk drive or controller, but we have most often seen it when the computer looks for a non-existent floppy drive.

If you have an XT machine, check for a bad or unformatted floppy disk. If you have an AT-class or EISA computer, note that the CMOS chip contains setup information about a drive. If you have removed the drive from the machine, or unplugged a data or power cable from the drive, the computer will report this error on bootup.

DISK DRIVE RESET FAILED

The floppy disk controller is unable to reset. Try turning off the power to the machine, waiting a few seconds, and then turning it back on. If the problem is still present, you will have to replace the controller card.

DISK ERROR READING (OR WRITING) FAT

There is a bad sector in the File Attribute Table. Luckily, DOS creates and stores two copies of the FAT and simply starts using the second copy.

This is a warning, though, that the fail-safe mechanism is already in use; you don't have any additional copies of the FAT if this second one goes bad.

If the problem is on a hard drive, use a disk repair utility such as PC Tools DISKFIX or SpinRite II on the drive. If the failing disk is a floppy, just save the data you want to a new floppy and trash this one.

DISK BOOT FAILURE

The boot disk in drive A: is probably bad. Try another boot disk. If that doesn't solve the problem, see "Disk Read Failure—Strike F1 to Retry Boot."

DISK DRIVE FAILURE

DISKETTE DRIVE X FAILURE

See "Disk Drive 0 Seek Failure" or "Disk Drive 1 Seek Failure."

DISK READ FAILURE—STRIKE F1 TO RETRY BOOT

DISKETTE READ FAILURE

Many things can cause this problem, beginning with a simple bad disk. Try several new known good boot disks; test them on another computer equipped with an equivalent drive.

Have you just been working inside the computer? In most cases, this error is caused by knocking loose a cable or by a mistake in installing the data or power cable. See "Floppy Drives" in Chapter 8 for full cable installation directions.

If the problem persists, a bad floppy drive is the most likely cause. Try swapping in a known good replacement floppy drive. If the machine still does not boot, replace the disk controller.

DISPLAY ADAPTER FAILED; USING ALTERNATE

DISPLAY SWITCH NOT SET PROPERLY

The mono/color jumper switch on many AT/286/386/486 motherboards has been set incorrectly. Check your manual for the location and proper setting for this jumper.

DIVIDE OVERFLOW

A numerical error has occurred in the processing of a software program. Reboot the computer; if you receive the error message again, contact the manufacturer of the software.

DMA BUS TIMEOUT

A message from an AMI ROM BIOS indicating that the reply to a signal on a bus. This may be a random or rare occurrence; reboot the PC and continue.

If you receive the message again, it may be a problem with an add-on card, or the DMA chip of your computer. If you have just added a new card, consider it a prime suspect. Turn off the computer, remove the covers and take out one card at a time (starting with the most sophisticated devices) and try running the machine until you have isolated the problem. You may need to install a known good video card in order to continue with your testing. If all of the cards appear to be working properly, the problem may lie with the motherboard. Some diagnostic programs can check on the status of the DMA controller.

DMA ERROR

DMA 1 ERROR

DMA 2 ERROR

The DMA chip has failed. In most cases the motherboard will have to be replaced because the DMA chip is usually soldered in place.

(.)(..) DOES NOT EXIST

(.)(..) ENTRY HAS A BAD ATTRIBUTE (or LINK or SIZE)

The (.) entry (current directory) of the (..) entry (parent directory) has been trashed. Run a disk repair utility such as SpinRite II or PC Tools DISKFIX.

Directory files should not fail in this manner. Read the information about the "Hard Disk Read Failure" error message; this may be an early indication of hard disk troubles. Back up your data, run hard disk diagnostic/repair utilities, and keep alert for possible new problems.

DRIVE NOT READY. ABORT, RETRY, IGNORE, FAIL?

DRIVE X: NOT READY. MAKE SURE A DISK IS INSERTED INTO THE DRIVE AND THE DOOR IS CLOSED

If drive X is a floppy, make sure a disk is properly installed. Try the disk in another drive to be sure it is working properly. If the error continues, the floppy drive cable may be damaged, or the drive's disk sensor may be broken. Try reinstalling the cable and retesting, then installing a new cable before you install a new disk drive.

If it turns out that thé floppy disk itself was damaged, use a disk repair utility like PC Tools DISKFIX or Norton's Disk Doctor to repair the disk.

This same error will occasionally be reported by a hard drive. In this case, a SCSI or ESDI controller may be having trouble talking to your motherboard—it's usually caused by a timing incompatibility. You will often be able to get past the problem by pressing **R** for Retry; the problem will often go away with the second attempt to read. If the hard disk does not respond after the first or second Retry, you should run a disk repair utility such as PC Tools DISKFIX (and make use of your PC Tools Recovery Disk, if you made one.)

EISA CMOS CHECKSUM FAILURE

EISA CMOS INOPERATIONAL

The data in an EISA bus CMOS setup chip is corrupted and has failed a Checksum test, or there has been a read/write error. The CMOS chip holds its information with the aid of a battery, and the first suspect is a low battery. Read the discussions under "Invalid Configuration Information" and "Invalid EISA Configuration Storage."

ERRORS FOUND; DISK X: FAILED INITIALIZATION

The hard disk has not reported back properly on initialization. The possible causes range from a simple CMOS configuration error to a major hardware catastrophe. As always, try to cure the problem with the simplest and cheapest fix. Run your setup program and enter correct hard disk configuration information; if this doesn't work, start checking the hardware.

Possible causes include:

- The power cable may not be connected to the hard disk properly
- The cables connecting the hard disk to its controller may be improperly installed or have come loose
- The drive select jumper on the hard disk may be set wrong
- The hard disk may be dead
- The hard disk controller may be dead

ERRORS FOUND; INCORRECT CONFIGURATION INFORMATION MEMORY SIZE MISCOMPARE

The CMOS memory has probably forgotten the setup information. Run the setup program and retest. If the error is still there, turn off the system, remove the case, replace the CMOS battery, and run the setup program one more time.

If the error continues, turn off the power, remove the case, and press down on all of the memory chips to assure they are firmly seated in their sockets. Then turn on the computer and retest; if the error is still present, remove all of the socketed memory chips and take them to a repair shop equipped with a memory tester.

If none of the RAM chips fail the memory test, or if all of the RAM chips are soldered into place, you may have to replace the motherboard. But first try swapping a known good power supply. If this doesn't work, the motherboard will have to be replaced.

ERRORS ON LIST DEVICE INDICATE THAT IT MAY BE OFF-LINE. PLEASE CHECK IT

An obscure message that refers to the printer; make sure it is not turned off or off-line. Next check the printer cable; it should be tightly plugged into the back of the printer and tightly connected to the printer port on the back of the computer. If you have a parallel printer, refer to Chapter 17 or to "Parallel Ports" in Chapter 16. If you have a serial printer, look at Chapter 17 and "Serial Ports" in Chapter 14.

ERROR WRITING FAT

See "Disk Error Reading (or Writing) FAT"

*nnn*K EXPANDED MEMORY

*nnn*K EXTENDED MEMORY

EXTENDED MEMORY SIZE = *nnnnnn*K

*nnn*K EXTRA MEMORY

These are informational messages. Your computer has successfully tested *nnn* kilobytes of expanded or extended memory.

EXPANSION BOARD DISABLED AT SLOT X

This is an informational message. The board in slot X has been disabled. Use the EISA configuration utility to disable or enable a board.

EXPANSION BOARD NMI AT SLOT X

The board in slot X generated a nonmaskable interrupt error, a significant problem. Remove the card and examine it for obvious problems. Consult your instruction manual for the card, and contact the manufacturer if necessary.

EXPANSION BOARD NOT READY AT SLOT X

The computer does not a see a board in slot X, but it is expecting to find one because of information in the EISA configuration utility.

FAIL-SAFE TIMER NMI

An EISA message that a device has gone wild and is hogging the bus. It may be a random event; try rebooting and retesting.

If you receive the message again, try isolating the offending card. Turn off the computer and pull out one of the cards. If you don't receive the message again, you can hope that the problem lays with the card you have removed. (One other possibility: the DMA controller chip on the motherboard.) If you have just added a new card, consider it a prime suspect. Turn off the computer, remove the covers, take out one card at a time (starting with the most sophisticated devices), and try running the machine until you have isolated the problem. You may need to install a known good video card in order to continue with your testing. If all of the cards appear to be working properly, the problem may lie with the motherboard.

FAIL-SAFE TIMER NMI INOPERATIONAL

The fail-safe timer on your EISA board has failed. You'll probably have to replace the motherboard.

FDD CONTROLLER FAILURE

FDD A IS NOT INSTALLED

FDD B IS NOT INSTALLED

These errors generally point to a bad floppy disk drive and floppy disk drive controller subsystem. Make sure the controller card is seated firmly in the bus slot. Check for missing or misinstalled cables before replacing the controller.

FILE ALLOCATION TABLE BAD

FILE ALLOCATION TABLE BAD DRIVE X:

There is a problem with the FAT. Try repairing the disk with a program like Norton Disk Doctor or PC Tools DISK-FIX. See Chapter 6 for information on data protection and recovery.

FIRST CLUSTER NUMBER IS INVALID, ENTRY TRUNCATED

CHKDSK has effectively deleted the file. It has zero clusters and now exists only as a name in the disk directory. The file is probably lost; you can try running a hard disk diagnostic or repair utility to see if it can be repaired. Next time use a more sophisticated disk diagnostic such as Disk Doctor, DISKFIX, or SCANDISK from DOS.

Truncating should not happen often and may be an indication of controller problems.

FIXED DISK CONFIGURATION ERROR

FIXED DISK CONTROLLER FAILURE

See "Hard Disk Configuration Error."

FIXED DISK FAILURE

See "Hard Disk Failure."

FIXED DISK READ FAILURE

See "Hard Disk Read Failure—Strike F1 to Retry Boot."

GATE A20 FAILURE

SHUTDOWN FAILURE

An error message that can be generated by an AT clone machine. The computer must switch into protected mode to count and check for extended memory in an AT clone (whether or not such memory is actually present). A bad motherboard or keyboard can cause a failure to switch into protected mode.

A faulty keyboard can cause the 8042 keyboard controller chip to keep sending signals to the processor on address line 20. Check the keyboard's switches to make certain they are properly set, and then try a known good keyboard. If that does not solve the problem, you will have to replace the motherboard.

GENERAL FAILURE READING (or WRITING) DRIVE X: (A)BORT, (R)ETRY, (I)GNORE?

Press **I** (Ignore) first. If the drive reads properly after then, run diagnostic tests on it. Some such errors are transient or random and do not cause a problem with corrupted data; in other cases you may have a failing controller or disk drive.

If **I** (Ignore) won't work, then press **A** (Abort) to get out of the error message; start looking for a hardware problem. Turn off the computer and remove the cover. Check the power cable and the ribbon cables to the drive. Make sure the disk controller is firmly seated in the bus.

The error can also be caused by a bad floppy disk. Try several known good floppy disks in the same drive, and run a diagnostics program. See "5.25-inch Floppy Disk Drives" in Chapter 10 for more testing suggestions.

If the problem drive is a hard disk, see Chapter 9 for testing and repair suggestions, and Chapter 19 for data protection and resurrection ideas.

HARD DISK FAILURE

The hard disk controller has not received the response from the hard disk it expected. The controller tries to do a seek on the last head on the last cylinder of the hard disk. If the head can successfully move to that last cylinder, the system BIOS assumes that the hard disk type has been correctly set, the hard disk is working, and all is well.

Sometimes, however, the system BIOS sends out the command but doesn't get the response in the maximum time allotted. So the BIOS gives a "time-out error" and displays the dreaded Hard Disk Failure message.

Possible causes include:

- The power cable may not be properly connected to the hard disk
- The data cables connecting the hard disk and its controller may be misinstalled

- The drive select jumper on the hard disk may be set wrong
- The hard disk may be dead
- The hard disk controller may be dead

In most cases, this message refers to the first hard disk (logical drive C), but it could be either hard drive.

HARD DISK READ FAILURE—STRIKE F1 TO RETRY BOOT

There are many possible causes for this message. If you've recently been working inside the computer, you may have knocked a cable loose or misinstalled one of the hard drive cables. See the installation information in your instruction manual, and in Chapter 9.

If you have not been under the covers recently, try pressing **F1** to see if the computer boots on the second try; if it does, the problem may be a transitory one. Run hard disk diagnostic/correction software such as PC Tools DISKFIX, Norton Disk Doctor, or SpinRite II that will read rewrite the boot segment on the hard disk drive. If the drive is getting slightly out of alignment, such software will often head off more serious and expensive data losses.

If the hard drive won't boot when you press **F1** a second time, you'll have to boot from a floppy disk with the system on it. Type **C:** to look at the hard disk. If you get an "Invalid Drive" message, the computer can't read the C: drive. Run the setup program to make sure the configuration information for the hard disk is correctly stored in the CMOS. Try to boot again. If it still won't boot, your next step depends upon your backup method for data.

If you are fully backed up, reformat the hard disk with system tracks and reload your programs and data. Retry booting. If the system does not work now, the hard disk and controller should be replaced.

If you are not backed up, you may still be able to rescue your data by sending it to a data recovery service. And next time, back up your data.

HAS INVALID CLUSTER, FILE TRUNCATED

CHKDSK has found an invalid cluster—a reference to a nonexistent cluster, for example. It has deleted the tail end of the file, from the bad cluster to the end. The end of the file is probably gone, but a disk repair program like PC Tools DISKFIX can sometimes recover it.

Use DISKFIX, Norton's Disk Doctor, SpinRite II, or the new DOS SCANDISK program regularly, instead of CHKDSK, to look for developing disk problems.

ID INFORMATION MISMATCH FOR SLOT *n*

An EISA message indicating that the computer believes that cards have been moved to a slot different from the one listed in Setup. Run the EISA Configuration Utility (ECU) to tell the computer what cards are where. If you haven't moved any cards, replace the backup battery for the CMOS memory and retest.

INFINITE RETRY ON PARALLEL PRINTER TIMEOUT

PRINTER DEVICE FAILURE

Your printer is not turned on or it is not on-line.

INSUFFICIENT MEMORY

NOT ENOUGH MEMORY

These are software errors generated if you try to use more memory than is physically installed in the machine.

INTERNAL CACHE TEST FAILED—CACHE IS DISABLED

Reboot your computer. If the message recurs, run a diagnostic program to test your motherboard. It is probable that your 486 or Pentium CPU chip is dead.

INTERNAL ERROR

This is a software error. Check your DOS manual for explanation.

INTERNAL STACK OVERFLOW

This is generally a software error. Check your DOS manual for assistance. If the memory persists, check the memory on your motherboard; it could be any kind of memory problem in the bottom 64K of memory.

INTR1 ERROR

INTR2 ERROR

The interrupt controller logic has failed; the motherboard must be replaced.

INVALID BOOT DISKETTE

See "Not a Boot Disk—Strike F1 to Retry Boot."

INVALID CONFIGURATION INFORMATION. PLEASE RUN SETUP PROGRAM

If you have additional error messages displayed along with this one, try to eliminate them. You can then deal with the message listed above.

Begin by running your setup program. Are you certain that you are entering the correct answers to the setup questions? (Check the video adapter information, disk description, keyboard specification, and other options.)

If the problem disappears when you run the setup program and then returns when you turn the computer off and on again, replace the battery and run the setup program again.

Another possible cause of this problem is a bad power supply. After you have replaced the battery for the setup memory and run the tests, try swapping a known good power supply and running setup one more time.

The final possibility—a rare event—would be the failure of the CMOS chip or chips themselves. In most cases the CMOS chips are soldered into place and you will have to replace the motherboard to solve a problem with them.

INVALID CONFIGURATION INFORMATION FOR SLOT X

INVALID EISA CONFIGURATION STORAGE. PLEASE RUN THE CONFIGURATION UTILITY.

Rerun the ECU, making certain that you have entered the correct information for the board and the correct slot number. Double-check your CMOS battery backup. If the battery power level is low, your computer can lose setup information.

I/O CARD PARITY ERROR AT XXXX (R)

I/O CARD PARITY INTERRUPT AT XXXX:XXXX. TYPE (S)HUT OFF NMI, (R)EBOOT, OTHER KEYS TO CONTINUE

I/O CARD NMI AT *XXXX:XXXX*. TYPE (S)HUT OFF NMI, (R)EBOOT, OTHER KEYS TO CONTINUE

I/O CARD PARITY INTERRUPT AT *XXXX:XXXX*. TYPE (S)HUT OFF NMI, (R)EBOOT, OTHER KEYS TO CONTINUE

There is a bad peripheral card. First you must figure out which card is bad. If you absolutely must continue work, press **S** to shut off the nonmaskable interrupt (NMI) and save the file. The message will go away, but you haven't fixed the source of the problem.

When you are ready, turn off the computer, pull out all the cards except the video adapter, and reboot. If the error message does not reappear, reinstall the cards one at a time—turning the computer off as you install each card—and test until you find the bad card. If the error remains with only the video card installed, you will have to replace the video card, then retest. The last possibility to check is a bad motherboard; before you do this, though, try installing a known good basic video card to eliminate that device as the source of the problem.

KEYBOARD BAD

The keyboard has failed the POST. Make certain the keyboard is properly connected to the PC. Turn off the computer, then turn it back on and reboot. If the message persists, you have a bad keyboard which must be replaced.

KEYBOARD CLOCK LINE FAILURE

KEYBOARD DATA LINE FAILURE

KEYBOARD CONTROLLER FAILURE

KEYBOARD STUCK KEY FAILURE

The keyboard controller chip tests the keyboard during POST. These messages indicate that the keyboard is not sending the right replies to the controller's POST signals. Either the keyboard cable or the keyboard itself is bad. Check for stuck keys. Check the AT/XT switch on the bottom of the keyboard and make sure it is in the proper position for your machine. Consult your instruction manual for information.

KEYBOARD ERROR

If your computer has an American Megatrends, Inc. AMIBIOS, the keyboard may be incompatible with the BIOS ROM. American Megatrends suggests that the keyboard may have a timing problem. One way to attempt to get around this problem is to set the keyboard in Standard CMOS Setup to **Not Installed** to skip the keyboard POST test.

LAST BOOT INCOMPLETE

This message is generated by a malfunctioning chip in the Intel 82335 chip set, which is used in some older AT clone motherboards. These chips have extended features that need to be set in the extended CMOS. Run your Intel 82335 setup program, with particular attention to the memory interweaving and EMS configuration parameters. Consult your PC's instruction manual for more details.

MEMORY ADDRESS LINE FAILURE AT *XXXX:XXXX*, READ HEX VALUE *XXXX*, EXPECTING *XXXX*.

The good news is that this error message is telling you a great deal of information about where it found a problem with your PC's bus; the bad news is that it is nearly impossible to repair such a problem. If the message recurs, the motherboard will have to be replaced.

MEMORY ALLOCATION ERROR. CANNOT LOAD DOS, SYSTEM HALTED

This is a software error. You may have a trashed DOS boot disk, or damaged boot files on your hard drive. Try booting from a new floppy drive. Run **SYS** to copy **COMMAND.COM** and boot tracks to the hard drive.

MEMORY DATA LINE FAILURE AT *XXXX:XXXX*, READ *XXXX*, EXPECTING *XXXX*"

MEMORY FAILURE AT *XXXX:XXXX*, READ *XXXX*, EXPECTING *XXXX*

MEMORY DOUBLE WORD LOGIC FAILURE AT (*hex value*), READ (*hex value*), EXPECTING (*hex value*)

This problem is caused by a bad or slow memory chip. The hexadecimal number in the first line of this error message tells you what row of memory chips contains the defective chip or chips. The message provides enough information to locate the specific malfunctioning chip.

You or a computer repair technician can figure out which chip is the problem by converting the hexadecimal number, or whole banks of memory can be pulled out and checked in a memory tester. (We suggest that memory be checked at 20 nanoseconds faster than the minimum speed recommended for your motherboard.)

Some diagnostic software programs, including CheckIt, can figure out the chip for you. Trust us, it's a whole lot easier than trying to figure out the chip's address manually.

Here's how to convert the hexadecimal address to a particular memory address in K (kilobytes) manually. In this example, we will use the hexadecimal address 1EAF:45FF.

APPENDIX B

1. Shift the segment—the first half of the number (before the colon) one place to the left. For example: 1EAF becomes 1EAF0 hexadecimal.
2. Add the offset—the second part of the number (after the colon) to the shifted number. Now remember, you are adding hexadecimal numbers, which are base 16 and used 0 through 9 plus A through F. You can use a calculator which handles scientific math; there is also a capable computer calculator that is a part of Windows that can do the work for you.

For example:

    1EAF0 hexadecimal
    +45FF hexadecimal
    230EF hexadecimal

The result is the address of the bad chip. The first numeral (number 2 in our example) tells you what bank of memory is the problem.

Here is a list of hex addresses and the associated memory chips:

    0xxxx = error in the first 64K of memory
    1xxxx = error in the second 64K of memory
    2xxxx = error in the third 64K of memory
    3xxxx = error in the fourth 64K of memory
    4xxxx = error in the fifth 64K of memory
    5xxxx = error in the sixth 64K of memory
    6xxxx = error in the seventh 64K of memory
    7xxxx = error in the eighth 64K of memory
    8xxxx = error in the ninth 64K of memory
    9xxxx = error in the tenth 64K of memory

Thus, in our example, the problem is in the third 64K of memory.

3. Locate the correct row of chips. When computers were built with nothing but 64K chips, this step was easy. Each bank of nine 64K chips corresponded to one segment. Now that 256K, 1 MB, and 4 MB are popular, you'll have to do a bit of figuring.

   Each 256K chip contains four 64K segments (64 x 4 = 256K)

   - A simple XT clone equipped with 640K of system memory may have two rows of 256K chips, each with four segments of 64K, and two banks of 64K for the final two segments.

   - A more modern 386 or better computer loaded with memory may have eight or more banks of 1 MB or 4 MB chips on the motherboard. The entire 640K (ten 64K segments) is in a single bank of 1 MB chips. Each motherboard maker handles memory mounting slightly differently; read your computer's instruction manual to determine which bank is the one with the problem.

4. Once you have located the correct row of chips, you can locate the specific bad chip using the hex data values in the second line of the error message. You do this by comparing the data the computer attempted to store with the hexadecimal number it read back from memory. The difference between the two numbers points to the bad chip.

For Example: If you have the error message, Memory Data Line Failure at Hex Value 1EAF:45FF, Read C3B6, Expecting B3B6, subtract the smaller number from the larger number:

C3B6
-B3B6
1000 (a hexadecimal number that must be converted to binary)

1000H (1000 hexadecimal) = $xxxx\ xxxx\ xxxx\ xxxx$ with each hexadecimal digit equal to a group of four binary digits. So 1000H is 0001 0000 0000 0000 in binary—the number that points to the bad chip.

Each digit of the 16-digit binary number corresponds to a particular chip. Counting from the right to left, we learn that the problem lies in the thirteenth (out of sixteen) chip in the row of RAM you have identified.

That was simple, right?

Once you have determined the bad chip, you must now physically locate it on the motherboard or the memory expansion card, if used.

Sometimes you will be lucky—some motherboard makers screen the bit numbers on the board. If so, you will see 0, 1, 2, 3, 4, 5, 6, 7, P. The next bank will be numbered 8, 9, 10, 11, 12, 13, 14, 15, and P. Other manufacturers use hex numbers. (P stands for "Parity," which is used on most older PCs as part of an error-checking algorithm; many modern PCs have dispensed with parity-checking.)

However, many board makers do not bother to print this information on the board; consult your instruction manual for assistance here.

MEMORY HIGH ADDRESS LINE FAILURE AT *XXXX:XXXX*. READ *XXXX*, EXPECTING *XXXX*.

MEMORY ODD/EVEN LOGIC FAILURE AT (*hex value*), READ (*hex value*), EXPECTING (*hex value*)

If either of these is a recurring error, your motherboard has failed and must be replaced.

MEMORY PARITY ERROR AT (*hex value*)

You have a bad memory chip. It could be either a data-storing memory chip or one of the memory chips dedicated to parity checking on most motherboards. Read the directions for the error, "Memory Data Line Failure at *xxxx:xxxx*, Read *xxxx*, Expecting *xxxx* remembering that the problem could be either the data-storing chip or the parity chip in the suspect bank of memory chips.

MEMORY PARITY NMI AT *XXXX:XXXX*. TYPE (S)HUT OFF NMI, (R)EBOOT, OTHER KEYS TO CONTINUE

MEMORY PARITY INTERRUPT AT *XXXX:XXXX*. TYPE (S)HUT OFF NMI, (R)EBOOT, OTHER KEYS TO CONTINUE

This error is most often caused by a bad memory chip, and that is the first solution that should be explored.

First, press **S** to shut off the NMI. Then save the file you have been working on. The error message will go away, but the error has not been fixed.

The bad memory chip will almost certainly *not* be at the address mentioned in the error message. You may choose to take all memory chips (from the motherboard and any memory expansion cards) to the repair shop for checking in a memory tester. You can also bring the entire machine to the shop for testing. We suggest that memory chips be tested at 20 nanoseconds faster than the minimum speed recommended for your motherboard.

If none of the memory chips test as being bad, there may be another unusual event causing the display of this message. We know of one computer which routinely displayed this message when it was formatting a disk; our guess is that the floppy disk controller card was drawing more power than expected, bringing down the power for the memory chips.

MEMORY TESTS TERMINATED BY KEYSTROKE

You are allowed to halt the initial POST memory tests on most computers by pressing the space bar during booting. When you do, the computer displays this message and proceeds with the rest of the POST routine.

MEMORY WRITE/READ FAILURE AT (*hex value*), READ (*hex value*), EXPECTING (*hex value*)

You have a bad memory chip. Read the directions for the error, "Memory Data Line Failure at *XXXX:XXXX*, Read *XXXX*, EXPECTING *XXXX*."

8087 NMI AT *XXXX:XXXX*. TYPE (S)HUT OFF NMI, (R)EBOOT, OTHER KEYS TO CONTINUE

The 8087 math coprocessor chip used with some 8088 CPUs has generated an NMI error. This means there is some problem with the 8087. Press **S** to turn off the NMI message and you will be able to proceed with your work for the moment. Do an orderly shut down of the system, saving your work.

Then test the 8087 thoroughly using a diagnostics program; replace it if it's bad.

NO BOOT DEVICE AVAILABLE—STRIKE F1 TO RETRY BOOT

The computer is unable to boot, a problem that may have many causes.

Many machines are set up to examine the contents of drive A first, looking for a bootable system disk. If a disk is found but the machine cannot find system tracks on that disk, this error message is displayed. If no disk is found in the A drive, the PC will try to boot from the C drive (the hard disk). If there is no hard disk, or the hard disk won't boot, then the ROM BIOS displays this message.

If you have recently been working inside the computer, you may have knocked a cable loose or misinstalled one of the hard or floppy drive cables. See Chapter XX (floppy disks) and Chapter XX (hard disks) for cable installation directions.

Make sure you don't have an unbootable disk in your A drive. If you're sure the disk in the floppy drive is bootable, try some other disks. If you still can't get the computer to boot, test the disks in another computer with a floppy drive of the same size and capacity.

What happens if you don't have a disk in the floppy drive, and you still get this error? When the computer sees no disk in drive A, it tries to boot from the hard disk. You can watch the machine turn on the red light in the floppy drive, look for a floppy, then turn off that light and turn on the indicator light associated with the hard drive.

Try pressing **F1** to see if the computer will boot on the second try. If it does, great. But you still haven't solved the mystery of why it failed the first time. Run hard disk diagnostic/correction software such as SpinRite II, Norton's Disk Doctor, or PC Tools DISKFIX. Any of these programs will read and rewrite the boot segment on the hard disk drive. If the drive is getting slightly out of alignment, using this software will often head off more expensive data losses.

If the hard drive won't boot even when you press **F1** several times to get the computer to retry the hard disk, you'll need to boot from a floppy disk with the DOS system files on it. If this works, you may be able to run a hard disk diagnostic/repair software program.

If you receive an "Invalid Drive" message, this is an indication that the computer can't read drive C. Run the setup program to make certain the configuration information for the hard disk is correctly stored in the CMOS. Try to boot again; if your PC still will not boot, your next step depends on whether you have made a recent backup of your data.

If you are fully backed up, reformat the hard disk with system tracks and reload your programs and data. Retry booting. If the system does not work now, the hard disk and controller should be replaced.

If you are not backed up, you may still be able to rescue your data by sending it to a data recovery service. And next time, back up your data.

NO FAIL SAFE TIMER NMI

The fail-safe timer on your EISA board has failed. Run a diagnostics program such as QA Plus or QA/WIN to check your system board. If the error is real, you will have to replace your motherboard.

NO SCAN CODE FROM THE KEYBOARD

This message is generated only by certain XT class machines, and indicates that the keyboard is locked out or not connected to the computer.

NO SOFTWARE PORT NMI

Run a diagnostics program such as QA Plus or QA/WIN to check your system board. If the error is real, you will have to replace your motherboard.

NON-DOS DISK ERROR READING (OR WRITING) DRIVE X:

The boot track on this disk is dead, so DOS is unable to recognize the disk. Disk repair software may be able to fix the problem. If not, you may have to boot from a floppy disk and either use SYS to add tracks to the hard drive or remove all data to a backup medium and then reformat the hard disk with system tracks.

NON-SYSTEM DISK OR DISK ERROR. REPLACE AND STRIKE ANY KEY WHEN READY

NON-SYSTEM DISK OR DISK ERROR. PRESS A KEY TO CONTINUE.

Normally these errors are caused by trying to boot from a nonsystem (nonbootable) floppy disk. If you receive one of these messages when trying to access your hard disk, use SYS to reinstall **COMMAND.COM** and system tracks to your hard disk.

NO TIMER TICK INTERRUPT

The timer chip cannot get the interrupt controller chip to send interrupt 0 (the timer interrupt). This means that you have a bad motherboard; it will have to be replaced.

NOT A BOOT DISK—STRIKE F1 TO RETRY BOOT

The computer is unable to boot from the floppy drive. Make sure there's a bootable disk in your A Drive. If you're sure the disk is bootable, try a couple other disks. Test all these boot disks in another computer equipped with a floppy disk drive of the same size and capacity.

   If the disks test as being good, the error may be caused by the floppy disk controller or by a bad floppy drive. Had you had similar problems in the past? For instance, have you occasionally received data error messages inside DOS—messages that pointed to read/write problems with this drive? If so, try replacing the drive first. The second step would be to replace the controller.

NOT READY READING DRIVE X:

NOT READY ERROR READING (OR WRITING) DRIVE X:

The drive door is probably not closed. If the error message persists after you close the door, try a couple of different known good disks. If that doesn't work, you might have a bad door-closed sensor on the drive; the drive itself can also fail.

If the disk is the problem, not the drive, or if drive X: is a hard drive, try a disk repair software program.

According to the DOS manual, you can also receive the "writing to" version of this error if the printer is off-line or turned off, and the computer is attempting to send data.

(hex value) OPTIONAL ROM BAD CHECKSUM = (hex value)

The ROM on an optional expansion card has been corrupted or destroyed. Likely candidates are ROM on the hard disk controller or a video card.

Check the instruction manual for the ROM location for your expansion card. Not all ROM locations for particular types of cards are standardized, and technicians or users can also reassign memory addresses to avoid conflict. The best defense is to keep a record of all assignments for all cards as they are installed; a good diagnostic program can also examine your machine and give you a listing of what is where in memory.

Typical assignments for equipment include:

- C800, CA00 and D800 for hard disk controllers
- C000 is often used for video cards
- CE00 is used for high-density floppy controllers
- DC00 is often taken by network cards

If the ROMs on your computer have other addresses and you cannot determine their location using a diagnostic program, you may have to experiment. Turn off the computer, remove the cover, and take out all cards except the video card. If you still have the error when the power is turned back on, the problem must be with the video card. If the error is not displayed, turn off the computer and reinstall and test the other cards one by one until you find the culprit.

OUT OF ENVIRONMENT SPACE

This is a software error related to a setting in your **CONFIG.SYS** file. See your DOS manual.

PARITY CHECK 1

PARITY CHECK 2

Check 1 is an indication of a parity error on an expansion card. Hard disk controller cards, memory expansion cards, and some other cards have memory on them, complete with parity checking for error detection. Turn off the computer, remove the cover, and take out all cards except the video card. If you still have the error when the power is turned back on, the problem must be with the video card. If the error is not displayed, turn off the computer and reinstall and test the other cards one by one until you find the culprit.

Check 2 indicates a problem with one or more of the memory chips on the motherboard itself. You can remove the memory chips and take them to a computer shop for testing, or bring the entire unit to the shop. In some cases, the memory is okay, but the motherboard has failed and must be replaced.

POINTER DEVICE FAILURE

Your mouse, trackball, pen, or other device attached to the PS/2-style mouse port on the motherboard is not responding properly to the queries of the computer. Check to see if it is properly attached. If the error continues, run the test program that comes with many peripheral devices.

PROBABLE NON-DOS DISK. CONTINUE (Y/N)?

The boot track on the disk has been erased or corrupted. This can happen as the result of an electrical spike or as the result of a misbehaving disk controller and occasionally by a poorly designed piece of software. And sometimes the culprit is a computer virus.

First check for viruses using an antivirus program on a floppy disk. Then try reinstalling the system tracks with the SYS command from DOS. Finally, you can try a disk repair utility like SpinRite II, PC Tools DISKFIX, or Norton's Disk Doctor. When all else fails, you may have to back up your data and reformat the disk. If you are unable to perform a backup, you can send the disk to a data recovery service.

PROCESSING CANNOT CONTINUE

You get this error when you try to run **CHKDSK** or other DOS utilities without enough memory; add more RAM.

RAM BAD

The RAM failed the POST. You will have to test the RAM and replace the bad chips. You can remove chips and bring them to a computer repair shop for testing, or bring the entire unit in for testing. This error is usually generated by the failure of one or two chips. Sometimes, though, the circuitry on the motherboard itself has failed and the motherboard must be replaced.

READ FAULT ERROR READING DRIVE X:

SECTOR NOT FOUND ERROR READING (OR WRITING) DRIVE X:

SEEK ERROR READING (OR WRITING) DRIVE X:

UNRECOVERABLE READ (OR WRITE) ERROR ON DRIVE X:

Double check your floppy disk? Is it installed in the drive correctly? It could be upside down, or not fully installed. Type **R** for retry.

If the error recurs, there is at least one bad spot on the floppy or hard disk. Run a disk repair utility.

This is not necessarily a significant error. All drives eventually go out of alignment and produce this error. Luckily, DOS gives this early warning. Disk utilities will cause the drive to rewrite the data, often moving it to a better-quality spot on the disk. Once rewritten, the data is in alignment with the aging drive's alignment, so you should have no more trouble with this particular disk until a bit further down the road.

REAL TIME CLOCK FAILURE

The real time clock or the battery that supports it has failed. See "Time-Of-Day Not Set Up—Please Run Setup Program."

RESUME=`F1' KEY

An error has occurred; press the **F1** key to continue processing.

ROM

If you're using an XT, this message means that the system ROM BIOS located on the motherboard has been damaged and you will have to replace it if possible.

ROM BAD SUM=

ROM BAD CHECKSUM=

ROM ERROR

A message from XT systems indicating that the BIOS ROM on the motherboard could not be read and must be replaced if possible. In some cases, the motherboard itself is damaged and must be replaced.

XX=SCANCODE, CHECK KEYBOARD

An erroneous scancode was received from the keyboard. A stuck key or a bad keyboard connector can send a bad scancode from the keyboard to the CPU. Try swapping in another known good keyboard. If the keyboard has an XT/AT switch, be sure the switch is properly set.

SHARING VIOLATION READING DRIVE X:

This is a software error; check your DOS manual.

nnnK STANDARD MEMORY

This is an informational message indicating that your computer has successfully tested *nnn* kilobytes of standard memory.

STRIKE THE F1 KEY TO CONTINUE

This message is an indication that an error was found during the POST. The computer will display an error message describing the problem. You can try to boot the system despite this error. Correct the problem (for example, a non-booting disk in drive A), then press **F1** to try booting the system.

STUCK KEY SCANCODE=XX

A key is stuck on the keyboard. Locate and repair the stuck key; if the stuck key is not obvious, try pressing each of the keys in turn. The stuck key will feel different when you press it.

TARGET DISK IS WRITE PROTECTED

This error message should appear only if you are attempting to **DISKCOPY** to a write-protected floppy disk. Occasionally, the part of the floppy drive responsible for detecting the write-enable notch (on a 5.25-inch disk) or the covered write-enable slide (on a 3.5-inch disk) is broken. If so, the disk will assume all disks are write-protected. It is not easy and rarely cost-effective to repair a floppy disk drive, which retail for about $50.

TIMER OR INTERRUPT CONTROLLER BAD

TIMER CHIP COUNTER 2 FAILED

Either time timer chip of the interrupt controller chip has failed. Both are soldered to the motherboard; therefore, the motherboard must be replaced.

TIME-OF-DAY CLOCK STOPPED

TIME-OF-DAY NOT SET UP—PLEASE RUN SETUP PROGRAM

Run the setup program that came with your computer or is resident in the ROM BIOS. If this error persists, try replacing the batteries that power the CMOS chip whenever the computer is turned off; then run the setup program again.

If the error message still appears, the error is probably caused by the power supply. Replace the power supply and run the setup program again. In rare situations this may be caused by a failing motherboard.

TRACK 0 BAD—DISK UNUSABLE

You may receive this error when you try to format a 1.2 MB floppy disk in a 360K drive, or the other way around.

Another possibility is that the floppy disk actually has a damaged track 0; throw away the floppy disk and use another one.

If you get this error on a hard drive, the news is worse: it means that the hard drive has gone bad and must be replaced.

If you do not have a backup for the data on the disk, you can send the disk to a data recovery service.

UNEXPECTED HW INTERRUPT *XXH* AT *XXXX:XXXX*. TYPE (R)EBOOT, OTHER KEYS TO CONTINUE

UNEXPECTED SW INTERRUPT *XXH* AT *XXXX:XXXX*. TYPE (R)EBOOT, OTHER KEYS TO CONTINUE

This is a Phoenix BIOS error that can be caused by many hardware or software problems.

The message means an interrupt is being sent on an interrupt line which has not been properly initialized.

For example, a poorly designed card that is installed without its accompanying software driver and one with malfunctioning driver software can cause this error message.

UNEXPECTED INTERRUPT IN PROTECTED MODE

This problem can be caused by a bad expansion card or a failed motherboard. Bad VGA or network cards can produce this error, since both can use the NMI line to communicate with the CPU. In either case, though, the card is sending interrupts during bootup, a time when it should not be using the NMI circuit.

Turn off the computer, pull out all the cards except the video adapter, and reboot. If the error message does not reappear, reinstall the cards one at a time—turning the computer off as you install each card—and test until you find the bad card. If the error remains with only the video card installed, you will have to replace the video card, then retest. The last possibility to check is a bad motherboard; before you do this, though, try installing a known good basic video card to eliminate that device as the source of the problem.

UNLOCK SYSTEM UNIT KEYLOCK

This message appears when you lock the key on the front of the computer that grounds out the keyboard to motherboard circuit. Unlock the keylock and reboot the computer.

UNRECOVERABLE ERROR IN DIRECTORY. CONVERT DIRECTORY TO FILE (Y/N)?

WAIT! Press **N**(No). If you press **Y**(Yes), you will lose everything in this directory and in all the subdirectories within it. Sometimes a disk repair utility will repair the error.

WRITE FAULT ERROR WRITING DRIVE X:

WRITE PROTECT ERROR WRITING DRIVE X:

The disk drive door may be open.

Occasionally, the part of the floppy drive responsible for detecting the write-enable notch (on a 5.25-inch disk) or the covered write-enable slide (on a 3.5-inch disk) is broken. If so, the disk will assume that all disks are write-protected. It is not easy and rarely cost-effective to repair a floppy disk drive, which retail for less than $50.

APPENDIX C
Beep Error Codes

How do you know what is going on inside your computer if the video monitor does not work? One answer is a series of sound codes that are built into the ROM BIOS of the PC.

There is no official standard for the use of the codes, but over the years the dominance of two BIOS makers—Phoenix and American Megatrends, Inc.—has created a common group of codes for PC clones; IBM's own BIOS is also widely used, and is close to AMI and Phoenix in its structure and syntax.

If you don't know the brand of your BIOS, check your computer's instruction manual or call its manufacturer. Or, you can take off the covers and examine the motherboard. The ROM BIOS consists of one or several chips near the CPU, usually marked with "AMI" or "Phoenix"; you may also see other chips identified as BIOS. (Ignore other ROMs on video cards, disk controllers, or other devices.)

AMI Codes

Computers using the AMI BIOS use an uninterrupted series of beeps to signal a *fatal error* (an error that halts the boot process before the video screen is usable). These AMIBIOS codes are listed in numeric order below. Count the number of beeps you hear—turn the machine off and on again to recount the beeps if necessary—then look up the error code in the list.

One Beep: DRAM REFRESH FAILURE

Many XT and some AT-class computers beep once or twice when booting up normally. If your computer shows standard information on the screen, you do not have a problem; if there is anything wrong, the computer will display a screen error message.

If you have no video display, check the simple things first. Is the video monitor plugged in and turned on? Did the video cable from monitor to computer become disconnected?

This single beep tells you there is fault memory refresh circuitry on your motherboard. The timer chip told the DMA chip to go into RAM and refresh the memory. The DMA chip did this, but the refresh process failed. The possible causes of this malfunction are: (1) bad memory chips, (2) a bad DMA chip, (3) bad memory addressing chips on the motherboard.

Turn off the computer. Reseat the memory chips or the SIMMs, then retest the computer. Since the DMA chip is almost always soldered to the motherboard—as are the memory address logic chips—any problems with these chips almost always requires replacement of the motherboard.

Two Beeps: PARITY ERROR/PARITY CIRCUIT FAILURE

Many XT and some AT-class computers beep once or twice when booting up normally. If your computer shows standard information on the screen, you do not have a problem; if there is anything wrong, the computer will display a screen error message.

If there is no video, check first that your monitor is turned on and plugged in properly. The double beep may be there to tell you of parity error in the first 64K of memory. (This is the same as the Phoenix BIOS error 1-4-2, described below.)

If you're lucky, a memory chip has simply worked itself loose on the motherboard. Reseat the chips or the SIMM memory strips; if that doesn't work, follow the directions for Phoenix error 1-3-3 below.

Three Beeps: BASE 64K MEMORY FAILURE

This error can be caused by bad memory chips or by a bad motherboard. Try reseating the memory chips or SIMM memory strips. If that doesn't work, follow the directions for Phoenix error 1-3-3 below.

Four Beeps: SYSTEM TIMER NOT OPERATIONAL

This code may indicate a malfunctioning timer 1, or failure in the first 64K of RAM memory. Turn off the computer, reseat any loose memory chips, and retest. If the beep error persists, you can try testing the motherboard with known good memory from a comparable computer. Replace the first 64K of memory (the single row of chips in an XT clone, two rows of chips in a 286-based computer, and from one to four rows of chips in a 386 or 486 computer). If you still receive the four-beep error message, replace the motherboard.

Five Beeps: PROCESSOR FAILURE

The CPU chip appears dead. Turn off the computer, reseat the memory chips, and then retest. If the error continues, you can consider replacing the CPU, although that may not be cost efficient—it may make more sense to replace the motherboard. If you transplant a CPU from another machine, it should ideally be the same speed as your old chip.

Six Beeps: 8042 KEYBOARD CONTROLLER/GATE A20 FAILURE

This error, like Phoenix 4-2-3, can be caused either by keyboard problems or a bad motherboard. A rare handful of keyboards have a fuse; check to see if it needs replacement or resetting. Try a different known good keyboard to see if it solves the problem.

If the keyboard seems okay, AMI recommends reseating the keyboard controller chip if it is not soldered to the motherboard. If it still beeps, replace the keyboard controller if possible. The last resort is a new motherboard.

Seven Beeps: PROCESSOR EXCEPTION INTERRUPT ERROR/VIRTUAL MODE EXCEPTION ERROR

The CPU is dead. Turn off the computer, reseat the memory chips, then retest. This probably won't help, but if it does, it's a lot cheaper than replacing the whole motherboard. If the error continues, you can consider replacing the CPU, although that may not be cost-efficient—it may make more sense to replace the motherboard. If you transplant a CPU from another machine, it should ideally be the same speed as your old chip.

Eight Beeps: DISPLAY MEMORY READ/WRITE ERROR

The video card is missing or bad. Check to make sure it is properly seated in the bus. Install a new video card or known good unit to see if it solves the problem. Another possibility is the failure of the memory on the video card itself, which may or may not be efficiently replaced.

Nine Beeps: ROM BIOS CHECKSUM ERROR

An indicator of a damaged ROM BIOS. It is not likely that this error can be corrected by reseating the chips. If it persists, the BIOS chips have to be replaced.

Ten Beeps: CMOS SHUTDOWN

REGISTER READ/WRITE ERROR

When an AT or later CPU chip boots up it transfers into protected mode, then transfers back to real mode (the mode it will use to run DOS). The chip has to reboot to transfer to real mode. Before it reboots, the CPU posts a note to itself in CMOS RAM saying, "I've just booted. I'm trying to get into real mode to do some work. Don't send me back into protected mode to initialize everything—I've just done that." The likely problem is that the CMOS shutdown register on the computer is broken, and the CMOS memory and associated chips will have to be replaced; it may be more cost-effective to replace the motherboard itself.

Eleven Beeps: CACHE MEMORY BAD—DO NOT ENABLE CACHE

This is an indicator that the cache memory test has failed and has been disabled. On many AMI systems, you *could* press <Ctrl> <Alt> <Shift> <+> to enable cache memory, but AMI recommends you do *not* do so. Instead, try reseating the cache memory on the motherboard and retesting. If the error persists, replace the cache memory.

No Beeps

If all you hear is silence, and there is no image on the screen, check the power supply with a voltmeter. Next, inspect the motherboard for loose components. A loose or missing CPU, BIOS chip, clock crystal, or ASIC chip will cause the motherboard not to function.

Next, eliminate the possibility of interference by a failed or improperly set up I/O card by removing all cards except the video adapter. At the least, the system should power up and wait for a drive time-out. Insert the cards back into the system one at a time until the problem occurs again. When the system hangs up again, you can assume the problem is related to the last expansion card that was put in.

If you cannot determine the problem in this way, the motherboard will have to be replaced.

Phoenix BIOS 3.X and Earlier

What do you do if your computer fails before it is able to display information on the video screen? The answer may lie in the audio signals generated by the PC's BIOS.

Computers using a Phoenix BIOS use a group of three or four sets of beeps separated by pauses. We have listed these codes as a sequence of three numbers. For example, "Beep <pause> Beep <pause> Beep Beep Beep" would be listed as 1-1-3.

There are also a few special codes that use short and long tones.

One Beep

This is ordinarily not an indication of a problem; the beep comes at the completion of the self-test just before DOS is loaded.

Two Beeps

A possible configuration error. The BIOS may be detecting that the video card does not match its settings, or some other configuration is invalid. This could indicate a video card failure, monitor failure, or loose monitor cable connection.

One Long Beep, One Short Beep

This indicates a video failure. Check the jumpers and DIP switches on the card or motherboard if any changes have been made lately.

One Long Beep, One Short Beep, One Long Beep, One Short Beep

A report of a double video failure, meaning that the BIOS attempted to initialize both a color and monochrome video adapter, and both failed or were not present.

1-1-3 CMOS WRITE/READ FAILURE

The computer is unable to read the configuration that should be stored in CMOS. If the error persists, replace the motherboard.

1-1-4 ROM BIOS CHECKSUM ERROR

The ROM BIOS has been damaged, and will have to be replaced if possible.

1-2-1 PROGRAMMABLE INTERVAL TIMER FAILURE

There is a bad timer chip on the motherboard, and the motherboard will have to be replaced.

1-2-2 D MA INITIALIZATION FAILURE

1-2-3 DMA PAGE REGISTER WRITE/READ FAILURE

The DMA chip is probably bad. Since this chip is usually permanently soldered onto the motherboard, you'll likely have to replace the whole motherboard.

There is a remote possibility that a bad expansion card is grabbing hold of one of the DMA lines and not letting go; you could try removing all cards except the video card and seeing if the error persists. If it does not, continue with the other cards to try to determine the very rare culprit.

1-3-1 RAM REFRESH VERIFICATION FAILURE

The timer chip told the DMA chip to go into RAM and refresh the memory. The DMA chip did this, but the refresh process failed. The possible causes of this malfunction include: (1) bad memory chips, (2) a bad DMA chip, or (3) bad memory addressing chips on the motherboard. Turn off the computer, remove all the memory chips, and test them. Replace any bad chips and retest the computer. Since the DMA chip and the memory address logic chips are almost always soldered to the motherboard, you will probably have to replace the motherboard.

1-3-3 FIRST 64K RAM CHIP OR DATA LINE FAILURE, MULTI-BIT

For some reason, the first 64K of RAM is not responding to the CPU. The memory chips may be bad; you can try switching the high and low memory on your motherboard to see if the problem goes away.

In 8086 and 8088 machines the first bank of memory contains the first 64K (or the first 256K if the computer is using 256K chips), so switching the first and second banks (or the third and fourth banks) may solve the problem. Read your PC's instruction manual to find out which is the first bank on your particular motherboard.

A bad motherboard can also cause this problem. If the memory chips all test good, you will have to replace the motherboard itself.

1-3-4 FIRST 64K ODD/EVEN LOGIC FAILURE

1-4-1 ADDRESS LINE FAILURE 64K OF RAM

A failure of address or logic chips on the motherboard, which will have to be replaced.

1-4-2 PARITY FAILURE FIRST 64K OF RAM

You have a bad memory chip, either a data-story chip or one of the chips dedicated to parity error checking. Read the directions for code 1-3-3.

There are also chips on the motherboard that are responsible for calculating the memory parity. If these chips go bad, the motherboard will need to be replaced. Test the memory chips thoroughly first, though, before replacing the motherboard.

1-4-3 FAIL SAFE TIMER FAILURE

The fail safe timer on your EISA motherboard has failed, and the motherboard will have to be replaced.

1-4-4 SOFTWARE NMI PORT FAILURE

The software port allows the EISA software to talk to EISA expansion boards; the motherboard will have to be replaced.

2-X-X FIRST 64K RAM FAILURE

2-1-1	BIT 0	2-3-1	BIT 8
2-1-2	BIT 1	2-3-2	BIT 9
2-1-3	BIT 2	2-3-3	BIT 10
2-1-4	BIT 3	2-3-4	BIT 11
2-2-1	BIT 4	2-4-1	BIT 12
2-2-2	BIT 5	2-4-2	BIT 13
2-2-3	BIT 6	2-4-3	BIT 14
2-2-4	BIT 7	2-4-4	BIT 15

These beep codes indicate there is a bad memory chip in the first 64K of RAM. Each word of data on an AT-class computer has 16 bits; since each bit in a particular word is stored in a different memory chip, there are 16 chips for each word. (386 and 486 computers also boot up as 16-bit computers, not as 32-bit machines, and the BIOS codes also apply for Phoenix ROMs.)

Unfortunately, when you look at the motherboard, it is not obvious which particular memory chip holds the indicated bit. Your computer's instruction manual may have memory chip location diagrams; some motherboards have the bit number printed alongside the chip sockets. *P* stands for parity chip, *1* for bit 1, and so on. You may also have to call the manufacturer for help. The last and most time-consuming resort involves a trial-and-error search for the bad chip.

3-1-1 SLAVE DMA REGISTER FAILURE

3-1-2 MASTER DMA REGISTER FAILURE

3-1-3 MASTER INTERRUPT MASK REGISTER FAILURE

3-1-4 SLAVE INTERRUPT MASK REGISTER FAILURE

You have a bad DMA chip or interrupt controller chip. Since both of these chips are almost always soldered onto the motherboard, you will likely have to replace the motherboard.

3-2-4 KEYBOARD CONTROLLER TEST FAILURE

The keyboard controller chip is not sending the right replies to the controller's POST signals when it tests the keyboard at boot-up. This is an indication that the keyboard cable or the keyboard itself has gone bad. Check the AT/XT switch on the bottom of the keyboard to make certain it is set properly. Check also for a stuck key.

Try swapping a known good keyboard before you purchase and install a new keyboard.

3-3-4 SCREEN INITIALIZATION FAILURE

The computer cannot find a video card. Is one installed? Is it properly seated in the bus? If you cannot bring it to life, try swapping a known good video card.

3-4-1 SCREEN RETRACE TEST FAILURE

The video chip on the video card is failing; the card will have to be replaced.

3-4-2 SCREEN RETRACE TEST FAILURE

There is a problem with your video card; it won't reset the retrace bit in the allotted time. The card will have to be replaced.

4-2-1 TIMER TICK FAILURE

The timer chip cannot get the interrupt controller chip to send interrupt 0 (the timer interrupt). You have a bad motherboard and will have to replace it.

4-2-2 SHUTDOWN TEST FAILURE

This code applies only to AT-class machines. The computer must switch into protected mode to count and check the extended memory in an AT, even if there is no extended memory (it must check and see there is zero kilobytes of extended memory). Once the computer performs this check, it shuts down and reboots itself in real mode.

A bad motherboard can cause failure to switch into protected mode, as can a failed keyboard controller chip on the motherboard; the easiest to check and replace is a bad keyboard.

4-2-3 GATE A20 FAILURE

An error message that can be generated by an AT clone machine. The computer must switch into protected mode to count and check for extended memory in an AT clone (whether or not such memory is actually present). A bad motherboard or keyboard can cause a failure to switch into protected mode.

A faulty keyboard can cause the 8042 keyboard controller chip to keep sending signals to the processor on address line 20. Check the keyboard's switches to make certain they are properly set, and then try a known good keyboard. If that does not solve the problem, you will have to replace the motherboard.

4-2-4 UNEXPECTED INTERRUPT IN PROTECTED MODE

Either a bad expansion card or a bad motherboard can cause this error. Bad VGA or network cards, for example, can produce this error since both can use the nonmaskable interrupt (NMI) line to communicate with the CPU. In either case, though, the card is sending interrupts during bootup, a time when it should not be using the NMI circuit.

Turn off the computer, pull out all the cards except the video card, and reboot. If the error is gone, reinstall the cards one at a time (turning the computer off as you install each card). Test each card in turn until you find the bad card. If the error remains with only the video card installed, you will have to replace the video card, then retest. The last possibility is a bad motherboard. Before you install a new motherboard, though, try installing a basic video card from another computer to make sure the problem is not in the original video card.

4-3-1 RAM TEST ADDRESS FAILURE

The chips that are responsible for memory address logic have failed. Since these chips are almost always soldered to the motherboard, you will likely have to replace the motherboard.

4-3-2 PROGRAMMABLE INTERVAL TIMER CHANNEL 2 TEST FAILURE

4-3-3 INTERVAL TIMER CHANNEL 2 FAILURE

The interval timer is used to refresh memory; the motherboard will have to be replaced.

4-3-4 TIME OF DAY CLOCK FAILURE

Run the setup program that came with the computer; if the error persists, replace the batteries which power the CMOS memory whenever the computer is turned off. Run the setup program again.

If the error is still there, the error is probably caused by the power supply. Replace the power supply with a known good unit and run the setup program again.

In some very rare instances, you will have to replace the motherboard to fix this problem.

4-4-1 SERIAL PORT TEST FAILURE

4-4-2 PARALLEL PORT TEST FAILURE

The serial or parallel ports have failed the POST tests. Run a system diagnostic program to check them. Ports on an expansion card can be replaced by installing a new card. If the ports are located on the motherboard, they can be disabled by placing a jumper; new ports can then be added with an add-in card.

4-4-3 MATH COPROCESSOR FAILURE

The math coprocessor chip used in some 8088, 286, and 386 systems may have failed. Use a coprocessor testing diagnostic program to double-check it. If the coprocessor is bad, it can disabled (only a few software programs require its presence) or replaced.

PhoenixBIOS 4.0 Error Beep Codes

More recent modern machines use an enhanced version of the Phoenix BIOS. Following are the beep codes, and the POST code that would be read on a POST readout card if one was installed into the system bus.

beep code	post code	test point
1-1-1-3	02	Verify Real Mode
1-1-2-1	04	Get CPU type
1-1-2-3	06	Initialize system hardware
1-1-3-1	08	Initialize chipset registers with initial POST values
1-1-3-2	09	Set in POST flag
1-1-3-3	0A	Initialize CPU registers
1-1-4-1	0C	Initialize cache to initial POST values
1-1-4-3	0E	Initialize I/O
1-2-1-1	10	Initialize Power Management
1-2-1-2	11	Load alternate registers with initial POST values
1-2-1-3	12	Jump to UserPatch0
1-2-2-1	14	Initialize keyboard controller
1-2-2-3	16	BIOS ROM checksum
1-2-3-1	18	8254 timer initialization
1-2-3-3	1A	8237 DMA controller initialization
1-2-4-1	1C	Reset Programmable Interrupt Controller
1-3-1-1	20	Test DRAM refresh
1-3-1-3	22	Test 8742 Keyboard Controller
1-3-2-1	24	Set ES segment to register to 4 GB
1-3-3-1	28	Autosize DRAM

beep code	post code	test point
1-3-3-3	2A	Clear 512K base RAM
1-3-4-1	2C	Test 512 base address lines
1-3-4-3	2E	Test 512K base memory
1-4-1-3	32	Test CPU bus-clock frequency
1-4-2-4	37	Reinitialize the chipset
1-4-3-1	38	Shadow system BIOS ROM
1-4-3-2	39	Reinitialize the cache
1-4-3-3	3A	Autosize cache
1-4-4-1	3C	Configure advanced chipset registers
1-4-4-2	3D	Load alternate registers with CMOS values
2-1-1-1	40	Set initial CPU speed
2-1-1-3	42	Initialize interrupt vectors
2-1-2-1	44	Initialize BIOS interrupts
2-1-2-3	46	Check ROM copyright notice
2-1-2-4	47	Initialize manager for PCI options ROMs
2-1-3-1	48	Check video configuration against CMOS
2-1-3-2	49	Initialize PCI bus and devices
2-1-3-3	4A	Initialize all video adapters in system
2-1-4-1	4C	Shadow video BIOS ROM
2-1-4-3	4E	Display copyright notice
2-2-1-1	50	Display CPU type and speed
2-2-1-3	52	Test keyboard
2-2-2-1	54	Set key click if enabled
2-2-2-3	56	Enable keyboard
2-2-3-1	58	Test for unexpected interrupts
2-2-3-3	5A	Display prompt "Press F2 to enter SETUP"
2-2-4-1	5C	Test RAM between 512 and 640k
2-3-1-1	60	Test expanded memory
2-3-1-3	62	Test extended memory address lines
2-3-2-1	64	Jump to UserPatch1
2-3-2-3	66	Configure advanced cache registers
2-3-3-1	68	Enable external and CPU caches
2-3-3-3	6A	Display external cache size

beep code	post code	test point
2-3-4-1	6C	Display shadow message
2-3-4-3	6E	Display non-disposable segments
2-4-1-1	70	Display error messages
2-4-1-3	72	Check for configuration errors
2-4-2-1	74	Test real-time clock
2-4-2-3	76	Check for keyboard errors
2-4-4-1	7C	Set up hardware interrupts vectors
2-4-4-3	7E	Test coprocessor if present
3-1-1-1	80	Disable onboard I/O ports
3-1-1-3	82	Detect and install external RS232 ports
3-1-2-1	84	Detect and install external parallel ports
3-1-2-3	86	Re-initialize onboard I/O ports
3-1-3-1	88	Initialize BIOS data area
3-1-3-3	8A	Initialize extended BIOS data area
3-1-4-1	8C	Initialize floppy controller
3-2-1-1	90	Initialize hard-disk controller
3-2-1-2	91	Initialize local-bus hard-disk controller
3-2-1-3	92	Jump to UserPatch2
3-2-2-1	94	Disable A20 address line
3-2-2-3	96	Clear huge ES segment register
3-2-3-1	98	Search for option ROMs
3-2-3-3	9A	Shadow option ROMs
3-2-4-1	9C	Set up Power Management
3-2-4-3	9E	Enable hardware interrupts
3-3-1-1	A0	Set time of day
3-3-1-3	A2	Check key lock
3-3-3-1	A8	Erase F2 prompt
3-3-3-3	AA	Scan for F2 key stroke
3-3-4-1	AC	Enter SETUP
3-3-4-3	AE	Clear in-POST flag
3-4-1-1	B0	Check for errors
3-4-1-3	B2	POST done—prepare to boot operating system
3-4-2-1	B4	One beep

APPENDIX C

beep code	post code	test point
3-4-2-3	B6	Check password (optional)
3-4-3-1	B8	Clear global descriptor table
3-4-4-1	BC	Clear parity checkers
3-4-4-3	BE	Clear screen (optional)
3-4-4-4	BF	Check virus and backup reminders
4-1-1-1	C0	Try to boot with INT 19
4-2-1-1	D0	Interrupt handler error
4-2-1-3	D2	Unknown interrupt error
4-2-2-1	D4	Pending interrupt error
4-2-2-3	D6	Initialize option ROM error
4-2-3-1	D8	Shutdown error
4-2-3-3	DA	Extended Block Move
4-2-4-1	DC	Shutdown 10 error
4-3-1-3	E2	Initialize the chipset
4-3-1-4	E3	Initialize refresh counter
4-3-2-1	E4	Check for Forced Flash
4-3-2-2	E5	Check HW status of ROM
4-3-2-3	E6	BIOS ROM is OK
4-3-2-4	E7	Do a complete RAM test
4-3-3-1	E8	Do OEM initialization
4-3-3-2	E9	Initialize interrupt controller
4-3-3-3	EA	Read in bootstrap code
4-3-3-4	EB	Initialize all vectors
4-3-4-1	EC	Boot the Flash program
4-3-4-2	ED	Initialize the boot device
4-3-4-3	EE	Boot code was read OK

IRQ, DMA, and Memory Assignments

Standard IRQ Assignments

XT-class fossils had eight available interrupts, numbered from 0 to 7; AT-class machines have eight additional IRQs, from 8 through 15.

IRQ	Device
NMI	RAM Memory Parity Error (Nonmaskable Interrupt)
0	Timer
1	Keyboard
2	XT Reserved
	AT Cascade IRQ 8-15
3	COM2/COM4
4	COM1/COM3
5	XT hard disk
	AT LPT2:
6	Floppy disk
7	LPT1:
8	Real-time clock
9	Redirected to IRQ2
10	Unassigned
11	Unassigned

IRQ	Device
12	Unassigned or PS/2 Mouse
13	Math coprocessor
14	AT hard disk
15	Unassigned

Standard DMA Assignments

XT-class machines have four DMA channels, while AT-class systems have eight.

DMA#	Device
0	Memory refresh
1	SDLC
2	Floppy disk
3	Unassigned
4	Unassigned
5	Unassigned
6	Unassigned
7	Unassigned

Standard I/O Addresses

Port	I/O Address	IRQ/DMA
Com1	3F8-3FF	4
Com2	2F8-2FF	3
Com3	3E8-3EF	4
Com4	2E8-2EF	3

Port	I/O Address	IRQ/DMA
Com5	2F0-2F7	4
Com6	2E8-2EF	3
Com7	2E0-2E7	4
Com8	260-267	3
LPT1	378-37F	7
LPT2	278-27F	5
System Timer		0
Floppy	3F0-3F7	6
Hard disk-AT	1F0-1F8	14
Hard disk-XT	320-32F	5
Key press	060-06F	1
Real time clock	070-07F	8
Math coprocessor	0F0-0FF	13
Mono card	3B0-3BF	
CGA card	3D0-EDF	
EGA card	2B0-2DF and 3C0-3CF	
DMA controller 1	000-01F	
DMA controller 2	0C0-0DF	
Interrupt controller 1	020-03F	
Interrupt controller 2	0A0-0BF	
Game port	200-207	
Unused		10, 11, 12
Used to reroute IRQs 8-15		2
Used to reroute other interrupts		9

Memory Segments

Most boards have jumpers to allow you to select the memory locations the board will use. It's a good idea to note the addresses taken up by the boards in your machine.

Segment	Used by
A000-A800	MDA display memory
B000-BFFF	MDA display memory
B800-BFFF	CGA display memory
A000-BFFF	EGA or VGA display memory
C000-C3FF	VGA, EGA BIOS
C800-CBFF	Hard disk BIOS
D000-D7FF	Cluster adapter BIOS
D800-DFFF	EMS bank switch areas
E000-EFFF	Expansion area for system BIOS (rarely used)
F000-FFFF	System BIOS
FF000-FFFFF	Copy system BIOS

APPENDIX D

Microsoft System Diagnostics

If you're still running a dinosaur, or if you have a modern machine running Windows 3.1, you may have a hidden utility called **Microsoft System Diagnostics** (MSD) that will help you understand the innards of your machine. (Some users who have upgraded to Windows 95 from an earlier version of Windows or DOS may also be in luck.)

This utility runs from the DOS prompt only, and is best used outside of Windows.

MSD is not as capable as a modern reporting utility like CheckIt, but it is free, and specific to the needs of Microsoft in troubleshooting problems with its software. I use MSD as a second diagnostic utility regularly.

To use MSD, exit to DOS. You should see the basic C: or C:\ prompt, indicating you are at the root directory (the portion of the disk that includes the basic elements of the operating system.)

Type **CD \DOS <Enter>** to change to the subdirectory containing the operating system utilities. You may have to change the name of the subdirectory if your DOS installation is nonstandard. Consult your DOS manual for assistance.

Now type **MSD <Enter>** to launch the program.

Click on **Computer** to see the details of the system; the report can also be output to a printer or saved to a file. If you are not running a current version of DOS, or if the machine won't boot, you'll have to do your own research, of course.

MSD may not properly identify a motherboard manufacturer. MSD refers to the BIOS for the information, and some system manufacturers may include their own BIOS chips or make adaptations to an industry-standard BIOS.

In the table that follows, we've included an edited version of part of the MSD report for one of the machines in the Word Association lab.

Summary Information

Computer: Gateway/Phoenix, 486DX

Memory: 640K, 15360K Ext, 15648K EMS, 8368K XMS

Video: 8514/A, ATI , Ultra

Network: No Network

OS Version: MS-DOS Version 6.22

Mouse: Serial Mouse 8.20

Other Adapters: Game Adapter

Disk Drives: A: B: C: D: E:

LPT Ports: 1

COM Ports: 2

Computer

Computer Name: Gateway

BIOS Manufacturer: Phoenix

BIOS Version: Phoenix SETUP Utility (Version 1.00) 02

80486 ROM BIOS PLUS Version 0.10 GJX30-05E

LOGITECH MOUSE DRIVER V6.40

BIOS Category: IBM PC/AT

BIOS ID Bytes: FC 01 00

BIOS Date: 01/15/88

Processor: 486DX

Math Coprocessor: Internal

Keyboard: Enhanced

Bus Type: ISA/AT/Classic Bus

DMA Controller: Yes

Cascaded IRQ2: Yes

BIOS Data Segment: None

Memory

Conventional Memory

Total: 640K

Available: 634K 649536 bytes

Extended Memory

Total: 15360K

MS-DOS Upper Memory Blocks

Total UMBs: 124K

Total Free UMBs: 34K

Largest Free Block: 16K

Expanded Memory (EMS)

LIM Version: 4.00

Page Frame Address: E000H

Total: 15648K

Available: 8368K

XMS Information

XMS Version: 3.00

Driver Version: 7.50

A20 Address Line: Enabled

High Memory Area: In use

Available: 8368K

Largest Free Block: 8336K

Available SXMS: 8368K

Largest Free SXMS: 8336K

VCPI Information

VCPI Detected: Yes

Version: 1.00

Available Memory: 8368K

Video

Video Adapter Type: 8514/A

Manufacturer: ATI

Model: Ultra

Display Type: VGA Color

Video Mode: 3

Number of Columns: 80

Number of Rows: 25

Mouse

Mouse Hardware: Serial Mouse

Driver Manufacturer: Microsoft

DOS Driver Type: Serial Mouse

Driver File Type: .SYS File

DOS Driver Version: 8.20

Mouse IRQ: 4

Mouse COM Port: COM1:

Mouse COM Port Address: 03F8H

Number of Mouse Buttons: 2

Horizontal Sensitivity: 50

Mouse to Cursor Ratio: 1 : 1

Vertical Sensitivity: 50

Mouse to Cursor Ratio: 1 : 1

Threshold Speed: 2

Mouse Language: English

Disk Drives

Drive	Type	Free Space	Total Size
A:	Floppy Drive 80 Cylinders, 2 Heads 512 Bytes/Sector, 18 Sectors/Track	3.5"	1.44M
B:	Floppy Drive 80 Cylinders, 2 Heads 512 Bytes/Sector, 15 Sectors/Track	5.25"	1.2M
C:	Fixed Disk, CMOS Type 49 988 Cylinders, 15 Heads 512 Bytes/Sector, 56 Sectors/Track CMOS Fixed Disk Parameters	65M	404M

Disk Drives (continued)

Drive	Type	Free Space	Total Size	
	768 Cylinders, 15 Heads			
	56 Sectors/Track			
D:	Fixed Disk	CMOS Type 48	262M	502M
	1021 Cylinders, 16 Heads			
	512 Bytes/Sector, 63 Sectors/Track			
	CMOS Fixed Disk Parameters			
	768 Cylinders, 16 Heads			
	63 Sectors/Track			
E:	Floppy Drive			
	265 Cylinders, 64 Heads			
F:	CD-ROM Drive			
	52355 Cylinders			
	SHARE Installed			
	MSCDEX Version 2.23 Installed			
	LASTDRIVE=G:			

NOTE

That the last two drives reported by MSD may seem nonsensical; if they don't now, they should after you've read a bit into the book. The reason is that these two devices are SCSI drives that purposely fool the system about their real configuration. On the test system examined here, Drive E is a 270 MB Syquest removable hard drive, and Drive F is a CD-ROM drive.

GLOSSARY

A

Access time The time required to read or write data to a storage device, including RAM or a disk drive. The nature of the device as well as the operating system settings can affect the access time.

Adapter ROM Read-only memory on an adapter card installed in the computer's bus. The ROM contains code to control the adapter device, such as a disk drive adapter, a video card, or a memory card.

Address A specific location in memory.

Address bus One or more lines that carry address codes from the microprocessor to other parts of the system.

Analog A means of recording values by use of a continuously variable representation, including voltage levels. Contrast with *digital*, which represents values with discrete numbers.

Anti-aliasing. Despite how it appears from a short distance, your computer screen is made up of straight vertical and horizontal lines. There are no real circles or diagonals. Instead, the graphics adapter draws shapes by stair-stepping up and over or down and across. The stair-stepping Etch-a-Sketch–like effect is called *aliasing* or *jaggies*. Advanced graphics cards deliver something called *anti-aliasing*, which makes edges appear to be smoother by reducing the intensity of pixels on the edges of a shape.

Application software The program your computer uses to do work, such as word processing or a spreadsheet program.

Arbitration A technique that permits devices to compete for possession of a channel. Devices are assigned levels of priority and can seize control from a lower-valued unit.

ASCII Code American Standard Code for Information Interchange. A definition for numerical codes that represent controls and characters used by many computers.

ASIC Application-Specific Integrated Circuit. A chip designed to perform a specific function. The chip starts out as a nonspecific collection of logic arrays. In the manufacturing process, a layer is added to connect the gates for a specific function. By changing the connections, the chip maker can adapt the ASIC to different purposes.

ASPI Advanced SCSI Programming Interface, defining a common language between SCSI host adapters and peripheral devices. It allows SCSI peripherals from many vendors to be easily used on a single SCSI chain.

AT Bus The 16-bit system first used in IBM's PC AT computer, which was based on the Intel 80286 processor. The basic AT bus has been extended for use in most modern PCs, and is now called the ISA (Industry Standard Architecture) bus.

AT command set A set of commands to control modems, originally developed by Hayes Microcomputer Products. Commands begin with an *AT* for *Attention*.

B

Bank A set of memory chips divided into segments for easy access; most modern-machine motherboards have two banks for memory.

Bank Switching A technology to expand available system memory by switching between banks of memory as needed. The "off" bank retains its memory when not in use, but it is not immediately available.

Baud A measure of the number of voltage transitions in one second in a communications link. It is often incorrectly interchanged with bits per second (BPS).

BBS Bulletin Board System. A computer equipped with a modem and attached to a phone line that can be contacted by other computers for the transfer of information.

Benchmark A utility program that calculates the speed of completion of a particular task. It can be used to compare the performance of systems.

Binary A base-two numbering system used by computers. All numbers are made up of 0s and 1s.

BIOS Basic Input/Output System. The BIOS ROM tells the computer how to boot, contains a Power-On Self-Test (POST) routine, and generally acts as the interface between the hardware and the software. Most modern video cards, hard disk controllers, and other internal devices also contain ROMs with accompanying instructions (firmware) to tell them what to do.

Bit The smallest piece of information in a computer. A bit is either ON or OFF; we say it has the value 1 or 0, or TRUE or FALSE.

Bitmap A representation of an image or font as a binary file. The memory bit is either ON (1) or OFF (0) to indicate the corresponding screen pixel is either on or off.

Bits Per Second. (BPS) The number of binary digits that can be transmitted in one second. A more accurate means of measuring the potential speed of a modem.

Boot The process the computer goes through to load the operating system. There are two kinds of boot, hard and soft. When you turn on the computer or hit the **Reset** button, the system performs a hard boot. A *hard boot* forces a check of all hardware and creates a table of devices on the machine, such as the number and type of floppy drives, the presence and size of the hard disk, and so on, before it loads the operating system. When you press **Control-Alt-Delete**, the computer performs a *soft boot* and only reloads the operating system.

Boot Drive The disk drive from which the operating system is loaded.

Boot Sector The portion of the disk reserved for the operating system, usually the first sectors in the first disk partition. When the computer starts, the machine looks in the boot sector for the operating system.

BPS Bits Per Second, a measurement of the speed of data transfer in a communications link.

Buffer An area of memory or space on a disk reserved for I/O processing.

Burst Mode A scheme for data transfer that permits a device to remain inactive as far as the bus is concerned, and then send large amounts of data in a rapid burst; this design is used for DMA transfers on the EISA bus.

Bus The main interconnecting highway in a computer through which most data flows. The structure of the bus determines what sort of devices can be added to a computer, and how fast the PC can perform certain types of functions. PCs using ISA (the original AT bus), EISA (the extended ISA bus), or Micro Channel (IBM's proprietary bus) run slower than the microprocessor and offer narrower data paths than the CPU could handle. Intel's PCI (Peripheral Component Interconnect) bus, used in Pentium-class systems, is capable of operating at full processor speed. See also *bus board* and *bus connector*.

Bus board Some manufacturers of older modern machines chose to put the bus and bus connectors on one board and the rest of the mainboard chips on a separate processor board. In theory this allows for easier upgrades, although proprietary designs sometimes make this unrealistic.

Bus connector Expansion cards are connected to the bus through bus connectors on the mainboard. XT clones and compatibles use 8-bit bus connectors, with a single 64-contact socket for each expansion card. Modern machines use either the IBM AT-style industry standard architecture (ISA) bus, the extended industry standard architecture (EISA) bus or the Micro Channel bus; a VL or PCI bus can be added as a second bus in these systems. ISA is a 16-bit bus with a double bus connector on the mainboard for 16-bit cards; most such machines also provide a couple of the short, XT-style, 8-bit connectors for older cards that won't physically fit into 16-bit slots. Some 386 and 486 computers also have a proprietary bus connector for the manufacturer's proprietary memory expansion card. EISA uses a 32-bit bus that is backward-compatible with ISA cards (the 8-bit XT-style and 16-bit AT-style cards used in ISA computers). EISA bus connectors fit either EISA cards or ISA cards. Micro Channel is IBM's proprietary 32-bit bus.

Bus Mastering An architecture introduced to the PC world with EISA and Micro Channel buses. The design permits add-in boards to perform complex tasks independent of the CPU; among devices that take advantage of this facility are some graphics accelerator cards and network adapters. The Micro Channel design permits multiple bus masters. The CPU arbitrates among contending bus master applicants.

Byte Eight bits, the smallest unit of data moved about in a personal computer.

C

Cache Memory used to store data that the computer can reasonably guess it will need next. It is a bridge between a slow device and a fast device, for example, a hard disk (slow) and main memory (fast). A hard disk controller with cache memory will store most-recently-used hard disk data in the cache. Main memory is slow by comparison to the CPU (microprocessor chip). The CPU cache stores most-likely-to-be-needed-next data from the main memory so the CPU can gobble it up quickly when the CPU is ready for another bite. Cache performance (how much it speeds up your work) depends on several factors including the speed of the cache chips, the size of the cache, and most importantly, the intelligence of the cache controller.

CD-ROM Compact Disc Read-only Memory. An adaptation of music CD technology used to store large amounts of data. A CD-ROM is fairly slow in transferring information, but can hold as much as 660 MB of data.

CGA Color Graphics Adapter. A dinosaur video standard, introduced soon after the arrival of the IBM PC. By modern standards, it is extremely limited in the number of colors and resolution.

Centronics interface A 36-pin connector used between a printer and the PC's parallel port. A 50-pin version is used for SCSI devices. It provides eight parallel data lines plus additional lines for control and status information.

Checksum An algorithm for error checking. The CPU adds the value of the binary information in a block of data; the number is compared with a checksum computed by another device or computer that has received the block of data.

Chip The name for a integrated circuit. Chips are silicon wafers with circuits photo-etched into the silicon surface in layers.

Chipset An integrated set of chips that performs the functions of a larger number of discrete logic devices on a PC.

CISC Complex Instruction Set Computing. One design for a microprocessor. CISC uses complex assembly language instructions that usually require many clock cycles to execute. Compare to *RISC*.

Clock doubling A CPU design that improves processor performance by speeding up internal processing while maintaining the original speed for operations outside the chip. Intel's DX2 series of chips include the popular 486DX2/66, which runs a an internal speed of 66 MHz while it communicates with the system bus and memory at 33 MHz.

Clock tripling Intel's DX4 series triple the processor's internal throughput. For example, the 486DX4/100 runs at 100 MHz internally and 33 MHz externally.

Clone A generic equivalent to an original design. In theory, all AT-class machines other than IBMs are clones of the original PC.

Cluster A group of sectors treated by the operating system as a unit. The operating system controls the number of sectors in a cluster.

CMOS Complementary Metal Oxide Semiconductor chips require very little electricity, and therefore are used to store information using battery power. On most modern PCs, a block of CMOS memory is used to store critical system setup information including drive configuration, memory settings, date, and time. CMOS memory must be edited when drives or memory and certain other elements of the system are added or changed.

Codec COmpression/DECompression hardware or software used to compress or decompress digitized audio or video information.

Cold Boot Starting or restarting a computer by removing all power to the system. A different kind of boot is a *warm boot,* which uses a reset button or combination of keystrokes to restart the system. In certain situations, a cold boot is necessary in order to reset some hardware devices.

COM port A serial communications port. PCs usually have two serial ports, can support as many as four. The ports are numbered COM1, COM2, COM3, and COM4.

COMMAND.COM The command processor program of DOS, a basic element of the operating system.

Compression See *CODEC* and *Disk Compression.*

Conducted noise Erratic fluctuations in the electric power running into your computer.

CONFIG.SYS The system's configuration file that is part of the boot disk. It is used to instruct the operating system about device drivers to be loaded, and provides settings for system variables such as memory.

Configuration The group of parameters and settings that control communication between the system, major system components, and adapter cards and peripheral devices. Configurations are established from the Setup screen on a modern machine and through choices made in some shells such as Windows 3.1 and Windows 95.

Conventional Memory Memory located between 0 and 640 KB. This is the only memory that DOS applications can directly address. See also *Expanded* and *Extended Memory.*

Coprocessor A chip that performs a function parallel with the processor. It has no responsibility for control of the machine. The usual example is the x87 (8087, 80287, etc.) math coprocessor that handles floating-point calculations for the microprocessor at a faster speed than the general-purpose CPU. The 80486 DX and Pentium CPUs contains an integrated math coprocessor.

CPU The Central Processing Unit is the part of the computer that executes instructions and manipulates information. PCs are based on Intel or compatible CPUs, including the original 8088 and follow-on chips such as the 80286, 80386, 486, and Pentium.

Cycle time The amount of time it takes to read from or write to a memory cell. Cycle time includes the precharge when the cell is prepared to accept information and the actual access when data is moved between the memory and the bus or directly to the CPU.

Cyclic Redundancy Check (CRC) A form of error-checking that uses checksums.

Cylinder Part of the computer's addressing scheme, used to locate data on a high-capacity hard disk. Data on a hard disk is stored in concentric circles, called *tracks.* Large hard drives have multiple platters with separate read/write heads for each; a cylinder is defined as the same track on each platter. (If you were to cut the hard disk with a circular cookie cutter, you would end up with a set of cylinders spread across more than one platter.) Large files are recorded across cylinders instead of across tracks to minimize the amount of movement the read/write heads have to make to retrieve data.

D

DAC Digital-to-Analog Converter. On a modern video adapter, this circuitry is used to convert digital information into an analog signal that can be used by an analog monitor.

Data separation circuit The circuit in the path between the controller and the heads on the hard disk. It encodes the data so it may be consistently read back from the media surface. See *encoding scheme.*

Default A value, setting, or option that is preassigned by a program or system. Most configuration programs permit the user to drop back to the default settings which are usually a good place to start when the user-selected configuration seems to be causing problems.

Density The number of bits or characters that can be recorded in a specified space.

Device driver A set of instructions to the computer that explains the commands a particular device understands. An extension of the BIOS, a device driver allows DOS to access specific hardware in a hardware-blind fashion. DOS doesn't need to know about the hardware details in a mouse, for example. Instead, the mouse device driver is located at interrupt 33, and DOS just interrupts at hex 33 to access this mouse-control subroutine.

DIN connector A European-developed round plug and socket system, used on many PCs to connect keyboards and mice.

DIP switch Dual Inline Package Switch. A little module containing several tiny switches. It is designed as a dual inline package (two rows of little legs) so it can be mounted on a circuit board exactly like a chip.

Disk Compression A system that reduces the size of data files stored on disk by applying an algorithm that substitutes codes for repeated characters. The efficiency is measured by the **Compression Ratio,** which compares the original size of the file to its compressed size. For example, a 2:1 ratio means the original file was twice as large as its compressed version.

DLL Dynamic Link Library programs are executable elements of many Windows applications.

DMA Direct Memory Access. Data is transferred inside a computer through the DMA chip, not through the microprocessor, thus increasing the transfer speed. The hard disk controller uses DMA to read data from the hard disk and store it directly into RAM. PCs have eight available DMA channels.

DMF Distribution Media Format is a special format developed by Microsoft for installation diskettes; it allows the disk to hold 1.8 MB of data rather than the standard 1.4 MB. DMF formatted diskettes cannot be copied with the DOS or Windows disk copy commands.

Dongle Specialized hardware used to prevent unauthorized use of a piece of software. The device (named after its inventor, Don Gill) includes an embedded serial number and typically attaches to a computer's parallel port; the software will only work if it finds the dongle in place.

DOS Disk Operating System. This operating system is a CP/M variant. It was originally written by Microsoft, at the request of IBM in 1979. It is an extension of the BIOS ROM. It allows simple access to peripherals by a higher (hardware-blind) program—for example, COMMAND.COM.

Double buffering A scheme used by 3-D graphics card that uses separate blocks of memory for the finished image and for another image that is in the process of being rendered. This allows smooth transitions from one scene to another or film-like animation.

DRAM Dynamic Random Access Memory. Memory chips that need to be refreshed regularly. While being refreshed, a DRAM chip cannot be read by the microprocessor, and therefore DRAM read and write accesses often require *wait states*. See also *SRAM*.

Driver See *Device Driver*.

DS/DD Double Sided/Double Density, the most common diskette form factor for older PCs. It includes 5.25-inch 360 KB and 3.5-inch 720 KB diskettes. The original IBM PC was shipped with single-sided 160 KB floppy disk drives, but these dinosaurs quickly became extinct.

DS/HD Double Sided/High Density, a diskette form used in most modern PCs. Fast fading from the scene are 5.25-inch 1.2 MB floppies; in common use are 3.5-inch 1.4 MB diskettes.

DSP The Digital Signal Processor chip is used on many sound cards and advanced video processors to speed up audio and video.

Dual Boot A configuration that allows a computer to be loaded with more than one operating system, with the user able to choose between them at boot-up.

DX2, DX4 See *Clock doubling, Clock tripling*.

E

EEPROM Electrically Erasable Programmable Read-Only Memory. A special type of integrated circuit that can be used to store BIOS and other programming; it can be erased and reprogrammed by a special device. Flash Memory is a form of EEPROM that can be updated in place within a PC using special programs.

EGA The Enhanced Graphics Adapter was a relatively short-lived video standard used between the CGA and VGA eras. It can displays resolutions as high as 640x350 with 16 colors from a palette of 64. EGA uses a digital (TTL) video signal.

EISA Extended Industry Standard Architecture, an improvement over the 16-bit AT (ISA) bus, adding a 32-bit path and bus mastering. It still runs at a slow 8 MHz, and is becoming surpassed by local bus and PCI designs.

EMS Expanded Memory System. Also known as (Lotus/Intel/Microsoft [LIM], for the vendors who defined the standard) and as bank-switched memory. See *expanded memory* for a complete definition.

Encoding scheme Used to process data before it is stored on floppy diskettes, hard disks, tape, or other media. The encoding scheme massages "raw" data and turns it into a stream of signals designed to make error detection easier. Encoding schemes are also used to compress data.

Energy Star A specification for power-saving designs.

Enhanced IDE An improvement to the IDE specification for disk drives and other devices, permitting data transfer rates up to 13 MB per second.

EPROM Erasable Programmable Read-Only Memory are erased through a burst of ultraviolet light. See *EEPROM*.

EPP The Enhanced Parallel Port is an improved standard that permits data transfers of as much as 500 KB per second, more than triple the 150 KB speed of the original Centronics interface.

ESDI Enhanced Small Device Interface. Interface for hard drives in which the data separation (encoding) circuit is in the hard drive, supporting a maximum transfer rate of 3 MB per second. The cabling scheme is the same as the ST412/ST506 interface, but in ST412/ST506 the data separation circuits are on the hard drive controller. ESDI allows the manufacturer of the hard drive to use any encoding scheme they wish, so the manufacturer can pack more data onto the physical drive surface.

Expanded memory The same as LIM, EMS, or bank-switched memory. This is a memory management scheme designed to get around the 1 MB memory barrier in 8088 CPU chips. It allows specially written applications to address as much as 32 MB of memory by switching multiple 64K banks. EMS exploits a window of available address space above 640K but below the 1 MB barrier. Banks of memory are switched into and out of the 16K window as needed, which provides effective access to as much as 8 MB of additional memory. Many application programs have been written to utilize LIM to store data or to store programs until they are needed.

Extended memory The memory in a modern machine with an address above 1 MB. It can be used under DOS by programs that throw the 286/386/486 CPU chip into protected mode, where it can take advantage of this memory. Up to 32 MB of extended memory can be accessed through a 64 KB window in conventional memory divided into four 16 KB memory pages.

F

FAT The File Allocation Table is a listing created by DOS that serves as a map to the location of files and other information including file name, creation date and time, and file size.

FCB File Control Block. DOS maintains information about the status of every file in this section of memory.

Fixed-frequency monitor A video display that is designed to work with only one type of video signal and must be matched to the proper video adapter. Compare to *Multisynchronous Monitor*.

Flash disk A storage device using flash memory, often used as PCMCIA expansions to portable computers.

Flash memory Special memory chips that can hold their contents without power. Used for updatable ROM BIOS and in Flash disks.

Floppy disk A storage device that uses flexible plastic disks with a magnetic coating. The most commonly used size on modern machines is the 3.5-inch disk, which adds a semi-rigid carrier and is capable of storing 1.44 MB of data. Older machines used 5.25-inch floppy disks, with top capacity of 1.2 MB.

FM synthesis A technology used to simulate the sound of musical instruments on older and lower-cost sound cards. A more advanced technology is *wave table synthesis*, which stores actual samples of musical instruments.

Format (high-level) The process of preparing the media (disk or tape) for addressing by DOS. DOS checks the media for defects and creates certain tables. These tables allow DOS to find the stored data.

Format (low-level) The process of placing marks on the media so data stored on the media can be found again.

FPU A Floating Point Unit is a portion of the CPU used to perform floating-point mathematical calculations.

Full-duplex A communications protocol permitting the sending and receiving of data signals at the same time. See also *Half-duplex*.

G

General MIDI A set of 128 standard sounds used in MIDI sound cards and output devices; see *MIDI*.

Gigabyte Informally, one billion bytes. The actual size of a gigabyte is 1,073,741,824 bytes.

Gouraud Shading. An advanced method for shading colors within a shape that works by averaging the color values at the edges of a shape and adjusting colors to evenly blend them across the shape. Without Gouraud shading, most graphics schemes fill shapes with *flat shading*—a color or gray scale that does not vary within polygonal elements of an image.

GPF General Protection Fault, a system crash under Windows 3.1.

H

Half-Duplex A communications protocol that permits only sending or receiving at one time. See also *Full-Duplex*.

Hard Disk A large-capacity storage medium that uses spinning platters coated with magnetic material.

Head The component of a floppy or hard disk drive that reads or writes data.

Head Crash A disastrous failure of a hard disk that occurs when the read/write head that ordinarily Aflies@ a few millionths of an inch above the platter comes to rest on the disk. In most cases, the hard disk is damaged beyond repair, although some data recovery services are able to extract data from the disk.

Head Load Time On a floppy disk drive, the amount of time required for the drive head to settle after it is lowered onto the drive surface.

Head Settle Time On a floppy disk drive, the amount of time required for the heads to settle after a Seek operation.

Head Unload Time On a floppy disk drive, the amount of time required for the drive head to settle after it is lifted from the drive surface.

Heat Sink An aluminum structure with vanes that radiates heat away from a hot component, helping to prevent failure of electronic devices. Most of the early Pentium CPU designs required heat sinks because of the amount of heat they produced.

Hercules Standard An older monochrome text and graphics display standard that uses a 720x348 screen.

Hexadecimal A base-16 numbering system. Digits are represented by 0 through 9 and the characters *A* through *F*.

High Memory Memory between the 640 KB and 1 MB plateaus of a DOS-based computer.

HIMEM.SYS A device driver that manages extended memory; it is included with current versions of DOS and Windows.

HMA The High Memory Area is the first 64 KB of extended memory, from memory address 1024K to 1088K.

Host In a SCSI system, the computer in which a host adapter is installed. The host adapter card permits connection of SCSI devices to the bus.

I

IBM clone A computer that is functionally the same as an IBM PC, XT, or AT. *Clone* and *compatible* mean the same thing since the Phoenix and AMIBIOSs came on the market. Some earlier IBM-compatible machines, such as the Sanyo, were unable to run standard software without modification.

IDE Integrated Device Electronics. A disk drive interface in which the electronic circuitry for the controller resides on the drive itself, eliminating the need for a separate controller card. The Extended IDE (EIDE) interface is also used for some CD-ROM drives and other devices.

Initiator On a SCSI system, the device that requests that an operation be performed by another SCSI device (the target).

Interleave Data is loaded onto the hard disk one sector at a time, but not necessarily in contiguous sectors. An interleave of two uses every other sector. An interleave of three uses one sector, then skips two, then loads one, skips two, and so on. Slow CPUs require higher interleave numbers if they are to successfully read a hard disk. Some hard disk diagnostics will find your computer's ideal interleave number and set up the hard disk for maximum access speed.

Interleaved Memory A method to reduce wait states for RAM chips by interleaving memory by placing odd-numbered and even-numbered bytes of memory in separate rows. When the processor accesses an even-numbered location, it can then access an odd-numbered location without waiting.

Interrupt A call for the attention of the CPU. A PC is called an interrupt-driven system; every keystroke from the keyboard and every other event generates an interrupt to the processor. Two devices cannot share the same IRQ. Current PCs have 16 IRQ channels. *Hardware interrupts* break in on the CPU's internal meditations and ask for attention from the CPU. *Nonmaskable interrupts (NMIs)* demand attention right now. The CPU must suspend operations for an NMI. Most hardware interrupts are maskable; they are mediated by an interrupt controller chip. The interrupt controller chip queues up the interrupts and asks the CPU to service each one in its order of priority. *Software interrupts* are a jump to a subroutine. The subroutine locations and the interrupt numbers assigned to each subroutine are stored in the Interrupt Vector Table.

Interrupt Vector Table A table of 256 interrupts, located in the first kilobyte of memory, which contains the subroutine address assigned to each interrupt.

I/O Address The memory location where a particular device such as a disk drive, port, mouse, or other component reserves its gateway to the processor. No two devices can occupy the same address.

I/O, Input/Output The name for the process by which the computer communicates with the external world. Input comes from keyboards, mice, scanners, modems, and digital tablets. Output goes to printers, monitors, modems, and so forth. The term *I/O* is very context dependent. For example, data that is output from one program may become input for another program.

IO.SYS An element of MSDOS.SYS. See *MSDOS.SYS.*

IRQ Interrupt ReQuest Line. Hardware lines over which devices can send interrupts to the CPU. IRQs are assigned different priority levels to allow the processor to determine the comparative importance of requests for service. See also *Interrupt.*

ISA The Industry Standard Architecture is the compatible update to the original IBM PC-AT bus.

J

Jumper A small plastic block that is put into place on metal pins to turn on or off a specific function or make a particular setting.

K

K Kilo, as in 1,000. In computers, K means 1024.

Kb Kilobits. 1,024 bits.

KB Kilobyte. 1.04 bytes.

Kbps Kilobits per second.

Keyboard buffer A block of memory that can store a particular number of keystrokes that have not yet been processed by the computer.

Keyboard controller A special-purpose microprocessor in the keyboard that interprets keyboard presses, relieving the PC's main processor from this task. The Keyboard controller BIOS, located on the motherboard, manages the interface between the keyboard and the system.

L

Landing zone On a hard disk drive, a particular cylinder where the read/write heads can be safely parked when the power is shut off. Data is not stored in the landing zone.

Laser printer Essentially, a photocopy machine that makes copies based on electronic signals from the computer, rather than reflected light patterns from a paper original. These boxes seem to be the greatest of mysteries in the electronic age—once set up, though, they are easy to use.

LCD Liquid Crystal Display. A display used on most laptop PCs that produces characters by changing the polarity of a filter in response to an electrical signal.

LED Light Emitting Diode. A highly efficient semiconductor that converts electrical energy to light.

LIM Lotus-Intel-Microsoft (for the vendors who developed the standard): A technique to expand the amount of memory the computer can use for data. This method only works with special LIM or EMS cards and programs designed to use this memory. See *expanded memory*.

Logic Name for the internal parts of the computer that perform functions defined by the rules of logic, as in philosophy.

Logical unit In a SCSI system, a physical or virtual device addressed through a target. Each logical unit of a device has a logical unit number (LUN) by which it is addressed.

Low level format The electronic markings placed on a hard drive as a road map; the operating system further refines the indexing of the disk when it formats the drive.

LPT1 The computer's name for the first parallel port. The term comes from the days of mainframes, an abbreviation for *line printer*.

M

Magneto-Optical disk drive A data storage device that combines a laser and a magnetic medium to store information.

Mainframe A computer that is able to handle hundreds of users at the same time. Prices start in the millions of dollars.

Main memory Another term for *Conventional memory*.

Math coprocessor See *Coprocessor*.

Mb See *Megabit*.

MB See *Megabyte*.

Mbps Megabits per second. The number of millions of *bits* moved in one second. *MBs* is millions of *bytes* per second.

MCA Micro Channel Architecture. The name of the bus in the IBM PS/2 Model 50s and up. This bus is supposed to allow multiple bus masters; MCA buses are not compatible with ISA cards. On any bus only one processor at a time can have control, but the MCA design allows any one of the processors in the machine to be in control. By comparison, ISA allows only the CPU to have control of the computer; all other processors are slaves to the CPU. EISA, like Micro Channel, is a 32-bit bus and allows other processors to take over the bus. See also *EISA, ISA,* and *PS/2*.

MDA Monochrome Display Adapter. The original video display standard for the IBM PC, it can produce only text at a 720x350.

Media The name for the actual channel of communication. Floppy disks and hard disks are magnetic media. Compact disk/read only memory (CD-ROM) is optical media.

Mega Computer engineering term for a million; actually equal to 1,048,576. Also abbreviated as MB (megabyte).

Megabit Approximately 1 million bits; actually 1,048,576 bits.

Megabyte Approximately 1 million bytes; actually 1,048,576 bytes.

Megaflops A measure, in millions, of the number of floating-point operations per second of a CPU.

Megahertz One million cycles per second, abbreviated MHz.

Memory The part of the computer that remembers things. Unlike human memory, it cannot remember any context or any emotion. It can only remember a past state. See also *expanded memory, extended memory, nostalgia, RAM, refresh, ROM,* and *system memory.*

Memory Management Unit Hardware that supports the mapping of virtual memory addresses to physical memory addresses.

Memory refresh See *refresh.*

MFM Modified Frequency Modulation. One of many possible encoding schemes. MFM uses clock bits interspersed with the data. The ST412/ST506 standard for MFM was the most common hard disk controller encoding scheme for years. See also *ESDI, RLL,* and *SCSI,* all competing hard disk controller designs.

Micro Channel Architecture See *MCA.*

GLOSSARY

Microprocessor The part of the computer that processes. In microcomputers, the chip that actually executes instructions and manipulates information. Also called the CPU or the processor.

MIDI The Musical Instrument Digital Interface protocol is a specification for the interchange of music data. MIDI consists of a set of instructions to be executed by a MIDI output device; since it does not store the sound itself, MIDI files are very small.

Minicomputer A computer smaller than a mainframe in both power and cost; they were widely used as servers for groups of terminals and then groups of PCs in the early years of the PC. They are now mostly supplanted by high-end PCs.

MIPS Million Instructions Per Second, a measure of the speed at which a computer executes instructions.

MMX A set of multimedia extentions added to the Pentium instruction set and introduced in new Intel Pentium chips in 1997.

Modified Frequency Modulation (MFM) An older method for recording data on a hard disk drive by varying the amplitude and frequency of a signal.

Modem MODulator/DEModulator. A device that converts digital data from a computer to analog data for transmission over telephone lines by modulating it into waves; at the other end, the modem converts the analog data back to digital form by demodulating it.

Motherboard The main board of the PC, holding the microprocessor, system BIOS, expansion slots, and other critical components.

Mouse A device used to control the location of an onscreen pointer that can be used to identify data or issue commands to the processor.

MPC The Multimedia PC specifications were set by a consortium of hardware makers and identify the minimum requirements for multimedia applications.

MSCDEX The Microsoft CD-ROM Extensions is a device driver that controls management of CD-ROM drives attached to DOS machines.

MSD The Microsoft Diagnostics is a utility, supplied as part of current DOS, that can report on memory availability and settings, interrupts, I/O ports, and other elements of your PC. It is an excellent beginning step to understanding your system.

MSDOS.SYS An essential element of the Microsoft operating system, it is a hidden file on the boot track. (In IBM's version of DOS, this same file is called IBMDOS.COM.)

MTBF Mean Time Between Failure is a measure by hardware makers that purports to show the average time a component can be expected to work before it fails.

Multifrequency Monitor A video display that is capable of adapting itself to different video adapters; also called Multisynchronous.

Multitasking An operating system that is able to do multiple jobs simultaneously.

Multiuser An operating system that allows many users doing different tasks to run on the same computer.

N

Nanosecond A billionth of a second.

NMI Nonmaskable Interrupt. An interrupt generated by the hardware that cannot be turned off; this usually indicates a serious memory or I/O problem.

Noise interference Noise from any source that interferes with your computer. Examples: erratic electrical, magnetic, or radio waves. Likely causes: the air conditioner compressor or a thunderstorm (electrical noise), the local radio station (magnetic/radio waves).

Nonvolatile memory Another name for *CMOS RAM*.

Null Modem Cable A specialized serial cable used to connect two serial devices directly, without the use of a modem.

Numeric coprocessor A special chip (8087, 80287, and 80387) designed to do floating-point calculations, logarithms, and trigonometry.

O

OEM An Original Equipment Manufacturer is a maker that produces equipment sold by another company under its brand name. For example, Intel and Micron are OEMs of motherboards to many PC makers.

Offset A way to address memory, using a numbering system that indicates the relative distance (offset) from the beginning of a memory segment.

Operating system The program that allows the computer to load programs and that controls the screen, the drives and other devices. The more the computer does, the more complex the operating system.

OS/2 Operating System 2, by IBM/Microsoft. (operating system 1 is DOS.) IBM originally intended this operating system for the 80286, but released it for PS/2s.

Overdrive CPU An add-on chip from Intel that can upgrade certain 486 chips to faster DX and DX/2 processors.

P

Paged memory See *expanded memory* and *LIM*.

Page Frame A physical address in Conventional Memory to which a page of virtual memory can be mapped.

Page Mode Memory Access A means by which the computer accesses data in RAM. In an ordinary scheme, the CPU activates a RAS (Row Address Strobe) and a CAS (Column Address Strobe) signal to specify the row and column of the data. In Page Mode Memory Access, the CPU assumes the data is located in the same page as the initial data and the CPU can obtain information more rapidly.

Parallel Port The I/O channel to a parallel device such as a printer.

Parity A system used to check each byte of data for errors. The parity bit plus the 8 bits in the byte must add up correctly. For even parity, the number of 1s in the byte plus the parity bit must add up to an even number—if they don't, the computer knows there has been an error transmitting the signal. For odd parity they must add up to an odd number.

Partition Under DOS, a disk can be divided into several partitions, each of which can be worked with as if they were a separate disk. This is one way to deal with a hard drive that is larger than DOS will recognize, a problem more common with earlier versions of the operating system. Some users prefer to divide their disks into separate partitions for organizational reasons.

Password Check Option A feature of some ROM BIOS systems, it can be used to prevent unauthorized use of the system or alterations to Setup.

PC Cards See *PCMCIA*.

PCI The Peripheral Component Interconnect is a high-performance bus designed by Intel that includes a 64-bit-wide data path and bus mastering. PCI bus systems have mostly supplanted VL local bus designs.

PCMCIA The Personal Computer Memory Card International Association specification for a credit card-sized addition to PCs, most often used in portable computers. In 1995, the group renamed the devices as PC Cards. The original Type I card is mostly used in handheld personal assistants; Type II cards are principally used for memory, network adapters, and modems, and Type III cards are thick enough to hold miniaturized disk drives and other devices.

Pentium The fifth major generation of Intel CPUs used in PCs. It uses a 64-bit internal architectures and runs at speeds of as much as 200 MHz. An advanced version of the Pentium is the Pentium Pro. And in 1997, Intel extended the Pentium to include MMX multimedia facilities.

Peripheral A hardware device connected to a computer. Typical peripherals include keyboards, monitors, printers, disk drives, and more.

PGA Pin Grid Array. One method of mounting chips on a circuit board, used by devices with a large number of lines to connect. Pins stick out of the bottom of the chip and are meant to mate with holes in a socket. PGAs are used for most microprocessors, for example.

Photo CD A technology, developed by Eastman Kodak, that permits the storage and retrieval of photographs on a CD-ROM for display on home TVs or through a personal computer.

Physical Address An actual memory location in hardware.

Picosecond One-trillionth of a second.

PIF A Program Information File is an element of Windows that contains instructions on how to run DOS applications.

Pinout A drawing or table that lists the nature of the signals that use particular pins of a chip or connector.

Pixel A picture element is the smallest addressable area of a computer image. Screen resolutions are expressed in pixels, such as the 640x480 VGA specification.

Plug and Play Part of the holy grail of PCdom, this is a specification for a ROM BIOS jointly developed by Intel and Microsoft and incorporated within Windows 95. It is intended to make peripherals self-configuring. A new device plugged into such a system would be able to set its own IRQ, DMA channel, and memory address and avoid conflicts.

POST Power-On Self-Test. The BIOS ROM contains a series of hardware test instructions (POST), which runs each time the computer is turned on. If hardware errors are found, POST either beeps or displays error messages.

Power supply A critical element of the PC that converts AC wall current to DC voltage. Electronic circuits run at 5 volts or less, while disk drive motors draw 12 volts.

PRN The DOS name for the LPT1 port.

Processor The part of the computer that executes instructions and manipulates information. In microcomputers, this is a single chip. It is also called the CPU or the microprocessor.

Processor interrupt An interrupt generated by the microprocessor, also known as a logical interrupt. One example is a Divide by Zero logical error.

PROM Programmable Read-Only Memory. A special type of memory that can be custom produced to hold information or programming. A PROM cannot be rewritten. See also *EEPROM, EPROM.*

Protected mode The mode of an 80286, 80386, or 80486 in which the processor executes instructions that are extensions to the original set of 8086 instructions. 80286/80386/80486 chips are capable of operating either in real mode, where they are limited to the 8086 instruction set, or in protected mode. The 80386 and 80486 also have a virtual mode which allows them to impersonate multiple 8086 or 8088 computers running on the big 386 or 486 machine. See also *Virtual Memory.*

PS/2 Personal System 2. This 1987 IBM family of microcomputers incorporates a patented bus called MCA. We classic-bus partisans feel IBM designed this line to thwart cloning. See also *MCA.*

R

RAM Random Access Memory. Any part of this memory can be used by the microprocessor. Each storage location in RAM has a unique address, and each address can be either written to, or read, by the processor. *System memory,* maximum 640K, is the area DOS uses to manipulate programs. *Expanded memory* or *Extended memory* (see these two terms in the glossary) are also RAM. When people are using the term RAM casually, as in "How much RAM does your computer have?" they are usually talking about the system memory, plus expanded and extended memory. Windows, unlike DOS, uses both system memory and extended memory. See also *DRAM, ROM, refresh,* and *SRAM.*

Real mode 80286 microprocessors can operate in two memory addressing modes: *real mode* and *protected mode.* 80386 and 80486 microprocessors also have a *virtual mode,* one where 386/486 computers can masquerade as multiple 8088 machines. In real mode these microprocessors pretend to be a very fast 8086 or 8088. These processors operate in real mode when running DOS; they operate in protected mode when running Windows. In real mode, the processor can only address conventional memory, using only the first 20 address lines of the processor.

Reboot Restart the computer. See *Boot, Cold boot, Warm boot.*

Refresh DRAM forgets the information stored unless it is refreshed (read and rewritten). DMA channel 0 is dedicated to continuous memory refresh in a microcomputer.

Register System addresses for storing program instructions, data, or addresses.

Resolution A measure of the sharpness of an image, usually expressed as the number of pixels that can be displayed horizontally and vertically.

RGB The Red, Green, Blue specification describes one way in which colors are displayed on a monitor. This is an additive scheme; if all three colors are displayed at full intensity, the screen will be white. **CMYK** is a subtractive technology used in many color printers, which mixes colors to produce darker shades.

Ribbon Cable A flat multiconductor cable used primarily under the covers of the computer to connect peripheral devices such as disk drives to controllers.

RISC Reduced Instruction Set Computing. A design for microprocessor logic that concentrates on rapid and efficient processing of a relatively small and simple set of instructions that can be executed in a minimum number of instruction cycles. See also *CISC*.

RLL Run Length Limited. This is a method of encoding data on hard disk surfaces. It is similar to MFM, but does not require clock bits, so it can record more data in the same space. Instead of clock bits, it uses a rule about the number of consecutive zeroes that are written in any data stream. The method was developed by IBM some 15 years ago for mainframe use. It is as reliable as MFM for recording data but the recording surface must be very good. If the hard disk is not RLL-certified by the manufacturer of the drive, don't use an RLL controller on the drive. See also *ESDI*, *MFM*, and *SCSI*.

ROM Read Only Memory. Recorded once, at the factory, ROM is the ideal way to hold instructions that should never change, such as the instructions your computer requires to access the disk drive. See also *BIOS* and *RAM*.

ROM address The memory location for an expansion card's ROM chip, this is also called Base I/O Address. When the computer boots up it searches for any additional ROM chips in the system, reading the setup information from each ROM chip as it finds it. A typical ROM is 8, 16, or 32K long. Therefore, it uses up an 8, 16, or 32K block of memory addresses beginning at the "ROM address" (the starting address). No two ROMs can be at the same starting address, and their blocks of memory cannot overlap each other. You'll find ROMs on your video card (EGA and above), hard drive controller and/or SCSI host adapter, and many other expansion cards. There are no ROMs for parallel or serial ports, game ports, or ordinary floppy controllers because the computer already knows how to use these simple devices—the instructions are stored in the computer's ROM BIOS on the mainboard.

ROM BIOS See *BIOS*.

ROM Shadow A technique in which BIOS code is copied from slower ROM to faster RAM at bootup; the BIOS is then executed from RAM.

RS-232C The recommended standard set by the electronics industry for serial data transmission.

GLOSSARY

S

SCSI Small Computer System Interface. An intelligent interface to exchange data. A 50-pin connector is used in SCSI devices. Up to seven devices, not including the computer, can be attached to the SCSI bus via a single SCSI connection. The interface allows the drive manufacturer to use any encoding scheme they choose. However, SCSI is not supported in a standard way by the BIOS in ATs, posing interesting installation problems at times.

Sector The smallest unit of storage that can be allocated by a hard disk. Common sector counts can be as little as 512 or 1,024 bytes.

Seek time The length of time it takes for a hard disk head to find a track; expressed in milliseconds (ms). Average seek time is how long it will take to find a track, on average. Though fast seek times are often touted as an indication of a fast hard disk, seek time alone is rather useless as an expression of hard disk speed. Transfer rate is more meaningful. See also *settle time*.

Segment An element of the processor's addressing scheme, a segment is a unit of contiguous, position-independent space.

Serial communications The transmission of information between devices one bit at a time over a single line. Serial communications can be *synchronous* (controlled by a clock or timing device) or *asynchronous* (managed by control signals that accompany the information.) For modern machines, nearly all serial communication is asynchronous.

Serial Port A connector on a computer to which a serial device is attached. Serial devices include modems, mice, and certain printers.

Settle time How long it takes for the heads to settle down to the process of reading the hard disk once the specified track is found. See also *seek time*.

Setup A program used to store hardware information in the CMOS chip of a modern machine.

SIMM Single Inline Memory Modules are units that can hold a group of individual memory chips—typically eight or nine—in a single unit that plugs into a socket. A common current design is the 72-pin SIMM, which can hold from 1 to 64 MB.

Single user An operating system that allows only one user to use the computer at a time.

Single user, single task A version of single user that allows only one user at a time to do one task at a time. DOS is an example.

Single user, multitask A version of single user (see above) that allows only one user to do multiple tasks simultaneously. Examples: OS/2, Windows 3.1, and VM/386.

SIP Single Inline Package. A design for holding an electronic component in which all connectors emerge from one side of the package. See also *DIP.*

Software Interrupt A request for service generated by a program.

SRAM Static Random Access Memory chips that do not require refresh as long as they are powered. They are very quick, but do not hold as much information as a typically complex DRAM chip. SRAMs are often used as cache memory.

Stack A scratch pad for the microprocessor. When the microprocessor is interrupted in the middle of a task by a more urgent task, it saves notes to itself about the contents of registers, and so on. These notes are essential if the microprocessor is to resume the first task where it left off.

State Condition, as in ON-OFF, HIGH-LOW, or ZERO-ONE. In computers this means the particular way all the memory locations, registers and logic gates are set, for example, "wait state." State is also used casually to indicate the particular condition and status of the computer.

Step rate On a floppy disk drive, this is the amount of time required for the read/write head to move from one track to another.

ST412/ST506 The names of the original hard drives in micros. The drives are no longer made, but the interface Seagate developed for them is still used. This interface is used on inexpensive XT and AT drives and controllers. See also *MFM* and *RLL.*

Surface mount A design for circuit boards in which chips are directly attached to the board instead of being soldered into place or attached through sockets. In theory a surface mount design is less susceptible to problems caused by bad connections; however, a failed chip often requires replacement of the entire circuit board.

System Boot parameters Many BIOS chips permit the user to specify a number of options at bootup. These include bus speed, whether the NumLock function is set on or off, and boot up sequence which establishes whether the BIOS goes to the A: or B: floppy drive or to the C: drive for boot.

System memory The memory in the computer that DOS (or the chosen operating system) can use to store information and execute programs. On most DOS computers this is a maximum of 640K. DOS 5.0 and DR DOS 6.0 tuck data in high memory (the last 64K of memory in a 286/386/486 computer) that we used to put in the first 640K of memory, so these operating systems have an effective system memory of 704K.

SYSTEM.INI A Windows file that contains information about the hardware environment. See *WIN.INI.*

T

Tape drive A storage device that records data on a moving tape, like an audio tape recorder in concept. Tape Drives are used for backup of data.

Target A SCSI device—including both peripherals and the SCSI host adapter—that performs an operation requested by an initiator.

Task The job (usually an application program) that the computer does. A task is not the same as a user—a task is what the computer is doing. One person can simultaneously perform multiple tasks on a single computer. See *Multitasking.*

Terabyte 1,000 gigabytes; more precisely, 1,099,511,627,776 bytes.

Termination The first and last device on a SCSI bus must have a resistor pack that indicates it is the end of the line.

Text Mode A video display mode where the adapter converts ASCII character data directly into display information.

Timeout The operating system or BIOS is usually instructed to end a process when a predetermined amount of time passes without response.

Track A magnetic ring of information on a disk drive, somewhat like a groove on an old phonograph record. On a sequential data storage device like a tape drive, tracks run parallel to the edge of the medium. See also *sectors.*

Track skew factor When a read/write head reaches the end of a track, and if information is sequential from one track to the next, the head has to move to the next track to continue. If the next track was to start at the same sector that the previous one ended at, the disk drive would have to wait until the disk spun nearly completely around before it could begin to read new information. Instead, most disk drives *skew* the starting point of each track from the other by a few sectors so that information can be read and written in a near-continuous stream.

Track-to-track access time How long it takes for the heads of a drive to move from one track to another. This number determines much of the speed with which data is read from the drive.

Transfer rate The amount of data, measured in bytes per second, the computer can read from the hard disk.

True color A term applied to video display adapters or monitors capable of displaying 24-bit color, a maximum of 16.7 million colors.

TSR Terminate and Stay Resident. A program that pops back into use when a hotkey sequence is pressed. Sidekick is an example. TSRs sometimes present problems when they clash with each other or programs loaded subsequent to them, and cause symptoms that you might think are hardware-related.

TWAIN An industry interface that stands between scanners and other capture devices and image-editing software.

U

UART The Universal Asynchronous Receiver Transmitter chip set manages communications through a serial port. The original PC used an 8250A UART, which proved incapable of handling high-speed data transfer; modern machines use the 16550 UART. Many older machines can be upgraded to use the new chip either through a direct swap of chips or by disabling the existing serial port and installing a new serial card in the bus.

UMA The Upper Memory Area is PC memory with addresses between 640 KB and 1,024 KB (1 MB).

UMB Upper Memory Blocks are located within the UMA.

UNIX An operating system developed by AT&T in the early 1970's to run their computerized phone switching system on PDP-11s. This operating system is known for low overhead with easy connecting of different tasks. Unlike DOS, UNIX is a true multiuser, multitasking system.

Upper Memory Memory located between 640K and 1024K (1 MB). Divided into blocks (Upper Memory Blocks), modern machines can use it for the system BIOS, video BIOS, video memory, adaptor ROM, additional device drivers, and TSRs. It is sometimes also called Reserved Memory or High DOS Memory.

USRT Universal Synchronous Receiver-Transmitter. A synchronous equivalent of the UART, it is only used on PCs adapted for use in synchronous communication applications.

V

VGA Video Graphics Array. An advanced analog video standard capable of displaying as many as 256K colors at 640x480 resolution. The Super VGA standard has superseded it in the market.

Virtual mode The mode of the 80386 and 80486 where it pretends to be multiple 8086/8088s. This is the mode used by Windows 3.1.

Virtual Address A calculated address used to reference memory locations. The Memory Management Unit translates the virtual address to a physical address.

Virtual Memory A means to allow the system to work with a larger memory than it is permitted to use, or larger than actually exists. Paged memory is one type of virtual memory.

VL-Bus The VESA local bus is a high-speed data connection between the CPU and peripheral devices, developed by the Video Electronics Standards Association. It has been largely replaced in modern machines by the PCI bus.

Voltage spike An electrical geyser.

Voltage surge A big electrical wave.

VRAM A special type of memory installed on a video display adapter which allows simultaneous read and write operations.

W

Wait state A pause programmed into the operations of a microprocessor while the CPU waits for memory to catch up with it; the faster the memory, the fewer wait states necessary.

Warm boot Restarting a computer without turning off the power, using the **Ctrl-Alt-Del** computer key combination or by pressing a reset button on the PC or keyboard. See also *Cold boot*.

Weitek Processor A non-Intel math coprocessor that can be used with some systems.

WIN.INI A file containing configuration information about Windows applications and the user environment such as fonts, colors, and general appearance.

Word The smallest unit of data the processor can work on. On Dinosaur 8088s, a word is 1 byte. For the 8086, 80186, 80286, 386/SX, and 486/SX a word is 2 bytes or 16 bits. For the 80386, 486, and Pentium chips, a word is 4 bytes or 32 bits.

WORM drive Write Once Read Multiple Times. A data storage device that can be written to once, and then read from as needed.

Write precompensation As the head on a hard disk starts to write on the smallest inner tracks, data errors can occur if the data is recorded exactly as it was on the large, outer tracks. Write precompensation—subtle timing changes as the data is recorded—provides clean, clear data storage even on the innermost tracks.

X

Xenix A version of UNIX developed for microcomputers. Slowly being replaced by UNIX as the microcomputers of today develop the power of minicomputers of ten years ago.

XMS Extended Memory Specification. See *EMS*.

XT Class A relic PC based on the 8088 or 8086 processor.

Z

Z-buffering Also called *Hidden Surface Removal*, Z-buffering is another assignment for the beefed-up processor of advanced graphics cards. In this case, it calls on the brains of the card to keep track of the depth of each shape and its hidden surfaces so that they will appear as the viewer changes perspective or as objects that may be in the foreground of background move.

ZIF Socket A Zero Insertion Force socket is used in many modern motherboards to allow easy removal and replacement of certain computer chips, including the CPU.

640KB 1 MB Relocation A setup option in the AMIBIOS that allows relocation of the 640KB 1 MB memory area. This area is usually reserved for ROM, but if shadow RAM is not enabled and the RAM in this area is available, it can be remapped to a location above 1 MB so that portion of RAM can be used as extended memory.

Index